THE SOCIAL STRUCTURE OF ISLAM

THE SOCIAL STRUCTURE OF ISLAM

BEING
THE SECOND EDITION
OF
THE SOCIOLOGY OF ISLAM

BY
REUBEN LEVY
Professor of Persian in the University of Cambridge

CAMBRIDGE
AT THE UNIVERSITY PRESS
1965

PUBLISHED BY
THE SYNDICS OF THE CAMBRIDGE UNIVERSITY PRESS

Bentley House, 200 Euston Road, London, N.W. 1
American Branch: 32 East 57th Street, New York 22, N.Y.
West African Office: P.O. Box 33, Ibadan, Nigeria

First Edition 1957
Reprinted 1962
1965

Printed in the United States of America

PREFACE

The present work was originally undertaken at the request of Mr Herbert Spencer's Trustees in continuance of his *Descriptive Sociology*. The Muhammadan communities of the world, possessing certain common characteristics traceable to their religion, are suited for treatment as a unity, and the purpose of this book is an endeavour to investigate the effects of the religious system of Islam on the life and organization of the societies which acknowledge it. Aspects of the social structure of the Muhammadan community in the classical period—generally under the Caliphate—have been treated in the past by such scholars of eminence as von Kremer, W. Robertson Smith and Goldziher. Here the basic principles of Islam are examined and an attempt is made to ascertain how Muhammadans of different periods and climes have adapted their way of life to them.

The first edition of the work appeared in two volumes, in 1931 and 1933 respectively, under the title of *The Sociology of Islam*. The materials have now been revised in the light of changed conditions and more recent work on the subject, rearranged, and collected into one volume for the sake of convenience and economy. In the original preface I acknowledged my indebtedness to my colleagues Professors A. A. Bevan and R. A. Nicholson and to Mr T. W. Hill, who was editor of the Herbert Spencer *Sociology*. All are now beyond the reach of my thanks, but my indebtedness to them remains. For criticisms and corrections to the first edition I am under an obligation to Professor J. Schacht, of the University of Leyden, and for new materials to Professor J. N. D. Anderson.

R. L.

CAMBRIDGE
28 April 1955

CONTENTS

MAPS

INTRODUCTION

The first occasion on which Muhammad, son of 'Abd-allāh of Mecca, merchant and former camel-driver, confided to any living soul that he was the recipient of visions from on high was, as tradition declares, in A.D. 610, when he had already attained the age of forty years. The earliest divine manifestations commanded him to "recite"[1] what he heard. It was followed by others which bade him denounce the idolatrous beliefs and practices of his fellow-townsmen, to whom he was to reveal a higher faith and a purer system of life. The central point of the new faith was that there is no God but Allah, a deity who was already known in the Arabian pantheon but who was henceforth to be not only supreme, but unique. From Muhammad's earliest utterances also it is clear that he claimed to be himself regarded as Allah's mouthpiece and the last of his prophets; the final link in that long chain of seers which went back through Jesus, Moses, Abraham and some others to Adam, the first. Affirmation of Allah's uniqueness and the divine origin of Muhammad's apostleship became the creed of Muhammadanism, and it has remained to this day the test of all who profess the creed. To Allah, the all-powerful and omniscient, "everyone who is in the heavens or on the earth resigns himself willy-nilly",[2] and such resignation—for which the Arabic term is *islām*—is the essence of the prophet's doctrines. Everyone who so "resigns" himself is a *Muslim.*

At first, probably from motives of expediency, Muhammad kept his errand a secret, confiding it only to the members of his own immediate household, who became his first disciples and converts. The traditional story is that the secret was closely guarded for three years, during which time, however, a number of new adherents were gained from amongst the younger men in Mecca. Most of them belonged to the humbler classes, but there were some, like Muhammad's future father-in-law, Abu Bakr, who were men of rank and substance.

Whether or not the Prophet from the beginning, or at all,

[1] Arabic *iqra'*, whence the word *Qur'ān*, Koran.
[2] Koran 3⁷⁷.

intended his message to apply beyond the confines of his own land of Arabia is a question which cannot be definitely settled. The evidence of his own utterances is vague and contradictory and eminent authorities may be found in support of either view.[1] It may be said, however, that the traditional stories of the messengers whom Muhammad despatched to the rulers of the then known world[2] have so much of the improbable in them that they must be accounted inventions of a later age. On balance it would appear that at the beginning of his career, at Mecca, there was no possibility of his having had the idea of a universal faith. All he desired then was to persuade his fellow-citizens of the truth and validity of the revelation he brought. The public declaration of his divine call had led to immediate opposition from his own clan of the Quraysh, who justifiably saw in his pretensions a grave danger to their own profit and prestige as hereditary guardians of the *Ka'ba*, the "cubical" shrine at Mecca, which thousands of pilgrims visited every year. His arguments, so far from persuading the Quraysh of his claim to prophethood—with the leadership of the clan that it implied—only aroused their fury, and led to such danger that in the year A.D. 622 he was compelled to leave Mecca. He took refuge with his handful of converts in the city of Yathrib, the later Medina, which lay about eleven days' caravan march to the north. This emigration (the *hijra* or *hegira*) marked a definite stage in the development of Muhammad's religion, and its importance was recognized some years afterwards when it was adopted as the epoch from which events in Muslim history were reckoned.[3]

At Medina Muhammad's apostleship found readier and more general acceptance, of which the consequence was a rapid increase not only in his religious authority but also in his political power; a phenomenon which is not unusual amongst a simple and democratic people. In theory, and even when the Prophet was in a position to assert his authority, there was no compulsion on the inhabitants of Medina or others to believe in his teachings, and

[1] The evidence was re-examined by F. Buhl in *Islamica*, II (1936). He supports the view that Islam was not in the beginning intended to be a universal religion.

[2] See Ṭabarī (Leyden, 1879–1901), I, 1559.

[3] The *hijra* took place on Thursday, 15 July, A.D. 622. The era begins on the day following, so that Friday, 16 July, A.D. 622, is equivalent to the 1st of Muḥarram A.H. 1 (i.e. year 1 of the *hijra*). The year is a lunar one of 354 days.

his mission is described as one of preaching only.[1] Yet many were soon persuaded to join his cause. The Jews who inhabited Medina and the surrounding country alone proved stubborn. It would seem to have been mainly from a feeling of superiority over a man who, in his revelations, could give such mutilated and confused versions of the Bible stories that he had heard from them or from the Christians. They claimed to have the original and authentic source of the stories: he retaliated by accusing them of falsifying the Scriptures. When that failed to have any effect, he eliminated the danger they represented by slaughter or banishment. As soon also as he had acquired a sufficient force of arms, he proceeded against the unbelievers at Mecca, partly for vengeance—which led him to urge believers to "fight in God's way",[2] partly also because it was essential to his prestige that he should capture the traditional sanctuary of his own people. His efforts succeeded, and though other cities followed Medina as the capital of the Muhammadan empire which grew up, Mecca always remained the spiritual centre of Islam. The effect of the Prophet's success and of his growing religious influence was to impose upon the various warring tribes of Arabia a bond far stronger though more subtle than that of kinship which they had hitherto recognized. Blood-relationship had been the strongest tie between man and man. Now Islam was to be an additional one; even more compelling and more comprehensive.

Before his death in A.D. 632 Muhammad had gathered to his banner most of the inhabitants of Arabia. The exceptions were Jews and a few Christians and Magians, whom he permitted to remain in their own faith provided they recognized his political overlordship by the payment of a poll-tax (*jizya*). But he excluded them and other unbelievers from the communal life by forbidding them all access to Mecca[3]—a prohibition which remains in force to this day.

The divine messages which were revealed to Muhammad from time to time as the necessity arose for the enlightenment and guidance of his flock, were collected several years after his death to form the Koran. It is the principal source of our knowledge of the Prophet's own views and aims. On a number of topics it speaks with more than one voice, because his ideas developed and changed but his abrogated utterances were nevertheless preserved along

[1] Koran 2^{257} and 3^{19}. [2] *Ibid.* 2^{245}. [3] *Ibid.* 9^{28-29}.

with the newer ones. On questions which could not have presented themselves to him, at any rate with any degree of urgency, it throws no light. Of these, as we have seen, one was the question whether Islam was intended for the universal acceptance of the whole world or for adoption only by the inhabitants of Arabia. From the fact that possessors of Scriptures, "People of the Book", were exempted from belief provided they paid the poll-tax, it is legitimate to assume that he had recognized the impossibility of turning every man into a Muslim, even in Arabia. Still more significant is the place accorded in Islam to Mecca. It could have had little meaning for anyone outside the tribes of the peninsula, and to have substituted it for Jerusalem[1] as the point to which all Muslims must turn in prayer indicates that the prophet's views were centred on Arabia. However the question be decided, Islam did spread beyond the confines of the peninsula, which nevertheless has retained a large and important place in the religion of Muhammad. Mecca was one contributory factor; its language was another, being the tongue not only of the Koran but of prayer for all Muslims. Arabic, in fact, became the sacred language of Islam as Hebrew did of Judaism, and its written characters were adopted, however unsuitably, to represent the languages spoken by Muslims, whatever their nationality or native tongue. Until, in 1928, Turkey made a modified form of the Latin alphabet compulsory for printed and official documents, it might have been said that, except in the case of the Syrian Christians, the normal use of the Arabic characters marked an individual or a people as Muslim.

In the world outside Arabia the Prophet during his lifetime made no converts. The historians[2] speak of envoys sent by him to Syria in the year 8/629, but what their purpose was is not clear, though it has been precariously assumed that they were instructed to summon the Emperor Heraclius to adopt Islam. The envoys were killed, and an expedition directed against the emperor's Arab subjects to avenge the murder was routed at the battle of Mu'ta. Another force was actually being made ready to wipe out this disgrace when the Prophet died (8 June, A.D. 632). In the

[1] Jerusalem (*al-Quds* "the Holy") remained the next most sacred city in Islam. The Temple was the scene of the prophet's legendary night-voyage (Koran 5[2]), and most Muslims believe that from it will be heard the Last Trump (Koran 50[40]).

[2] Cf. Ṭabarī, I, 1610.

chain welded by Islam, Muhammad himself had been the strongest link, and his disappearance meant disruption. The Bedouin tribes, upon whom their recently assumed Islam sat very lightly, promptly revolted in every direction and many deserted to one or the other of the numerous pretenders to the Prophet's mantle.[1] Medina, with Mecca and the neighbouring town of Ṭā'if remained loyal, but they were faced by the difficulty of finding a suitable leader. The man whose word had most weight in the Muslim community was Omar; but he was not a native of Medina, being only a *muhājir*, an "emigrant", one of the group who had accompanied Muhammad from Mecca to Medina at the *hijra*. The Medinese, meanwhile, insisted on having a chief from amongst their own number, and Omar, who was strong enough to dominate the situation, compromised by causing allegiance to be paid not to himself but to Muhammad's father-in-law, Abu Bakr, who thus became the first Caliph (*Khalīfa*) or Successor of the Prophet.

The force which had originally been intended for dispatch to Syria had remained at the disposal of the first Muslim commander able to use it. The most obvious use for it would have been to send it against the Arabian tribes in revolt, but the Caliph, in spite of advice to the contrary, insisted on carrying out what he considered to be the Prophet's intention. Accordingly, the force, numerically no stronger than a raiding party, advanced swiftly against the Roman emperor's Arab subjects living on the confines of Syria, and then promptly returned to relieve Medina, which was in a state of siege[2] owing to the fact that Abu Bakr was engaged in the task of subduing the rebellious Bedouin and reimposing Islam. By repeated sallies from Medina he was able to rout the malcontents, though he did not succeed immediately in the task of regaining the Muslim solidarity that had prevailed in Arabia in Muhammad's later days. That was achieved only when the Caliph began to send expeditions into neighbouring lands, thereby utilizing his army's appetite for war but also rewarding them for their past services. Their despatch on such tempting business had the effect of recalling many of the rebel tribes to their loyalty. On three sides it was possible for armies to advance without need of

[1] The most prominent was Maslama, known by the satirical diminutive Musaylama, "little Maslama".

[2] Ṭabarī, I, 1851.

sea transport. To the north lay provinces belonging to Byzantium and Persia, far enough from the centres of authority to be attacked without too great danger and rich enough to promise fair booty. The first raid was made in the year 12/633, under the leadership of Khālid ibn Walīd, "The Sword of God", against the Persian province of 'Irāq 'Arabī, which lay nearest. Along the Euphrates lay a number of rich cities; amongst them Ḥīra, which had a large Christian community and was the seat of a bishopric. Most of them submitted with little opposition and agreed in return for a guarantee of immunity against further assault to pay an annual tribute. In the event they failed in their compact, with results that shall be seen.

While Khālid ibn Walīd was operating along the Euphrates, the Caliph Abu Bakr had despatched a force of about 7000 tribesmen against Palestine and Syria. They came mainly from tribes in southern Arabia and took their women and children along with them as though for permanent emigration rather than for a warlike expedition.[1] In spite of this handicap and the strength of the opposing Byzantine phalanxes, the force was able to penetrate as far as the Sea of Galilee and even beyond. There, however, the Roman general outmanœuvred the tribesmen, who were sent flying in retreat. By the time that news of the defeat reached Medina, Khālid ibn Walīd had returned from Iraq, and he was at once sent with supporting troops to the aid of the army in Palestine. His arrival restored the courage of the defeated warriors, who again advanced along the Jordan valley, this time without encountering any but the feeblest opposition.

Khālid's fame as a general undoubtedly contributed to the withdrawal of the Syrians from the fight, but it was probably due in still greater measure to the fact that the inhabitants of the villages and open country, as distinct from the city populations, were of the same kin as the invaders, in whom they recognized fellow-Semites. Although they professed Christianity, they had never properly assimilated its doctrines, and the bitter quarrels of rival churches over mystical teachings which the peasants found impossible of comprehension drove them into the arms of the invading Muslims. These men spoke a language closely allied to their own, and the new faith which they brought, when they made

[1] A. von Kremer, *Die herrschenden Ideen des Islams* (Leipzig, 1868), p. 325.

any reference to it at all, seemed to make few demands in the way of belief, while its adoption was an easy mode of release from the burdens of plunder or taxation.

Politically, submission to the Arabs meant only the substitution of one master for another, and, since Roman ways of life and thought had touched the Syrians only very lightly, it required no great effort to make the change.

Khālid's advance brought him in March 635—by which time Omar had succeeded Abu Bakr as Caliph—before the walls of Damascus, which capitulated after a six months' siege. The fall of the city provided the invader with the key to Syria, but Palestine proper still remained in the hands of the Roman troops, who, having access to the sea, could gain reinforcements from Byzantium. In 636 they attempted to cut the Muslim line of communication between Damascus and Arabia. The effort, however, failed. In August of that year, at the battle of the Yarmūk (an eastern tributary of the Jordan, flowing into it just below the Sea of Galilee), the Byzantines were utterly routed, leaving the Muslims a way open into Palestine. There the Roman posts were stormed one after another, and though a stand was made by the garrison at Jerusalem, that too had capitulated by the end of 636.

Simultaneously with the expedition into Syria large raiding parties—they were little more—were advancing in other directions. By sea a small fleet even ventured in 637 from Oman in eastern Arabia to Tānah near Bombay. Like similar expeditions to India dispatched within the next fifty years the raid achieved nought beyond gaining some booty, and the Caliph Omar so little approved of it that on its return he wrote to the leader that if there had been any casualties amongst the raiding party an equal number of his kinsmen would have been sacrificed to avenge them.

The case was different in Persia. After the first Muslim success, there had been a check at the Euphrates in 634, when the invaders, under the leadership of Muthannā, were repulsed by Persian troops. The check proved to be only temporary, for after a number of raids had been carried out under the direction of Omar, with the object of wearing down the opposition, a new advance was made, and a victorious battle in October 635, at Buwayb near Kūfa, succeeded in restoring Muslim confidence. Further south in Iraq, at a point near the mouth of the combined Tigris and

Euphrates stream, the riverside town of Ubulla[1] was captured in the same year, thus preventing the Persians from receiving reinforcements from the province of Fārs. The Byzantine defeat at the Yarmūk released a considerable body of Muslims for service elsewhere, and a number of them were sent by Omar to reinforce his army now fighting east of the Euphrates.

Their first action was to recapture the city of Ḥīra, which had failed to keep the pact made with the first Muslim raiders under Khālid ibn Walīd, "the Sword of Allah". This success was followed by the storming of the immensely strong fortress which the Persians had at Qādisīya, and the way now lay open to the Persian winter capital of Madā'in (the twin cities of Seleucia and Ctesiphon). It fell after a siege in July 637, and the Muslim commander found it a convenient centre for numerous profitable raids into surrounding territory. However, the Caliph Omar, who tempered his genius for tactics with a large amount of discretion, considered that Madā'in was too far advanced into enemy territory to form a good base for operations, and he commanded a withdrawal to a point nearer the Arabian frontier. By this step the lines of communication were considerably shortened and he was able to enforce his instructions that no further raids were to be made to the east of the Tigris.

The order did not prevent an advance along the Tigris banks to the northward. Accordingly, by 641, the whole of western Iraq and Mesopotamia as far as Mosul was in Muslim hands, and raiders had advanced into Armenia. They could have done little more than rob the Armenians of their movable property; for the conquered people retained not only their religious liberties, feudal institutions and system of land-holding, but even a certain power to defend themselves against oppression. However, their social system, which made every family an independent unit, prevented the country from organizing and permitted the Arabs to pour in.[2] For similar reasons, in other parts of Mesopotamia force compelled submission to the Arabs, who allowed those of the inhabitants of the raided territories who so wished to remain in their old faiths —Zoroastrianism, Christianity or idolatry.

[1] Near it in 17/638 Omar founded the city of Baṣra.

[2] See J. Laurent, *L'Arménie entre Byzance et l'Islam depuis la conquête arabe jusqu'en* 886 (Paris, 1919).

In the rest of the belt of territory lying between the Caucasus and the Taurus the inhabitants eagerly embraced Islam, and there the faith made rapid strides. West of the Taurus, however, it found as many difficulties as in Armenia. Possibly the comparative nearness of Byzantium heartened the men of Asia Minor to resist the invaders, and in any event long familiarity with Greek domination must have made them unwilling to adopt new masters. The first raid into Asia Minor would appear to have been made in 20/641[1], and resulted in the capture of some booty. Successive years saw other expeditions, each penetrating further into the peninsula until in 652 the Arabs came within sight of Constantinople. But the Muslim base never advanced further than Antioch, into which the Caliph Mu'āwiya (661–80) put a Persian garrison, and, in spite of the fact that for several years Muslim troops wintered in the heart of Asia Minor and even on one occasion attacked Smyrna, their foothold was a precarious one. So far as permanent occupation was concerned, no progress was made in the years following, and no serious attack was made on Constantinople until 717, when an attack was launched by Maslama, brother of the Caliph Sulaymān.

After a march through Asia Minor, in which he had stormed a number of cities, the Arab commander wintered in Roman territory and after reinforcement by some fresh troops sent by the Caliph from Mesopotamia advanced on the capital. Simultaneously a fleet of ships commanded by 'Umar ibn Hubayra approached from the west so as to cover the shores of the Dardanelles and the approaches to the Bosphorus. This fleet was of service in ferrying a large number of troops across to the European side of the Straits, where Maslama entrenched himself strongly, with a view to starving the capital into surrender if he could not achieve his purpose by direct assault. Although during the siege he had the assistance of naval reinforcements from Egypt and Syria, his force was inadequate. His vessels were destroyed by fire-ships employing the mysterious and awe-inspiring "Greek fire", and an exceptionally hard winter combined with the difficulty of obtaining supplies of food and clothing to slay his men by hundreds. The siege had lasted thirteen months when its hopelessness was realized by the new Caliph, Omar II (717–20), who ordered

[1] Ṭabarī, I, 2594.

a retreat. "The March of the Arabian cavalry over the Hellespont and through the provinces of Asia", says Gibbon, "was executed without delay or molestation; but an army of their brethren had been cut to pieces on the side of Bithynia, and the remains of the fleet was so repeatedly damaged by tempest and fire that only five galleys entered the port of Alexandria to relate the tale of their various and almost incredible disasters."[1]

The Arabs never gained either Byzantium or Asia Minor, though other Muslims did so in due course. In the tenth century, a succession of three great Byzantine generals, Nicephorus Phocas, Zimisces and Basilius—forced them to retreat from various cities in Asia Minor and Syria. The ninth-century historian Balādhurī, in his *Futūḥ al-buldān*[2] ("The Conquest of the Lands"), speaking of the limits of Syria on the north, says that in the days of Omar and 'Uthmān the frontier was marked by Antioch and other cities of the kind afterwards called *'awāṣim* ("defences" or "strong points") by Hārūn al-Rashīd. "The Muslims", he continues, "used to raid the territory beyond as they now raid the country beyond Tarsus. And between al-Iskandarūna (Alexandria by Issus) and Tarsus, the Romans had fortresses and armouries like those by which Muslims pass today." The tenth-century Byzantine generals were able to drive the Muslims out of some of these "strong points" which had been in Arab hands since the days of the first Caliph Omar, and they were not regained until the arrival of the Seljūq hordes in the century following.

In dealing with the fortunes of the Muslims in Asia Minor, we have gone ahead in time more than three centuries and we must return to see how it fared with them in other lands. The Caliph Omar's cautious policy in the advance into northern Persia had induced him to order a withdrawal to the Euphrates after the successful attack on Ctesiphon. The effect was to encourage Iranian counter-attacks of such fury that he was soon forced to come to a decision whether he would retreat entirely from his project or take active measures to secure the gains he had already made. If he meant to crush the enemy and retain Muslim prestige, the only course open to him was to resume the invasion of Persia. His army's eagerness for action encouraged him to this decision,

[1] *Decline and Fall*, ed. J. B. Bury (London, 1896–1900), VI, 9.

[2] Ed. de Goeje (Leyden, 1866), p. 163.

and he accordingly gave his men on the Euphrates authority to advance and ordered the governor of Baṣra to invade Khūzistān, the province watered by the Kārūn river at the head of the Persian Gulf. From Oman the governor sent an expedition across the Gulf to seize the islands lying off the coast of Fārs, and then to advance on to the mainland. Both projects were successful. The large island of Abarkawān was captured and also a number of cities on the mainland, amongst them Tawwaj, Sābūr, Iṣṭakhr (the ancient Persepolis) and Arrajān.

To the north, in Iraq, the advance into Persia was pressed by the forces from the Euphrates base at Kūfa along the ancient highway leading from Babylon to Khurāsān. The year 640 saw the capture of Ḥulwān, a city lying in the pass which carried the road across the Zagros range on to the Persian plateau. Then by slow stages the Arab invaders moved forward, keeping to the line of the Khurāsān highway, until they had passed the mountain of Behistūn (with the famous inscription carved upon it by Darius), and had reached the plain of Nihāwand. It lay at the foot of the Alwand mountain which guards the approach to Hamadān on the west and south, and here they were met by all the forces that the Persian king, Yezdigird III, could muster. His troops had already been defeated by the Arabs at Qādisīya on the Euphrates, and the reverse, with the loss of his capital at Ctesiphon, had warned him of what the result might be if he failed to stem the advance. Nihāwand would settle the fate of his empire, and accordingly every city and village had been compelled to send all its males of fighting age to swell the ranks of his army. The men came reluctantly, and, although greatly outnumbering the Arabs, fought unwillingly and were easily routed by the invaders, who were wild to plunder the rich country and all the more eager to destroy the Persians because of their hatred of an enemy differing in faith and blood from themselves. Yezdigird's difficulties were at the same time increased by the simultaneous attack which was being launched against his territory in the province of Khūzistān by Arab warriors under Abu Mūsā al-Ash'arī, governor of Baṣra. When battle was joined at Nihāwand, therefore, the Persian troops broke and fled, and the panic-stricken king fled into hiding.

Persia, however, was too large a country and its population too unyielding in nature to be conquered immediately by the forces of Islam. Besides, the various local dynasties and the priests of the old Zoroastrian faith had too firm a hold to be overthrown at the first assault. The Caliph Omar soon discovered the fact, and after the battle of Nihāwand no immediate effort was made at systematic subjugation. Instead, Omar found it expedient to divide the conquered provinces between the commanders of the military camps at Kūfa and Baṣra, who were to hold the defeated Persians in check, to collect tribute from them, and, if possible, extend the area to be put under contribution. There was no wholesale conversion to Islam. Although they were not entitled to the privileges of "The People of the Book", the Zoroastrians were too numerous to be denied them, so that payment of poll-tax for long relieved them of the necessity of changing their faith. Yet many became Muslims either for reasons of expediency or because they were weary of the tyranny of the Magian priesthood, and their numbers gradually increased. But it was not until the tenth century or even the eleventh that the whole of Persia became Muslim.

Though it was not possible immediately to secure the absolute submission of the whole country to the central government in Arabia, the military occupation of Īrān was pressed steadily forward. After Nihāwand, the commander sent out by the authorities at Kūfa continued the advance along the Khurāsān highway, and after crossing the Alwand range by what is now known as the Asadābād Pass, he seized the important cities of Hamadān and Rayy. His raids off the main path of communication extended far to the north and north-west. Thus, in 643 he invaded the province of Ādharbayjān, routed at Qazwīn a force of Daylamites who had left their homes on the southern shores of the Caspian Sea to stem his advance, and raided Erivān and Ararat in Armenia.

In 644 Omar was assassinated by a Persian Christian who had applied to him without success for protection against the general who commanded the Muslim force in northern Persia. But neither the change of Caliphs nor the frequent revolts in the recently occupied territories interrupted the spread of Islam. The east of Īrān was conquered in the Caliph 'Uthmān's reign by a number of simultaneous expeditions sent and directed from Baṣra. One after another the greater cities in the vast province of Khurāsān submitted, until, by 652, the towns of Herāt, Nīshāpūr,

Bādghīs and Sarakhs had been occupied and the province of Sīstān overrun. Two years later, Fāryāb, Jūzjān and Tukhāristān had fallen.

Possession of lands in the invaded territories was subject to two rules. Where the inhabitants had submitted peacefully they were allowed also to keep their lands, for by a wise stipulation no Muslim warrior was permitted to seize and possess conquered territory for his own purposes. The occupiers were allowed to retain their possessions on payment of a land-tax (*kharāj*) and a head-tax (*jizya*). They could even sell their estates to one another, though not to one of the conquering Muslims. Where the inhabitants had had to be subdued by force, their lands became confiscate to the public purse for the common benefit of Muslims, of whom no individual was allowed to possess any, the original occupiers remaining to cultivate the soil—which could not be sold—on condition of surrendering a portion of the yield. The only stipulation made with the conquered peoples was that once Islam was embraced there could be no return to the old faith. Apostasy meant death.

As has been indicated, the invaders were not uniformly successful. Here and there diplomacy had to come to the aid of armaments, and a Persian *marzubān*, or district overlord, would be allowed to retain a modified sovereignty on payment of the poll-tax, or even without, if his position were strong enough. Apart from the official operations, there was going on all the time a good deal of lesser campaigning. Arab clans fought on their own account for plunder, and without caring very much what happened in the semi-pacified regions they left behind them, and with a certain amount of independence at that distance from home Arab generals pushed ever further eastward. In 661 or 662, after the Caliph Mu'āwiya—the first of the new dynasty of the Umayyads—had come to the throne, there was launched the first Muslim raid on Kābul, followed by an expedition which brought Balkh, the ancient Bactria, to its knees.

As a measure of the fluctuating fortunes of the invaders, it must be noted that in the four years following 640, the annals record persistent outbreaks of rebellion in Khurāsān, coupled with native opposition so strong as to put a stop to the progress of conquest for the time. It is probable, though there is no record of it, that the Arab forces may have had to withdraw temporarily to ground which they held more securely. By the year 644, however, they had recovered sufficient strength to subdue the rebels and to advance again. Ghazna was taken, and a year later Kābul was more decisively stormed, yielding twelve thousand converts to Islam. Even so, Khurāsān could not be considered anything more than raiding territory, and it remained as a whole unsubdued in spite of the efforts of Ziyād, "the son of his father", who governed both Baṣra and Khurāsān with the same mailed fist.

To the west of Arabia, the riches of Egypt and also its vulnerability had been very evident to the Muslim leaders from the first, and a descent upon it at the earliest opportunity was inevitable. As in Syria, the inhabitants of the land had been left sullen and resentful by Roman rule and by ecclesiastical tyranny from which they were eager to escape by any means possible. It was with relief, therefore, that they heard of the advance of a Muslim force, and they made scarcely a show of resistance. The attackers were under the command of 'Amr ibn al-'Āṣ, who had left to his son the siege of the city of Caesarea in Cilicia (which fell in 640) and advanced on Faramā (Pelusium), the key of Egypt, with an army of 3500 mounted men. There a stand was made by the Byzantine garrison, but the place was soon occupied. It is not certain if 'Amr had the support of the Caliph Omar for what he was doing. One account declares that the Caliph rebuked his general for leaving his post without permission in order to undertake what promised to be a more lucrative campaign. This would be in the right tradition of Omar's policy of cautiousness. But another account definitely states that the Caliph himself ordered the advance on Egypt. In any case, after the temporary check at Faramā, the small Muslim force marched rapidly across country to the Nile, which they reached at a point named by them "al-Fuṣṭāṭ", now Old Cairo. Reinforced there by drafts numbering ten to twelve thousand men, they finally defeated the Romans in battle near Heliopolis and having marched down the Nile occupied Alexandria, the capital, in 641.

Certain correspondence that passed between the Caliph and his general in Egypt is quoted by the historian Ṭabarī and throws a considerable light on the Muslim attitude to the conquest of Egypt, as well as other foreign lands. There is no reason to doubt the general truth of the letters, and even if Omar is not the writer of the one attributed to him, its tone is appropriate to what we know of his policy. In reply to a question sent to him by the Arab commander as to whether he ought to accept an offer made by the defeated governor of Alexandria to pay tribute in exchange for Alexandrian prisoners, Omar tells the general to accept. "I prefer tribute", he says, "to loot, which is divided up and soon disappears." But also he bids his general lay down the condition that the Alexandrian Christian prisoners, who, like the majority of the Egyptians, were Copts, are to be given the choice of adopting or rejecting Islam. If they chose the former alternative they were to be treated in all respects as Muslims; if the latter, they were to pay the poll-tax demanded from Christians. The general wrote back to say he had complied with the orders sent to him, and at the same time described his feelings and those of his men while the prisoners were deciding whether to keep their old faith or adopt the new one. When a man chose to become a Muslim the Arabs "cheered louder than when they captured the city of Alexandria"; when one remained steadfast in his Christianity, they were as gloomy and angry as if one of their own men had deserted to the enemy.[1]

Many Copts living in the neighbourhood of Muslim camps were doubtless persuaded to the step of conversion by a desire to escape both heavy fiscal dues and definite social disabilities, which became greater with the passage of time. Yet the majority of the inhabitants of lower Egypt were still Christian in the ninth century. By the middle of the fourteenth, the position had changed, and by the census of 1947 fewer than a million out of Egypt's nineteen million inhabitants were Copts.

To the west the territory between the North African desert and the Mediterranean Sea offered no obstacle to Muslim advance. The Berber inhabitants of the Pentapolis (Cyrenaica), whose religion was still in the stage of animism, were utterly distinct from the Greek colonists of the cities in civilization and outlook. To them one conqueror was no worse, and could be no better, than another. They submitted to the Muslim terms without any great struggle, although some of the inhabitants of cities such as Barqa, which in 642 fell to 'Amr ibn al-'Āṣ, the general in Egypt, were compelled to sell their children in order to find money to

[1] Ṭabarī, I, 2582 f.

pay the poll-tax on non-Muslims. In 643 'Amr besieged the city of Tripoli, which fell in the following year. Shortly afterwards, the death of the Caliph Omar removed the ban which he had placed on further movements westward. In 647 and the next year, Muslim raiders were able to descend on North Africa and Waddān, and, within the twenty years afterwards, the Pentapolis had become territory settled almost exclusively by Muslims. Greek colonies were repeatedly attacked and steadily the Muslim forces moved north and west. In 675 they founded the city of Qayrawān, whence after hard fighting they occupied the city of Ifrīqiya[1] in 681. Every step now made was against strong resistance. The Berber inhabitants of the region today known as Tunisia, the majority of whom are said to have been Christians or Jews, fought the invaders with determination, and those upon whom Islam was forced are said to have apostatized a dozen times.[2] An outbreak at Qayrawān is typical of many. There a Berber "sibyl"[3] roused such animosity against the Muslims that they were forced for a time to evacuate the city, which was destroyed. Her triumph only lasted until reinforcements could reach the Muhammadans, who routed her and her supporters and reoccupied the city. It took twelve years from the first occupation of Qayrawān to reach the city of Carthage (which did not fall until 687), whose Greek inhabitants fled to Sicily or Spain.

The year 708 marks an epoch in the military occupation of North Africa. It was then that Mūsā ibn Nuṣayr, who had been appointed its governor, launched the first of his attacks on the territory allotted to him. By his day, Islam had come to mean something more to the Arab warriors than an adjunct to plundering expeditions. Accordingly, when Mūsā appointed his freed slave, Ṭāriq ibn Ziyād, to the governorship of Ṭanja (Tangier), he sent with his army, which was composed almost entirely of Berbers, a teacher to instruct them in the Koran and the essential duties of Islam.[4] Its influence, when it once took hold in this territory, was powerful enough to make North Africa one of the most fanatical of Muslim lands, and such it has remained ever since.

[1] Froissart's "Africa"; also called "Mahdīya" by the Moors.
[2] Cf. Ibn Khaldūn, *Al-'Ibar*, tr. MacGuckin de Slane in *Histoire des Berbères*.
[3] *Kāhina*. Ibn Khaldūn says she was a Jewess (*op. cit.* p. 208).
[4] Ibn al-Athīr, under A.H. 89.

Up to the time which we have now reached in the narrative, the Arab raiders had confined themselves, with few exceptions, to campaigns which did not involve any long passage by sea. They were not good sailors and they lacked transport. These handicaps, however, had not prevented them from making short dashes across the sea when any material advantage was to be gained. Thus, the island of Rhodes was raided in 32/652–3, the capital city being attacked and the famous "Colossus" carried off. Later on, for a period of about eight years (673–80),[1] a Muslim "colony" was established on the island, provisioned from Syria and apparently a thorn in the side of the Byzantines, whose ships were attacked at sea and cut off from their base. The cause of its withdrawal was that its protection proved too difficult, so that it was a constant source of anxiety to the Muslim authorities. The coast of Sicily was raided in the same year as the first attack on Rhodes, and the raid was repeated in 45/665, when the Muslims are said to have penetrated to Syracuse, from which they carried off a number of prisoners as well as gold and silver images from the churches.[2] At an even earlier period (in 27/647–8), Cyprus had been raided, and in 653, after the Cypriots had aided the Greeks in an attack on Muslim settlements on the Syrian coast, the Caliph Mu'āwiya stationed a garrison of twelve thousand men on the island.

Mūsā ibn Nuṣayr also, in the same year (708) that he launched his campaign against the Berbers of the western portion of North Africa, had sent a successful expedition against Majorca.[3] Consequently, it is no cause for wonder that when he reached what are now called the Straits of Gibraltar he refused to consider them an obstacle to an attempt on the riches of the Iberian peninsula.

The first raiding party was sent to the Andalusian coast in 710, and the spoils which it brought back from Algeciras were such as to encourage a renewal of the venture in the following year, when Mūsā sent his Berber freedman Ṭāriq with a stronger force. So greatly had the country been weakened by jealous quarrels between reigning princes and by the corruption of the priesthood, that leadership was entirely lacking, and so little opposition was made to the invaders that they were allowed to penetrate far into

[1] See Ṭabarī, II, 158.
[2] L. Caetani, *Chronographia Islamica* (Rome, 1912 ff.), A.H. 45.
[3] Ibn al-Athīr, IV, 427.

Andalusia. They swept aside the feeble attempt of Roderick of Toledo[1] to stay their advance, and in a very few years they overran all the peninsula with the exception of the mountainous province of Asturias on the southern shore of the Bay of Biscay.

The year 719 saw them pouring over the southern part of Gaul (Septimania) and occupying the cities of Carcassonne and Narbonne. When Avignon fell in 730, its new governor, 'Abd al-Raḥmān, envisaged a prospect of himself as conqueror of the whole of Gaul, and began the process of conquest by leading an army down the Garonne and capturing Bordeaux. From there he was marching across to the Loire with the object of seizing Tours, when Charles "The Hammer", son of Pépin d'Héristal, met him at a place "between Poictiers and Tours",[2] and defeated him (732) so decisively that no further Muslim effort was made to subdue France. Usually, the result of the battle of Tours is declared to have been that the Saracens were driven permanently out of the country. As a matter of fact they retained Narbonne for a time, and its governor was able in 734 to cross the Rhône, sack the city of Arles and even recapture Avignon. According to the historian Maqqarī, the Saracens of Languedoc also established themselves in strong positions on the Rhône, and from Narbonne made raids into the Dauphiné, where they destroyed a number of churches. No further expeditions across the Rhône are reported after 739, but Narbonne continued in the hands of the Muslims until, after twenty years more of their domination, the natives revolted, killed the garrison, and definitely ended the alien rule of their country, although raids from Spain still continued.[3]

We have noted the farthest limits to which Muhammadan arms penetrated in the west, and we must now return to the east in order to observe what progress was being made there by the armies and the faith of Islam. It has been seen that in the province of

[1] Until lately, historians accepted the traditional view which placed the site of the battle on the banks of the Guadalete (Wādī al-Ladhdha) near Jerez de la Frontera. Recent scrutiny of the evidence has shown that the site of the battle-field was much further south, at the junction of the little river Barbate (or Guadbeca) with the lake of La Janda. Cf. *Cambridge Medieval History*, II, ch. vi and xii.

[2] The cities are seventy miles apart, but no research has yet discovered the exact site of the battle.

[3] For the Muslims in France, see M. Reinaud, *Invasions des Sarrazins en France* (Paris, 1836).

Khurāsān their success was by no means uniform. The province was, in fact, never completely settled and pacified by the Arabs nor were its boundaries properly defined, for the reason that the garrisons by which the land was held were constantly being called upon to repel the attacks of Turks from across the Oxus river or of dissatisfied native Persians. They, in their turn, were not free of their own difficulties. For them Islam had come to cut across, or even displace, older loyalties, and those who embraced the new faith were ready to side with their new brethren in religion rather than with their blood relations or their old quasi-feudal lords and masters. Yet the older loyalties continued strong enough to deter many from conversion to Islam, and it was only when the cities of Nīshāpūr, Merv and Herāt became established strongholds of Muhammadanism and began to exercise an influence as nurseries of Muslim teaching, that the conquerors were able to move with any confidence out of their well-guarded fortresses. Even so, the risks they ran were great and they had to keep close watch on their lines of communication. With proper precautions, al-Ḥakam, the amīr of Khurāsān, was able in 47/667 to invade the territory of Khūr in the south-east of his province, and also to lead an expedition against Khwārazm (Khīva), to the south of the Aral Sea. Two years later Balkh was taken, and being the nearest great city to the Oxus river, which so far had set a bound to Muslim endeavours in that direction, it became a base for operations in Transoxiana. That territory was at the time composed of five parts; Sughd (the ancient Sogdiana) with its two capitals of Bukhārā and Samarqand; Khwārazm, covering the Oxus delta; Saghāniyān on the Upper Oxus, to the south-east of Khwārizm; Farghāna on the upper Jaxartes; and Shāsh at the river's outflow into the Aral Sea.[1]

The first raid across the Oxus was made in 671, after which year forays became frequent, although the raiders did not venture to winter in Transoxiana until Salm ibn Ziyād's governorship of Khurāsān (681–3). Very largely, the difficulties of the Muhammadans in these campaigns, launched against objectives so far removed from their base, were due to physical reasons. The majority of the attacking troops were unaccustomed to the severe cold they encountered and were hampered by the amount of warm

[1] Cf. le Strange, *Lands of the Eastern Caliphate* (Cambridge, 1905), p. 443.

clothing they had to carry with them, whilst in Bukhārā they had to fight in mountainous territory—a form of campaigning with which they were unfamiliar. In a measure also the inter-tribal jealousies of the Arab warriors who undertook these campaigns were responsible for the tardiness of their progress. On the other hand, they were helped by the dissensions amongst the invaded peoples, who had for long been split into two by difference in race between the governing and the governed. The subjects were Iranians in origin, speech, and ways of life, while the rulers were Turks, whose home was east of the Jaxartes river and who came only for the purpose of exacting tribute.[1] It was with them that the newcomers had to contend for supremacy, and the reason is accordingly clear why no combined front was presented to the Muslim invaders, who found a number of small principalities at feud with one another. Even so, the results so far as the spread of Islam and the Muslim empire were concerned were at first negligible, for the Arabs, like the Turks, were content with plunder, leaving more permanent concerns to take care of themselves.

More than anyone else it was the commander Qutayba ibn Muslim (appointed governor of Khurāsān in 705), who consolidated the Muhammadan position in Transoxiana, and it was he who first definitely established the Arab power there. Usually he waived Omar's rule that only Muslims could bear arms in invaded territory, and he incorporated in his troops fighting men of the conquered peoples. Further, he permitted the native rulers to continue in their office so long as they paid tribute, only stipulating that each prince must be supervised by an officer appointed by him (Qutayba). In various districts the governor placed "colonies" of Arabs, which became centres of Arab and Muslim life and teaching but in which the original inhabitants were allowed to remain, even with some kind of independence under their own authorities. Amongst the most important stations of the kind were Samarqand, Khwārizm and Bukhārā, where strong garrisons were lodged. Arab tolerance here did not go to the extent of leaving intact the Magian fire-temples, which were destroyed wholesale. During the progress of the war, the storming of Paykand (765)—a market town containing large stores of arms and armour—proved of immense benefit to the Arabs, only very few of whom

[1] Cf. J. Wellhausen, *Das arabische Reich* (Berlin, 1902), pp. 261 ff.

were sufficiently equipped with the accoutrements of war. In addition to the material gain, the victory provided encouragement for further efforts, which were successfully made in spite of stubborn opposition from the Turks. It ought not to be forgotten here that Ḥajjāj, the masterly and determined governor of Iraq, to whom Qutayba was responsible, was carefully watching events in the distant campaign and used all his influence to urge his general on. Qutayba's first attack on Bukhārā was, however, repulsed and he returned across the Oxus to Merv. In further attempts he had to face the prince of Sughd, who came to the aid of the Bukhāran king, but the Arab general's own pride, stimulated by Ḥajjāj's commands, at last (in 709) forced a victory, the Sughdians making peace independently and agreeing to payment of tribute.

In 711, the year in which Spain was invaded, Qutayba led an expedition into Sīstān, the easternmost province of Persia. While there he received a call for help across many hundreds of miles of territory from the king of Khwārazm, who had been attacked by a younger brother eager for power. The Arab general undertook the long march, and having successfully given his aid on terms satisfactory to himself, he set out again on another expedition, this time against the Sughdians, who had remained consistently hostile. He hoped to take them unawares and break through their lines to their capital of Samarqand. But his hopes were not altogether fulfilled; for though he was able to storm the city and capture a large amount of treasure he had to encounter fierce opposition and lost a great many of his men. In part, the defence was due to the princes of Shāsh and Farghāna, whose territory lay beyond the Jaxartes. Despite the terms of peace laid down after the storming of Samarqand, Qutayba could not forget the hostile part played by these princes, and determined to exact vengeance at the earliest opportunity. This came in 713, when Muslim troops were, for the first time, led across the Jaxartes. They overran the lands of the two enemy princes and some are even said to have raided Kāshghar, which was then in Chinese territory, and to have penetrated even further into China.

The historian Ṭabarī,[1] who is the authority for this statement, explains that when Qutayba approached the Chinese frontiers,

[1] II, 1275 ff.

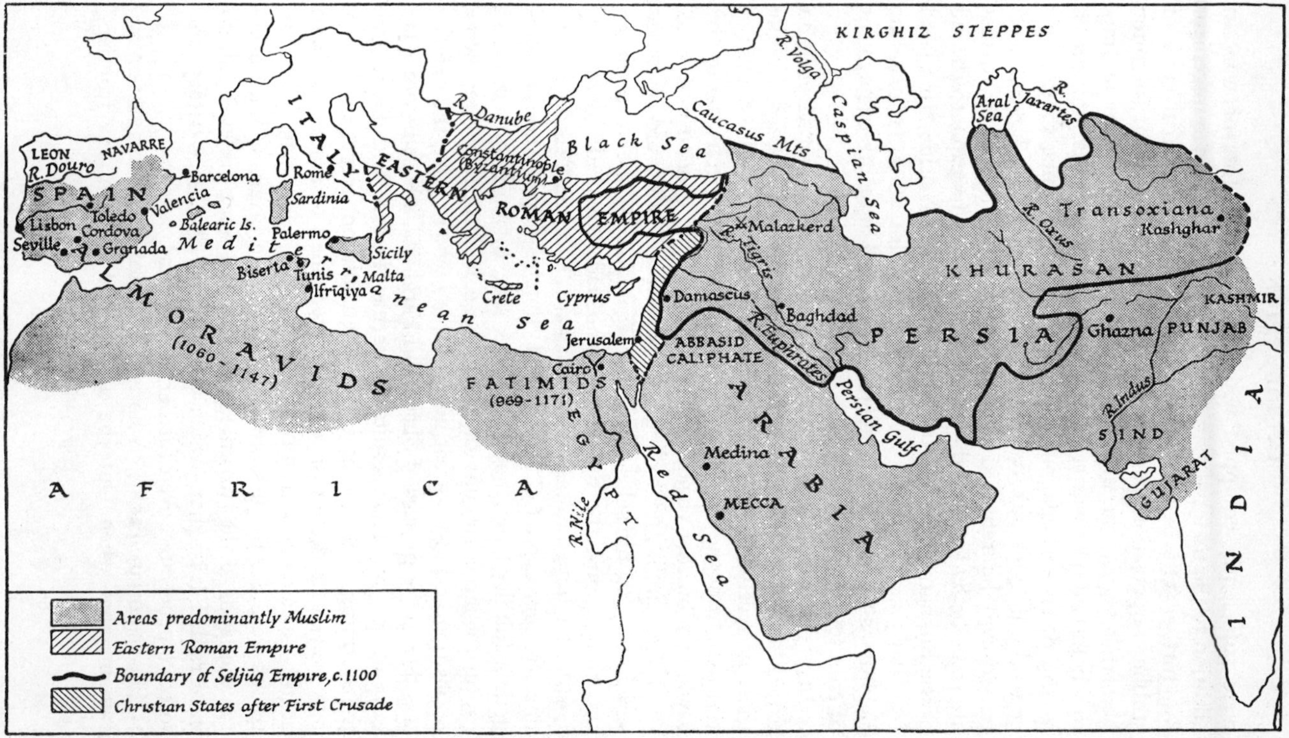

I. The Extent of Islam *c.* A.D. 750

the Celestial Emperor sent him a message with the request that he would dispatch to the Chinese court twelve men of rank who could expound the faith of Islam. If Ṭabarī's statement is to be believed, the reception of the emissaries by the Chinese emperor was by no means friendly, for he dismissed them with the threat that if his land were invaded the consequences would be terrible for the invaders. However that may be, it is certain that no regular invasion of China was attempted from the direction of Persia, and Qutayba's incursion marks the furthest limits to which Muslim troops advanced into central Asia. Not long after it was made, the new Caliph appointed his own nominee to be governor of Khurāsān. Qutayba refused to yield his place and was slain in battle as a rebel.

Like nearly all the earliest expeditions of Muhammadan forces into unconverted territory, Qutayba's campaigns in Khurāsān and Transoxiana had achieved very little for the faith of Islam. The spread of the religion had to be encouraged in ways other than that of force, and we find the Umayyad Caliph Omar II [717–20], a zealous Muslim, offering a remission of taxes to converts. To Jarrāḥ, his governor in Khurāsān, he wrote: "Remit the poll-tax to anyone who turns in prayer towards Mecca". This step seemed so simple a method of avoiding taxation that numbers of the population hastened to adopt the new faith—with disastrous results to the revenue. Jarrāḥ reported the unexpected and undesired consequences of this simplification of the religious demands on converts, and suggested that circumcision should be the test. Omar, however, refused to follow the suggestion, replying that "Allah sent Muhammad to summon men [to Islam] and not to circumcise".[1] When Jarrāḥ further persisted in his belief that only the sword would pacify Khurāsān, the Caliph removed him from office.[2]

A similar conflict between the claims of the faith and those of the royal treasury took place in 728, under the Caliph Hishām, when a governor of Khurāsān, Ashras ibn 'Abdallāh, planned to convert all the inhabitants of Transoxiana to Islam by offering freedom from taxation as an inducement. The Muslim missionaries

[1] Ṭabarī, II, 1354.

[2] Balādhurī, *Futūḥ al-buldān*, p. 426. For a full discussion of the measures taken by Omar II to reconcile the claims of the faith and the state revenues, see H. A. R. Gibb, "*The Fiscal Rescript of 'Umar II*", in *Arabica*, II (Leyden, 1955), 1–16.

who were sent out were so successful that protests were raised not only by the revenue officials, whose perquisites depended on the sums they collected, but also by the local chieftains (the *dihqāns*), who had reason to fear considerable harm to their own prestige if the democratic faith of Islam took too firm a hold on the peasantry. The arguments of the treasury officers were at last able to convince the governor that since the Arab garrisons in Persia depended on the revenues collected locally, they would soon be reduced to starvation if all taxes were remitted. He accordingly reimposed the *kharāj*, or land-tax, on everyone who had formerly been liable to it and whether they had submitted to the test of circumcision or not. The result of this change of policy was wholesale rebellion, which for some years lost the Arabs the whole of Transoxiana except small regions about Dabūsīya and Samarqand. Some of the lost territory was regained for Islam—though not for the Umayyad Caliph Hishām, then reigning at Damascus—when in 734 the supporters of the claims of the Prophet's family, the 'Alids, rose in revolt against Hishām and gathered adherents by promising "to observe the contract made with the adherents of the 'protected' religions [here mainly Zoroastrians], not to levy tribute on the Muslims, and not to oppress anyone".[1]

Once the earliest campaigners had made good their foothold in the invaded territories, these gradually ceased to be mere treasure-houses for plunder. In the great camps such as Bukhārā and Samarqand in Transoxiana, as earlier at Kūfa and Baṣra in Iraq and at Fusṭāṭ (Old Cairo) in Egypt, there were teachers and legists, and soon schools of ecclesiastical law and of grammar were set up to answer the demands of those who wished for a true interpretation of the meaning of the Koran. These schools eventually became the nuclei from which Islam derived its strength and from which gradually the occupied regions were converted.

By the time the Abbasid Caliphs were settled on the throne, the first powerful wave of Muslim conquest had spent itself. It was not long before the inhabitants of great stretches of occupied territory began to realize that they were remote enough from the capital, Baghdad, for the Caliph's authority to be disregarded with impunity. At the extremities of the Caliphate, in Persia, Spain, and North Africa, usurpers who could find military support set

[1] W. Barthold, *Turkestan* (London, 1928), p. 190.

themselves up as independent monarchs, though in Persia at any rate nominal allegiance continued to be paid to the Caliph, whose name was still mentioned in the *khuṭba* (bidding-prayer) during the Friday assemblies in the mosques and was still impressed on minted coins. Loyalty here did not go to the extent of paying tribute or acknowledging the Caliph's guidance in any matter that affected local interests.

The decline of the temporal power of the Caliph at Baghdad did not diminish the power of the faith of Islam as a whole, which kept on multiplying the number of its adherents. At the same time, the total area submitted to Muslim domination was continually on the increase, reaching its maximum in the sixteenth and seventeenth centuries of our era, even though some of the gains were counterbalanced by losses, both of territory and adherents.

The rise and decline of Islam in the Mediterranean islands are typical as showing how political conditions have affected the numerical strength of its adherents. The early raids on Rhodes, Sicily, Cyprus, and Majorca have already been noticed. Crete was attacked in 54/674 by 'Abdallāh ibn Qays, who remained on the island with his troops during that winter. Thereafter, however, it was left alone except for periodical raids until 210/825, when a party of Moors took refuge there after an unsuccessful rising against the Umayyad Caliph al-Ḥakam at Cordova, and overwhelmed the inhabitants of the island. It remained in Muslim hands until 961, when Nicephorus Phocas restored it to Byzantium. For the best part of the following seven centuries Crete was Christian, and then, between the years 1645 and 1669, Turkish invaders once more subjugated the island to Islam, although some of the inhabitants persisted in their Christianity. The Turks have always been amongst the most active of the Muslim peoples, and if they are not greatly given to pious exercises, they are bigoted believers in their faith and excellent fighters in its cause. Possibly for that reason they have not, until the most recent times, shown great capability in the art of government, so that subject peoples, whether of the same faith or not, have suffered at the hands of the ruling classes. The Cretans were not exempt from their misgovernment, and therefore when in 1821 the Greeks broke out in revolt against Turkish domination, the non-Muslim Cretans headed by the Sfakiot mountaineers rebelled in sympathy with them. Turkish efforts to subdue the outbreak were unsuccessful, and when at last peace was made the island was transferred for a period of ten years (1830–40) to the government of Muhammad 'Alī of Egypt. It was then restored to Turkey, in whose power it remained until August, 1920, when, by the Treaty of Sèvres, it was put once more into the hands of its old masters the Greeks. With every change of master the dominant faith has changed, and at the present time the great majority of the islanders are non-Muslim.

By a parallel series of events, Cyprus, first raided in 27/647, remained subject to Muslim depredations until 966, when Nicephorus Phocas regained it. Various changes of fortune transferred it from the hands of the Byzantines to those of the Venetians, who were in their turn compelled, in 1571, to yield it to the Turks, whose government here was no better than in Crete. Finally, under a convention arranged with the Sulṭān 'Abd al-Ḥamīd II in 1878, Cyprus was handed over for administrative purposes to England, who formally annexed it on the declaration of war with Turkey on 5 November, 1914. At the census of 1946, the number of Muslims on the island was less than a fifth of the total population, the proportion having been very greatly reduced since Turkey resigned its full dominion.

Further west, Sicily was subjected to raids from the Muslims in Egypt between 652 and 670, and even Syracuse was laid under tribute, but the island continued to owe allegiance to the Roman Empire until 826. In that year the rebel Euphemius, who had risen against Roman authority, was himself thrust aside by Moors from North Africa.[1] They chose Palermo as the base of their operations, and during the next fifty years gradually reduced the western part of the island. It took longer to drive all "Christianity and loyalty to Cæsar" out of Syracuse and to exterminate the religion and language of Byzantium. That end was achieved in 962, when with the fall of Taormina the island became entirely Muslim.[2] It then provided a convenient base for operations against Italy. Ships from Palermo engaged with others from Biserta and Tunis in North Africa in transporting Moorish and Berber

[1] Cf. Ibn al-Athīr, A.H. 201.
[2] Cf. *ibid.* A.H. 351.

warriors against the cities of Calabria and Campania, and if there had been any efficient or united leadership of the Muslim forces there can be little doubt that the whole of Italy would have fallen to them. As it was, the amīrs of Sicily insisted on their own independence, while the Moors had long before thrown off the authority of the Baghdad Caliph. Accordingly, to use the words of Gibbon, "the design of conquest was degraded to a repetition of predatory inroads",[1] and Italy escaped even temporary occupation by the Moors. In Sicily their dominance remained until the coming of Roger of Normandy in 1060, since which time the faith of the island has been Christianity.

Malta fell to Muslim attacks at about the same time as Sicily. But the hold of the Muhammadans on Malta was stronger than on Sicily, and their influence more firmly established, for until the present time the language of the Maltese continues to be a dialect of Arabic. The island was lost to Islam in 1090, when the Normans conquered it, but they were permitted to continue living there until the middle of the thirteenth century.[2]

It will be appropriate after this cursory glance at the history of Islam in the Mediterranean islands—which traditionally are included in Europe—to examine how Islam fared on the mainland of the continent from the time when the adherents of the faith were driven out of France. Their failure to hold the territory they had won was in great measure due to their numerical weakness and to the fact that they always regarded the south of Spain as their base. It was only there that they ever achieved real strength and had any degree of permanence, and nowhere else in the peninsula were they able to parallel the brilliance of the Umayyad dynasty (founded by a member of the house that had ruled at Damascus) which held sway at Cordova over a period of nearly

[1] There had been previous attacks on Italy. In 846, a fleet from the African coast sailed up the Tiber, and Muslim warriors actually entered Rome, whose churches, including that of St Peter, they plundered. The invaders were driven out by Guy of Spoleto, but three years later another attack was launched by the Aghlabid monarch, Muhammad I (840–56), who sent a fleet from Sardinia. The ships cast anchor sixteen miles from Rome and prepared to land troops. By the efforts of Pope Leo IV, an alliance of maritime states was hastily formed to counter the threatened attack, and the defenders, aided by a great storm, were able to rout the Muslim fleet at the battle of Ostia. Cf. Gibbon, *Decline and Fall*, ed. Bury, II, 40 f.

[2] Cf. *Encyc. of Islam*, s.v. and *Z.D.M.G.*, LVII, 905, n. 2.

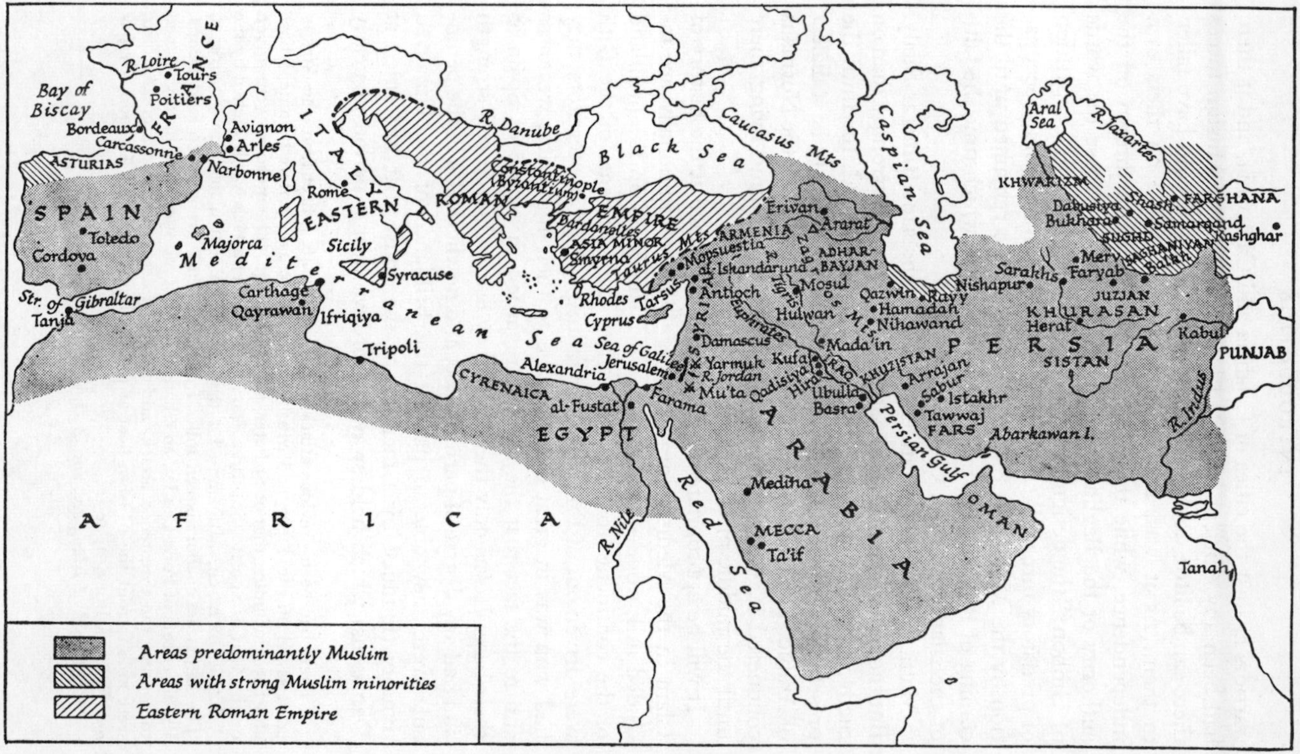

II. The Extent of Islam *c.* A.D. 1050

three centuries, from 756 to 1031. The achievements of the members of this dynasty more than compensated for the comparative smallness of their empire. Particularly under 'Abd al-Raḥmān III, who ascended the throne in A.D. 912, their country prospered. "Agriculture, industry, commerce, the arts and the sciences, all flourished. . . . Cordova with its half-million inhabitants, its three thousand mosques, its superb palaces, its hundred and thirteen thousand houses, its three hundred bagnios, and its twenty-eight suburbs, was inferior in extent and splendour only to Baghdad."[1]

In the north of Spain and in Castile the conquered territory was held in subjection by means of military camps and there was never any peaceful settlement of Muslims here as there was in Andalusia and Valencia. In Cantabria Islam gained no foothold at all, and it was there that as early as 751 the Gothic prince Alfonso, joined by the Galicians of the Atlantic coast, began his counter-campaign to drive out the Moors. He succeeded in dislodging them from the provinces of Old Castile, Leon, Asturias and Galicia, territory which they never regained in spite of a serious effort made early in the tenth century. The work of pressing back the intruders was continued with the aid of the Christians of Toledo and Navarre until, at the beginning of the tenth century and mainly by the endeavours of Alfonso III of Leon, who died in 910, the Muslim power had retreated as far south as the Douro and even, in one direction, as far as the Guadiana.

It must not be understood that even in northern Spain there was unremitting conflict between Spaniard and Moor. Friendship between them was common, often leading to intermarriage, and before the power of the Church began to assert itself many a Christian knight adopted Islam out of motives of policy or economy, since being a Muhammadan meant comparative freedom from the burdens of taxation. It was only when the influence of the Spanish church grew strong that Muslim opinion hardened in opposition and religious antagonisms lent bitterness to the racial differences between the two peoples, both of whom regarded Spain as their home.

The Moorish retreat was as slow as its advance had been rapid. Not until the fall of the Umayyads had the Muslims weakened sufficiently to give the Christian Spaniards any hope of dislodging

[1] R. Dozy, *Spanish Islam*, tr. Stokes (London, 1913), pp. 445 f.

them. But then, in 1085, under Alfonso VI of Leon and Castile, the Christians regained Toledo, for which there was great mourning amongst all Muslims. The loss was not brought about by force of arms, but by a treaty that had been arranged between the Christian king and Yaḥyā, who was ruler of Seville and a member of the 'Abbādid dynasty, into whose hands the power of the Umayyads had fallen on their collapse. By the terms of the treaty, Yaḥyā was to have received Valencia in return for Toledo, but before this part of the bargain could be carried out, Yūsuf the Almorāvid, a North African prince, had appeared on the scene with ambitions of his own. He had been summoned by the 'Abbādid prince to aid against the Christian encroachments, but discovering the weakness of the dynasty which he had come to help, he seized the crown from them (1090) and turned the fight against the Christians to his own advantage. Within the next twelve years he had asserted his authority over the whole of Moorish Spain,[1] with the exception of Toledo, which remained permanently in Christian possession. Spanish territory in Muslim hands now became a province of North Africa, with which connections had always been close and from which came members of the dynasty of the Almohades, between 1145 and 1150, to oust the Almorāvids from the throne. They did more than that, for they succeeded in recapturing for Islam large tracts of territory ravished from their predecessors by the kings of Castile, Aragon and Portugal. Their continued success so alarmed the Pope, Innocent III, that he proclaimed a Crusade against the infidel. The Almohades were unable to oppose the combined Christian forces brought against them and, in 1212, at the battle of Las Navas de Tolosa (in the Sierra Morena), they were routed.

The Iberian peninsula, north of a line drawn from Lisbon through Sierra Morena to Barcelona, was now freed from Muslim domination. Thereafter the centres in which Muhammadan princes held sway were confined to Seville, Cordova, Jaen, Granada and Valencia.[2] Their rivalries helped the Spaniards to still

[1] He seized Valencia in 1102.

[2] The history of the Balearic Islands (Majorca, Minorca and Yābisa (Ivissa)) is bound up with that of Spain at this period. An expedition was made against them by the amīr Abu'l Ḥasan al-Mujāhid, who had charge of the city of Dānia (Denia) in 407/1016 (Ibn al-Athīr, IX, 405), and the islands were subjected to Muslim domination. They remained so until 1228, when Jayme I of

further reconquests and between the years 1238 and 1260, Fernando III of Castile and Jayme I of Aragon were able to seize the districts of Valencia, Cordova, Seville and Murcia, leaving to the Moors only the province of Granada, which comprised the country about the Sierra Nevada and the sea coast from Almeria to Gibraltar.[1] Their independence in these circumstances could not long be maintained, even though assistance was forthcoming from other provinces which were now nominally Christian but could not forget how recently they had acknowledged Islam. The Castilian crown imposed its suzerainty on the remaining Moorish princes, who exercised now only a shadow of their former authority. With the marriage of Ferdinand and Isabella and the union of the kingdoms of Aragon and Castile, no hope remained of continuing even a show of Muslim sovereignty. In 1492, Granada, the last Moorish capital in Spain, was overthrown and its prince Boabdil (Abu ʿAbdallāh) exiled himself to Africa. The vast majority of his subjects, unable to follow the path he chose, had perforce to remain behind and acknowledge allegiance to their Christian Majesties. Many, either from choice or compulsion, were converted to Christianity, but, where force had been used to obtain conversion, any conformity could only be outward. Such nominal Christians, who in secret practised the ritual of their old faith came to be known as Moriscoes, and it was only with their expulsion in 1610 that Islam was finally banished from the Peninsula.[2]

While the Muhammadan faith was slowly retreating from the west of Europe, it was finding an increasingly stronger foothold at the other end of the continent, where the ʿUthmānlī (Osmanli) or Ottoman Turks were fighting their way in. To understand how this was made possible, it is necessary to retrace our steps, in time between three and four centuries and in space across the Asiatic continent to the furthest limits of Persia. There the weakening of the Caliph's authority had permitted the rise of more than one small kingdom which claimed independence of him and had begun

Aragon captured Majorca, the other islands being retaken within the following three or four years. It was from the Balearic Islands that the last great Muslim raid on Sardinia was led, by al-Mujāhid, who subjugated the island after decimating the Christian population (Ibn al-Athīr, *ibid.*).

[1] S. Lane-Poole, *Moors in Spain* (London, 1887), p. 218.

[2] For details of the history of the Moors in Spain, cf. Lane-Poole, *Mohammadan Dynasties* (London, 1894), and Dozy, *Spanish Islam*.

to contend with one another for leadership. By the latter part of the tenth century we find the independent dynasty of the Sāmānids, who had ruled over a large part of Khurāsān, already losing their hold over their vassals. One of these, Subuktagīn, had been the slave of Alptagīn, himself a slave of the Sāmānids; but by the exercise of his considerable military talents, he had achieved freedom and taken possession of a very large tract of territory. This he bequeathed to his son Maḥmūd, who at first continued, as his father had done before him, to acknowledge the suzerainty of the Sāmānids. But the young warrior possessed an even greater share of soldierly talent than his father. Before many years were over he had extended very considerably the area of his possessions, which stretched on both side of the Indo-Iranian frontier, and he had thrown off all allegiance to his overlords. He was now a king in his own right and with a capital established at Ghazna, in what is now Afghanistan, he began the series of campaigns into India which has made his name famous in Muslim history. His victories resulted in the permanent accession of the Punjab to the realm of Islam and the subjection of the kingdom of Gujarāt to Muslim raiders.

To the north Maḥmūd overran Kashmir and added Transoxiana to his other possessions. In these lands across the Oxus, a certain family of Turks, known as the Seljūqs, had come into prominence during his reign. Originally inhabitants of the Kirghiz steppes of Central Asia they and the Turkoman tribes over whom they held authority had migrated to Transoxiana during the days when Islam was establishing itself there, and had embraced the new faith with enthusiasm. In the struggles between the Sāmānids and Maḥmūd, complicated by the hostile operations against him of the Īlak Khāns of Turkistan, the Seljūqs also had intervened to their own profit. The death of the great amīr of Ghazna in 1030 gave them an opportunity for further acquisition, and within seven years they had driven the Ghaznawid Mas'ūd out of his father's possessions in Khurāsān, Transoxiana and other provinces of Persia, leaving him the lands east of the Indo-Persian frontier and themselves reaching westwards until in 1055 their chieftain Tughril Beg entered Baghdad itself and received from the feeble Caliph, to whose office he paid allegiance, the title of Sulṭān.[1]

[1] Cf. the admirable summary of Seljūq history in Lane-Poole's *Mohammadan Dynasties*, pp. 149 ff.

Tughril Beg's horde had possessed themselves of territory whose inhabitants had in great majority embraced Islam. Another section of the Turkomans, under the leadership of Sulṭān Alp Arslān in Asia Minor invaded Roman territory. At the battle of Malāzkerd (Manzikert) (1071) they routed the Byzantine forces which attempted to oppose their march and captured the Roman emperor Romanus Diogenes, with the result that, as Gibbon says, "in this fatal day the Asiatic provinces of Rome were irretrievably sacrificed",[1] and the way into Asia Minor lay open. Between the years 1074 and 1081, Sulaymān ibn Qutulmish succeeded in founding the powerful kingdom of Rūm or Qonya in the centre of Asia Minor, which has remained Muslim ever since.

In the course of two centuries after Sulaymān, the kingdom he had founded was dismembered, parts for a time being recaptured for Christianity by the armies of the First Crusade or of the Byzantine rulers, the Comnenoi. The rest was divided up amongst various claimants, one of whom was the Osmanli amīr Ertughril. He and his clan, as a reward for services rendered in battle to the Seljūq sulṭān Kaykobād II (1245–54), had been granted a small tract of territory near the ancient Dorylæum in Phrygia. The diminutive kingdom grew and prospered, until, in 1308, the Mongols of Persia overran the whole of western Asia, wiping out all independent authority and leaving a trail of desolation behind them. But the Osmanli Turks retained the germs of recuperation, and in 1326 Ertughril's descendant 'Uthmān, the eponymous ancestor of the dynasty, was able to re-establish the kingdom. His son Orkhān extended his territory to Brusa, which he made his capital, and restored to Islam the city of Nicæa, which had been lost to it since the days of the First Crusade.

Islam had now reached the middle of its eighth century, when its possessions in western Europe had shrunk to the Kingdom of Granada. But it was to have its revenge in eastern Europe. Orkhān's son Murād I (Amurath) came to the throne in 1360. Three years previously the Ottoman standards had been carried across the Dardanelles into Europe and the Byzantine emperor Palæologus brought to his knees. Murād, after fighting and winning the battle of the Maritza in 1371 overran nearly the whole of the country south of the Balkans, including the greater part of

[1] *Decline and Fall*, ed. Bury, VI, 240.

Thrace, Bulgaria, Macedonia and Serbia. His success decided him to transfer his seat from Asia to Europe, and accordingly Brusa was forsaken in favour of Adrianople, which remained the Ottoman capital for ninety years. By 1386 his generals had subdued the territory as far west as the river Vardar and as far north as Nish in Serbia and Monastir in Bulgaria. The loss of the battle of Kossovo in 1389 cost the Serbians all the rest of their country. Murād died the same year, leaving his empire to his son Bāyazīd I (Bajazet), known as *Yilderim*, "The Thunderbolt", who continued his father's successes, invading the northern part of Bulgaria along the Danube and overthrowing the fortresses that had barred his way across the great river into Hungary. In spite of a crusade which had been declared against him he was able to raid the country, incidentally defeating the crusaders at the battle of Nicopolis in 1396.

There was then no obstacle in the way of Bāyazīd's invasion of Greece, which within the next three years he added to his empire. But he had now to call a halt to his career of conquest, and retrace his steps to face an opponent more formidable than any he had yet encountered. This was the bloodthirsty Tīmūr-i Lang (Tamerlane) the Tartar, who had marched across Persia with his hordes and had overrun the Turkish province of Anatolia. With very little effort he routed Bāyazīd at the battle of Angora in July 1402, and took him prisoner. The story that the conqueror put his captive into an iron cage and carried him about with him wherever he went is well known, but probably has little truth in it.[1]

Tīmūr's ravages utterly destroyed more than one kingdom, but Turkey was not amongst them. With astonishing vitality it once more asserted itself within the next half century, and in 1453 Constantinople was at last captured for Islam by the Sulṭān Muhammad II. There the Turk still retains his foothold in spite of the numerous efforts made, down to the most recent times, to oust him, and it remains a monument of Islam's past imperial greatness in Europe.

The capture of Byzantium was but a step to further acquisitions in Europe. In 1475, the Crimea was annexed and the islands of the Ægean became Turkish territory, as also, for a time, a part of

[1] Cf. E. G. Browne, *Persian Literature under Tartar Dominion* (Cambridge, 1920), p. 198.

Italy which included Otranto. Under Sulaymān the Magnificent (1520–66) the Ottomans came further westward, penetrating deep into Christian Europe. Belgrade fell to them in 1521, and after "The Destruction of Mohács" (1526), in which King Louis of Hungary attempted "with a mere handful of hastily levied troops, consisting mainly of unarmed peasants",[1] to oppose Sulaymān's numerous and highly disciplined forces, Hungary was reduced to the state of an Ottoman province. In spite of a long siege (1529), however, Vienna stood firm against the invader, but he was able, nine years later, to defeat "pope, emperor and doge together" in a naval battle off Trevesa. Sulaymān also drove the Spaniards out of North Africa, where they had presumed to lay their grasp on Muslim territory.

The lands won by Sulaymān in Europe were retained for over a century, and the map of Europe after the Peace of Westphalia (1648), which brought the Thirty Years' War to a close, shows the Turks in possession of territory stretching from the Asiatic side of the Crimea almost to Vienna. It was rarely that they forced Islam upon their newly acquired subjects, to whom, as a rule, they proved tolerant masters, though always regarding Christians as an inferior caste. And yet, except in Hungary, where Ottoman occupation was purely military and Islam never took hold, the inhabitants of the conquered lands, whether from political motives or out of conviction, eagerly embraced the faith of the dominant race. Indeed, the Muhammadans of Bosnia, Bulgaria and Albania came to be known as highly fanatical devotees of their faith, with Islam as the factor dividing them from their Christian fellow-countrymen, though they were of the same blood.

It was not to be expected that the European powers would submit without a struggle to the supremacy of the alien. Even if religious differences had not led to revolt in the conquered countries, the inefficiency of Turkish administration must have provoked it, for the central authority was far too occupied with military projects to concern itself greatly with the government of acquired territories, and much was left to officials, who feathered their own nests at the expense of both the sulṭān and his less fortunate subjects. Hungary was first to throw off the yoke,

[1] *The Turkish Letters of Ogier Ghiselin de Busbecq*, tr. Forster (Oxford, 1927), p. 72.

striking at the Turks in 1664, when they had been defeated in battle by the Austrians at St Gothard. Next, John Sobieski of Poland drove them out of Podolia after their second—and disastrous—attempt to gain Vienna by siege (1683). This defeat was followed successively by the loss of Croatia to the Austrians (1684) and of Buda-Pesth to the Hungarians, who regained their capital after it had been in enemy hands for a hundred and forty-five years. The second battle of Mohács (1687) resulted in another Austrian victory, by which Hungary was freed from the Muslim. An Ottoman counter-attack a year later was repulsed, and the Austrians succeeded in capturing Belgrade and occupying the greater part of Bosnia. After a national revolt in Dalmatia they also captured various Danube fortresses, Nish too falling into their hands.

While the Turks were having to face Austria on the north, they were being simultaneously attacked from the south by the Venetians, who successfully invaded Greece, capturing the Morea in 1686, and, a year later, the Piræus and Athens, together with a large tract of surrounding country. By the two treaties of Karlowitz (on the Danube) signed in 1698 and Passarowitz, signed in 1718, between Austria and Venice on the one side and Turkey on the other, the latter was forced to surrender all that remained in her possession of Hungary, together with large parts of Wallachia, Serbia and Bosnia. As compensation, however, she received back the Morea from the Venetians.

The results of the war with Austria made it evident to the Turks that any further adventures into Europe would be bitterly opposed and that in future they would have to be content to remain on the defensive if they wished to hold what was left of their European possessions. It was not long before their strength was put to the test by Russia, with whom they were nominally at peace. The Russians seized a number of forts near Azoff and after invading the Crimea captured that fortified town itself. The surprise war was ended by the Treaty of Belgrade (1739), by the terms of which Azoff was destroyed. Turkey, however, this time gained more than she lost, Belgrade, and much of Serbia, Bosnia and Wallachia being restored to her. As might have been expected, the terms were not palatable to Russia, who waited her opportunity to reverse them. It did not arrive for thirty years, when Catherine II, in spite of Turkey's protests, agreed with Frederick the Great of Prussia on the partition of Poland, causing Turkey to attack. But the results on this occasion were not favourable to the Muslim power, which lost the Crimea to the Russians and had also to accord them the right, which they eagerly sought, to protect the Christians in Constantinople. In return, the Treaty of Kainarji (1774) guaranteed the freedom of the Tartar Muslims in the Crimea and Bessarabia, while various parts of Wallachia, Moldavia, Bessarabia and Georgia which had been previously taken from Turkey, were restored to her suzerainty. Still another attack on her ended, after the Treaty of Jassy (1792), in fixing her eastern boundary along the line of the river Dniester.

To summarize the position of affairs at the beginning of the nineteenth century it may be pointed out that the Turkish empire in Europe consisted of the stretch of territory known as European Turkey together with (1) the modern kingdom of Greece, except the Ionian islands, and (2) the present states of Bulgaria, Albania and Yugoslavia, while across the Danube, Moldavia and Wallachia acknowledged her protection. The total area was estimated at 238,000 square miles with a population of 8,000,000.[1] Since then, by one treaty after another following wars of aggression, these possessions have very greatly diminished. Out of all the lands once held in Europe, Turkey now (1955) owns Eastern Thrace with her old capitals of Adrianople and Constantinople,[2] and of the islands in the Ægean only Imbros and Tenedos; most of the rest, including Crete, having been handed over to Greece.[3] In the latter country the number of Muslims has been greatly reduced, mainly by the interchange of populations carried out in accordance with the Mudania convention of 1922, and Hellas has become almost totally Christian and European.

The foregoing survey of the history of Islam in Europe will have shown that the warriors of the faith advanced in two great waves which very rapidly reached the flood and then very slowly receded. Both waves left their traces, but of different kinds. In Spain not a

[1] W. Miller, *The Ottoman Empire* (Cambridge, 1936), p. 16.

[2] In 1950 the population of European Turkey numbered 1,626,229.

[3] After some military and diplomatic vicissitudes, the islands were assigned to Italy by the Treaty of Lausanne (24 July 1923), and her possession of them, including Castelrosso, was subsequently recognized by the Great Powers. There were still Muslim schools in the islands, but Italian was taught in them for four hours a week, as in the schools of other denominations (*The Times*, 20 May 1929). Greece regained the occupied islands from Italy in 1947.

Muslim has survived, but Moorish architecture and many Arabic elements in the Spanish language remain as monuments to the magnificence and power of Muhammadan rule. In eastern Europe, the evidences of Turkish dominion are to be sought in the various populations who have remained true to Islam. The earlier Turks were a fanatical people whose one enthusiasm was their religion, and sooner or later the peoples subject to them embraced their faith, either from reasons of expediency and influenced by the zeal of the dominant race, or, more rarely, under pressure, as was the case with the Janissaries, all of whom were originally sons of Christian parents.[1]

The greatest body of Muhammadans left in Europe today are people of mixed Turkish or Turcoman and Tartar origin, subjects of Russia. The majority of them inhabit the Kirghiz Qazaq steppes from the Caspian to the Sea of Azov, and many till recently lived in the Crimean peninsula and in the Caucasus, as well as at Kazan, Orenburg, Ufa and other cities.[2] There are also some Polish-speaking Muslims of Tartar origin in Lithuania. Their ancestors, the Golden Horde, under the leadership of Bātū, the grandson of Chingīz Khān, about 1240 occupied the lands watered by the lower and middle Volga. On that river they placed their capital, Sarāy, after a campaign during which they had entered Moscow and Novgorod, burned Cracow and besieged Pesth.[3] In 1272 they embraced Islam, and they have ever since preserved their faith and maintained some kind of national spirit by the cultivation of the Tartar language. Nevertheless, except for the nomads, their ways of living and thinking appear to be entirely Slav; their names are formed after Russian models and they all speak or understand the Russian language.[4]

[1] Apart from the Muslims under Turkish rule in Europe, there are strong Muslim communities in Bulgaria (14 per cent Turks and Pomaks, although 160,000 Turks were expelled in 1951), Yugoslavia (12 per cent, mostly in Bosnia), Rumania and Albania (68 per cent). See further L. Massignon, *Annuaire du Monde Mussulman* (Paris, 1955). The Georgians, on the other hand, have always remained Christian.

[2] Since the first edition of this work was published there have been movements of populations and changes in the U.S.S.R. The Muhammadan press at Kazan on the Volga from which numerous Arabic, Turkish and Persian works at one time issued, is no longer in existence.

[3] Lane-Poole, *Mohammadan Dynasties*, p. 208.

[4] The most recent converts to Islam in Europe are the Abkhazes of the Caucasus, who, until the edict of toleration of 1905, had been nominally

Apart from a few small communities attracted by the teachings of some of the "reformed" sects such as those of the Bābīs, Bahā'īs and adherents of the Aḥmadīya movement, Islam is at a standstill in the western world, or is actually retreating. Political considerations apart, it would seem that the creed of Muhammad the Prophet is not suited to peoples reared in the Greek and Roman traditions and codes, which have shown themselves sufficiently elastic to permit of adaptation to varying needs. As Islam stands at present, purposing to regulate and determine the minutest actions of everyday life, the faith appears on the one hand not to find approval where the individual is allowed a large measure of choice in his social conduct and of liberty in his thinking, or, on the other, where its tenets conflict with strongly held local or native tradition and doctrine.

Elsewhere, in Asia and Africa, where vast numbers of the population submit themselves to the voice of religious authority, the case is different. There the rigidity of the Islamic code is in its favour as conducive to simplicity, and it is there that the strongholds of Islam must be sought, amongst peoples either not given to speculation or else content to regard fulfilment of ritual as an end in itself. Not all such peoples, of course, are Muslim, but it is they who, having been once acquainted with Islam, have most eagerly adopted it and helped in its propagation. The largest groups of Muhammadans today are to be found in Pakistan, India and the Republic of Indonesia.

The new faith came to these regions at a comparatively late date. The earliest Arab expeditions were in extent little more than plundering raids, having scant effect in making new accessions either of territory or converts. Only when Khurāsān was conquered did the Muslim troops gain a way of access to India which they could use with some degree of ease. In that province, as has been described, was laid the foundation of the Ghaznawid empire, which, begun by Subuktagīn, was built up by his son Maḥmūd of Ghazna. After annexing the Punjab he began the process of conversion which turned more than half of its population from Hinduism to Islam. Maḥmūd's idol-breaking exploits at Hindu temples such as Mathurā (1018) and Somnāth (1024) probably

Christians, though of Muslim origin. See T. W. Arnold, *Preaching of Islam* (London, 1913), p. 101.

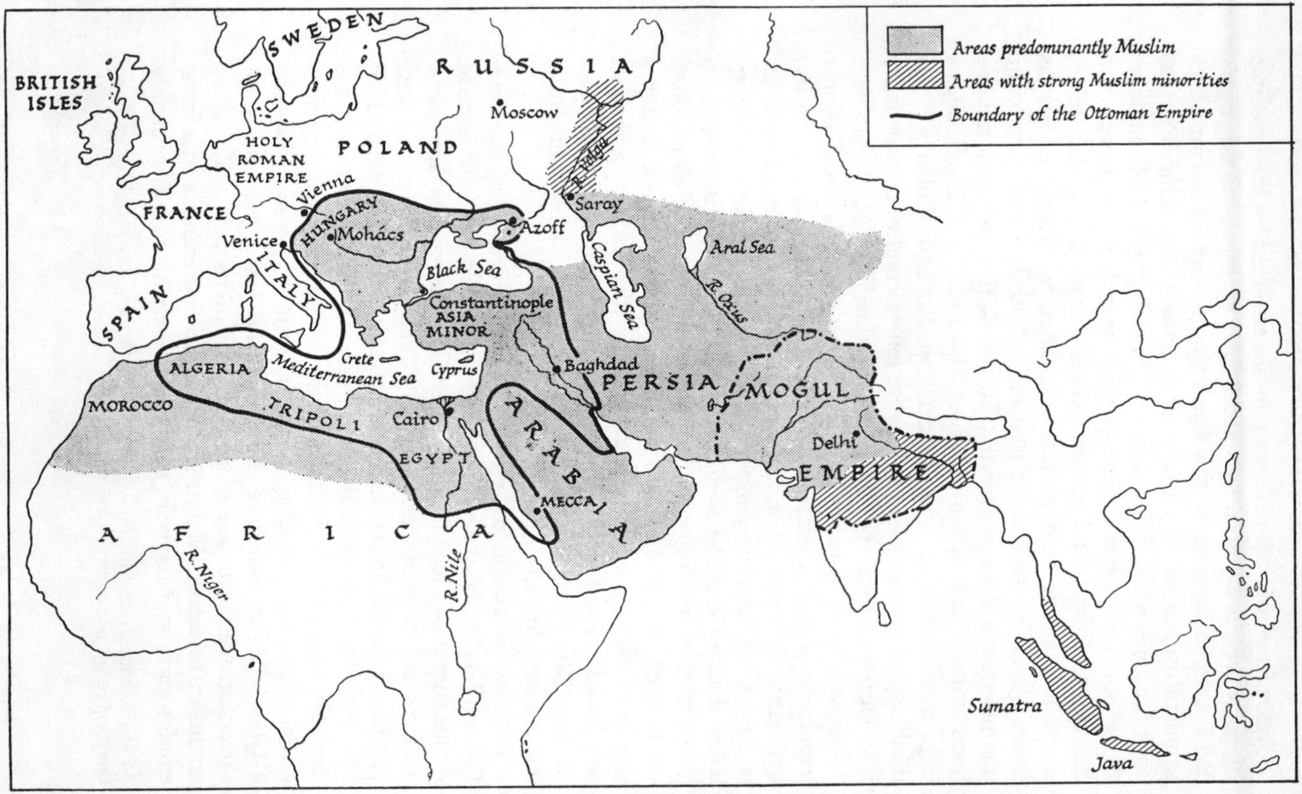
Areas predominantly Muslim
Areas with strong Muslim minorities
Boundary of the Ottoman Empire
BRITISH ISLES
SWEDEN
RUSSIA
Moscow
HOLY ROMAN EMPIRE
POLAND
FRANCE
Vienna
HUNGARY
Mohács
Venice
ITALY
SPAIN
R. Volga
Saray
Azoff
Black Sea
Caspian Sea
Aral Sea
R. Oxus
Constantinople
ASIA MINOR
Crete
Cyprus
Mediterranean Sea
ALGERIA
MOROCCO
TRIPOLI
Cairo
EGYPT
Baghdad
PERSIA
MOGUL
EMPIRE
Delhi
ARABIA
MECCA
AFRICA
R. Niger
R. Nile
Sumatra
Java

III. The Extent of Islam *c.* A.D. 1650

helped very little towards this result, and indeed the stories of them which have passed into Muslim legend may well be in great part apocryphal. However, he made it possible in the Punjab for Muslim traders to sell their wares and expatiate at the same time on the advantages of their faith. His invasions of Kashmīr and Gujarāt effected very little, and were practically forgotten after his death in 1030. The empire too which he founded did not long survive him, the Seljūqs wresting the Persian and Transoxine portions away between the years 1037 and 1045. Still more was lost when the Afghan family of Ghūrids, members of which he had himself dispossessed on his way to the throne, seized and burned Ghazna in 1061. After considerable vicissitudes the Ghūrids were able to extend their acquisitions, and a member of the family, Muhammad Ghūrī marched into India and reduced Sind and Multan (1175). He then took Lahore, where he extirpated the surviving Ghaznawids who had taken refuge there, and advanced against the Chohān Rājputs and their allies. They were able to withstand his first attacks, but in 1192 a victory on the battlefield of Thanesar over nearly all the Rājput princes who had assembled to protect northern India resulted in their territory being subjected to his power. From Peshawar to the Bay of Bengal Hindustān was now under Muhammadan rule. In 1193 the capital was placed at Delhi, whose sulṭāns, beginning with the "Slave Kings" that succeeded Muhammad Ghūrī's short-lived dynasty, held sway as far as the Vindhya mountains in the south.

In the Deccan and Southern India the process of Muslim conquest was begun by the Khaljī Turks, who followed the Slave Kings on the throne in 1290. Most progress was made by 'Alā al-Dīn, but even he did not succeed in converting more than a few Hindus in spite of ferocious regulations designed to crush opposition. It was under him that Gujarāt definitely submitted to Islam, but it took centuries to find many adherents in Bengal and it was not until the reign of Sulṭān Akbar (1556–1605) that it became strong. In Ceylon Islam spread slowly but now (1955) has over four hundred thousand members, generally of Madrasi origin.

After the days of definite conquest the Muslims in India multiplied at a proportionately greater rate than the Hindus, and by 1941, the date of the last census taken before British India was divided into Pakistan and India, the invading force of the early eleventh century had by natural increase, intensive conversions of the local inhabitants and the inflow of other Muhammadan invaders, come to represent nearly one quarter of the total population. As a rule, the provinces situated nearest to western Asia, whence Islam came, or to central Asia, whose vigorous populations embraced and propagated the faith, became more rapidly and more thoroughly Muhammadan than the provinces further south and east. Thus, according to the census of 1921, the Muslims in the North-West Provinces and Baluchistan constituted more than 90 per cent of the population, in Kashmir they were over 75 per cent, and in the Punjab they exceeded 50 per cent, while in Assam only one inhabitant in three hundred was a Muslim.

Bengal proved exceptional. There, according to the 1951 census, more than half of Pakistan's Muhammadan population is domiciled. Geographical proximity to other Muslim lands is, therefore, only one of the causes of the comparatively greater growth of the Muhammadan communities as compared with those of the Hindus. Even more potent causes are the higher vitality of the Muslims (due in some measure to their diet, which does not exclude meat), and the fact that being as a rule town-dwellers and not cultivators in so large a proportion as the Hindus, they are less liable to be caught by famine. Moreover, premature marriage is not so common as amongst Hindus and no restriction is placed on the remarriage of widows. A still more significant cause is a social one, for many of the "untouchables", the outcast group of Hindus, find in Islam a refuge from the stigma attaching to their birth.[1]

The mountainous region of Nepal appears not to have been touched by the Islamic invasion, probably for the reason that the rigours of warfare and of winter in the Himalayas proved too severe for the invaders. Yet there are numerous families of Muslims in Tibet, settled in Lhasa and other towns. Some of them are of Chinese origin and act as butchers for the Buddhist population; others—a more numerous body—have penetrated from Kashmir and gain their living by commerce or in trades of various kinds.[3]

[1] It is interesting to find that for a similar reason Muslim propaganda has found some measure of success amongst the Negro population of the U.S.A. (*The Moslem World*, July 1926, pp. 263–6).

[2] H. Landon, *Nepal*, II, p. 24.

[3] Sir Charles Bell, *People of Tibet* (Oxford, 1928), p. 217; *Journal of the Royal Central Asian Society* (1952), XXXIX, 233–40.

On the Pamir plateau too, there is a small Ismā'īlī community and, if the Soviet Press is to be credited, agents of the Aga Khan penetrated to it in 1952 in order to collect dues.[1]

It was from India that Islam spread to Malaya and the great neighbouring islands of Sumatra, Java and Borneo. The evidence lies in the fact that the "Arabic" alphabet used for Malay is of the Indo-Persian form, and the Muhammadanism of Malaya contains pantheistic and Ṣūfī elements characteristic of Islam in India or Persia and foreign to the orthodoxy of Arabia.[2] There are, however, indications that Arabian traders, probably as early as the ninth century, found their way to the Malacca coast,[3] and when Marco Polo visited Sumatra, which he calls Lesser Java,[4] he found in the seaport towns on its north coast numerous Muhammadans who had been converted by the Saracen merchants that constantly visited these places.[5] The Moroccan traveller Ibn Baṭṭūṭa, on that part of his voyage between India and China, about 1346, found that the inhabitants of the city of Sumuṭra, capital of the island which came to be called Sumatra, were Muslims.[6] Also, Chinese annals of the year 1409 record that the Malays of Malacca were then Muhammadans.[7] From Malacca Islam was introduced into Johore and Achīn, whence it spread in the seventeenth and eighteenth centuries to the Sumatran coast-towns and into the interior.

The first Arab missionary to come to Java after the earliest Indian Muslims was a certain Mawlānā Malik Ibrahīm.[8] He died in 1419 at Grisek, where he had settled, and his name has been preserved on a monument. Like the traders that followed him, he was an inhabitant of Haḍramaut in southern Arabia, and it is they who, by their unofficial missionary activities, were mainly responsible for the spread of Islam in the island. They had been

1 A Bennigsen in *L'Afrique et l'Asie* (Paris, 1952–3).

2 Ibn Baṭṭūṭa, arriving in the port of Sumuṭra, about 1346, was met by notables who bore Persian names: Dawlasa [? Dawlatshāh], Sayyid al-Shīrāzī and Tāj al-Dīn al-Iṣpahānī (*Voyages d'Ibn Batoutah*, ed. Defrémery and Sanguinetti (Paris, 1874), IV, 230).

3 Cf. H. Yule, *Cathay and the Way Thither* (2nd ed., London, 1913), I, 127.

4 Marco Polo's "Great Java" would seem to be the island which we call Java. Ibn Baṭṭūṭa's name for it is "Mul Java" (*op. cit.* IV, 239).

5 *Travels*, ed. H. Yule (3rd ed. London, 1903), II, 284.

6 *Voyages d'Ibn Batoutah*, IV, 229.

7 Cf. R. O. Winstedt, *Malaya* (London, 1948).

8 In Java proper the inhabitants were still unconverted in Ibn Baṭṭūṭa's day (*op. cit.* IV, 239, 245).

driven by scarcity out of their original homes, and having settled in Java and the neighbouring islands of Borneo and Celebes they there founded small states in which their faith spread rapidly. The Dutch settled in the territory in the early part of the seventeenth century and held the government until December 1949, when the Republic of Indonesia was proclaimed, with a Muslim as its first president. Out of an estimated population of eighty millions the majority are adherents of Islam. All the Malays of Malaya are Muhammadans.[1]

The seeds of Islam sown by Qutayba ibn Muslim and his Arab warriors in central Asia towards the end of the first century of Islam took firm hold and the faith became established throughout the immense region afterwards known as Turkistan, comprising Khīva (Khwārazm), Bukhārā, Samarqand, Farghāna and other lands stretching to the frontiers of China and beyond.[2] Even the destruction caused by the Mongol invaders under Chingīz Khān failed to destroy the hold which Islam had upon its adherents, so that in time the Muslim khanates grew up and retained their independence until they were subdued by Tsarist Russia in 1873. Under the Union of Soviet Socialist Republics Muslim territory in central Asia has been divided into the five Republics of Uzbekistan, Kazakhstan, Turkmenistan, Tajikistan and Kirghizia, a sixth being that of Āzarbaijān. In Russia itself there are recognized Muslim areas in the Autonomous Republic of Bashkiria, with its capital at Ufa and the district of Northern Caucasus.

Since the apparent aim of Soviet policy is to make the State the sole object of loyalty and its laws the sole guide to living, there is inevitably some conflict with Islam, which is strong and of long standing in rural and agricultural areas of the Muslim Republics. The Soviet Press is especially critical of the observance of Ramaḍān and Muslim feasts, of pilgrimages to the shrines of saints, and of polygamy. In the old nomadic regions and districts previously industrialized and "Russianized" (e.g. Baku and Ashkabad), the younger people are becoming more and more ignorant of Islamic matters.[3]

In Northern and far-eastern Asia, Islam, mainly because these

[1] Winstedt, *The Malays* (London, 1950), pp. 33 ff.

[2] See Barthold, *Turkestan* (London, 1928), pp. 180 ff.

[3] Bennigsen, *op. cit.*

regions are very difficult of access, has not been adopted to any great extent. The few Muslims are the descendants of Tartar invaders, e.g. the Shaybānī Khāns of Tioumen, who were converted at a comparatively recent date and are best known as the Uzbegs. The nomad Kirghiz, in spite of an earlier conversion, retained their original Shamanism until the middle of the eighteenth century, and their Islam was merely nominal until Tartar mullahs from Kazan—usually sent by Russia for political reasons—built mosques and encouraged a more definite adoption of the faith.[1]

China in some regions proved rather more susceptible to Muslim propaganda, although Chinese hatred of foreign interference has affected its success. The earliest account of Islam would appear to have been brought into the country by traders who came by sea along the coast as far as Hang-chou-fu (Kansu) and founded colonies on the sea-board. They did not penetrate into the interior, where Islam was probably introduced first by the Turks of central Asia, who had racial affinities with the Chinese. The Turks themselves for the most part did not adopt Islam until 960,[2] when many of their clans were converted, doubtless to one or other of the mystical forms of Islam rather than to orthodoxy. The converts imported their new faith into China, but it is highly improbable that it made any considerable advance until Chingīz Khān had extended his empire across Asia.[3] Although he himself was a Shamanist he treated all religions with equal indifference and placed no obstacles in the way of conversions. Even when the road was thus left open, and although Muslims are now to be found in every Chinese province, they only achieved considerable numbers in the west and north, i.e. in Kansu, Sinkiang (Chinese Turkistan), Shensi, Shansi, Chihli and Yunnan.

The latter province would appear to have been the starting-point of Muhammadanism in the empire, for it was here that Qūbilāy Khān (Kubla Khan, 1260–94) appointed as his governor a Muslim named Sayyid-i Ajall, who claimed to be a descendant of the prophet Muhammad. The Sayyid and his son, Naṣīr al-Dīn, seem to have been active missionaries for their faith, which gained numerous adherents.

[1] Cf. *Annuaire du Monde Mussulman* 1955, pp. 56 ff.

[2] Ibn al-Athīr, VIII, 396. Cf. Barthold, *op. cit.* p. 255.

[3] Cf. *Encyclopædia of Islam*, s.v. *China*.

It would appear that some communities were established during the latter part of the Mongol Yüan period and the early days of the Ming dynasty (i.e. during the second half of the fourteenth century); others followed even as late as 1939, when there was an infiltration of Muslim railway-workers. In Inner Mongolia some communities consist of the descendants of native Chinese who defied Manchu laws forbidding emigration beyond the Great Wall and acquired their new religion from Muhammadans who accompanied them. The number of Muslims in China today cannot be established, but it is stated that they form about one-ninth of the population.[1]

Although in dress, appearance and mentality[2] the Muhammadans are said to be indistinguishable from their fellow-countrymen of other religions, and have long been cut off from Muslims elsewhere, Islam has never been regarded in China as a native religion.[3] There are two main sects, the "Old" and the "New", of which the latter appears to be more actively interested in the practice of the faith.[4]

In Japan Islam has made no headway, and probably for reasons similar to those suggested for other peoples not susceptible to Muslim doctrines. The few Muhammadans in the empire are usually emigrants returned from Java.

Following after Asia, the continent of Africa has the largest groups of Muslims, whose numbers there have of late been steadily increasing. Here, as elsewhere, the cause is not to be sought in organized missionary labours, but in the unsponsored voluntary efforts of Muhammadan travellers and traders, whose main object is commerce but who enter into discussion of their faith with everyone they meet in the course of their business. In particular the faith is spread by marriage with native women, who, with

[1] *China Handbook*, 1953–4.

[2] They favour certain occupations such as the keeping of horses for posting. Many are innkeepers and display a water-jar as a sign, betokening that they are Muslims and serve no pork.

[3] It was not until 1931 that the first complete translation of the Qur'ān was made directly from Arabic into Chinese.

[4] See further M. Hartmann, *Zur Geschichte der Islam in China* (Leipzig, 1921); *Oriente Moderno* 1935, pp. 353–64, 425 ff., 483 ff., and 1939, pp. 241 ff.; *Revue des Études Islamiques* 1933, pp. 153–84; Wing-tsit Chan, *Religious Trends in Modern China* (New York, 1953).

their children, become converts to the religion of the pacific invaders.

From the first century of Islam, when the Egyptians and Berbers were converted, the process continued with greater or less speed according to political circumstances and the physical obstacles that were encountered. Along the Nile the faith spread with rapidity as far as Aswān. For some reason, however, it took a considerable time to permeate beyond that, although as early as the year 31/651 the governor of Egypt, ʿAbdallāh ibn Saʿd, invaded Nubia, whose inhabitants had been converted to Christianity in the sixth century and who had retained their independence when the Arabs invaded Egypt. Beyond taking some booty and battering down the church at Dongola the invaders did very little, and whether it was owing to lack of Arab effort or to the tenacious hold of the Sudanese on Christianity, the negroes were still steadfast in their faith well on in the fourteenth century when Ibn Baṭṭūṭa visited them.[1] Even by the beginning of the fifteenth century the Arabs had not pushed their conquests inland further than Aswān and the First Cataract.

On the coast of East Africa Islam had made its mark much earlier. Proximity to Arabia had attracted traders from the peninsula from very early times, and some of the first Meccan converts to Islam had taken refuge in Abyssinia from the persecutions of their fellow-citizens. It was inevitable that the country should come, sooner or later, to attract Muslim attention. By the tenth century, Muhammadans were arriving in strength, and the simplicity of their cult won them the favour of the common people in spite of the fact that these were nominally Christians. Occasionally the chieftains also were attracted to Islam although the rulers tried in various ways to counteract its influence by enforcing Christianity. A struggle between the two faiths could not be avoided and grew to be especially fierce during the reign of the King Ameda Zion (1314–44), who attempted to reimpose Christianity upon those who had shaken it off and to drive the enemy faith into the sea. However, a powerful Muhammadan kingdom, Adal, had grown up on the coast in a part of what is now Eritrea, and its king bitterly opposed the Abyssinians efforts,[2] without much success. For a

[1] *Voyages*, IV, 396.
[2] Cf. G. K. Rein, *Abessinien* (Berlin, 1918), I, 41 f.

time Islam lost ground, but it recovered again to the extent that in the sixteenth century the Muslim king of Adal was able to invade Abyssinia and make converts. From that time the faith has made steady progress, although the rulers have always remained Christian, and many chieftains for social reasons have forsaken Islam. In Somaliland Muslims form the bulk of the population, in Eritrea and the Harar Province about half, in Galla-Sidāma about one-third; but in Abyssinia proper only about ten per cent of the people are Muhammadans.[1] Among the causes given for the spread of Islam among the common people in later times, one is that the Christian priesthood was corrupt and ignorant, and another that the Church had abandoned large tracts of territory and was therefore unable to fulfil its charitable obligations. Further, the superiority of Muslim officials over the Christians in the employ of the Government led to their being treated with greater respect, and persuaded many of the subject people to join the faith which they regarded as having more claims to consideration than the official one.[2] The reforms being made in the Christian church today by the importation of Coptic priests may make a difference to the future of Islam, but for the present it would appear to be finding increased favour in the country.[3]

In a neighbouring part of Africa we find that it was not until late in the fifteenth century that nomad Arabs, following up the course of the Nile, introduced Islam to the negro population of the Sudan. Westward they advanced as far as Lake Chad, while from the sultanates of Zanzibar, Mombasa, Mozambique and elsewhere on the coast, Arab traders forced their way into equatorial Africa. In the Egyptian Sudan the more highly endowed Hamitic-speaking tribes occupying the region between the Nile and the Red Sea in the northern and middle provinces, adopted the faith almost as soon as they became acquainted with it. Amongst them as amongst the Arabic-speaking tribes Muhammadan culture is spreading, and knowledge of it as well as of the Arabic language is gradually finding a way up the Nile and its tributaries.[4]

[1] J. S. Trimingham, *Islam in Ethiopia* (Oxford, 1952), p. 15.

[2] Arnold, *Preaching of Islam*, 2nd ed. (London, 1913), pp. 117 ff.

[3] Rein, *op. cit.* I, 422 f.

[4] The population of the Sudan Republic numbers about eight millions, of whom the majority are Muhammadans. The negroes of the south are generally pagans. Cf. *Annuaire du Monde Mussulman* 1955, p. 280.

In Sudan territory further westward, in the vast region stretching between the Sahara and the coast of Upper Guinea and Kamerun, Islam, in the primitive and schismatical form of Khārijism, came to be known through Berber emissaries from the Sahara, although the Berbers themselves showed little enthusiasm for the faith until the eleventh century of our era. The efforts of the early Muslim conquerors, such as 'Uqba and Mūsā ibn Nuṣayr, had been directed mainly to securing the safety of the invading troops and pressing on the work of filling the Caliph's treasuries. Repeatedly, as has already been noted, the Berbers attempted to drive the invaders back and more than once might easily have succeeded if there had been any cohesion amongst them. As it was, the Muslims remained, and their faith covered the whole of North Africa. Legend says that in the angle between the Mediterranean and the Atlantic (modern Morocco) the natives were converted in comparatively early days by the sons of the 'Alid saint and ruler Idrīs II (died 828), who founded Fez.[1] In fact it took place in the twelfth century, when a general movement of the Berbers southward and westward overwhelmed the native populations, with the result that nearly all the inhabitants of the Saharan regions of the north-west Sudan (i.e. negro) territory adopted the faith of the invaders and became Muslims.[2] In what is now French Sudanese territory, the Mauritanians, Peuhls (Fūla) and Tuareg all profess Islam, although the negro Sudanese properly so called until recent times were animists. Reckoned by districts it may be said that Mauritania, Senegal and French Guinea are predominantly Muhammadan, while the region of Upper Volta is animist. In French West Africa Islam has not yet reached its full development and so far only about a third of the population are Muslims, but they form a vigorous and active community which, from indications available, seem destined to draw further recruits from the tribes professing older beliefs.[3]

In Nigeria, where it dates from the fifteenth century, Islam is the religion of the northern part, the country of the Hausa culture and language. Except for the Kano, the numerous small Hausa

[1] *Annuaire du Monde Mussulman*, 1955, pp. 250 f.

[2] Cf. D. Westermann, 'Islam in the Sudan', *International Review of Missions*, I (1912), 618–53.

[3] Cf. P. J. André, *L'Islam Noir* (Paris, 1924).

kingdoms were not properly converted until the Fūla (or Fūlanī) tribe, under the leadership of 'Uthmān Foudie (? Fawḍī), who was a member of the Qādirī order, took advantage of the internal dissensions in the country, and in 1804, after proclaiming a *jihād* descended upon the heathen from the north. His success resulted in the conversion to Islam of many of the Hausas in the north-west, and his own tomb at Sokoto has come to be regarded by the local adherents of the Qādirī order as a sacred shrine, although the country still contains peoples holding animist beliefs. The Hausa tongue is the *lingua franca* in the eastern parts of West Africa, and partly for that reason the spread of Islam has been facilitated there. The Hausa and Fūla peoples, who are distributed over the northern territory of Nigeria, are nearly all Muhammadan, and through them and the Kanurī practically the whole of Northern Nigeria and the neighbouring French territories with their mixed Berber and negro population, are now Muslim. In southern Nigeria, however, the Ibo elements of the population have proved indifferent to Islam.[1]

Similar conditions have prevailed in the Mende territory of Sierra Leone where also a section of the Fūla people is to be found. With the Mandingo, who are of Bantu descent and also inhabit other parts of West Africa, they have proved to be the apostles of Islam in this region, where the faith is making steady headway amongst the animist population.[2]

The predisposing causes for the advance of Islam in Africa are not different in the main from those which affected its dissemination elsewhere. The inhabitants, whose culture ranked low in the scale of civilization, were easily led to respect the cultural, political and military supremacy of the Muslims who came amongst them, and hence to adopt their social and religious institutions. Thus, to take an example, in Africa as in Java, the Ḥājjī who has returned from pilgrimage to Mecca comes to be regarded with exceptional respect, and excites emulation. Soldiers and traders, intermarrying with the native population, convert their wives and children to Islam, which finds the readier acceptance also amongst the men of the native tribes by recognizing polygamy as necessary, both as

[1] *Annuaire du Monde Mussulman*, IV, 344.

[2] Cf. H. C. Luke, *A Bibliography of Sierra Leone* (Oxford, 1925); K. L. Little, *The Mende of Sierra Leone* (London, 1951).

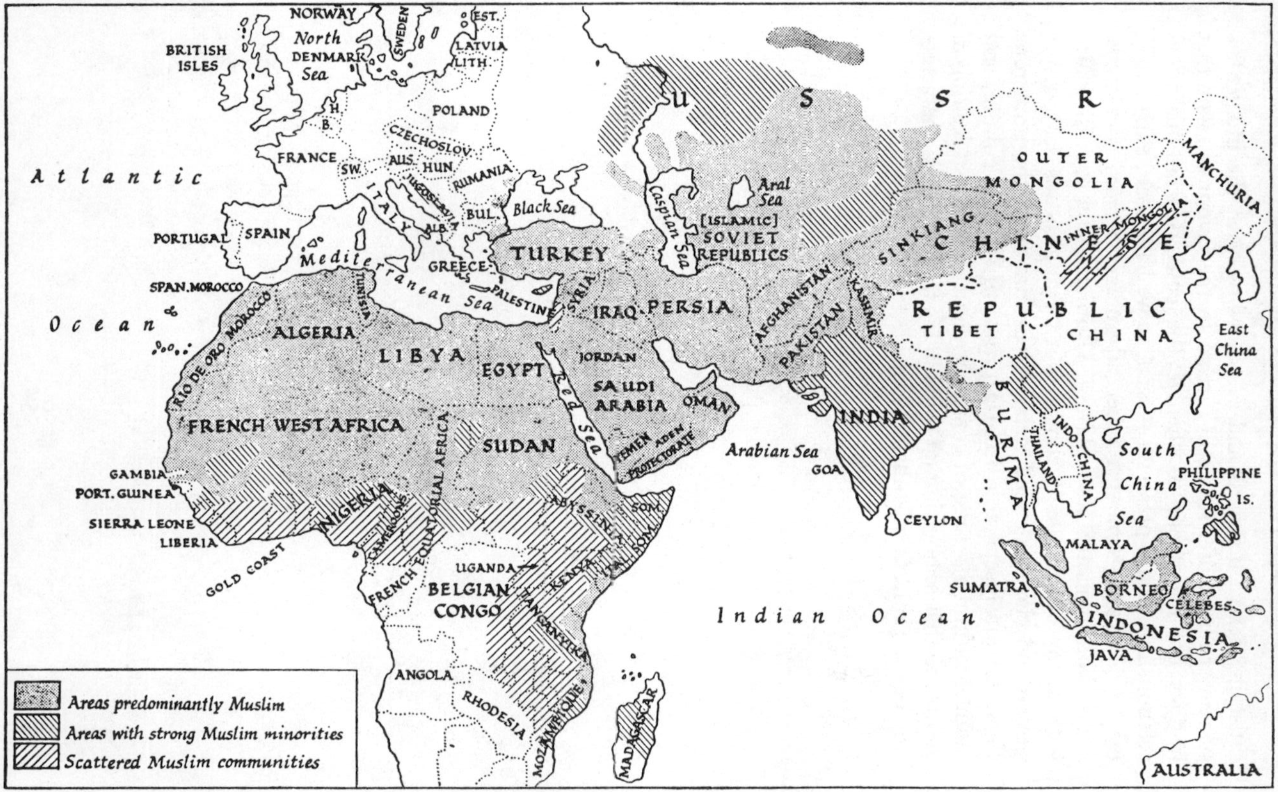

IV. The extent of Islam in A.D. 1955

satisfying sexual demands and as according with the indigenous system of family life. It is still further in the favour of Islam that it does not endeavour to alienate the convert from his tribal relationships, and it preserves—even, as we have seen, enhances—his social status. Amongst other advantages it may sometimes secure him immunity from slavery. Ultimately, by providing him with a way of life which, though not by any means easy, is yet simple and clearly defined, Islam frees him from the numerous vague terrors inseparable from a primitive state of culture, and induces in him a feeling of confidence and self-respect leading in its turn to that unquestioning pride in his faith which is characteristic of the professing Muhammadan.

CHAPTER I

THE GRADES OF SOCIETY IN ISLAM

Adequately to estimate the part played by Islam in the communities which adopted it would require an exact investigation into the social conditions prevailing in each community before and after the introduction of the new faith. It is sufficient criticism of such an undertaking to point out the magnitude of it. Yet much was done by such scholars as W. Robertson Smith[1] and Ignaz Goldziher[2] in clearing the ground, and the results of their labours have been laid freely, and inevitably, under contribution. No attempt will here be made to do more than indicate the principal changes wrought by Islam in the various strata of society amongst the peoples who accepted that faith, and to note the social legislation introduced by Muhammad together with some of the modifications made in it by his interpreters.

The population of Arabia, outside of the few settled communities embedded in it, has throughout historical times been so constituted as to form a number of groups or tribes, very loosely held together either by loyalty to a particular leader or by the assumption of descent from a common ancestor, whether real or legendary. Within each of such groups or tribes, the independence of the individual units—the tents or families—has always been taken as a matter of course, and the head of each unit has been regarded as being in status the equal of every other. In the hands of the heads of families lies the power to elect the *shaykh* or tribal chief, of whom, in theory, no special qualification is required. In actual practice, however, there is normally a strong prejudice in favour of choosing the shaykh from amongst the members of particular families. At the time of the rise of Muhammad, such families held a position of great influence within the community, so that in any claim to authority the factor of birth was considered of paramount importance. Noble ancestry was the supreme test of nobility, and no person whose genealogy was not entirely free of

[1] Cf. *Kinship and Marriage in Early Arabia* (Cambridge, 1885, 2nd ed., 1903). The references in the present work are to the 1st edition.

[2] Cf. *Muhammedanische Studien* (Halle, 1889), I.

hereditary taint—for example ancestors of servile or negro origin[1]—could be regarded as conforming to the requisite standard. Such persons were relegated to the humbler ranks of society and were thus compelled to undertake careers that inevitably marked them as inferior beings.

The concept of tribal aristocracy as one of birth persisted after the coming of Islam, and has continued to be valid. The fourteenth-century philosopher-historian Ibn Khaldūn,[2] basing his generalization on examples drawn from history, lays it down that where tribal *esprit de corps* is strong, no one who is unable to boast of his genealogical connections in the tribe can ever hold command in it; and certainly no stranger can do so. Accordingly, when the Prophet Muhammad first proclaimed his new dispensation, even though he was a full member of his tribe of the Quraysh, his lowly origin, coupled with his humble occupation as a camel-driver, put a serious obstacle in the way of his success. His primary task was that of convincing his meagre following—made up largely of humbler members of society—that the new faith was to make them the equals, if not the superiors, of the unbelievers who had hitherto been regarded with awe as the aristocracy. The latter, however, were in the stronger position at the moment through having all the weight of established custom and tradition behind them.

The Prophet's religious fire was able ultimately to vanquish the chiefs of the old régime, and Ibn Khaldūn proceeds to argue from the subsequent history of Muhammadanism that Bedouins cannot found an empire unless they have been filled with religious enthusiasm by some prophet or saint.[3] Here Muhammad was the prophet and leader—last and greatest prophet of all, according to his own claims—but though he persuaded some of his fellow-Arabs to concede his claims, the older aristocracy of his own tribe, whose supremacy he so obviously threatened, refused for long to yield. Even when Islam had taken hold and he had attained sufficient power to capture Mecca from the Quraysh nobility, their opposition continued. It was then that the definite "revelation"

[1] Cf. *Aghānī* (Būlāq, A.H. 1285), VII, 177.

[2] *Prolégomènes*, ed. Quatremère (Paris, 1858), I, 239 *ad fin.*; tr. de Slane (Paris, 1863–8), I, 276.

[3] *Ibid.* text, 273; trans., 313.

was made to him that birth counted for nothing and that zeal for the faith was the only criterion of honour. "O ye folk, verily we have created you of male and female . . . Verily the most honourable of you in the sight of God is the most pious of you", says the Koran (49[13]) in a section which, although judged by modern critics to have been revealed at a comparatively late date in the career of the Prophet,[1] voices what must have been an essential doctrine from the beginning. The explanation given by the thirteenth century commentator Bayḍāwī is typical of most Muslim opinion on the verse. His comment is: "We have created every one of you by means of a father and mother. All are equal in this and there is no reason therefore for boasting of one's lineage [the old Arab view being that in lineage lay honour] . . . Through piety are souls brought to perfection and persons may compete for excellence in it; and let him who desires honour seek it in piety."[2]

So intangible an element in social organization as a feeling of pride in ancestry was not to be destroyed by edict at one stroke. Equality even amongst all Arabs—and Muhammad could scarcely have had in mind any broader application of this rule at the time when he made his pronouncement—was not conceded by the representatives of the old order until after a bitter struggle. A story told in the *Kitāb al-Aghānī*, the great storehouse of early Islamic anecdote, illustrates the new and the old points of view to a nicety. The prince Jabala ibn al-Ayham of Ghassān, while on pilgrimage to Mecca, had his cloak trodden upon by an Arab tribesman in the crowd that was thronging to carry out the ceremonies of the *ḥajj* and struck the Bedouin a blow in the face. He complained to the Caliph Omar, who summoned the offender and told him he would give his victim leave to retaliate in kind for the blow. "How can that be possible?" asked the astonished Ghassānid. "He is a man of the people and I am a prince." Omar replied: "Islam made you one with him, and you can have no superiority over him except in piety and good works." "I thought that in Islam my rank would be even higher than in the days of

[1] See Nöldeke-Schwally, *Geschichte des Qorans*, 2nd ed., I, 221. Ṭabarī, I, 1642, says that the Prophet read this verse at his entry into the Ka'ba at Mecca in the year 8/630. This statement implies that the "revelation" of the verse was of earlier date.

[2] Bayḍāwī, *Anwār al-tanzīl*, ed. Fleischer (Leipzig, 1846), II, 276.

Barbarism [*al-Jāhilīya*—the name given to the time before the coming of Muhammad]", remarked the prince. "Rid yourself of that idea ...", was Omar's reply.[1]

Later days brought *ḥadīths* [sayings attributed to the Prophet] in support of the theory of equality. "There are no genealogies in Islam" is one well-known *ḥadīth*, while others forbid emulation and boasting over ancestry.[2] But in spite of the Prophet's own desires and the weight of learned authority, the claims of birth remained strong, tempering the equality which rules in principle.[3] Far from destroying the regard paid to hereditary greatness, the effect of the Prophet's own success was to create a new object of veneration amongst a people in whom the instinct to pay homage to birth was strong. Henceforward kinship with him was regarded as the touchstone of true nobility, and even the slight degree of relationship to him which was implied in fellow-membership of his tribe—that of the Quraysh—was regarded as a patent of high distinction. A Qurashite could command a place of honour higher than that of any notable from a different tribe,[4] and even a *da'iy*, an adopted member of the Quraysh, was held to be of nobler station than the offspring of an old shaykhly family.[5] It is not strange, therefore, that it came to be said that no woman of the Prophet's tribe could be a slave[6]; certainly no male Qurashite could be a bondman.

The historians attempt to illustrate the theory of equality at work among the early Muslims by showing how Abu Bakr, the first successor of the Prophet, divided the spoils of war equally

[1] *Aghānī*, XIV, 4. The Caliph Omar is credited with having practised religiously the doctrine of the equality of Muslims. Tradition says he clothed himself in coarse linen and wore sandals of fibre in which he walked in the streets, refusing to ride, and he would address the humblest of his subjects, using the most vulgar dialect. In early times all Muslims shared alike in the spoils gained by the raiding of unconquered territory, and once when he was accused by one of his subjects of having taken more than his share, he was put to the trouble of proving the man wrong (Ibn al-Ṭiqṭaqā, *Fakhrī*, ed. Ahlwardt (Gotha, 1860), pp. 33 and 89).

[2] E.g. *Musnad* of Aḥmad b. Ḥanbal (Cairo, A.H., 1313) I, 301; II, 366; IV, 134, etc. See also A. J. Wensinck, *A Handbook of Early Muhammadan Tradition* (Leyden, 1927), s.v. Birth.

[3] Cf. Lady Anne Blunt, *Beduins of the Euphrates* (London, 1879), II, 229 ff.

[4] Cf. *Aghānī*, IV, 103, and Jāḥiẓ, *Bayān*, in Nicholson's *Elementary Arabic, Second Reading-Book* (Cambridge, 1909), p. 30.

[5] *Aghānī*, XVIII, 198, line 3 from bottom.

[6] *Aghānī*, XIV, 110.

amongst them all, whether young or old, slave or free, male or female.[1] The Caliph Omar, who succeeded Abu Bakr, although insisting that Islam levelled all distinctions of birth, was not prepared to concede that in the matter of the faith all Muhammadans were on equality. When dividing the spoils of war he gave precedence to those whose conversion to Islam was of longest standing. "I will not make him who fought against the Prophet the equal of him that fought with him", he said. Beginning with those who had been earliest associated with Muhammad, he gave to the *Muhājirūn* and *Anṣār*—respectively the Prophet's fellow-emigrants to Medina and his helpers there—who had fought with him at the battle of Badr, the sum of 5000 dirhams each. Those who had not fought there received 4000 dirhams, their sons 2000, their wives between 200 and 600 each, Meccans 800 and other Muslims between 300 and 500.[2] The sums in themselves have no significance, but they indicate the kind of distinctions that Muslims began to recognize.

Once Islam was adopted by peoples beyond the confines of Arabia, the ordinary full-blooded free Bedouin tribesman, the *ṣarīḥ*, inevitably regarded himself as the superior of the new foreign converts. In the same way that the old nobility resisted the assumption of equality by other Arabs, so the inhabitants of Arabia as a whole refused to consider foreigners as being their peers, in spite of the demand of their common faith that social and genealogical inequalities were to be wiped out and all tribal jealousies were to cease—seeing that all "believers are brothers".[3] Yet the Koran, by insisting that God was the creator of the diversity of tongues and colours amongst the believers,[4] made it logical for any Muslims—including negroes and others traditionally regarded in Arabia as inferior beings—to consider themselves the equals of any other Muslims, whoever they might be.

The battle was fought out in the three centuries following the prophet's death. On the one side stood the Arabs, on the other the new Muslims of non-Arab extraction, the *mawālī*,[5] or "clients", as they came to be called. Under the old customary law of the Arabs the *mawlā* was a tribesman or occasionally even a non-Arab

[1] Ya'qūb b. Ibrāhīm (Abu Yūsuf), *Kitāb al-Kharāj* (Būlāq, A.H. 1302), p. 24.
[2] *Ibid.* [3] Koran 49^{10}. [4] *Ibid.* 30^{21}.
[5] Its singular is *mawlā*.

foreigner who had, after a period of probation, become affiliated to a tribe not his own and with the members of which he stood on an equal footing as regards duties and privileges.[1] When the conquests of Islam became extensive, the name *mawālī* was applied to such inhabitants of the subdued territories outside Arabia as were converted. These, being freed from captivity or war or from slavery, became affiliated to some Arab tribe amongst the conquerors,[2] but were not independent of their patrons, forming their retinue in peace and war and in return receiving their protection.[3] This was not always of value, for the *mawālī* were treated with rigour by the military authorities, who would seldom allow them even such a trivial privilege as that of transferring their "clientship" from one Arab tribe to another.[4] The bloodthirsty, though able, governor of Iraq, Ḥajjāj b. Yūsuf, and his lieutenant Qutayba b. Muslim, in Khurāsān and Transoxiana imposed on them the *jizya* or poll-tax, to which strictly only non-Muslims were liable. When the inhabitants of the province of Iraq rebelled in protest, Ḥajjāj drove them out of the towns in which they had settled, called them barbarians and confined them to the villages, decreeing further that every *mawlā* should have the name of his village branded on his hand.[5] Even greater injustice was done to the *mawlā* when changing circumstances led to the abolition of Omar's enactment that no Muslim among the conquering armies could acquire land or houses in invaded territory; for while the Arab escaped with a small income-tax known as *zakāt*, "alms", the non-Arab *mawlā* was made to pay the *kharāj*, a land-tax that might amount to as much as a fifth of the product of his fields, in addition to the *jizya*.

Yet taxation was probably not so damaging to the self-esteem of the clients as the contempt with which the Arab treated them.

[1] There were occasional exceptions, e.g. at Medina the bloodwite exacted for an affiliate was only half that for a full member. Cf. Caussin de Perceval, *Essai sur l'histoire des arabes avant l'Islamisme* (Paris, 1847–8).

[2] There was also another class of *mawālī*, namely, slaves who had been manumitted and become "clients" of their late masters. They are not in question here.

[3] J. Wellhausen, *Die religiös-politischen Oppositionsparteien in alten Islam* (Berlin, 1901), p. 79.

[4] Goldziher, *Muhammedanische Studien* I, 141.

[5] Mubarrad, *Kāmil*, ed. Wright (Leipzig, 1864 ff.), p. 286, and cf. van Vloten, *Recherches sur la domination arabe* (Amsterdam, 1894), pp. 17 and 26 f.

In the cities which arose from the military camps of the early days of the conquest, no Arab would be seen walking with a *mawlā* in the street. If he had any dealings with him he called him by his *ism* or ordinary name, or by a *laqab*—a nickname or trade-name—while he himself insisted on the *kunya*, or patronymic title of respect, "Abu so-and-so," or "Ibn so-and-so."[1] On festive occasions also, when there were public gatherings, the last and humblest seats were allotted to the clients,[2] and in at least one place, Kūfa on the Euphrates, they even had a mosque of their own, while in Khurāsān they had their own administration and official corporate existence. Under the Umayyad regime, even when they took part in the wars for Islam, many were deprived of the share of the booty to which they were entitled.

The earliest and most important of the clients were inhabitants of Persia, including among them many men of learning and culture who took their new faith seriously, making themselves proficient in its doctrines and traditions. It was not long before the non-Arabs—Persians, Turks and others—came to be known as having the most learned doctors of Islamic theology and jurisprudence; and in fact, these sciences were almost exclusively in their hands. The historian-philosopher Ibn Khaldūn explains that since law and divinity were cultivated in the great cities of the Muhammadan empire, and since their chief inhabitants were Persians long accustomed to the arts of civilization, it followed that the earliest and most eminent of the professors of the learned arts in Islam were Persians. But the chieftains that led the various tribes composing the Arab invading armies, true to their traditions, regarded the conquering peoples as inferior beings and looked upon letters and the sciences as fit only for underlings. Those who had an

[1] Goldziher, *op. cit.* I, 267, and von Kremer, *Culturgeschichtliche Streifzüge*, (Leipzig, 1873), p. 21 f. Compare the similar treatment accorded in the southern states of the United States of America at one time to negroes. In public vehicles where white and coloured people were carried, the latter were confined to a particular compartment, and negroes were as a rule addressed by white fellow-citizens by their Christian names, without regard to any appellation or title of courtesy of the kind normally in use.

[2] Mubarrad, *op. cit.* p. 712. Their position is succinctly described in a couplet quoted in the *Murūj al-dhahab* of Mas'ūdī (ed. de Meynard and Pavet de Courteille, VI, 154):

"He that seeks shame, ignominy and opprobrium,
Will find all combined [literally neck and extremities] amongst the *mawālī*."

appreciation of these matters went so far as to deny to the Persians any claim to scholarship or skill in the field of Arabic literature, although in fact the most learned investigators into Arabic grammar, the most assiduous commentators on the Koran, and not a few compilers of creditable Arabic poetry, were men of Persian origin.[1]

The obvious disadvantages of the *mawlā* led to a regular system of subterfuges by which non-Arab Muslims sought to improve their lot. The less courageous of them changed their Persian names to Arabic ones, even going to the length of fabricating Arab genealogies for themselves. Where the fact was discovered the culprit was bitterly satirized, but the practice nevertheless continued. It may be added that even comparatively late in the history of Islam, entire peoples sought to enhance their status in the eyes of the Muslim world by claiming kinship with the Arabs of Arabia, and providing themselves with Arab ancestry. At one time, the Kurds and Berbers and even African negroes, e.g. the Bornu and the Fūla, wished either themselves or their rulers to be considered as having an Arab origin.[2] The Persians saved their national pride in somewhat different fashion by claiming that the Prophet's grandson Ḥusayn married Shahr-Bānū, a daughter of Yezdigerd III, the last Sasanian king of Persia.[3]

So long as the rule of the purely Arab Umayyad dynasty continued, the *mawālī* were forced to endure their inferiority. The piety of Omar II (717–20), it is true, induced him to make an attempt towards carrying out the principles of the Koran in the spirit, and in spite of much opposition he appointed two *mawālī* as qāḍīs at Cairo.[4] But the criticism which his action aroused was extreme, and it was not until the rise of the Abbasid Caliphate in the middle of the eighth century, when Persian political influence became strong, that any regular amelioration came in client status. It was then, with the access of political importance to the non-Arabs, that their apologists, who came from their own ranks, began to be active. Using the literary sources they had at their

[1] The references for the foregoing are to be found in Goldziher, *op. cit.* I 120 f.

[2] Goldziher, *op. cit.* I, 141–4.

[3] Ya'qūbī, *Historiae*, ed. Houtsma (Leyden, 1883), II, 293. Cf. E. G. Browne, *Literary History of Persia* (Cambridge, 1928), I, 130 ff.

[4] Maqrīzī, *Khiṭaṭ* (Būlāq, A.H. 1270), II, 332.

command, they pressed that the theoretical equality of all true believers in Islam should be put into practice, and demanded that men of Arab origin should in public and private recognize the brotherhood of all Muslims of whatever race. Various *ḥadīths* were invented and statements put into the mouth of the Prophet[1] to supplement the pertinent sections of the Koran[2]; while older traditions were adapted to include some expression of his opinions on the matter. The famous oration said to have been delivered by Muḥammad on the occasion of his "farewell pilgrimage" to Mecca may be taken as an instance of how earlier material was modified to suit the purposes of *mawālī* propaganda. Nearly all the biographies of the Prophet contain some version of this speech. In that of the ninth-century historian Ya'qūbī[3] there is inserted a passage which reads: "[All] men are equal in Islam. Men are but the outer margins of the ground that Adam and Eve cultivated. The Arab has no superiority over the foreigner (*'ajamī*) nor the foreigner over the Arab, save in the fear of God.... Bring me not your genealogies, but your [good] deeds." It is interesting to note that the versions of the speech given by the Prophet's biographers, Ibn Hishām[4] and Wāqidī,[5] who predeceased Ya'qūbī by half a century or more, do not contain this passage.

That the efforts of the apologists had some effect in the desired direction is doubtless true, but the political power of the numerous Persians who flocked to the capital during the reign of the Caliph Ma'mūn would seem to have been the real means of establishing the position of the non-Arab on a plane of equality with that of his Arab fellow-Muslim.

A class of *mawālī* who created special difficulties amongst upholders of the theory of equality were the negroes, whose ancestors, and even sometimes they themselves, had been imported from Africa into Arabia as slaves. It was clear in the Koran for all to read that God was himself the creator of the diversity of tongues and colours amongst believers. Faith, if not logic, therefore demanded that the negroes should be permitted to regard themselves as the

[1] Cf. Goldziher, *op. cit.* I, 114 ff.

[2] 49^{10},13.

[3] *Historiae*, II, 123. Cp. Jāḥiẓ, *Kitāb al-Bayān* (Cairo, A.H. 1313), I, 164, and see Goldziher, *op. cit.* I, 72, where further references are given.

[4] Wuestenfeld's edition, p. 821.

[5] Wellhausen, *Muhammed in Medina* (Berlin, 1882), p. 431.

peers of other Muhammadans. But those Arabs who had been brought up in the older tradition, which was reluctant to concede equality even to free men of their own kind and colour, were still more reluctant to recognize the parity of a people foreign in origin and, in their eyes, of definitely inferior status. The negro himself, though he might be a Muslim, claimed no privileges, and was perhaps scarcely in a position to do so. The point can be well illustrated from a story, told in the *Kitāb al-Aghānī*,[1] of the negro Ibn Musajjiḥ, who lived under the régime of the Umayyad Caliphs, descendants and representatives of the old pagan aristocracy of Arabia. He had gained a reputation as a poet and singer at Mecca, but, having been banished by the governor Ibn Zubayr on the grounds that he was corrupting the youth of the Quraysh, he fled to Damascus. In the mosque, on his arrival, he saw a group of young men engaged in discussion, and being without means and at a loss where to turn, he addressed himself to them. "Generous people", he said, "is there one amongst you who will give hospitality to a stranger from the Ḥijāz?" They looked at one another—for they had made an appointment to visit a singing-girl—and hesitated. One of them, however, rectified this show of bad manners by offering him hospitality, saying to his friends, "You proceed; I will go with my guest." But they answered: "No. Come with us and let your guest come too." Accordingly they all departed together. When the mid-day meal was brought, Ibn Musajjih said: "I am a negro. Since I may be offensive to someone amongst you, I will eat and drink apart." With that he rose, causing them to feel ashamed.

When the singing-girl and her friends appeared, he recited a complimentary verse, whereupon she flew into a rage at what she regarded as his presumption. "Shall a negro like this be permitted to utter parables about me?" she cried, causing the company to look at him disapprovingly. Their anger, however, did not restrain him from applauding as before when a second girl appeared and sang. This time it was the owner of the girl who was enraged at his presumption. He cried out: "Shall a negro like this embolden himself toward my slave-girl?" For the sake of peace the youth who had first offered hospitality to the negro poet suggested that he should go home to his lodging, but the rest of the company

[1] III, 87.

regarded this as unnecessarily discourteous, and the poet was finally permitted to stay, being warned to better his manners.

The problem of equality was raised in its acutest form when the question of marriage had to be faced. By long-established custom, the father or other nearest kinsman of the girl asked in marriage, acted as her *walī* or guardian. It was his business to see that the suitor was of equal birth with the girl he desired to marry and that in other ways also the match was a suitable one. When Islam insisted that it levelled all distinctions of birth there was more than a danger that such requirements might be disregarded. It became possible, for example, for a slave with perfect legal justification to ask to marry a free woman, possibly one belonging to a distinguished family.

The task of reconciling the law with ancient custom was not, however, beyond the ingenuity of the jurists, even if by the time they came to formulate their rules the difficulty had not been in great measure solved for them by what was actually taking place. For about a century and a half after Muhammad the *mawālī* had not ventured on offering marriage to the parents of pure-blooded Arab maidens.[1] Those who did so were liable to severe rebuffs, and it is probable that most of them knew their place.[2] During that time practice had crystallized; the Quraysh had come to be recognized as the new aristocracy, and the rest of the Muslims had worked out a scheme of social grades of their own. It was comparatively easy for the general rule to be evolved by the school of Abu Ḥanīfa that all Qurashites were of equal standing in a class by themselves, and that all other Arabs were equal irrespective of their tribes. Amongst non-Arab Muslims, a man was by birth the equal of an Arab if both his father and grandfather had been Muslims before him, but only then if he were sufficiently wealthy to provide an adequate *mahr* (or marriage endowment).[3] It is obvious that even thus the full equality of non-Arab with Arab Muslims is not admitted by the Ḥanafites; and they are followed by the Shāfi'ites, though the Mālikites, a great many of whom are negroes, stand by the spirit of the Koranic doctrine.[4]

[1] The marriage of the Arab with a non-Arab woman was equally frowned upon in early Islam, which was still very conscious of pre-Muhammadan practice.

[2] Goldziher, *op. cit.* I, 128–30.

[3] Shaybānī, *Jāmi' al-ṣaghīr*, on margins of *Kitāb al-Kharāj* (Būlāq, A.H. 1302), p. 32.

[4] Goldziher, *op. cit.* I, 130 ff.

Where the question was one of marriage between a free Arab and a slave-girl, the problem created was not so serious. The children of such a marriage were regarded as legitimate, although the Arabs of the old order refused, as we have seen, to regard the offspring of a slave-girl as having any claims to nobility. This was directly contrary to the Koranic doctrine that marriage with slave-girls was as valid as with free-born Arab women.[1] However, long before the middle of the Abbasid period it had ceased to matter who a man's mother was, and all after the first three Caliphs of the line had slaves for mothers.[2] Ibrahīm, son of the Caliph Mahdī, was born of a negress, but was not thereby debarred from receiving the allegiance of many fellow-Muslims, who considered he was more worthy of the Caliphate than his nephew, Ma'mūn, the son of Hārūn al-Rashīd.[3]

Like other *mawālī*, the negroes were not without their supporters, who pressed their claim to equality. Jāḥiẓ of Baṣra, a man of liberal mind who died in 869, himself a *mawlā*, wrote a treatise in their defence, in which he put forward various arguments to show how the negro could often boast of being the superior, and not alone the equal, of the white man.[4] In another work devoted to the defence of the *mawlā* he boldly stated that "the Lord is able to make of his servant an Arab or a non-Arab, a Qurashite or a negro, as he wills".[5] There were even *ḥadīths* designed to support the case of the negro and display him in a favourable light.[6]

During the time that the non-Arab was bearing his burden of inferiority and struggling to assert his rights as a Muslim, an important change was taking place in the character of the population throughout the lands which owed allegiance to the faith. In the conquered territories, such places as Baṣra and Kūfa which originally had been military camps for the purpose of keeping the surrounding country and its inhabitants in subjection, had grown by the end of the Umayyad period into large cities, while older towns such as Damascus in Syria, Ḥīra and Anbār in Iraq, and

[1] Koran 4³.

[2] Cf. Goldziher, *op. cit.* I, 124.

[3] Cf. R. Levy, *A Baghdad Chronicle* (Cambridge, 1929), pp. 80 ff.

[4] *Kitāb Fakhr al-Sūdān 'alā al-Bīdān* in *Tria Opuscula Auctore . . . al-Djahiz*, ed. van Vloten (Leyden, 1903).

[5] *Manāqib al-Atrāk*, tr. Walker, in *J.R.A.S.* (1915), p. 656.

[6] Goldziher, *op. cit.* I, 74 f.

Bukhārā and Samarqand in Transoxiana, had increased enormously in importance and in population. In 762 Baghdad was founded to become the capital of the Abbasid Caliphs, the half-Persian dynasty which succeeded that of the Umayyads. The growth of the cities brought with it a definite cleavage of the population into town-dwellers, who established themselves in houses and had settled homes, and the people who clung to the nomadic ways of life. One great consequence was that with the increase in urban populations and the establishment of the centre of government in such cities as Damascus or Baghdad, political power in the Caliphate came to be more usually wielded by inhabitants of the towns than by the nomad tribesmen.

A still further change was the evolution undergone by public sentiment on the question of what constituted aristocracy. Something of this we have already seen. Instead of the old tribal nobility, basing their claim to honour on kinship with heroes of a semi-legendary past, there had arisen a new class, whose boast was that either they or their ancestors were *Muhājirūn*—i.e. "fellow-emigrants" who, on the occasion of the *hijra*, had with Muhammad left their homes in Mecca and migrated to Medina; or else that they were *Anṣār*—i.e. "Helpers", natives of Medina who enrolled themselves among his followers and pledged themselves to his support. Still another group who regarded themselves as having claims to lofty rank were the Hāshimites, who were kinsmen of the Prophet by right of common descent from Hāshim, his great-grandfather. Their claims were, in the Abbasid period, recognized by the State, to the extent that they received pensions from it and were exempted from the "alms"-tax.[1] In the large cities they were also granted the privilege of being under a jurisdiction of their own, and having a magistrate, the *naqīb*, specially appointed by the Caliph.

A similar but rival group to the Hāshimites, and included with them amongst the *Ashrāf* or nobility, were the 'Alids, who traced descent from the Prophet's son-in-law 'Alī, through his martyred son Ḥusayn. Their modern representatives are the *Saiyids* who, in the eighth/fourteenth century, adopted as the outward sign of their claim to distinction the green turban which was so noticeable

[1] Māwardī, *Constitutiones Politicae*, ed. Enger (Bonn, 1853), p. 165.

in some Muslim lands.[1] The claim to the honour of being an 'Alid or a Sharīf was often made with little justification, a point made by Sa'dī in his *Gulistān*, in one of the stories of which he tells of an impostor whose father was a Kurdish Christian.

The divisions of society at about the middle of the second century of Islam are fairly accurately represented by the "Testament" described as containing the death-bed injunctions of the Caliph Omar to his successor; though as he died before a successor was appointed, the ascription to Omar would appear to be false. The document reads:

I commend to you the fearing of God, with whom is no associate; and I commend to your favour the early *Muhājirūn*, that you may recognize their past services; and I commend to your favour the *Anṣār*—approve their good deeds and pass over their misdeeds; and I commend to your favour the inhabitants of the cities, for they are [the support of Islam][2] against the enemy and the gatherers of tribute. And exact no tribute from them except by their favour and consent. And I commend to you the inhabitants of the open country, for they are the originals of the Arabs; and it is of the essence of Islam that you should take part of the superfluities of the wealth of their affluent ones and remit it to the poor among them; and I commend to your favour the people under "protection". Do battle to guard them and put no burden on them greater than they can bear, provided they pay what is due from them to the Muslims, willingly or "under subjection, being humbled"[3] . . .[4]

The people described as under "protection" were non-Muslims who legally had no rights in the State at all, and were permitted to exist only on the payment of the *jizya*, or poll-tax, as was provided by the Koran (9^{29}) whereby peoples "to whom the Book had been brought" were to be exempted from attack on payment of such a tax.[5] The "People of the Book" were at first

[1] Turkey and Persia have forbidden the wearing of turbans except by those who are, by examination, qualified to perform quasi-priestly functions.

[2] Thus the *Tāj al-'Arūs* (A.H. 1287), I, 75, I. I, which omits the words "against the enemy".

[3] Koran 9^{29}.

[4] Jāḥiẓ, *Kitāb al-Bayān*, I, 168.

[5] In Bukhārā the *jizya* was still exacted from infidels, except Russians, in Tsarist times (F. H. Skrine and E. D. Ross, *Heart of Asia* (London, 1899), p. 380).

defined as the Jews, Christians and Ṣābians, who could produce or claimed to have "Scriptures". Later, by a comprehensible analogy demanded by circumstances, the Zoroastrians were included amongst the "protected" peoples. They performed indispensable functions, particularly in the realm of commerce and finance, and they were also in demand for their skill in medicine and the embryonic sciences of the time. Probably for that reason they were noticed in "Omar's Testament", although at times they were permitted to exist only on sufferance and subject to numerous restrictions.

By the end of the ninth century A.D., when the Caliphate and the offices attached to it had suffered considerable modification in power and function, a further change, though a slight one, had come about in the social order. The geographer Ibn al-Faqīh, writing about 903, quotes the Abbasid courtier al-Faḍl b. Yaḥyā as having divided mankind into four classes: "Firstly, rulers elevated to office by their deserts; secondly, viziers, distinguished by their wisdom and understanding; thirdly, the upper classes, elevated by their wealth; and fourthly, the middle classes, to which belong the men marked by their culture. The remainder are filthy refuse, a torrent of scum, base cattle, none of whom thinks of anything but his food and sleep."[1]

It is worthy of note that the pre-Islamic Arabian ideals of birth had almost entirely vanished, for by the time that Ibn al-Faqīh wrote, the struggle for "equality" had been won, and either money or political office were titles to aristocracy. Not without its influence on the change of attitude is the fact already quoted that all the Caliphs after the first three were the sons of Turkish, Greek or even negro slave-girls.

In modern Arabia the *Ashrāf*[2] or descendants of the Prophet hold a position of some importance as landowners,[3] and often form separate communities. They have been acknowledged by all Arabs since the seventh century as persons of the highest nobility, and the proudest Bedouin chief kisses the hand of the poorest of them. As a rule a *Sharīf* will give his daughter in marriage to no one but

[1] *Kitāb al-Buldān*, Bibliotheca Geographorum Araborum, ed. de Goeje (Leyden, 1885), V, 1.

[2] Plural of *sharīf*.

[3] See references in H. St J. Philby, *The Heart of Arabia* (London, 1922), I, 180, 194, 199, 215; II, 92, 94.

a *Sharīf*. Yet in no sense do the *Ashrāf* form a separate priestly caste or any particularly pious community.[1] Out of their ranks have arisen such secular monarchs as the kings of present-day Iraq and Jordan, who, as far as their religious origins are concerned, stand no higher in public esteem than the ruler of Sa'ūdī Arabia, whose kingdom was gained largely by the sword.

Beyond the confines of Arabia, Islam brought similar changes in the estimate of what constituted a claim to honours, so that relationship to the Prophet, however remote, and also wealth and political power have all counted. In modern Egypt those who reckon themselves descendants of the first Caliphs Abu Bakr and Omar are included amongst the *Ashrāf*.[2] The Bakrīs (or Ṣiddīqīs), descendants of Abu Bakr, have since the beginning of the nineteenth century been the holders of the most lucrative of the religious appointments.[3] Political prestige was, however, until the abolition of the monarchy in Egypt (1953), retained by the families of Turkish origin, many of the ministers being drawn from the old Turkish ruling caste. They still form the real aristocracy, and in spite of their common religion they do not mingle with the tribesmen or the *fellāḥīn*, marrying almost exclusively amongst themselves.[4]

The influence of the Saiyids is perhaps strongest to this day in Persia, where the traditional reverence for the Prophet's son-in-law 'Alī and his sons, Ḥasan and Ḥusayn, was crystallized when, in 1502, a self-styled descendant of theirs (Ismā'īl I) founded the

[1] Amongst the Shī'a, however, in southern Iraq, the Saiyids (*Sāda*—also often called *Mīrzās*) live together in fairly large communities and often exert considerable political influence, being regarded by the rest of the population as holy men.

[2] "A shereef or descendant of the prophet is called 'the seyd' or 'the seyyid' (master, or lord), whatever be his station. Many shereefs are employed in the lowest offices: there are servants, dustmen, and beggars of the honoured race of Mohammad; but all of them are entitled to the distinctive appellation above mentioned, and privileged to wear the green turban: many of them, however, not only among those of humble station, but also among the wealthy, and particularly the learned, assume neither of these prerogatives, preferring the title of 'Shaykh' and the white turban." (E. W. Lane, *Manners and Customs of the Modern Egyptians* (Everyman ed., London, n.d.), ch. v, p. 135.) In Egypt the green turban is now very rarely seen.

[3] *Mitteilungen d. Seminars für Orientalischen Sprachen* (Berlin, 1909), p. 81.

[4] Cf. A. B. Clot Bey, *Aperçu général sur l'Égypte* (Paris, 1840), and M. Harris, *Egypt under the Egyptians* (London, 1925).

dynasty of the Ṣafawī Shāhs. The early Ṣafawīs combined in themselves both spiritual and temporal distinction, and Persian Saiyids, who received a reflected glory from them, continued in possession of a hierarchical status even when the Ṣafawīs had departed from the throne.

In pre-Islamic times it was aristocratic connection with princes and warriors that had formed a claim to honours amongst the Persians, amongst whom it was as valid as amongst the Arabs; and priests and holy men stood in a subordinate place. The often-quoted essayist Jāḥiẓ of Baṣra, writing about the middle of the ninth century A.D., tells us that the Persian king Ardashīr (Artaxerxes) divided his subjects into four classes and kept them rigidly in their separate divisions, for the reason, he explained, that nothing more swiftly leads to the destruction of empires than the transfer of one class to another, whether it be the elevation of the humble into a higher class or the degrading of the noble into a lower one. His classification was into first, knights and princes; second, religious leaders and guardians of the fire-temples; third, physicians, scribes and astrologers; and fourth, cultivators, menials etc.[1]

With the coming of Islam any regular priesthood that existed in Persia and elsewhere disappeared, but in its place there arose a class of interpreters of the Koran and prophetic "traditions" and of the laws derived from these two sources. These "learned men", *'ulamā* and *qāḍīs*, held high place, but still ranked under the shāh and his administrative officials. The *Siyāsat-nāma* or "Treatise on Government" compiled about A.D. 1092 by the famous Niẓām al-Mulk, the vizier of the Great Seljūqs, deals with the various officers of the State in the following order: (1) the king, (2) the provincial governors or tax-gatherers, (3) the vizier, (4) feudal landowners, (5) the peasants subject to them, and (6) *qāḍīs*, preachers (*khaṭībs*), police officers (*muḥtasibs*) etc.

That the aristocracy of Persia in Niẓām al-Mulk's time laid great store by birth and ancestry is indicated in the *Qābūs-nāma*, the book of moral and practical instruction which Kai Kā'ūs ibn Iskandar, prince of the South Caspian province of Ṭabaristān, composed for his son Gīlān-shāh in 1082–3. In it he speaks at length of his ancestry and explains to his son how distinguished

[1] Jāḥiẓ, *Kitāb al-Tāj*, ed. Ahmed Zéki Pasha (Cairo, 1914).

his forbears were, and what cause he has to be proud of them. The position had not greatly changed five centuries later, under the Ṣafawid rule, except that first of mankind are now put the Prophet, his Companions and the Imāms—or the twelve "leaders" of Islam in direct descent from him. After them in order come princes, amīrs, viziers and other state officials, wits and epistolographers or secretaries, Bedouin (*sic*) grammarians and orators, shaykhs, *'ulamā* (learned teachers and legists) and finally philosophers. This is the order in which 'Alī b. Ḥusayn b. al-Wā'iẓ al-Kāshifī, the author of *Laṭā'if al-ẓarā'if* or "Subtleties of Witticisms" (composed in 1532–3) deals with the various classes of mankind.[1]

A peculiar class of the Persian nobility in the early centuries of Islam were the *dihqāns*, or subordinate landowners, who stood at the head of the peasantry and varied in status from important chieftains to mere village headmen.[2] By timely conversion to Islam they preserved their power and influence, materially helping the Arab conquerors by acting as their agents in the collection of taxes, a function which they continued to perform until well on in the reign of the Caliph Ma'mūn (813–33).[3]

At the present time there are no sharp divisions of society or any castes in Persia. There are, of course, differences of wealth and political status, partly, though not exclusively, linked with the possession of landed estates, large or small. But there is no stable landed aristocracy which passes its estates relatively undiminished from father to son—a situation due largely to the provisions of Islamic law.[4] Besides the descendants of the Qājār shāhs only a few nomad chiefs have any regard for genealogy, which some trace back to Chingīz Khān, to Tamerlane or even to the Sasanians. If the words *najābat*, "nobility", and *najīb*, "noble", are heard, they refer only to the rank which an individual may hold; there is no allusion to birth.[5]

In the regions beyond the Oxus that were once Persian territory,

[1] Cf. Ethé, in *Grundriss d. Iran. Phil.* II, 332.

[2] Nöldeke, *Geschichte der Perser* (Leyden, 1879), p. 440.

[3] Jāḥiẓ, *Maḥāsin wa 'l-aḍdād*, ed. van Vloten (Leyden, 1898), p. 11. Ibn al-Athīr, IV, 116.

[4] Cf. Lambton, *Landlord and Peasant in Persia*, ch. XIII and *passim*.

[5] Polak, *Persien* (Leipzig, 1865), I, 35 f. Cf. Morier, *The Adventures of Hajji Baba of Ispahan*.

princes set themselves up independently of the Caliphate at a comparatively early period in the history of the Abbasid Caliphs of Baghdad. The longest-lived of the minor states so established was that of the Sāmānid princes, who were the actual rulers, although they had a host of officials under them. Yet the Muslim "learned", who took the place of the Zoroastrian priesthood, held great honour and power in Transoxiana, being, for example, exempted from certain humiliating formalities, such as that of kissing the ground in front of the prince.[1] The traditional place of importance accorded to the quasi-priesthood was continued in the Transoxine amīrate of Bukhārā, where next to the amīr himself the Saiyids, *'ulamā* and others who held religious authority ranked highest in the social order. They included amongst themselves even such persons as merchants and better-class artisans who had attended the *madrasas* or mosque schools. There was no aristocracy or privileged class with inherited rights, and any man of ability amongst the *fuqarā* (lit. "the poor"), or non-official class, could rise to be a "beg" or provincial governor. In the days immediately before the Russian occupation, various high officials in the state were either the sons of Persian slaves or themselves freed slaves. The only exception to the general absence of hereditary privileges was that the legitimate son of a "beg" inherited his father's title, though not his office; for the son of a highly placed official might often be found following a very humble occupation, as often happened in Persia during the reign of the Qājār dynasty.[2]

Further east still, amongst the Muslims of China, it is equally the case that birth confers no privileges, and even Saiyids have not achieved the influence which is theirs elsewhere in the realms of Islam; the reason being a general recognition of the fact that the conversion of most Chinese is of comparatively recent date.[3] Amongst the officials concerned with the faith there would appear to be no differences in rank nor any "hierarchy", any more than there is—in theory at any rate—elsewhere in Islam. In China each *A-hong* (Persian *ākhūnd*) or ministrant,

[1] Cf. Barthold, *Turkestan* (London, 1928), pp. 226–32.

[2] Cf. O. Olufsen, *The Emir of Bokhara and his Country* (London, 1911), pp. 399, 576.

[3] *Encyclopaedia of Islam*, s.v. China, pp. 849 f.

is concerned only with his own mosque and those who worship there.[1]

Amongst the huge Muslim population of Pakistan and India, although Sunnīs predominate largely in numbers over the Shī'ites, who are by tradition the upholders of the hereditary principle in Islam, the class of Saiyids is an important one. As elsewhere, they trace descent from the Prophet's grandson Ḥusayn and form a distinct group, the name *pīrzāda*, i.e. "of saintly descent", which they give themselves, marking them off as holy men. The title *Saiyid* or *Mīr* is always accorded them, and their women add the title *Begam* ("lady") after their names.[2] The honour paid to the *Ashrāf* is of early date in India, and the tradition of it was introduced by Indians into Sumuṭra (Java) with Islam, for when Ibn Baṭṭūṭa visited that island in the middle of the fourteenth century, the notables who received him included a number of the *Shurafā* or *Ashrāf*.[3]

Rather lower in the scale of honours is the class of the "shaykhs", who, if their title is not merely one of courtesy, claim descent from the first two Caliphs or from 'Abbās, the prophet's uncle. Other honoured classes also are the Afghans and Mughals (Moguls), persons of foreign descent whose privileged position is due to their being by origin natives of a land nearer than India to the source of Islam.

In spite of the theoretical equality in Islam of these classes with one another and with their fellow-Muhammadans of native origin, the influence of the Hindu caste system has brought certain distinctions of its own, and the so-called "hypergamous" system[4] is in vogue amongst the *Ashrāf*. Thus "a sayid will marry a sheikh's daughter, but will not give his daughter in return; and intermarriage between the upper circle of *soi-disant* foreigners [e.g. Afghans and Mughals, who claim social distinction on account of their foreign descent] and the main body of Indian Muhammadans, is generally reprobated, except in parts of the country where the

[1] d'Ollone, *Recherches sur les Mussulmans Chinois* (Paris, 1911), p. 4, and Wing-tsit Chan, *Religious Trends in Modern China* (New York, 1953).

[2] G. A. Herklots, *Islam in India*, ed. Crooke (London, 1921), pp. 114 f. and 10.

[3] Ibn Baṭṭūṭa, *Voyages*, ed. Defrémery and Sanguinetti (Paris, 1874), IV 230.

[4] By which a woman must always marry into a class above her own, though a man is permitted to marry a woman of any class to which he has access.

aristocratic element is small and must arrange its marriages as best it can".[1]

Amongst the Bengal Muhammadans the *Ashrāf* or upper class include all undoubted descendants of foreign Muslims (Arabs, Persians, Afghans, etc.) and converts from the higher castes of Hindus. "Like the higher Hindu castes, they consider it degrading to accept menial service or to handle the plough",[2] and they look with contempt upon all other ranks of Bengal Muslims whom they call *Ajlāf*, "coarse rabble". These include the "functional groups" such as weavers, cotton-carders, oil-pressers, barbers, tailors, etc., as well as all converts of originally humble caste. "In some places a third class called *Arzal* [*sic*][3] or 'lowest of all' is added. It consists of the very lowest caste such as the Helakhor, Lalbegi, Andal and Bediya, with whom no other Muhammadan would associate, and who are forbidden to enter the mosque or to use the public burial ground."[4]

It may here be remarked that something of the nature of a pariah caste exists in the Arabian peninsula, where the "gypsy" groups of the Ṣulaib and Hutaim (whom Doughty in *Arabia Deserta* calls "Solubba" and "Heteym") are regarded as *kuffār* ("unbelievers") and inferior beings by the rest of the inhabitants.[5]

A class of human beings that has formed an integral part of Muslim society up to the present day is that of the slaves. Muhammad took over the slavery system, upon which ancient society was based, seemingly without question and regarding it as part of the natural order of the universe. His injunctions recommending humane treatment[6] of slaves and making it a meritorious act to emancipate them[7] indicate that he intended some amelioration in their condition, but neither from the Koran nor from the "Traditions" is it possible to infer that the abolition of slavery was intended. The doctrine that Islam bestowed equality on all

[1] *Indian Census Report*, 1901, I, 543.

[2] *Ibid.* They correspond to the Brahmans; and their traditional occupation, if they are Saiyids, is the "priesthood". The Mughals and Pathans correspond to the Kshatriya (warrior) caste of the Hindus.

[3] Arabic, *ardhal*.

[4] *Indian Census Report*, 1901, I, 544.

[5] Cf. Taqī ed-Dīn al-Hilālī, *Die Kasten in Arabien*, in *Die Welt des Islams*, XXII (1940), 102 ff.

[6] Koran 16[73], 4[40].

[7] Koran 24[33], etc.

who accepted it can have meant no more than that the Arabs of Muhammad's time need no longer pride themselves on their ancestry, but it is nevertheless a fact that as Muhammadanism grew older, the stigma attaching to the status of the slave gradually disappeared. Liberty, however, could not have been granted through conversion to Islam any more than "economic" equality could be imposed on all Muslims by their common faith.

In certain circumstances some slaves had opportunities for acquiring wealth and power even greater than those that were within the reach of free men. Thus Subuktagīn, the confidential slave of a Sāmānid prince in Transoxiana, was able to acquire a large tract of territory and found the dynasty of the Ghaznawids, to which belonged the famous conqueror Maḥmūd. Aybak, the favourite slave of the chieftain Muhammad Ghūrī, the real founder of Islam in India, was the first of the Slave Kings of Delhi, and the Mamlūk[1] sulṭāns of Egypt were of similar origin. Whole series of dynasties were founded in the Middle East during the twelfth and thirteenth centuries by the Turkish Aṭābegs. Originally purchased as slaves to be the bodyguard of the Seljūq sulṭāns, they were appointed to the highest offices in the state, and, says Lane-Poole,[2] "the great slave vassals of the Seljūks were as proud and honourable as any Bastards of mediæval aristocracy; and when they in turn assumed kingly powers, they inherited and transmitted to their lineage the high traditions of their former lords".

These favoured individuals rose from the ranks of the white Turkish slaves who were bought by princes for their self-protection. The human chattels underwent a regular course of training, as may be gathered from the account of the system in vogue under the Sāmānid princes given in the *Siyāsat-nāma* ("Treatise on Government") of Niẓām al-Mulk.[3] In the first year after his purchase, the slave (*ghulām*) was trained as a foot soldier, and was never permitted, under penalties, to mount a horse. In his second year, on the recommendation of the tent commander (the *withāq-bāshī*) to the royal chamberlain (*ḥājib*) the slave was given a horse

[1] *Mamlūk*="owned", generally applied to a white (Turkish or Circassian) slave.

[2] *Saladin* (New York, 1898), pp. 22 f.

[3] Ed. Schefer, p. 95; tr. Schefer (Paris, 1891–3), pp. 139–40. Cf. Barthold, *Turkestan*, pp. 227 f.

with plain saddle and equipment. After another year's training he received an ornamental belt, and in his fifth year a better saddle and a mace. In his seventh year he became *withāq-bāshī* (tent commander) himself, in which office he was entrusted with work of considerable importance.

These Turkish slaves were, however, on a very different plane from other slaves, of whom the vast majority belonged to an inferior class and suffered under considerable disabilities. Before Muhammad's regime, slaves were by origin either prisoners taken in war or in raids into hostile territory, or else the offspring of slaves. It was still possible in those days for Arabs to enslave their fellow-countrymen by capture in war[1] or to recoup themselves for a debt—at any rate for a gambling debt. Thus the *Kitāb al-Aghānī*[2] tells how Abu Lahab al-'Āṣī—whose infidel grandfather fought against the early Muslims at the Battle of Badr (624)—lost all he had in gambling with Ibn Hishām, to whom he said: "I see the arrows [of the kind used for gambling] are in league with you. I will play you once more, and the one of us that loses shall be slave to the other." Abu Lahab agreed and won, but disliking the thought of carrying off his friendly opponent as a slave he approached the latter's tribe and asked them to redeem him for ten camels. They refused, however, to give so much as a single hair for him, and Abu Lahab thereupon carried him off to be his slave.

By the Islamic legists the theory was evolved that all men were free except such as acknowledged themselves slaves or could be proved on good evidence to be slaves.[3] Quite early in the history of the faith the principle was established that there was to be no taking of captives from amongst Muslims and no enslavement of Muslim Arabs,[4] although the Koran does not say so, the principle being doubtless evolved from actual practice. But it was not invariably respected. Thus, in its biography of the talented slave-girl Shāriya, the *Kitāb al-Aghānī*[5] has two versions of how she came to be a slave at all. The first says that she was born at Baṣra, that her father was a member of the Banū Sāma tribe, and her mother a slave. Further, that on the birth of Shāriya her

[1] *Aghānī* XI, 79 f. [2] III, 100.

[3] Ibn Bābūyah, *Man lā yaḥḍuruhu al-faqīh*, British Museum MS. Add. 19,358, fol. 45 a. [4] *Aghānī*, XI, 79 f. [5] XIV, 109.

father repudiated her, so that she took her mother's status and was sold. The second account says that she was stolen as a child and sold to a woman of the Hāshimite clan.

In later days (at the beginning of the tenth century A.D.), the Carmathian "heretics" of southern Iraq enslaved other Muslims whom they had captured in battle or acquired in other ways. Their reason, however, for so doing was that they regarded themselves as the only true believers, the rest being no better than pagans.[1] A similar argument was used in the nineteenth century by Sunnī Turkomans, who carried off Shī'ite Persians and Tājiks into slavery without compunction.

As in the *Jāhilīya* so in Islam, property in slaves can be acquired by sale,[2] gift or inheritance, as well as by capture. But since, after the coming of Islam, the only persons who could be legally enslaved were unbelievers captured in hostile territory,[3] it became illegal to sell a free Muslim into slavery for any reason whatever. Parents therefore were forbidden to sell their children, though the practice has not been unknown in modern times.[4] Persons already in slavery were regarded merely as chattels, and Islamic legislation provides for their sale and purchase as for any ordinary goods,[5]

[1] Cf. Yāqūt, *Irshād al-arīb* (*Mu'jam al-udabā*), ed. Margoliouth (London, 1908–27), VI, 299.

[2] The distinguished Muslim lawyer Ameer Ali held (in his *Personal Law of the Mahommedans* (London, 1880), pp. 38 f.) that slavery by purchase was unknown during the reigns of the first four Caliphs. But purchase was so obvious and regular a method of acquiring slaves in all countries—even in Arabia—immediately before and after them, that it does not seem probable it was suspended for the period of these Caliphs. With regard to legal provision for the sale of slaves, cf. Sachau, *Muhammedanisches Recht* (Berlin, 1897), pp. 286 f.

[3] Cf. Koran 47⁴. The technical name for them is *raqīq* (plural *ariqqā*). Armenian girls are said to have been sold in the open market in Palestine during the war of 1914–18, before the British occupation. They were *ariqqā*, and could be legitimately bought by Muslims (Père J. A. Jaussen, *Coutumes palestiniennes: Nablus* (Paris, 1927), p. 129).

[4] Lane, *Modern Egyptians*, ch. VII, and A. Mez, *Die Renaissance des Islams* (Heidelberg, 1922), p. 154. The sale of their daughters by Circassian fathers was still prevalent in the early part of the twentieth century, although illegal. Jaussen (*loc. cit.*) declares that in 1925 in Palestine there were Arabs who sold their daughters for debt.

[5] Jews and Christians therefore could in theory own Muslim slaves. Cf. Shāfi'ī, *Kitāb al-Umm* (Būlāq, A.H. 1321), IV, 188. Free Jews and Christians who had paid the poll-tax could not be taken as slaves. For a "buyer's guide" to the slave market see *Qābūs-nāma*, ed. R. Levy, and translation, *A Mirror for Princes* (London, 1951), ch. XXIII.

with certain restrictions in the case of female slaves who have borne children by their masters and of these children themselves. Actually, and aside from the law, sentiment often played a part in the relationships between master and slave, and if the latter was born and brought up in his master's house he was never sold except for some special fault, e.g. habitual drunkenness. The adoption of slaves as members of the family was common. Cruelty to them was forbidden, there being numerous "traditions" enjoining kindly treatment of slaves. In spite, however, of the disapproval of the Koran and the traditions, emasculation of slaves was frequently practised, the employment of eunuchs having arisen as a necessary adjunct of the harem system.[1]

The legal disabilities of slaves in Islam arise from the fact that in theory they have no more rights than other chattels. On this question the schools of law are substantially in agreement, and the authorities quoted in what follows are taken at random from any school, only divergencies being noted.

With regard to the satisfaction of their bodily needs, slaves are classed with domestic animals.[2] There are, however, the restrictions already mentioned on the sale by a master both of the slave (*umm walad*) by whom he has had children and of his children by her. Apart from them the slave-owner can sell, bequeath or give away his slaves, he can use them as pledges, put them out at hire

[1] The Koran (4^{118}) regards mutilation of God's creatures as instigated by Satan. Bayḍāwī in his commentary on the verse explains that mutilation includes emasculation of slaves, branding them or filing their teeth, and unnatural offences. It was the duty of the *muḥtasib*, or police-officer, to see that the law was not broken. Young slaves often were castrated before their importation and brought high prices (Māwardī, ed. Enger, p. 431).

[2] Khalīl b. Isḥāq, *Mukhtaṣar*, tr. Guidi and Santillana (Milan, 1919), II, 166; Sachau, *op. cit.* p. 18; Shīrāzī, *Tanbīh*, ed. Juynboll (Leyden, 1879), pp. 258 f. "Sustenance must be provided for slaves and domestic animals in sufficient measure, and they may not be put to more labour than they can perform." Food, clothing and shelter, doctors' fees and physic are included in the term "sustenance" (Khalīl, p. 101). In general the provision made must be that which is normal in the country in which the slave lives. It is not necessary, though praiseworthy, for the slave to have the same food and clothing as his master (*ibid.* p. 102). If sustenance is not provided by the master, the slave may complain to the judge, who is empowered to sell so much of the master's goods as is necessary for the slave's keep. If the master has not the means he must by the judge's orders sell, hire out or manumit the slave. If all this is impossible the slave becomes a charge upon the public purse.

It is expressly laid down that the slave has the right to a period for a siesta during the hottest part of the day in the summer season.

or compel them to earn money for him in other ways. They can own no property, and must hand over to their master any they may acquire. It follows that, except as his master's agent, no slave may carry on a trade or business, but the contracts made by him as agent are valid and binding on the owner to the extent he has authorized.[1] Similarly no slave may inherit property, even if he or she (for example an *umm walad*) is to be freed on the owner's death.

Morally as well as physically the slave is regarded in law as an inferior being. His evidence is rarely valid in a court of law,[2] and being held not entirely responsible for his actions his crimes are punished by half the penalty inflicted on the free man, though vengeance (*talio*) is exacted from him if he kills another person, whether bond or free, of set purpose. The Koran,[3] dealing with the question of the *talio*—more especially where a blood-feud is concerned—lays it down that the life of a free man is exacted for that of a free man, a slave's for a slave's and a woman's for a woman's. Bayḍāwī, commenting on the passage, says:

There was in the *Jāhilīya* a blood-feud between two tribes, and one of them, claiming superiority over the other, swore they would kill a free man for any slave of theirs and a man for a woman. When Islam came they brought the matter to Muhammad for decision. The present verse was thereupon revealed, and he further ordered that they were to be equal in their retaliations. This verse, however, does not indicate that a free man may not be slain for a slave . . . nor yet the contrary. . . . Mālik and Shāfi'ī[4] denied it was legitimate to slay a free man for a slave—whether his own or another's—but it was only because of a tradition that once, when a man killed his slave, the Prophet scourged him, and banished him for a year, but did not put him to death for murder. It is reported of 'Alī that he declared: "It is the practice in Islam that no Muslim is slain for a protected non-Muslim and no free man for a slave".

[1] Khalīl b. Isḥāq, *Mukhtaṣar*, II, 329 ff. Cf. Juynboll, *Handbuch des Islamischen Gesetzes* (Leyden, 1910), pp. 204 f.

[2] Since every witness must be free, a Muslim, and of sound mind (Khalīl b. Isḥāq *op. cit.*, II, 616, and Sachau, *op. cit.* p. 739). On some matters, tradition admits the evidence of slaves who are of good character. (Cf. Bukhārī, *Ṣaḥīḥ*, ed. Krehl, (Leyden, 1862–8), II, 153; Bk. 52, 13.)

[3] 2[173].

[4] Cf. Khalīl b. Isḥāq, *op. cit.* II, 662, and Sachau, *op. cit.* p. 776. The Ḥanafites, on the other hand, make the free man liable to *talio* for the deliberate killing of a slave.

Normally a free man who kills the slave of another is liable to pay him as compensation not blood-money[1] but the slave's value at the time of death. It would appear therefore that a man might kill his own slave with impunity, notwithstanding the law-books.[2]

Marriage is permitted to a slave, but requires the owner's consent.[3] The Ḥanafī and Shāfi'ī codes allow him only two wives, bond or free; but the Mālikites permit him four, making no distinction in this matter between the slave and the free man.[4] Views differ as to whether a master may compel his slave to marry. It is agreed, however, that he in his turn, cannot be compelled to give consent to his slave's marriage.[5] Like the free man, the slave on marriage is required to provide a *mahr* (endowment), which he must earn by his own labour, and which becomes the property of the wife's owner if she is a slave. The children of the marriage of two slaves are slaves and belong to the owner of the woman. If a free man marries a female slave not his own, the children become the property of the woman's master.[6]

In spite of the permission given to the free Muslim in the Koran (4[29]) to marry his own slave-girl if she is of his own faith, marriage of this kind is hedged about with restrictions by the jurists. The Shāfi'ite school even hold that if a man wishes to marry his own slave he must first free her.[7] There are no restrictions, however, upon concubinage with slave-girls. The children of the married slave-girl (not an *umm walad*) will be slaves and belong to her owner, whether their father is a slave or a free man. If, on the other hand, the master takes his own slave for a concubine by virtue of his right of ownership and she bears children by him, she becomes *umm walad*, and her children by him are free,[8]

[1] Cf. Shīrāzī, *Tanbīh* (p. 271), which declares that a master is not liable to payment of blood-wite for killing his slave. See also Sachau, *op. cit.* p. 783.

[2] See Lane, *Thousand and One Nights* (London, 1841), I, 63.

[3] There is a "tradition" to the effect that without this consent a slave's marriage is no more than fornication.

[4] Cf. Goldziher, *Muhammedanische Studien*, I, 130 f. It is interesting to note that the Mālikite school is most widespread in north and central Africa.

[5] Khalīl b. Isḥāq, *op. cit.* II, 4; Shīrāzī, *op. cit.* p. 190.

[6] This is the case also if the children of a slave-girl are born of an irregular union.

[7] Sachau, *op. cit.* p. 24. The story of Ibrahīm ibn al-Mahdī and the slave-girl Shāriya provides a case in point (*Aghānī*, XIV, 110). See below, pp. 111 f.

[8] Shīrāzī, *op. cit.* p. 180. Cf. Juynboll, *Handbuch*, p. 236. This regulation is directly due to Islam, for previously the rule held that "the child follows the

though any children that she may previously have borne by another man are slaves and the property of her master. He may not sell, pledge, or give her away as a gift, but he is entitled to demand service from her; and he has power, if he is a Muslim, to give her in marriage to another man, even against her will.[1]

It has already been indicated that the Koran[2] and the *ḥadīth* make it a commendable act for masters to emancipate slaves in expiation for certain misdeeds, e.g. involuntary manslaughter, or if the slaves demand it and are worthy.[3] There were various ways in which a slave might become free.[4] The *umm walad* becomes free on his death with all the children she has borne after becoming his wife or concubine.[5] The slave who comes into the possession of an owner who is related to him or her in the direct line, either ascendant or descendant, is free.[6] For example, if a father who is a freed man is granted his slave son by a master's bequest, that son is free. The slave may also be manumitted by a promise of his master, given either verbally or in writing, that when he (the master) dies, the slave shall be free.[7]

Freedom may be bestowed as an act of piety by an owner, as recommended by the Koran, or by an unequivocal declaration, whether made in jest or earnest, by the master to the slave that he has freed him. Similarly, if the master declares to a third person that the slave is free, then the declaration is legally binding.[8] The slave may redeem himself if his master agrees and contracts to let him go on payment of a stipulated sum of money, which may be paid in two or more instalments, or on the giving of stipulated

womb" so far as its status is concerned. According to Lane (*Thousand and One Nights*, I, 62 f.) the master may recognize them as his children, or not, as he pleases. If recognized by him they are free and enjoy all the privileges of other children; if not recognized by him they are his slaves.

[1] Khalīl b. Isḥāq, *op. cit.* II, 4; and Sachau, *op. cit.* p. 173.

[2] E.g. 4[94]; 5[91]; 58[4].

[3] Koran 24[33].

[4] The slave bequeathed as *waqf*, i.e. endowment for the benefit of some pious foundation such as a mosque, can never become free. A *waqf* is something determined for all time, and to free a slave means to deprive some future beneficiaries of his services (Sachau, *op. cit.* p. 133).

[5] Khalīl b. Isḥāq, *op. cit.* II, 782; Sachau, *op. cit.* p. 127.

[6] Khalīl b. Isḥāq, *op. cit.* II, 752; Sachau, *op. cit.* p. 125.

[7] Sachau, *op. cit.* p. 126. But the master may sell the slave and so invalidate the promise (*ibid.*).

[8] *Ibid.* p. 133. The slave is then called ʿ*atīq*.

services or other consideration. If the consideration is a sum of money, the master must grant the slave the right to earn and to own property.[1]

The slave on emancipation becomes the *'atīq* (freedman) or *mawlā* (client) of his late master, who becomes his *walī* (patron). He receives certain benefits, mainly pecuniary, from the client, and owes him protection and "patronage" in return. The patron cannot refuse his patronage nor alienate it in any way and it passes on to his heirs on his death.[2] The client, on the other hand, cannot change his patron. If the former dies without heir, the patron (or his heir) inherits from him, except when the patron is a Christian or Jew and the client a Muslim, in which case the public purse benefits, since no non-Muslim can inherit from a Muslim. With that exception the relationship of patron to client holds, whatever the respective faiths of the two.[3] The patron may be a Christian and the client a Muslim, or both may be of the same faith. The duty of clientship to his late master is not confined to the freedman, but devolves also upon his heirs and even upon his own freedmen.[4]

We have said that Muhammad found slavery a regular element of society in his day, and though he brought about a considerable amelioration in its conditions, like other religious leaders before him, he took slavery for granted as an ordinary part of the social system. It has continued in Muslim lands ever since, except where for a time European powers held authority. During the Caliphate, on account of the great profits to be derived from the trade, thousands of slaves, both black and white, were imported annually; the negroes coming from Fezzan in Libya and from Upper Egypt, while the white slaves, who were scarcer than negroes and hence more valuable, were brought from central Asia or from Syria. Some of the most beautiful slave-girls were sent to the harems of the Baghdad Caliphs from Europe, particularly from Spain,[5] and there was a brisk trade from Italian

1 Sachau, pp. 150 f. The slave thus emancipated is called *mukātab*.

2 *Ibid.* pp. 125 f.

3 *Ibid.* p. 141.

4 A. W. T. Juynboll, *Handbuch* (Leyden, 1910), p. 208.

5 Ibn Khurdādbih, new ed. p. 97. They were called *Saqāliba*, i.e. Spanish *Esclavo*.

harbours, the Venetians having a slave-market of their own in Rome in the eighth century.[1] In the tenth century the most valuable commodity imported into central Asia from the Volga lands was that of the slaves, who were brought into the Oxus region and especially to Samarqand, where the best were sold.[2] At Samarra, on the Tigris, the slave bazaar invited the special interests of the geographer Ya'qūbī, who saw there the long lanes of houses for the exhibition and sale of slaves.[3]

Egypt, South Arabia and North Africa were the chief markets for negro slaves from the centre of Africa, and Islamic rulers never legally abolished the trade. Between the sixteenth and eighteenth centuries Christian Europe was ravaged by the Turks and Barbary corsairs, who not only enslaved the crews and passengers of ships sailing to Mediterranean and Spanish ports, but sacked parts of Ireland and threatened Bristol, as well as carrying off hundreds of British captives.[4] Gruesome pictures were painted by travellers and by monks sent to ransom the unfortunate captives[5] of the cruelties practised on galley-slaves and others. Yet the lot of many, both in private possessions and in the public service, was in some respects tolerable enough, and reports of some travellers and monks seem to be exaggerated, if comparison is made with those of others who visited the corsairs' headquarters.[6] Perhaps the most famous of the pirates' captives was Cervantes, who spent five years loaded with chains and in circumstances of the greatest wretchedness.

Muslim slaves were better treated than Christians. Writing about 1862, the English traveller W. G. Palgrave[7] says that in Arabia he constantly met with negro slaves in large numbers. The effects of concubinage with negresses were apparent in the number of people of mixed race, and emancipation of slaves he found to be common. "These new possessors of civil liberty", he says, "soon marry and are given in marriage. Now, although an emancipated negro

[1] Cf. Von Kremer, *Culturgeschichte des Orients* (Leipzig, 1875–7), I, 234; II, 152.

[2] Maqdisī (ed. de Goeje (2nd ed.), Leyden, 1906, p. 325.

[3] *Kitāb al-Buldān*, ed. de Goeje (Leyden, 1892), p. 259.

[4] See Lane-Poole, *Barbary Corsairs* (London, 1890), pp. 265 ff.

[5] E.g. Father Dan, quoted in Lane-Poole, *op. cit.* pp. 236 ff.

[6] *Ibid.* p. 242, and the literature there quoted.

[7] In his narrative of *A Year's Journey Through Central and Eastern Arabia* 5th ed. London, 1869), pp. 270 ff.

or mulatto is not at once admitted to the higher circles of the aristocratic life, nor would an Arab chief of rank readily make over his daughter to a black, yet they are by no means under the ban of incapacity or exclusion which weighs on them among races of English blood."

About a quarter of a century after Palgrave, Doughty[1] speaks of the condition of slaves as he saw it. He describes it as always tolerable and often happy: "Bred up as poor brothers and sons of the household they are a manner of God's wards of the pious Mohammadan householder." . . . It is not many years, "if their house-lord fears Allāh, before he will give them their liberty and then he sends them not away empty".

Doughty remarks that slave-holding was harsher in the "mixed" holy cities, and that Mecca was the centre from which returning pilgrims brought slaves for all the north-west of the Muhammadan world, "but gazing all day up and down", he says, "I could not count five among them".[2] The Dutch scholar and traveller, Snouck Hurgronje,[3] who spent six months among the *'ulamā* at Mecca as one of themselves, bore out Doughty's statements. The great part of the slaves were Africans and they were important "both for the trade in slaves and for the composition of Meccan society". They were divided into classes. The shining black "Nubians", as they were called, were used for the heaviest tasks, such as building, quarrying and the like. Others, employed in general labour and normally imported from the Sudan, were called simply "black slaves"[4]. They also often began on bricks and mortar, their owners putting them as boys to work on building in order to make them learn Arabic properly. The less skilled amongst them remained common labourers like the Nubians, and were hired out as such to builders and others. Their education was usually confined to teaching them the most essential ritual performances of Islam. Although they were not seldom neglectful of these, the Muhammadan feeling of these grown-up children was fanatical. Their food was sufficient, for supplies were ample and cheap. Clothes and housing, owing to the climate, were superfluous, but what was necessary of these was given to them. When freed they sought employment as water-carriers, or day

[1] *Arabia Deserta* (Cambridge, 1888), I, 554 f.
[2] *Ibid.* I, 209.
[3] Writing before 1888. Cf. *Mekka* (Leyden, 1888).
[4] *'abd aswad.*

labourers. Mostly they preferred a continuance of supervision, especially when their master had permitted them to marry.

Other negro slaves, better equipped, found employ as house-workers or shop assistants. Merchants of good position liked to fill their houses with slaves, for whom life became very easy; but even the "slave of all work" did not find life too difficult, and all were members of the family they served. The better slaves in shops became trusted assistants who retained only the name of slave. House slaves, almost as a rule, were freed at the age of twenty, probably because their work brought them into the presence of the many women, bond and free. The respectable owner felt himself bound to supply his slave with a house whenever possible; emancipation was regarded as meritorious and the familiar relationships remained on the same footing as before it. Practically no office or position was closed to such freedmen. They competed on equal terms with the free-born and results showed that they were by no means always beaten in the competition, for many of the most influential citizens, owners of houses and shops, were ex-slaves. The colour of their skin was (and is) no handicap to them because the citizen had swarthy children by his slave concubines.

Negresses were used for services about the house and in the kitchen; occasionally they were concubines, while Abyssinian women, amongst whom were all shades of colour from pale yellow to dark brown, were concubines first, though they sometimes undertook light housework. Male Abyssinians were considered more delicate and more intelligent than the negroes and were better reared and educated accordingly. They were used as servants or as assistants in business.

Circassians, male and female, came via Istambul. Because of their high price their number was small and they were never sold in the open market at Mecca.

"Improbable as it may seem," the author says in another section of his work,[1] "even India and the Dutch East Indies supply considerable numbers of slaves to the Meccan market. The Javanese slaves come from the pagan region of Celebes and Borneo, or from the island of Nias. They are also sold to Egypt. I saw many young slaves from India and also four freshly-imported

[1] *Mekka*, II, 15.

Indian slave-girls. Whether they were stolen from their parents, or from what district they came, I could not ascertain."

It is probable that the Indian children were sold by their parents who had come to Mecca on pilgrimage. There would appear to have been a regular trade carried on in this fashion, involving the sale of some 5000 boys and girls each year by parents who came from India,[1] the East Indies and Africa, taking their children to Mecca for sale.[2]

In 1925 slaves were being bought and sold at Mecca in the ordinary way of trade. "A number of new slaves still reach Mekka from the Yemen and from Africa and occasionally from Asia Minor, but the majority are children born of slaves in Mekka."[3]

By the Treaty of Jedda, May 1927 (art. 7), concluded between the British Government and Ibn Sa'ūd (the Wahhābī king of Nejd and the Ḥijāz), it was agreed to suppress the slave-trade in Arabia. So far the efforts made in that direction have not met with entire success,[4] although by a decree issued in 1936, the importation of slaves into Sa'ūdī Arabia was prohibited unless it could be proved that they were slaves at that date. The Yemen regards slavery as entirely legal since it is an institution recognized by the sharī'ah. In Oman and south-east Arabia in quite recent times, slaves were common and suffered from the disabilities which have always been theirs. Bertram Thomas, who travelled in south Arabia in 1928, says that when passing through the territory of the Hināwī tribe it was necessary to be accompanied by a *rafīq* or representative from the tribe, whose presence was a guarantee of the traveller and showed he was not a member of the hostile tribe of the Ghāfarī. A traveller amongst the latter tribe would be similarly protected. "Only amongst the Qara is a slave acceptable

[1] "Slavery as far as established by law was abolished in India by Act V, 1843, but the final blow was dealt on 1 January, 1862, when the sections of the Indian Penal Code dealing with the question came into operation" (W. Crooke, *Islam in India* (Oxford, 1921), p. 112 n.).

[2] See the report of a conference organized by the League of Nations Union in *The Times*, Friday, 8 March 1929.

[3] E. Rutter, *The Holy Cities of Arabia* (London and New York, 1928), II, 93 f.

[4] An article written by a naval officer in the *Sunday Express* of 3 February 1929, stated that slave traffic still went on in the Red Sea and off the North African coast; also that there were regular slave-markets in Arabia, where thousands of natives from the Sudan were bought and sold. Abyssinian traders, further, landed cargoes in southern Arabia.

as a *rafīq*; elsewhere it is the custom to kill the free man and take captive the slave. In truth it would appear that the slave has a commercial value, and as such shares the privilege of the camel taken in the raid."[1]

As for slavery in Muslim lands other than Arabia, it exists today in the deserts of Iraq bordering on Arabia,[2] and in 1908 "in the borderlands between Egypt and Palestine slaves were to be found amongst all tribes. Not negroes alone were slaves but also members of other tribes particularly from North Africa."[3] In the Sudan also there are slaves with certain tribes. But

only negroes are slaves. . . . Owing to the action of the Government, slaves cannot be made at the present day, and any man who demands it must be given his freedom. As a matter of fact slaves are so well treated and their bondage is so light that they seldom wish to change their condition. . . . The only difference between a slave and a free Arab is that the former would not be allowed to marry a daughter of the latter. A master would see to it that his slave should have as wife a good and reliable woman, chosen from among the daughters of slaves. In times of peace slaves occupy positions of trust, and in warfare ride by the side of the master.[4]

Further to the west, among the Sunūsīyah inhabiting the oases of the Libyan desert, slavery is a regular part of the social system. The Egyptian explorer Hasanein Bey, writing in 1924, said that in recent years the price of slaves had advanced because no more were coming up from Wadai (French Sudan), in which province the French authorities were showing great vigilance to counteract the trade.

Occasionally the Beduins get round this by contracting a marriage with a slave girl in Wadai, and then when they come back, divorcing and selling her.[5] The Beduins sometimes marry

[1] "Among some Unknown Tribes of South Arabia", *Journal of the Royal Anthropological Institute*, LIX (January–June 1929), 98.

[2] The present writer when engaged (1920) in Government service at Sūq al-Shuyūkh on the Lower Euphrates, was visited by a negro slave (ʻ*abed* in the Iraq dialect) who brought certain title-deeds from his master, a member of the well-known Saʻdūn family.

[3] A. Musil, *Arabia Petræa* (Vienna, 1907–8), III, 224 f.

[4] C. G. and B. Z. Seligman, "The Kababish", *Harvard African Studies*, II (1918), 116.

[5] A. M. Hasanein, *The Lost Oases* (London, 1925), p. 179.

their slave girls, and if one bears a male child she automatically becomes free. The Beduins have no prejudice against colour; if a slave bears a son to the head of a tribe, that child becomes the head of the tribe, however black he may be. Whereas the children of slaves are slaves, the children of a free man and a slave girl are free, and even though their father dies leaving them poor, they can never become slaves. . . . The lot of a favourite slave is a pleasant one. . . . He is generally his master's confidant and is well treated. A male slave is permitted to buy a girl slave.[1] The shabbiest slave that you see in an oasis is generally the freed slave, who curiously enough is looked down upon by the other owned slaves, and himself feels ashamed he belongs to no one.[2]

Further west still, and in spite of the fact that in French territory slavery has legally been abolished,[3] the veiled Tuaregs of the Sahara have their slaves. They fall into two categories: (1) the household slaves, and (2) outdoor slaves. Both are regarded as chattels in local customary law. The negro slaves, the Ikelan, who belong to the first category, are primarily concerned with garden cultivation and indoor tasks. One half of the produce of their labour goes to their masters and the other half to support themselves and their families. They also perform all the domestic duties, and if they live in the neighbourhood of the pastures, they herd their masters' sheep and goats. The slaves in the second class, the Buza, are employed in herding livestock, especially camels. Often they are negroes, but they are reckoned of higher status than the Ikelan of the first category. Slaves of either class do not wear the face-veil which is the peculiar and characteristic article of Tuareg male attire. Despite their legal status as chattels, they are in practice permitted to own property. They always have a hope of manumission, with a change to the status of the serf—a step upward in the social scale which does in fact often occur.[4]

In central Asia, Turcoman activity in man-stealing and trading

[1] A. M. Hasanein, *ibid.*

[2] *Ibid.* p. 181.

[3] There were slaves in Morocco earlier in this century. Cf. E. Übach and E. Rackow, *Sitte und Recht in Nordafrika* (Stuttgart, 1923), p. 16.

[4] F. R. Rodd, *People of the Veil* (London, 1926), pp. 134 f. The author concludes his observations on Tuareg slavery by commenting that it was in slave-trading and not in slave-owning that the Tuareg sinned against the ethical standards of Europe.

in slaves was notorious until the Russians conquered Bukhārā, Khiva and other "khanates", and abolished slavery.

At Constantinople the sale of women slaves, both negresses and Circassians, continued to be openly practised until the granting of the Constitution (1908).

Slavery was also rife in the East Indies towards the end of last century. In Singapore, in 1891, there was a regular trade in Chinese slaves, both men and women, and official protection was given to the trade. Chinese slaves were converted to Islam by the Muhammadan buyers, and girls and women were used for concubinage. The Chinese alone—that is, non-Muslims—did the actual trading, but most of the slave-owners were Muslims.[1]

In 1939 a periodical reported the request by the *'ulamā* of Java for a *fetwā* from the competent authorities at al-Azhar on the question whether a Muslim father might sell his young son and whether the purchase by a Muslim buyer would be legal. The answer was in the negative, but the matter until recently was one of controversy.[2]

A form of virtual slavery was practised in the Straits Settlements by Arab planters in the island of Cocob, belonging to the Rajah of Johore, where the slaves were natives of the Dutch East Indies who had made the pilgrimage to Mecca. There they spent all their money and having no means of paying for their return passage, were approached by Arab planters who offered them enough for their passage in return for their labour, and so practically bound them for life.[3]

The competent observer who noted these facts about slavery in the East Indies, and has been quoted at some length above with regard to the system at Mecca, remarks[4] that "slavery in Muhammadan lands is an age-old institution required by circumstances. It provides the negro with better treatment than exploitation by Europeans." He is supported by many travellers—of whom some have been quoted—who speak of the lot of the slave in Muslim lands as being in general a comfortable one. Whether the public conscience of the Muslim world would now be satisfied by that

[1] S. Hurgronje, *Verspreide Geschriften* (Bonn, 1923), II, 11 ff.

[2] Cf. J. Jomier, *Le Commentaire Coranique du Manar* (Paris, 1954), pp. 231 ff.

[3] S. Hurgronje, *ibid.*

[4] *Op. cit.* II, 11.

fact is no longer a question of debate, and internal reform in Islamic lands may be expected with the spread of political self-consciousness.[1]

Within the broad classes of Islamic society and sometimes drawing from all of them are groupings which have at various times and places come about on the basis of some common interest, that might be a handicraft, a sport, a religious "reform", a political impulse, trading expediency or a combination of two or more. The occupational groups, or trade guilds, probably date from long before Islam and illustrate their history by the manner in which bazaars are disposed in almost any city of the Middle East or North Africa, where the workshops or trading booths of any particular craft are generally to be found assembled in a quarter recognized by tradition as theirs.[2] The guilds had their own officers who saw to internal discipline, but the religio-political authorities also appointed the *muḥtasib*, whose function it was to see that all trading was honest and the laws of Islam not infringed.

The continuity of guild tradition may be illustrated by comparison of the social activities of the Anatolian *akhīya* (? "fraternities", sing. *akhī*) in the fourteenth century A.D.,[3] with those of the ancient guild of wrestlers in Persia, who in each town have their own *zūr-khāna*, or gymnasium, where they practise their traditional exercises—referred to by Sa'dī in the *Gulistān*—under the aegis of a large portrait of 'Alī b. Abi Ṭālib, their patron saint.

Of much greater significance in community life are the religio-political confraternities (*ṭuruq*; sing. *ṭarīqah*) which have been a feature of Islamic society in every land. The most familiar are those of North Africa, the best known being that of the Sunūsīyah[4] although the Jam'īyat Ikhwān al-Muslimīn, founded in 1929 by Shaikh Ḥasan al-Bannā (assassinated in 1949), has achieved notoriety in Egypt.[5] In the Sudan there are few Muslims who do not belong to one ṭarīqah or another. All have orthodox tenets,

[1] Most Muslim states have abolished slavery, but it still flourishes in some of the Arabian Peninsular States such as Sa'ūdī Arabia, the Yemen and Oman, though it has been abolished in Kuwait and Qatar.

[2] Cf. *Encyclopaedia of Islam*, s.v. *ṣinf*, and, for the modern guilds of North Africa, C. S. Coon, *Caravan* (New York, 1951), pp. 227 ff.

[3] Cf. Ibn Baṭṭūṭa, *Voyages*, II, 260 ff.

[4] C. A. Nallino, *Raccolta di Scritti* (1940), II, 387.

[5] Cf. J. Heyworth-Dunne, *Religious and Political Trends in Modern Egypt* (Washington, 1950).

but the Mahdīyah—rivals of the Khatmīyah or Mīrghanīyah, numerically the strongest—also acknowledge the claims of Saiyid Sir 'Abd al-Raḥmān al-Mahdī (posthumous son of the Mahdī who fought General Gordon) to being the forerunner of the Messiah.

Frequently there have been close associations between such fraternities and Sūfism or dervishism. In Turkey relationships were intimate between the corps of Janissaries and the Bektashi dervishes, members of whose order accompanied the troops as "chaplains".[1] In central Asia, to judge from criticisms in the Soviet Press, there has in recent times been an increase of *murīdism* (apparently a reaction amongst the poorer Muslims against over-energetic secularization), which takes the form of association in religious orders.

[1] Cf. J. K. Birge, *The Bektashi Order of Dervishes* (London, 1937), pp. 46 ff.

CHAPTER II

THE STATUS OF WOMEN IN ISLAM

Islam has throughout its history inevitably borne the marks of its Arabian origin; yet in so fundamental a matter as the position held by women and children in his community Muhammad was able to introduce profound changes. Evidence is scarce of how exactly matters stood in the Prophet's day, but much may be inferred from the Koran and from books, mainly anthologies, compiled in the Muhammadan era but containing older materials. In the work by Robertson Smith that has already been frequently quoted, it is deduced from the evidence there collected that among many of the tribes of ancient Arabia a form of polyandry had existed in which government was by matriarchy. As a rule, such a state of society implies a scarcity of women, but if there had been a scarcity of the kind it would appear to have been remedied by the time of Muhammad's coming. Artificial restriction of the number of females was then being practised and consisted in the burial of unwanted girl children at birth. It is not known what proportion of children was destroyed, but the motives leading to the practice are fairly clear from the Koran, which unconditionally forbade its continuance. None of the motives can be considered as supporting the theory that in Muhammad's time women held a position of paramount importance in the public affairs of the community.[1]

Though it is not improbable that originally, and at a fairly remote period, the idea of sacrifice may have lain at the root of female infanticide,[2] yet in later times rational explanations were found for it. Poverty sometimes was given as the cause, by parents of the poorer class who were afraid they might not be able to find the means for feeding their offspring. At other times, and by parents of higher standing, the reason given was fear of the

[1] Cf. J. Zaydān, *Umayyads and 'Abbāsids*, tr. Margoliouth (Leyden, 1907), pp. 6 f.

[2] Cf. the passage in the Koran 6[137]: "Their associates have made seemly to many of the idolaters the killing of their children, to destroy them and to obscure for them their religion. . . ."

possibility of disgrace and loss of prestige in having one of their own flesh and blood married to a stranger. Alongside the idea that it is humiliating to beget daughters[1] would seem to have lain the thought that in a society where marriage by capture was common, girls might be carried off in war to become the wives or concubines of enemies.[2] How strong the feeling was on this question may be gathered from the commentary on a verse in the *Ḥamāsa*[3]—an anthology that contains much of pre-Islamic Arabic origin—which quotes an early saying to the effect that the grave is the best bridegroom and that the burial of daughters is demanded by honour. Whatever the reason for the practice, Muhammad denounced and forbade it in more than one Koranic revelation,[4] with the result that it disappeared in Arabia in early Islamic times. Within a fairly short time also, Islam succeeded in partly removing some of the ostensible causes of it. From poverty, which was probably regarded as a vice, Muhammadanism took away the stigma by making almsgiving compulsory and praiseworthy, while the doctrine that there were "no captives in Islam"[5] prevented the taking of Arab prisoners and led to the gradual disappearance of marriage by capture. That custom was still widespread in the Prophet's own time, and though, once taken into captivity, women might be treated with great regard and consideration, the possibility of capture reduced the general status of women to that of chattels. The point is well illustrated by a story told of 'Arwa b. al-Ward, who carried off a married woman of the Muzayna tribe. On his way home, coming to an encampment, he was plied with wine by the men of the place, who asked him to give the woman to them; and he consented. He was, it would appear, completely within his rights so to dispose of her, although in fact he regretted his action when he recovered his sober senses.[6]

The captured woman and any children she had by her captor became members of his tribe. He himself exercised complete

[1] See Koran 16^{50-61}.

[2] Cf. W. Robertson Smith, *Kinship and Marriage in Early Arabia* (Cambridge, 1885), p. 279.

[3] Ed. Freytag (Bonn, 1828–47), I, 141, v. 2.

[4] Cf. 6^{141}. "Losers are they who kill their children foolishly . . . they have erred . . . "; 6^{152}. " . . . Ye may not kill your children through poverty; we will provide for you and them." Cf. also 17^{33} and 81^{8}.

[5] Cf. Zaydān, *op. cit.* p. 29.

[6] *Aghānī* (Būlāq, A.H. 1285), II, 191.

authority over her, and, except that he might not sell her in the open market, she was virtually no better than a chattel.

For women generally this would appear to have been the rule. It is to be doubted whether more than a very few had any degree of personal independence to the extent of being able to choose husbands for themselves, or even to have the disposal of property of any value. The cases which are often quoted to prove that the status of women was a high one are of exceptional people, and have for that very reason been preserved.[1] Several are quoted in the *Kitāb al-Aghānī*. There is, for example, that of the daughters of Aws of the tribe of Ṭayy. The two elder ones in turn had refused marriage to Ḥārith b. 'Awf, who had come to their father as a suitor. The third and youngest, Buhaysa, consented to the marriage. When, however, he attempted without ceremony to assert his conjugal rights, she refused consent. "Am I", she asked, "to be treated like a slave-girl or like a captive taken in war?" Before she finally consented to be his wife in more than name, she imposed on him the difficult task of making peace between the tribes of 'Abs and Dhubyān, who had for long been fierce rivals.[2]

Another case quoted is that of Sukayna, daughter of the prophet's grandson Ḥusayn. She married four husbands in succession, choosing them herself.[3] Her exalted origin undoubtedly placed her in a favourable position, but we also hear of a certain 'Ātika, daughter of Zayd, whose only claim to notice is that she was thrice married.[4]

Other instances are given of married women who without hurt to themselves were able to leave their husbands for offending against the marital laws. Thus Umm Salma, who parted from her husband when she found he had a *liaison* with a slave-girl.[5] It was possible, further—at any rate amongst the Bedouins—for a woman to refuse to marry again when her husband died. She indicated her wishes by standing during the mourning ceremonies which were held for him.[6]

As an offset to marital tyranny, some degree of security was

[1] Cf. Nöldeke's review of Robertson Smith's *Kinship* in *Z.D.M.G.*, 40 (1886), 142 f.

[2] *Aghānī*, IX, 149–51.

[3] *Ibid.* XIV, 170 f.

[4] *Ibid.* XVI, 133.

[5] *Ibid.* IV, 89.

[6] *Ibid.* II, 138 *ad fin.*

normally afforded to a married woman by the fact that her blood-kinship with her own tribe was not forgotten and that she could claim its protection in case of necessity. Where her family was influential, a check was undoubtedly placed on the husband's powers.[1] Thus 'Ā'isha bint Ṭalḥa, niece of the Prophet's wife 'Ā'isha, not only kept her lover Muṣ'ab waiting for a considerable period before she consented to marry him, but insisted on her own way over the question of veiling.[2] These instances may at most be taken to indicate that in Muhammad's time there remained traces of an old system in which marriage did not necessarily mean the husband's definite mastery over his wife.[3]

In general, the woman of Arabia in the early Muslim era was in subjection either to her nearest male kinsman—father, brother or whoever he might be—or to her husband, whose right over her was regarded in the same way as his right over any other property.[4]

So far as morality was concerned, the wife's honour was entirely in the keeping of her husband, whose business it was to see that it was not violated. She was his *muḥṣana*, his "woman to be guarded", and if he failed in his duty no stigma attached to the woman for alliance with another man. There were in fact no legal or "moral" sanctions to enforce observance of the laws of proprietary marriage ("*ba'al* marriage", Robertson Smith has called it), and though within a man's own tribe it was regarded as normal and honourable to respect his rights in his wife as in any other property,[5] yet if a man from another tribe seduced a married woman he committed no unlawful or dishonourable act, and poets constantly boasted of their stolen amours.[6] Seducers were, however, open to the vengeance of the outraged husband and of his kinsmen as well as to that of the wife's kinsmen. The latter also were quick to resent an accusation of adultery, for though no

[1] See R. Smith, *Kinship*, pp. 100 ff.

[2] *Aghānī*, x, 54. The chronicler comments incidentally: "So also the women of the Banu Tamīm were the most perverse of God's creatures, yet they were the greatest favourites of their husbands."

[3] Cf. Th. Nöldeke, *Z.D.M.G.*, XL, 142.

[4] Cf. *Aghānī*, XI, 17, 44.

[5] Cf. Wellhausen, *Die Ehe bei den Arabern* (Nachrichten von der Königl. Ges. der Wissenschaften zu Göttingen, 1893), pp. 433 f.

[6] Cf. *ibid.* R. Smith (*Kinship*, p. 71) regarded the stealthiness of these loves as being in the same category with the secrecy which etiquette in some savage tribes demanded from the husband visiting his newly married wife.

dishonour attached to it there was the practical consequence that it gave the husband grounds for repudiating his wife. Thus, in the story of Hind bint 'Ataba we are told that she was married to al-Fākih of the tribe of Quraysh, and that he dismissed her to her home after catching sight of a man in suspicious circumstances near her tent. When she arrived at her father's house he urged her to tell the truth. "If the accusation is a true one," he said, "I will set someone on to kill al-Fākih and prevent people from talking about you. If it is false, I will have him arraigned before one of the *kāhins* (soothsayer-priests) of Yemen."[1]

Alongside marriage by capture there also existed, before and in Muhammad's day, a system that would appear to have been a comparatively late introduction, namely, marriage by purchase or contract. The status of women did not greatly alter under this newer system. Here the suitor paid a sum of money (known as the *mahr*) to the father or nearest kinsman of the girl he wished to marry, and another sum (the *ṣadāq*) to the girl herself. No definite amount was fixed for either payment, but it was possible, where the woman was regarded as the prospective mother of warriors, for the *mahr* to be very large. By Muhammad's time the system had undergone some slight change from its original form. Payment by the bridegroom was still made, but it was to the bride only and not to her father or near kinsman, so that *mahr* and *ṣadāq* became interchangeable terms. The woman's position and the conditions under which she lived were, however, scarcely altered. She was still regarded as the property of her husband, who, having in fact paid for her, regarded himself as entitled exclusively to her services.

The fact that in Islam the *mahr* or *ṣadāq* was paid to the wife[2] has a bearing on the question whether women in pre-Islamic times and in early Islam could own property. The evidence is contradictory, but it appears that in Muhammad's own time women were not allowed the uncontrolled disposal of possessions. In support of this view is adduced the fact that in ancient Medina, according to the commentators on the Koran,[3] women could not

[1] *Aghānī*, VIII, 50 f.

[2] Koran 4³ (latter part) which grants the husband full enjoyment of any portion that the wife may remit.

[3] E.g. Bayḍāwī, on 4⁸, ¹²⁶ dealing with the laws of inheritance.

inherit—presumably from a near kinsman who died intestate. Caution is necessary in accepting the evidence of Muslim doctors of any but the earliest time, for the reason that their statements are sometimes made with the deliberate intent of contrasting the blessedness of Islam with what went before. It is undoubted that under Islam, as shall be seen, the law enacts that women are entitled to a share of inheritance from husband or kinsmen, whereas the statement is constantly made that in the *Jāhilīya*, "the Time of Barbarism", on the other hand, only they could be heirs who took their share of duty in tribal battle and in guarding tribal property.[1] There is some ground, therefore, for thinking that women were then excluded from inheritance. Weight is lent to this view by the story of Qays b. al-Khaṭīm who, when he went off to battle, provided for his mother by leaving with a kinsman a palm-garden, of which the produce was to be for her maintenance.[2] To place against this is the case of the widow Khadīja, who became Muhammad's wife. She was a wealthy woman and able to give the Prophet a great deal of assistance in his efforts to feed and support his early converts.[3] According to tradition, Muhammad, when she died, encountered serious difficulties, being at one time reduced almost to beggary. This would indicate that her property, instead of being at her disposal to bequeath to her husband and daughter as would have been natural, had, on her death, reverted to her nearest male kin, her brothers and their sons or her cousins, as rigid custom demanded.[4]

To his laws of inheritance, as to many others, Muhammad was undoubtedly compelled by the exigencies of the moment. When men fell in battle fighting for his cause he could not have allowed the old custom to prevail and so leave the wives and children of believers destitute in order to benefit kinsmen who were probably hostile to him. Tradition relates[5] that after the battle of Uḥud, in which a certain Aws ibn Ṣāmit had fallen, his widow complained to Muhammad that two cousins of her husband claimed his estate and that if they were permitted to have it she and her three

[1] Cf. Bayḍāwī on Koran 4^8. [2] *Aghānī*, II, 160.

[3] Similarly, the husband of Umm Salma was able to use her great wealth for his own purposes (*Aghānī*, IV, 89).

[4] Cf. Th. Nöldeke, *Z.D.M.G.*, XL, 153.

[5] Cf. Bayḍāwī on Koran 4^9.

young daughters would be left destitute. Thereupon the Prophet received the revelation: "Men should have a portion of what their parents and kindred leave, and women should have a portion of what their parents and kindred leave, whether it be little or much, a determined portion."[1]

Further instructions of a more definite nature are given in the same chapter for the disposal of the property of a person dying intestate. "God instructs you concerning your children: for a male the like of the portion of two females, and if there be women [i.e. daughters] above two, then let them have two-thirds of what [the deceased] leaves. If there be one, then let her have a half."[2] This is followed by particular mention of the portion allotted to a mother, "a third, and if he [the deceased] have brethren, let his mother have a sixth after payment of the bequest he bequeaths and of his debt."

The husband is entitled to a half of what his wife leaves if she has no child; otherwise to a fourth, after payment of any bequests she may make or of any debts.[3] The wife's privilege of making testamentary bequests is here plainly assured, and her power to inherit from her husband is shown in another verse.[4] There is, however, no community of property between husband and wife. He retains full possession and control of his belongings and she of hers, but she is entitled to be properly fed and clothed at his expense, and, furthermore, a married woman is allowed to retain the *mahr* as her wedding-portion and her exclusive possession.[5] It is probable that in this matter Muhammad simply gave sanction to what was becoming the normal practice; but he established it and extended its force by forbidding any coercion of women in respect of their property, making it illegal for a husband to withhold divorce from a woman who was entitled to it if his action was induced by reluctance to lose her possessions.[6] The Koran made it equally illegal to divorce a wife on a false charge whereby the husband might retain some of the property lawfully belonging to her.[7] To all women Muhammad permitted the inheritance of "a portion of what their parents and kindred leave";[8] though in general, it is true, the male was to receive "the like of the portion of two females".[9]

[1] Koran 4[8]. [2] *Ibid. v.* 12. [3] *Ibid. v.* 13. [4] *Ibid. v.* 14.
[5] *Ibid. v.* 3. [6] *Ibid. v.* 23. [7] *Ibid. v.* 24. [8] *Ibid. v.* 8. [9] *Ibid. v.* 12.

In practice, ancient usage has sometimes proved stronger than the law of Islam, as amongst certain tribes of Morocco where daughters do not inherit,[1] and amongst the Kababīsh of the Sudan where only males in a family inherit. In the latter case, however, the widow, daughters, sisters and mother of a man dying intestate would expect to receive some small part of his estate though not in the proportion fixed by the Koran.[2] Apart from such exceptions as these, it is on the whole clear that Muhammad succeeded in bringing about a definite reform when he permitted to women the handling of their own property.

Where other aspects of women's life were concerned, long-established practices and traditions could not have failed to influence the Prophet's views when he came to formulate new laws. Quite clearly he adhered to the traditional estimate of the female as a lesser being. In denouncing the idolators who worshipped the goddesses Allāt, al-'Uzza and al-Manāt, hẹ asks ironically: "Shall there be male offspring for Him (Allah) and female for you? That were an unfair division".[3] "Verily," he says in another place, "those who believe not in the hereafter do surely name the angels with female names."[4] Even more definitely stated is his view of unaccommodating women, particularly married ones, whom he regards as entitled to no better treatment than that given to unruly and obstinate children. "Men stand superior to women in that God hath preferred the one over the other. . . . Those whose perverseness ye fear, admonish them and remove them into bed-chambers and beat them; but if they submit to you then do not seek a way against them."[5]

In his interpretation of this passage, the thirteenth-century commentator Bayḍāwī, whose word is respected by Sunnites to the present day, sets out categorically the different fashions in which men stand superior to women. Allah has preferred the one sex over the other, he says,

[1] E. Übach and E. Rackow, *Sitte und Recht* (Stuttgart, 1923), p. 39.

[2] C. G. and B. Z. Seligman, "The Kababish", *Harvard African Studies*, II (1918), 144.

Halide Edib (*Inside India* (London, 1937), pp. 135 f.) declared that "the Muslems at Lahore have adopted the (Old Hindu) custom-law in place of the Muslem law in regard to women's status and inheritance. . . . One hundred and seventy Muslem women had become Christians in order to be able to inherit."

[3] Koran, 53^{21}. [4] *Ibid.* v. 29. [5] *Ibid.* 4^{38}.

in the matter of mental ability and good counsel, and in their power for the performance of duties and for the carrying out of [divine] commands. Hence to men have been confined prophecy, religious leadership, saintship,[1] pilgrimage rites, the giving of evidence in the law-courts, the duties of the holy war, worship in the mosque on the day of assembly [Friday], etc. They also have the privilege of electing chiefs, have a larger share of inheritance and discretion in the matter of divorce.[2]

Very definitely here is the common Muslim view of women as creatures incapable of and unfitted for public duties.[3] Yet they are reckoned as a part of the community of Islam and the reward of Paradise is offered equally to believing women as to believing men.[4] The private virtues are not denied to women by the Prophet himself, whatever his interpreters may have felt on the matter. His humanity recognized their claim to considerate treatment from parents and from husbands; and on the latter point his interpreters have followed the spirit of his legislation and enacted that a wife is entitled to be fed and clothed at her husband's expense. She is never asked to earn for him, nor to spin or weave for the household. If she has been accustomed to the help of a servant and her husband is able to afford one, he is required to provide such help for his wife as is necessary. No one wife, moreover, is to be favoured at the expense of another, if the husband has more than one, and for him to undertake a vow of abstention from marital intercourse is counted equivalent to an intention of divorce.

From the wife who has not been accustomed to the help of a servant it is expected that she will look after the cleanliness of the household and prepare meals for her husband, though not for his guests. Further, if it is the custom of the country, she may be

[1] On this particular, see below, p. 132.

[2] Cf. Ibn Khaldūn, *Prolégomènes*, text, ed. Quatremère (Paris, 1858 ff.), I, 354.

[3] "The Mufti of Egypt, Shaikh Muhammad Ḥasanayn Makhlouf, issued in June this year a *fatwa* which declared that there was no authority in the Islamic social system for giving women the right to vote or to be elected to parliaments on the ground of their inherently unsuitable nature on the authority of Islamic law . . . " (*The Islamic Review* (Woking), August 1952). Editorial comment on this was that the dignitaries of al-Azhar had failed here to differentiate "between what is customary and what is Islamic".

[4] Koran 97^8.

required, as she very often is, to occupy herself with outdoor work in the fields or with domestic animals.[1]

The greatest of Muhammad's reforms affecting the status of women came in the matter of their relationships with the opposite sex. From the Koran it would seem that his enactments on the question of marriage were designed to bring Islamic practice into line with what held in Judaism and Christianity as he knew them, though there were features—notably the fact that in Islam marriage is a secular contract and not a religious rite—which made for differences. The most important of the new rules was the restriction on the number of wives which the Muslim might at any one time hold in lawful marriage. Before Muhammad, the capacity of the Arab's purse would appear to have provided the only limitation to the number of his wives, and though there were established conventions about the status of women he married, there were neither conventions nor laws to dictate to him how many they should be. The Koran[2] enacted that a man might marry two, three or four wives at one time, although it also recognized that he might find it difficult to treat more than one wife with impartiality.[3] Presumably it is free women that are being spoken of, for the recommendation is made that if financial hardship is involved in marriage with more than one free woman, then either only one should be married or else female slaves should be taken, the indispensable *mahr* and maintenance of the latter not being so costly as that of free women. Muhammad himself received a special "revelation" permitting him to dispense with all limitations and enabling him to marry "any believing woman if she gave herself to the prophet".[4] As was pointed out long ago by Lane,[5] the Prophet may have been actuated in this matter by the want of male offspring[6]—for he had no son who reached manhood—rather than compelled by voluptuousness. But of this he cannot be entirely acquitted when it is noted how he wrested his own laws in his favour and abrogated a long-established custom[7] (namely the convention of regarding an adopted son as equal to a

[1] Khalīl b. Isḥāq, *Mukhtaṣar*, tr. Perron, *Exploration scientifique de l'Algérie* (Paris, 1877), XIII, 130.

[2] 4[3].

[3] 4[128].

[4] Koran 33[49–51].

[5] *Modern Egyptians* (Everyman ed. London, n.d.), ch. III, "On Civil Laws."

[6] Koran 33[40].

[7] *Ibid.* v. 4.

real son in all respects) when he desired to marry the divorced wife of his own adopted son.[1]

Certain *ḥadīths* on the subject of marriage are deserving of notice in this connection, and the substance of them may well be genuine. Thus the Prophet is traditionally credited with having declared it meritorious to marry numerous wives, who should for preference be free women and virgins. Another *ḥadīth* proclaims that no woman should be married without her consent.[2]

For marriage with more than the permitted number of wives no punishment is specified beyond the general threat of hell-fire for wrongdoers. But the position of the offspring of an illegal marriage was probably taken into consideration, although the Koran says nothing of it. In actual practice in modern times economic conditions make it comparatively rare in most Muslim countries for a man to have more than one wife at a time; for not every man can provide the separate establishments which the law-books as well as custom and expediency demand for each. Moreover, the growth of public conscience and the spread of western education have in some Islamic countries led to legislation of a restrictive character which has made the marriage with more than one wife at a time difficult without definitely forbidding what the Koran sanctioned. The famous modernist reformer, Muhammad 'Abduh (1849–1905), on the strength of his interpretation of the Koranic passages (4^{3}, ^{128}) which declared it difficult for a man to act with impartial justice to a plurality of wives, considered that the Prophet himself imposed monogamy, a view which has not found many followers. Polygamy was abolished in Turkey with the introduction of the Swiss Civil Code in 1926,[3] and it has become more difficult in Egypt, Syria, and Persia, where restrictive legislation has been introduced.[4] In the U.S.S.R. and China polygamy is illegal, but there is evidence that in the Muslim states of central Asia the law is frequently evaded. In countries

[1] Koran 33^{37}.

[2] For further examples cf. A. J. Wensinck, *Early Muhammadan Tradition* (Leyden, 1927), s.v. Marriage.

[3] Polygamy persists, being lawful according to Islam, but only the first wife is recognized by the State.

[4] See further J. N. D. Anderson, "Recent Developments in Sharī'a Law", *The Muslim World* (1950–52), and "The Syrian Law of Personal Status", *Bulletin of the School of Oriental Studies* (1955), pp. 34 ff.

where Islamic canon law is the law of the land, frequent changes of wives are common, being only limited by the husband's liability to pay alimony for the woman he divorces.

Proceeding on the assumption that the Koranic enactment about polygamy applies only to free men, the Shāfi'ite school of legists declare that a slave is entitled only to two wives.[1] The Shī'ites, whose position will be discussed later, agree with this decision if the wives are free women, but their number may be increased to four if they are slaves.[2]

From the provisions of the Koran, it follows that for women a plurality of marriages is impossible and that for them monogamy was always the rule.

As to *whom* a man may marry both custom and Koranic law have their say. In pre-Islamic times a form of endogamy, expressed in the marriage of cousins, prevailed amongst a majority of the Arabian tribes. A man's *bint 'amm*, i.e. his father's brother's daughter, was, as a rule, his first wife, who remained mistress of the household even when other women who might be greater favourites were introduced into it. Such marriage within the tribe was preferred probably for the reason that the bride's kin were the better able by it to keep control over the bridegroom and prevent the loss of any property to the tribe. It had the further advantage for the tribe that the woman's children remained within it.

A woman was not compelled in pre-Islamic times by anything more than custom to marry her cousin, and it was possible, without any legal sanction being involved, for her to refuse her consent. But the presumption that he had a right to her was very strong and was generally recognized. The case is quoted of a father, who, when rebuking his daughter for not wishing to marry his brother's son, said to her: "He is your uncle's son and of all men has first claim to you."[3]

Islam has perpetuated the practice, which has thus acquired the force of law, except amongst Chinese Muslims, where local custom forbids it. According to the Ḥanafite school of legists, if a man gives his daughter in marriage to his brother's son while she is still

[1] Cf. E. Sachau, *Muhammedanisches Recht* (Berlin, 1897), p. 5.

[2] A. Querry, *Droit Musulman: Recueil des lois* (Paris, 1871), I, 673.

[3] *Aghānī*, XIV, 161 f.

a minor, she has no right on reaching puberty to claim annulment, whereas the spouse may, though some legists dispute it.[1]

In general the Koran makes it lawful to marry any woman except an idolatress,[2] mentioning specifically "chaste women of those to whom the Book has been given".[3] From its use in other connections this qualification refers to people who have received revealed Scriptures, i.e. Jews, Christians and, by a curious misunderstanding of the Prophet, Ṣābians.[4] In this sense the Ḥanafite school have taken the text and accordingly allow a Muslim to marry Jewish or Christian women to the full number permitted him. The Shāfi'ites, on the other hand, make it virtually impossible to wed non-Muslim women, basing their restrictions on the verse of the Koran which forbids a man to "retain a right over misbelieving women".[5] In this they are supported by a *ḥadīth*, although the Prophet himself by no means confined his marriages to believing women.

So far as Muslim women are concerned they may marry no man but a believer. Apart from the custom that would enforce this rule, sanction for it is derived from the verse of the Koran[6] which forbids a believing woman to marry an idolator and which enforces an earlier revelation forbidding Muslims to send back believing women who have escaped from unbelieving husbands.[7] The new Turkish Civil Code does not prohibit the marriage of a Muslim woman to a non-Muslim man, but custom strongly urges the bridegroom's prior conversion to Islam.[8]

The persons with whom Islam forbids marriage are, with some exceptions, those who come within the prohibited degrees of kinship as set out in the priestly code of the Old Testament.[9] It was in this matter that Muhammad's most drastic change in established practice was brought about. In the *Jāhilīya* the barriers placed on marriage were comparatively few. A man could inherit his father's widow (i.e. his own step-mother), and either marry her himself or give her in marriage to another. The story is recorded of Abu 'l-'Arṣī, who, acting as his mother's *walī*, or

[1] Shaybānī, *Jāmi' al-ṣaghīr* (Lucknow, 1893), p.

[2] Koran 2²²⁰. [3] *Ibid.* 5⁷ [4] Cf. *ibid. vv.* 72 f.

[5] *Ibid.* 60¹⁰. [6] 2²²⁰. [7] 60¹⁰.

[8] G. Jäschke, "Die Eheschliessung in der Türkei", *Die Welt des Islams*, II (1953), 143 ff.

[9] In particular, Leviticus XVIII, 7–18.

sponsor, gave her in marriage to her step-son, his own half-brother Abu 'Amr.[1]

It was never lawful, however, for a man to marry his own mother. That is clear from the commentaries on certain passages in the Koran[2] dealing with the question of the remarriage of a divorced woman. The formula of divorce in ancient times was, according to the native commentators, "Thou art to me as the back of my mother", the pronouncement of which euphemistic formula made it illegal for a man to resume cohabitation with his wife.[3]

The Koran makes it unlawful for a man to marry either the widow or the divorced wife of his father, although where such a marriage has already taken place it remains valid. The phrase used in the Koran[4] to express this latter condition is "except what is already past", i.e. except what is in force already. The same words are used in connection with the marriage of two sisters,[5] which accordingly would appear to have been lawful in pre-Islamic times though the Koran forbade it.[6] Muhammad's legislation further prohibited a man from marrying his daughters, his sisters,[7] his aunts on both his father's and mother's side, his brothers' and sisters' daughters[8] and his sons' wives.[9] Moreover, a man is forbidden to marry a woman and her daughter; nor may he take in marriage a woman who is already lawfully married to, and in the possession of, another man.[10] An ordinance peculiar to the Koran is that forbidding marriage between two persons reared at the breast of the same foster-mother, or between the foster-mother and the youth who has been suckled at her breast.[11]

The law-books amplify the Koranic provisions—and incidentally bring them further into lines with Biblical precedent—by forbidding a man to marry his grandmothers or granddaughters or

1 *Aghānī*, I, 10 (top). 2 33^4 and 58^2. 3 Cf. Smith, *Kinship*, pp. 163 f.

4 4^{26}. 5 4^{27}. 6 Cf. Leviticus XVIII, 18.

7 This made a change in the social customs of Persia, where Zoroastrianism permitted and even encouraged the marriage of brother and sister.

8 The Old Testament code does not mention them as within the prohibited degrees of kinship, and marriage with a niece is accordingly permitted by Rabbinical law. By Iranian law a man may not marry a niece of his wife's without the latter's consent.

9 Koran 4^{26-27}.

10 The latter enactment ensures the monogamy of women.

11 4^{27}.

to marry a woman and her niece at one time.[1] A special clause is reserved in the law-books for the form of marriage known as *shighār*. By it a man contracted to take another's daughter in marriage, giving his own in return and without any other valuable consideration as dowry being demanded by either father, the persons of the wives being regarded as the *mahr*. The law-books forbid this kind of marriage, which seems to have been frequent in pre-Islamic times; although no ban is placed upon it if a separate *mahr* is provided for each of the two women.[2] By Iranian law a man who has had sexual relations with another man may not marry the latter's mother, sister or daughter.[3]

In spite of the Koranic sanction of the marriage of a free man with a female slave, the law-books place certain restrictions on it, as we have had occasion to note in the previous chapter. No restriction is placed on the possession of unmarried female slaves in concubinage by their owner, but the Ḥanafī code forbids a (free) man to marry his own or his son's female slave and a (free) woman to marry her male slave. Accordingly,

> When a man, from being the husband, becomes the master of a slave, the marriage is dissolved and he cannot continue to live with her but as her master, enjoying, however, all a master's privileges; unless he emancipates her; in which case he may again take her as wife with her consent. In like manner, when a woman, from being the wife, becomes the possessor, of a slave, the marriage is dissolved and cannot be renewed unless she emancipates him, and he consents to the re-union.[4]

According to most of the jurists a man may marry another's female slave provided:

(*a*) that he is unmarried and does not already possess a slave-girl to be his concubine;
(*b*) that he is too poor to afford a *mahr* for a free woman;
(*c*) that he is exposed to the danger of unchastity if he remains unmarried; and
(*d*) that the female slave is a Muhammadan.

[1] Cf., for example, Qudūrī, *Mukhtaṣar* (Bombay, 1886), p. 150.
[2] Querry, *op. cit.* I, 687 f.; cf. Lane, *Arabic Lexicon*, s.v. *shighār*.
[3] R. Aghababian, *Législation Iranienne* (Paris, 1951), II, 1056.
[4] Lane, *Thousand and One Nights* (1st ed.), I, 63.

There is no bar to the possession as concubines of Jewish or Christian slaves. The Ḥanafites, moreover, permit marriage with them and demand only that the man shall not be married already to a free woman.[1]

A still further reform made by Muhammad, and a closer approximation to the Biblical code, was when he stipulated certain times at which a woman might not be married. It was lawful in the *Jāhilīya* for a woman immediately on the death of her husband, or after divorce by him, to be married to another man without regard to her physical condition. Islam made it necessary for a divorced woman before remarrying to wait "three courses",[2] and for a widow to wait four months and ten days[3] in order to allow sufficient time for it to be made clear whether she is with child or not.[4] If she is pregnant, the new husband must wait for cohabitation until the child is born. Similarly, when a man comes into possession of a female slave, he must wait until he is certain she is not pregnant.[5] If she is pregnant, he must wait until she is delivered of her child. It is not unlawful, however, during the time of waiting, for a man to propose marriage to the woman, although it must be done in veiled words and not openly, and the marriage must not take place until the end of the time.[6]

There is no period of waiting for a free woman not divorced or a widow.[7]

No age limits have been fixed by Islam for marriage, and quite young children may be legally married, although a girl is not handed over to her husband until she is fit for marital congress.

[1] Shīrāzī, *Tanbīh*, ed. Juynboll (Leyden, 1879), p. 195; Sachau, *Muhammedanisches Recht*, p. 24, and *Encyclopaedia of Islam*, s.v. '*Abd*.

[2] The period known as the '*idda*, Koran 2^{228}. Compare the similar Talmudic law that a divorced or widowed woman must wait at least 90 days before remarriage in order to ascertain if she is with child (Talmud Babli, *Yebāmoth*, 41–3).

[3] Koran 2^{234}.

[4] The periods given are for free women. For slaves the durations are respectively two "courses" and two months and five days (cf. Sachau, *op. cit.* p. 16).

[5] The period of waiting for a slave-girl is known as *istibrā'*.

[6] Koran 2^{335}. Cf. Sachau, *op. cit.* p. 17.

[7] This fact provides the point of the story told of Hārūn al-Rashīd, who wished to have immediate union with a slave-girl he had acquired. He consulted his qāḍī, Abū Yūsuf, as to how he might satisfy his desires and yet remain within the law. The qāḍī replied that he could do so by manumitting the girl, for there is no *istibrā'* for a free woman (Ibn Khallikān, in the biography of Abu Yūsuf).

The Ḥanafite code lays it down that a wife must not be taken to her husband's house until she reaches that condition. In case of dispute on the matter between the husband and the bride's *walī*, who is her nearest male kinsman and her guardian, the qāḍī is to be informed, and he is to appoint two matrons to examine the girl and report on her physical preparedness for marriage. If they decide that she is too young, she must return to her father's house until she is judged fit. Betrothal may take place at any age. Actual marriage is later, but the age for it varies in different lands.

In Islamic Soviet Republics the State fixes eighteen as the minimum for either sex, but in 1950 Uzbek school-directors were favouring the marriage of girl pupils at the age of twelve or thirteen.[1] Turkey by its national code has fixed eighteen completed years as the lowest age for men and seventeen for women, although in certain circumstances the courts can be asked to sanction marriage at fifteen for either sex, but no earlier. In some other Muslim lands, with the growth of the feeling that child-marriage is undesirable, recent legislation has made it more difficult, not by direct prohibition—which would have conflicted with the *sunna* of the Prophet—but, as in Egypt, by procedural regulations such as the refusal to register marriages in which the parties have not reached a specified minimum age. Lack of official registration makes it impossible to obtain judicial relief in the event of matrimonial litigation.

In Persia no woman can contract marriage before the age of fifteen and no man before the age of eighteen. In certain circumstances dispensation from the observance of these limits can be obtained from the courts, but not if the woman is below the age of thirteen and the man under fifteen.[2]

In Egypt the custom has been for girls to marry at twelve or thirteen. Not many remain unmarried after sixteen years of age[3] and nineteen is "the age of an oldish old maid".[4] In Persia and Chinese Central Asia the marriage age for girls was from twelve to fourteen years,[5] and similar ages are usual amongst the Berbers

[1] V. Monteil, *Revue des Études Islamiques*, XX, 1952.

[2] Aghababian, *Législation Iranienne*, II, 1041.

[3] Lane, *Modern Egyptians*, ch. VI.

[4] Burton, *Thousand Nights and a Night*, I, 195.

[5] Cf. Bayhaqī, *Ta'rīkh-i Mas'ūdī*, ed. Morley (Calcutta, 1862), p. 301; and Skrine, *Chinese Central Asia* (London, 1926), p. 194.

dwelling in the oases of the Libyan desert.[1] So also amongst the Kababish of the Sudan, where betrothal of girls takes place when they are about nine to eleven years old, and marriage three or four years later. The bridegroom is usually older than the bride.[2] Amongst the Tuareg of the Sahara the age would appear to be later than is usual amongst Oriental women.[3] As a general rule, however, it must be taken that when marriage for a girl is being discussed it is not age but physical fitness for matrimony which is the decisive point.[4]

The preliminaries to a first marriage are, with some few exceptions, fairly similar in most Muslim lands and depend largely upon the fact that as a rule a man keeps the female inmates of his house veiled. In Baghdad, to take an instance, although amongst modernized and educated families the young man desirous of a wife chooses her for himself, yet in general it is still the rule for a prospective bridegroom to inform his mother or other near female relative of his wishes. Accompanied by friends and relations she calls on the mother of a girl she thinks suitable and begs her to speak of the proposed match to her husband. If the girl's mother has any reason for not wishing the match she gives an evasive reply which conveys what she means, otherwise she consents to do what she is asked. If all then goes well, she communicates with the mother of the young man and tells her that the formalities of the betrothal can be carried through. More often than not, the girl, if she is being married for the first time, is ignorant of the negotiations that are proceeding, and her parents may promise her to a man she has never seen. It would appear, however, that no young woman well brought up ever refuses a match agreeable to her parents. On a day fixed, the prospective bridegroom goes in company with the *imām* (prayer-leader) of the quarter in which he lives and a number of his friends to ask the girl's father formally for his daughter's hand in marriage. In the course of the visit the question of the *mahr* is discussed and settled.[5] The imām then

[1] A. M. Hasanein, *Lost Oases* (London, 1925), p. 101.

[2] Seligman, "The *Kababish*", p. 132.

[3] F. R. Rodd, *People of the Veil* (London, 1926), p. 170.

[4] Cf. *Revue internationale de législation musulmane* (Cairo, 1895), p. 104.

[5] Amongst some tribes of Morocco and Tunisia the amount of the *mahr* is known and determined by custom, and it is not therefore discussed (Übach and Rackow, *Sitte und Recht* (Stuttgart, 1923), p. 37).

recites prayers and sends to a qāḍī to ask him to grant the necessary permission to marry, after which the two people concerned are considered officially betrothed.

The custom in Egypt and other lands is very similar.[1] There are, however, as in all such matters of tradition, some exceptions to the general practice. Amongst the Bedouins of the Libyan desert, boys and girls mix freely except amongst the higher classes, whose women are all kept in seclusion. "As a rule, the boy knows his sweetheart, and he goes to her camp and sings to her, generally in verse of his own making. If she likes him, she comes out and answers his song, not rarely in words of her own composition, too. The boy then goes and asks for the girl from her people, paying a dowry if an agreement is reached. Cases of elopement leading to blood-feuds are known."[2]

Similarly, in Chinese Turkistan, the practice of not allowing a boy to see his betrothed until the wedding-day is not followed, for the children have known and played with each other from early childhood.[3] Amongst the Tuareg, with whom women enjoy a position of exceptional freedom, marriages are not arranged as amongst the neighbouring Arabs, and the women choose their own husbands.[4] How the custom stood in ancient times may be gathered from the case of a youth at Medina who was able to see and fall in love with a girl out walking with friends. However, when he sent his father and some of the elder members of his family to sue for her hand, her father refused to consider the match.[5]

The Shīʿa law permits a man to see the hands and face of his prospective bride,[6] but it would appear that the privilege was rarely granted in practice until Shah Rizā enacted his unveiling laws in Persia. Since his death the old restrictions appear to have been reimposed except in Europeanized families.

In arranging the terms of the marriage, the *walī* of the bride plays a special role, his function dating from the time when the *mahr* was the price paid for the bride by the bridegroom to her

[1] Compare the account given in Lane, *Modern Egyptians*, ch. VI.
[2] Hasanein, *Lost Oases*, p. 101.
[3] Skrine, *Chinese Central Asia*, p. 195.
[4] Rodd, *People of the Veil*, p. 170.
[5] *Aghānī*, XII, 169 f.
[6] Querry, *Recueil*, I, 642.

nearest kinsman. Even in Muhammad's time the function had a marketable value. The different schools of law differ about who should perform the duty of the *walī*. According to the Shāfi'ī rite he should be her father, grandfather or other relative in the ascendant line. Failing them, her brother, nephew, uncle or male cousin (in that order) may act. In the absence of any male relative, the qāḍī undertakes the duty.[1] According to the Ḥanafī rite the *walī* should be the woman's father or else her son or other relative in the descendant line, if she has one; if not, then some other male relative may act. In the last resort the Caliph or Sulṭān is the *walī*, a duty which the prophet himself fulfilled in his own day. Whatever his relationship to the bride, he is required by the law-books to be (*a*) a Muhammadan,[2] (*b*) of full age, (*c*) male, (*d*) a free man, (*e*) of sound mind, and (*f*) of blameless character.[3] His chief duty is to see that the principle of the equality of the parties[4] is maintained, and that the woman over whom he has charge does not make an unsuitable or undesirable match which may bring dishonour on the tribe. It is he who, on payment of the agreed portion of the *mahr*, hands the bride over into the control of the husband, who may now take his bride home if he wishes. There is a *ḥadīth* that no woman may be given in marriage without her consent; but, according to the Ḥanafī code, the *walī* may give in marriage a girl who is a virgin and also a minor, after informing her that a suitor has presented himself, even if he (the suitor) is a slave. Her silence gives consent, but even if she says that she does not consent, the marriage is lawful.[5]

[1] Sachau, *Muhammedanisches Recht*, pp. 6 f.

[2] Thus, if a Christian has a daughter who has become a Muhammadan, he cannot legally give her in marriage as her *walī*. On the other hand, a Jew or Christian may act as the *walī* of a Jewish or Christian woman.

[3] The last condition is not enforced where the bride is a slave.

[4] Shīrāzī, *Tanbīh*, p. 192; in this it is laid down that no *walī* may arrange a humble match for his ward except by her consent and that of the other *walīs*. "Equality is to be maintained in birth (lineage), religion, occupation and degree of personal liberty. And no Arab woman may be married to a Persian, no Qurashite woman to a non-Qurashite, no Hāshimite woman to a non-Hāshimite, no chaste woman to a libertine, no merchant's daughter to a weaver, etc." "Parity of rank is much regarded. A man is often unable to obtain as his wife the daughter of one of a different profession or trade, or a younger daughter when an elder remains unmarried" (Lane, *Thousand and One Nights*, I, 318).

[5] Shaybānī, *Jāmi' al-ṣaghīr*, p. 37. The *walī* must be the kinsman who has actual right to the office. In a marriage made by anyone else the girl's refusal is upheld and the marriage would be invalid.

Under Shāfi'ī law, the marriage of a virgin is impossible without father or grandfather to act as *walī*.[1] But since Islam attaches great importance to marriage the difficulty may be circumvented by the girl's changing of the rite under which she was brought up. This permits a wider set of relatives to be included amongst the *walīs*, giving a chance that a suitable one may be found.[2] According to the Ḥanafī rite a free woman of full age can never be given in marriage without her consent even if she is virgin,[3] but by all the codes, if a woman is not a virgin, whether lawfully or otherwise deflowered, her consent is required for her marriage. Once the *walī* has completed his duty, his concern with the marriage and the married woman legally comes to an end until such time as the question of her remarriage arises.

In the matter of the *walī*, as in other matters in Islam, deviations from the general rule are noticed, for the demands of the law-books are not always carried out in everyday practice. Thus, when the qāḍī Iṣṭakhrī went to take up his duties in Sīstān, he found that the services of the *walī* were dispensed with.[4] According to the modern Persian code a woman under the age of eighteen cannot contract a marriage without the consent of her legal guardian, and even if she is over that age she cannot do so for the first time unless her father (failing whom her grandfather) agrees. If consent is refused, she can carry out her wishes through the intermediation of a bureau especially appointed.[5]

The owner of a female slave—as has been noted in a different connection[6]—might give her in marriage to anyone that he pleased without asking her consent. If he wished to marry her himself he had first to emancipate her, and that done, her consent to the marriage was necessary. This is clear from the history of Shāriya, the slave of Ibrahīm ibn al-Mahdī. Becoming possessed of a desire to marry her, he summoned a number of his friends and called Shāriya to unveil in their presence. He then asked her to give them her name, and she replied, "I am Shāriya, your slave." After this he commanded those present to look at the girl's face

[1] See *Encyc. of Islam*, s.v. *Nikāḥ*.

[2] See S. Hurgronje, *The Achehnese*, tr. O'Sullivan (Leyden, 1906), I, 330.

[3] Qudūrī, *Mukhtaṣar*, p. 151.

[4] Ibn Khallikān, ed. Wuestenfeld, no. 157 (II, 88); cf. I. Goldziher, *Zeitschr. für vergleichende Rechtswissenschaft*, VIII, 409.

[5] Aghababian, *Législation Iranienne*, II, 1042 f.

[6] See p. 80.

and said, "I call you to witness that she is free, before God, and that I am marrying her and giving her a dowry of ten thousand dirhams". Then turning to the girl said, "O Shāriya, freed-woman of Ibrahīm ibn al-Mahdī, dost thou consent?" She answered, "Yes, my master. And praise be to God for the bounty He has bestowed upon me." Thereupon he bade her go within and caused food to be set before his guests.[1]

Considerable importance is attached amongst all Muslim peoples to the formalities of the actual wedding, which usually takes place a few days after the betrothal and proceeds according to a set form. The custom that prevails at Baghdad, for example, is that on the day before the wedding, the bridegroom informs himself of the number of women in the house of his betrothed and sends to each a pair of shoes or some other small gift, together with sweets and a number of silk handkerchiefs, which are used for their distribution amongst the wedding guests. This gift, carried in trays on the heads of several men, is sent with as much ceremony as the status of the bridegroom allows. It is preceded by a band consisting of an Arab clarinet and a drum, while following it come a number of women who from time to time emit ululating cries of joy. On the same day the bridegroom sends out invitations to the people who are to witness and sign the contract of marriage—which fulfils a very important part in the ceremony.

On the wedding day, the invited guests repair to the house of the bride's father; the women remaining in the harem and the men in the apartment reserved for them. When all are assembled, an imām who is invited to attend summons a representative each from the families of bride and bridegroom, and they constitute the two witnesses whose presence at a wedding is rigorously demanded by custom. It is by custom also that the imām officiates, for since in essence a Muslim marriage is a secular contract his presence could be dispensed with. It is the witnesses, and not the bride and bridegroom, who sign the wedding contract, and their importance is shown by the conditions they must fulfil in order to be eligible for their office. They are required, like the bride's *walī* himself, to be males, free men, adults, of full understanding and Muslims. If two such men are not available, two Muslim women

[1] *Aghānī*, XIV, 110.

may take the place of one of the men, though at least one of the witnesses is required to be a man.[1]

At the signing of the contract the imām formally asks the representatives of the two families if they consent to the terms of the marriage and then puts the hands of bride and bridegroom together so that their thumbs touch. In this position he holds them while he recites a prayer. All present then recite the *Fātiḥa* (the opening chapter of the Koran), and the formal part of the wedding is over. The feast which follows is, however, an integral part of it, being a custom that dates from pre-Islamic times and probably originating in an ancient sacrificial meal. No man who is invited to the feast may absent himself without good and sufficient cause, and the host—the bride's father or *walī*—is recommended to invite not only the rich and influential but the pious and learned as well. It is commendable for the host to sacrifice a sheep, if he has the means, and he must see to it that no ritually unlawful food is set before his guests and that no forbidden luxury (e.g. the use of gold or silver vessels) is indulged in.[2]

The central feature of the marriage is, however, the contract. Its most important clause concerns the *mahr*, the value and character of which must be specified.[3] The law-books generally name no sum as a maximum, and according to the Shāfi'ites there

[1] If a man marries a Jewish or Christian woman, the marriage is legal if performed in the presence of two women of the bride's faith (Abu Ḥanīfa, according to Qudūrī's *Mukhtaṣar*, p. 150).

[2] Bukhārī, *Saḥīḥ*, ed. Krehl (Leyden, 1862–8), III, 436 ff (Bk. 67, 67 f.). Cf. Juynboll, *Handbuch des Islamischen Gesetzes* (Leyden, 1910), pp. 164 ff.

[3] The following written contract, which may be regarded as typical, is quoted in F. H. Ruxton's *Mālikī Law* (London, 1916), p. 94:

> Glory be to God, the Lord of the worlds!
>
> The honourable Kaddūr, being of age and living in Algiers, a trader by calling, son of Sulaymān, has contracted a marriage by God's blessing . . . with the noble virgin Fatima, now passed the period of puberty, 18 years of age, daughter of Md. b. Ali, weaver, domiciled in Algiers. The marriage is contracted in consideration of a dower of blessed augury amounting to 30 douros, of which half is at once due, before consummation of the marriage, and the remaining half payable within four years. The husband will only be acquitted of this debt by lawful means. The bride's father has contracted in her name, and this by virtue of the powers conferred on him by God and after obtaining her consent, expressed by silence, which is considered as the equivalent to consent. The husband has appeared in person; he has accepted the contract, the offer and the acceptance have been made as required by Law.
>
> All that precedes has been witnessed [by two witnesses].

is no specified minimum.[1] The Ḥanafites,[2] however, do not permit a marriage where the valuable consideration to the bride is less than one dīnār (or ten dirhams).[3] This sum is given because, according to one "tradition", Muhammad gave to several of his wives a dowry of ten dirhams and a number of household necessities, such as a hand-mill, a water-jug and other furniture.[4]

The *mahr* is paid to the bride only if she is a free woman.[5] If she is a slave the *mahr* belongs to her master whether her husband is a slave or a free man. As a rule, the amount of it is considerably higher if she is a virgin than if she is a divorced woman or a widow. A woman, however, who has had experience of marriage and is beyond the average in good looks and wit is much more sought after and commands a good *mahr*, whether it be in Mecca or Chinese Turkistan.[6]

Usually the whole *mahr* is not paid at once, although this is a matter of arrangement with the woman's *walī*, and custom differs in various regions as to the portion payable before consummation. It may be half or two-thirds, the balance being held in reserve to be paid to the wife if the husband dies or divorces her. Until the agreed instalment of the *mahr* is paid, the wife may deny herself to her husband or refuse to go on a journey with him.[7] The *mahr* may be of only the most moderate value, but if it is not mentioned in the contract of marriage, there is strongly accredited tradition to the effect that the marriage is invalid. Amongst some tribes in North Africa the husband pays the *mahr* only when he divorces his wife, although, as a general rule there, it is paid on the morning after the marriage.[8]

[1] See Sachau, *op. cit.* p. 9.

[2] Abu Ḥanīfa, *Jāmi' al-ṣaghīr*, p. 41.

[3] The sum quoted is in an archaic and entirely obsolete denomination. The value of the coins mentioned was never constant. In Baghdad during the early Abbasid Caliphate the dirham was a silver coin and worth about five pence.

[4] This "tradition" is especially unreliable. According to Ibn Hishām's "Life" of the Prophet, the latter usually gave 400 dirhams as *ṣadāq*. The articles of furniture mentioned were given to his wife Umm Salama (Ibn Hishām, *Sīrat Saiyidnā Muḥammad*, ed. Wuestenfeld (Göttingen, 1858–60), pp. 790, 1001 f.).

[5] No *mahr* is demanded in concubinage.

[6] Cf. S. Hurgronje, *Mekka* (Leyden, 1888), II, 109 f., and Skrine, *op. cit.* p. 202.

[7] Abu Hanīfa, in *Jāmi' al-ṣaghīr*, p. 41.

[8] Übach and Rackow, *op. cit.*

The marriage contract often declares whether the bride is being married as a virgin or not. In Morocco, frequently, if a bride is found not to be a virgin, though claiming to be one, she is sent away by the bridegroom. In some tribes she may even be killed by her own father or brother.[1]

So far, that form of marriage has been discussed to which Koranic regulations on the subject of marriage have reference, and in which the wife is placed entirely under the domination of her husband.[2] This form perpetuates some of the features of the old marriage by purchase, in which the *mahr* was the payment made to the father or nearest kinsman of the woman, who became the chattel of her husband. Under Islam, as has been noted, the *mahr* became the woman's dowry and was paid to her, but otherwise her position did not become greatly better than under the old system. Alongside this *ba'al* marriage, there existed in Arabia in pre-Islamic times another form which has been called *mut'a* marriage, from an Arabic phrase which is used in the Koran (4^{28})[3] in connection with marriage, and which denotes "enjoyment" or the "reward for enjoyment". *Mut'a* marriage differed from *ba'al* marriage in that its object was not the establishment of a household or the begetting of children, but simply to provide a man with a wife when he was away from home on military service or for other reasons.[4] The characteristic mark of such a temporary marriage was that the contract specified for how long it should hold. It was a purely personal arrangement between the two parties and it was arranged without any intervention on the part of the woman's kin. Accordingly, no *walī* was necessary. At the end of the specified period both parties were free, without any further ceremony, to part, provided that the woman had received the dowry or fee due to her. The system obviously lent itself to abuses and it differed so little from prostitution that the "traditions" declare that Muhammad made it unlawful. The Koran

[1] Westermarck, *Marriage Ceremonies in Morocco* (London, 1914), ch. VII, p. 270.

[2] Robertson Smith called it *ba'al* marriage, the Hebrew word *ba'al* denoting "lord", "master" or "possessor", and being the term used in the Old Testament for "husband".

[3] "But such of them (women) as ye have enjoyed, give them their hire as a lawful due; for there is no crime in you about what ye agree between you after such lawful due."

[4] Cf. Juynboll, *Handbuch*, p. 228.

itself, however, is evidence to the contrary, and there are other "traditions" which seem to permit the practice. Probably the fact is that Muhammad gave reluctant permission for the hire of prostitutes, a class of persons who had always existed and could not be abolished at a word.

The character of the *mut'a* marriage and the attitude of orthodox Islam towards it is shown in a story of "the Ḥimyarite Sayyid".[1] He once met on the road a woman who offered him marriage there and then. He replied: "It would be like the marriage of Umm Khārija[2]; before the arrival of *walī* or witnesses." She then asked him who he was and, on hearing his reply, made in boastful verse, her answer was that marriage with him was impossible seeing that he was a Yemenite and of the Rāfiḍī (heretic) sect, while she was of the rival Tamīmī tribe and a Khārijite by religion. "Be of good sense and let your soul be generous towards me," he answered, "and let neither of us remember our ancestry or religion". "When a marriage is made public, are not private concerns revealed?" she retorted. Whereupon he said: "I have a different suggestion to make to you . . . namely, *mut'a*, of which no one need know anything." "That", she replied, "is the sister of harlotry". "I conjure you by God", he protested, "not to misbelieve in the Koran, having once believed in it".[3] The woman finally consented to the union, thereby risking death at the hands of her clansmen, who, not knowing it was simply a *mut'a* marriage, accused her of having married a misbeliever.

The Caliph Omar attempted to abolish the practice of *mut'a* marriage, which is regarded as illegal by the Sunnites,[4] but the Shī'ites find in the verse quoted of the Koran full permission to take a temporary wife. Accordingly, in Persia and other Shī'ite countries, it is common for a Muslim to take a woman of his own faith, or a Jewish, Christian or (though some contest this) a Magian woman,[5] for a fixed period of time, which may vary from

[1] *Aghānī*, VII, 18.

[2] Proverbial for her swiftness in arranging her numerous marriages (*Aghānī*, XII, 79).

[3] Presumably referring to 4^{28}, already quoted.

[5] The Caliph Ma'mūn legalized it, but he was compelled by public opinion to withdraw his edict (Ibn Khallikān, s.v. *Yaḥyā b. Aktam*, tr. de Slane, IV, 36).

[5] Some Shī'ite lawyers insist that *mut'a* is only lawful where the woman is known to the man. Cf. Ibn Bābūyah, *Man lā yaḥḍuruhu al-faqīh*, B.M. MS. Add. 19,358, f. 140a.

a fraction of a day to a year or several years.[1] Respectable persons will only contract such a marriage for a term of ninety-nine years, thus making it the equivalent of a permanent one.[2] In Persia the woman is known as a *ṣīgha*, although properly speaking that term belongs to the contract[3] drawn up by the officiating *mullā*. In this contract the *mahr*—which may be as little as a handful of corn—and also the term must be specified; but no phrase or expression may be used in it to imply that the woman is being given into the possession of the man for a valuable consideration, or as a gift for hire. Any such phrase or expression nullifies the contract, which merely serves to limit the absolute freedom of the man to separate from the woman, for though the marriage may be dissolved before the expiry of the stipulated period, it must be by mutual consent, and the husband has no power to divorce the wife without it.[4] The children of such a marriage are legitimate and have a right to a share of inheritance from their father, but, unlike the ordinary wife, the *ṣīgha* has no legal claim to maintenance or to anything more than the gift stipulated in the contract, and she does not inherit from her husband. Similarly, he does not inherit from her.

Concubinage is expressly differentiated from marriage in Islam, mainly by the fact that female slaves alone, and not free women, are held in concubinage. As has already been noted above, the owner of a female slave may not marry her unless he first emancipates her. The law places no limit on the number of concubines that a man may possess either in addition to or in place of a wife or wives. Certain bounds are, however, placed to the right of unrestricted cohabitation with them. They must be Muslims, Jewesses or Christian women, and not already married. Their owner may not cohabit with two or more who are sisters or who stand in such relationship to one another that marriage with them at the same time would be impossible to him if they were free.[5] Also he must delay cohabitation with a newly acquired slave for

[1] Querry, *Recueil*, I, 689 f; E. G. Browne, *A Year amongst the Persians* (London, 1893), p. 462.

[2] C. J. Wills, *Land of the Lion and the Sun* (London, 1893), p. 326.

[3] For ordinary marriage the contract is called *'aqd*.

[4] The husband has a right to refuse marital union, which in ordinary marriages would give the woman claim to divorce. If the marriage is dissolved before consummation, the woman has a right to half the *mahr* stipulated in the contract.

[5] Cf. Lane, *Modern Egyptians*, ch. III, p. 104.

a period during which it may be ascertained if she is pregnant.[1] A still further restriction on the full powers of the master over his female slaves is this, that although he may himself use them as concubines, or may give or sell them to other men for that purpose, he may not force his female slaves to prostitution for his gain "if they desire to keep continent".[2]

There is a *ḥadīth* to the effect that the wages gained by the prostitution of a slave-girl may not be enjoyed by her owner.[3] Yet the qualification attached in the Koran to the decision about harlotry seems to imply either that Muhammad was not convinced of the rightness of his interdict, or that prostitution was too firmly established to be at once removed. The latter is more probably true. Of the fact of public prostitution in the days before Muhammad there can be no doubt, and the attempt has been made to show that the pre-Muslim Arabs considered it no shame to have traffic with whores.[4] If that was so, Islam brought about a change. In connection with the history of the short-reigned Umayyad Caliph Marwān b. al-Ḥakam, the chroniclers relate that persons who wished to insult him spoke of him as "The son of al-Zarqā". The latter, his ancestress, was one of those women of Arabia "who hung out a flag, whereby in the *Jāhilīya* the houses of prostitutes were indicated".[5]

Prostitutes never lived with their own clan; almost certainly because their profession was regarded as dishonourable. Where they did not keep to special houses they were to be found at markets and fairs and the more frequented parts of the public streets. A member of the class of whom many stories were told

[1] That this rule is not always obeyed is clear from more than one source. Cf. S. Hurgronje, *Mekka*, II, 135.

[2] Koran 24[33].

[3] Cf. Wensinck, *Early Muhammadan Tradition*, p. 217.

[4] Cf. R. Smith, *Kinship*, p. 143.

[5] Cf. Ibn al-Athīr (ed. Tornberg), IV, 160; and *al-Fakhrī* (ed. Ahlwardt, p. 144). The latter also tells how Ziyād ibn Abīhī (Ziyād Son of his Father) was born of a public prostitute called Sumayya (p. 133). The same term is applied to her as to Zarqā. According to Robertson Smith, *Kinship*, p. 143, these women belonged to those who, after the coming of Islam, adhered to the old lax system of polyandry; and at the time it was no disgrace to frequent their houses. The evidence to the contrary is comparatively late, but there can be no doubt of the disgust expressed by Mu'āwiya's contemporaries when he claimed Ziyād, the prostitute's son, as his half-brother. Ṭabarī, at any rate, knows of her as "Sumayya, the whore" (II, 133; III, 478).

was Kharqā of the Banū 'Āmir tribe, who kept herself for pilgrims and considered herself as "one of the pilgrimage rites". She would unveil only before strangers and kept her face covered in the presence of any man she knew.[1]

There is no need to say more on this subject than that in spite of the official disapproval of Islam, public prostitution has never been abolished[2]; and although public women and their procurers are regarded as law-breakers, they are to be found in practically all Muhammadan lands.[3]

The nature of the relative status in marriage of men and women would appear to discourage marital infidelity amongst wives. If, nevertheless, a charge of adultery is laid, the evidence required by the Koran[4] is such as to be practically impossible to obtain. The text reads: "Those who cast imputations [of adultery] on chaste women and then do not bring four witnesses,[5] scourge them with eighty stripes", upon which the relevant part of Bayḍāwī's comment is as follows: "Chastity here implies being free, of full age and sound mind, professing Islam and abstaining from fornication. And there is no distinction made in it between male and female. (Chaste) women are specified in order to give actual examples, or because accusation against women is graver and more culpable."

In the unlikely event of the evidence being produced, the Koran demands a severe penalty for the culprits, but contains two different views of what it shall be. In Sūra 24^2, which may be presumed to be the earlier passage dealing with the subject, the punishment for both the adulterer and the adulteress is specified as a hundred strokes; in Sūra 4^{19} only adulterous wives are mentioned, and they are to be "kept in houses" until they die.

[1] *Aghānī*, XVI, 123 ff.; XIX, 26; XX, 140 f. Cf. Wellhausen, *Die Ehe bei den Arabern*, p. 470.

[2] Cf. Ibn Qutayba, '*Uyūn al-akhbār*, ed. Brockelmann (Berlin, 1900–8), p. 436.

[3] Cf. Ibn al-Athīr: X, 63. Ibn Baṭṭūṭa, *Voyages*, II, 227 f.; Sir J. Chardin, *Travels in Persia* (London, 1927), p. 205. J. L. Burckhardt, *Arabic Proverbs* (London, 1875), pp. 173 ff.; Burton, *Thousand Nights and a Night*, VI, 268, X, 85; Skrine, *Chinese Central Asia*, p. 203. Rodd, *People of the Veil*, p. 177; Lane, *Modern Egyptians*, p. 361; Hurgronje, *Mekka*, II, 109 f.

[4] 24^2. Cf. G. Zaydān, *Ta'rīkh al-tamaddun al-Islāmī* (Cairo, 1902–6), V, 129 f.

[5] In Koran 4^{19}, the demand is specifically made: "If any of your women be guilty of fornication, then bring four witnesses against them from among yourselves."

According to the commentators on the latter passage, women taken in adultery were, in the early days of Islam, literally immured; a penalty which in later times was changed to stoning.[1] In order to reconcile the two passages, the interpreters of the law divide offenders into two classes: (*a*) those who are *muḥṣan* and (*b*) those who are not *muḥṣan*. The former are persons, either male or female, who, being free men and women, of full age and understanding, have been in a position to enjoy lawful wedlock.[2] The penalty for such persons is death by stoning. The persons in the latter category are such as do not fulfil the conditions mentioned.[3] For them the penalty is a hundred strokes if they are free men and women, and half that number if they are slaves.

A husband who accuses his wife of adultery without being able to bring all the necessary evidence, may, according to the Koran,[4] "testify four times that, by God, he is of those who speak the truth; and the fifth testimony shall be that the curse of God shall be on him if he be of those who lie". If the wife by her silence admits the charge, presumably she suffers the penalty. The Koran, however, provides that "it shall avert the punishment from her if she bears testimony that, by God, he is of those who lie; and the fifth that the wrath of God be on her if he be of those who speak the truth".[5] Even if the woman is prepared to swear this five-fold oath, the marriage is annulled and she is separated by a

[1] An authority of the second century of the *hijra* reports that a woman once confessed her adultery. 'Alī, Muhammad's son-in-law, and one of his "successors" (Khalīfa or Caliph), imprisoned her until her child was born; he then dug a pit, into which she was let down as far as her breasts, and cast a stone at her, after which he commanded the bystanders to stone her. *Majmū' al-fiqh*, attributed to Zayd b. 'Alī, ed. E. Griffini (Milan, 1919), pp. 218 f.

[2] See Bayḍāwī on Koran 24^2. He adds that Shāfi'ī makes adherence to Islam a further condition. Against this the objection is raised that since Muhammad stoned Jews for adultery this further qualification would appear to be unnecessary.

[3] It is not clear what process of logic is used to make the distinction. Probably, as Snouck Hurgronje has claimed, the matter has to be considered as *ta'abbudī*, i.e. one which the pious must take as an article of faith without too close investigation of its intelligibility. Cf. *Z.D.M.G.*, LIII, 161, in a review of Sachau's *Muhammedanisches Recht*.

[4] 4^{6-9}.

[5] The special oath of accusation here in question is known as *li'ān*, lit. "the calling down of a curse upon someone". The law-books specify certain holy places at which these oaths may be sworn. When it is considered that an oath at a sacred shrine is not lightly undertaken by the vast mass of Muslims even at the present day, the test may be said to be on the whole a good one.

perpetual divorce from her husband, who may never in any circumstances resume cohabitation.[1]

Of divorce in general the Koran has much to say, but it deals rather with the actual procedure to be followed and with the husband's financial and other responsibilities towards the divorced woman and her children than with the grounds for divorce. It is here that the interpreters of the law have profoundly influenced Muslim life. Since no justification for divorcing his wife is demanded from the husband by the Koran, he is permitted to divorce her at his own will or caprice.[2] But no such privilege is accorded to the wife, an inequality which has had the consequence of gravely lowering the status of women in Islam. In some respects the facility of divorce permitted to the husband derives from pre-Islamic times, when a man, having purchased his wife, could discharge his total obligation to her by payment of any portion of the *mahr* that might remain due to her father or *walī*, and be rid of her by pronouncement of the formula of dismissal.[3] In token of his definite purpose to divorce her, he repeated the formula three times, either at one and the same time or at intervals. This simple procedure was retained in Islam, with the difference that the first and second times a man may repudiate his wife and take her back without any ceremony and without her permission, if he so wishes, providing that he does so before the end of the period of waiting required by law prior to her marriage with another man.[4] If, however, the husband has pronounced the formula of divorce a third and final time, and thus proclaimed that he has lost all further right in her, he cannot resume marital relationships with her until she has first been taken in marriage by another man and been divorced by him.[5] If this man was a slave, the marriage to

1 Thus the Shāfi'ites (cf. Bayḍāwī on Koran 24^7 and Sachau, *op. cit.* pp. 14 f. and 73–7). The Ḥanafites, however, declare that this is a case for the ordinary "divorce of dismissal" pronounced by a judge (Bayḍāwī, *loc. cit.*).

2 "A man can repudiate his wife at any time at which he thinks fit" (Aghababian, *Législation Iranienne*, II, 1133).

3 *Anti ṭāliq*, "thou art dismissed", whence this form of divorce is known as *ṭalāq*, "dismissal".

4 Koran, $2^{228, 232}$. Cf. the Rabbinical law that permits a man to remarry his wife, after divorcing her, without waiting for the period of 90 days which is otherwise required (Talmud Bablī, *Yebāmōth*, 43a).

5 Koran 2^{230}. It sometimes happens, particularly where the triple formula has been pronounced at once through anger or other cause, that a couple wish to be remarried. The law is then satisfied by the woman's marriage—which must

him was dissolved by his being presented to her as a gift, since a woman could not legally be the wife of her own slave.

The period of waiting before remarriage is an innovation made by Islam and forbids divorced women, "until they have had their courses thrice",[1] to take other husbands.[2] During the period of suspended divorce a woman continues to be regarded as her husband's wife, and if he already has four wives he cannot marry another. It is during this time that he is permitted to take back his provisionally divorced wife without further ceremony. After the final divorce, if it becomes apparent during the period of waiting that she is pregnant, the husband is recommended to take her back and treat her with consideration until the child is born.[3] Unless conceived in adultery the offspring belongs to the husband, and the woman is forbidden to marry anyone else until after her delivery.

If, during the period of suspended divorce, the husband takes back his wife, all the declarations of divorce are annulled and the parties resume cohabitation. By this method of pronouncing a quasi-divorce and then taking back his wife, a husband, wishing to practice extortion from her, may keep her in a state of being neither properly married to him nor properly divorced so long as she refuses to agree to his demands. The Prophet expressly forbade this practice[4] and further permitted a woman to ransom herself from her husband, for a sum agreed upon by them both, after he had twice pronounced divorce against her.[5] In pre-Islamic times it had been possible for a woman to buy her freedom from her husband by resigning her *mahr* to him.[6] The obvious openings for abuse which the practice created led Muhammad to restrict it,[7] but it was apparently too well established for him to

be consummated (Bayḍāwī on Koran 2^{230})—and divorce by a second man, who is willing to go through the double ceremony for a fee (cf. Juynboll, *Handbuch*, p. 231). The process is known as *taḥlīl* ("making lawful").

[1] Koran 2^{228}. The law-books extend it to four months from the date of the husband's pronouncement of his intention.

[2] In the *Jāhilīya* the divorced woman could remarry immediately after divorce even if she were pregnant, and the child belonged to the new husband.

[3] Koran 2^{228}.

[4] *Ibid. vv.* 231 f.

[5] *Ibid. v.* 229.

[6] Cf. R. Smith, *Kinship*, p. 92. This kind of divorce is called *khul*ʿ, "divestiture".

[7] See Koran $4^{24\,f.}$ and 2^{229} (first part).

abolish, though it was only permitted "if the parties fear they cannot keep within God's bounds". Once the husband receives back his *mahr* he loses all rights over the woman, who must, however, wait the usual period before remarrying. If the husband wishes to take her back it must be after making a fresh arrangement with her.

Another case where a woman may claim a divorce[1] from her husband is when, both being non-Muslims, she adopts Islam and her husband fails to be converted with her. If, on the other hand, the wife remains non-Muslim when her husband becomes a convert to Islam, the qāḍī is to decide between them. There need be no divorce, but if there has been no cohabitation and divorce is ordered, the husband need pay no *mahr*.[2]

The law-books make provision for the annulment of marriage on the grounds of physical imperfections in either husband or wife. Either may, for example, claim to have the marriage annulled if the other is sexually incapacitated. Other grounds for the dissolution of marriage would be the non-fulfilment by either party of the terms of the marriage contract. A common case is where the bride, claiming to be a virgin, is held by the bridegroom not to be so.[3] Since the tests of virginity imposed by custom are frequently misleading, and public opinion on the matter is strong, it is a common practice for friends of the virgin bride to provide her with artificial means of producing the necessary tokens to avoid difficulty. Among certain tribes in Abysinnia and the Sudan girls are subject to infibulation in order to assure pre-marital chastity.[4] In Egypt in the past century public defloration was practised, if the evidence of the French physician Clot Bey is accepted.[5]

On the woman's side, it is grounds for annulment of marriage if the woman can prove before a qāḍī that her husband is not in a position to pay the *mahr* specified in the marriage contract or cannot provide her with necessities. Failure to fulfil other conditions set out in the contract of marriage can lead to its dissolution. Thus by recent Persian legislation the wife can, with the consent of the courts, claim divorce from her husband if he breaks an

1 It is *ṭalāq*, i.e. "dismissal".
2 Qudūrī, *Mukhtaṣar*, p. 151.
3 Cf. Westermarck, *Marriage Ceremonies in Morocco*, ch. VII.
4 Cf. Gray in Hastings, *Enc. Rel. Eth.* (Edinburgh, 1908 ff.), III, 667, 669.
5 *Aperçu général sur l'Égypte* (Paris, 1840), II, 44.

agreement not to marry another wife, or absents himself beyond a specified period, or fails to provide maintenance or maltreats her. The Turkish National Civil Code places women on a par with men both for marriage and divorce. It also contains provisions for judicial separation, a state introduced from Swiss law and criticized on the ground that it originated in the Catholic idea of the sanctity of marriage which has never been recognized by Muslim law.

Finally, the marriage contracted by a slave without the permission of his master is void, as also is a marriage in which either husband or wife, after having been free, becomes the slave of the other.

Closely bound up with the subject of marriage in Islam is that of the veiling and seclusion of women.[1] In ancient Arabia custom appears to have varied; the women of the desert-dwellers going unveiled and associating freely with men[2] while women in the cities were veiled. Amongst the Prophet's own tribe of the Quraysh, veiling was in general the rule. Thus, in ancient Mecca, according to the historian Fākihī, the citizens used to dress their unmarried daughters and their female slaves in all their finery and parade them with faces unveiled around the Ka'ba, in order to attract possible suitors and buyers. If this performance succeeded in its object, the women resumed their veils once and for all.[3] Possibly there is a reference to this heathen custom in a passage of the Koran[4] directed by Muhammad to his own wives and bidding them remain in their houses and not go around in public decked out as in the time of Barbarism.[5] In an early revelation, made at a time before his rise to power and when many of his supporters were liable to insult and outrage, he commanded his own wives and daughters and also the wives of believers to protect themselves by wearing long veils when they had occasion to go out in public.[6]

[1] Cf. S. Hurgronje, *Verspreide Geschriften* (Bonn, 1923), I, 305 ff.; A. von Kremer, *Culturgeschichte des Orients* (Vienna, 1875–7), II, ch. III.

[2] Cf. *Aghānī*, VII, 174.

[3] Wuestenfeld, *Chroniken der Stadt Mekka* (Leipzig, 1858–61), II, 4 f. See Lane, *Modern Egyptians*, ch. VI, on Marriage.

[4] 33[33].

[5] Bayḍāwī (who, however, speaks with little or no authority on this matter) says that before Muhammad, women were in the habit of adorning themselves with pearls and of walking in the public highways, displaying themselves to men.

[6] Koran 33[59 f.] Ṭabarī's *Tafsīr* (p. 29, part 22, of the Cairo ed.) on this verse reads: "God says to his prophet, 'Tell your wives and daughters and the

In the same chapter[1] he requests his followers not to make familiar use of his house and not to enter it except by his permission. If they have any request to make of his wives, they are to ask it "from behind a veil".[2]

So far as the women of his own household were concerned, it seems clear that Muhammad wished to follow the ordinary custom of his tribe. Even so, there was at least one member of his family who refused to be bound either by convention or by his desires. We are told that a niece of his wife 'Ā'isha asserted her independence and went unveiled before all men in spite of her husband's protests.[3]

At a date later than that of his revelation on the subject of veiling, the Prophet enacted some general rules of modest conduct and chastity, applicable to both men and women. For the latter some extra regulations were added bidding them not to display their charms openly, except in the presence of their husbands or of persons so closely related to them by blood as to come within the prohibited degrees for purposes of marriage, or the wives of such persons.[4] The pertinent paragraphs read: "Say to the believers that they cast down their looks and guard their privy parts. . . . And say to the believing women that they cast down their looks and guard their privy parts and display not their ornaments, except those of them that are external; and let them pull their veils over the opening of their chemises at their bosoms and not display their ornaments save to their husbands or their fathers", etc. On these paragraphs the pertinent comments of Bayḍāwī are illuminating so far as the custom of his own day

wives of believers when they go out of doors not to be like female slaves in their garb, leaving their hair and face uncovered; but let them let down part of their robes that no miscreant may expose them to harmful comments when he discovers them to be free-born women'. The interpreters differ (however) on the meaning of 'letting down (the veil)'. Some say it means they must cover their faces and heads, showing nothing but one eye." (Others say the forehead only need be covered.)

1 *v*. 53.

2 Bayḍāwī's comment is, "It is related that Omar said, 'O Apostle of God, there come into thy house men who may be simple or wicked. It were well if you commanded the veil for the mothers of believers.' This verse was then revealed."

3 *Aghānī*, x, 54.

4 Koran, 24[30 f.] Others excepted are slaves (eunuchs in particular), and children too young to be conscious of differences of sex.

(thirteenth century) and later times are concerned. He explains the injunction to guard the privy parts as an exhortation to chastity, or alternatively as a command that they are to be properly covered. Until the most recent times the command was interpreted literally, so that except for the very few who were brought up in, or aped, the European fashion, no respectable Muslim male would wear the occidental garb of short coat and trousers, which were not regarded as sufficiently decent. The command to women not to display their ornaments "except those of them that are external", Bayḍāwī explains as meaning "except the face and the two hands, for they are not pudendal". "But it is more probable", he continues, "that this [uncovering] is only for purposes of prayer and not to permit [people] to gaze. Indeed the whole of the body of a free woman is to be regarded as pudendal and no part of her may lawfully be seen by anyone but her husband or close kin, except in case of need, as when she is undergoing medical treatment or giving evidence."

Until the third century of the *hijra*, and even later, women enjoyed with men the right to pray in the mosque: Omar is said to have appointed a Koran reader especially for them at public worship.[1] They were not required then to be veiled; but the law-books prescribe the kind of dress to be worn, which consists of at least two pieces—a chemise, and a cloak for the upper part of the head and the body. The face, hands and upper side of the feet need not be covered, though on the last detail there is some controversy.[2]

In the same way as the Rabbinical commentators of the Pentateuch placed "a fence about the Law" by requiring a precautionary margin in order to ensure the entire fulfilment of its dictates, so the interpreters of the Koran demanded more than their original. In the matter of veiling they imposed upon all women what was laid down for the Prophet's own wives and daughters, presumably justifying their action by the argument that as it was laudable for men in all matters to follow the practice (*sunna*) of the Prophet, so for women it was commendable to follow the customs of his womenfolk. The one occasion when the jurists permitted a man who was not a physician to see a woman not related to him was

[1] Ṭabarī, I, 2649.
[2] Cf. Querry, *Recueil*, I, 50; and Bukhārī, *Saḥīḥ*, pp. 553, 555, 567.

before betrothal,[1] and even that permission was withdrawn in practice.[2]

It is not possible to say when the harem system and the seclusion of women began to be general. The early interpreters of the Koran were men who originated in Persia, a land in which the women had long been secluded, and it is probable that their authority in Islam began to make itself felt after the close of the rule of the Umayyad Caliphs of Damascus.[3] By the time of Hārūn al-Rashīd, one-and-a-half centuries after the death of the Prophet, the system was fully established, with all the appurtenances of the harem, in which, amongst the richer classes, the women were shut off from the rest of the household under the charge of eunuchs. By the middle ages the system had normally taken so firm a hold that pious visitors were shocked when they came to lands where there was free social intercourse between men and women. The Moorish traveller Ibn Baṭṭūṭa found amongst the Massūfa tribe at the oasis of Iwālatan in the Sahara that, although they were Muslims

their women showed no modesty in the presence of men and did not veil. Yet they were assiduous in their prayers. Anyone who wished to marry them could do so, but they would not go a journey with a husband. Even if one of them wished it, her kinsfolk would prevent her. The women there have friends and companions amongst the men who are related to them. So also the men have friends amongst women not related to them. A man may enter his house and find his wife with her [male] friend and yet will not disapprove.[4]

Presumably Ibn Baṭṭūṭa is describing the women of the Tuaregs, who to this day enjoy a position of perfect freedom and wear no veil.[5] In other places where the women go unveiled economic conditions have prevented strict adherence to the law. The inconvenience of having the face covered is obvious where the women do hard manual work in the house or out of doors. Accordingly,

[1] Koran 33[59].

[2] Cf. Juynboll, *Handbuch*, p. 163.

[3] According to Ibn Taghribardī (I, 148) the harem system was introduced by them; but this is not probable, for they were men who held in large measure to the ideas of pagan Arabia.

[4] *Voyages*, IV, 388 ff.

[5] Rodd, *People of the Veil*, p. 167.

amongst Bedouin women in Arabia, amongst the Kurds, and elsewhere, veiling has generally been the exception. In Egypt the women of the *fellāḥīn* use the veil mainly as an instrument of coquetry. So also in central Asia the women of the nomad tribes are not restricted in their social intercourse with men by the veil, and the harem system is unknown,[1] though amongst the Kirghiz, women take the veil on marriage.[2] The settled populations of the region now included in the Muslim Soviet Republics have, however, for long been strongly orthodox in their observances and have kept strictly to the traditional practices with regard to the seclusion of women. In spite of the Soviet Union's being pledged to a policy of complete emancipation for women, these practices persist, so that even in large cities women go veiled, using, it is said, a perforated tablecloth as a substitute for the regular veil, which is no longer made in the U.S.S.R. and cannot now be imported.[3]

In the Caspian provinces of Persia the countrywomen are never veiled.[4] Amongst the poorer classes in the towns of Persia, on the other hand, and where ecclesiastical influence is strong, as in Qum for example, the feminine part of the population goes carefully veiled, and married or marriageable women are rigorously secluded. Further east, in Malaya, the former Dutch East Indies and China, the rules about veiling are very generally disregarded. The Malay woman goes abroad with her face uncovered, "takes part in her husband's affairs and exhibits her finery at festivals".[5]

At Mecca, the Dutch traveller Snouck Hurgronje found that women regularly attended the mosque and were separated from the men only by a grille. Not infrequently their faces were unveiled, but their hair was always covered with scrupulous care so that not a strand escaped, on peril of the grave disapproval of the fanatical, who look on straying tresses as the most damnable coquetry. During the *iḥrām* or ceremonial robing for the rites of the pilgrimage, men bare their heads and women their hands and faces in accordance with the regulations laid down by the law-

[1] A. Vambéry, *Sketches of Central Asia* (London, 1868), p. 80; Skrine, *Chinese Central Asia*, p. 194.

[2] Skrine, *loc. cit.*

[3] *Central Asian Review* (London, 1953), pp. 47 ff.

[4] *The Times*, 23 October 1929, p. 17.

[5] Winstedt, *Malaya*, p. 91. Cf. Hurgronje, *Verspreide Geschriften*, I, 306.

books.[1] Even then, however, many women of high rank, finding their unveiled state embarrassing, put on a kind of mask and wear the veil over that, thus carrying out the letter of the law.[2]

As part of his programme of Europeanization, Mustafa Kemal Ataturk forbade Turkish women to wear the veil in public, and his example was followed by Shāh Riza in Persia in 1936. Within the past few years the practice has been abolished by decree of the Yugoslav government. In the larger cities of Egypt, Iraq and other countries of the Middle East, Muslim women have for the past quarter of a century gone about dressed in European garb and unveiled without any official action having been taken.[3] On the other hand, the appearance of women unveiled in public was forbidden by the Wahhābī 'ulamā of Sa'ūdī Arabia in 1926.[4]

On the whole, the exceptions that can be enumerated to the general practice of the veiling and seclusion of women are comparatively few, and the practice is entirely in keeping with the supremacy of the male over the female postulated by the Koran. But the vagueness of its provisions placed great authority in the hands of the Muslim doctors of law, who frequently interpreted them as local custom demanded,[5] particularly where no pertinent *ḥadīth* existed. Yet it was not unknown for *ḥadīth* to have been deliberately manufactured in order to bolster up a particular interpretation, many of such "traditions" being in direct conflict with Koranic statements or else seeking to twist their significance. Women were obviously not meant by the Koran to be excluded from religious duties, and, so far as they are good believers, they are regarded as the equals of men, being like them offered the reward of Paradise for true faith.[6] A significant passage in the Koran[7] enumerates the persons whom the prophet regards as possessing

[1] According to [Zayd b. 'Alī] *Majmū' al-fiqh*, p. 126, the *iḥrām* for men consists in (baring) the head, for women the face.

[2] S. Hurgronje, *loc. cit.*

[3] Cf. *Oriente Moderno*, April 1948, June 1953.

[4] *Ibid.* 1926, pp. 338 f.

[5] Ancient Arabian custom followed that of Babylonia, Assyria and Persia in permitting the husband to repudiate his wife at his own whim. In Persia, if not also in the other two countries, the system of the harem had existed from very ancient times.

[6] Koran 9[73] and 48[5]. Cf. 3[193], "I will not suffer the work of him among you that worketh, whether male or female, to be lost."

[7] 33[35].

the qualities of the faithful. They are, "the men and women who resign themselves [to Allah], believing men and believing women, devout men and devout women, truthful men and truthful women, patient men and patient women, humble men and humble women, almsgiving men and almsgiving women, men who fast and women who fast, chaste men and chaste women, and men and women who often call upon the name of God—and God has prepared for them forgiveness and a mighty recompense." Trustworthy historical tradition shows that even after the prophet's time all Muslims without regard to sex were treated alike by authority. Thus the prophet's "substitute" (*Khalīfa*), Abu Bakr, divided the spoils of war equally between all the members of the community of Islam, young or old, bond or free, male or female.[1]

Later, in spite of the clearly expressed intentions of the Koran, its interpreters—frequently men of Persian or Turkish origin—who had been brought up in an environment in which men avowedly ruled, imposed their own views and traditions upon the Muhammadan world. It is thus that in most of the standard collections of "traditions"[2] a *ḥadīth* is to be found to the effect that most of the inhabitants of Hell are women, and that, "because of their unbelief". The orthodox interpreters of the Koran, of whom Bayḍāwī is typical,[3] further attempted to reconcile with their own views the Prophet's offer of Paradise to women by adducing a *ḥadīth* which says that although men innumerable have been able to attain religious perfection—with the consequent reward of Paradise—only four women have ever done so.[4]

In estimating the status of women in Islam, their liability to undertake duties is perhaps of even greater importance than their privileges. In the passages recently quoted from the Koran there can scarcely be any doubt that women were meant to do what they could in the way of carrying out the statutory duties.[5] Yet almost as soon as there was any question of their emerging from the harem to fulfil their tasks they were faced by the hostility of the learned. The simplest and most obvious method of declaring oneself a true

[1] Abu Yūsuf, *Kitāb al-Kharāj* (Būlāq, 1302), p. 24.

[2] E.g. Bukhārī, *Saḥiḥ*, XI, 13.

[3] See his commentary on Koran, 66^{11} f.

[4] Another form of the *ḥadīth* is given in Damīrī, *Ḥayāt al-ḥayawān* (Cairo, A.H. 1311), II, 142, s.v. Ghurāb.

[5] Ibn Khaldūn, *Prolégomènes*, ed. Quatremère (Paris, 1858 ff.), I, 354.

believer is that of praying in public. According to one early tradition, Muhammad himself was not averse from allowing women to pray in his company,[1] and declared that they could go to the mosque regularly if their husbands permitted.[2] That tradition would seem to be corroborated by another in which the Prophet is shown disapproving any hindrance placed in the way of the "handmaidens of God" who wished to pray in the mosque.[3] A work wrongly ascribed to Zayd ibn 'Alī (second century A.H.) declared that women were forbidden to pray in public assembly,[4] and in fact attendance at mosque soon became the prerogative of males. There have always been exceptions, of course. As late as the twelfth century A.D., the Moorish traveller Ibn Jubayr found women as well as men gathered together to hear a famous preacher at Baghdad. The women, amongst whom was the Caliph's mother, were stationed behind a latticed window in the royal palace, while the general mass of the congregation were assembled in the courtyard below. The preacher, however, knew of the presence of the august lady, for he called down blessings upon her and pronounced a eulogy in which he called her "The Most Noble Veil" and "The Most Compassionate Presence".[5]

Where women in Muslim lands still attend prayers at the mosque it is at festivals only, although at Mecca they come regularly but are separated by a grille from the men. Further, at Agades, amongst the Tuaregs, while the men pray—presumably in the open—the women stand at one side listening.[6] This is the case also in a good many other places in the realms of Islam.

For the most part, however, the harsh disapproval of the learned has succeeded in driving women out of the mosque,[7] a contributory cause of the restrictions placed upon their attendance at public worship being the extreme sensitiveness of the Muhammadan to the opinion of his fellows, and the fear of fathers and husbands lest their womenfolk should by some lapse of conduct disgrace them.

[1] Bukhārī, *op. cit.* x, 161, and [Zayd b. 'Alī] *Majmū' al-fiqh*, p. 43.
[2] Bukhārī, *op. cit.* x, 166.
[3] *Ibid.* xi, 13. Cf. Ṭabarī, i, 2649.
[4] [Zayd b. 'Alī], *ibid.*
[5] Ibn Jubayr, *Travels*, ed. Wright and de Goeje (Leyden, 1907), pp. 222 f.
[6] Rodd, *People of the Veil*, p. 167.
[7] Cf. von Kremer, *Culturgeschichte des Orients*, ii, 101, 104.

It is a fact worthy of note that despite their disabilities, women could, before the disapproval of the later authorities prevailed, achieve saintliness. "There are few dictionaries of the biographies of saints that do not under each letter of the alphabet contain a row of holy women, whose miracles are not in the least inferior to those of the male saints that come to be their neighbours in the same books."[1] The fact that there is no organized priesthood in Islam, and no priestly caste, may the more easily have permitted the rise of women saints,[2] but the great majority of them are to be found amongst the Ṣūfī devotees and others of mystical tendencies, who set little store by differences of the outward form. Of Rābiʿa the saint, the biographer of Ṣūfī saints, Farīd al-Dīn ʿAṭṭār, remarks:

If anyone should ask me why I note her amongst the ranks of men, I reply that the master of all prophets has said, God looks not to your outward appearance. Attainment of the divine lies not in appearance but in [sincerity of] purpose. . . . If it is possible to have learnt two-thirds of the Faith from ʿĀ'isha the Righteous [the wife of Muhammad], then it is possible to learn some of the truth of religion from one of her handmaidens. Since a woman on the path of God becomes a man, she cannot be called a woman.[3]

This is significant in the light of the opinion of Bayḍāwī (quoted above)[4] that prophecy, leadership in public prayer, and saintship are reserved exclusively for men.

Farīd al-Dīn ʿAṭṭār's own anticipation of criticism for mentioning Rābiʿa, is itself indicative of the normal attitude of later Islam towards any assumption by women of careers that might attract public attention towards them. Earlier in the history of the faith it was possible for a *ḥadīth* to be recorded which made it incumbent upon every Muslim man and woman to seek learning.[5] For any woman to have carried out the behest and achieved distinction, must inevitably have led her to a position that would have attracted the attention of learned persons of the opposite sex, who

[1] Goldziher, *Muhammedanische Studien*, II, 300.

[2] Cf. M. Smith, *Rābiʿa the Mystic and her Fellow-Saints in Islam* (Cambridge, 1928), p. 3.

[3] *Tadhkirat al-awliyā*, ed. Nicholson (Leyden, 1905–7,) I, 59.

[4] Pp. 98 f.

[5] Goldziher, *op. cit.* II, 302.

looked upon scholarship as their own prerogative. And that is indeed what happened. Yet not only were their women saints, who might perhaps have owed their position of eminence to popular sentiment, but there were also women scholars who, by the ordinary methods, acquired learning and in their turn attracted large numbers of students and received the praises of male colleagues. Thus the famous "writer" Shuhda bint al-Ibarī, "the pride of womankind", by her attainments acquired a great reputation and ranked amongst the first scholars of her age.[1]

Part of Shuhda's fame rested on her profound knowledge of *ḥadīth*. This was a branch of Muslim science which might have been expected to be exclusively a pursuit for men, but was in fact not so. In earlier times women had often been themselves reckoned as competent links in the chains of authorities that guaranteed the genuineness of various "traditions" of the prophet. In some of the collections of *ḥadīth*, e.g. in that of Bukhārī, their evidence is indeed of prime importance. They continued sporadically to appear as authorities until the tenth century of the *hijra*.[2]

In the sphere of practical affairs it was not often that women's capacity was openly recognized. In the harem and behind the throne it obviously existed very frequently, though it was rarely acknowledged outside. But during the Abbasid Caliphate several instances are known of royal ladies whose influence extended beyond the throne. Thus at Baghdad the name of the Sitta Zubayda, wife of Hārūn al-Rashīd, acquired such renown that to this day great reverence is paid to the tomb which—albeit not authentic—is said to be the depository of her remains. About a century after her, the mother of the Caliph Muqtadir, who was a weakling, ruled the empire of Islam—somewhat shrunken by that time. It was she that held public audience to redress wrongs and receive petitions, summoned governors and qāḍīs to render account of their doings, and who herself signed and issued state edicts.[3]

Yet the names of women of such outstanding character occur

[1] She died at Baghdad in 574/1178 (Ibn Khallikān, ed. Wuestenfeld, no. 295). Cf. Goldziher, *op. cit.* II, 406.

[2] See further Goldziher, *ibid.*

[3] Cf. Levy, *A Baghdad Chronicle* (Cambridge, 1929), p. 140.

infrequently enough in Muslim annals to excite comment whenever they appear. That might indeed be true of women in history generally; but outside Islam the obstacles deliberately and officially put in the way have not been so formidable. Though pressure from without is having its effect in Islam, the obstacles still exist; and they must continue until either the rigid attitude of the doctors of the faith yields or else loses significance for the general body of Muslims owing to the decay of religious authority.[1]

[1] See further, "Al-Azhar, Islam and the Role of Women in Islamic Society," in *Islamic Review* (August 1952).

CHAPTER III

THE STATUS OF THE CHILD IN ISLAM

Within the tribal organization of Arabia the smallest unit is that of the *ahl*, "the tent" or household. It consists of a single family, of which the father is the head and the other members are his direct descendants. In their own interest and that of the society amongst whom they live they are reckoned as belonging to his stock, and his actual physical paternity therefore is a matter of importance. There was a time before the coming of Muhammad, when, according to Muslim tradition, the principle ruled that "the child follows the bed", i.e. that the child reckoned paternity from the man, whoever he might be, who was married to its mother at the time of its birth.[1] Islam modified the principle by declaring that a pregnant woman, when her husband dies or divorces her, cannot be remarried until the birth of her child, which is reckoned by Muhammadan law as begotten by him and as legitimate.

As a general principle a child born in wedlock is regarded in Islam as legitimate[2] and as being the child of the wife's husband, provided it is born not less than six months after cohabitation of husband and wife.[3] However, if the father wishes to acknowledge a child born less than six months after his cohabitation with his wife, it is legitimate. The extreme limit of four years after cohabitation is allowed for the birth of a child by the Shāfi'ite and Mālikite codes, which within that limit would regard such a child as legitimate, provided, of course, that the mother had not in the

[1] *Tāj al-'arūs* (A.H. 1278), v, 461; R. Smith, *Kinship and Marriage in Early Arabia* (Cambridge, 1885; 2nd ed. 1903), ch. II (latter part) and ch. IV.

[2] So far as the religion of the child is concerned, if one of its parents professes or embraces Islam, it is presumed to be Muslim (A. Querry, *Droit Musulman: Recueil des lois* (Paris, 1871), II, 331).

[3] *Jāmi' al-ṣaghīr* (on margin of *Kitāb al-Kharāj* of Abu Yūsuf (Būlāq, A.H. 1302), p. 51); and Querry, *Recueil*, I, 739. The figure is arrived at by a combination of two verses of the Koran, 31^{13}, which says that the period of a child's weaning is two years, and 46^{14}, which says the bearing and weaning take thirty months. (See Baydāwī on the latter verse.)

meantime contracted another union.[1] Ḥanafī law makes the limit two years.[2] The Shī'ites, however, refuse to accept any child as legitimate if born more than ten months after the last union of husband and wife.[3]

The principle that the "child follows the bed" is coupled in the *ḥadīth* with the declaration that "the adulterer gets nothing"[4]; that is, that the child belongs to its mother's husband at the time of its birth even if he should not be the father. Shī'ite law goes so far as to say that the paternity of a child conceived adulterously is attributed to the husband unless he disavows it formally by pronouncement of the *li'ān* against his wife.[5] If a father repents of his disavowal later and desires to acknowledge his paternity, that is permitted. In any event, the adulterer cannot claim paternity of the child.[6]

Where there has been any doubt about paternity, Islam followed the custom of the *Jāhilīya* in calling in a *qā'if*, a member of a class of seers whose business it was to assign paternity according to the child's physical features.[7] The traditionist Bukhārī[8] declares that the man to whom the *qā'if* allotted a child had to acknowledge paternity of it. But the point is disputed.

In Islam it is sufficient for the father to acknowledge cohabitation with his wife or slave to establish the legitimacy of the child. If circumstances (such as the question of succession) should require the mother to prove a child to be hers, her statement must be supported by that of the midwife or some other respectable Muslim woman present at the birth. Seeing that concubinage is lawful in Islam, it is not necessary for the mother of a child to be married to its father in order for it to be declared legitimate.

[1] Nawawī, *Minhādj aṭ-Ṭālibīn*, ed. Van den Berg (Batavia, 1884), III, 28. Even if there should be a doubt whether (during the period of four years after the last congress of the husband and wife) the latter has cohabited with some-one else, the child remains legitimate.

[2] *Jāmi' al-ṣaghīr, loc. cit.*

[3] Querry, *loc. cit.*

[4] Bukhārī, *Ṣaḥīḥ*, ed. Krehl, II, 34.

[5] Querry, *Recueil*, I, p. 657. See p. 120 above, n. 5.

[6] *Ibid.* 739.

[7] Smith, *Kinship*, pp. 143 f. In pre-Islamic times a prostitute who bore a child was allowed to declare who its father was. Not uncommonly he claimed it (so *al-Fakhrī*, ed. Ahlwardt (Gotha, 1860), p. 135). Cf. Goldziher, *Muhammedanische Studien*, I, 184 f.

[8] *Ṣaḥīḥ*, VI, 124.

Children born of a marriage which is subsequently declared irregular remain legitimate if the parents can prove that they contracted the marriage in good faith and believing they were entitled to be married. Also, in case of error, or where there is a doubt that the child was begotten in wedlock or during a master's lawful ownership of a slave-girl, the child is declared legitimate.[1]

Cases of repudiation of children by parents are rare, for sons in particular are regarded as a precious possession.[2] If, however, a husband, suspecting that a child borne by his wife is none of his, does not wish to acknowledge it, he must denounce it immediately it is born, and follow up his denunciation with an accusation of adultery against his wife in accordance with the procedure of the *li'ān*[3] described under the section on adultery. He cannot, however, denounce the child simply on the ground that it does not resemble him in appearance. The extreme case is quoted, or invented,[4] of a Bedouin Arab who came to the Prophet declaring that his wife had given birth to a negro child, and hinting that he wished to repudiate it. Muhammad, however, refused him permission to do so, and the remark of a commentator on the "tradition" is: "Difference [even] of colour does not prove adultery, and the woman's husband is not entitled to divorce her."[5] Another *ḥadīth* makes it definitely unlawful for a man to disavow on insufficient grounds any child born to him.[6]

From the time when Islam became firmly established, the law has placed very few difficulties in the way of recognizing the legitimacy of children. The main bars to such recognition have been quoted. By them a child born within less than six months after the marriage of the mother would be presumed not to have been begotten by her husband in lawful wedlock, and similarly a

[1] "Les Orientaux vivant souvent en commun, cette erreur est assez fréquente, il arrive que le mari ou le maître, croyant entrer dans le lit de sa femme ou de son esclave, est admis dans le lit de la femme ou de l'esclave d'un autre."

"Another case is where a woman who has been declared a widow or divorced finds herself really still married" (Querry, *op. cit.* I, 742).

[2] Cf. Koran 18^{44}, "Wealth and sons are the adornment of this life." Cf. 8^{28} and 63^{9}. A. von Kremer (*Culturgeschichte des Orients*, II, 120), shows how proud a good father could be of his daughters.

[3] Cf. p. 120 n., and E. Sachau, *Muhammedanisches Recht* (Berlin, 1897), p. 77.

[4] Muslim, *Ṣaḥīḥ* (Stamboul, A.H. 1331), IV, 211 (=Bk. XIX, 18–20).

[5] Nawawī, commentary on passage quoted in preceding note.

[6] Nasā'ī, *Sunan* (Cairo, A.H. 1313), XXIV, 47, and Aḥmad b. Ḥanbal, *Musnad* (Cairo, A.H. 1313), II, 26.

child born more than the specified period after cohabitation of husband and wife would be declared illegitimate. Apart from such instances the only case in which the law requires a child to be declared illegitimate is when it was conceived in circumstances where the man, being a Muslim, knew he could have no semblance of a right to the woman either by marriage or by ownership of her as his concubine.[1] From the fact that the Muhammadan law universally forbids the marriage of a Muslim woman with a non-Muslim, it follows that the children of such a union are regarded as illegitimate.

The stigma which attaches to the illegitimate child in Muslim lands could be legally justified in very few instances, since it is very rarely that no argument at all could be found for assuming the validity of a particular marriage. At the present day though "son of a whore" is a common term of abuse, "bastard"[2] is not heard except in Persia, where the implied insult can seldom have a legal backing, for the reason that the usual penalty for adultery is death both for the mother and the child.[3] In the Dutch East Indies, when a child was in danger of being born in doubtful circumstances, some means or other, whether legal or not, was generally provided of giving it a show of legitimacy.[4]

If a child is disavowed by the husband of the mother it reckons descent from her alone[5]; and similarly if the husband's kinsfolk dispute, with a show of proof, that the child is his. Normally, indeed, the legitimacy of a boy is a matter of some concern to the father's family or tribe,[6] and where there is a special reason for

[1] Cf. *Fatāwi-yi ʿĀlamgīrī* (compiled in India for the emperor Awrangzīb), tr. Baillie in *Digest of Moohammudan Law* (London, 1865), p. 3.

[2] *Ḥarāmzāda*. See J. E. Polak, *Persien* (Leipzig, 1865), I, 217 f.

[3] The story of Zeenab, the Kurdish slave in Morier's *Hajji Baba of Ispahan*, is almost certainly drawn from life, and may be taken as an illustration.

[4] S. Hurgronje, *Verspreide Geschriften* (Bonn, 1923), II, 352.

[5] Muslim, *Ṣaḥīḥ*, Bk. XIX (Stamboul ed., IV, 208); and Shīrāzī, *Tanbīh*, ed. Juynboll (Leyden, 1879), p. 236. Cf. *J.R.A.S.* (1915), p. 655.

[6] The Tuaregs in this as in other matters are exceptions to the rule. Amongst them a woman's children belong to her own tribe, whoever their father may be. If the wife and husband belong to different tribes and the husband dies, the wife returns with her children to her own tribe. Should inter-tribal hostilities break out, the children fight for their mother's kin, although normally they live with their father until his death or his divorce of their mother. It is the law amongst the Tuareg that the child must follow the caste of the mother and not of the father. However, where a noble father who has married a "servile" wife is sufficiently powerful, he will often succeed in passing off his children as of noble birth (Rodd, *The People of the Veil*, pp. 103, 148 ff.).

guarding the purity of the family, claims to belong to it are scrutinized with some care. The following example from the early period of Islam is quoted from the *Kitāb al-Aghānī*. The family of 'Alī b. Jahm al-Sāmī, court poet to the Caliph Mutawakkil, claimed that they were descended from a member of the Quraysh known as Sāma. The genealogists of the Quraysh, however, refused to accept the family of the poet as kin to them, saying that when Sāma died his widow married a man from another tribe, and that the person from whom the poet's family claimed descent was a child of this second marriage.[1]

The law refuses to recognize external claims to paternity of a child which its mother's husband has disavowed, and in such case no blood relationship between the child and the person claiming to be its father is in law recognized. Some legists would accordingly permit marriage between a man and his illegitimate daughter, but others (in particular the Shī'ites) pronounce against this.[2]

On the question of responsibility for the support of children the Koran makes few regulations. It is conceivable that where the parents lived together there was no need to formulate any laws on the subject, particularly where children were regarded as precious possessions. The need for legislation arose when matters were complicated by the divorce of the mother. While the possibility is nowhere envisaged by the Koran that a father may be guilty of neglecting his children, the mother would appear not to be free of that suspicion. The two pertinent sections of the Koran follow immediately on passages dealing with divorce, and lay it down that a mother should suckle her child for two full years at least,[3] during which time she should be fed and clothed by the father, though neither parent can be unduly pressed for the support of the children.[4] The earlier passage[5] relating to the maintenance of children definitely imposes no compulsion on the divorced mother to suckle her child, and if she undertakes it she is entitled to a fee for her services like any other wet-nurse who may be hired. That is the opinion of some of the legists.[6] Others, basing their opinion

[1] *Aghānī*, IX, 104 f. Cf. Goldziher, *op. cit.* I, 188.

[2] Juynboll, *Handbuch des Islamischen Gesetzes* (Leyden, 1910), pp. 193 f. Querry, *op. cit.* I, 656.

[3] Cf. Koran 31^{13}. [4] *Ibid.* 2^{233}; cf. $65^{6\text{ f.}}$ [5] 65^{6}.

[6] E.g. Abu'l Qāsim Ja'far al-Ḥillī, translated by Querry (*op. cit.* I, 745).

on the later passage,[1] hold that mothers, whether married or divorced, are compelled to suckle their children. Still others, for example the Mālikites, are of the opinion that a married mother is compelled to suckle her child for the specified period, but that a divorced woman need not. Both, however, ought to suckle their children should these refuse to go to anyone else.[2] The adherents of the various schools are content to follow their own codes without reference to any other. It may be added that the period of two years laid down by the Koran may be lessened to a time agreed upon by both parents.[3]

When parents are married and are living together they are jointly responsible for the upbringing of their children, the father providing the material necessities, and the mother caring for the welfare of their bodies and for their mental and religious training.[4] In the case of dispute the mother has the right to custody of the children during their infancy. How long that period may extend is not specified in the Koran, and the various schools of law accordingly provide their own ideas on the subject. In the view of the Shī'ites, the mother, provided she is a free woman and a Muslim, has charge of a child for the first two years of its life, while it is at the breast. After weaning, a boy is to be entrusted entirely to the custody of his father, a girl until she is seven years old to that of her mother. After that age the father takes charge of the daughters too. If the mother dies before the son is two years old or the daughter seven, then the father takes charge; as he does also if he divorces the mother. If the father dies, the mother takes charge.[5]

The Shāfi'ite school agrees that the mother has first right to the custody of the child until the age of seven years. It is considered that at that age the child has power to discriminate,[6] and it can then choose with which parent it will live for the future. However,

[1] 2²33; cf. Bayḍāwī on this verse.

[2] Khalīl b. Isḥāq, *Mukhtaṣar*, ed. Guidi and Santillana (Milan, 1919) II, 168.

[3] Thus the Koran 2²33. In Egypt the agreed time is a year or eighteen months (E. W. Lane, *Modern Egyptians* (Everyman ed. London, n.d.) ch. II). Shī'ite law holds twenty-one months to be an appropriate period (Querry, *op. cit.* I, 745).

[4] This kind of charge is technically known as *ḥaḍāna*.

[5] Querry, *op. cit.* I, 746.

[6] At that age a boy is required to begin the duty of saying his prayers. At the age of ten he may be beaten if he is remiss in his duty.

the mother must be a free Muslim woman, in full possession of her senses, innocent of misdemeanour, trustworthy, having a fixed abode and not married to a man other than the child's father.[1]

According to the Mālikites, guardianship of a boy continues with his mother until his puberty; of a girl, until the obligation to maintain her ceases, i.e. until the consummation of her marriage. The mother may even be an infidel, a divorced woman or a widow.[2]

The law-books set out at great length lists of the persons who by reason of kinship are responsible for the maintenance of orphans. The Koran itself says little about it, but the matter must often have presented itself in an urgent form, as when a father died leaving his widow without sufficient provision for herself and her children. Among tribes where, in spite of the freedom given by Islam, endogamy was the rule, orphans or the children of a divorced woman still remained part of the tribe. But there can scarcely have been any communal obligation to take care of them until they were of an age to provide for themselves and become assets to the tribe. Even if the widow or divorced woman married again, the new husband, if he did not wish it, could not be compelled to burden himself with extra mouths. Where exogamy ruled, the woman who was left a widow with young children doubtless took them with her to her own tribe. The husband's tribe would not concern itself with them until they were of an age to be useful.[3]

For children without parents or kinsmen to take charge of them the prophet seems to have made no regulations, but pious foundations (*awqāf*, plur. of *waqf*) provide for the poor, and foundlings are an express charge on the whole community.[4]

Muhammad in the Koran determined no age for puberty, although he indicated (24^{56}) that a youth reached manhood when nocturnal emissions began. The majority of the legal schools agree upon the age of fifteen as being for a boy the age when he reaches manhood. A *ḥadīth* invented to settle the point is to the effect that 'Abdullāh, son of the Caliph Omar I, once told a

[1] Sachau, *Muhammedanisches Recht*, pp. 18 f.

[2] Khalīl b. Isḥāq, *op. cit.* II, 169.

[3] Cf. J. Wellhausen, *Die Ehe bei den Arabern* (Göttingen, 1893), pp. 459 f.

[4] Nawawī, *Minhādj aṭ-Ṭālibīn*, II, 209.

freedman of his that the Prophet, after the battle of Uḥud, had refused him a share of the spoils because he was too young to participate, he being then fourteen years old. But a year later, after the battle of the Trench, he was granted his share.[1]

The particular age of fifteen years is set as the legal term of manhood if there is doubt about the physical signs of puberty. If these physical signs can be proved, then an earlier age may be accepted; though nine years is the lowest limit. For a girl similarly, either the legal age of fifteen or the regular physical indication of puberty is taken to mean the definite attainment of womanhood.[2] Abu Ḥanīfa preferred the age of eighteen as the legal age of manhood,[3] and declared that where a youth was in the care of a guardian whom he could not satisfy about his capacity to have the disposition of his own property, the period of minority might be deferred for seven years longer, i.e. until the age of twenty-five.[4]

During the period of their minority, children have no power to dispose either of their persons or their property. Accordingly they are then nominally in the charge of an elder whose tutelage may be of three kinds. The first kind, already discussed, is that concerned with the care and upbringing of infants, and here the parents are jointly concerned. If the mother is divorced, it is she who is, as we have seen, entrusted with their care until they reach a particular age—either two years old or seven, according to the different schools. If the mother dies before the child has reached the age of seven, her mother, or failing her, her maternal grandmother, takes charge. Only if these relatives are not available is

[1] Bukhārī, *Ṣaḥīḥ*, II, 158.

[2] Cf. Bayḍāwī on Koran 4⁵. The legal punishment for theft (cutting off the hand or foot) is not inflicted on a youth below the age of fifteen (Abu Yūsuf, *Kitāb al-Kharāj*, p. 106). The *Mejelle*, the Civil Code of Turkey from 1876 to 1926, made fifteen years the full age of puberty, though it was possible, if all the physical signs were present, to accept the age of twelve. (*Mejelle*, Tyser *et al.* (Nicosia, 1901)). See also Sachau, *Muhammedanisches Recht*, pp. 26 and 344.

[3] Mālikī agrees with this (Perron, "Jurisprudence Mussulmane" (translation of the *Mukhtaṣar* of Sīdi Khalīl) in *Exploration scientifique de l'Algerie*, XIII, 60). Eighteen is the legal age of majority in Turkey and also, except for marriage and divorce, for which separate regulations are made, in Persia (cf. Aghababian, *Législation Iranienne* (Paris, 1951), II, 111). According to the Constitution of the Republic of Syria promulgated on 10 July 1953, citizens both male and female have power to vote if they have completed their eighteenth year on 1st January of a year in which an election takes place.

[4] See Bayḍāwī on Koran 4⁵. Von Kremer, *Culturgeschichte* (I, 517, 533), regards this as a sign of the influence of Roman on Muhammadan law.

the father entrusted with the care of the child up to the age of seven. If the parents are both living but are divorced, those schools of law which consider seven years to be an age at which a child has power to discriminate, permit it then to choose whether it will live with its father or its mother. Only if the parent chosen is a Muslim of full age and free can he or she undertake the guardianship of the child. If the mother marries a man outside the circle of the child's kinsfolk she is incapacitated from acting as guardian.

Closely bound up with the first form of guardianship is the second, which is concerned with providing children with spouses[1] when they have reached the right age. The guardian from this aspect is the *walī*, whose functions and powers have been discussed already in the section on marriage. It is the father here who has first right to the office and then the nearest male kinsman. As *walī* the guardian must be a Muhammadan of full age. A Christian father who had a Muslim daughter could not dispose of her in marriage.

The third form of guardianship is that which is connected with the care and management of the property of minors. Here, too, it is the privilege of the father to exercise guardianship;[2] failing him, it falls to the grandfather or a person appointed in the grandfather's will. Males alone have the right to the office, but some legists consider that the claim of an infant's mother to be the guardian is entitled to consideration.[3]

Under any of these forms of tutelage the powers of the father over his children are very great. He cannot sell them into slavery, but he can, according to most codes, give his virgin unmarried daughters in marriage to whomsoever he pleases, and he can contract marriage for a son that has not reached puberty.[4] He can further banish from home a disobedient son who is married but has not set up a household for himself, and can thereby deprive him of a full share in the family possessions, over which he himself has absolute power as head of the household, though custom sets a limit to the amount of the family possessions which he may

[1] And is hence called *wilāyat al-nikāḥ*, "marriage tutorship".
[2] Known as *wilāyat al-māl*, "guardianship of property".
[3] Sachau, *op. cit.* p. 351; and Juynboll, *Handbuch*, pp. 198 f.
[4] Cf. Wellhausen, *Die Ehe bei den Arabern*, p. 459.

bequeath to persons outside. Normally, parents have little difficulty in enforcing their authority, for they are treated even by married children with the greatest respect, this being a duty constantly recommended by the Koran.[1]

The guardian of an orphan has powers which are similar to, though less extensive than, those possessed by a father. A marriage contracted by the latter for his infant son is valid when the latter reaches marriageable age; but any other *walī's* contract could be set aside by a ward at his coming of age. A minor, however, may not alienate his property without permission of his guardian, who himself may have no dealings with the property of his charge, except it be in the latter's interests.[2] But the Koran permits a guardian who is in need to use for his own purposes a portion of his ward's possessions.[3] When he reaches the age of marriage, the orphan, after being tested with respect to his fitness to manage property, should be given his possessions if the test is found satisfactory.[4] According to Abu Ḥanīfa, the orphan's property, whatever the results of the test, must not be retained after he has reached the age of twenty-five, provided he is not mentally deficient.[5]

So far as we have considered it, the status of the child in Islam is not greatly different from that of children under western systems. There is a distinct difference, however, when it comes to the question of inheritance. The Koranic regulations on this subject, although failing to provide for all the contingencies that might arise, introduced the novel and outstanding reform of permitting women to inherit from their kinsmen; while, as was inevitable, retaining some of the features of pre-Islamic custom. In the *Jāhilīya* new possessions were not acquired, as a rule, except from booty taken in raids or battles, in which the whole clan or tribe participated. When the shaykh had received his special portion (one-fourth), the rest was distributed equally amongst all who had helped to acquire it. In some measure, therefore, the clan had some claim to the possessions which a man left at his death. Muhammad recognized this in principle when he formulated his laws of inheritance.[6] But he inserted into them a remark expressing doubt concerning the relative value a man might put on parents

1 E.g. $17^{20\,f.}$; 29^{7}; 31^{13}. 2 *Ibid.* 6^{153}; 17^{36}. 3 *Ibid.* 4^{6}.
4 *Ibid.* 4^{5}. 5 Cf. Bayḍāwī on Koran 4^{5}. 6 Koran $4^{8-12,\,15,\,175}$.

and children; and he lent force to this doubt in his new laws, whereby all sons without regard to age are assured of a portion of inheritance, but by which fathers, brothers, mothers, wives and daughters also secure their portion. The amount of inheritance to be taken by a son is not specified in the Koran, which, however, allots definite "shares"[1] of a deceased person's estate—without distinction of movable and immovable—to members of his family other than the sons. "Shares" being fixed by the Koran, have first claim on the estate after debts and special bequests have been paid. The Muslim lawyers have, on the basis of the Koranic regulations, evolved elaborate tables of them, which may be studied in most manuals of Muhammadan law.[2] Our concern here is only with the rights of sons and daughters. A testator may, by established custom based upon tradition, make bequests to the extent of not more than one third of his or her property remaining after payment of all debts.[3] Out of the rest, or if he dies intestate out of the balance left after payment of all debts, the persons mentioned in the Koran as being entitled to "shares" receive them, and the remainder then goes to the sons, if there are any.[4] There is no mention in the Koran of any right accruing to a first-born son, with the result that according to Muslim law sons all inherit equal portions of their father's estate. Where, in addition to sons there are also daughters, the latter, by the Koran, receive "shares" in the proportion of one to every two received by the sons.

Daughters are amongst the persons who are specially mentioned by the Koran as entitled to "shares". Where there are no sons, an only daughter receives one half of the estate after the necessary deductions have been made for debts, etc., and two or more daughters receive between them two thirds. Where there is no

[1] They are known as *farā'iḍ*, i.e. "obligatory shares", and the part of the law dealing with them is known as *'Ilm al-Farā'iḍ*. "The Science of *Farā'iḍ*."

[2] E.g. E. Clavel, *Droit Musulman* (Paris, 1895); R. K. Wilson, *Digest of Anglo-Muhammadan Law* (London, 1908); Nawawī, *Minhādj aṭ-Ṭālibīn*, II; Ameer Ali, *Mahommedan Law* (Calcutta, 1894), II; Querry, *op. cit.*; A. A. A. Fyzee, *Outlines of Muhammadan Law* (Oxford, 1955).

[3] Bukhārī, *Ṣaḥīḥ* II, 185 f. (bk. 55, 3).

[4] By Mālikite law the testamentary dispositions of a minor are valid provided that he includes nothing that may be offensive to the law of Islam (*Mukhtaṣar* of Sīdi Khalīl, tr. Perron, *loc. cit.* p. 63). Shāfi'ī law, on the other hand, declares the will of a minor invalid (Sachau, *op. cit.* p. 236).

other legal heir, some codes assign the remainder of the estate also to the daughter or daughters, though others deny their title to it. According to the law-books no son or daughter can be excluded from inheritance by any mistaken calculation of the amount of the "shares" allotted by a testator or by the law. In practice, however, not seldom daughters receive no part of their father's estate. Thus amongst some tribes in Morocco only sons inherit,[1] and from a married woman it is her husband who inherits and not her children.[2] Amongst the Kababish, property passes to a man's sons, failing them to his brothers and so forth; neither daughters nor other female relatives receive any "share" as laid down in the Koran.[3] Nevertheless they expect to receive some part of the estate in which they have an interest. So also amongst the Bedouins of Palestine daughters did not inherit, although the Turks attempted to enforce the canon law.[4]

Where the law is regarded, keeping in view the fact that there is no recognition of primogeniture, a deceased person's son, however junior, takes precedence over a grandson—even if he is the eldest son of the eldest son.[5] Thus in the matter of succession to the Caliphate the genealogical tables show that very often brothers succeeded one another on the throne. The three sons of Hārūn al-Rashīd—namely Amīn, Ma'mūn and Mu'taṣim—occupied the sovereignty as sixth, seventh and eighth Caliphs respectively, to the exclusion of the son of Amīn, who was the eldest son of Hārūn. Amīn made great efforts to place his own son on the throne and exclude Ma'mūn, but he was not successful. On the other hand, amongst the later Caliphs son succeeded father with great regularity. Each of the Ottoman sulṭāns, further, down to Muhammad III (who died in 1595) was able to arrange for the succession of his own son, although after his time it was the senior male agnate who succeeded. Amongst the Shī'a, however, primogeniture is in some respects recognized. For example, in the

[1] E. Übach and E. Rackow, *Sitte und Recht in Nordafrika* (Stuttgart, 1923), p. 39.

[2] *Ibid.* p. 43.

[3] C. G. and B. Z. Seligman, "The Kababish", *Harvard African Studies*, II (1918), p. 144.

[4] A. Jaussen, *Coutumes des arabes au pays de Moab* (Paris, 1908), pp. 20 f.

[5] In practice the eldest son has the advantage that he stays in his father's house—especially amongst the Bedouins (Jaussen, *op. cit.* p. 21).

Qājār dynasty of Persia, each shāh in succession transmitted the throne to his own son.

A curious divergence from practice is recorded by Ibn Baṭṭūṭa,[1] who says that the heir to the Sulṭānate of Takadda was always the son of the ruler's sister. That coincides with what we know of Tuareg custom in other respects, although hereditary office is rare amongst the Tuaregs of today.

Certain disabilities have been invented by the legists and the interpreters of the Koran, to preclude undesirable persons from inheritance. Thus no person can inherit from another whom he has slain, either by design or by accident.[2] The apostasy of an heir excludes him from any legacy, and so also would the fact of his being a slave or an unbeliever.[3] Bastardy only excludes from inheritance from the father but not from the mother, between whom and whose children, however begotten, the ordinary rules of kinship hold. The child, therefore, can also inherit from its mother's kinsfolk. This is the law according to the Sunnī schools. The Shī'ites hold that the illegitimate child does not inherit from its mother or mother's kin, nor they from it.[4] If, however, the child is one that was conceived during wedlock, but has been disavowed by its mother's husband by the *li'ān*, then it has a claim to inherit from its mother.[5]

Adoption gives no right to inheritance under Islam. In pre-Islamic times, a *da'iy*, or adopted member of a clan or family, stood on an equality with true-born members of it, sharing in booty and inheritance as well as in the duties of the raid. Even women could be legally adopted and share in inheritance, sometimes in face of the opposition of other heirs.[6] Since adoption also gave a clan the right to inherit from an adopted member, persons who owned property were sometimes invited to membership, even though they were regarded as of humble status. Occasionally such a person, suspecting the motive of the invitation, would refuse, as Nuṣayb the Singer did.[7]

[1] *Voyages*, IV, 388, 443.

[2] By Shī'a law murder must be proved before a person can be excluded from inheritance. The accidental causing of death is no bar.

[3] Unbelievers, however, are permitted to inherit from one another (Querry, *op. cit.* II, 331). Muslims are not permitted to inherit from them (Sachau, *op. cit.* pp. 206 f.).

[4] Querry, *op. cit.* II, 365.

[5] *Ibid.* II, 363.

[6] Cf. the story of Ṣuraym's slave-girl (*Aghānī* XVII, 94).

[7] *Aghānī*, I, 134.

The Prophet Muhammad himself, in the days before he preached Islam, had a slave known as Zayd ibn Ḥāritha. Of him it is told that when one day his father and uncle arrived at Mecca to ransom him, Muhammad proposed that Zayd should choose between staying with him and going back to his kinsfolk. The youth chose to stay and thereupon the Prophet said to the bystanders: "I call you to witness that Zayd is my son; I inherit from him and he inherits from me." Until the coming of Islam the youth was called Zayd "son of Muhammad". Some time afterwards there occurred an event which brought about a complete change in the status of the adopted child. Muhammad was attracted by the wife of Zayd, whom he persuaded to divorce her so that he could marry her himself. This aroused a great deal of scandalous talk to the effect that the Prophet, having forbidden marriage with a son's wife, himself took in marriage the wife of his son Zayd. To put a stop to these accusations, "revelations" were sent down justifying his action; one[1] to the effect that the Prophet was father to no individual man and another[2] saying that God had not made adopted sons real sons, and that they were to be called by the name of their father. Thereafter Zayd was called "son of Ḥāritha" (Ḥāritha being his father's name) and not "son of Muhammad".[3]

The Ḥanafī legists have interpreted the Koranic story so as to exclude adopted children—they are always sons—entirely from any rights of inheritance and from any of the duties of true children. The only recognition of any special relationship is that marriage between adoptive parent and child is not encouraged. Apart from this restriction, adoption—with the consent of the child to be adopted, if he is old enough—is free to any Muslim man of full age and to any Muslim woman who has the permission of her husband. If one or both of the parents of the adopted child are known, there is no legal obligation on the adoptive parent to support him, though the moral obligation remains.

The Mālikites, as opposed to the Ḥanafīs, permit an adopted child to inherit from adoptive parents, but restrict adoption to such persons as would not otherwise be entitled to a share of inheritance. The restriction would appear to have for its object

[1] Koran 33^{40}. [2] *Ibid.* $30^{4\,f.}$

[3] Ṭabarī, III, 2299–3301 (cf. Ibn Hishām, ed Wuestenfeld, II, 54).

the prevention of any kinsman's acquiring a share of inheritance greater than the law grants in the ordinary way.

Amongst some of the tribes of southern Palestine there is a form of partial adoption by which, when an individual from outside has for some time been a member of a household, he comes to be regarded as part of it and can receive part of the common property, though he could not *inherit* from individual members. There is also true adoption, in which the adopted son comes to be regarded as offspring by blood and is declared by the adoptive father to be his son, *damawy*, "by blood" and *samawy*, "by name", and he may marry within the tribe if its permission is first granted.[1]

[1] Jaussen, *op. cit.* p. 25.

CHAPTER IV

ISLAMIC JURISPRUDENCE

According to the predominant view in Islam, *fiqh* or "jurisprudence" is defined as "Knowledge of the practical rules of religion"[1]; or, more fully, as "Knowledge of the rules of God which concern the actions of persons who own themselves bound to obey the law respecting what is required [*wājib*], forbidden [*maḥẓūr*], recommended [*mandūb*], disapproved [*makrūh*] or merely permitted [*mubāḥ*]. Such knowledge is acquired from the Book [i.e. the Koran], the *Sunna*, and such arguments as the legists may adduce for the necessary comprehension of the laws contained in them. It is the body of rules derived by these legal arguments that is called *fiqh*."[2] This science combines with that of *kalām*, or dogmatics and scholastic theology, to form the science of the *shar*ʿ or *sharīʿa*, which means literally the "path" or "road" (of the theocracy of Islam, of which Allah is the head and inspiration), and hence "the Law" of Islam. But it does not correspond merely to the "canon" law of Christianity, for it comprises, by definition, all the laws compiled in Islam by those competent to act in this matter.

Now the theoretical basis of Islam is the book known as the Koran, or more strictly Qur'ān, i.e. "the Reading". The name is derived from the Arabic root *qara'a*, meaning "he read" or "he recited", and it is applied in the text of the book itself either to a single "reading" or passage[3] or to a collection of several.[4] It is to be inferred that the Prophet regarded the book as containing a series of "revelations"[5] made to him at irregular intervals as necessity demanded[6] and as dictated from an original code, "the Mother of the Book",[7] which is preserved in Heaven.[8] The intermediary which brought the revelation to earth was "a faithful spirit",[9] later identified with the angel Gabriel.[10]

[1] Subkī, *Jam' al-jawāmi'* (Būlāq, 1283), I, 23 (margin).

[2] Ibn Khaldūn, *Prolégomènes*, ed. Quatremère (Paris, 1858), III, 1. See further *Law in the Middle East*, ed. M. Khaddury and H. J. Liebesny, I, *Origin and Development of Islamic Law* (Washington, D.C., 1955).

[3] E.g. 72^{1}, 10^{62}.

[4] 15^{87}, 17^{84}.

[5] *Tanzīl* = "a sending-down".

[6] 25^{34}.

[7] *Umm al-Kitāb*.

[8] 43^{3}, 13^{39}, 3^{5}, 85^{22}.

[9] 26^{193}.

[10] 2^{91}.

By the frequent exhortations in the book bidding the Prophet to "recite" or "say", it is implied that the heavenly messages are being dictated by God, to be "a guide for him who should do right" and "a decision on all matters".[1] The book claims further that it contains the essence of truth which had existed from all time past, and that it was preceded on earth by the book given to Moses, which where necessary it now confirms.[2]

Several times the book proclaims itself to have been revealed in Arabic, or in the Prophet's own tongue,[3] and is therefore, it implies, entirely lucid and comprehensible.[4] "Had we made it a Koran in a foreign tongue they [its opponents, or perhaps its recipients] would have said, Unless its signs be made clear... [we will not receive it]. What! a foreign Koran and [for] an Arab?"[5]

As it now stands, the Koran is a collection of *sūras*, or chapters, of very mixed content. Taken together, they are a series of reports —in essence genuine—of discourses delivered by the prophet Muhammad in the course of his career. It is probable that he himself did not write down his speeches, either before delivery or after, and indeed Muslim tradition holds that the Prophet was illiterate.[6] The historians preserve the name of the secretaries whom he employed at one time or another; yet it can scarcely be imagined that the earlier chapters of the Koran were set speeches which had been rehearsed before delivery, for the impression they make is one of wild spontaneity. There may have been, and

[1] 6^{155}. I.e. "a detailed exposition of every question that may arise concerning the faith" (Bayḍāwī). In fact it is not so even by the commentators' standards; for, to take an exmple, it contains no word about circumcision, which, though not universally practised in Islam, is generally regarded as the mark of the Muhammadan.

[2] 46^{11} and 6^{155}. [3] 19^{27}. [4] 42^{5}, 20^{112}, 26^{195}, 13^{37}, 41^{2}.

[5] 41^{44}. Out of this arises the question whether the Koran could be lawfully and validly recited in a foreign tongue. Ṭabarī, in his commentary on the Koran (I, 5), remarks: "God sends revelations in the tongues of His own apostles. Since Muhammad spoke Arabic the Koran is in Arabic." Another commentator, Zamakhsharī, elucidating the statement that the Koran is in the Arabic tongue, "and it is in the scriptures of the ancients" (Koran $26^{195\,\mathrm{f.}}$) says: "Either the Koran or the themes treated therein [are meant]. Hence Abu Ḥanīfa decides in the affirmative the question whether it is permitted at prayer to recite the Koran in Persian. For the Koran remains the Koran even if translated into a tongue other than Arabic . . . for the themes treated therein remain unchanged" (*Kashshāf*, ed. Lees (Calcutta, 1856–9), II, 109).

[6] This is an inference made from the verses $7^{156,158}$ and 29^{47}.

probably there were, some written notes on points of law involving figures, which might have been difficult to retain in the memory, but the great mass of the "revelations" lived in the memories of the hearers. It was from reports which survived and from odd written notes that the Koran was, after the Prophet's death, officially compiled.[1]

So far as the arrangement of the *sūras* is concerned, length has been the factor deciding which should take precedence. After the first or "opening" chapter, the *fātiḥa*, which has a liturgical significance, they are arranged with the longest first and the numerous short ones at the end. Whether each chapter as it stands represents a single discourse, or is a compilation of several discourses, must remain open to some doubt; for even some of the longer ones, though of considerable extent and dealing with a variety of subjects, might have been delivered at a single session.[2] That the method of arranging in order of length rather than according to the period of delivery was not employed out of ignorance of the latter, is shown by the fact that the great majority of the *sūras* are labelled, with every likelihood of accuracy, as belonging either to the Meccan or the Medinese period of the Prophet's career.[3]

For the reason that even good memories must have failed to retain all the details of subjects heard perhaps only once and at some considerable distance of time, the number of obscurities in the Koran is fairly large. There are also, to complicate matters, variations in the received text of the book, due to the imperfect character of the Arabic script, which, in its early stages, was a very inadequate instrument for the recording of the language. Not only was it unprovided with the short vowels on which mainly depend the inflexions of nouns and verbs, but it also contained several letters that, until distinguished by diacritic points, might easily be confused with one another. Finally, there are disputed readings which may be due to the dialectical

[1] This is not the place for a history of the Koran, for which see R. A. Nicholson, *Literary History of the Arabs* (London, 1907; 2nd ed., Cambridge, 1930) and the authorities there quoted.

[2] Speeches lasting the best part of a day are not uncommon in Muslim and other lands. The variety of the contents may be paralleled in discourses of the Hebrew prophets.

[3] Muhammadan scholarship has even preserved a tradition of differences of date within one and the same *sūra*. Thus Bayḍāwī, on 2[241], says it was revealed earlier than another verse in the same *sūra* to which he refers.

peculiarities in the speech of those who heard and reported the Prophet's words.

Frequently, however, it is the thought itself which is obscure, seeing that the Prophet must often have been called upon at short notice to deliver judgment upon questions of importance, and to make regulations upon complicated and difficult matters—such as that of inheritance—which might have far-reaching issues. Moreover, the Prophet insisted on retaining the poetic form and speech of his "revelations", even in the later stages of his career when he was dealing with prosaic matters of law and there was need for plain and clear direction.

The early *sūras*—those delivered at Mecca—and also the earlier Medina chapters, are filled with impassioned harangues delivered by the Prophet to his newly converted followers to encourage their belief, with fiery denunciations of his enemies, and with vivid descriptions of Hell, Heaven and the judgment of the Last Day to point his remarks.[1] There are, in addition, narratives derived from the Jewish and Christian Scriptures or Apocrypha quoted with the same purpose of encouraging belief, but told with such changes and discrepancies as make it obvious that the Prophet had gathered the stories from hearsay.[2] Here and there comes a moral behest inculcating such virtues as continence,[3] the guarding of trusts and covenants, honest testimony,[4] giving just and generous weight,[5] and kindness and gratitude to parents.[6] Instruction about conduct too is not forgotten.[7] More frequent, as illustration of divine power and dominance of the world, is a description of creation and an exposition of the Prophet's ideas, which were presumably those ruling amongst the learned of the time, with regard to cosmogony and the construction of the universe.[8]

So far as the religious, ritual, and what may be called the civil duties and obligations of the true believer are concerned, direction is to be found in an occasional hint rather than in any clear

[1] See especially *sūras* 52 and 56.

[2] Some of the longest of these stories are those concerning Joseph (*sūra* 12), Jonah (*sūra* 10) and Moses (*sūra* 7^{101-60}).

[3] 70^{29}, 26^{165}.

[4] 70^{32} f.

[5] 55^{8}, 26^{1}, 11^{86}.

[6] 29^{7}, 46^{14}, 31^{13}.

[7] 31^{16-19}.

[8] E.g. 21^{31-34}, 25^{55}, 38^{39} f., 41^{8-11}, 11^{9}, 54^{47} f, $15^{16, 19, 22, 26}$ f.

statement of what is required. An example may be taken from *sura* 70, "the Ascents".

Man was created avaricious; when evil toucheth him [he is] impatient, but when good toucheth him [he is] grudging. Not so the prayerful, who are ever constant in their prayer, nor those out of whose wealth there is a known and rightful share for the beggar and the unprosperous; nor those who believe in the day of judgment; nor those who are on their guard against the chastisement of their Lord—none is secured against the chastisement of their Lord—nor those who guard their privy parts, save for their wives or the [slave-women] which their right hands possess (for these they are blameless, and those whose demands are beyond this are transgressors); nor those who are true to their trusts and compacts; nor those who are upright in their testimonies; nor those who are on their guard concerning their prayers.[1]

Even in the Medina period, when the Prophet might have been expected, from the growing size of the Muslim community and the spread of Islam throughout Arabia, to have devoted himself to providing a code of legislation, there is still little of straightforward direction, and while the Medina *sūras* are more prosaic than those of Mecca, they continue to deal with the same topics. So far as the religion is concerned, his views are still so little fixed that he contents himself with repeating an early formula of his laying down the duties of the believer as being regular prayers, paying the poor-rate[2] and being convinced about the next world.[3] Yet he was compelled by circumstances to make regulations, even if he did nothing more than formulate a code of the most meagre description.

There has been occasion in previous parts of the present work to refer to Koranic regulations touching slavery, marriage and inheritance—nearly all of such regulations belonging to the Medina period. It must now be shown how the legislative portions of the Koran were developed and supplemented in the course of the growth of Islam, and what place they have in the vast structure of Muslim jurisprudence. A fair example is to be found in the

[1] 70^{19-34}.

[2] *Zakāt*, as opposed to *ṣadaqa*, the free-will offering of alms, though often the two terms are used interchangeably.

[3] 31^{3} and *passim*.

regulations for what are regarded by every believer as amongst the most important of his religious duties: namely, worship, payment of the poor-tax, fasting and pilgrimage. For three of these duties the Koran has made what is, for it, a fair amount of provision. Accordingly, since they have the authority of the "word of God", the pertinent regulations have obtained almost universal validity amongst Muslims and every treatise on Muhammadan jurisprudence gives them pride of place. Each of these duties is known as a *farḍ al-'ayn*, i.e. an "essential duty imposed" on the individual, as opposed to *farḍ al-kifāya*, which is a duty, such as that of the election of a sulṭān, incumbent on the community. From the comparisons which follow it will be seen how the basic regulations of the Koran[1] on these subjects have been expounded.

I. WORSHIP: THE STATED TIMES

Give praise in adulation of thy Lord before the rising of the sun and before sunset. And part of the night give praise to him . . . [2]

Observe prayer at the setting of the sun up to the darkening of the night and the reading at dawn . . . and part of the night hold vigil for voluntary prayer.[3]

Observe worship at the two ends of the day and at portions of the early part of the night.[4]

Take heed to the services of worship and the middle service.[5]

It would appear from these verses that only three appointed times of worship are indicated. But to have decided that definitely would have meant to ignore the repetition of the wording, which came to be regarded with the utmost reverence as the actual utterance of Allah, and therefore as having in itself some significance. It was remarked that the wording differed each time the regulation was repeated, implying to the Muslim jurist that something was added on each occasion. For a century or more after the death of the Prophet it was not definitely known, or decided, actually how many periods of worship were laid down nor at what hours worship was to be performed.[6]

The uncertainty of the law in the first century of Islam, it may

[1] The passages are given without regard to chronological order.
[2] 50^{38} f. [3] 17^{80} f. [4] 11^{116}. [5] 2^{239}.
[6] Cf. I. Goldziher, *Muhammedanische Studien*, II, 30 f.

incidentally be said, was not confined to worship.[1] Even such immediate and practical questions as those of lawful foods and the way in which inheritances should be divided were by no means certainly defined even in the minds of those who might have been expected to be authorities on such matters. Thus, when the son of Omar II is asked whether fish thrown up by the sea may be lawfully eaten, he replies in the negative, but when a copy of the Koran is brought to him and he is shown a passage declaring "the spoils of the sea"[2] to be lawful food, he changes his answer and says there is no harm in it.[3] Similarly, the widest differences of opinion prevailed as to whether horseflesh was permitted, a question which has never been authoritatively decided for the whole of Islam.[4]

An instance of how opinion fluctuated on a matter of such elemental importance as the disposal of a deceased man's estate amongst his relatives is described by the historian Mas'ūdī.[5] In his version of the story a certain man of learning, by name Shu'bī, is asked by Ḥajjāj, the famous governor of Iraq, in what proportions an estate ought to be divided between a man's mother, sister and grandfather. Shu'bī replies that five companions of the Prophet had all delivered different judgments on the point.[5]

It was only when the authorities at Medina, the Prophet's own capital city and the seat of traditional learning, had begun to exert some influence on the faith, that a final inference was made from all the Koranic verses on prayer taken together, to the effect that five periods and not three were indicated.[6] The means by which this result was reached is stated most succinctly in the remarks of the thirteenth-century Persian commentator Bayḍāwī on one of the verses above quoted [50[38f]]. He says: "By the giving of praise is meant worship: and the worship before sunrise means the

[1] See J. Schacht, *Origins of Muhammadan Jurisprudence* (Oxford, 1950), *passim*.

[2] 5[97].

[3] Mālik b. Anas, *Muwaṭṭa'*, with commentary of Zurqānī (Cairo, A.H. 1280), II, 357. Cf. Goldziher, *op. cit.* II, 74.

[4] See below, pp. 172 f.

[5] *Murūj al-dhahab*, ed. and tr. B. de Maynard and P. de Courteille (Paris, 1861 ff.), V, 335.

[6] See further Goldziher, *Revue de l'Histoire des Religions* (1901), pp. 1 ff.; Mittwoch, *Abhandl. d. Preuss. Akad.* (1913), XV, 2.

'morning'[1] [service]; that before sunset comprises the [services] of 'noon[2] and 'after-noon',[3] while by 'part of the night' is meant the two periods[4] of 'evening' and 'night'." By his interpretation the commentator is obviously reading into the text of the Koran a justification for the custom ruling in his own day, which has continued to be valid to the present time.[5]

Further legislation on the subject of prayer concerns ritual ablution, on which the Koran makes these regulations:

You who believe! Come not to prayer being drunk, [but wait] until you can understand what you say; nor polluted—except you are travelling on the road—until you have washed yourselves. And if you are sick or on a journey, or if one of you has come from the privy or you have touched women, and you have not found water, then cleanse yourselves with some pure part of the surface of the ground, rubbing it upon your faces and hands.[6]

You who believe! When you address yourselves to prayer, wash your faces and your hands up to the elbows and wipe your hands and feet up to the ankles.[7]

As for orientation for prayer, there seems to have been originally no special direction ("The East and the West are God's: therefore whichever way you turn, there is the face of God").[8] Later, in the widely held traditional view, Jerusalem was chosen, possibly in order to conciliate the Jews.[9] But Jerusalem is in fact not mentioned in the Koran, the passages which speak of the "sacrosanct place of worship" (2^{145}) or "most distant place of worship" (17^1) having been later interpreted as referring to it.[10] However that may be, the mosque at Mecca was very early made the point of orientation of the Muhammadan's worship.

All Koranic regulations were expanded and multiplied in the books of *fiqh* so as to provide answers to the widest possible range of queries that might be addressed to the legist, many of the points raised being casuistical in the extreme.

1 *Ṣubh.* 2 *Ẓuhr.* 3 *'Aṣr.*
4 *Al-'ishā'ān*, i.e. *maghrib* and *'ishā*.
5 See Lane, *Modern Egyptians* (Everyman ed., London, n.d.), ch. III, pp. 73 f. 6 4^{16}.
7 5^8. For the modern practice see Lane, *op. cit.* pp. 69–72.
8 2^{109}. 9 Thus Bayḍāwī on 2^{138}.
10 Cf. Barthold, in *Der Islam*, XVIII, 245 ff.

In what follows, only the title of the chief sections in the law-books are given. Thus, under the heading of "Ritual Purity", which logically precedes that of "Worship", the *Majmū' al-fiqh*[1] treats of these subjects:

Ablutions for prayer, ceremonial washings after defilement, *tayammum* or cleansing with sand where there is no water, on menstruation, etc.

On the subject of "Worship" there are the following headings:

The call to prayer [*adhān*], times of prayer, who leads the community in prayer, prayer on a journey, etc.

In another work of more regularly jurisprudential form but of similar date, the *Jāmi' al-ṣaghīr* of the Ḥanafite Muhammad ibn Ḥasan al-Shaybānī,[2] the section-headings under "Worship" are as follows:

What voids ablution; what may be used for ablution; impurity which befouls a garment, a stocking or shoe; on the prayers of a woman having [by inadvertence] a quarter of her thigh uncovered [whether they must be repeated from the beginning]; on the *adhān* or call to worship; on the formula *Allāhu Akbar*; on a man who finds himself in a company at public worship when he has already recited part of the service in private; what voids worship; on reading the Koran during worship; actions disapproved during worship; on faults in worship and what corrects them; an invalid who worships sitting down; on worship at the festivals; on the carrying of a corpse and the appropriate prayers; whether a person slain innocently need be washed; the law concerning [proprietorship of] mosques.

In still another law-book which may be quoted for illustration, the *Tanbīh* of Shīrāzī,[3] the section-headings under "Ritual Purity" are:

On waters; vessels used for ablutions; description of *wuḍū'* [ritual ablution for worship]; what voids the *wuḍū'*; ceremonial washing; *tayammum*; menstruation; the cessation of the state of impurity.

[1] A compilation of *ḥadīths* with legal bearing and of Shī'ite, or schismatic, origin. It was traditionally attributed to one Zayd b. 'Alī (second century A.H.) but that ascription has been proved doubtful.

[2] Būlāq, A.H. 1302 (margins).

[3] Composed in 452/1061. The author belonged to the Shāfi'ī rite. The edition used here is by Juynboll (Leyden, 1879).

Under "Worship" the section-headings are as in the *Majmū' al-fiqh*, with the addition of the following:

On covering the privy parts; on purity of the body and garments and the place of worship; on the true direction (the *qibla*) for worship; what is obligatory in worship and what is customary; on supererogatory prayer; prostrations during recital of the Koran; on what voids worship; on omissions in the number of prostrations; the times at which worship is forbidden; on communal worship; on the qualities required in the imāms; on the positions at worship of the leader [the imām] and the led [*ma'mūm*]; on worship by an invalid; on worship by a traveller; on prayer uttered in fear; clothes which are disapproved and those which are allowed; on Friday worship; on the ordering of Friday; worship at the two festivals; prayer at the eclipse of the sun; prayer for water.

2. ALMS OR POOR-RATE

On this subject, although there are numerous verses in the Koran exhorting the believer to give alms,[1] yet there is none which specifies how, to whom, or in what amounts the rate is to be paid. The only piece of legislation approaching exactness on the question is contained in the verse[2] which says that of booty one-fifth part is to go "to God and his apostle, to near of kin and orphans, and to the poor and the wayfarer". This absence of a precise scale of payments is, however, not to be wondered at, seeing that the idea of the empire of Islam as an organized state did not arise until after the Prophet's death; and only then can any validity have been attached to the figures given in all the law-books in the section on *zakāt*. There are not lacking "traditions" that the prophet himself laid down a scale of revenue charges which his agents in various parts of Arabia were to levy on the population.[3] These traditions are probably spurious, although it cannot be doubted that some of the statutory demands may date from early in the history of the Muslim empire.[4]

1 (*a*) *Zakāt*, 41^{6}, 19^{56}, 30^{38}, etc., or (*b*) *Ṣadaqa* 2^{280}, 4^{114}, 9^{58}, etc.

2 8^{42}.

3 Cf. Goldziher, *Muhammedanische Studien*, II, 50.

4 See Bukhārī, *Ṣaḥīḥ*, ed. Krehl, I, bk. 24, nos. 38 ff.; and cf. below, the chapter on Government, pp. 271 ff.

The sections under the heading of *zakāt* included in the three books of *fiqh* already mentioned are as follows:

(*a*) The amount levied upon camels, oxen and sheep; on gold and silver; land liable to tithe and other impost; the merit of granting loans and the persons entitled to alms; the curse inflicted by the Prophet upon persons who refused alms or delayed payment.[1]

(*b*) The alms-tax on property; the "fifth" and the poor-rate; the person who evades the collector of tithe; tithe on [the produce of] land; other taxes upon land and the poll-tax upon "protected" peoples [i.e. Jews and Christians]; the tax on minerals and the alms payable at the end of the fast of Ramaḍān.[2]

(*c*) The persons liable to payment of *zakāt*; the alms-tax levied upon cattle [including camels]; the *zakāt* payable on growing crops, coin, merchandise and minerals or metals extracted from the earth; the alms payable at the close of Ramaḍān; amongst what persons the alms is divided, etc.[3]

3. FASTING

The regulations on this subject, which were almost certainly derived from pre-Islamic practice, are fairly comprehensive, and the bearing which they have on modern usage is easily traceable. The salient points are contained in a single passage:

> O believers, fasting is prescribed to you as it was prescribed to those who were before you . . . for [certain] numbered days. But if any of you is sick, or upon a journey, then a number of other days. . . . [4] The month of Ramaḍān . . . he among you who witnesses [the new moon of] the month, let him set about fasting. But he who is sick or upon a journey, then a number of other days. . . . [5]

This is supplemented by the following:

> It is lawful to you on the night of the fasting to have intercourse with your wives . . . and eat and drink until by the [light of] dawn a white thread is distinguishable by you from a black thread. Then make your fasting strict until the night, and have no commerce with them, secluding yourselves in the mosques. . . . [6]

[1] *Majmū' al-fiqh.* [2] *Jāmi' al-ṣaghīr.* [3] The *Tanbīh* of Shīrāzī.

[4] "This is permissive; others say it is compulsory" (Bayḍāwī, *ad loc.*).

[5] $2^{179-181}$.

[6] 2^{183}. For modern usage, see Lane, *op. cit.* ch. XXIV, pp. 478–84.

Again, the sections under the heading of "Fasting" in the three works of *fiqh* already quoted are as follows:

(*a*) On the merit of fasting; on breaking the fast; what voids the fast; who may break the fast; expiation for deliberately breaking the fast; the evidence that the new moon [of the month following Ramaḍān] has been seen; expiation due for taking false oaths.[1]

(*b*) Fasting upon a day about which there is a doubt as to its belonging to Ramaḍān or not; whether persons lying unconscious or demented, youths just reaching puberty, Christians about to become Muslims, and travellers who have broken their fast before the due time are compelled to complete the month of fasting; persons who are compelled, and those who are not, to complete the fast and make expiation.[2]

(*c*) Who must fast in Ramaḍān and who need not [this is included under the general heading of "Fasting"]; supererogatory fasting; on secluding oneself for worship during Ramaḍān.[3]

4. PILGRIMAGE

The largest amount of space devoted in the Koran to any one of the four duties is that given to pilgrimage. For this there is set out a well developed ritual that was undoubtedly taken over with little change from the practice of the pagan Arabs of the pre-Islamic period. The pertinent verses are as follows:

> The first house [temple] that was founded for mankind was that at Bakka.[4] . . . In it are clear signs; even the standing-place of Abraham: and he who enters it is safe. And a duty to God incumbent upon all mankind is pilgrimage to the house—all who can perform the journey thither.[5]

> Verily Ṣafā and Marwa are of the places of God's rites, and whoever makes a pilgrimage to the house or visits it [ceremoniously] shall commit no fault if he circumambulate them both.[6]

[1] *Majmū' al-fiqh.* [2] *Jāmi' al-ṣaghīr.* [3] *Tanbīh.*

[4] I.e. Mecca. [5] 3^{90} f.; cf. 22^{27-30}.

[6] 2^{153}. The implication in the last part of the verse is that a pagan practice is being retained, but that its retention is approved.

Fulfil the pilgrimage and the ceremonious visitation unto God; and if ye be prevented, then [send] what is available to you by way of gift. Shave not your heads[1] until the gift shall reach its destination. . . . The pilgrimage is [in] months well known; and whosoever makes the pilgrimage incumbent on himself, then there is [for him] neither sexual intercourse, nor lewdness, nor strife. . . . "[2]

Under the heading of "Pilgrimage" the books of *fiqh* contain such sections as the following:

(*a*) The duty of pilgrimage; the meeting-place for pilgrim trains; [on various ceremonies to be carried out at Mecca]; hunting on pilgrimage; the pilgrimage to be performed by youths, slaves and Bedouins; pilgrimage by proxy; the prayers to be uttered at the sacrificial slaughtering of beasts; sacrifices; the eating of sacrifices; game animals [as sacrifices], etc.[3]

(*b*) [Expiatory deeds by] persons who miss the specified time of pilgrimage or who enter Mecca not being clad in the ceremonial dress appointed to be worn; the penalty on a pilgrim who kills game; the pilgrim who pares his nails or cuts his hair; [various problems connected with faulty or irregular performance of the pilgrimage ceremonies]; pilgrimage by proxy, etc.[4]

(*c*) [Upon whom pilgrimage is incumbent]; the appointed place of assembly for pilgrim-trains; ceremonial dress to be worn at Mecca; expiation for faulty dressing; the ceremonies to be fulfilled at the *Ḥajj*; sacrifices; game and other animals slaughtered [for food]; foods [lawful on pilgrimage]; vows.[5]

Other enactments in the Koran, though dealing with as great a variety of subjects as the books of Leviticus or Deuteronomy in the Old Testament—subjects which occidental systems would place in the categories of theology, ritual, ethics and law, both civil and criminal—are yet very scanty. A whole topic may be disposed of in a sentence or two inserted, almost casually it would appear, in the middle of a long discourse on some other subject. Moreover, even when an enactment was made it was not always final; for naturally enough Muhammad had occasion at times to change his mind. With each change of mind came a new

[1] In practice this meant letting all the hair on the body grow, and also the nails, during the whole of the pilgrimage. See R. F. Burton, *A Pilgrimage to Al-Madinah and Meccah* (London, 1893), ch. XXV–XXXI.

[2] 2[192] f. [3] *Majmūʿ al-fiqh.* [4] *Jāmiʿ al-ṣaghīr.* [5] *Tanbīh.*

"revelation" contradicting some older one already in existence. This uncertainty in the revealed code laid the Prophet open to accusations that the changes were dictated by expediency, charges which required special "revelations" to be sent down to refute the calumniators, e.g.:

When we change one verse for another—and God knows best what he reveals—they say thou art only a fabricator.[1]

And

Will they not examine the Koran with care? If it came from anyone but God, they would find many contradictions in it.[2]

The principle involved in these changes was that of *naskh* or "abrogation", which is explained in such verses of the Koran as the following:

What he pleases God will blot out or confirm; and with him is the "Mother of the Book".[3]
If we abrogate any verse, or cause it to pass into oblivion, we bring a better one than it, or one as good.[4]

Bayḍāwī's comment on the latter verse is illuminating on the significance of the principle of "abrogation" for Islam. "The verse", he says, "is proof that abrogation and the deferring of revelation—since the original revelation is qualified by 'if'—and any commands that the latter may include, are valid. The reason for it is that laws are formulated and verses revealed as they are required, to suit the good of mankind. . . . This varies with the time and the individual; as, for example, the necessities of life, which may be beneficial at one time and harmful at another."[5]

Unfortunately, when, after the Prophet's death, the Koran was compiled, both "abrogating"[6] and "abrogated"[7] verses were included, since no one but Muhammad himself could have decided which was to remain valid. Accordingly, the text which says that prayer may be uttered in any direction is closely followed by one which declares that it is on Mecca that all eyes should be focused

[1] 16^{103}. [2] 4^{184}. [3] 13^{39}. [4] 2^{100}.
[5] Earlier in the same passage he has said: "Abrogation of a verse indicates that it has ceased to be a pious act to recite it, or that any law based upon it has ceased to be valid—or both."
[6] *Nāsikh*. [7] *Mansūkh*.

in prayer.[1] For the example which Bayḍāwī gives of the "necessities of life etc", he may have had in mind the prohibition of wine,[2] which had at one time been associated not only with the "healthful nutriment" derived from the palm,[3] but also with the sensuous delights of Paradise itself,[4] amongst them being rivers of wine as well as rivers of pure water, milk and honey.[5]

Of greater moment were abrogations on such matters of social importance as inheritance, penalties for adultery, etc. Thus at one time the Prophet had published the "revelation" that men who died leaving wives must bequeath to them sufficient to maintain them for a year.[6] This was abrogated by another, which made it compulsory for men who died leaving no issue to bequeath to their wives a fourth of their estate, or an eighth if there were a child.[7] In this connection also, the vague prescription to leave one's estate at death equitably to parents and kinsmen[8] is to be contrasted with the later passage in which specific regulations are made for the division of inheritance.[9]

The question of punishment for adultery has already been discussed,[10] and it has been shown how the Muslim commentators reconcile one verse,[11] which prescribes death as the penalty, with a later one[12] in which the punishment is reduced to a hundred stripes.

To explain such discrepancies and contradictions in the sacred text needed all the ingenuity of those whose business it was to know and interpret the law and whose powers of dialectic had to be pressed into service in order to facilitate the business of everyday life. Later jurists argued that either "abrogation" meant substitution of one law for another which was abolished, or that it meant expansion and elucidation of the earlier law.[13]

Yet this matter of contradictory directions in the Koran was of less serious import to those who had to administer the law than the fact of the utter inadequacy of Koranic legislation to meet practical contingencies. Within twenty years after the death of the Prophet, a great belt of territory from the Indus to the Atlantic

1 See above, pp. 4, 157.
2 Koran 2^{216}, 5^{92}.
3 16^{69}.
4 78^{35}, 83^{25}.
5 47^{16} f.
6 2^{41}.
7 4^{14}.
8 2^{176}.
9 4^{8} f. 12, 15, 175.
10 Pp. 119 f. above.
11 4^{19}.
12 24^{4}.
13 E.g. Subkī (d. 771/1369), *Jam' al-jawāmi'* (Būlāq, A.H. 1285), II, 65 ff. (margin).

Ocean had been overrun by Arab tribesmen, the rank and file of whom were interested for the most part in little more than the prospect of plunder. In every one of the newly subdued territories, the conquerors met with a civilization vastly superior to their own, but about which their sacred book said little or nothing. The culture of both the Persian and the Roman provinces therefore provided the Arab leaders with constant matter for wonder and the exercise of ingenuity. Having in the Koran, even if they knew or studied it, no comprehensive guide either in political emergencies or when social or legal problems arose, the Muslim governors were driven to adopting local usage or else to applying their own reason and common sense as a way out of their difficulties. In the first stages of their career of conquest it may be assumed that the Arab generals and administrators at times of necessity used their own judgment without any hesitation. There is even some measure of historical support for this assumption. Thus it is reported that when the qāḍī of Egypt referred to Omar II (717–20) a case dealing with an assault of a particular kind by a youth on a girl, the Caliph replied that he could find no precedent for such a case and that the qāḍī must use his own judgment.[1] This exercise of judgment or opinion is known in Arabic as *ra'y*, and it has become a technical term in Muslim jurisprudence. In later times, the resort to *ra'y* received some sanction from a tradition that the prophet himself exercised his own opinion when no revelation was forthcoming on a matter in dispute.[2]

As the non-Arab Muslims during the second century of Islam increased in numbers and devoted themselves with growing ardour to the study of Islam, their piety persuaded them that they must look to the Koran as the spring and origin of all the regulations which concerned their religion. Accordingly the free and unrestricted use of *ra'y* or arbitrary opinion was checked by the introduction of a rule that such *ra'y* must be controlled by reference to the Koran. If the latter should contain no precedent on any particular point, it yet contained—such was the theory—a precedent on a similar point from which the correct inferences could be drawn. Thus was evolved the principle of *qiyās*, "measurement" and hence "analogy", the second of the four roots of

[1] Al-Kindī, *Kitāb al-Wulāt*, ed. Guest (Leyden, 1912), p. 334.
[2] Cf. Ibn Ḥazm in Goldziher, *Zahiriten* (Leipzig, 1884), pp. 212 f.

Muhammadan jurisprudence; the first, of course, being the Koran itself.

This form of reasoning is generally connected with the name of a Persian scholar known as Abu Ḥanīfa, who died in 767. He was born at Kūfa in Iraq, and in the struggles for the Caliphate that arose with the decline of the Umayyad house, he, being imbued with the legitimist sympathies of a Persian, supported the losing side of the 'Alids, the descendants of Muhammad the prophet. During his lifetime he gathered about him a band of disciples who were to become the nucleus of the earliest school or rite[1] of Muslim jurisprudence, that which was known after him as the Ḥanafī school. He himself constructed no formal code and did not write any systematic work of jurisprudence or any manual of law; seeming, in fact, to have troubled very little about general principles and to have made decisions on such questions only as were propounded to him. From a compendium of his sayings which was compiled by his disciples it may be inferred that he had small liking for the practical side of the law, and something of the kind might be gathered from the description of him given by the biographer Ibn Khallikān, namely, that he seldom spoke, but that when he did so his words poured forth in a torrent.[2]

In applying the principle of *qiyās* or analogy, Abu Ḥanīfa was not content to seek for verbal resemblances between the written provisions[3] of the Koran and those he desired to evolve, but he endeavoured to penetrate behind the wording of the text to the '*illa*, or motive, of the provisions made. In the new application[4] of the text, or in the law derived from it, there must be the same '*illa* as in the Koranic revelation or traditional usage. Thus, to take an illustration, the Koran forbids wine on the grounds (or '*illa*) that it causes intoxication; therefore when by analogy fermented date-juice is forbidden it must be on the same grounds.[5]

Some of the successors of Abu Ḥanīfa sought to win sanction for the use of *ra'y* and *qiyās* by holding that every derived law was implicit in the text of the Koran, and that all they did by their

[1] *Madhhab.*

[2] Ibn Khallikān, ed. Wuestenfeld, no. 775; tr. de Slane, III, 553 f.

[3] *Nuṣūṣ* (singular, *naṣṣ*).

[4] Known as the *far'*, i.e. "the branch".

[5] Subkī, *Jam' al-jawāmi'*, II, 180 (margin).

reasoning process was to elicit what was already contained in the text. Others modified this position by holding that it was only the "worldly" laws which could thus be elicited by reasoning, the theological laws being entirely clear and explicit and therefore not in any need of exposition by the methods of derivation or analogy. Abu Ḥanīfa would have sympathized with neither position, holding as he did that the basic text contained some, but by no means all, of the regulations and laws required by society. From the basic text and laws these fresh ordinances were to be derived by *qiyās*. Thus the Koran[1] contains provision for the punishment of theft—which is "taking secretly the possessions of another"[2]—but says nothing about burglary, which means breaking into a building for the purpose of stealing. By *qiyās* it is established that the penalty for the latter offence is the same as for the former; namely, cutting off the miscreant's hand.[3]

"The truth is", says an authority,[4] "that *qiyās* supplies the argument, or reason, underlying the normal and patent actions of the [Prophet's] companions. . . . However, *qiyās* will not apply to natural functions or ancient practice; thus it cannot be used to specify what shall be the shortest period of menstruation or accouchement or gestation, since particulars of that kind cannot be derived from the written text [of the Koran]. Long-established laws also cannot be held to derive any force from *qiyās*, for there are some that cannot be [reasonably] explained; as, for example, the necessity for the kin of a man-slayer to pay blood-wite. Nor can *qiyās* be based upon an abrogated verse of the Koran."

Reliance on "opinion" led to differences, and even immediate disciples of Abu Ḥanīfa sometimes refused to follow him unquestioningly on the path of *ra'y* and *qiyās*. Various instances of this are given in Abu Yūsuf's work on revenue, the *Kitāb al-Kharāj*, which he compiled for his patron the Caliph Hārūn al-Rashīd. One case may be taken as typical. In this Abu Yūsuf argues before the Caliph that if a man has put into cultivation, or otherwise utilized, "dead" land—i.e. land that was until then untilled or unused and had no discoverable owner—then that man (who has restored the land to use) has a claim to ownership of it.

[1] 5[42]. [2] Bayḍāwī, *ad loc.*

[3] Subkī, *op. cit.*, with the commentary of Muḥillī, II, 176 (margin).

[4] Subkī, *op. cit.* II, 176–8.

It was objected that although this was also Abu Ḥanīfa's ruling on the question, he had inserted the proviso that the imām's (i.e. the Caliph's) permission to work the land was necessary for the claim to ownership to be recognized as valid; and further, there was a *ḥadīth* bearing on the question to the same effect. Abu Yūsuf replied that his teacher had made the Caliph's permission a necessary qualification simply in order to facilitate decision between possible rival claimants. He therefore adhered to his own view.[1]

It is obvious that the unfettered employment of personal opinion by the judges might lead to abuse; but in the last resort it was the consensus of the opinion of the learned in any one period—what came to be known as *ijmā'*—which decided whether any law obtained by *qiyās* had valid force. *Qiyās* indeed only received its place as one of the four "roots" of jurisprudence after long battles had been fought over its admissibility as a source of Muslim law alongside the Koran and *ḥadīth*.

One of the dangers of *qiyās* is that it encouraged casuistry. Abu Yūsuf, for instance, was notorious for the way in which he twisted the laws to suit expediency, until even his own co-religionists viewed his decisions and even his reports of *ḥadīth* with distrust. Ibn Khallikān quotes the historian Ṭabarī to the effect that the traditionists were suspicious of any *ḥadīth* delivered by Abu Yūsuf, for the reason that he was too greatly addicted to the use of *ra'y* and because of the way in which he contrived new applications of laws.[2] In particular Abu Yūsuf applied a principle developed by his teacher which gave him great freedom of interpretation and allowed him to adopt local customs and prejudices as part of the general laws of Islam. This principle was that of *istiḥsān* or "regarding as better", which provided him with a convenient way of escape from a difficult situation if *qiyās* strictly applied should prove inconvenient or inexpedient. Thus,

Suppose a man from the "abode of war" [i.e. from a non-Muslim territory] comes to us under a promise of security for his life, or as an ambassador, and commits fornication or steals. Some of our jurists would say he is liable to punishment. . . . But the author

[1] *Kitāb al-Kharāj* (Būlāq, A.H. 1302), p. 36; cf. p. 39. See Goldziher, *Muhammedanische Studien*, II, 77.

[2] Ibn Khallikān, (Cairo, A.H. 1310), II, 303.

holds that, as the man did not come to us in the ordinary way as a member of one of the tolerated cults, our laws do not apply to him. . . . There are some who say that he must be punished in the ordinary way . . . and suffer all the regular penalties of wrong-doing. They argue that if a Muslim stole from him, that Muslim's hand would be cut off and *qiyās* demands that *his* hand likewise should be cut off. But I hold it better [to rule as I have done].[1]

An example of *qiyās* from a later period, and made on grounds other than Koranic doctrine though of the theoretical kind beloved by Abu Ḥanīfa, is given in the case quoted of two men who fell into a well, one of the men being in full possession of his eyesight, while the other was blind. The blind man had fallen on top of the other in the well and killed him. When the case was put before the Caliph Omar for his decision on the matter of compensation, he decided that the blind man was guilty of homicide and hence liable to pay. He appealed against the decision and the matter was argued backwards and forwards, some saying that the blind man could not be held responsible for the seeing one, since it was the latter who had led the way to the well, and he was therefore the cause of their both having fallen in. If he had gone there of set purpose (to make them both fall in) he would have been responsible had the blind man been killed, but if he had not gone there for that purpose then no responsibility would attach to him. (By analogy, therefore, the blind man, who was himself led to the well, and did not go there for the set purpose of causing the accident, could not be held responsible.) Others, however, argued that the Caliph's decision was right, because the blind man permitted himself to be led to the well and the man who led him was fulfilling a duty. Yet he that is summoned to do an act which he must carry out cannot be made responsible for what arises out of his act. "Now as for this blind man, [admittedly] he fell upon the seeing one and killed him. Therefore responsibility rests with the blind man; the analogy being with the case of the man who in falling from a roof alights on another."[2]

The followers of Abu Ḥanīfa represented in the main the holders of the provincial point of view, particularly that of Iraq,

[1] Abu Yūsuf, *Kitāb al-Kharāj*, pp. 116 f. Cf. another example of *istiḥsān* on pp. 108 f. of the same work.

[2] Ibn Taymīya, *Al-Qiyās fi'l-shar' al-islāmī* (Cairo, A.H. 1346), p. 80.

as opposed to that of the holy cities of Arabia, in which the memory of the Prophet Muhammad had been perpetuated by numerous accounts—some authentic, others certainly not so—covering all the incidents of his career. Especially at Medina, where he spent the later and more influential period of his life, the part played by "tradition" in justifying local custom was an important one. The learned of Medina, in fact, being compelled by circumstances to supplement the legal provisions of the Koran, did so not as the provincial Muslims had done, by an avowed resort to reason, but by deliberately inventing *ḥadīths* of the prophet to justify their new regulations or fresh ways of applying Koranic laws.

The *ḥadīth*, properly speaking, is the report of the Prophet's *sunna* or course of conduct, or of his doings and sayings,[1] to any one of which a particular *ḥadīth* may refer. The obvious way out of the dilemmas provided by the Koran or by the need for reconciling Koranic doctrine with conflicting but ineradicable alien practice, was to refer to what the Prophet had done in similar circumstances, and consequently the *sunna* acquired an authority only a little less than that of the Koran itself. In the later times of Islamic theology the *sunna* came to be held as of equal origin and equal validity with the Koran. Thus the commentator Bayḍāwī, expatiating on the passage, "Remember God's favour to you and the Book and the Wisdom which he hath sent down to you",[2] equates "the Book and the Wisdom" with the Koran and the *sunna*. As for the individual *ḥadīths*, they consist firstly of the *isnād* or the chain of authorities who have transmitted the report, and secondly, of the *matn*, the text or substance of the report. The usual form taken by the *ḥadīth* is that the relator says: "It was told by *A*, who had it from *B*, who had it from *C*, who had it from *D*, that the Prophet—upon whom be peace!—said [or did] . . . [here follows the *matn*]." Now the great body of Muslims recognize a number of persons as having been in a position to report the *sunna* of the prophet. They are such persons as 'Abdallāh b. 'Abbās, the Prophet's uncle and one of his "Companions", Ibn 'Umar, 'Ā'isha, the Prophet's widow and daughter of Abu Bakr (his first successor), and Abu Hurayra, a friend of the Prophet's. Muslims

[1] Subkī, *Jam' al-jawāmi'*, II, 83 (margin).
[2] Koran 2^{231}.

who accept the *sunna* as transmitted by these are known as "Sunnites", while those who do not are the "Shī'ites", who originally were a political party but became also a religious community. According to their views, the community of Muslims has no power to elect its head, who is an *imām* always divinely appointed from the stock of Muhammad or his immediate kin. He had no surviving son, therefore his daughter's husband 'Alī was alone entitled to succeed him; and the three "Caliphs", or "Successors", who ruled in Islam after him—as well as all other "Caliphs"—were usurpers and impostors. Moreover, since Ibn 'Abbās, 'Ā'isha, Abu Hurayra and the rest consistently refused to report those *ḥadīths* which would prove 'Alī to have been appointed to the headship of Islam by the Prophet himself, the Shī'ites rejected the whole body of *ḥadiths* originating from these sources, which in their view are tainted, and they allow as genuine only those *ḥadīths* for which 'Alī himself is the authority. The Sunnite *ḥadīth* therefore is not onc of thc "roots" of *fiqh* recognized by the Shī'ites.

On the face of it, the experiences of a single lifetime, even if it were that of the Prophet—who, it must be emphasized, was never regarded as divine by Islam—could not furnish precedents in more than a limited number of cases. The fact appears to have been recognized by Islam in the years immediately after Muhammad's death and before legend had obscured his entirely human character. Thus, at one point in the civil war which raged at the beginning of the reign of the Caliph 'Alī, his opponents Ṭalḥa and Zubayr, while discussing how to put an end to the difficult situation in which they found themselves, are declared to have said: "We and they are Muslims, and this is an emergency which has never occurred before today, and so no Koranic revelation could have been made about it nor could there be any 'tradition' of the Prophet. It is a new thing."[1]

It is not intended here to inquire into the question of the authenticity of *ḥadīth*, but rather to examine its place as one of the "roots" of Muslim jurisprudence: yet, seeing the number of *ḥadīths* in existence, it is obvious—and was so quite early to Muslims themselves—that many must be forgeries in spite of an impressive chain of authorities. In fact, at a distance in time or

[1] Ṭabarī, I, 3166. Cf. D. S. Margoliouth, *Early Development of Mohammedanism* (London, 1914), p. 75.

space from the companions of the Prophet or the members of his family who were the sources of tradition, in an emergency the inducement was great to invent some helpful *ḥadīth*. In course of time, and in spite of the fact that the Muslim doctors recognized the existence of a great body of forged "traditions", *ḥadīth* grew into a valid source or "root" of the laws of Islam. Often these invented *ḥadīths* merely crystallized and gave sanction for the purposes of Islam to local practices or adapted laws of an alien or older civilization.[1]

The revolt of Medina, the stronghold of *ḥadīth*, against the free and arbitrary use of *ra'y* and *qiyās*, was led by Mālik ibn Anas, a native of the city, who died there in 795. In later times he came to be regarded as the representative of their views by large numbers of people who were therefore grouped together as belonging to the Mālikite *madhhab* or school. Mālik's aims were similar to those of Abu Ḥanīfa, and the results differ in details only. Yet for the Medinese doctor it was tradition, either that of the Prophet or local custom, which had first claim to consideration after the Koran. If *ḥadīths* differed he gave preference over them to local practice (*'amal*).[2] But it was only when neither *ḥadīth* nor the weight of Medinese learning could provide him with authority in deciding a point that he resorted to his own "opinion"; and he appears to have preferred even a "doubtful" *ḥadīth* to that. His method is shown in his work the *Muwaṭṭa'*, "The Well-trodden (or Smooth) Path", a collection of *ḥadīths*, local traditions and customs arranged under headings, as a guide to legal decisions. Usually he states the case at issue, quotes the passage of the Koran that applies, and then the pertinent *ḥadīths*. The latter may be omitted where the Koran is the authority. Thus, in discussing whether certain domestic animals may lawfully be eaten, he says: "The best opinion expressed about horses, mules and asses is that they may not be eaten, because God [in the Koran] has said, 'Horses, mules and asses for you to ride upon',[3] thus specifying horses, mules and asses as being for riding, and cattle either for riding or eating."[4] Where there is no Koranic

[1] *Ḥadīths* have for this reason been compared with the *Novellae Constitutiones*, the "Novels", by which Justinian supplemented the Roman Codex.

[2] Ṭabarī, III, 2505 f.

[3] Koran 16[8].

[4] Cf. Koran 16[5–7]. The passage quoted is to be found in the *Muwaṭṭa'* of Mālik b. Anas (edited with Zurqānī's commentary, Cairo, A.H. 1280), II, 359.

precedent Mālik adduces *ḥadīth*. For example, in deciding whether carnivorous beasts are lawful eating—a point on which the Koran gives no direct guidance—he says: "The apostle of God said, 'The eating of all fanged animals is forbidden'."[1] It may be significant of the origin of this *ḥadīth* that the commentator on the text of the *Muwaṭṭa'* quotes its author as having confessed to a dislike for eating hyenas, foxes, wolves, wild cats and all other beasts of prey. In connection with this, it may be of interest to quote a statement of the great annalist and commentator Ṭabarī, who in his elucidation of the verse, "Horses, mules and asses for you to ride upon and for ornament",[2] remarks: "Some learned doctors are of the opinion that this verse is proof of the prohibition of horseflesh. Now Ibn 'Abbās[3] used to dislike the flesh of horses, mules and asses and used to say: 'God's word is, "The cattle he created for you . . . to eat of them". These therefore are for eating. "And horses, and mules and asses for you to ride upon". These therefore are for riding'. Others, however, traverse this view and say that the juxtaposition of the verses does not imply prohibition, but only that God is making manifest to his servants the favours he has bestowed on them."[4]

It is comprehensible that local tradition and custom in Mālik's system should have played an important part when prophetic *ḥadīth* was lacking, but they persisted even when the *ḥadīth* on a point had been created and was apparently decisive. An example of the method followed in the *Muwaṭṭa'* in an instance of this kind may be illuminating. On the question of the right of a non-Arab child born amongst Arabs to inherit, Mālik quotes first a tradition that the Caliph Omar refused to allow any non-Arab to inherit unless born amongst the Arabs; then comes Mālik's own opinion, that if a woman with child comes from enemy territory and has her child amongst the Arabs, it inherits from her; thirdly, Mālik says, "the point agreed upon amongst us and the practice (*sunna*) about which there is no dispute, is, as I have gathered from the learned of our city, that a Muslim does not make an unbeliever his heir".[5]

[1] *Muwaṭṭa'* of Mālik b. Anas, II, 358 (misprinted 332). [2] Koran 16^8.

[3] 'Abd-allāh b. 'Abbās, the prophet's uncle, normally accounted the principal source of *ḥadīth*. [4] Ṭabarī, *Tafsīr* (Cairo, A.H. 1320–21), XIV, 52.

[5] Mālik b. Anas, *op. cit.* II, 378. For cases where no *ḥadīth* is quoted, cf. *ibid.* 315, 365, 378, etc. See further, Goldziher, *Muhammedanische Studien*, II, 214.

There are instances when the practice quoted by Mālik is simply pre-Islamic custom taken over unchanged. Thus, on the question of revenue, the case is quoted of the Caliph Omar's levying tithe on the first waters of a newly opened well, that having been the practice of pre-Islamic days.[1] In such instances too, it was possible for usage to be at variance with *ḥadīth*. The case is quoted of the *'umrā*, i.e. a gift made for the lifetime of the recipient, on whose death it reverts to the donor or his heirs. This kind of gift would appear to have been common in pre-Muslim days, and Mālik recognized it as lawful in spite of the fact that there is a whole series of *ḥadīths* against the conditions accompanying such gifts and the fact that some of these *ḥadīths* are quoted in the *Muwaṭṭa'* itself.[2] Where usage or the consensus of local opinion (*ijmā'*) contradicted or differed from *ḥadīth*, and where the former was followed in preference to the latter, since it could not be admitted that the Prophet's word had been outweighed or abrogated by that of ordinary mortals, the theory came to be evolved that somewhere there existed another prophetic *ḥadīth* abrogating the inconvenient one, and that upon it the *ijmā'* is based.[3]

How tradition and usage entered into Muslim jurisprudence when it was already well developed may be further illustrated from the *Ḥayāt al-ḥayawān* or "Life of Animals" by Damīrī, an Egyptian naturalist of the fourteenth century A.D. The work is almost as much concerned with what the law says about animals as with the legends it reports of their habits and characteristics. Thus of the *waral*,[4] which is a reptile of the lizard species, he remarks:

It has already been decided of the serpent that it is unlawful for food. This would be the obvious ruling in accordance with the opinion of the early jurists. But Rāfi'ī prefers to go further back and to discover whether the Arabs found it to their taste or not. This would be in agreement with the verse, "They will ask you what is lawful to them. Say, Lawful to you are the good things. . . ."[5] The Arabs are the prime authorities in any consideration of this subject, for the reason that the faith is an Arab one, and

[1] Mālik b. Anas, *op. cit.* II, 76.
[2] III, p. 224. Cf. Goldziher, *op. cit.* II, 80.
[3] Goldziher, *op. cit.* II, 86.
[4] II, 329 f.
[5] Koran 5^6.

the prophet was an Arab. But the question can only be referred to the inhabitants of towns or villages and not to uncivilized dwellers in the desert, who eat without discrimination anything that creeps or crawls. . . . Some say that the persons who are to be regarded as authorities are the Arabs of the prophet's day, because they were those who were addressed [by the Koran].

A little further under the same heading Damīrī continues in what he calls "an important note": "Know that in this book mention has been made of animals concerning which the Companions [of the Prophet] expressed no opinion with respect to their being lawful or unlawful [for food]. . . . But they propounded certain general rules of universal application and others of special application. From amongst these rules is derived that which concerns the *waral*." He then says that if a question about an animal has been referred to the Bedouins for their opinion and contradictory answers have been received, then those who are in the majority are to be followed. If the two sides are equal in numbers, some authorities would follow the Quraysh, who are the "pole" of the Bedouins and hold the prophetic office amongst them. If the Quraysh differ amongst themselves or refuse to make a decision, then the animals most closely resembling the one under discussion must be examined. If no conclusion is to be reached by that method either, then there is room for two opinions.

Before the differences in the methods of interpreting and expanding the law had crystallized into codes, each with its "school" of adherents,[1] no hard and fast distinction was made between those who relied mainly on *ra'y* and those who put *ḥadīth* immediately after the Koran as a main "root" of *fiqh* or jurisprudence.[2] With the passage of time, and as the importance attached to authority increased, *ḥadīth* was pressed into the service of *ra'y* and *qiyās* in order to lend greater countenance to them. The annalists even state that the prophet had himself declared that he used *ra'y* when no revelation was vouchsafed to him on any

[1] A highly critical account of the early history of the *madhāhib*, and one which alters the whole story of their origins as given by tradition, is furnished by Bergsträsser in *Islam*, XIV, 76 ff.

[2] Cf. Ibn Qutayba (d. A.D. 889), (*Kitāb al-Ma'ārif, Handbuch der Geschichte*, ed. F. Wuestenfeld (Göttingen, 1850), pp. 248–251), who calls Abu Ḥanīfa, Mālik b. Anas, Abu Yūsuf al-Qāḍī and al-Awzā'ī (d. A.D. 774, the founder of a short-lived *ḥadīth* school), all *Aṣḥāb al-Ra'y*, i.e. users of *ra'y*.

particular question. Parallel with this may be placed the *ḥadīth* that the prophet once, when sending a qāḍī to the Yemen, asked him how he proposed to decide his cases. He replied that he would be guided by what he found in the Koran; if that contained nothing to the point he would refer to the *sunna*, the Prophet's practice, and if that failed too, he would exert his own judgment, *ra'y*.[1]

In more than one story also the Caliph Omar is declared to have given instructions to qāḍīs that they were to use their own opinion in the absence of precedents. Such stories are probably apocryphal for the reason that Omar can have had neither the knowledge nor the temperament suited to giving instruction on points of law, if only because he was constantly occupied as a soldier with his campaigns and the task of bringing the newly conquered territories of Islam into more thorough subjection. Still, specimens of these "instructions" will serve to show what their inventors regarded as the proper "roots" of jurisprudence. In a letter sent to Abu Mūsā al-Ash'arī, the famous qāḍī and companion of the prophet, Omar is made to tell him that on matters which he has to consider and for which there is no precedent either in the "written word" [i.e. the Koran] or in any "tradition", he must ascertain the parallels and from them draw an analogy "relying [then] on what is closest to God['s word] and most like the truth".[2] Another qāḍī is instructed in the following terms: "About what you find in the book of God consult no one; what you cannot perceive in the book of God refer to the *sunna*: if it is not in the *sunna*, exert your own judgment."[3]

In the elastic character of *ḥadīth* lay the germ of much conflict and confusion out of which grew some further *madhhabs*, "rites" or "schools". By the very character of its growth the *ḥadith* inevitably harboured contradictory "traditions" which were due either to the different opinions which the various provinces of Islam had on even the most elementary points of the law, or to the divergent requirements of the various parts of the Muslim empire. The 'Iraqīs and the Ḥijāzīs, for example, held different views on a *ḥadīth* which declared that the prophet, being asked what a recent convert to Islam should do if he had more than four

[1] Ibn Ḥazm in Goldziher, *Zahiriten* (Leipzig, 1884), pp. 212 f.
[2] Mubarrad, *Kāmil*, ed. Wright, p. 9; II, 9–11.
[3] *Aghānī*, XVI, 36.

wives, replied that he should keep four only and divorce the rest. The Ḥijāzīs, keeping to the letter of the "tradition", said it was a matter of indifference which of the wives were divorced so long as no more than four were retained. The 'Iraqīs, on the other hand, seeking after the spirit and intention of the *ḥadīth*, insisted that only the first four wives were lawful, for in Islam marriage with the remainder could never have been legally contracted.[1]

Grave difficulty arose when *ḥadīth*, which by the middle of the second century of Islam had come to be regarded as of equal authority with the Koran, contradicted some of its provisions. If both Koran and *sunna* were given by God, then logically a rule of the Koran might be abrogated by a later one of the *sunna*. Further, there were old customs everywhere in the Muslim empire running counter to *ḥadīth*, and yet so much a part of the life of the community that they could not be abolished. Some solution of the problem which this presented had to be discovered, and the task was undertaken towards the end of the second century of Islam by a man who had been trained in both the *ra'y* and the *ḥadīth* schools. He was Muhammad al-Shāfi'ī,[2] a man of Arab birth, who began his studies with Mālik ibn Anas at Medina and followed them up by learning the methods of Abu Ḥanīfa from his disciple and younger colleague al-Shaybānī. Consideration of their systems led him to be dissatisfied with both; with Mālik's for its rigid adherence to tradition—and perhaps also for the doubtful character of some of its expedients for reconciling with the *sunna* of Muhammad the law and custom as they actually stood—and with Abu Ḥanīfa's for what he considered the excessive scope for personal prejudices which "opinion" allowed to the arbitrary decisions of individual jurists. He set himself, therefore, to elaborate a system that should be free of the faults contained in the methods already in existence; and it is this evidence of a deliberate purpose in his work which makes him the first to present a clear idea of what the system of Muslim jurisprudence and its "roots" ought to be. He appreciated and acknowledged for the first time the fact that custom and long-established usage had to be taken into consideration in any code of law, and he therefore placed them definitely amongst its "roots".

[1] Cf. Goldziher, *Muhammedanische Studien*, II, 81.

[2] He died in 208/820.

This he did on the principle that *ijmā'*, or the consensus of Muslim learned opinon—which Mālik, as we have seen, had applied, though restricting it to the opinions of the Medina scholars—was a manifestation of the will of God. Shāfi'ī, however, expanded the idea of *ijmā'* to include all the immense body of ideas and decisions which those competent to do so in Islam—apart, of course, from the Prophet Muhammad himself—had formulated and agreed upon.[1] The principle proved to be one of immense importance, for in fact it was that which decided Muslim opinion in each emergency and in each matter which affected the attitude of Islam as a whole. Immediately after the Prophet's death, *ijmā'* had naturally been confined to his companions, who had formed an aristocracy of opinion. When they died it was held that the learned of the two sacred cities of Mecca and Medina were the authorities whose *ijmā'* ought to be decisive. But in course of time, as non-Arabs came to study the law and their general political status improved, the learned doctors outside Arabia had to be accorded the right to an authoritative opinion. *Ijmā'* therefore came to mean the common opinion of the accredited jurists (*faqīhs*) of Islam in each era.[2] It was they alone who had the faculty to interpret the books of the law and to give decisions on doubtful points,[3] and they derived their exclusive authority so to do from the Koran itself.[4]

There were adherents of some early rites, e.g. the Ẓāhirīs, who would recognize the validity of no *ijmā'* but that of the Companions of the Prophet. The great majority of jurists, however, were compelled with the passage of time to the position that the *ijmā'* of one age modifies that of any preceding one except that of the Companions, also that *ijmā'* must be regarded as infallible, otherwise there could be no ultimate human authority for legislation in

[1] Cf. Subkī, *Jam' al-jawāmi'* (Būlāq, ,1283) II, 156 (margin).

[2] "*Ijmā'* is the agreement of those whose opinion is regarded in the *umma* concerning legal decisions and any matter of religious importance." Thus al-'Āmilī in his *Ma'ālim al-dīn* (Lucknow, A.H. 1301), p. 99, a Shī'a work on the principles of *fiqh*. The statement is quoted as a preliminary to a refutation of *ijmā'*.

[3] The decision on a point of a law is the *fatwā* and the person who gives it is the *muftī*.

[4] E.g. 16[45], "... Ask the people who have the monition ..." i.e. "the People of the Book, *or*, they that are learned (*'ulamā*) in the traditions" (Bayḍāwī). Cf. Koran 3[5].

Islam. This must not be taken to imply that there is, or ever has been, anything corresponding to a Sanhedrin or Council which decides what is valid for Islam universally. All that can be said is that opinion, following practice, slowly formulated and took a particular direction in each age.

Three of Shāfi'īs "roots" of jurisprudence, to sum up, were the Koran, the *sunna* of the Prophet, and *ijmā'*. In his view they were insufficient for all the requirements of the law, and he found a fourth root in *qiyās*, "analogy", which he used when the others failed.[1] He frowned upon the unrestricted liberty of *ra'y* or "opinion" and its offshoot *istiḥsān*, but felt that in *qiyās* he had an instrument which could be kept under control, since he insisted that, before any valid deduction could be made, the *'illa* or underlying motive in the Koranic "premisses" must be taken into consideration. Because of the greater rigidity of the Shāfi'ite system, the deductions made by its *qiyās* have not always agreed with those drawn by the more liberal Ḥanafī school. An instance is the question which has already been discussed of the guardianship of a girl still legally a minor who is no longer a virgin. According to the Ḥanafīs, the man who is the guardian in charge of her property should also be her *walī*, or guardian for purposes of marriage, as he would certainly be if she were still an unmarried virgin. The Shāfi'īs, however, reject this view, saying that in the case of the virgin who is not of age, her property is entrusted to him by the law because her person is already in his charge, and not vice versa. If the girl is not a virgin, she has the right to say whether or not she will be married again, even although as a minor her property is entrusted to a guardian, and he therefore requires her consent before he can act as her *walī* and give her in marriage.[2]

From the moment when *qiyās* obtained the open approval of the learned it had as a principle been attacked and opposed. A pupil of al-Shāfi'ī, namely Aḥmad ibn Ḥanbal,[3] Ibn Ḥanbal as he is commonly called, was one of the bitterest of its critics. According to him, rationalist interpretation of the Koran and tradition is

[1] He equated it with *ijtihād*, i.e. personal "effort" to obtain guidance. *Risāla fī uṣūl al-fiqh* (Būlāq, A.H. 1321), p. 66.

[2] Cf. Abdur Rahim: *The Principles of Muhammedan Jurisprudence* . . (London, 1911), pp. 25 f.

[3] He died in 241/855.

permissible, and he with those of like mind refused to recognize or to sanction what they termed the unlawful "innovation" (*bid'a*) of the *ijmā'*. Ibn Ḥanbal, however, was not primarily concerned with jurisprudence and interested himself in the sources of *ḥadīth* rather than in its juridical aspects. It was from this point of view that his great collection of "traditions", the *Musnad*, was compiled. Also, he founded no original system of *fiqh* and was therefore regarded by the historian and jurist Ṭabarī as not being an authority in jurisprudence, but only a traditionist.[1] He had, however, given expression to his views on points of law in expounding the *ḥadīth*, and in the eleventh century A.D., when the adherents of his way of thought had become a powerful body, the *ijmā'* of the Muslim world came to recognize them as one of the orthodox schools of jurisprudence, with him as its founder. On the whole, the Ḥanbalī school is the most reactionary of all, and the fact explains why it declined in the course of the centuries until it is now also the least strong in numbers. It might have died out almost entirely if in the eighteenth century an offshoot of its adherents, the Wahhābīs of Arabia, who then achieved political power, had not revived it.[2] The rite spread to parts of India, and in its own territory gathered strength with the rise in the political fortunes of Ibn Sa'ūd, the Wahhābī king of Nejd and the Ḥijāz.

There has been occasion to notice, in connection with *ḥadīth*, that the Shī'ites refuse to accept Sunnite authority. They hold that in the Koran and their own *ḥadīth* the whole of the law is implicit, and that there is no need either for *ra'y*, with its offshoot *qiyās*, or for *ijmā'*. In the Shī'ite view, if *qiyās* had been lawful the prophet would himself have employed it, but he found it unnecessary for the reason that the Koran declares explicitly what is demanded of the faithful. "We have sent down to thee the Reminder [i.e. the Koran]," it says, "that thou mayst explain to men what has been sent down to thee and perchance they may reflect."[3] What the prophet did not explain, in accordance with this, would inevitably have disappeared from the world; but the right "path" of the law is still extant and can be known.

[1] For references see F. Kern, *Z.D.M.G.*, LV, 67, and A. Mez, *Die Renaissance des Islams*, pp. 202 f.

[2] Cf. H. S. J. Philby, *The Heart of Arabia* (London, 1922), I, xvii.

[3] 16^{46}.

Incidentally, the Shī'ites accuse the Sunnites of having suppressed passages favourable to them in the Koran, and otherwise to have "falsified" it in accordance with their own views. To prove the futility of *ra'y* as well as its unlawfulness, the Shī'ites point to the *ikhtilāf*, or differences brought about by "opinion" amongst the "orthodox" schools, and a *ḥadīth*, obviously of partisan origin, is adduced to the effect that "innovation" brought about in the law by means of "opinion" is the nearest approach man can make to idolatry. Moreover, it is pointed out that legislation by *qiyās* is only a step removed from producing "revelations" like those of Allah himself.[1]

For the benefit of the ages after the Prophet, say the Shī'ites, there has been a series of twelve imāms, or divinely inspired "leaders", descended from the Prophet, and their purpose has been to give mankind guidance to the truth. It is declared further that since his mysterious disappearance in the third century of Islam, the last of the imāms, the Mahdī, has been "occulted" and hidden from the eyes of mankind. But he remains in the world and his authority is in every age the only valid one for the *shar'*,[2] of which he is the guardian. Without his ruling being given, no *ijmā'* can be complete, and it must be invalid even if it had been possible to collect all true opinion in Islam from the days of Abu Bakr to the present day—which is not the case.[3]

While the last imām remains occulted his agents are the *mujtahids* who arise in each age, and who are able by their "supreme effort and endeavour" [i.e. *ijtihād*] to arrive at a complete knowledge of the Koran and the "traditions". So long as the imām continues to exist in the world the "Gate of *ijtihād*" remains open to favoured persons. Adherence to this dogma by the Shī'a world explains why it is that in Persia[4] the people who are able by their

[1] Ḥasan b. 'Alī al-Ṭabarī, a Shī'a apologist of the thirteenth century A.D., *Kāmil-i bahā'ī* (Bombay, A.H. 1323), p. 31, and Abu'l-Qāsim b. Ḥasan al-Jīlānī, a Shī'ite *faqīh* of the late eighteenth century, *Qawānīn al-uṣūl* (Tabriz, 1858), pp. 303 and 311.

[2] Cf. Muhammad al-'Āmilī, *Bidāyat al-hidāya* (Shī'ite) (Lucknow, 1885), pp. 1 f.

[3] 'Āmilī, *Ma'ālim al-dīn* (Lucknow, A.H. 1301), pp. 99–101.

[4] Shī'ism became the official religion with the accession of Ismā'īl Safawī in A.D. 1501. When Ḥamdallāh Mustawfī wrote (740/1340) his *Nuzhat al-qulūb* a great many cities of Persia had Sunnite populations. See the translation by G. le Strange (London, 1919) *passim*.

learning and their personal qualifications to gain popular esteem have been able to exercise powerful religious, and consequently also political, influence.

The doctrine of *ijtihād* also prevails amongst the Sunnites, but they maintain that the "Gate" was closed after the death of Ibn Ḥanbal, the founder of the last of the four orthodox *madhhabs*. During the third and fourth centuries of Islam, however, there was still a possibility of the pursuit of *ijtihād*. During those centuries there was a stage when the four "rites" were not alone, alongside them being numerous groups whose leaders were men of more than local fame. Those which disappeared did so for causes generally political, but often too, as the geographer Maqdisī has suggested,[1] because most of the wandering scholars who travelled in search of famous teachers kept fairly well to the beaten and frequented paths, such as those used by the pilgrims on their way to and from the sacred cities of the Ḥijaz. Teachers who lived in out of the way places failed to secure that succession of disciples which ultimately led to the foundation of a "school". Otherwise, such schools as those of Dā'ūd al-Ẓāhirī, Sufyān al-Thawrī, and the latter's disciple al-Awzā'ī, which in the tenth century of our era stood on an equality with the Ḥanafites and Shāfi'ites,[2] might well have survived.

The *madhhabs* which are still in existence cover the Sunnī world between them, and to one or other of them every Sunnī belongs. The Shāfi'ites are to be found mainly in southern Arabia, Malaya, Tanganyika Territory in East Africa and some parts of central Asia; the Mālikites predominate in North Africa —as they once did also in Muslim Spain—in western Africa and the Sudan and at various places along the Arabian shores of the Persian Gulf; the Ḥanafites hold the former Turkish empire and the subcontinent of India and Pakistan, while the Ḥanbalites are mainly to be found in central Arabia and in a few places in India.[3]

It was probably accident that in the first place determined to what *madhhab* a man belonged, but his descendants continued in it by a natural process. For the last five centuries at least the four

[1] Ed. de Goeje, p. 44. Cf. S. Hurgronje, *Verspreide Geschriften*, II, 307.

[2] For references cf. Mez, *Renaissance des Islams*, p. 202.

[3] So far as numbers are concerned it would seem probable that about half the Sunnites in the world belong to the Ḥanafī rite.

madhhabs have by *ijmā'* been regarded as of equal orthodoxy; yet in spite of this it is rare for the member of one "rite" to change to another. A transfer may sometimes be made, as has been seen, in order to facilitate marriage, which Islam regards as a serious duty. Even in comparatively early days, however, the person who changed his *madhhab* for material reasons, or changed too frequently, was regarded with disapproval.[1] There have sometimes been forcible and wholesale removals from one "rite" to another, generally for political reasons; as when the Ottoman Turks, having gained power in Iraq and the Ḥijāz in the sixteenth century, compelled the Shāfi'ite qāḍīs either to change to the Ḥanafī "rite" to which they (the Turks) belonged, or to relinquish office. With this may be compared the displacement of "orthodox" officials throughout Persia when the Shī'ite dynasty of the Ṣafawīs came to the throne.

At one period in the history of Islam the arguments between the four rites were such as to lead frequently to bloodshed. Particularly in the fifth and sixth centuries of the *hijra*, Shāfi'ites fought bloody battles with Ḥanbalites in the streets of Baghdad and Ḥanafites slaughtered Shāfi'ites at Isfahan. When the period of active recrimination ceased, the jurists of each school engaged in verbal contests in which legal arguments were the weapons used.[2] Even earlier the importance of *ikhtilāf* or "difference" had almost converted it into a branch of philosophy in which all the minutiæ of the variations in the results of the *fiqh* of the "schools" were examined with close attention. That the differences were not very great, even in the view of Islam itself, is indicated by the fact that with the change of mental attitude brought about by the passage of time Muslims can now regard with toleration what once would have aroused them to bloodshed.

Some of the differences between the "rites" have been exemplified in previous chapters, in the sections dealing with slavery and marriage. Largely they turn on points of interpretation in questions often casuistical in the extreme, such as whether the formula of *Bismillāh*, "In the name of God", which is a phrase from the opening verse of the Koran, may be used out of its

[1] Cf. Levy, *A Baghdad Chronicle*, pp. 245 f.

[2] Cf. Subkī, *Mu'īd al-ni'am*, ed. D. W. Myhrman (London, 1908), pp. 106–9.

context for the ritual of worship. The Mālikites, as opposed to the other three schools, deny that it may be so used. Even more detached from reality are questions concerning the lawfulness for food of certain animals which are in fact never used for human consumption. The way in which the "rites" differ concerning the lawfulness of horseflesh has already been indicated; the Shāfi'ites[1] and Ḥanbalites[2] admitting it, while the Ḥanafīs[3] and Mālikīs[4] do not.

Sometimes, however, the question involved may have some practical significance, as, for example, that which decides whether a person unfamiliar with Arabic may recite the Koran in his native tongue. If the question is answered in the negative, many a non-Arab convert might be prevented from performing the rites of worship, in which the *Fātiḥa*, the opening chapter of the Koran, has a prominent part and is recited in the ordinary worship of Muslims all over the world. Yet the school of Abu Ḥanīfa alone concedes that a Persian, for example, may lawfully say the whole of his prayers, including the portion from the Koran, in his own tongue.[5]

Another difference of a similar kind may be illustrated from the ritual of fasting. Abu Ḥanīfa takes no account of an accidental or involuntary breaking of the fast; Mālik and Ibn Ḥanbal, however, demand that other days of fasting shall be substituted for those made void.[6]

All four schools agree that within Islamic territory neither Jews nor Christians may erect new places of worship in towns or large villages. Whether their erection is also forbidden outside such centres of population is a question on which the schools differ. Mālik, Shāfi'ī and Ibn Ḥanbal refuse to permit it anywhere; Abu Ḥanīfa, however, on this question as on many others shows himself sane and humanitarian[7] and permits the erection of churches

[1] Shīrāzī, *Tanbīh*, ed. Juynboll, p. 89.

[2] Juynboll, *Handbuch*, p. 177.

[3] Cf. Nasafī (d. 710/1310), *Kanz al-daqā'iq*, with commentary of al-'Aynī (Būlāq, A.H. 1285), II, 259.

[4] Khalīl, *Mukhtaṣar*, tr. Guidi, I, 329.

[5] Thus Nasafī, *op. cit.* I, pp. 38 f.

[6] For references see Goldziher, *Vorlesungen über den Islam* (2nd ed. Heidelberg, 1925), p. 55.

[7] This opinion has been controverted (*Islamica*, III, 219) on evidence which appears to have been insufficiently well weighed.

and synagogues, though at a distance of at least a mile from the outer wall of towns and villages. On the question of the restoration of dilapidated churches and synagogues, Abu Ḥanīfa is joined by Mālik and Shāfi'ī in declaring it to be lawful, provided that the ground on which the building stands was in the first place granted freely by the Muslim conqueror. If the ground had originally been seized from Islam[1] it would be against the law to permit its restoration. Of Ibn Ḥanbal's view of the matter there are different versions. The one best supported teaches that neither the restoration of partly dilapidated buildings used for non-Muslim worship nor the rebuilding of totally ruined ones is ever permitted. Another version permits the one but not the other, while the least credible version allows both.[2]

Another example of a difference in the attitude adopted towards unbelievers is provided by two members of the Ḥanafī school. Nasafī, the author of the *Kanz al-daqā'iq*[3], holds that the word of an unbeliever may be accepted in deciding whether a particular article of food or drink is lawful to the Muslim. The commentator, however, insists that the author's statement must have been made in error, for the reason that religious doctrines are involved, and upon them the unbeliever is not competent to decide. All that can be meant, the commentator argues, is that the unbeliever's word may be taken on such a question of fact as whether he himself bought a particular piece of meat at the shop of a Jew, a Christian, or a Muslim.

Normally, so long as the various *madhhabs* continue to base their laws on the teaching and practice of the imāms recognized by the *ijmā'*, there is peace between them. The fundamental bases of agreement between all Muslims have remained substantially unchanged since the rise of Muhammadanism, and there has never been any dispute about such questions as the unity of God and the eternal validity of the Koran. The Shī'ites may part company from their "orthodox" brethren on such serious questions of political theory as the succession to the Prophet, but all four Sunnī "schools" are at one over these. Where there are

[1] This might often have occurred in Spain or in the Turkish empire in Europe.

[2] Ṣadr al-Dīn al-Dimashqī, *Kitāb Raḥmat al-umma*, quoted by Goldziher, *Z.D.M.G.*, xxxviii, 673 ff.

[3] ii, 266.

differences between them, the points at issue are seldom of practical importance. Much indeed of the whole body of *fiqh* is detached from reality, for though all books of law purport to regulate not only the acts of the individual Muslim but also the governance and transactions of the state, yet ruling princes and conquerors have generally applied such methods as expediency dictated rather than those which authority demanded. Consequently only the ritual and personal laws and those dealing with the administration of *awqāf*, or pious foundations, have in fact had consistent practical application, and the rest of the *shar*ʿ has been regarded by those religiously engaged in studying it as an ideal to be brought into actual use only at the coming of the Mahdī, the last precursor of the Resurrection.[1]

The religious or ethical origin and character of the provisions of the *fiqh* have been illustrated by some of the enactments concerning ritual purity, prayer, *zakāt* and the pilgrimage, and the way in which the framing of them differs from that of a strictly lay and civil code like that of Roman law is clear. In the latter, enactments are made either commanding or forbidding, and penalties are decreed for any infringement. In the Muslim law, on the other hand, it is often left to the individual to decide how he will act in particular circumstances. The five-fold division of acts into required, forbidden, recommended, disapproved and permitted, the last without any expression of authoritative approval or disapproval, is in itself an indication that only in two categories out of five can there be any question of a specific penalty for omission or commission. Even then, the retribution demanded is often of the expiatory nature characteristic of a religious code. Lastly, the very arrangement of the law-books, which treat ritual and ceremonial regulations as being on precisely the same footing, and belonging to the same parts of the *fiqh*, as what may be called civil and criminal enactments and even military ordinances, points in the same direction.

With the compelling need to make their laws conform to actual conditions and also to make them approximate to international standards, modern Islamic States have supplemented the sharīʿa from other sources, generally secular. Thus in Egypt a Civil Code promulgated in 1949 gives governmental legislation first place as

[1] Cf. Shaʿrānī, *Mīzān*, tr. Perron (Algiers, 1898), pp. 32 f.

a source of law, with customary law (*'urf*) and the sharī'a following it. Similar enactments were put into force in Syria in 1949 and in Iraq in 1953.[1]

ISLAMIC JURISPRUDENCE: APPENDIX

For further study a conspectus of the contents—other than those dealing strictly with ritual and religious ceremonies and requirements—of some books of *fiqh* is here appended. The three chosen are (A) the *Majmū' al-fiqh* of [?] Zayd ibn 'Alī, (B) the *Tanbīh* of Shīrāzī and (C) the *Jāmi' al-ṣaghīr* of Muhammad ibn Ḥasan al-Shaybānī; all of which have been quoted in connection with the portions of the present chapter dealing with ritual etc.

In method the three works differ from one another, the *Majmū'* being mainly in the form of question and answer, the *Tanbīh* a systematic treatise dealing in formal paragraphs with the various requirements of the law, while the *Jāmi' al-ṣaghīr* is a series of answers to questions not formally stated and generally of a casuistical nature.

The main interest of the works at the present time is an historical one, for apart from the *Tanbīh* of Shīrāzī they are seldom consulted for decisions on points of law. The law-books of each era sooner or later reach a stage when they require elucidation and commentaries, with the result that the interpretative works of the newer authorities gradually displace the older ones.

In this connection it may be said that the various "rites" will seldom use any but their own law-books, for each adheres to a particular sense of the laws, many of which can be interpreted in a number of ways, and in their own compilations the learned of the different "schools" dictate to their followers what sense it is to which they must adhere.

Before the chapter on the alms-tax, the *Majmū'* (A) has a section on "[Duties to] the dead", of which the main headings are:

Washing of the corpse; its transport for burial; prayers for the dead; the method of placing the body in the grave; conduct to be observed on meeting a funeral; mourning; embalming; on a

[1] See an article on modern legislative activity in the field of personal law in some Islamic countries, in *Oriente Moderno*, July 1953.

Jewess who dies having a Muslim child in her womb, and on a woman who dies having any [living] child in her womb; various questions on prayer.

The *Tanbīh* (B) begins with a general section: "On what is to be done with the dead", and continues as A except that it omits the casuistical sections at the end. The *Jāmiʿ al-ṣaghīr* (C), omits the chapter.

The parts strictly concerned with civil and criminal law begin with the chapter on sales.

A. The main heads are: on the advantages of lawful gain, consultation of the *fiqh* before transacting business, the curse upon the chief who trades on behalf of his people, [the sin of] usury, exchange of goods by measure or weight, selling for profit, articles of which the sale is forbidden, deceit in selling, defects, sale of fruits before [the date of] ripening, the sale of objects outside one's possession, e.g. an unborn slave or an unborn animal, fish still to be caught, etc., the sale of food-stuffs, that the separation by sale of slaves related by blood is an offence, the period to be observed by a purchaser before congress with a female slave, the sale of slaves who will be freed by their master's death and of female slaves who have borne him children, of the slave who is permitted to carry on trade, sale of goods for future delivery, pre-emption, profit-sharing, partnership, wages, pledges, loans and securities, gifts and charitable grants, wrongful seizure and the responsibility therefor; transfer, security, surety, etc.

B. What constitutes complete sale, what may and what may not be sold, profit [i.e. upon what goods it may be taken], the sale of roots and fruits [included in any land sold], the sale of milch cattle and their return because of blemishes, selling for mutual profit, etc., disputes between buyer and seller, selling for future delivery, loans, pledges, bankruptcy, guardianship [of the property of a minor], etc. Then, as in (A), with the addition of the following sections: On contests [competitions between men armed with weapons of war, races between animals, etc.], on restoring "dead" lands to cultivation, etc., on property found, on foundlings,[1] on pious foundations, on gifts, on wills, on emancipation of slaves, etc.

C deals with the above sections in a different order in different parts of the work. In the order in which they appear the subjects

[1] They are regarded as free.

of the sections are as follows: Selling for future delivery, what is forbidden and what permitted for sale, articles sold by measure or weight, dispute of buyer and seller over price, option stipulated [at the time of the bargain], defects [in goods], rights connected with [purchase of] a house, payments that fall due [and are not made], pre-emption, a slave permitted to trade and then sold or freed by his master, guarantee for property, seizure of joint property by one of two owners, pledges.

On Testimony.

A. On oaths, evidence and judicial decisions.

B divides the contents of this book into two parts which are placed towards the end of the whole work. The first deals with judicial decisions, the office of judge and judicial procedure; also on the division of property and on claims and evidence. The book on testimony deals with the qualifications of persons permitted to give evidence, the admissibility of evidence, conflicting evidence and confessions.

C has sections on claims, decision by oath, decision on evidence and decision in cases of inheritance. It also has a separate book dealing with the question of agency, and others dealing with deposits, loans, gifts, hiring, etc.

On Marriage.

A. On the virtue of marriage, the *mahr*, the *walī* and witnesses to a marriage, persons whose marriage is permitted, the marriage of slaves, equality of status for marriage, marriage of unbelievers, equity of treatment for a man's several wives, allowances for wives, physical imperfections discovered in a wife, kinship by fosterage, etc.

B. What persons ought and ought not to marry one another, what marriages are forbidden, option of marriage and return [of a wife] for physical faults, marriage of unbelievers, the *ṣadāq* [or marriage gift], the *mut'a* marriage, the marriage-feast, on equitable dealing between wives.

C. On the giving in marriage of a virgin and of minors, on equality of status for marriage, irregular marriage, on the *mahr* [or marriage-gift], on the marriage of a slave—male or female.

On Divorce.

A. Regular divorce, the period to be observed by a divorced woman before remarriage, irrevocable divorce; the husband's abstention from marital intercourse, denunciation of a wife for adultery, etc.

B. [In which these sections are included in the book of marriage.] On dismissal of either spouse by the other, on divorce, on the number of times the formula of divorce is uttered, on conditional divorce, on doubtful divorce, on the return of a divorced wife, on abstention from marital intercourse, on the form of divorce known as *ẓihār*, on denunciation of a wife for adultery, on admission of affiliation.

C. Regular divorce, repetition of the formula of divorce, oaths concerning divorce, the utterance of metaphors for the divorce formula, dismissal of one spouse by another, on marital abstention, the period to be waited by the divorced woman before remarriage, on establishing paternity and the fact of birth, which parent [on divorce] has more right to a child, disputes concerning household goods, etc.

(*Ḥudūd*) Penal Offences[1] [punishable by death, mutilation, etc.].

A. Adultery, falsely accusing of adultery, sodomy, wine-drinking, theft, witchcraft and heresy. A section is devoted to discussion of the blood-wite.

B. This contains the following heads: who may and who may not be punished in retaliation for offences, offences liable to retaliation, on forgoing retaliation, from whom blood-wite may not be exacted, from whom blood-wite is to be exacted, on blood-wite, the slave's kinsmen liable to pay blood-wite, atonement for slaying, on combating rebels, the slaying of renegades, the combating of unbelievers, division of spoils and booty, the covenant of protection and imposition of the poll-tax, the covenant of truce, revenue from the *Sawād* (Mesopotamian lands), the penalty for adultery, the penalties for theft, highway robbery and wine-drinking, correction for minor offences. [Attached to this book is a section on the qualifications of the sulṭān.]

C. On theft, what entails the penalty of cutting off the hand and what does not, on [intoxicating] liquors, on penal offences—what demands retaliation and what does not but is satisfied by blood-wite, evidence of slaying, consideration of the circumstances of slaying, on wounding that is not fatal, on offences by a slave, on wrongful seizure of a slave, on [threatening] display of weapons, on damage to walls or parts of buildings, etc.

[1] For discussion of the general question see below in the chapter on Government.

On expeditions [into non-Muslim lands].

A. This contains sections on raiding and expeditions against unbelievers, the merit of the *jihād* or "effort" for the cause of Islam, the merits of being martyred, division of spoils, treaties and "protection", banners and standards, the leader's choice of spoils before division, renegades, misappropriation of common stores, the combating of rebels, etc.

B includes most of the material here discussed in the book of penal offences.

C under this heading includes sections on renegation and the validity of the civil actions of a renegade, on tribute to be levied on conquered Greek cities, on Muslim slaves and their property retained by the enemy, etc.

On Inheritance.

The contents of this section have in large measure been discussed in Chapter III. With it is included the strictly legal portion of the *Majmū' al-fiqh* (A). The *Tanbīh* of Shīrāzi (B), however, contains more Books which are of interest. The first is on oaths and includes sections on persons whose oath is valid and those whose oath is not, on prevarication, on penance for a false oath and also on the period of waiting necessary for a divorced woman before remarriage, and other headings usually included under divorce. The second book deals with the expenditure to which the head of a household is liable for its maintenance. The headings are: Maintenance for wives, maintenance for close kin, slaves and domestic animals and the responsibility for rearing children.

The *Jāmi' al-ṣaghīr* (C) also has a book on oaths and devotes another two books to the various forms of the emancipation of slaves and the question of clientship.

CHAPTER V

MORAL SENTIMENTS IN ISLAM

Ethical doctrine in Islam is intimately connected with the law. In the official expositions of the faith, such as are contained in the books of *fiqh*, no special distinction is made between rules regarding conduct and those which concern ritual or what other systems would regard as appertaining to the province of civil and criminal law. The moral teaching of Muhammadanism, therefore, is an integral part of a practical code designed to instruct the true believer concerning the path he must follow to win the approval of Allah and the reward of Paradise. Failure to obey the instructions of the *fiqh*, whatever their concern, is to incur the wrath of Allah and punishment of Hell.[1] Such is the view of the doctors of Islam, based, as all *fiqh* is based, on the "roots" of jurisprudence.

From those who accepted his message, Muhammad himself demanded adherence to certain beliefs and practices of which he was the exponent, and the Koran, in keeping with the cultural circumstances of its origin, makes it clear that primary importance was attached to faith, conduct being a secondary consideration. The most widely followed "orthodox" teaching in Islam, namely, that of Abu 'l-Ḥasan al-Ash'arī, formulated at a time when the tendency to crystallization was becoming manifest, declared that faith means "justification in the heart", i.e. recognition and acknowledgment by the mind of the truth of the doctrine that "there is no God but Allah and Muhammad is his apostle".[2] Verbal utterance of the creed and the fulfilment of the statutory duties, the "pillars" (*arkān*), of the religion (namely, almsgiving, worship, fasting, and pilgrimage), are "branches" (i.e. secondary offshoots) of the belief "in the heart". A man does not cease to be a true believer if he refrains from carrying out the "branch"

[1] A government warning erected near some cotton-fields outside Cairo in 1942 read: Beware of wetting cotton (before weighing), for it is fraud, of which the consequence is loss in this world and punishment in the next.

[2] According to Ibn Ḥazm, *Kitāb al-Fiṣal* (Cairo, A.H. 1317), III, 188, the argument is based on the premiss that the Koran was revealed in Arabic, in which tongue *īmān* ("faith") means *taṣdīq* ("proclaiming true"). "Works" would not be called *taṣdīq*, nor would *tawḥīd* ("the assertion of the 'oneness' of God"), which is another synonym of *īmān*.

duties but only if he denies the "oneness" of Allah and the truth of the message of the prophets.[1]

The Koran itself is not concerned any more than other Scriptures to present an abstract view of moral values, and no general and theoretical criteria are provided for the distinction of right and wrong. Even if Muhammad had been capable of formulating them they would have been out of place in the circumstances in which the revelations were made. Once the believer was convinced that Allah alone was God and possessed of all the transcendant powers of Godhead, the subject-matter of conduct could be peremptorily dictated to him.

As was his general policy, whether deliberately or not, Muhammad in his demands made comparatively few changes in the ordinary mode of life of his converts, and although he introduced certain important reforms, particularly in the matter of sexual relationships, he was content to accept the common moral ideas of his tribe. What they were is comprised in the term *muruwwa* (literally "virtue"), to which "chivalry" in many respects corresponds, but which is more fully represented by "honour and revenge". There is a *ḥadīth* that the Prophet said to Sā'ib, who had been his friend in the *Jāhilīya* (i.e. before the revelation of the Koran): "Look to those moral practices you had in the *Jāhilīya*, and apply them in Islam; give security to your guest, be generous toward the orphan and treat your *jār* (the stranger who is under your protection) with kindliness."[2] The same sentiment is to be found in the Koran,[3] in a verse that, characteristically, begins by bidding the believer to serve Allah and associate nought with Him, and continues: Show kindliness towards parents, kinsfolk, orphans, the poor, the *jār*, whether kinsman or alien, to fellow-workers, wayfarers and slaves.

The Koranic teaching confines itself to the more generous side of *muruwwa*, and omits any reference to vengeance, more particularly the blood-revenge, an obligation that "lay heavy on the conscience of the pagan Arabs".[4] In this matter the religion (*dīn*) of Muhammad brought some of its most significant reforms. It

[1] Shahristānī, *Kitāb al-Milal*, ed. Cureton, I, 73.
[2] Aḥmad b. Ḥanbal, *Musnad* (Cairo, A.H. 1313, 6 vols.), III, 425.
[3] 4⁴⁰.
[4] R. A. Nicholson, *Literary History of the Arabs* (Cambridge, 1930), p. 93 ff.

taught that instead of its being cowardly and ignominious to forgo revenge, true nobility lay in forgiveness, that in Islam those who restrain their anger and pardon men shall receive Paradise as well-doers.[1] From the earliest *sūras* the prophet is concerned with the quality of the relationships that obtain between adherents of the faith. Belief is essential and the kindly acts of an infidel will not be regarded as an equivalent;[2] but next to piety or fear of God come equity and just dealing.[3] Allah himself is "*al-raḥmān al-raḥīm*" ("the compassionate, the merciful"),[4] and He guides man to the "two highways" of good and evil. In an early passage the good is described as a "steep" which is attempted only by "those of the right hand", i.e. those who are righteous and achieve the reward of Paradise. It is defined as consisting of the ransom of captives, giving food on the day of famine to the orphan who is near of kin or to the poor man who lies in the dust, and, besides this, of being among those who believe and who enjoin patience on one another and "urge each other to compassion".[5] Elsewhere,[6] the man "that denies the faith" is equated with him "that thrusts away the orphan and gives no encouragement to feed the poor".

It is significant of the position of Muhammad's teaching in relationship to the practice current in the *Jāhilīya* that he appears to have adopted the tribal terminology for good and evil. When he has occasion to refer in a single term to the beliefs and conduct accepted as good, he speaks of them collectively as *al-ma'rūf*, literally "the known" and probably, like *'urf*, "what is customary and approved"; misbelief and misconduct being *al-munkar*, i.e. what is disapproved, or more literally, "what is regarded as unknown or foreign". Tribal societies in a state of civilization parallel to that of the Arab tribes of the *Jāhilīya*, would, in the same way as they did, regard the known and familiar as the good and the strange as the evil. In the Koran there are frequent general exhortations to enjoin the *ma'rūf* and forbid the *munkar*.[7] The commentators, as for example Bayḍāwī,[8] explain the former term

1 3^{128}. 2 9^{19}. 3 5^{11}.

4 Bayḍāwī (on Koran 1^{1}, ed. Fleischer, I, 5) says that the former term is the wider in its scope, since it implies that Allah is the benefactor of all men whether Muslims or unbelievers, whereas the term *raḥīm* is confined to God's especially beneficent attitude towards believers.

5 90^{10-18}. 6 107^{1-3}. 7 E.g., 31^{16}. 8 2^{176}.

as being equivalent to equity, while the other is defined as anything which the *shar'* calls evil (*qabīḥ*). *Munkar* is also taken to mean "that which all just men would judge to be evil".[1]

The teaching adapted from the older society is combined in the Koran with ethical doctrine which is more specifically Islamic. Thus the reward of Paradise is promised to believers who restrain their lusts, abide honourably by their compacts and are careful to observe the ritual of worship.[2] There is even a passage in one of the Meccan *sūras*, which is of the nature of a code, although informal and unsystematic:

Thy Lord has decreed that ye shall not serve ought but him; and to parents kindness.[3] . . . And give the kinsman his due, and the poor and the wayfarer. But do not lavish wastefully. Do not keep thy hand fettered to thy neck, nor yet spread it to full width. . . . And slay not your children in fear of poverty. We will provide for them. Beware: to slay them is great sin. And approach not to fornication; it has always been vileness and evil as a practice. And slay not the soul that God has made inviolable, save for just cause.[4] As for him that is slain unjustly, we have given his *walī*[5] authority.[6] But let him not exceed in slaying: he shall be aided. And approach not the possessions of the orphan, except for what may be better, until he reach his full strength. And fulfil your compact. Verily your compact shall be required. And give full measure when you measure and weigh with just balance. This is best and most excellent in [its] interpretation. And make no accusations of foul deeds where thou hast no knowledge: verily hearing, sight and mind, all these shall be questioned about it. And walk not on the earth with self-conceit: thou wilt neither split the earth nor touch the mountains in height.[7]

Women as well as men are recommended to ways of modesty (in distinction to their allegedly flaunting manners in the *Jāhilīya*), and also to be steadfast in prayer, to give alms and obey God and

1 *Tāj al-'Arūs*, s.v.

2 E.g. 70^{29} ff, 79^{40} f.

3 But only, presumably if they are believers. Cf. Koran 9^{23}.

4 "Save for one of three things; misbelief after faith, harlotry after chastity and the slaying deliberately of an innocent Muslim." (Bayḍāwī, *ad loc.*).

5 Nearest kinsman.

6 ". . . to exact what is demanded for the slaying from him who is liable, or to exact retaliation from the slayer." (Bayḍāwī, *ad. loc.*).

7 17^{24-40}. The same doctrines are more succinctly expressed in 2^{172}, 25^{64} ff, and 31^{16-18}, where the moral exhortations are combined with instructions in manners.

his apostle.[1] Further they are directly associated with men in a verse which assures believers of both sexes that, if they are truly "resigned" (Muslims), devout, truthful, patient, humble givers of alms, punctilious in fasting, heedful of sexual modesty and constant in remembering God, then they shall receive his forgiveness and reward.[2]

The Prophet guarded himself against speaking of mere ritual performance as good. "Piety", he says, "is not that ye shall turn your faces towards the east or the west, but the pious man is he who believes in God and the last day and the angels and gives his wealth for his love of kinsmen, orphans, the poor and the wayfarer."[3] Further, good is rewarded with good,[4] but not unconditionally; for hypocritical ostentation[5] in obeying the law, as well as cynical adherence to the mere letter (as when a man accompanies the giving of alms by insult and outrage of the recipient) destroys the likelihood of recompense.[6] Furthermore, evil is to be kept at bay (or, possibly, paid for) by "what is better",[7] for neither good nor ill has its exact equivalent and by the return of good an enemy becomes "as though he were a warm friend".[8]

These precepts are not applicable to all mankind without distinction, but only to believers, faith in Allah being the first requisite in the brotherhood of Islam.[9] The pre-Islamic virtues with which legend endowed Muhammad show most clearly what Islam regards as the ideal of conduct, for to imitate him as closely as possible is the height of the pious Muslim's ambition. He is the arbiter of right and wrong in every act of life, whether it concerns the relationship of man with his neighbour (and all such acts, however personally regarded, have their social aspect), or of man with Allah. Like the Koran, the *ḥadīth* deals with ceremonial, ritualistic and ethical requirements of the faith, but there can be perceived in it a development in the conception of piety and an advance towards a high standard of moral values.

A comprehensive view of the character of the Prophet himself as seen through the spectacles of tradition is provided by Ghazālī in his *Iḥyā 'ulūm al-dīn* ("The Revival of Religious Knowledge"). The author, after describing Muhammad's table-manners and his personal likes and dislikes, all of which had their effect on the

[1] $33^{32\text{ ff.}}$ [2] 33^{35}. Cf. $24^{30\text{ f.}}$ [3] 2^{172}. [4] 55^{60}. [5] $107^{6\text{ f.}}$, 4^{4}.
[6] $2^{265\text{ f.}}$ [7] 23^{98}. [8] 41^{34}. [9] 16^{99}.

manners and tastes of Muslims, proceeds to give in detail an account of his moral qualities and his opinions on questions of ethics. "The apostle of God was of exceeding humility and self-abasement, praying ever to God to favour him with goodly qualities and generous character. He used to say in his petitions, O God, make me by nature (*khalq*) and by habit (*khulq*) good. And he used to say, O God, keep away from me all unlawful habits." And God answered his petition, fulfilling his promise which says, "Call me and I shall answer you favourably."[1] And he revealed unto him the Koran, and this character was as (required by) the Koran.

Ghazālī's quotations from the *ḥadīth* picture the Prophet as the gentlest, bravest, most just and most continent of men. His hand never touched a woman's unless he owned her or was married to her or was too closely related by blood to marry her. Also he was the most generous of men. Not a single *dīnār* or *dirham* remained with him at night. If he had anything over and he had not found anyone to whom to give it when night came upon him, he would not return home until he had delivered himself of it to some person in need. Of what God sent to him he took nothing but the provender allotted him for the year, the simplest that could be found of dates and barley. He used to patch his own sandals and repair his clothes. He would do duty with the menials of his people and would eat with them, and being the most modest of men he would not stare in any person's face and would grant the request of slave or free man. Also he would accept any gift, however humble. He carried out what was right even if it were to his own detriment; he would not ask the help of idolators even when he had need of every man he could win[2]; and he was patient of anything that annoyed him.[3]

In reporting what tradition regarded as the Prophet's own conception of morality, Ghazālī quotes the story of the maid captured at the Islamic conquest of pagan Arabia, who addressed him and said, "O Muhammad, if you saw your way to free me and not let

[1] Koran 40^{62}.

[2] Ghazālī, *op. cit.* II, 314. The list of the Prophet's good qualities concludes with the statement that he was superlatively endowed by God with all the virtues even though he was unlettered, being able neither to read nor write, since he had grown up in a land of ignorance in the open fields, where, orphaned and in poverty, he had herded sheep.

[3] *Ibid.* p. 320.

the Arab tribes rejoice at my misfortune [it were well], for I am the daughter of the lord of my people. My father protected those whom it was his duty to defend, relieved those in distress, fed the hungry, spread peace abroad and refused none that had need. I am the daughter of Ḥātim of Ṭayy." The Prophet answered, "Maiden, that is the character of true believers."[1]

In speaking of Islam he declared that Allah had included in it the noblest virtues and the finest qualities, which are: kindliness in intercourse and generosity in the dealings between man and man, accessibility, free giving of what is lawful, feeding the poor, the dissemination of peace, visiting the sick Muslim, whether he be upright or a transgressor, escorting the bier of the dead Muslim, being a good neighbour, whether one's neighbour is a Muslim or a *kāfir*, honouring the aged Muslim, granting requests for food and accepting invitations to eat with others, granting forgiveness, making peace between men, open-handedness, generosity and liberality; being the first to give greeting and restraining one's anger. To be avoided are what Islam forbids, namely frivolous pleasures, singing and the playing of musical instruments of any kind (whether stringed or otherwise suited for the making of music), slander, lying, meanness, coarseness, intrigue, treachery, calumny, disloyalty in friendship, disavowal of kinship, ill-nature, arrogance, boasting, sly scheming, overreaching and haughtiness, insult and obscenity, spite and envy, inconstancy, aggressiveness and tyranny.[2]

The first *ḥadīth* reported in the collection of Bukhārī is that it is not the act but the intent that counts for reward, a sentiment that may be a generalization from several passages in the Koran denouncing hypocrisy.[3] He that practises cunning and deceit ("two-faced conduct") is declared to be regarded as the "worst of men" at the Resurrection.[4] The workings of conscience are described in another tradition which declares that virtue means the possession of goodly qualities, whereas sin is that which disturbs the soul and "of which you do not wish others to know".[5]

The emphasis placed in the *ḥadīth* on the ethical side of Islam

[1] Ghazālī, *op. cit.* II, p. 213. [2] *Ibid.* p. 314. [3] E.g. 107^6.

[4] Bukhārī, *Ṣaḥīh*, Bk. 78 (*Adab*), no. 52.

[5] Nawawī, *Arba'īn* (The "forty" traditions), no. 27. Quoted by Goldziher, *Vorlesungen*, p. 16.

is illustrated by the tradition that no Muslim is truly a believer unless he desires for his brother what he desires for himself,[1] a declaration which is paralleled by that of Omar, sent by him in reply to the "Greek" king's request for a formula containing the sum of all knowledge.[2] Bukhārī has a rubric declaring that loyalty to a compact is part of the faith, but he quotes no accompanying *ḥadīth*.[3] Mas'ūdī, however, sets down a similar doctrine and reports that the prophet declared that his people would always be blessed as long as it refused to regard loyalty as a source of enrichment (and almsgiving as a burdensome debt), that a believer's word is as good as his bond and that Muslims must keep their promise, except it be to treat as lawful what is forbidden and treat as unlawful what is permitted.[4]

The Prophet hated untruth[5] and although he was ready to accept cowards and misers as believers he refused to regard a liar as a true Muslim.[6] He classed liars with promise-breakers, and called men guilty of treachery to their covenants, or who litigated in bad faith, hypocrites.[7] Of them there is constant denunciation in the Koran, but lying as such is nowhere in it specifically condemned, with the result that later authorities have on that question as on others, to form their own conclusions.

According to the Ẓāhirī ("literalist") Ibn Ḥazm there are men who hold that falsehood is in all cases evil. But there are five instances in which lying may be good, as, for example, when a believer is in hiding from a cruel and tyrannous ruler. All Muslims would agree that in such circumstances the man's fellow-believers may lie to protect him and his possessions, and anyone who betrayed him would be a transgressor against God, whereas if he disclaimed knowledge of the fugitive and his whereabouts, he would be worthy of reward as a benefactor.

[1] Nawawī, in *Kitāb Jāmi' al-'ulūm wa'l-ḥikam fī sharḥ khamsīn ḥadīth* (Amritsar, 1887), no. 23, p. 84. The commentators dispute concerning the meaning of this *ḥadīth;* there would appear to be room for doubt, since another tradition in the same collection declares that even major sins are as though they had not been committed, if the transgressor is a true believer.

[2] Ṭabarī, I, 2822.

[3] Bukhārī, ed. Krehl, IV, 116.

[4] *Murūj al-dhahab*, IV, 169.

[5] Ibn Sa'd, I, ii, 99.

[6] Ibn Qutayba, '*Uyūn al-akhbār*, ed. Brockelmann, p. 416.

[7] Bukhārī, ed. Krehl, II, 101 f. (no. 17).

Other examples are those of a man's uttering a falsehood in order to secure his wife's affection; or a man's telling lies during the course of a war against idolators, in order to secure the release of Muslim captives. In the latter instance a lie could only be evil if accounted so by God; reason could not designate it as evil.[1]

According to Ghazālī, speech is a means towards certain ends. When a lawful end may be achieved by truth as well as by falsehood, then lying is forbidden (*ḥarām*). If, however, that end can be achieved only by the telling of a lie, then that becomes lawful; it is even imperative if the end is imperative (*wājib*).[2] But it is necessary to guard oneself in the practice of lying, because once the door of falsehood is opened there is a danger that it may be used for purposes in which it is unnecessary.

There is an opinion, he continues, that all lying is a transgression except that by which a Muslim may be benefited or be delivered from harm. When a tyrant questions a Muslim about his possessions he may deny having them; also if a prince seizes a Muslim and questions him about any sins he may have committed against God, he may deny their commission. There is a Tradition saying: "He who commits a foul sin, let him conceal himself under God's veil; for disclosure of the transgression is in itself another transgression".

Even where the object to be attained by falsehood is lawful there may arise out of it what is forbidden. A man must therefore weigh expediency against truth in the balance of justice. If he knows that the forbidden thing that may arise from the truth is, from the point of view of the *shar*ʿ, more grievous than a lie, then he may choose the lie. If the contrary is the case, then the truth is imperative. Most men utter falsehoods for money or place; warning is given that the furtherance of selfish objects does not permit falsehood.[3]

In this connection the matter of swearing oaths in evidence is one of importance. To swear falsely is to commit a sin demanding expiation, *kaffāra*.[4] This rule is applied mechanically so that it is permitted in some cases to make expiation before the oath is

[1] Ibn Ḥazm, *Kitāb al-Fiṣal* (Cairo, A.H. 1317), part III, 109.

[2] E.g. where the life of a Muslim is at stake; or where the objects of a war cannot otherwise be achieved; or if a broken alliance cannot otherwise be cemented.

[3] *Iḥyā*, III, 121 f.

[4] Shīrāzī, *Tanbīh*, ed. Juynboll, p. 239.

broken and in anticipation of the offence.[1] So extreme an application of the letter of the law would appear, however, to be rare, and it must in any event be considered in conjunction with the accepted teaching about *niyya* or "intent".[2]

The general weight of Islamic thought is against lying, despite Sa'dī's famous declaration that a lie concocted for good is better than a truth which arouses strife. The better conception is expressed by the pseudo-Jāḥiẓ: "Keep to the truth; for a sharp sword in the hands of a brave man is not more powerful than the truth. And the truth is an honour even if it contain that which you dislike; a lie is humiliation even if it involves something dear to you. Moreover, he that is known to lie is suspect even when telling the truth."[3]

Another aspect of the morality of *ḥadīth* and one in close accord with the general character of Koranic teaching is a report by Abu Dharr, one of Muhammad's associates, to the effect that the Prophet gave him the seven-fold charge; to love the poor and be accessible to them, to look always to them that were below and not to those above him, to demand nought of any man, to preserve his loyalty towards his kin even when he was enraged against them, to speak the truth always even if it was bitter; not to let himself be frightened when engaged in any cause for the sake of Allah, and to cry out frequently, "There is no power and no strength save in Allah."[4] Parallels are frequent. Thus: "He that believes in Allah and the Day of Judgment should speak what is good or remain silent, and should honour his neighbour and his guest"[5]; and "Fear Allah, let a good deed follow an evil deed in order to cancel it. . . . "[6]

There would seem to be more authority than can usually be attributed to *ḥadīth* for assuming that the Prophet was of a mild and forgiving disposition,[7] and disliked unpleasantness and cruelty.[8] The choice of two courses was never laid before him but

[1] Shīrāzī, *Tanbīh*, ed. Juynboll, p. 246.
[2] Cf. *infra*, pp. 219 f.
[3] *Le Livre des Beautés et des Antithèses*, ed. G. Van Vloten (Leyden, 1898), p. 43.
[4] Ibn Sa'd, IV, i, 168 *ad fin*. Cf. the report of the speech at the "Farewell Pilgrimage". (Ya'qūbī, *Historiae*, ed. Houtsma, II, 123.)
[5] Nawawī, *Arba'īn*, tr. J. Schacht in *Der Islam* (*Religionsgeschichtliches Lesebuch*, Tübingen, 1931), p. 18, no. 15.
[6] *Ibid*. p. 19, no. 18.
[7] Ghazālī, *Iḥyā* II, 313 ff.
[8] See Bukhārī, ed. Krehl, IV, 116–9, 120.

he chose the easier, and he never took vengeance from any man unless he had been harmed in a matter touching the faith (*fī sābīl Allāh*).[1] He held it to be wicked to eat alone, to beat a slave, to refuse forgiveness, or to hate his fellow-men[2]; and he accounted kindness to animals as a virtue to be rewarded by forgiveness of all sins.[3]

A tradition whose sentiments are not greatly different from those attributed to Muhammad is ascribed to his cousin and son-in-law 'Alī ibn Abi Ṭālib, the fourth of the "Orthodox" Caliphs. It concerns a verse which he composed proclaiming that nobility consists of ten "pure" qualities: reason, religion, knowledge, clemency, liberality, understanding, piety, patience, gratitude and compassion.[4]

These expressions of moral sentiment culled from the Koran and the *ḥadīth*, propound the ethical principles upon which, according to Muhammad and his orthodox interpreters, the associations of Muslims with one another should be based. Like the other requirements of the faith, namely, those which affect the believer's relationships with Allah, they have been reduced by the *fiqh* to a series of practical regulations intended to ensure that Muslims shall not be in doubt concerning the demands of the *shar'*. But it is to be understood that although fulfilment of the rules as they stand may content some Muslims, others with higher ideals of piety have regard to the spirit of the *ḥadīth* and are aware that "intent" counts for more than outward performance. The practical rules are to be found in any work of *fiqh*, and according to them acts are classed as belonging to one of the following five categories:

(*a*) *farḍ* or *wājib*, essential duties, fulfilment of which is rewarded and neglect of which is punished;

(*b*) *mustaḥabb*, *sunna*, *masnūn* or *mandūb*, duties recommended but not essential, fulfilment of which is rewarded, though they may be neglected without punishment;

(*c*) *jā'iz* or *mubāḥ*, actions lawfully or legally indifferent, being neither rewarded nor punished;

1 Ibn Sa'd, I, ii, 94.
2 Mubarrad, *Kāmil*, ed. Wright. p. 39.
3 Bukhārī, *Ṣaḥīḥ*, ed. Krehl, II, 103 (no. 23).
4 Ibshīhī, *Mustaṭraf* (Cairo, n.d.), I, 19.

(*d*) *makrūh*, actions disapproved but not forbidden; and
(*e*) *ḥarām* or *maḥẓūr*, actions forbidden and punishable.[1]

In the first class are those duties prescribed by the Koran, namely those of worship, alms-giving, fasting and pilgrimage.[2] These duties alone are universally recognized in Islam as indispensable. The class of other actions is variously estimated by different schools of Muslim opinion, although a measure of agreement exists concerning certain deeds classed as *ḥarām*, namely those which the *fiqh*, with the Koran as its authority, regards as sins without distinguishing whether the laws transgressed are concerned with ceremonial or morals. A disquisition on them is provided by a commentator, al-Bannānī,[3] on the *Jam' al-jawāmi'*[4] of al-Subkī, and it may be considered as reflecting orthodox, Sunnī, opinion.

The greatest of all sins is *kufr*, "misbelief", which stands alone for heinousness. Then come, as major offences, wilful slaying, fornication, sodomy, the drinking of wine and the use of intoxicants generally, theft and unlawful seizure, wrongful accusation of adultery, calumny, slander, false witness, lying oaths, disavowal of kinship, disobedience to parents, fraudulent measure and weight, anticipating or postponing the time of worship without proper excuse, uttering falsehoods against the apostle of Allah, striking a Muslim without just cause, defamation of the "companions" of the apostle, suppression of evidence, bribery, cuckolding, pandering, delation, refusal of alms, despairing of the mercy of God, reliance upon cunning (i.e. procuring others to commit an offence and relying for indemnification upon God's pardon), *ẓihār* (use of a pre-Islamic formula of divorce with incestuous implications),[5] eating the flesh of swine or of animals that have died of themselves, breaking the fast of Ramaḍān, treachery, making war against believers, sorcery, usury and persistence in minor sins.

In ordinary works of *fiqh* a not inconsiderable amount of space is devoted to commercial law, in which many of the provisions are framed so as to prevent infringement of rights, damage to persons or property, gambling and speculation. Thus, it is not

[1] See above, p. 150. [2] See above, pp. 155 ff.
[3] Died 1198/1784 (Brockelmann. *Ar. Lit.* II, 89).
[4] Būlāq ed. (A.H. 1285), II, 135 ff. (margins).
[5] Cf. Bayḍāwī on Koran 33^4.

lawful to sell *waqf*-property (permanent endowments for pious objects), or the *umm walad*, i.e. the female slave who has borne a child to her master and is therefore entitled to freedom on his death. It is unlawful to sell what will cause cruelty to animals or damage to other property (e.g. the wool from the back of a live sheep or a length of stuff out of a garment already made up).[1]

The setting of animals to race against one another is not forbidden—indeed the *fiqh* contains rules for its regulation—but gambling on the results is prohibited and so also is speculation in all forms. Thus it is not lawful to sell that which is not yet in existence (e.g. crops of a future year or a slave as yet unborn) or that of which the weight, measure or value is not known (e.g. an unmeasured heap of grain or the milk in an udder).[2]

The *fiqh* as it stands represents the formalism characteristic of the founders of the "rites" and of their subordinates but also of the more recent authorities who, by close imitation (*taqlīd*) of the methods of the early masters, exposed Islam to the danger of becoming a rigid system of commands and prohibitions. Alongside its standards of morality, however, there exist certain higher ones which are to be found in the *ḥadīth* and elsewhere. In the fifth century of the faith far-reaching reforms were brought about by Ghazālī (d. 1111), surnamed from his influence *Ḥujjat al-Islām*, "The Proof of Islam". He had himself been reared in the methods and results of scholastic theology, which had driven vitality out of the orthodox form of the religion and reduced it to a set of ritual observations. Contemplation drove him to cast form aside and to seek a solution for his difficulties elsewhere. With this end in view he plunged into the study of Greek philosophy and so was brought under the influence of Aristotelianism and neo-Platonism. But he ended in revolting against pure reason as a guide to life and found satisfaction in the mystical doctrines of Sufism. Past training, nevertheless, could not all be shaken off. Its effects combined with those of his newer studies to make a syncretism, established primarily upon the direct study of the basic sources of the *fiqh*, namely the Koran and *ḥadīth* free of their commentators, but moulded by his new studies and convictions and suffused by humanism. In his *Iḥyā 'ulūm al-dīn* ("The Revival of Religious

[1] Shīrāzī, *Tanbīh*, ed. Juynboll, pp. 94 f.
[2] *Loc. cit.*

Knowledge") he elaborated an entire system of life for the believer; one that might cover every aspect of conduct and belief.

Before proceeding to examine the work, it is necessary to consider further the influences working upon its author and the ideas which he had absorbed during his career. As a man of deeply religious feeling he was much concerned with the problem of good and evil in the world and the responsibility for sin, and the sources available to him did not satisfy his desire for certainty. In the Koran it was only after the link of faith had been forged between man and God that regard was paid to the ethical consequences of the relationship. On the side of Allah the Prophet could postulate no obligations due to man.[1] Allah does what he wishes.[2] He is all-powerful, all-knowing and all-decreeing. And here a difficulty arises which has led to serious debate in Islam, for the Koran speaks with two voices. With one, the believer is told that Allah guides aright those whom he wishes so to guide,[3] leading them to true belief and the subsequent reward of Paradise,[4] while He leads others astray,[5] not desiring to guide them aright.[6] With another voice the believer is told that God does not desire unbelief in his servants,[7] that what betides them of good is from Allah and what comes upon them of evil is from themselves,[8] and further, that those who do wrong on earth will endure his curse and an evil abode in Hell.[9] There is also an indication that the Prophet attributed sin to the Devil, who misguided believers.[10]

The argument which turned about these incompatibles involved wider theological considerations upon the nature of God. Orthodoxy, which had found its best-known exponent in Abu 'l-Ḥasan al-Ash'arī, maintained that God, being He that has power, who knows and decrees, has willed all things good and ill, the beneficial and the harmful. That which He has willed and knows, He has desired from His servants; and He has commanded the pen to write it on the "guarded tablet", which is preserved in Heaven. This is His immutable decree and inexorable judgment to which man is subject. Allah therefore is Lord of all: He does what He wishes and decides as He desires, and if He were to send

[1] Cf. Shahristānī, *Kitāb al-Milal*, ed. Cureton, I, 74, I, 2.
[2] Koran $22^{14, 19}$, etc.
[3] 2^{136}, 22^{16}.
[4] 22^{14}.
[5] $13^{27, 30, 33}$, $14^{4, 32}$.
[6] 16^{38} f.
[7] 39^{9}.
[8] 4^{81}.
[9] 13^{25}, 4^{18}.
[10] 24^{21}.

all created beings to Paradise there would be no injustice done, or if He sent them all to Hell there would be no wrong (*ẓulm*). Wrong consists in usurping rights over that which one does not own or cannot justly claim, and since He is the absolute possessor of all created things, no wrong can be predicated of Him. Further, all the duties incumbent upon man are the subject of revelation from God. No essential duty can be dictated by the mind, which cannot in itself determine that an action is good or evil. Nevertheless the knowledge of God comes through the mind, upon which His commands are imposed by revelation. Ignorance of the law therefore cannot be pleaded in excuse of sin, for the Koran says: "We punished not before we sent an apostle".[1] On that account, gratitude to the benefactor, reward for the obedient and punishment for the transgressor are made necessary by revelation and not by reason. Yet reason can conceive no duty which is incumbent upon God, since He derives neither benefit nor harm from man's actions and has power over all without question.[2]

This raised the question whether God can impose on his servants duties which they cannot fulfil, and punish them for their failure. Ghazālī replied in the affirmative,[3] but orthodoxy generally evades the onus of attributing evil to God by declaring that He, being compassionate and merciful, rewards His servants, not according to their works but by His good will.[4]

Aḥmad Ibn Ḥazm, who died in Spain in 456/1069, a member of the sect of the Ẓāhirīs ("Literalists"), attacked the Ash'arite doctrine concerning the nature of God and carried his arguments from the Koranic texts to their logical conclusions. According to him, anyone that says that God would do nothing save what is good according to our understanding and would create nothing that our understanding classes as evil, must be told that he has regarded the matter from his own standpoint and perversely applied human argument to God.[5] Nothing is good, but Allah has made it so, and nothing is evil, but by His doing.[6] Nothing in the

1 17^6. Cf. $2^{140\text{ f.}}$

2 Shahristānī, ed. Cureton, pp. 73 f.

3 *Iḥyā* (Būlāq, A.H. 1289), I, 141.

4 Tha'ālibī, *Qiṣaṣ al-anbiyā* (Cairo, A.H. 1310), p. 16, l. 22. Cf. also Koran 22^{10}.

5 Ibn Ḥazm, *Kitāb al-Fiṣal* (Cairo, A.H. 1317), III, 100.

6 *Ibid.* pp. 101 f.

world, indeed, is good or bad in its own essence; but what God has called good is good, and the doer of it is virtuous; and similarly what God has called evil is evil and the doer of it is a sinner. All depends upon God's decree, for an act that may at one time be good may be bad at another time. Thus at one time it was accounted good to turn towards Jerusalem in prayer, then Mecca was made the *qibla* (the point to which all must turn in worship) and the former practice became evil. Conversely, an act may at one time be evil and become good with change of circumstances: thus, for example, sexual intercourse before marriage and after, or the enslavement of a "foreigner" who, after having been a client under protection and free, breaks his convenant and lays himself open to captivity and sale as a slave.[1]

Still further, no person has by right any claim to privilege from another unless God has established it. For example: if God so willed, a child might be produced out of the earth, but it is born of parents instead and they derive pleasure from it. Gratitude and piety towards them should be no more necessary than towards the earth, but God has enjoined it; otherwise it would not be necessary.[2]

Some people say that tyranny (*ẓulm*) is evil. If you ask in what tyranny consists, the answer will be that it means slaying or torturing men, or seizing their property. Further, suicide and self-mutilation are sins. But God permitted the seizure of the property of their enemies by the Muslims in Khurāsān, and the exposure of oneself to slaughter "on the path of Allah" (in holy war) is expressly approved by the Koran.[3] So also the ceremonies of the pilgrimage would be accounted madness if God had not ordained them. Even *kufr*, "misbelief", the greatest of all sins, would not have been evil if God had not declared it to be so. Indeed He allows a profession of it when there is need for "prudence" (*taqīya*),[4] but declares it a capital sin otherwise. Connected with

[1] Ibn Ḥazm, *Kitāb al-Fiṣal* (Cairo, A.H. 1317), III, 66.

[2] *Ibid.* p. 108.

[3] 2⁵¹. A similar argument is used by Ibn Ḥazm to prove that it is only God's behest that would make a man's exposure of his wife to all men a sin.

[4] Cf. Koran 3²⁷. The doctrine of *taqīya* was evolved owing to the religious differences between rulers and their subjects, which made dissemblance a virtue, especially to Shī'ites, who may in hostile territory disavow their beliefs in order to secure their personal safety.

this point is the question of wine-drinking. If a man before its prohibition in the Koran[1] had regarded it as unlawful he would have been a misbeliever. After its prohibition he became a misbeliever if he regarded it as lawful.

It is clear therefore that only that is *kufr* which God declares to be so. Similarly nothing is *ẓulm* ("wrong") except what God forbids. God himself can do no wrong, and if He punishes a man for not carrying out a command of which he is incapable, then that cannot be a wrong since God does not declare it so.[2]

An unorthodox view at the opposite extreme from that of Ibn Ḥazm concerning good and evil was that of the Mu'tazilīs, a sect who were prominent in the third century of Islam as the exponents of "free-will". According to them, God can do no evil and does not will the existence of *kufr* nor of wickedness, desiring neither the misbeliever to misbelieve nor the wicked to commit wrong, nor that He should himself be subject to vilification, nor that the prophets should be slain. They base their argument on verses in the Koran which declare that God takes no pleasure in the "misbelief" of his servants[3] and that sinners follow a course which angers Him and reject what pleases Him.[4] According to the Mu'tazilīs, moreover, if God himself desired misbelievers or sinners to act as they do, then they are deserving of reward for having carried out His commands.[5] God does in fact do nought but good, since He is the all-wise, and it is a part of His wisdom to guard His servants,[6] but the human being nevertheless "creates" all his own actions, good or evil, and will deserve reward or punishment according to his deeds.[7] Both good and evil necessitate a certain knowledge and a capacity in the mind to distinguish them,

[1] 5^{92}. Another verse (2^{216}) concedes some good to wine but declares the evil of it outweighs the good.

[2] Ibn Ḥazm, *op. cit.* III, 109.

[3] 39^{9}.

[4] 47^{10}.

[5] Cf. Ibn Ḥazm, *op. cit* III, 142. His reply to the Mu'tazilī argument is that God could have prevented the misbeliever from his *kufr* and the sinner from his sin if He had desired. To deny this is to imply that God is not omnipotent and amounts therefore to misbelief.

[6] Shahristānī, *op. cit.* p. 30.

[7] *Loc. cit.* "This wicked and accursed saying has led a man of high rank amongst the Mu'tazilīs to declare that God did not create *kāfirs* ('misbelievers'), because they are compounded of human bodies and *kufr* together, but that He created only their bodies and not their *kufr*." (Ibn Ḥazm, *op. cit.* III, 54.)

and this capacity came before any revelation, although instruction in the duties demanded by Allah came by His favour through the prophets, in order that man might be proved and informed.[1]

In this connection it may be remarked that the Shī'a teaching concerning responsibility for good and evil corresponds to a large extent with that of the Mu'tazilīs. In the first place God stands clear (*munazzah*) of any evil action,[2] and all His acts are in accord with wisdom and righteousness.[3] Moreover, He is all-powerful, although all things within His power are not necessarily produced.[4] God does no evil, and indeed no evil can issue from Him because (i), the doer of evil is either conscious of the evil of his actions, or (ii), he is not conscious of it, or (iii), he is unable to avoid commission of the evil act or needs to do it, or (iv), he is able to avoid it and has no need to do it but nevertheless does it without purpose. If the first be the case, then God's ignorance is postulated; if the second, His impotence; if the third, His need; and if the fourth, His folly. And none of these can be postulated of God.

So far as man's actions are concerned, the Imāmī (Shī'a) belief is that he is a free agent, that good and evil are matters for judgment by the reason and that an act must be considered by itself in respect of its goodness or badness, without reference to any *shar'* or law.[5] Goodness (*ḥusn*) is here defined as that which the

[1] Shahristānī, *op. cit.* p. 31. Ibn Ḥazm accused the Mu'tazilīs, who argued in this fashion, of sophistry in their use of Koranic texts (*op. cit.* III, 142). He also attacked the views of those "free-thinkers" who declared the actions of men to be "natural" to them in the same way that it is the "nature" of fire to burn or of snow to be cool. Such views, he asserted, might be true even if men were dead. There are some men, he continued, that say all man's actions are "created" and all that he need do is to exercise his will. "Now we have found", he says, "that as for the will, man is unable to control or manipulate it in any way. All that is manifest in a man is the alternation of his movement and his resting. As for his will, he has no power over it; for we may often find a man sound in body who would desire to possess any comely woman, but refrains only from fear. He prefers sleeping to praying on cool nights and hot afternoons, he longs to eat on fast-days and he would rather keep tight hold on his money than give it away in alms. He does the opposite of what he desires only by suppressing his will with violence. As for directing it, he has no means of doing that." (*Op. cit.* III, 55.)

[2] Mullā Muhammad Bāqir Majlisī, *Ḥaqq al-yaqīn*, (Tehran, A.H. 1241), p. 1a.

[3] *Op. cit.* p. 3a *ad fin.*

[4] The Shī'a thus attempt to guard Allāh from the charge of creating evil.

[5] Cf. also Ḥillī, *al-Bāb al-Ḥādi-'Ashar*, tr. W. M. Miller (London, 1928) pp. 40 f.

free and competent agent does whereby he becomes deserving of praise in this world and reward in the next, while badness (*qubḥ*) is that which incurs blame and punishment.[1]

Judgment of the goodness or badness of an act may sometimes be made immediately; as for instance concerning the goodness of a truth from which benefit accrues or the evil of a lie which brings harm. Sometimes, on the other hand, the judgment is the result of reflection, as in the matter of an expedient lie or the utterance of a truth that may bring harm. In the latter circumstance, knowledge of the goodness or badness of the act comes by thought and contemplation. There are certain things, however, of which the goodness or badness is not to be judged by man but can only be known after the formulation of a law (*shar*ʻ). Thus, for example, the goodness of fasting on the last day of Ramaḍān and the badness of fasting on the next day, which is the first of the month of Shawwāl.[2]

A slightly different statement of the Shīʻa view is that

> God alone can create, and it is heresy to believe with the Zoroastrians that God creates only what is good and the Devil what is evil. But God can and does use means to this end, and can delegate His creative powers to angels or other agents. The good or evil manifested through God's plenipotentiary servants is not God's act but their act, wherefore they are the recipients of reward or punishment, by reason of the option which they enjoy, so that they themselves, by their own volition, do those things which God hath commanded or forbidden. For although they act by virtue of a power and strength which they do not in themselves possess, but which God hath conferred upon them, yet, since He hath given them this option, He hath also assigned to them rewards and punishments. Yet God is the Creator of Good and Evil, while His servant is but the agent and doer thereof.[3]

All debate of this kind was swept aside as irrelevant to the true issue by the mystical teaching of Sufism. Evil to it was unreal and in itself non-existent, since it was no more than the obverse aspect, or the foil, of the goodness of God.[4] Nevertheless there

[1] *Ḥaqq al-yaqīn*, p. 6a. [2] *Loc. cit.*

[3] ʻAlī Aṣghar b. ʻAlī Akbar, *ʻAqāʼid al-Shīʻa*, tr. by E. G. Browne in *Literary History of Persia*, IV, 384.

[4] Cf. Jalāl al-Dīn Rūmī, *Mathnawī*, ed. Nicholson, I, l. 3204, "Not-being and defect, wherever they appear, are the mirror which displays the excellence of all crafts." Cf. also I, ll. 3210 ff. "Vileness is the mirror of power and glory."

were Ṣūfīs, deceived perhaps by the double meaning possessed in Arabic by the word *nafs* (the lower "soul" or "the flesh"), who declared that the soul of man was created with an inclination towards evil and possessed two properties, the first being what prevented it from the good and the second what spurred it on to lust.[1] Both transgressions and base qualities like pride, envy, avarice, anger, hatred, etc., which are to be commended neither by law nor reason, are caused immediately by it, for it is the seat of evil.[2] The only hope for man is to wean his soul from its accustomed ways and to curb its desires with the bridle of piety.[3]

In treating Sufism the authoritative manuals generally contain some discussion concerning the elements of the good life as conceived by various schools, but the fact that the basic principle of the system is the reality of God alone led adepts to frame their own corollaries. The result is a mass of conflicting thought even on so important a question as that of the place of the law in life. The antinomianism of that strange personage Ḥusayn Manṣūr-i Ḥallāj would seem to have been more obvious than his conformity,[4] for he insisted that though the *shar'* was decreed by God, the practice of it was another matter. Sin was, therefore, disobedience of the law and not of God's will.[5] According to the Persian mystic Abu Sa'īd ibn Abi 'l-Khayr (d. 1048) also, the varieties of positive religion mattered nothing in the last resort.[6] Qushayrī (d. 1074), on the other hand, held that the *sharī'a*, the law, was a mode of revealing the truth (*ḥaqīqa*) and was God's own command to men, informing them how they were to behave in His service.[7] The

[1] Qushayrī, *Risāla* (Būlāq, A.H. 1287), p. 57. Jalāl al-Dīn Rūmī, though convinced of the goodness of God, was equally certain of the sinfulness of man, and while denying evil in relation to its Creator affirmed it in relation to His creatures. (Cf. *Mathnawī*, ed. Nicholson, I, ll. 3188 f.) Even this was a manifestation of the all-pervading nature of Godhead, seeing that all man's actions, good or ill, were for God's sake. (*Mathnawī*, I, ll. 3800 ff.)

[2] Hujwīrī, *Kashf al-maḥjūb*, ed. Zhukovsky (Leningrad, 1926), p. 246; tr. Nicholson (Gibb Series), p. 196.

[3] Qushayrī, *loc. cit.*

[4] Cf. his statement that he belonged to no *madhhab* ("religion" or "rite") but had chosen the most difficult features of them all; also the fact that in his practice of *dhikr* (constant indulgence in the ritual of worship) he transgressed the rules of the *fiqh* ('Aṭṭār, *Tadhkirat al-awliyā*, ed. R. A. Nicholson, II, 138).

[5] Cf. R. A. Nicholson, *Studies in Islamic Mysticism* (Cambridge, 1921), p. 158.

[6] Cf. R. A. Nicholson, *The Mystics of Islam* (London, 1914), p. 90.

[7] Qushayrī, *Risāla*, p. 50. Cf. Hujwīrī, *Kashf al-maḥjūb*, pp. 498 f.; tr. Nicholson, pp. 383 f.

mystic Junayd of Baghdad, who had immediate influence on Ghazālī, also held that all paths to God were closed for men unless they followed the prophet, and definitely stated that Ṣufism was bound up with the principles of the Koran and the *sunna*.[1] "This path (of Ṣufism)", he declared, "is for him who has taken the Book of God in his right hand and the *sunna* of Muhammad in his left and walks by their light so that he falls not into the pit of doubt or the darkness of heresy."[2] Nevertheless, the early Ṣūfī Abu 'l-Ḥusayn Nūrī (d. 908) had asserted that Ṣufism did not lie in the practice of any forms nor in knowledge, but in morality and the acquirement of a godly character.[3]

Since morality, in large measure though not entirely, concerns man as a social being, some of the more enlightened of the Ṣūfīs insisted that the true saint lives among his fellow-men, trades with them, marries and takes part in social activities without ever forgetting God for a moment.[4] There were those, however, who regarded ascetic seclusion as the means of achieving goodness. Furthermore, in an early stage of the history of Ṣufism, Koranic teaching concerning predestination developed logically, into *tawakkul*, "absolute reliance" upon God, and therefore into quietism. It meant complete indifference to personal affairs and resignation to the will of God, in whose hands men are as the corpses in the hands of the corpse-washer,[5] utterly without will or participation. From some of their sayings it is clear that these Ṣūfīs took no care for the ordinary means (*asbāb*) of livelihood but left it "to God" to provide them, since "His are the treasures of heaven and earth".[6] It was amongst the principles of *tawakkul* not to beg, nor to refuse, nor to keep anything.[7] The phase of quietism passed, except amongst the most extreme, after protests of the community generally against this form of obtaining public assistance, and even amongst Ṣūfīs themselves there were those who held that it was virtue to earn one's daily bread, and that the doctrine of *tawakkul* was vitiated when a man had to take active measures to secure the aid of his fellow-man, as happened, for example, when he had to resort to remedies in sickness.

[1] Qushayrī, *Risāla*, p. 22.
[2] 'Aṭṭār, *Tadhkirat al-awliyā*, II, 8.
[3] *Op. cit.* II, 55.
[4] Cf. Jāmī, *Nafaḥāt al-uns*, ed. N. Lees, p. 345.
[5] Qushayrī, *Risāla*, p. 89, l. 7 ff.
[6] *Ibid.* p. 89, l. 25 f.
[7] *Ibid.* p. 89, l. 2.

It was not necessary, according to the more sober adepts, either to withdraw from the society of men or to refrain from the ordinary functions of life. Ascetism (*zuhd*), however, was a virtue, though Ṣūfīs disputed about the form it was to take. According to some, it meant abstention from what was *ḥarām* (forbidden by the *shar'*); for God permitted to all men what is *ḥalāl* (lawful according to the *shar'*) and if He blessed a mortal with a wealth of goods and imposed on him only the duty of thankfulness, leaving him free to do what he wished with his property, then there were no grounds for criticism of him, since he held it by divine right. Others said that abstention from what is *ḥarām* is commanded to all and is therefore no merit; real merit lies in abstention from what is *ḥalāl*. The truly pious man is patient and contented whatever his worldly circumstances. General opinion seems to be in favour of this view and asserts that *zuhd* consists in forsaking worldly possessions without regret.[1] Another opinion sees in it "freedom" (*ḥurrīya*) from care or concern about any created thing.

Other virtues inculcated by Ṣūfīs are hope, sincerity and gratitude, trust in the goodness of God and awareness of His watching all human actions, true piety, steadfastness, truth, modesty and *futuwwa*. The last is defined in a number of ways which make it equivalent to chivalry, generosity, and unselfishness. The spirit of it is indicated by the story of Abu 'Alī al-Daqqāq who said: "This people has no protection save in the Prophet; every one else on the Day of Resurrection will say: 'Me, Me', but he will say: 'My people, my people'."[2] Of the definitions supplied, one by Faḍl (ibn Rabī') asserted that it lay in ignoring the faults of the brethren of Islam; others called it not seeing in oneself any superiority over one's neighbour, and granting equitable treatment without demanding it. Another equated it with *ḥusn al-khulq*, "good-nature". One definition was that it meant to eat with anyone, whether saint or unbeliever, and to make no distinction. A story adduced to illustrate this definition received wide currency because it was used by the Persian moralist Sa'dī in his *Būstān*. It ran to the effect that Ibrahīm, "the friend of Allah", would never sit down to food without inviting a guest to share it. On one occasion he discovered that his guest was a Magian and thereupon refused him food unless he became a Muslim. Immediately a

[1] Qushayrī, *Risāla*, pp. 65 f. [1] *Ibid.* p. 121.

Divine revelation came to Ibrahīm, saying: "We have fed him for fifty years, despite his misbelief; and if you had given him a morsel without demanding his conversion [no harm would have come]."[1]

The opposites of *futuwwa* are the vices which must be shunned. They are pride, lust and envy, and the latter is particularly to be avoided for it implies God's having been unjust in the allotment of fortune.[2]

We may now return to the subject of Ghazālī's teaching. Orthodox Islam, in protest against the antinomian views of many adherents of Sufism, had for long regarded it as a form of heresy. It was the achievement of Ghazālī to have reconciled its mystical teachings with the doctrines of the *shar'*, so that it was accepted as a part of Islam, with the result that a truer conception of ethics permeated the dominant formalism. Like Socrates he based his teaching on knowledge, declaring that where there is knowledge, right action follows. But he was not content like the Greek philosopher to give the final authority to mere science. Knowledge was supplied by God through His prophets, and for the ordinary man who is incapable of delving for himself, the teachings of the "sources", namely the Koran and the "traditions", are authoritative. Beyond them the ordinary man should not go. One of the sins of the tongue, said Ghazālī, is

> too close inquiry by the common herd into the qualities of God and the *kalām* ("scholastic theology") and the *ḥurūf* (the mystical truths concerning the "Essentials"). The duty of the common run of men is to occupy themselves with fulfilling what is in the Koran. But this is a burden upon their souls, whereas officiousness lies easily on the heart. Moreover, the vulgar delight in delving into philosophy (*'ilm*), for the devil deludes them into thinking they are amongst men of learning and understanding and he ceases not to indulge their liking for such matters until they give utterance, with a pretence of scholarship, to what is pure heresy, although they remain in ignorance of the fact. Any major sin committed by the common run of mankind is indeed preferable to discussions on *'ilm*, particularly if it concerns God or His qualities.[3]

[1] Qushayrī, *Risāla*, p. 121. Cf. Sa'dī, *Būstān*, ed. Graf, pp. 142 f.

[2] *Ibid.* p. 85, cf. *Tadhkirat al-awliyā*, I, 27 *ad fin.*

[3] *Iḥyā* (Cairo, A.H. 1302), II, 141 f.

In another passage Ghazālī declared that piety had no great need for deep knowledge, and if any man desired a teacher as a substitute for the Prophet, then he must choose one who was capable of self-discipline, who ate and slept little, prayed much, gave much in alms and had the moral qualities of endurance, gratitude, reliance upon God, tranquillity of soul and the like. That kind of man would be a ray from the effulgence of the Prophet and imitation of him would be of advantage. "But," remarks the author, "men with such qualities are rarer and more precious than red sulphur."[1]

When, in the course of the exposition of his system, Ghazālī came to treat in detail the question of morals, he adopted, in spite of his attacks upon the philosophers, their psychology of the subject, though shielding himself behind a liberal use of Koranic texts and *ḥadīths* to defend his arguments. In particular the Platonizing doctrine of the trichotomy of the soul and that of the four cardinal virtues appealed to him as throwing a light on the matter.

In introducing the subject he begins in orthodox fashion by quoting the views of the traditionists and others of recognized opinion concerning what constitutes good morals. Appropriate verses from the Koran come first, then an exhortation given by the angel Gabriel to Muhammad the Prophet which reads: "Be the friend of him that would deny you, give to him that has deprived you and forgive him who has wronged you". Then come such aphorisms as that good morals are the foundation of Islam and that only by goodness of character can a man elevate himself.[2] The author, however, then proceeds to say that the mere quotation of opinions and aphorisms does not reach the true inwardness of morality. They deal only with its "fruit" of external manifestations and not even with all of them. The truth is this, that "constitution" (*khalq*) and qualities (*khulq*) are two expressions that must be employed together. You may say that so-and-so is a person excellent by nature and in manner; that is, both inwardly and outwardly. This is so because man is compounded of body perceptible to the eye, and of spirit and soul, apprehended by

[1] *Ayyuhā 'l Walad* (*O Kind!*), ed. Hammer-Purgstall (Vienna, 1838), pp. 21 f.

[2] *Iḥyā*, III, 46–8.

means of mental perception. Each has its own form. The body is merely of clay, but the soul is associated with the spirit of God and is, therefore, the nobler of the two. It has a definite "composition", out of which actions arise spontaneously without need for thought or consideration. If they are good and generous actions then the source from which they derive is a "good nature", and it is an "ill nature" in the opposite event. The matter depends not at all upon knowledge or external actions.

Now, in the same way that perfect facial beauty demands the beauty of each individual feature, so the inward beauty of the soul is not perfect unless the qualities which constitute it are perfect and equally balanced. They are the four "faculties" (*quwwa*), namely those of knowledge, temper and appetite, with justice as the fourth in a combination of the other three. In the faculty of knowledge, soundness consists in the power to distinguish easily between truth and falsehood in statements and beliefs, and between the good and evil in actions. If this faculty is sound, there are to be obtained from it the fruits of wisdom, which is the chief part of good morals (*akhlāq*). As for the faculty of "temper" the test of its goodness is that its "contraction" and "expansion" shall be controlled by wisdom. So also the appetitive faculty, the goodness of which consists in obeying the dictates of wisdom, by which are meant the principles of reason and the *shar*ʿ. The function of the fourth faculty too, that of justice, consists in the regulation of appetite and temper by reason and *shar*ʿ. Reason here plays the part of the counsellor, while justice is the executive force, being like a dog in hunting, which needs to be trained so that its fetching or its halting shall be as is commanded and not as its own impulse dictates. Desire similarly is like a horse ridden in pursuit of game, being sometimes under control and disciplined and sometimes allowed the rein.

Then follows the Aristotelian doctrine of the "mean". The man in whom each of the aforementioned qualities attains an even balance is of absolutely good character. Excess or deficiency in any one of them leads to vices, which are at the extremes of the qualities; virtue lying in the middle between the extremes. And of all the virtues there are four "mothers" and "roots": wisdom, courage, prudence and justice; all others being derived from these.[1]

[1] *Iḥyā*, III, p. 48.

Ghazālī then propounds the doctrine equally attributable to Aristotle that good can be achieved by training and practice. Thus, if a man wishes to acquire the virtue of generosity his way lies in practising the art of giving lavishly of his wealth, exerting himself in it until it is part of his nature. And so with other virtues. Vices similarly can by training be cured or even turned into good habits.

Certain persons, whom wickedness has conquered and who find discipline of the soul and improvement of morals a matter of difficulty, have contended that the natural characteristics of the soul can no more be changed than the features of the body. The short man, they say, cannot make himself tall nor the ugly man make himself handsome. Similarly, inward ugliness cannot be eradicated. Moreover, say they, to have good morals means to quench appetite, temper, love of the world and the other ingrained qualities, and they affirm that they know from long experience that it is a waste of time to endeavour to eradicate these qualities, which are of the very stuff and nature of mortal man. This argument, however, replies Ghazālī, is erroneous and is put forward by people who think that the object of the effort of discipline is to suppress and destroy those qualities entirely. That is far from the truth. Appetite was created for a beneficent purpose and is an essential part of man's constitution. If the desire for food were cut off, man would perish; if desire for sexual intercourse were destroyed, the human race would cease to exist; and if temper were entirely blotted out, man could not defend himself against destructive perils and he would perish. Now, to take an instance, so long as the root of appetite remains there will of necessity remain the love of wealth which induces desire and leads on to acquisitiveness. The purpose of discipline is not to eradicate this entirely but to reduce it to a just proportion, which lies in the middle between excess and defect.[1]

The true balance of any or all of the moral characteristics which the *shar*ʿ holds praiseworthy is achieved either through divine favour at birth, or failing that by submission to the discipline of reason and to the *shar*ʿ itself. In the latter event the desired end, which is the happiness to be derived from good character, is not to be attained merely by avoiding what is forbidden but in

[1] *Iḥyā*, III, p. 52.

persistent practice of what is good, until the doing of it becomes natural and pleasurable.[1]

Training should be lifelong and it should begin at birth, for then the child's mind is a precious jewel, free of all mark or figure. By education there can be engraved upon it all that is necessary to incline him either towards the good (which will give him happiness in this world and the next, and bring him reward in which his parents and teachers will share), or towards the evil (indulgence in animal sloth), when he will be unhappy and perish. It is the father's duty to guard him from the fire in this world; how much more so is it to guard him from the fire of the next. The way lies in educating and training him, teaching him good manners[2] and morals,[2] keeping him from evil companions, not accustoming him to ease nor permitting him to love finery and luxurious equipment, in the pursuit of which he may waste his life when he grows older and incur everlasting destruction. A good and pious nurse should be chosen for him, one who will eat lawful things, for any other may bias him towards those things which are forbidden. The first signs of the power of discrimination should be watched; they will consist of shyness and modesty and the refusal to do certain things. These signs will denote the dawning of reason in him and he will begin to regard some actions as distinct from others as being evil. This will indicate God's bounty to him and be a sign of a well-balanced character.

The earliest habit he will have formed will be that of gluttony. He must be educated therefore in table-manners; to eat with the right hand only, to pronounce the name of God over food, to eat what is nearest to him, not to hasten to food in advance of others, not to keep his glance fixed upon the food but upon those who are eating, not to eat quickly but to masticate well, not to add one mouthful uninterruptedly to another, and not to eat to excess. It should be pointed out that eating to excess will put him on a par with the beasts. Therefore contentment with little and with what is poor should be instilled. Then he should be taught to be content with simple, white garments rather than with coloured or silken ones, and it should be impressed upon him that these are worn only by women and effeminate men and that if he wears them men

[1] *Iḥyā*, III, p. 54.

[2] *Akhlāq* includes both meanings.

will hold him in contempt. And further training should continue in similar fashion.[1]

After external training comes self-discipline, based upon the thesis that hunger is preferable to satiety and that bodily lusts must therefore be controlled. For the Ṣūfī, the postponement of marriage is desirable that he may be able to devote his energies to the duties of the mystic "path".[2]

The faults which will require to be eradicated in training are many. To begin there are those of the tongue. Silence is a virtue and speech is conducive to numerous moral faults; talking to excess, engaging in vain words, wrangling, disputing, abuse, cursing, singing, the reciting of poetry, jesting, ridicule and satire, betrayal of secrets, lying, false swearing and others of the same kind.[3] Now as for lying, there are circumstances in which it may be permitted. It is not forbidden in essence, but only because of the harm it may bring to the hearer or another. Sometimes it may be necessary, and better than the truth; for example, when utterance of the truth might mean the exposure of an innocent person to danger of death.

In all actions, what is ethically important is the "intent" (*niyya*). It is synonymous with "will" and "purpose" and comprises two essentials, knowledge (conception) and action. Conception comes first and is the root condition; action is the fruit and therefore follows. This must be so, since every deliberate deed (all voluntary action or refraining from action) is made up of three elements, conception, will and capacity, and a man does not will that which he does not conceive. Intent cannot be omitted from the scheme, and it is defined as the attraction of the mind towards some object which is regarded as being in accord with its purposes, near or remote.[4]

"The 'intent' of the believer", says a *ḥadīth*, "is of more account than his doing." Ghazālī explains it as meaning that "doing" and "intent" must be considered in relation to the object to be attained. Even if the "execution" is an act of good, the real good lies in the obedience to the law of God implied by

[1] *Iḥyā*, III, 66–9. [2] *Ibid.* pp. 93 f. [3] *Ibid.* pp. 99–120.

[4] In a later section (*Iḥyā* III, 337) the author contradicts himself by saying "intent" is not a matter for a man's free choice. It is spontaneous and unreasoning like falling in love or satisfying hunger. Strictly speaking, therefore, the question of morality does not enter.

the good intent. Nevertheless, a rightful intention is vitiated if the means taken to accomplish it is unlawful. It would be an evil act to build a mosque with extorted money, whether the builder was conscious of the source of the money or ignorant of it.[1]

In his exposition of the practical applications, which precedes his discussion of the general principles of ethics, Ghazālī touches upon numerous aspects of everyday life and deals with manners, morals and laws. A typical section may here be taken to illustrate his point of view. In the portion dealing with the laws of commerce he prefaces his essay by remarking that business is transacted according to certain rules. These may, in the opinion of the *muftī* (the jurisconsult), be valid as law and yet may leave opportunity for wrong and injustice which will provoke God to anger, since a (moral) prohibition will not always invalidate a legal contract. An example is that of a commercial contract which permits a man to purchase food in time of famine and hoard it in order to sell at high prices. This kind of contract is commercially valid, but is wrong according to the *shar*ʿ (i.e. morally) since it permits the commission of a wrong against the community.

An example of another kind is the putting into circulation of false coin. Even if both parties in a commercial transaction know that the coin is spurious, harm is done; for the recipient will pass it on to another, and he to another, and so it will cause general and widespread loss. But the first utterer of the coins will be to blame and the burden of the harm done will rest upon him. It is the duty of the Muslim merchant to know what his duty is with regard to false coin. If any come to him he must cast them into a well and beware of putting them into circulation again. As a merchant he must recognize and understand coinage, not alone to escape loss himself, but in order that he may not pass bad coin to a Muslim who will *not* recognize it and become a transgressor by his (the first giver's) fault. All action indeed should be based upon knowledge. Thereby the welfare of Muslims may be safeguarded, and it is consequently a duty to acquire this knowledge.

Of a different kind is a transaction in which one of the parties is harmed and not the general public. Now, any transaction implies a tort if either of the parties suffers harm, and justice means nought but this, that no man shall harm his

[1] *Iḥyā*, III, 330 ff.

brother-Muslim. The general principle is that he shall not desire for his brother anything that he does not desire for himself. With particular application it means that he shall not praise a commodity for a quality which it does not possess, that he shall not conceal its faults, that he shall not withhold declaration of the weight or quantity and shall not conceal, over the question of the price, any fact which would prevent the sale.[1]

Concerning the general question of social obligations Ghazālī has much to say. They are not alike for all men. Within the community, a brother has many special claims, a non-related fellow-Muslim has fewer, all of them deriving from the "Golden Rule". Lastly comes the *jār*, the "protected foreigner" from an outside tribe, or a "neighbour". He has still fewer claims, although they are regarded as very strong. Into the discussion of the rights of the "protected foreigner" are introduced certain features which illustrate the attitude of Islam towards those who are not of the faith but are on a friendly footing with believers. A *jār* may be a kinsman and a fellow-Muslim, in which case he will be accorded the privileges to which his triple claim (arising from kinship, Islam, and the position as *jār*) entitle him. A Muslim *jār* has two of these claims and a *jār* who is a non-Muslim has a single claim on the "protector". Much stress is laid on these rights of the *jār*, and numerous "traditions" are quoted to support the behest that he is to be treated with favour rather than with cold justice. The majority appear to deal with the non-Arab Muslim, but Jews and Christians are also mentioned in *ḥadīths* which, however, confine the matter to recommending consideration, when food is being prepared in the household, for dependants who belong to these alien faiths.[2]

The recommendations on the treatment of slaves are summarized in a *ḥadīth* which bids the believer be God-fearing in his dealings with them. "Give them such food", the Prophet is made to say, "as you eat yourselves, clothe them in such garments as your wear yourselves, and burden them not with labours too heavy for them. Those of them that you like, keep; those you dislike, sell; but do not torment God's creatures."[3]

[1] *Iḥyā*, II, 59–61. The general principle is elaborated in a subsequent chapter of the work (II, 168 ff.). The Muslim should desire for fellow-Muslims what he desires for himself and reject for them what he rejects for himself.

[2] *Iḥyā*, II, 181 f.

[3] *Ibid.* II, p. 185.

Before leaving Ghazālī's treatise, a discussion contained in it on the subject of the *muḥtasib* (the "censor") is worthy of mention. The functions of this officer, whose business it was to prevent infringement of the provisions of the *shar'*, will be described later.[1] Here the discussion turns on the point of his moral qualifications, and the question to be determined is whether a man who is not himself entirely immaculate may be appointed to the office. Ghazālī is of the opinion that to demand entire freedom from sin is to close the door of *iḥtisāb*, i.e. to make the censorship impossible. Even the Prophet's companions, he says, were not sinless, and the prophets of old were themselves not without blame, for the Koran refers to Adam's contact with sin. Some authorities are willing to make exception, Ghazālī continues, in favour of a man who has committed no more than a minor sin (such as, for example, that he dresses in silk in contravention of the *shar'*), and would grant him authority to prevent fornication or wine-drinking. This concession, in Ghazālī's opinion, does not go far enough. He supposes the question asked whether a wine-drinker should be permitted to fight in a *jihād* in order to convert *kāfirs* from unbelief. If the answer is "No", then that is opposed to what is well authenticated practice, since everyone knows that the armies of Islam have been of mixed composition, containing both righteous men and sinners; and neither wine-drinkers nor the oppressors of orphans have been prevented from fighting in holy wars in either the Prophet's time or later. If the answer is "Yes", then surely, says Ghazālī, a man who has worn silk may prevent another from drinking wine and one who has drunk wine may be appointed to prevent murder?[2] The section ends with a discussion on the relative gravity of the transgressions against the *shar'*.

Despite his theoretical discussions, the *fiqh* itself remained for Ghazālī, as for other Muslim theologians and students, a sufficient guide to practical conduct. Only amongst the very few, most of whom orthodoxy (not perhaps without reason) reckoned as heretics, did moral doctrine achieve a rank of its own as a science. In the pseudo-Aristotelian fashion it was regarded as one of the three branches of practical philosophy, the other two being economics and politics. According to an opinion quoted by

[1] Cf. pp. 334–8. [2] *Iḥyā*. II, 269 f.

Ḥājjī Khalīfa the bibliographer, "Ethics (*'Ilm al-Akhlāq*) is the knowledge both of the virtues and the means of acquiring them for oneself so that the soul may be adorned by them, and of the vices and the means of warding them off so that the soul may be free of them. The subject-matter of this science concerns the moral qualities and characteristics and the reasoning soul." To his definition Ḥājjī Khalīfa, in true orthodox fashion, attaches an expression of doubt concerning the practical value of this science, which would be of use if morals and character could be altered, but is in fact useless, seeing that they are apparently unalterable. This view is supported by *ḥadīths*, of which one is to the effect that the moving of mountains is more credible than the changing of human nature.[1]

The ethics of the Muslim philosophers derives immediately from the Greek systems, but much labour was expended in order to reconcile it with the Koran. One of the earliest to deal with the subject of morals in a spirit different from that of the *fiqh* was al-Fārābī, a native of Turkistān (d. 950), whose system was not without influence on western thought. He did not especially devote himself to ethical science, but in treating of the function of the soul elaborated his philosophy with respect to good and evil. According to him, every mortal has within him two "forces", the one "rational" and the other "animal". Each of these has a will and a power of choice; each, moreover, has a bias in a particular direction and their possessor stands as though he were between them. Now the bias of the animal force is towards immediate sensual pleasures, while that of the rational force is towards praiseworthy, ulterior, aims such as the acquisition of the sciences and engaging in activities that foster these aims.[2] Further, says al-Fārābī, man in the course of his activities will meet both what is laudable and what is blameworthy. He may derive advantage from either by making it an exercise for his (lower) soul, either by directing it towards good or in restraining it from evil.[3] In the final resort it is reason which distinguishes good and evil, and by observation of the actions of his fellow-men a man will obtain practical demonstration of the difference.[4]

[1] Ḥājjī Khalīfa, ed. Fluegel, I, 200.

[2] *Traités inédits d'anciens philosophes arabes*, ed. L. Malouf *et al.* (Beirut, 1911), p. 19.

[3] *Ibid.* p. 20.

[4] *Ibid.* p. 19.

Al-Fārābī's great successor, Avicenna (Ibn Sīna) (d. 1037), best known in the west of all Muslim philosophers, paid no great attention to the pragmatic subject of morals, which, presumably, he left to the *fiqh*. In his introduction to the *Kitāb al-Siyāsa* ("Book of Politics") nevertheless, he thanks God for the noble qualities which permit man to distinguish between good and evil and between falsehood and truth.[1] In a later passage in the same work, speaking of man's control of the flesh, he says that before a man can govern ought else he must govern that. "The first thing that he must know who would govern himself is that he has a mind, which has control and a fleshly spirit which impels to evil and which of its nature includes all evils. He that would undertake to improve another, who is a wrongdoer, must first know all the faults. So also he that would control, govern and improve himself cannot begin until he knows all the defects in his own self."[2]

More specifically devoted to the science of ethics are works by two Persian authors, separated in time by about two centuries. The earlier, Ibn Miskawayhi (d. 1030), was a scholar and scientist in the employ of the Buwayhid Sulṭān 'Aḍud al-Dawla; the other, Naṣīr al-Dīn of Ṭūs, was associated with the Ismā'īlī heretics, who numbered amongst them the notorious sect of the Assassins. After the capture of their stronghold at Ālāmūt by the Mongol Hūlāgū, he accompanied the victor to Baghdad, where he died in 1274.

Ibn Miskawayhi's thesis deals with the improvement of morals and he follows the Socratic teaching that the foundation of a good character is knowledge. The special activities of the soul, he says, are concerned with the various forms of wisdom and knowledge, and according to the energy with which a man seeks after them so will be his merit. It is a merit which increases with the degree of a man's care for his soul and his avoidance of those matters which prevent attainment of his object. These obstructive matters are man's sensual, bodily preoccupations.[3] Now man shares the qualities of all created things, but he also has one quality which is peculiar to himself, namely, that of volition, with which is associated the faculty of thought and discrimination.[4] These matters of

[1] *Traités inédits*, p. 19. [2] *Op. cit.* p. 6.

[3] *Tahdhīb al-akhlāq* (? Cairo, A.H. 1298), p. 6.

[4] "The study of this is called 'practical philosophy'."

volition which concern man are divided into goods and evils, which are to be explained as follows. Goods are those things which are attained by man by his own will and effort out of the number of things for which man was created, and evils are the things which stand as obstacles in the way of achieving those goods or which frustrate his will and effort. In this respect sloth and indifference may be evils. The man who is successful in his efforts is called happy and he that is unsuccessful unhappy.[1]

There is a multiplicity of forms of happiness and no man alone can achieve them all. Men, therefore, must live together in societies in order to aid one another in attainment of them. Every good and every happiness indeed is derived from association, attaining perfection only in society, and when achieved it is common to all who have partaken in the effort leading to it. Each individual in the society helps the others as the members of the body help one another. True morality, then, is a social virtue, and is not to be attained by the solitary and the recluse.[2]

The individual soul is described in Platonizing fashion as possessing four virtues: wisdom, temperance, courage and justice. Of these a man may boast, but of nought else. The virtues are qualities which the soul has in different spheres of action: thus wisdom is a quality of the reasoning power of man, teaching him to ascertain what he may do and what he ought not to do; courage is a quality of the "temper" and is the active principle which carries out what reason dictates as necessary and aids in overcoming fear where the object of a deed is good and laudable; temperance is a quality of the appetitive soul and consists in controlling desire by reason; and lastly, from a combination of these qualities arises justice.[3]

Virtue is then defined as being the (Aristotelian) "mean", the middle point between extremes, which are the vices. They may be taken as represented by the ends of the diameters of a circle with virtue as the centre. To find this centre and to retain it when found are both difficult, for any movement towards the circumference must be regarded as vice.[4]

A man's characteristics are a part of his constitution at birth; but, says the author, they may be altered by training and the formation of habit. He takes this view, in opposition to that of

[1] *Tahdhīb*, pp. 7 f. [2] *Ibid.* p. 9. [3] *Ibid.* pp. 10 f. [4] *Ibid.* p. 15.

persons who deny the possibility of changing natural characteristics, because he claims to have had practical demonstration of it, and because, if it were not true, the existence of any power of discrimination and reason would be denied; and further, the education of children would be a futile undertaking. "As for the 'People of the Porch' (the Stoic philosophers), they considered that men were born good but degenerated through association with wicked men and by natural inclination towards vice." Aristotle, however, thought that vice could by training be transformed into virtue.[1]

Like all creatures, man has a form of perfection peculiar to himself and to be attained by no one but himself, in the same way that a horse has its own kind of perfection not to be attained by man. His perfection is of two kinds, corresponding to two faculties in him, the one speculative and the other practical; for his aims, on the one hand, are learning and the acquisition of knowledge and, on the other, the conduct of practical affairs. When man attains perfection in both he achieves perfect happiness.[2] In the pursuit of knowledge he will develop until his opinions are exact and his vision true, so that he will not err in his belief nor have doubts concerning the truth. In the end he will have knowledge of things as they are, in their order, and having attained the highest stage, which is that of knowledge of God, he will remain, serene and confident in heart, whence all perplexity has departed. This is perfection in the speculative faculty.

As for the practical faculty with which the *Tahdhīb al-akhlāq* especially deals, it is concerned with the perfecting of character (*khulq*). Its beginning lies in so ordering faculties and activities that none of them may dominate the others, and in disciplining them in such fashion that activities may be controlled by reason. The end will be a well-ordered State in which all activities and powers will be properly shared amongst men, all of whom will share in the common happiness.[3]

Now there are some who believe that the function of man's reasoning faculties, e.g. memory and imagination, is the recollection and repetition of feelings and pleasure. Thereby they turn the noble soul into the mean slave of their sensual desires, to do service for them in their eating and drinking and sexual

[1] *Tahdhīb*, p. 19. [2] *Ibid.* p. 23. [3] *Ibid.* p. 24.

intercourse. This is the view of the majority of mankind, the rabble. Mention of Paradise and proximity to their Creator merely stirs within them the desire for such goods as these. It is for these that they pray to their Lord in their petitions, and if they devote themselves to religious works, forsaking the world and practising asceticism, it is but a kind of trading and chaffering for profit on their part, as though they gave up the less valuable in order to acquire the more valuable and turned aside from the goods that perish in order to attain those that abide.[1]

It is possible for a man to determine for himself in which grade of mankind he would be. For there are three "spirits" in man, the bestial, the feral and the reasonable; and the noblest man is he in whom the endowment of the reasonable spirit is highest and whose desire for it is greatest, while men in whom either of the other "spirits" prevails are below the highest degree.[2] He that had not the advantage of early training, or who had it and was then perverted by his father, who reared him upon the recital of immoral poetry, teaching him to accept its falsities and approve its content of immoralities and its bias towards pleasure (such, for example, as is to be found in the poetry of Imr' al-Qays, Nābigha and the like), or he that was brought up in contact with elders who approved such poetry and gave him lavish presents, and who is tempted by men of his own age that are his allies in the pursuit of bodily pleasures, and he who has wealth which disposes him to over-indulgence in food, clothes, horses and ornament, let such a man account all these as evils and as not conducive to true happiness, and let him strive gradually to wean himself from them.[3]

What the individual's good and happiness is, he must find out for himself by experience, for there is both an absolute good and a good which is good in relation to the individual, and the perfection of happiness becomes greater according to the measure of its approximation to the supreme and absolute good.[4] Therein lies supreme happiness, which is constant and unfluctuating; but we know that man suffers many chances, so that it may happen that the most affluent of mortals is overtaken by misfortunes. It is

[1] *Ibid.* p. 25. Cf. Sa'dī, *Gulistān*, bk. II. "The pious demand the reward for their piety."

[2] *Tahdhīb*, p. 27.

[3] *Ibid.* p. 30.

[4] *Ibid.* p. 45.

therefore only when a man's life has ended that it is possible to judge whether he has been happy (fortunate) or not.[1]

In the *Akhlāq-i Nāṣirī* of Naṣīr al-Dīn Ṭūsī, the Greek antecedents of the work are as clear as in the *Tahdhīb al-akhlāq* of Ibn Miskawayhi, but the effort of harmonization with the Koran is more determined. Naṣīr al-Dīn, before entering on the actual presentation of his thesis, anticipates criticism by declaring that what he has included in his work is no more than a transcription from treatises on practical philosophy and it is to be regarded as the mere reporting of traditions of ancient and modern philosophers without any attempt at estimating their truth or falsehood. He insists, further, that he is not to be held responsible for the religious significance of his citations or of what is implied in them, for he is merely a transmitter and neither justifies nor blames.[2]

After discussing the question of the soul and its indestructibility, as contrasted with the evanescence of matter, the author proceeds to describe the three faculties of the soul through which all actions are initiated. They are the faculty of reason, which discriminates between good and evil deeds; the appetitive faculty, wherein is initiated the desire for goods and the seeking after physical pleasures; and the faculty of "temper", which induces man to repel harm, to advance against terrors and to desire domination and superiority. These faculties cannot be increased at will, but remain as they were created.[3]

Because of his soul, which is in contact with the Divine, man is the highest of created beings. The lower grades of men, however, who are the inhabitants of the fringes of the lower world, are in contact with the grade of the most intelligent of the beasts. Above them are the various higher grades of men, distinguished by their intellect and skill and culminating in the prophets, who, by inspiration and without physical means, have acquired a knowledge of eternal truths. They are the medium whereby comfort and happiness are brought to the inhabitants of the world. Beyond the highest ranks of men are the ranks of the angels, then comes the realm of reason and the heavens; lastly the "Place of Oneness" is reached. There the circle of being is completed, like a line begun at a particular point and brought back again to it.

[1] *Tahdhīb*, p. 56.
[2] *Akhlāq-i Nāṣirī* (Lucknow, 1891), p. 25.
[3] *Ibid.* p. 44.

Man is, by creation, of the middle grade of beings. He has a way open through his will to a higher grade, though by nature he inclines to a lower one. Man's superiority over the lower beings lies in his reason, and the key of his happiness or unhappiness, his perfection or lack of it, is entrusted to the power of his own competence. If he will choose to walk upon the straight path of good deeds and of knowledge he can advance himself stage by stage, because of the striving towards perfection which lies in his nature. Thus, he may reach the place in which the light of God shines upon him, where he finds approach to the highest asylum. If, however, he is passive and allows his nature to have control over him, then he will follow the downward path and his destructive passions will take possession of him.[1] What he chooses is left to man's reason. He may succumb to the lowest "spirit" in him, namely the bestial, or to the middle, which is feral, or to the highest, which is that of the angels. These are mentioned in the Koran as the "commanding", the "blaming" and the "confident" spirits respectively.[2]

The aim and object of man's life is the attainment of perfection. It is an aim that lies within the compass of man's powers and if he interprets his conceptions in action to the limit of his capacity, then perfection is attained.[3] The perfect or complete man is he who has achieved enduring existence in happiness and finds his felicity in God's commands. Between him and God there will be no veil interposed and in the glory of God's proximity he will find the greatest extreme of happiness.

According to the pre-Aristotelians, continues Naṣīr al-Dīn, happiness was purely a function of the soul. The post-Aristotelians, such as the Stoic philosophers, made happiness a function of the body as of the mind. But that is to make happiness, which is the most noble of things and utterly free from any hint of change or evanescence, depend upon a contemptible thing like the body and so make it contingent upon chance and accident. Aristotle

[1] *Akhlāq-i Nāṣirī*, p. 53.

[2] The terms in the text are taken from the Koran 12^{53}, 75^{2} and 89^{27}, respectively, but they can scarcely be made to bear the significations placed upon them.

[3] *Ibid.* p. 63. The principle is illustrated by the Aristotelian figure of the house which has lain in the imagination of the builder. That is the goal or concept. When its "objective" existence has been brought about, then the degree of completion or perfection is achieved.

himself, who had observed the variety of mankind and the differences of men's views with regard to happiness, saw that each man had his own ideal of it and the same man at different times had different ideals. He therefore divided happiness into five parts (health of body being the first), the lack of any one of which made perfect happiness impossible. This same philosopher, Aristotle, moreover said, "that without material prosperity and numerous friends, it is difficult for a man to carry out noble works, and that therefore philosophy has need of employment by the State for its noble qualities to find display". "We say (in reply) that if a gift comes from God to man, happiness consists purely in that alone."[1]

On the question whether happiness is to be attained in this world or is to be looked for in the next, the author quotes the opinion of the older philosophers that the body is the veil of the soul, which alone could appreciate happiness and that therefore it is only with the destruction of the body that happiness can be achieved. Aristotle said it would be a vile thing were we to say that in this world a man may be a true believer in God and constant in well-doing and yet can be accounted happy only when he and his good deeds perish. The philosopher's view is that there are grades of happiness to be achieved here below varying according to one's effort. Naṣīr al-Dīn himself draws the moral that every pleasure should be pursued in accordance with wisdom so that good habits are formed and remain permanent. The absolutely happy man is he whose happiness does not cease or change and who preserves his equanimity under the vicissitude of fortune. The possessor of such happiness, so long as he is in this world, is in the power of external influences (*ṭabā'i'*) and of the heavenly bodies, and the stars of his good or ill fortune are all about him. But although he may be associated with his fellow-men in misfortune, no ill can cast him down, for he is immune against harm from outside influence.[2]

Since virtue is the source of happiness, Naṣīr al-Dīn in the course of his work gives his reader counsel as to how he may acquire it. The foundations of all activities undertaken with a view to acquiring perfection are either natural or are artificially contrived. Nature is, so to say, the germ out of which "animal"

[1] *Akhlāq-i Nāṣirī*, pp. 83–6.

[2] *Ibid.* p. 99.

perfection grows through various stages, whereas art is like the working of wood by means of tools until it becomes a chair. The natural is higher in kind and degree than the artificial, since it springs from God's own wisdom, whereas the artificial arises from human strivings and desires; also, nature stands in the place of a teacher and art in the place of the disciple. Further, the perfect form of anything is that predisposed for it by its origin. Therefore perfection achieved by art must resemble that which is achieved naturally and has been predetermined by God. Now since the regulation of morals and the acquisition of the virtues are the functions of art, it must in this sphere imitate nature. We must therefore observe how our powers and faculties are ordered in the first instance and then discipline them, keeping the original measures. The development successively of the different faculties of a newly born infant is an example for study. It has various natural capabilities, such as the power to absorb nourishment or to cry when it is deprived of it, and these various powers are trained until the child reaches manhood. In morals, similarly, a beginning should be made by disciplining the appetitive faculty, then the faculty of temper should be ordered and so forth. Thus will a man by daily training achieve virtue and happiness.[1]

Such philosophic writings as have here been cited have had little importance in the practical shaping of Islamic morals, and even in popular literature it is the orthodox dogmas that are taught. These are to be found almost everywhere (the rare exceptions remaining for further consideration below), so that even in contexts that might otherwise appear unsuitable there is reference to them. To take the classic instance of the *Arabian Nights*, many of the stories bear upon them the marks of having been "edited" in the interests of the faith. In some there are inserted long passages of an edifying character that stand in sharp contrast to the general spirit of the stories. A passage of this kind, though its wording approximates less than most to the ordinary contents of the *fiqh*, is contained in the homily placed in the mouth of the dying merchant Majd al-Dīn.[2] In it he bids his son not to associate familiarly with men and to avoid all things that will cause harm and ill. "Do good", he insists, "when you are able, and be con-

[1] *Akhlāq-i Nāṣirī*, pp. 193 ff.

[2] *Arabian Nights*, 308 f., ed. Macnaghten, II, 312 ff.

stant in generous dealings with mankind; avail yourself of opportunities for dispensing kindness (*ma'rūf*). Be mindful of Allah; he will then be mindful of you. Guard also your wealth and do not expend it to excess. If you are extravagant you will come to have need of the lowest of men. Remember that the value of a man lies in what he possesses. Be compassionate to them that are below you, that he who is above may have compassion on you. Wrong no man, lest God put over you one who will wrong you."

More nearly approaching the form of the technical works of *fiqh* is the long debate, or rather catechism, in the story of Shammās the vizier and the prince.[1] It begins by discussion of the dilemma caused by the conflict of the instructions that exist in Islam with regard to the claims of this world and the next. If a man sets himself to seek his livelihood it is harmful to his soul, which he must neglect; if he devotes himself to the next world, it is to the detriment of his physical welfare. The answer given is that in the quest of his livelihood man gains power for the world to come. Another problem treated is that of man's ability to sin against the Creator, whose supreme might could compel man eternally to love him. To this, answer is given that Allah has shown them that are worthy to love him the path of good and has granted them the power to do what good they will. They that nevertheless do evil are transgressors; but the path of repentance remains open to them. The power to do good or evil rests with the five senses. Man was in the first place created to love God, but the soul in man has an innate inclination towards lust and the five senses are the instruments through which good and evil are accomplished. Of the vices there are three, the vileness of which none can wipe out. They are folly, meanness of character and falsehood. Some falsehoods, namely those which avert harm and bring benefit, may be condoned, though all are vile; and some truths, though they must all be accounted fair, are vile; namely, those by which a man vaunts himself of what he has and which express his self-conceit. The vilest of all men is he who boasts of what he has not.[2]

The general character of the stories depicts the popular conception of morality, which seldom conforms with the spirit of these

[1] *Arabian Nights*, 909 ff., ed. Macnaghten, IV, 394 ff.; tr. Burton (1894) VII, 143 ff.

[2] *Ibid*. 416 ff.; tr. Burton, VII, 163 ff.

edifying insertions. No wonder, therefore, that the reading or recitation of the tales is frowned upon by the learned of the faith, or that in many parts of Islam the reading or hearing of them is regarded as unlucky.[1] Although it is a well established fact that many of the stories originated outside of Islam, yet all have been worked over and been in some measure adapted so as to show some agreement with the requirements of the faith. They are all, moreover, admittedly fictional even when they are not concerned with the extra-mundane and the supernatural. A feature of them in this respect is that they, and most others of their type, lack the element of poetic justice. This is not to imply that the conception of "fair play" is absent from them, but that transgression is not shown as being inevitably followed by punishment. Wealth may, with impunity, be acquired by means no matter how criminal; men may slay, and by murder attain to fortune and high honours; the dishonesty and tyranny of those in high office is depicted in glaring colours yet without any indication that their misdeeds are in the long run avenged on earth or remembered for the reckoning in the hereafter.

This characteristic must be ascribed to the non-moral atmosphere of most of the stories, and cannot be attributed to deliberate immorality. To the same reason must probably be ascribed the fact that intoxication, the use of drugs such as opium and hashish, and the enjoyment of music and dancing, all of which are forbidden by the *shar'*, are mentioned as though they were normal and are spoken of without any expression of disapproval.[2]

It is not clear to what extent the incidents of sexual irregularity which are frequently mentioned in the stories are deliberately designed for erotic and licentious purposes. In some of the stories the point obviously lies in the description of the obscenity. Yet there is in the telling of many of the incidents an absence of stress and comment that implies a non-moral attitude also towards sexual questions. It is an attitude officially disapproved by the authorities of the faith, but it is to be observed elsewhere than in the *Arabian Nights*. With regard to such matters it may be said in this context that Muslims regard sexual intercourse in no different

[1] Cf. O. Rescher, "Studien über den Inhalt von 1001 Nacht", *Der Islam*, IX, 9.

[2] Cf. Rescher, *art. cit.* pp. 9–19; and E. W. Lane, *The Arabian Nights' Entertainment* (London, 1841), I, 214 ff.

light from other natural functions of the body. They discuss it freely,[1] even when children are present, and there appears to be little about it that the latter even do not know and discuss. Provided that it is *ḥalāl*, i.e. when the parties are by the *shar'* lawful to one another, satisfaction of the sexual instinct is encouraged. *Ḥadīth*, which here as in other matters is used in argument for or against, declares that the best of the Muslim community is he who contracts most marriages.[2] Celibacy is against the *sunna*,[3] and except amongst Ṣūfīs would appear to be unknown. Excess, however, is a matter for comment,[4] though satisfaction of the sexual instinct may be mentioned in prayer or thanksgiving along with other blessings.[5]

It is in the interest of purity that the *shar'* forbids the remarriage of a woman for a definite period after the death of her husband or after her divorce by him, but it commands that before a man may re-marry a woman whom he has divorced she shall have consummated a marriage with another man.[6] The law was probably enacted in the first place as a check upon ease of divorce, but it runs counter to the general ideas of sexual purity held in Islam.

Extra-marital intercourse is lawful only in concubinage; prostitution, though practised, is held in contempt. Pederasty is, by implication in the story of Lūṭ, forbidden,[7] but would appear to be common and not greatly deprecated by popular opinion, to judge both from the *Arabian Nights* and other evidence.[8] Ibn Khaldūn attributed to it and to fornication, as well as to the growth of the demand for pleasures of all kinds, the decay of civilization.[9]

1 *Arabian Nights*, ed. Macnaghten, IV, 413; tr. Burton, VII, 161 n. 10.

2 Ibn Sa'd, I, ii, 95, l. 20.

3 *Ibid.* V, 70, l. 6.

4 Cf. Ibn Khallikān on the traditionist Abu 'Abd al-Raḥmān al-Nasā'ī, who had four wives and a number of concubines.

5 Cf. Ṣubkī, *Ṭabaqāt al-Shāfi'īya* (Cairo A.H. 1324), III, 219, l. 18 f.; Yaḥyā b. 'Abd al-'Aẓīm b. al-Jazzār, *Fawā'id al-mawā'id* ("The Boons of the Table(s)") B.M. MS. Or. 6388, fol. 5 a. (For this reference I am indebted to Mr A. S. Fulton.)

6 See above, p. 121.

7 Cf. Koran 26¹⁶⁵.

8 Cf. Rescher, *art. cit.* pp. 11 f.; E. Westermarck, *Wit and Wisdom in Morocco* (London, 1930), pp. 86 ff. *Qābūs-nāma* (Gibb Series XVIII), ch. XV.

9 *Prolégomènes* (ed. Quatremère, II, 260; tr. de Slane, II, 302 ff.). He appears to imply that only the Mālikīs recognized the gravity of the offence; but the Shāfi'ites, too, regard it as a major sin. Cf. *Jam' al-jawāmi'*, II, 135 (margin).

This is not to say that either true modesty or the prudery which pays lip-service to it are absent. The *shar'ī* regulations concerning veiling were not without their effect, and even where secular law have officially forbidden it, the practice continues, especially in poorer communities. The psychological effects of unveiling are part of the stuff of Islamic literature. Thus the story is related of how a physician used the sudden removal of a veil as part of the "shock treatment" of a patient,[1] and an example of true modesty is quoted by Farīd al-Dīn 'Aṭṭār in his biography of the Ṣūfī Ḥasan of Baṣra. He related that one day a woman came to him with her face unveiled and both her hands uncovered, to make a complaint against her husband. But Ḥasan bade her first veil her face. She replied: "I have been created by a Friend [God] in such fashion that my wits have left me, and if you had not warned me, I should have gone into the bazaar as I am. But as for you, with all the friendship that you claim to have with Him, what would it have mattered to you if you had not noticed my being unveiled?"[2] A rebuke to prudery is administered by Ibn Qutayba, who exhorts his readers not to let modesty make them frown or turn away their faces at mention of the pudenda, male or female. The names of parts of the human body hold no sin, he says, but sin lies in besmirching the good reputation of others and in slander.[3]

A branch of Muslim literature in which didactic morality is a frequent subject for treatment is that concerned with *adab*, manners and "professional" etiquette. In most works included in in this class, generally regarded as *belles lettres*, treatment goes at any rate to the extent of quoting the moral sentences of the Prophet, and of his companions and others of authority in Islam. The spirit of such works is indicated with rare precision by Ibn Qutayba at the beginning of his '*Uyūn al-akhbār* ("The Sources of Traditions"), where he says:

This book, even though it be not concerned with the Koran and the *sunna* and the law of the faith or knowledge of *ḥalāl* and *ḥarām*, is a guide to lofty conduct, in that it gives direction to the man of noble character and prevents ignoble conduct. . . . There is not merely one way, and no more, open to God, nor is all good

[1] *Chahār Maqāla* (Gibb Series XI) p. 73.
[2] *Tadhkirat al-awliyā* (ed. Nicholson, I, 36, ll. 2–6).
[3] '*Uyūn al-akhbār* (ed. Brockelmann, pp. 7 f.).

comprised in nocturnal vigils or in prolonged fasting, or in the knowledge of *ḥalāl* and *ḥarām*. Nay, the ways unto Him are many, the gates of good are wide, and the prosperity of the faith lies in the prosperity of the age, which in its turn is dependent on the prosperity of the sulṭān. His prosperity, after Allah's blessing, depends upon righteousness and clear understanding.[1]

The moral tone of Ibn Qutayba's work is orthodox and formal except, at rare intervals, for a flash of sincerity such as that quoted above. His attitude, which is illustrative of that of most writers on *adab*, is shown by his comment on the prohibition of something which to the eye appears pleasant: "We should not have been forbidden it if there had not been in it something [to make the prohibition necessary]."[2]

The general result of the constant repetition of moralizing sentiments is that the most notable of them are as well known in Islam as in other communities. Juwaynī, the recorder of Mongol history, speaking of the "Nom" of the Buddhists, says that they have in it "goodly counsels corresponding to the doctrines and beliefs of *all* prophets. Amongst them are such that exhort man to guard himself against committing wrong, doing harm and the like, and bidding him to requite evil with good and avoid cruelty to animals."[3]

The extent to which the moral behests of a religious code are carried out by its adherents cannot be determined with any degree of accuracy. The ideals of the learned would appear to be seldom approached, and writers such as Shaykh Sa'dī of Shīrāz have caught the popular fancy because they pitch their ethical requirement at a lower level than those of the best part of the *fiqh*. Sa'dī's counsels indeed are based on expediency rather than on true morality. To him a lie which brings peace and profit is better than a truth which stirs up strife; a king is always in the right and must be told so, for to oppose him is to take one's life in one's hands. So also it is wise to keep on amicable terms with your friends, but not to entrust them with all your confidences. It may be that some day their friendship for you may cease and they will use their knowledge against you. To return good for evil is folly and to be merciful to the wicked is to wrong the good. When your enemy

[1] *Op. cit.* p. 5. [2] *Ibid.* p. 394.
[3] *Ta'rīkh-i Jahān-Gushā* (Gibb Series XVI), I, 44.

is at your mercy, take advantage of the opportunity. To pardon the oppressor is to do injury to the oppressed. On the other hand, loyalty to friends, gratitude to benefactors and kindness and consideration to subordinates, contentment and sincerity are the virtues which Sa'dī esteems and which he preaches with all the eloquence at his command. Like all the orthodox teachers, he is caught in a dilemma when he speaks of the reward and punishment for men's actions, since there is much which he must attribute to Fate, which is inexorable and incomprehensible, and the decisions of which are inevitable and not to be questioned.

A point of view similar to that of Sa'dī is to be found in the collection of fables ascribed to Luqmān the Sage, and many of which correspond to the fables of Æsop. Their Muslim editor has provided each with a moral in which it is rare to find any influence of the *fiqh*. In these fables of Luqmān it is not Paradise but the present life that is worth living, even if it be accompanied by hardship and poverty.[1] Death ends all joy. Expedient cunning and deceit have their immediate reward, and righteousness is an ideal, beyond the reach of most of mankind. Most men, indeed, are slothful when they hear the voice of duty, but their ears are keen for the sounds of pleasure. There is in many of the stories an element of despair, indicating a doubt concerning the value of goodness. In any event the good man cannot improve the wicked man, but may himself be spoiled by contact with him, and to do him a kindness is merely to increase his wickedness.

The rare Muslim critics of Islam share with its equally rare social satirists in representing that the state of morals amongst most adherents of the faith falls short of the ideals of the *shar'*. One such critic, the blind poet Abu 'l-'Alā (d. 1058) of Ma'arra, in Syria, indeed boldy denied that obedience to the *shar'*, or to any form of religion, implies real morality. True religion, he says, is to accord justice to all men without distinction and to pay every man what is due to him.[2] "You call yourself pious," he gibes in one of his epigrams, "but I swear by God you have no religion if you go to the holy house and yet give some miserable underling

[1] Cf. *Locmani Fabulae*, ed. A. Roediger (Halle, 1839).

[2] A. von Kremer, "Die philosophische Gedichte des Abu 'l-'Alā", in *Sitzungsberichte der Kaiserlichen Akademie der Wissenschaften zu Wien* (*Phil.-hist. Kl.*), CXVII, 27.

of yours cause for complaint against you."[1] In another epigram he calls down divine blessings upon any man who refrains from injuring him, even if that man should "read the book of Moses or conceive in his heart a devotion to Isaiah".[2] Virtue for him lies not in fasting nor any office of worship, nor in wearing rough garments of wool such as the Ṣūfīs used, but in renouncing and casting away evil and sweeping the breast clear of malice and envy.[3]

To protect himself from charges of heresy he is not averse on occasion from advocating conformity to the external practices of the faith, but he insists that they must be accompanied by ethical conduct in ordinary life. "When men worship," he says, "do you worship also; and pay the alms-tax, but keep free from vain gossip. Sharpen no knife to slaughter any beast therewith for flesh, nor draw sword against your fellow-man."[4]

Generally, however, for him as for the philosophers, reason was the source of right knowledge and then of right action.[5] It is the mind that acquires virtue and is able to defeat the inclination to evil, which is inborn in man.[6] Yet he places conscience above reason. "If in the mirror of your reason you see something different from that which your conscience shows you, then it is wrong."[7] Like other moralists he teaches men to do to others what they would desire done to themselves, and to let others hear what they would themselves choose to hear. But he protests that good must be sought for its own sake, and that it is no true morality to expect a reward for doing good. Any other conduct is mere trafficking in good deeds.[8]

For Abu 'l-'Alā life is weariness and men are evil by nature. It is better, therefore, to withdraw oneself from the world and to refrain from procreation, for that is to impose upon others an unnecessary burden.[9] But if men must live together and satisfy their natural impulses, let them work and earn their own

1 Cf. R. A. Nicholson, *Studies in Islamic Poetry*, p. 190, no. 300.
2 *Ibid.* p. 196, no. 309.
3 *Ibid.* p. 198, no. 312.
4 Von Kremer, *art. cit.* p. 33.
5 Cf. Nicholson, *op. cit.* pp. 142 f., 197.
6 *Ibid.* p. 153 n. 1, p. 198, no. 313; von Kremer, *art. cit.* p. 27.
7 Von Kremer, p. 30; cf. Nicholson, *op. cit.* p. 178, no. 311.
8 Von Kremer, *art. cit.* p. 34.
9 Nicholson, *op. cit.* p. 139.

livelihood, expecting no untroubled life and doing good whenever it is possible without hope of reward, except it be that of God.[1] Above all, God will on the Day of Reckoning pardon the women who, when other means of livelihood fail, will work at their spindles, earning by them what will sustain life. Patience grows stout and strong in lean days, and such women as these will give away in charity what they earn with their sewing. They will go out into the burning rays of the sun and give away to the poor and the hungry the food they need. They that do this will have achieved the highest degree of virtue.[2]

Above all in life Abu 'l-'Alā places kindness to living creatures, and would appear in this respect to have come under Indian (Jain) influence. Whatever the truth of that may be, he adopted as a result of his creed the most absolute form of vegetarianism, refusing to eat not alone meat and fish, but milk, eggs and honey. On the same grounds he prohibited the use of animal skins and furs for clothing, and recommended the wearing of wooden shoes.[3]

The Persian satirist 'Ubayd-i Zākānī, writing in 1340, takes Abu'l-'Alā's main thesis as a commonplace. The old theory, he says, was that the good and generous man might be of any religion, and that it was better to combine unbelief and a noble spirit than Islam and a bad character.[4] Moreover, the old philosophers held that wisdom, courage, temperance and justice were virtues to strive after, since they procure the happiness of this world and Paradise hereafter. But all that, he ironically remarks, has been changed. The moderns do not believe in the eternity of the soul. Life is a matter of this world; once the body is destroyed man is annihilated for ever. Therefore eat, drink and be merry.[5] Further, the products of the three faculties of reason, temper and appetite have also, according to the "moderns", assumed a different aspect since olden days. That kind of courage which leads a man to take up arms against danger and terror, ends, they say, either in the shedding of innocent blood or in suicide and the torments of hell.[6] In the old days the honourable man was he who restrained his eyes from seeing what was unlawful to him, his ears from

[1] Von Kremer, *art. cit.* p. 34.
[2] Von Kremer, in *Z.D.M.G.*, XXXVIII, 515, no. xxii.
[3] Nicholson, *op. cit.* pp. 134–7.
[4] *Laṭā'if* (Kāviānī edition, Berlin, A.H. 1343), p. 14.
[5] *Op. cit.* p. 20.
[6] *Op. cit.* p. 26.

hearing slander, his hands from grasping the property of others, his tongue from speaking vileness, and his lower soul from desiring unworthy objects. Such a man was held in esteem. "My contemporaries hold", says 'Ubayd, "that their predecessors were utterly mistaken in this matter, and spent their days in folly and ignorance without deriving any pleasure from life." The moderns knew better. They interpreted in their own way the verse of the Koran which says: "This world's life is only a sport and pastime and show, and a cause of vainglory among you; and the multiplying of riches and children, etc. . . . "[1] They declared that sport and pleasure could only be enjoyed through means forbidden by the law, and no wealth acquired without inflicting trouble and injustice upon others. He, therefore, who is temperate and honourable in his conduct cannot be regarded as being amongst existing creatures, for he lives a life of futility.[2] In this strain the author continues to let his satire play around those who advocate a disregard for the dictates of morality.

Direct observation of the life lived by Muslims today appears to show that the ideals of their faith have affected their conduct in some ways and not in others. In general it may be said that men who combine true piety with a tolerably high standard of morals are as frequently to be found amongst Muslims as amongst men of other faiths. The *shar'* itself is observed to the extent that in most lands of Islam there is little drinking of intoxicating liquors, and that public opinion strongly condemns indulgence in them. The use of drugs such as opium is more common, for although from the nature of it it is an indulgence not frequently to be observed, there is a flourishing trade in opium and hashish which is openly carried on.[3] The attitude towards sexual morality, is, as seen above, different from that normally prevalent in the west, yet judged by the standards of Islam itself there is much sexual irregularity, the remains of ancient custom, which arouses no popular comment but is strongly deprecated by the authorities of the faith. It is universally regarded as dishonourable to seduce innocent women or girls, and also prostitution and consorting with prostitutes are considered contemptible. In matters commercial,

[1] 57^{19}.
[2] *Op. cit.* pp. 26 ff.
[3] It must be remembered that in Muslim lands scientific means of relieving pain are still rare.

individual character plays a part, but Koranic teaching condemning unlawful gain has had its effect. In some lands also, as in Pakistan, there is still considerable hesitation concerning the taking of interest, although more frequently only the letter of the law is honoured. In general, great stress is laid on truth-telling, but Islam, it has been seen, has left the matter of telling the truth to the individual conscience.

In one particular, that of the vendetta, Muhammad's attempts at reform appear to have failed. Except where it is checked by European control, the blood-feud is active and frequently leads to murder. On the other hand, in the respect of the law of retaliation, actual practice is more humane than the law. The taking of an eye for an eye can never have been literally carried out, and the provisions made by the *fiqh* for monetary compensation in lieu of the exaction of a *talio* has probably obviated much unnatural cruelty.

CHAPTER VI

USAGE, CUSTOM AND SECULAR LAW UNDER ISLAM

The theory of Islam, as there has been occasion to indicate, regards the empire of Islam as a theocracy, in which Allah as supreme ruler is also the only true law-giver. Muhammad the Prophet was the agent through whom believers were made aware of the divine laws, which were explicitly or implicitly embodied in the Koran and his (the Prophet's) *sunna*—the sum total of his ordinary doings and sayings. Upon them in turn the *shar*ʿ or *sharīʿa* is, by hypothesis, founded. The Koran by itself was never after the death of Muhammad, who was its best interpreter, adequate as a code of laws, and even when "tradition" was pressed into service the temporal rulers of Islam's new possessions were thrown upon their own resources whenever a new political or administrative difficulty demanded solution. The ways open to them were either to make fresh regulations as reason or expediency dictated or else merely to continue local custom without questioning too closely whether it conflicted with Islam.

It has been noted above that except for a few striking reforms affecting sexual relationships and the position of women, Muhammad the Prophet had himself interfered little with the principles of the social system of his environment. For the tribe he substituted the Muslim community, but in essence his regulations continued to be applicable to the tribal mode of life. They were based in the main on the customs of his own tribe of the Quraysh and were imposed upon other peoples and communities possessing habits and social laws as firmly established as those of the Prophet's own clan. In many instances the older system would not be displaced by the newer one, or at any rate a considerable part of the older system survived and played its part in the life of the people equally with Islam.

Following the period of conquest and disturbance in which the general character of the *fiqh* was established, there came a time of theorizing and formulation during which the legists devoted themselves to the elaboration of laws by logical or speculative methods from the "sources". It was then that the *madhhabs* arose. Local requirements and the personal predilections of the legists led to the differences between them, but in essentials the codes tallied. From their nature, however, many of the rules elaborated had little of a practical nature about them and had small contact with the ordinary lives of believers, who nevertheless regarded them as the pattern of ideal conduct, seeing that in essence they were the laws of Allah. When, therefore, the requirements of the *fiqh* could be fulfilled without undue disturbance to everyday requirements they were carried out, even at the cost of considerable effort and expense, so that believers have in general worshipped, fasted, given alms and made the pilgrimage to Mecca.

Yet the law has in numerous places been overridden by traditional usages. It is well established further that in many tribal and other communities in Islam there are native codes of unwritten laws and traditions by which the members have continued to regulate their lives, and this in spite of a thrice-repeated declaration in the Koran[1] that those who do not determine their disputes in accordance with Allah's revelation are misbelievers and wrong-doers. Thus in southern Palestine there existed as late as the middle of the nineteenth century, a *fellāḥ* code which was called *sharī'at Khalīl*, i.e. "the law of Abraham", as distinct from the Muhammadan *sharī'a* or *shar'*.[2] Amongst the Bedouin of Arabia also there have always existed, as distinct from the qāḍīs of the *sharī'a*, special judges possessed of the customary lore of their tribe, to which recourse is had in all matters affecting tribal interests.[3] And examples could be multiplied.

In special particulars the tribal law may differ widely from the *shar'*. The important instance of the vendetta may be quoted as showing how Muhammad's regulations failed to displace established custom, for the Koran[4] declares that no Muslim, under penalty of everlasting torment in Hell, may slay another who is innocent of offence. Yet to this day the exaction of blood-revenge remains an important part of tribal life. In another instance, that of

[1] 5[48, 49, 51].

[2] *Palestine Exploration Fund, Quarterly Statement*, January 1879, p. 38.

[3] Cf. J. L. Burckhardt, *Notes on the Bedouins and Wahabys* (London, 1831), I, 120–2; A. Musil, *Arabia Petraea* (Vienna, 1908), III, 209, 337 f., 346, 365.

[4] 4[94] f.

theft, it has been no offence amongst numerous tribes of Arabia, and may even have been regarded as a mark of prowess, to steal horses or other property from those with whom the thief has not broken bread.[1]

Where family life is concerned, in marriage, divorce and the distribution of inheritance, the provisions of the *shar'* would appear to be very widely neglected. This is strikingly apparent amongst the numerous peoples living south of the Himalayas who profess Islam but nevertheless cling to indigenous social practices which are indistinguishable from those of neighbouring non-Muslim peoples. Despite the *shar'*, which counts Hindus amongst idolators and their women therefore unlawful believers, inter-marriage between them and Muslims is common; Hindu women being taken in marriage by men declaring themselves Muhammadans,[2] and, more remarkably, Muslim women marrying Sikhs,[3] although the *shar'* definitely forbids the marriage of believing women to unbelievers. On the other hand, the remarriage of widows, to which Islam takes no exception—indeed, the example of the Prophet encourages it, for his first wife was the widow Khadīja—is deprecated by certain Muhammadan sects of Hindu origin.[4] Under the influence of Hinduism similarly, divorce is, amongst some Muslim communities in India, an occurrence of considerable rarity.[5]

In the remoter districts of Indonesia, not completely Islamized, a man could not take a second wife without the consent of the first, who frequently gave it because in spite of the *shar'* the second wife was by local custom subordinate to her.[6]

Closely bound up with the topic of marriage is that of property.

[1] Cf. Burckhardt, *op. cit.* I, 325; A. H. Layard, *Nineveh and Babylon* (London, 1853), p. 296; Musil, *op. cit* III, 347. Elsewhere amongst tribal communities theft may be considered the worst of crimes and the thief be universally despised. Cf. J. W. Crowfoot, "Customs of the Rubāṭab", *Sudan Notes*, I, 121.

[2] C. L. Tupper, *Punjab Customary Law* (Calcutta, 1881), II, 122. The explanation offered is that the women are technically Muslims, having become converts immediately before marriage.

[3] *Ibid.* II, 195.

[4] Sir H. H. Risley, *People of India* (Calcutta, 1915), p. 214; Tupper, *op. cit.* IV, 48. For local reasons also, the remarriage of widows is rare in Morocco. Cf. Übach and Rakow, *Sitte und Recht in Nordafrika*, p. 44.

[5] Tupper, *op. cit.* II, 124, 130.

[6] Jan Prins, "Adatlaw and Muslim Religious Law in Modern Indonesia", *Die Welt des Islams*, n.s. I (1951), pp. 283 ff.)

In India, in the Gurgaon district of the Punjab, certain Muhammadan tribes follow a rule prevalent amongst Hindu tribes which demands that a woman must marry out of her own *got*, or clan, into another, to which thereafter she and her children belong. By the same rule, which rigidly decrees that property may not leave the *got*, she and her children will have no right to inherit her father's property, their rights of inheritance being confined to the property of the husband's family.[1] This practice may be paralleled by the Minangkabau custom of Malaya, which forbids marriage between persons of the same *suku*, descendants of the same women through the female line. Children too do not inherit from their father.[2] The capacity to contract marriage, which is almost invariably monogamous, is limited rigidly by the laws of exogamy, and all questions of property are governed by the matriarchial rule. During married life, property acquired belongs jointly to the pair. On the death of the man, his personal estate goes to the nearest female relatives on the mother's side, the rest of the property remaining with the widow and going, after her, to the issue. Both male and female children inherit portions of this, but custom strictly defines what kind of property may go to each sex.[3] Among the Tuaregs of the Sahara also, children belong to their mother's kin and inherit from them rather than from the father's side.[4]

A peculiar system of inheritance prevails amongst the tribes of the Qara mountains in southern Arabia. Here a man's widows take one-tenth of his estate. If one of them should have a daughter or three daughters and no son they would appear to inherit, to the exclusion of the deceased's male kin. This rule does not hold, however, if there are two daughters and no son.[5]

In most lands of Islam it is the exception rather than the rule for daughters to inherit, in spite of Koranic prescription. Accounts

[1] Tupper, *op. cit.* II, 145. The Māpillas (Moplas) of North Malabar follow the Marummakatháyam system of inheritance, which makes property heritable only through the female line. Cf. *Census of India* (1911) *Report*, XII, 171.

[2] Snouck Hurgronje, *The Achehnese*, tr. A. W. S. O'Sullivan (Leyden and London, 1906), II, 316. Cf. G. A. de C. de Moubray, *Matriarchy in the Malay Peninsula* (London, 1931) *passim*.

[3] E. N. Taylor, "The Customary Law of Rembau", in *Journal of the Malayan Branch, Royal Asiatic Society* (1929), pp. 16 f., 26.

[4] F. R. Rodd, *The People of the Veil*, pp. 148 ff.

[5] Bertram Thomas, *Arabia Felix* (London, 1932), pp. 56 f.

of the customary laws prevalent amongst the communities of Pakistan and Muslim India show that where there are sons or sons' sons, female children, and often both parents too, are excluded from succession to property, particularly if it consists of land or other immovable possessions. In the Sirsa district of the Punjab, the widow gets a life interest in the whole estate if there are no sons, but even then daughters and sons' daughters get no share, being excluded by agnates.[1] In the Gurgaon, Sialkot and other districts of the Punjab, in general, if there is both male and female issue, the sons alone inherit,[2] although sometimes the daughters are excluded from inheritance of land only and take what their father may have set aside for them as a marriage portion. Where there are no lineal descendants of the male sex, the widow inherits in preference to all others. Even there custom may differ and the widow, as amongst certain Baluch families, receives only maintenance for life.[3]

It has already been noted above[4] that this exclusion of daughters from inheritance is as prevalent in Palestine and North Africa as it is in India. In general it may be said that the *shar'ī* laws of inheritance, which are based upon the rules of tribes owning easily divisible property consisting of flocks and herds and movables of other kinds, cannot be successfully applied amongst peoples whose property is chiefly or partly in land. Such laws therefore are commonly disregarded, so that in the sub-continent of India, for example, it is seldom that a qāḍī is called upon, should there be any dispute, to determine "shares" in accordance with the *shar'*. Outside India it is not unknown, e.g. amongst the Rubāṭab tribe of the Sudan, for the inheritance not to be divided at all but to be held by all the heirs jointly.[5] There are places also where the *fiqh* is disregarded in other respects. Thus, although theoretically by the *shar'* all sons inherit equally, whether born of free women or slaves, it is the custom amongst the Rajput Muslims in the Gurgaon district of the Punjab that the sons of a slave-girl, even if legitimately married to the father, do not inherit.[6]

Irregular unions of the kind regarded by the *shar'* as unlawful,

[1] Tupper, *op. cit.* IV, 59. [2] *Ibid.* pp. 137, 204, 218, 221, etc.

[3] *Ibid.* II, 142.

[4] Cf. T. Canaan, "Unwritten Laws affecting the Arab Women of Palestine", *Journal of the Palestine Oriental Society*, XI (1931), 194.

[5] J. W. Crowfoot, in *Sudan Notes*, I, 121. [6] Tupper, *op. cit.* II, 161.

have, in various parts of Islam and at different times, been permitted by local custom. Thus the *mut'a* marriage, discountenanced by the Caliph Omar, has generally been regarded as forbidden to Sunnīs, although it is practised amongst the Shī'a. Yet in recent times it has been unofficially acknowledged as valid by certain Sunnīs in the sacred city of Mecca itself.[1] Even the prohibition against the marriage of two sisters together has not always been obeyed. A certain Mu'tamid al-Dawla Qirwāsh, at one time lord of Mosul, disregarded the law in this respect, and when he was told of this replied: "What then is there which we do that the *sharī'a* allows?"[2] In Arabia up to the time of the Wahhābīs, a husband of the 'Asīr tribe might lend his wife to an honoured guest, and there was a time when a man might enter into a partnership of conjugal rights with another man in return for his services as a shepherd.[3] There is evidence for believing that, in one of the lesser and obscurer tribes living in Baluchistān, until recently a host might provide an unmarried, but nubile, girl for the better entertainment of a guest.[4]

On the general question of the observance of the written laws of Islam, a competent observer compiled in tabular form a statement of the extent to which the public conscience in a particular region of India (the United Provinces) disagreed with the *shar'* in its estimate of a number of acts unlawful and lawful. Eating pork was entirely sinful according to both the *shar'* and the public conscience. The consumption of wine or spirits, on the other hand, though unlawful by the *shar'*, was not regarded as seriously sinful by the upper classes, but was a comparatively grave offence in the eyes of the other classes. Bazaar immorality although legally sinful, was a venial offence to the majority. On the other hand, divorce, permitted by the *shar'*, was regarded as "a beastly act". The reason given was that "people are often married among their own relations. A wife who is divorced brings the greatest possible shame on all her people who happen to be also the people of her husband."[5]

1 S. Hurgronje, *Mekka*, II, 156.

2 Ibn al-Athīr, A.H. 444.

3 Robertson Smith, *Kinship and Marriage*, pp. 139 f.

4 Sir Denys Bray, *Census of India* (1911) Report, IV, 104 f.

5 Sir R. Burn, *Census of India* (1901) Report, XVI, 104. For further references cf. Indian Census Reports generally and *Revue des Études Islamiques* (Paris,

In the following pages further evidence is collected from other parts of the various regions of Islam of the manner in which the provisions of the *fiqh* have been disregarded, in some respects through indolence but mainly by reason of the retention of ancient practices or by the development of customs arising from changing circumstances.

The unwritten laws of such local custom and practice are known collectively as '*Urf* ("What is commonly known and accepted")[1] or '*Āda* ("Custom"). They have generally been the produce of long-standing convention, either deliberately adopted or the result of unconscious adaptation to circumstances, and they have therefore been followed where practical considerations have been uppermost. There have not been lacking attempts to regard '*urf* as one of the "roots" of the *fiqh*,[2] but except in the works of the early Sunnī *mujtahids* the customary laws have generally gone unrecorded by the legists. Yet they have not gone unrecognized, for by some *faqīhs* they were preferred to laws derived by means of *qiyās* ("analogy" or "reason") and where local influences have been strong, custom has frequently been held to be decisive.[3]

Of '*urf* amongst the nomad populations of the Islamic world, amongst whom ancient tradition rules strongly, it is difficult to speak in general terms, for customs differ from tribe to tribe and there is a vagueness about them as well as a liability to sudden modification which prevents even trained observers from setting them down with certainty. Yet there are undoubtedly codes and standards apart from the *shar*' to which application is made in case of necessity. Such tribal laws, in territories subject to European domination, are called '*urfī*, in contradistinction to the civil laws of the state, and are generally recognized as valid for local cases except when there is serious contravention of the civil law, as, for example, where a feud would lead to manslaughter. In Wahhābī Arabia, tribal laws, if contrary to the rigid Islamic code followed by the rulers, are stigmatized as *ṭaghūt*,[4] i.e. "mistaken

1927). Sir Denys Bray pointed out that the catalogue of acts lawful and unlawful was wholly inappropriate to (other Muslims of India, e.g.) the Pathans of the Frontier Province.

[1] It may mean also "common sense", and is only equivalent to "custom" when synonymous with '*Āda*.

[2] For references see Goldziher, *Zahiriten*, p. 204.

[3] *Ibid.* p. 205.

[4] H. St J. Philby, *The Heart of Arabia* (London, 1922), I, 26.

conduct", a term applied to the ungodly ways of the *Jāhilīya*. How far the characterization is true and in what way tribal ways contravene the *shar'* must for the present remain uncertain for lack of investigation. The repository of such traditional laws in each tribe is the shaykh, or sometimes, as indicated above, a body of specially elected elders who act as judges when cases arise and whose decision is respected when those of the civil courts might not be.[1]

On the question of how far the *sharī'a* is deliberately neglected a great deal of investigation remains to be done. Clearly it is sometimes impossible to fulfil its behests. The Egyptian *fellāḥ*, the Anatolian peasant and the Javanese cultivator can seldom be able, however much inclined, to break off their work in order to perform five times a day the ceremonies of worship, with all the lustrations prescribed as being essential to ritual purity. At other times the failure to carry out the law must be ascribed to indifference: Kurds, town-bred Turks, Egyptians and Indians of European training are notoriously careless of the ritual of worship. But the fast of Ramaḍān would appear to have acquired a special importance, and even though the vagaries of the Muslim calendar[2] may cause the fast to occur in the height of the hot weather and so bring special hardship, failure to observe this fast publicly is rare, particularly among the poor, upon whom it must fall with the greatest severity.

In the matter of payment of *zakāt*, it ceased to be possible to carry out the terms of the *fiqh* once the community passed outside the control of an individual ruler who would be responsible for collection of the tax and make the right use of the proceeds.[3] The regulations governing the amounts payable can scarcely ever have been applied literally once large fortunes began to accrue, as they did in the hands of nobles and merchants at Damascus, Baghdad and other capital cities in Islam, as well as with important tribal chiefs. The great amounts that would have been involved can scarcely ever have been collected, or the sums actually taken

1 See further: F. Schwally, "Beiträge zur Kenntnis des Lebens der mohammedanischen Städter Fellachen und Beduinen im heutigen Ägypten", *Sitzungsberichte d. Heidelberger Akad. d. Wiss., Phil.-hist. Kl.* (1912, pp. 34 f.), and A. Kennett, *Bedouin Justice*, p. 63 and *passim*.

2 It consists of twelve lunar months, as required by the Koran (9[86]).

3 See above, pp. 159 f.

applied wholly to those pious purposes which the Koran sets out, namely: maintenance of the poor, the orphan and the wayfarer. Other taxes, legal or illegal,[1] were levied and large fines extorted by Caliphs and sulṭāns from their wealthier nobles, who in turn squeezed the peasantry for any sums they could wring out. Wealth so gained was not used for charitable object. Nevertheless the law holds in spirit, and the pious Muslim regards the giving of charity as compulsory[2] upon him as leading to felicity hereafter.

The fourth main duty of the Muslim as set down in the Koran, namely the *ḥajj*, the pilgrimage to Mecca, is in the majority of the lands of Islam regarded as of outstanding importance and incumbent on every Muslim, male or female, free and of full age who is physically capable of undertaking it.[3] Yet as early as the fourth century of Islam, Abu 'l-'Alā al-Ma'arrī says that to cry *Allāhu Akbar* twice at a certain tomb he mentions containing the bones of two 'Alids is equal in value to some of the ceremonies at the Ka'ba.[4] In Persia and Iraq today a "visit" (*ziyāra*) to the shrines of the imāms at Mashhad, Kerbelā, Najaf and Kāẓimayn, is by the people considered as having a merit not inferior to that of the *ḥajj*, and in south Arabia credulous tribesmen regard three visits to the "Mazār al-Walī", a well-known shrine, as equivalent to the pilgrimage to Mecca.[5] The Zikrīs of Baluchistan also, instead of performing the *ḥajj* go on the ninth day of the pilgrimage month to Koh Murād, a hill in Kech.[6]

The varying stress laid upon requirements of the *sharī'a* by different classes of believers is an indication of the influence of local custom. Both swine's flesh[7] and wine[8] are forbidden to Muslims, yet while the former is regarded with such abhorrence that no believer will approach the carcase of a dead pig, the latter, except amongst the most rigidly orthodox, is regarded with

[1] See on *kharāj*, *jizya* and *mukūs* below, pp. 309 ff.

[2] Shīrāzī, *Tanbīh*, pp. 50 ff.

[3] By the Shāfi'ī rite it is permissible to send a substitute, whose expenses must be paid by the sender (Shīrāzī. *op. cit.* p. 70).

[4] Goldziher, *Muhammedanische Studien*, II, 314.

[5] Bertram Thomas, "Among Some Unknown Tribes of South Arabia", *Journal of the Royal Anthropological Institute*, LIX (1929), 104.

[6] *Census of India* (1911) *Report*, IV, 59.

[7] Koran 5^{4}, 16^{116}, 2^{168}.

[8] 2^{216}, 4^{46}, $5^{92\,f}$. The *fiqh* implies the prohibition by forbidding under penalty of corporal punishment all consumption of intoxicating liquors. Cf. Shīrāzī, *op. cit.* p. 310.

toleration. The *Kitāb al-Aghānī* and the *Arabian Nights* are full of references to drinking and intoxication, generally to the accompaniment of music, which is equally reprobated.[1] In Persia its consumption is common and poets have been loud in its praise, Ḥāfiẓ having even gone to the length of protesting that the drinking of wine was no sin.[2] The practice has always been so ordinary a part of life there that a guide to manners and morals, such as the *Qābūs-nāma*, contains a chapter on the etiquette of wine-drinking (though it must be added that this work was intended in the first place for a young prince), and a whole prose work (the *Ḥalbat al-kumayt*) as well as the "wine songs" (*Khamrīyāt*) of Abu Nuwās are, in Arabic literature, devoted to the art of toping.

So far we have dealt with the extent to which obedience is given to the Koranic behests which are *farḍ* or *wājib*, i.e. incumbent as a bounden duty on all Muslims. They concern ceremonies and duties that distinguish the believer from the infidel, forming the outward tokens of adherence to Islam. Yet one of the most important of all rites in Muhammadanism is that of circumcision (*khitān* or *ṭahāra*), which is not mentioned in the Koran at all. It was practised by the Arabs of the *Jāhilīya* and adopted without question by Muhammad, and though the "schools" differ as to whether it is indispensable—the Shāfi'ites call it *wājib*[3] and its neglect punishable, while Mālikīs regard it as no more than *sunna*, i.e. as commendable[4]—Muslims, with a few doubtful exceptions, in practice regard it as an essential of the faith. The exceptions would seem to base their neglect on the lack of a positive ordinance in the Koran. Thus the pious Caliph Omar II is said to have declared that circumcision was not demanded from converts, for "Allah sent Muhammad to summon men [to Islam] and not to circumcise".[5] In Asia Minor, amongst the Yuruk tribes, whose

[1] Cf. E. W. Lane, *The Arabian Nights' Entertainment* (London, 1841), I, 214 ff., 242.

[2] Rosenzweig-Schwannau, *Dīwān* I, 270: "What matter if I and you should quaff a cup or two of wine? Wine is the grape's blood, not yours. This is not a fault from which comes aught of harm. And if it be a fault; what then? Where will you find a man without a fault?"

[3] Cf. Shīrāzī, *Tanbīh*, p. 3.

[4] Cf. Khalīl ibn Isḥāq, *Mukhtaṣar*, tr. Guidi (Milan, 1919), I, 339. The Zaydīs similarly regard the rite as *sunna* and class it with a number of "recommended" toilet practices. (Zayd ibn 'Alī, *Majmū'*, ed. E. Griffini (Milan, 1919), p. 298.)

[5] Ṭabarī, II, 1354. See p. 23, *supra*.

religion is a heterodox form of Islam, circumcision is not infrequently omitted, as also amongst the Qizilbāsh in the Hermus valley. These latter, like the nomad Qizilbāsh, do not conform to orthodox Muhammadan custom in the details of veiling women, polygamy, abstention from wine and worship in the mosque. They fast twelve days in the Spring, and their women are called by Christian names.[1] In Gujarāt, in Western India, the Shī'a Momnas of Cutch do not practise the rite of circumcision.[2] In the Chinese province of Yun-nan it is intermittently practised[3] and amongst several Berber tribes it is reputed not to have been introduced.[4] Normally it is justified by *faqīhs* as being part of the religion of Muhammad or of the natural primitive religion (*fiṭra*) into which a man is born.[5] By some it is regarded as being one of the rites of the religion of Abraham, which agreed with Islam,[6] and since he is known from the Scriptures to have been circumcised, the good Muslim also should be so. In pre-Islamic Arabia some tribes circumcised their women. The custom, of which official Islam says nothing, is still widespread, being found in Islamic lands from India to Morocco.[7]

Another non-Koranic regulation of some importance concerns images and paintings. There is no prohibition of them in the Koran and the evidence appears to be that painting, at any rate, was not rigorously condemned in the earliest period of Islam.[8] Images of living beings would appear to have been in a different category, although the Koran concerns itself only indirectly with idolatry, which might have provided a reason for prohibition. At a later stage in the history of the faith, the influence of the learned, stimulated perhaps by memory of the Old Testament,[9] led to the

1 F. W. Hasluck, *Christianity and Islam under the Sultans* (Oxford, 1929), I, 130, 143, 152.

2 *Census of India* (1911) *Report*, VII, 59.

3 G. D'Ollone, *Recherches sur les Musulmans chinois* (Paris, 1911), p. 9.

4 G. Rohlfs, *Adventures in Morocco* (London, 1874), p. 75.

5 Bukhārī, *Ṣaḥīḥ*, 77^{63}, 79^{51}.

6 Cf. Koran 4^{124}.

7 Robertson Smith, *Kinship* (London, 1903), p. 76 n.; A. Musil, *Arabia Petraea* (Wien, 1908), III, 219; J. A. Jaussen, *Coutumes palestiniennes* (Paris, 1927), pp. 40 f.; *Census of India* (1911) *Report*, IV, 61; J. S. Trimingham, *Islam in the Sudan* (Oxford, 1949).

8 See further, Snouck Hurgronje, "Ḳuṣejr 'Amra und das Bilderverbot", *Z.D.M.G.*, LXI (1907), 186 ff.; and Lammens in *Journal Asiatique*, XIe série, VI (1915), 239–79.

9 According to Sir T. W. Arnold, *Painting in Islam* (Oxford, 1928), p. 159, it was Jewish converts to Islam who were responsible for the ban on representation.

disapproval of all representation of living things, and "traditions" were invented to lend force to the doctrine of prohibition. Thus the Prophet is credited with having said that the angels will not enter a house in which there is a dog or an image[1] and that the worst punishment on the Day of Resurrection will be that meted out to painters.[2] This latter tradition was reported by a man who entered a friend's house and saw pictures on his cushion (*ṣuffa*). The ultimate reason of the prohibition would appear to be that Allah is the only "creator" or "fashioner", so that the *ḥadīth* implies that all human "fashioners" are imitators of Allah and therefore guilty of pretending to divine qualities.[3]

In spite of the very clear official discouragement of representational art, for centuries there was considerable patronage of it by men who could afford such luxuries in the Caliphate and the succession provinces, more especially Persia and in India. In Mesopotamia and Persia frescoes were common on the walls of public baths and would appear by some legists to have been tolerated there, as also in carpets and cushions made to be put on the floor and either trodden or sat upon, though pictures and rugs made to be hung on walls in private houses were forbidden.[4] Photographs were for long under the same ban, but they are now almost everywhere in Islam tolerated as mere "reflections". In Egypt the statues of Muhammad 'Alī in Alexandria and of Ibrahīm Pasha in Cairo have long been accepted, while in Persia there are statues of Firdawsī in Tehran, of Avicenna in Hamadan and of Riẓā Shāh Pehlevī in the capital and other large cities. In recent times there has even been produced an illustrated copy of the Koran.[5] It was, however, meant for non-Muslim tourists, part of the text having been removed.[6]

[1] Bukhārī, *Saḥīḥ, Kitāb al-Libās*, ed. Krehl, IV, 104 (ch. 77, no. 88).

[2] "Painters" in this connection has been interpreted as meaning "idol-makers". Cf. A. Enani, "Beurteilung der Bilderfrage im Islam nach der Ansicht eines Muslim", *Mitteilungen des Seminars für Orientalische Sprachen*, XXII, (1919), p. 21.

[3] Cf. Bukhārī, ed. Krehl, II, 41, *Kitāb al-Buyū'* 104: "He that fashions an image, Allāh will punish him by making him breathe into it the spirit [of life] a task in which he will never be successful."

[4] Cf. Shīrāzī, *Tanbīh*, p. 206.

[5] A paper on the subject was read by R. Gottheil at the Congress of Orientalists at Leyden, 1931.

[6] Cf. *Revue des Études Islamiques* (1931), pp. 21 ff.

Both the Koran and the actually observed *sunna* of the Prophet were obsolescent as a guide to practical life within thirty years after his death, by which time there remained no survivor amongst his companions. Since then, Muslims like the Wahhābīs and Sunūsīs, who have declared themselves adherents of the Koran and *sunna* alone, have been regarded by others of the faith as schismatics and heretics, suffering thus a fate similar to that which befell the Samaritans and the Qara'ites in Judaism and the Puritans in Christianity. Furthermore, since the great mass of the *fiqh* is elaborated on theoretical principles from the Koran and the *sunna*, the necessity arose almost from the beginning for rules to meet actual situations. Ancient custom, economic and political conditions, contact with non-Muslim peoples and the penetration of alien thought had their effect in making the *sharī'a* an ideal only possible of achievement when the Mahdī, the forerunner of the Resurrection, comes to bring righteousness upon earth.[1]

A telling example of adaptation to circumstances is that of the *jihād*. The combating of unbelievers by the *jihād* is a duty of the community as a whole, and the *fiqh* declares that the imām is to muster men and horses and to decide which of them are fit to enter hostile territory. He is to begin with the nearest unbelievers and the most important of them. Also he is to fight Jews, Christians and Magians until they accept Islam or pay tribute. Others are to be fought, without conditions, until they become Muslims.[2] It is clear that these laws have for some time been in abeyance, for although it is true that where the Muslims are weak, attack may be delayed,[3] yet even when they have been in the majority they have not in recent times fulfilled the command.

Practical disregard of the *shar'* is particularly noticeable in regard to the treatment to be accorded to *dhimmīs*, "protected" peoples (i.e. those possessing Scriptures, and the Magians), who are to be allowed to live in Muslim territory provided they pay a poll-tax and submit to certain humiliating conditions with regard to dress, housing and possessions, intended to distinguish them from Muslims. No dealings at all are permitted with other unbelievers, idol-worshippers being particularly abhorrent to the law.[4] Yet in India Muhammadans by convention include Hindus

[1] See Sha'rānī, *Mīzān*, tr. Perron, p. 32.
[2] Shīrāzī, *Tanbīh*, pp. 287 ff.
[3] *Ibid.* p. 288, l. 3.
[4] *Ibid.* p. 295.

amongst the *dhimmīs*, although a strict adherent of the faith like the conqueror Maḥmūd of Ghazna regarded them as idolators. It must be added, however, that circumstances have made the entire question of the disabilities of *dhimmīs* in India one of theoretical interest only.

It is in the sphere of trade and commerce that the greatest gap is visible between theory and practice. For example, the *shar'* entirely forbids the sale of certain goods because they are ritually unclean and because the consumption of them is forbidden. Thus (according to the Shāfi'ī code) it is forbidden to sell dogs, pigs, wine, dung or (ritually) unclean olives, though it is lawful to sell an unclean robe.[1] Further it is disapproved (*makrūh*), though lawful, to buy grape-juice from one who has extracted wine, weapons from one who has used them "against Allah" or any goods from a man whose property is illicitly acquired.[2] It is illegal, further, to sell anything for which no use can be found, e.g. vermin, or wild animals not useful for hunting,[3] and it is illegal also to sell things not actually in existence, e.g. the fruit still to be borne by a tree.[4] The completion of any sale, and delivery, must take place within three days of the making and acceptance of the contract.[5] Possession does not lie with the purchaser until the goods have been actually transferred to him, and until the transfer the seller is responsible for the goods sold; if the buyer dies before delivery the sale is void.[6] It is illegal to sell that which cannot be delivered, e.g. birds in flight, a runaway slave, etc., or that which would cause harm in the delivery, e.g. wool from a sheep's back or an ell of stuff out of a garment of which the value would be destroyed by cutting,[7] and the sale is also illegal of any goods of which the exact quantity or description is unknown, e.g. an unmeasured heap of grain, the milk in an udder, an animal in the womb, etc.[8]

There are numerous other restrictions upon commercial transactions, mainly designed to prevent speculation. Thus there are two views about the sale of commodities which the purchaser has not seen, the first being that it is illegal, the second that it is legal if a description of the thing is given and the buyer has the option of purchasing if the goods when he sees them agree with the

[1] Shīrāzī, *Tanbīh*, p. 94. [2] *Ibid.* p. 97. [3] *Ibid.* p. 94. [4] *Ibid.* p. 95.
[5] *Ibid.* p. 93. [6] *Ibid.* p. 94. [7] *Ibid.* [8] *Ibid.* p. 95.

description.[1] A sale made on conditions serving no useful purpose is unlawful, e.g. the sale of an animal on condition that the purchaser rides it, or of a house on condition that the purchaser dwells in it for a month.[2] Conditions in general (except where they are of the essence of the contract, e.g. the sale of a garden on condition that it is kept watered) nullify sales. Thus if one says: "I sell you this slave for ten if you sell me your house for twenty" or "I will sell you this for ten in cash or for twenty if payment is postponed", the contract of sale is void.[3]

It is lawful, however, to sell goods for a profit if the cost price and the amount of profit are disclosed.[4] According to the *fiqh* this applies generally if one commodity is bartered for another; for example, grain for gold. The Koran[5] forbids as a deadly sin all taking of increment (*ribā*, interest or rent) as distinguished from *bay*ʿ, "transfer for equivalents". The commentators, however, limit the prohibition to the taking of interest on, or the making of a charge for the loan of, gold and silver and articles of human consumption[6]; the *ḥadīth* further limiting the latter to wheat, barley, dates and raisins.[7]

These various restrictions upon normal commerce have either been openly disregarded by many Muslims, so that trade has been carried on according to local custom, or have led to the adoption of subterfuges and legal fictions in order that the letter of the law might be observed while transactions went forward as necessity and custom demanded. Thus, to deal first with the question of interest, while many pious Muslims adhere to the law, so that—to take an instance—the unclaimed interest on deposits made by Muhammadans in the Post Office Savings Bank in India amounted to lakhs of rupees,[8] others take what they may get, and the Punjabī Muslim moneylender demands interest like others of his class. If he has a conscience he takes the interest indirectly, in service or in kind, but sooner or later he finds it convenient to take the

[1] Shīrāzī, *Tanbīh*, p. 95. [2] *Ibid.* p. 97. [3] *Ibid.*

[4] *Ibid.* p. 104. [5] 2^{276}, 4^{159}, 30^{38}.

[6] See Shīrāzī, *op. cit.* p. 98, and Bayḍāwī on Koran 2^{276}.

[7] Cf. Goldziher, *Zahiriten*, pp. 41 f. It would appear that the prohibition dates from pre-Islamic times, when abuses were frequent owing to the practice of postponing the date of repayment of a loan in order to exact greater quantities of the commodity lent. (Cf. Bayḍāwī, *loc. cit.*)

[8] M. L. Darling, *Rusticus Loquitur* (Oxford, 1930), p. 368.

cash.[1] A common way of evading the law is for the lender to hand over to his client a sum of money in return for some object of value, such as a house or a horse, which the client then buys back for a sum greater than he has received, the amount of difference representing the interest.[2]

In Egypt, pious Muslims will lend cash to peasants and take payment in grain, or *vice versa* as the season renders advantageous; the conversion rate including the equivalent of one hundred or two hundred per cent. on each transaction. Even Muslim women will lend out their dowry money or the proceeds of their domestic poultry-keeping "without pangs of conscience".[3]

Similar expedients are adopted for other transactions which may be forbidden, or for which no provision is made by the *shar*ʿ. Thus, although the sale of fruit which has not yet appeared on a tree is unlawful, it is permitted to sell the leaves and blossoms and anything that may arise out of them and is dependent on them.[4] The sale of commodities in the mass without weighing or measurement is unlawful, but holds good if a price is specified for each part individually. Thus it is unlawful to sell a heap of grain without weighing, but not if a price is fixed for each unit of weight.[5] The direct sale of an unclean thing such as a dung-heap or a dog may be avoided by a formula which purports merely to transfer the owner's right of user for a consideration, for although the sale is unlawful the owner has a right of possession (*taṣarruf*) or a special interest (*ikhtiṣāṣ*) which may be given to another for value received.[6] The requirement of the *shar*ʿ that a contract must be fulfilled in three days is impracticable in the case of the manufacture of a large number of goods. One of two expedients therefore is adopted for evading it. The first is the making of an advance payment (*salam*), in order to secure an option on the

[1] M. L. Darling, *Rusticus Loquitur* (Oxford, 1930), p. 368. "The duty of every Muslim is to invest in industries. Invest in the shares of the Pan-Islamic . . . Co. Ltd., which offers you a golden opportunity to serve the Nation as well as to earn Dividends." Advertisement in the *Islamic Review* (London), August 1953.

[2] E. Sachau, *Muhammedanisches Recht*, p. 281.

[3] *The Times*, 17 November 1931.

[4] See *The Mejelle* (Ḥanafī Code), tr. C. R. Tyser and others (Nicosia, Cyprus, 1901), p. 26.

[5] *Ibid.* pp. 27 f.

[6] Cf. Sachau, *op. cit.* p. 279 n. 1, and p. 609, n. 1.

goods to be made, which may be rejected if they do not agree with the description.[1] The second is to invoke the clause concerning *istiṣnā'*, the arrangement of a contract with a skilled workman to make an article. In the latter case there is no need either to specify a time for delivery or to pay money in advance.[2]

In most trades and branches of commerce, indeed, use and custom have created their own rules, many of them dating from long before the advent of Muhammad. By them the dealings of individuals with one another are regulated, as also are the relationships of individuals with the community and, frequently, of ruler with subject. It is seldom in a commercial contract that all the details are specified. Much is left to the *bona fides* of the parties and everything customary is regarded as being included.[3]

Even in the realm of religion, local influences are sometimes strong enough to overrule the *fiqh*. This is particularly true where a local object of veneration may be called upon in sanction of a statement. Almost everywhere in Islam there are local saints, whose tombs are, despite the spirit of Islam, regarded with the greatest awe and respect. According to the *fiqh*, oaths invoking the sanction of anyone or anything other than Allah are *makrūh* ("disapproved"), and are not regarded as valid even if the Prophet or the Ka'ba at Mecca be invoked.[4] Yet the most solemn oath that may be taken by many Muhammadans is upon the tomb of a local saint. Thus various (Shāfi'ī) tribes of south Arabia swear by the shrines of their own saints,[5] and the oath most binding upon the (generally Shī'ite) inhabitants of lower Iraq is *bi 'l-Ḥusayn*, i.e. "by the [tomb of] Ḥusayn" at Kerbelā, or *bi 'l-'Alī*, i.e. "by the [tomb of] 'Alī" at Najaf.[6]

Linked with *'āda* and *'urf* as a powerful factor in governing life in Islamic countries has been the arbitrary will of the ruling

[1] Shīrāzī, *Tanbīh*, pp. 107–9. [2] *Mejelle*, p. 53.

[3] C. Hamilton, *Hedaya*, ed. S. G. Grady (London, 1870), p. 496.

[4] Shīrāzī, *Tanbīh*, p. 239.

[5] Bertram Thomas, "Among some Unknown Tribes of South Arabia", *J.R.A.I.* LIX (1929), 104. See also A. Kennett, *Bedouin Justice* (Cambridge, 1925), p. 41.

[6] Instances might be multiplied indefinitely. See further, Goldziher, *Muhammedanische Studien*, II, 275 ff. ("Die Heiligenverehrung in Islam.")

potentate. The fact has long been recognized by *ijmā'*, and although the Prophet never envisaged the event of his death, or in any event left no instructions about a successor, a number of sayings concerning the temporal rulers of Islam have been put into his mouth. Thus he is reported to have said: "There are two classes of my community who are such that if they be upright the people will be upright, and if they do wrong the people will do wrong. These two classes are those of the *amīrs* and the *faqīhs* [legists]."[1] Another tradition has it that Allah deters more people from transgressions through the governing power (*sulṭān*) than through the Koran.[2] All that is implied thereby is that the sulṭān is the agent charged with the duty of enforcing the provisions of the *shar'*. But it is obvious that the temporal rulers of Islam never confined themselves to that duty alone, and their activities included legislation for their own purposes independently of the *shar'*.

Neither *'āda* nor the independent enactments of princes could be recognized as valid by the orthodox doctors of the faith[3] once the position of the "schools" was established. Yet the existence of these secular and unauthorized forms of law and the fact that they had actual importance could not be ignored. Māwardī, who was himself an acknowledged authority on orthodox constitutional theory, as long ago as the fifth century of Islam let fall a hint that *'urf* was at least as well recognized amongst Muslims as the *shar'* itself.[4] Later in the same century, Ghazālī confessed himself compelled to admit that the acts of the secular administration were valid in view of the circumstances of the time.[5] This attitude may be paralleled in modern times from the work of the Moroccan author, Aḥmad ibn Khālid al-Nāṣirī, who, in the course of a history of his native country, quotes with approval the argument of al-Qarāfī on the question

[1] Ghazālī, *Iḥyā* (ed. Cairo, A.H. 1282), I, 6.

[2] Māwardī, *Kitāb Adab al-dunyā wa 'l-dīn* (Stambūl, A.H. 1299), p. 99. Cf. *Tāj al-'Arūs* s.v. *waza'a*.

[3] Even the philosophic mind of Ibn Khaldūn rejected the validity of secular legislation, declaring it to be concerned only with this world, fleeting and vain, whereas the laws of the *shar'* are designed to secure man's welfare both here and hereafter (*Prolégomènes*, ed. Quatremère, I, 342 f.).

[4] *Constitutiones Politicae*, ed. Enger, p. 5.

[5] *Iqtiṣād fī 'l-i'tiqād* (Cairo, A.H. 1327), pp. 98 f.

of regulations based on custom and precedent.[1] The argument is as follows:

If you ask what is the true position of *aḥkām* (government ordinances) acknowledged by the "schools" of Mālik, Shāfi'ī, etc., and based on practices still current, the answer is that the *'ulamā* have made them valid. But supposing that there has been a change in customary practice and that what now prevails is the contrary of what was formerly held, will the jurisconsults' decisions which we find set forth in books now be false, and must we formulate new decisions in accordance with the new practices; or shall we say that we are bound to accept the decisions as they stand, and that we may not innovate in matters of religious law and must therefore rule in accordance with what we find in the books of the *mujtahids* which have been transmitted to us? The answer is, that the enforcement of government ordinances, based on customs which have changed, would be opposed to *ijmā'* and would imply ignorance of the Faith.[2]

In another passage[3] the author admits that it is possible to regard a question of law in the light of reason and political expediency (*siyāsa*) as well as that of *fiqh* and the *shar'ī* law, although he guards himself from possible suspicion of heresy by adding that even then regard must be had to the *fiqh*, which is, by hypothesis, the final and infallible criterion of right and wrong in Islam.

Further examples may be culled from the intermediate centuries. The Persian philosopher Sayyid al-Sharīf al-Jurjānī, writing in the eighth century A.H., included amongst his *Ta'rīfāt* ("Definitions") the term '*Urf*, which he defines as "that upon which minds have agreed because of the evidence of reason, and in accepting which men of all dispositions concur". "Similar", he says, "is '*Āda*, which is the course normally followed by man."[4] The hint of conflict with the *shar'* is not the less obvious in the definition for being veiled.

At about the time at which Jurjānī wrote, the historian Maqrīzī was deploring the decline of the temporal powers possessed by the

[1] The title of al-Qarāfī's work which is quoted is significant. It is "Judgment in the Disagreement between *Fatāwī* (Jurisconsults' Decisions) and *Aḥkām* (Government Ordinances)".

[2] *Kitāb al-Istiqṣā* (Cairo, A.H. 1304), IV, 297.

[3] *Ibid.* pp. 396 ff.

[4] Cf. Fluegel's edition (Leipzig, 1845), p. 154.

spiritual authorities of his native Egypt. "People are in our day, and have been ever since the beginning of the Turkish (*Mamlūk*) regime in Egypt and Syria," he says, "under the impression that laws are of two kinds, the first that of the *shar'* and the second that of the *siyāsa* (i.e. the State)." The *sharī'a* he defines as the body of laws on prayer, fasting, pilgrimage and other acts of piety, while he derives the *siyāsa*, using popular etymology, from the Mongol *Yāsā* or code of laws, introduced into Egypt and Syria, as he claims, by Baraka, son of Tūshī (? Jūjī), son of Chingīz Khān. The Mongol practices, he continues,

were spread abroad in Egypt and Syria, and through fear of their masters the inhabitants of these lands permitted the chief qāḍī to have oversight of matters connected with the faith—for example prayer, fasting, alms and pilgrimage, to which they added the business of *awqāf*, the care of orphans and jurisdiction in marital and commercial disputes. But in all other matters they submitted themselves to the ways of Chingīz Khān and the rule of the *Yāsā*. For this reason they appointed the *ḥājib* (the chamberlain) to decide disputed issues which concerned everyday affairs. In this manner, by the provisions of the *Yāsā* they could obtain justice for the weak against the strong. They further entrusted to the chamberlain the oversight of affairs if the royal *dīwāns*, when disputes arose over grants of land in fief, and his officers could decide on matters involving revenue. The chamberlain's office indeed reached such a degree of power that even Copts in its employ could judge exchequer and land-revenue cases. They passed judgment in the *dīwān* in ways such as Allah can never have sanctioned, consuming what is His right and ignoring what is His due.

Maqrīzī is, however, compelled to admit that the most important cases were referred to the *nā'ib* or the sulṭān himself, although there were exceptions even then. He quotes the instance of the *ḥājib* Sayf al-Dīn Jurjī, who, in the days of the Sulṭān Ṣāliḥ b. Muhammad b. Qalā'ūn was given permission to try cases of debt according to government ordinances—though never before had a *ḥājib* been allowed to decide matters coming within the jurisdiction of the *shar'*.[1] Thence onwards, the author proclaims, the division of legal authority was established.

[1] Maqrīzī, *Khiṭaṭ*, II, 220.

In the tenth century A.H. a Jewish rabbi noted the dichotomy of jurisdiction in Egypt. "They have", he says, "two kinds of justice, the one *shar'ī* and the other *'urfī*. The *shar'ī* justice is in the hands of the chief qāḍī, who decides what is the religious law [Hebrew *dīn*], the princes being charged to carry out his decisions, while the *'urfī* justice is entrusted to the prince of the country, who may put a man to death by the *'urf* even if it be contrary to the religious law and without the knowledge of the chief qāḍī".[1] Under the "democratic" regime of modern times the *shar'* has greatly declined in authority in Egypt. Not alone are matters of personal law, such as marriage, divorce and inheritance, regulated by civil enactments, but even the *awqāf*, the endowments of pious foundations, are now under political control.[2]

Indian history provides parallels to these instances. Thus the *Ta'rīkh-i Fīrūz-Shāhī*, dealing with the history of 'Alā al-Dīn, the Khaljī sulṭān of Delhi, says that he regarded polity and government as one thing and the rules and decrees of the *shar'* as another; royal commands belonging to the king, while decrees of the *shar'* rest upon the judgment of the qāḍīs and muftīs. In accordance with this opinion, he judged all questions that needed his decision in the light of the public good, without considering whether his mode of dealing with them was lawful or unlawful. Nor did he ever ask for the legal advice of the muftī on matters of political import.[3]

The emperor Bābur illustrated the important place held in his realms by the code of traditional justice when he spoke in his memoirs of a certain act of blood-vengeance as being in accord with both the *shar'* and the *'urf*.[4] In British India customary law was of special importance in questions regulating revenue and the public life of the individual, so that in the Punjab and elsewhere local practice was used by the administration as a basis for legal codes. In the province mentioned, local, native sources such as the *wājib al-'arḍ*, which was a record of village administration, and the *rawāj-i 'āmm*, which embodied the system of tribal and

[1] R. David b. Abi Zimra. (For the reference see Goldziher, *Zahiriten*, p. 205.)

[2] See J. Schacht, "Šarī'a und Qānūn im modernen Ägypten", *Islam*, XX, (1932), 209 ff. For the place of customary law in Islam in British territory in Africa see J. N. D. Anderson, *Islamic Law in Africa* (H.M.S.O., London, 1954).

[3] Elliot and Dowson, *History of India*, III, 183.

[4] *Bābur-nāma*, ed. A. Beveridge (Gibb Series I), p. 124 b, l. 7 (tr., p. 194).

local usage, were employed in the formulation of a code for native requirements.[1]

The influence of the "extra-canonical" sources of law, namely imperial will and local custom, is as apparent in Persia as elsewhere under Islam. There, however, it is best illustrated not by the extent of positive legislation enacted through it but by the way in which justice generally is administered. Under the Ghaznawids, according to the orthodox historian Bayhaqī, the qāḍīs administered the law, namely, the *shar'*. But occasionally special officers were sent here and there to hear petitions and complaints of injustice.[2] Generally it was regarded as the duty of the ruler himself to hold two sessions a week at the capital for the purpose.[3] When thus acting in a judicial capacity the *amīr* was assisted by a counsellor and some court official, presumably that the interests of the prince might be the more carefully watched.[4] In the reign of Mas'ūd, at the trial and impeachment of Ḥasanak, who had been vizier of the usurping prince Muhammad, the judges were the great chamberlain and a number of qāḍīs, and there were also present many of the chief officers of the state, the qāḍīs and notables of Balkh. The accusation against the prisoner was that he was a Carmathian and a heretic. His real crime, however, was that of having been instrumental in selling royal property while he was in office, and the chief evidence produced against him was a list of estates which he had sold. The trial consisted mainly in denunciations and vituperation by the witnesses for the prosecution and he was condemned without any hearing of his witnesses, who were present, though he himself was permitted to plead on his own behalf.[5] It is obvious that the interests of the ruler here entirely overrode those of the faith.[6]

Further instances which may be quoted from the later periods of Persian history indicate that the ruler and his agents took the law into their own hands when their interests were affected. The

[1] Cf. C. L. Tupper, *Punjab Customary Law* (Calcutta, 1881), I, 161.

[2] Bayhaqī, *Ta'rīkh-i Mas'ūdī*, ed. W. H. Morley, p. 295.

[3] *Ibid.* pp. 39 f., *Siyāsat-nāma*, ch. III.

[4] Bayhaqī, *ibid.* p. 535.

[5] *Ibid.* pp. 213 ff.

[6] The qāḍī might on occasion be used as an instrument of the *shar'*. Thus the Caliph al-Ẓāhir, in a burst of reforming zeal, instructed his qāḍī at Baghdad to restore to persons who could produce proof of claim any property which had been unlawfully seized from them. (Ibn al-Athīr (A.H. 622), XII, 288.)

English traveller Anthony Jenkinson, who travelled to Persia in 1562 with a letter of recommendation from Queen Elizabeth to Shāh Ṭahmāsp, says: "if any man offend the prince he punisheth it extremely, not only in the person that offendeth but also in his children. . . . Theft and murder are often punished, yet none otherwise than pleaseth him that is ruler in the place where the offence is committed and as the partie offending is able to make friends or with money redeeme his offence."[1]

Sir John Chardin stated that the Persians in his day made distinction between *Cheray* (i.e. *sharā'i'*, plural of *sharī'a*) and *ourf* (i.e. *'urf*), a fact which he noted as remarkable. *'Urf*, he says, is founded solely on the arbitrary will of the sovereign and is regarded by the majority of the devout and especially by the ecclesiastics, as a kind of tyranny but nevertheless no great injustice would be done if it were not for the authority of the civil tribunals, which frequently bring before themselves cases held over by the ecclesiastical courts. Especially in commercial cases and in criminal cases affecting foreigners or non-Muslims their influence is felt.[2]

The seventeenth-century German traveller Olearius further testifies that in his day civil causes were commonly tried before the secular judges—"whom they call *Oef* [i.e. *'urf*]. They are a kind of Lawyers according to their way, and they have for their chief the *Diwan-beki*, who ought to be well versed in the Law of Mahomet."[3] "Criminals", says Don Juan of Persia, "are judged and punished by being brought before the Grand Vizier. He gives injunction to his Deputy or Wakil, who is, as we say here, the President. . . . The matter is then brought before the king, but the king has deputed all minor details of justice to the governors and ministers of the various cities."[4]

These instances must not be held as implying that the qāḍīs and 'ulamā are without importance. They have always been a powerful body in the country, exercising, particularly in settled

[1] *Early Voyages and Travells to Russia and Persia*, by Anthony Jenkinson and other Englishmen (Hakluyt Society, 1886), II, 436.

[2] *Voyages du Chevalier Chardin en Perse*, ed. L. Langlès (Paris, 1811), VI, 70–6.

[3] A. Olearius, *Voyages and Travells*, tr. J. Davies (London, 1669), pp. 273, 275.

[4] *Don Juan of Persia*, tr. G. Le Strange (London, 1926), pp. 46 f.

times, a decisive voice in the direction of affairs. In Ṣafawī times indeed the *Ṣadr* corresponded in rank and importance with the *Shaykh al-Islām* or Grand Muftī of Turkey—a personage whose power in the State was such that it might override that of the sulṭān himself. Yet as a rule the cases left to the qāḍī were those of "debt and division of inheritance, contracts and purchases". Also he took cognizance of marriages and divorces.[1]

Murder came only in special circumstances within the jurisdiction of the qāḍī. Olearius[2] quotes the case of an unfortunate Christian clock-maker who killed a burglar that had broken into his house. "The friends of the deceased went immediately to the Ecclesiastical Judge and made complaints of the Murther, committed by a Stranger and an Infidel, upon one of the Faithful." The clock-maker was arrested and, in spite of the efforts of the foreign ambassadors, condemned to die. He was given the choice of embracing Islam or being handed over to the relatives of the burglar for execution, but chose the latter.

According to John Fryer[3] punishment for theft was immuring, and for petty larceny "drubbing of the soles of the feet"—both penalties being peculiar to Persia and contrary to those recognized by the *shar'*.

[1] R. du Mans, *Estat de la Perse en 1660*, ed. Schefer (Paris, 1890), p. 172.

"To the Cadi's cognizance," says John Fryer, who visited the court of Shāh Sulaymān (1666–94), "belongs all manner of Contracts, Conveyances and Settlements; to which purpose near his Door are such as make Instruments ready written for sale in the Stile of their Law, to be presented for the Cadi's perusal; into which inserting the Names of John-a-Nokes, and John-a-Stiles, Zeid [Zayd] and Ambre ['Amr], the Cadi calls aloud, Zeid, where art thou? Who answers here, upon appearance, When the Cadi proceeds: This House, Garden or Land, or any thing of that kind, Dost thou sell willingly, and of thy own accord to Ambre? He, affirming, yes. Is the price agreed between you? Yes. Where are your Witnesses? says the Cadi. Then he replies, I have brought them, who answer for themselves; the Cadi asks them, Do you know this to belong to Zeid? Who affirm, it is known to all the Town, even to the Children.

The Cadi after these interrogatories, lifts up his Voice, and says, Does no one forbid this Contract? At which they jointly cry aloud no one forbids. Whereupon the Cadi calls for his seals, which are words engraven on silver, and dipping it in Ink, stamps it three or four times, in three or four places, especially at the junction of the Indenture, that no room may be left for fraudulent dealing, they not putting their own Hands, nor delivering it as their Act and Deed; but the Cadi makes the Obligation firm in this wise." John Fryer's *East India and Persia* (Hakluyt Society, 1915), III, 108 f.

[2] *Voyages and Travells*, p. 208.

[3] John Fryer, *op. cit.* III, 105.

The dual legal system continued in Persia almost to the present day. In the nineteenth century, the Shāh's German physician, Dr Polak, described the *'urf* as being administered by the king, governors and the royal *dīwān-khāna*. He says rightly that it could not be called case-law because it rested neither on precedents nor fixed regulations, but on the requirements of the moment or the needs of the State. There was no rule to decide which cases went to the *shar'ī* courts administered by the qāḍīs and which to those of the *'urf*. Mainly it was political cases that went to the *'urf* courts—rebellion against the Shāh or a governor, spreading of false reports about the government, debasing the coinage, offences against law and order, rowdy conduct in the streets, card-playing, etc., as well as theft, murders and highway robberies.[1]

With the political reconstruction that has occurred within recent years, the secular power has assumed greater control of law and of legislation, so that even those matters which were acknowledged as being within the purview of the *shar'* are now regulated by the civil law. Thus, by recent enactments, all marriages and divorces must be registered before a governmental officer. Any man who contracts a polygamous marriage must declare the fact, and a wife may take the initiative for seeking divorce on proper grounds.[2]

In asserting the right of the temporal power to legislate independently of the doctors of the *shar'*, the rulers of Turkey have from the beginning of the Ottoman rise to power been especially prominent. Like other Muslim princes they found that the religious code did not satisfy all the requirements of a living State and had to be supplemented from other sources. It was inevitable that the sovereign's own enactments, formulated as occasion demanded, should become law, and the theory within the Ottoman State came to be that every manifestation of the "royal will" (*irāda sanīya*) was a valid command, provided it did not run counter to those provisions of the *shar'* which were generally recognized and in force in the country. A distinction was, however, made in practice between (*a*) a manifestation of the royal

[1] Polak, *Persien*, I, 328 f. Cf. Curzon, *Persia*, I, 454 f., and C. J. Wills, *Persia as it is*, ch. V and VI.

[2] *Oriente Moderno* (Rome), October 1931, pp. 494 ff.

will promulgated after deliberation in the council of ministers and (*b*) an arbitrary expression of the royal will. The former was called a *qānūn* or *niẓām*[1] while the latter was an *irāda sanīya* properly so called. The sovereign's power thus to establish laws was in Turkey called *'urf*, here distinguished from *'āda*, established custom, which was recognized as another source of law.[2]

In distinction from the practice elsewhere in Islam the Turkish sulṭāns, except in the early period of their dynasty, published their enactments, using their own language (and not Arabic) as being proper for secular decrees. In early times the enactments were not publicly issued but took the form of separate instructions sent to officials as occasion demanded.

The true creator of *qānūn* legislation was Muhammad II, conqueror of Constantinople, whose first *qānūn-nāma*, or collection of statutes, is the first known to us.[3] But it was Sulaymān I, "Qānūnī", who made the completest use of his legislative opportunities, and his laws cover every branch of the civil and military requirements of his administration. A number of his successors followed his example in having their enactments collected and published as *qānūn-nāmas*, which are still extant.

In spite of protestations to the contrary, the royal will was on occasion at variance with some well-known provision of the *shar'*. A notable example is to be found in the decree that led to the formation of the corps of the Janissaries. According to the *shar'*, it was established that no *dhimmī* (a member of a "protected" community) who paid a poll-tax, could be enslaved[4] or be compelled to give up his children to be slaves. By act of *'urf* nevertheless, the Christian subjects of the sulṭān in Macedonia and Thrace were forced to surrender such children as the sovereign demanded in order that they might be converted and used to form the slave-corps of the Janissaries.[5] The initiation of the system is attributed

[1] It was sometimes also called a *Niẓām-nāma*; Cf. Cambridge University MS. Dd. II, 20⁴, f. 134 b, *Qānūn-nāma sulṭān fī aḥwāl iḥtisāb* (*sic*).

[2] See M. D'Ohsson, *Tableau général*, I, p. xxiii, "Discours préliminaire".

[3] It is given in translation by von Hammer, *Staatsverfassung*, I, 87 ff.

[4] See above, p. 76.

[5] Cf. *Hans Dernschwam's Tagebuch einer Reise nach Konstantinopel, 1553–55*, ed. Franz Babinger (Munich, 1923), p. 60. The statement that there was compulsory, or at any rate officially authorized, conversion is denied by D'Ohsson, *Tableau général*, VII, 327. It is true that the grand vizier and other most important ministers were appointed from amongst the Janissaries.

to Murād I, whose law of drafting (*devshirmeh*) thus arbitrarily provided that in the conquered districts of Europe Christian youths should be denied the exemption from military service implied by the payment of *kharāj*.[1]

Another example of a *qānūn* which runs contrary to the requirements of the *shar*ʿ is to be found in a *qānūn-nāma* of Muhammad II. It enacts that a man who commits adultery—the fact being established according to the requirements of the *shar*ʿ—shall pay a fine if he is married and possessed of means. According to the Koran, however, the punishment for adultery is either death or corporal punishment,[2] and there is some reference to this original penalty in the rule which accompanies the *qānūn*, namely, that where a woman is convicted of adultery she must pay the bloodwite for a man, i.e. the amount payable if he were slain on account of his adultery.[3]

It is because the *shar*ʿ code existed and had its validity alongside the *qānūns* that the fact of the existence of incompatible secular regulations requires comment. In theory indeed, the Ottoman law was based on the *shar*ʿ according to the Ḥanafī interpretation, the standard authority after the middle of the sixteenth century being the *Multaqā al-abḥur*, compiled in Arabic, as were all works of *fiqh*, by Ibrahīm al-Ḥalabī, who died in 1549. The chief interpreter of the *shar*ʿ code in Turkey was the Grand Muftī or Shaykh al-Islām, whose *fetwā* might on occasion override the will of a sulṭān. A classic instance of the powers of this dignitary was provided when the Sulṭān ʿAbd al-ʿAzīz (1861–76) proposed to substitute succession by primogeniture for the old system under which the eldest surviving male of the royal family succeeded. The Shaykh al-Islām of the day declared that the proposed change would not be lawful (*jā'iz*) according to the *sharīʿa*, and it was accordingly not introduced although it had been the rule earlier, until the death of Sulṭān Aḥmad I in 1617.

Owing to the influence of the Grand Muftīs and other religious authorities, and because of the claim to the Caliphate made by each successive Sulṭān, *qānūns*, whatever their content, purported

[1] This method of recruiting was given up in the reign of Murād IV, about A.D. 1637.

[2] See p. 120.

[3] Babinger, *Mitteilungen d. Osmanischen Geschichte*, 1, 13 ff. (quoted from Kraelitz-Greifenhorst, *Verfassungsgesetze des Osmanischen Reiches*).

to be in accordance with the *shar'*,[1] and as late as 1337/1921 the Great National Assembly enacted that all laws and rules were to be elaborated according to the canonical "roots" of the *shar'*, though they were also to bear close relationship to the ordinary life of the people and be compatible with the needs of the time and the traditions and habits of the country. By 1924, however, political events had advanced so far that the temporal authorities felt strong enough to disregard tradition, and on 20 April of that year the Great National Assembly declared that all legislative and executive powers in the Ottoman empire were concentrated in its hands and that it, and it alone, had the power to initiate, modify or abrogate laws. The term used for the making of laws in the decree is *tashrī'* (i.e. the formulation of *shar'*), which hitherto had not been used except in speaking of the law-making of the Prophet, and which was in Persia in similar circumstances carefully avoided by the legislators, who did not venture beyond *taqnīn* (i.e. the making of *qānūns*) to designate their powers. There appears indeed to have been a deliberate attempt to reduce the power of religious authority, and the abolition of any privileges held by the doctors of the *shar'* was made complete by the adoption for the nation of the civil and penal codes of Switzerland and Italy respectively.[2] A preface to the published version of the decree of the Assembly states clearly the attitude of the temporal rulers of Turkey. It was written by the Minister of Justice in the Republic and declared that attempts made in the past to modernize Turkish law had failed because their authors believed in the existence of two separate jurisdictions. In their view, says the decree, "the Caliphate and the Sultanate were two distinct authorities united in the same person.[3] There resulted two distinct jurisdictions, of which one was regarded as belonging to the representative of the Sultanate—namely, the Grand Vizier—and the other to the repre-

[1] The formula was *Shar'ī sharīf muwāfiq qānūn-nāma dir*. Cf. British Museum MS. Add. 7834, fol. 1.

[2] *Code Civil turc*. Law No. 743 of 17 February 1926. The new Civil Code came into force on 17 October 1926, and the new Penal Code on 21 August 1929. Albania adopted a Penal Code based on that of Italy in place of the old Ottoman Code on 1 January 1928.

[3] I.e. the Sulṭān, whose principal lieutenants are here said to be the Grand Vizier and the Shaykh al-Islām. In actual fact the latter would never have acknowledged his spiritual authority to be subordinate to that of the Sulṭān.

sentative of the Caliphate—namely, the Shaykh al-Islām." It came to be seen that this position of affairs developed a State within the State, whence the Great National Assembly determined to subject all law, civil, personal and criminal, to its own control henceforward.

CHAPTER VII

THE CALIPHATE AND THE CENTRAL GOVERNMENT

Perhaps the profoundest change wrought by Islam in the conditions of life in Arabia was the demand that adherence to the faith should henceforth be the factor deciding whether an individual was to be included within the community or not. Hitherto, the groups into which society had been divided had reckoned birth to be the criterion. Tribe was distinguished from tribe by difference of traditions and clash of material interests; but it was the assumption of separate ancestry that told most, just as within each tribe it was the idea of common descent which held the members together. Through this assumption of blood relationship, there was probably no question within a particular group of any hereditary difference in status. Chieftainship amongst Bedouins was never restricted to particular families, and it was rare for the headship of a tribe to remain in any one family for more than a few generations.[1]

Those who became chieftains were chosen by popular voice, for their strength of character, courage or experience, and generally at a time of crisis, when war or raiding expeditions were afoot. When these qualities were present, birth was an additional advantage. After election, except during periods when men voluntarily submitted to his authority, the chief could impose his will on the members of his tribe. He had no power to lay duties or to inflict penalties on them, and because he represented the united will of the tribe in war and peace, he normally followed rather than led public opinion, though a strong shaykh doubtless had it in his power to influence the collective will. His duties were numerous. It was he who decided small disputes over property or quarrels between husband and wife, and it was he also who provided hospitality for visitors to the tribe. All this, of course, in addition to leading raids and forays for plunder. As compensation, he had an extra share of any booty taken, he occupied the place of honour in all assemblies of his

[1] Ibn Khaldūn, *Prolégomènes*, tr. de Slane, I, 289.

tribe, and when it changed camp he had the choice of position for his own tent.

The individual member had a completely independent position in relationship both to the chief and the tribe in general. The head of a household could rebuke his chief for what he considered presumptuous conduct or could withdraw from the group if he felt himself aggrieved. Whilst he was with the tribe he owed it only those duties which he voluntarily offered; he shared in its counsels and was accorded its protection if ever he needed it. He conformed to certain rules (mainly concerned with rights of property) and traditional practices concerning marriage, but otherwise he was free. If he withdrew, he forfeited his right of protection and hence stood in danger from hostile tribes unless he deliberately sought refuge with a member of some tribe which would receive him. In the latter event, he became the *mulṣaq* ("attached" member) or *ḥalīf* ("one who has taken an oath") of the protecting tribe. His rights were about the same as those of the *mawālī*, who were the freedmen of the various members of the tribe and the descendants of such freedmen.[1]

The tribe, then, consisted firstly of the chief and his family; secondly, of the group of free families who acknowledged him; thirdly, of the *mawālī* and attached members; and, finally, of the slaves.

The tribal system prevailed in the towns as well as in the less settled regions. Thus, at Mecca, Muhammad's own tribe of the Quraysh formed the great majority of the inhabitants, and the chief men of the tribe were also the city notables. This was the case too at Medina, where, however, the city was divided among two powerful and rival tribes, the Aws and the Khazraj.

It was at Medina that Muhammad was able to put into practice his teaching that Islam must take precedence over all other loyalties. When he arrived, the Aws and Khazraj were violently at enmity with one another. Once Islam had begun to grow strong, the cleavage became not one between rival tribes but between believers and non-believers. The former consisted of the *Muhājirūn*, the Prophet's "fellow-emigrants" from Mecca, and the

[1] Ibn Khaldūn, *Prolégomènes*, tr. de Slane, I, 276. For the political constitution of the Arab tribe in modern times see Lady Anne Blunt, *Bedouins of the Euphrates*, 2 vols. (London, 1879), II, 229 ff.

Anṣār, his "Helpers" from amongst the Medinese; the non-believers were those who remained hostile to him and his religion, a body numerically strong amongst whom were many Jews.

The situation required careful handling, and as soon as he felt sufficiently well established to achieve his purposes Muhammad drew up a charter defining the position with regard to rights and duties of each party in his small State.[1]

Its main provisions are said to be as follows:

This is a charter of Muhammad the prophet [applicable] amongst the believers and Muslims of the Quraysh and of Yathrib [Medina], and amongst those who follow them and attach themselves to them and fight along with them.

They are one *umma* (community) over against mankind.

The Muhājirūn of the Quraysh remain in their former [tribal] constitution. They pay in common [any blood-wite, etc. incurred by any members of theirs] and they ransom their own prisoners—aided by what is considered right and equitable amongst believers.

The five groups forming the Khazraj tribe and the three forming the Aws were similarly to preserve their old constitution and be responsible each for the same collective payments as before and for redeeming their own prisoners.

Believers do not forsake any one of their number who is burdened with debt. They support him in such manner as is right when there is a question of ransom or blood-wite.

No believer conspires with the *mawlā* of another believer against him.

Pious believers are against any one amongst them who rebels or commits an act of deceit, hostility or wickedness against believers. Their hands jointly are against him, even if he be the son of one of them.

A believer will not slay a believer for an infidel nor will he aid an infidel against a believer.

The security [given by God's community] is collective. The protection granted by the least of believers involves [all] in the duty. Also believers are "clients" of one another against [other] men.

Any one of the Jews who follows us has our support and aid. They are not to be wronged nor their oppressors supported.

[1] Ibn Hishām, ed. Wuestenfeld, pp. 341–4. Wellhausen, *Medina vor dem Islam*, pp. 67 ff.; and *Das arabische Reich*, etc., pp. 1 ff.

The peace made by believers is single and collective; no believer may agree to a proposal for peace separately from other believers in any fighting on an errand of God. There must be the same conditions for all.

Every raiding party that raids with us will permit others [who have no mounts] to ride.

Believers hold each other responsible to avenge blood spilt on an errand of God.

Pious believers follow the best and most correct guidance. No heathen has the privilege of granting protection either to the property or the person of Qurashites (the prophet's own fellow-tribesmen, as yet unconverted) nor may take their part against a believer.

Should anyone deprive a believer of his life by murder, and the fact is clearly proven, then *talio* is involved, except if the next of kin of the slain man be satisfied with blood-wite. All believers will be against him and no course is open to them but to oppose himself.

No believer who acknowledges the truth of what is contained in this document and believes in God and the Last Day, may give support to any scandalous person nor grant him refuge. He that supports or grants him refuge shall have God's curse and his wrath on the Day of Resurrection and no fine or reparation shall be accepted from him.

If you dispute over any matter, then your recourse is to God and to Muhammad.

The Jews shall pay the costs of war with believers.

The Jews of the Banu Awf (and other tribes) are a community alongside the believers (the Jews keeping their faith and the Muslims theirs); they with their clients, except anyone of them who has committed a wrong or an offence—and he does not involve anyone but himself and his household in destruction.

The friends of the Jews stand on the same ground as they themselves.

None of them shall take the field in war except with Muhammad's leave. None shall be hindered from avenging a wound.

He who attacks another does so at his own cost and that of his family, unless he is the victim of a wrong; and God watches over [?] him who is justified in such matter.[1]

No man gains aught except for himself. Allah watches over what is most just and pure in this document, and this charter

[1] The text is not altogether clear.

avails not the wrongdoer or transgressor. He that goes forth is secure and he that stays at home is secure in Medina; except such that do wrong or transgress. Allah is the protector of him that is innocent and God-fearing and Muhammad is the apostle of Allah.

By this charter it is made clear that the Prophet's desire was not to abolish the old tribal constitution, but simply to expand and reform it in order that it might be less inadequate for the larger community of Islam. The charter contains the germ of the Islamic State, if that can be called a State in which the organization is so entirely haphazard and in which the machinery for carrying out the functions of government is left in such a rudimentary condition. Of these functions the legislative one alone was adequately provided for, and even then only so long as Muhammad himself remained alive, though Allah stands behind the Prophet to provide guidance for the community when necessary. So far, however, as other functions such as the judicial and executive are concerned, the charter provides no better organization than that already existing in the tribes. The old chiefs are left with some part of their internal authority; law and order are still maintained within the family group by its being held liable to pay, as before, for the delinquencies of its members and for the ransom of kinsmen who are prisoners. But there is now the important addition that the tribe is required also to produce, for vengeance to be exacted, any one of its members who has committed a wrong against a member of another group.

To outward seeming, then, little change immediately affecting the lives of Muslims was introduced by the charter. In reality, however, as the document itself makes clear, there had been made the great change that henceforward ultimate authority for the doings of the community rested not with the chiefs or the collective voice of the people, but with Muhammad, and, beyond him, with Allah. This introduced an idea hitherto foreign to the Arabs, namely, that of an overlord. The individuals who compose the Islamic community are made to resign a good part of their ancient freedom, to forgo their free choice of a leader and to bow to divine authority. They had, in fact, become a theocracy, a "community of God", a State in which the political power was held by Allah and his apostle Muhammad. There could be no distinction here of Church and State. The *Umma*, the "Community", partook of the nature of both and the purposes of one were the purposes of the other. Similarly, the Prophet derived his political power from his divine office and nothing else.[1]

How the religious and the political came to be intertwined may be seen from the copy of a letter purporting to have been sent by the Caliph Omar to Abu Mūsā al-Ash'arī, his governor at Baṣra. It read:

People have an aversion from their rulers, and I trust to Allah that you and I are not overtaken by it, stealthily and unexpectedly, or by hatreds conceived against us. See to the execution of the laws even if it be for only one hour in the day, and if two matters present themselves to you, the one godly and the other one worldly, then choose as your portion the way of God. For the present world will perish and the other world remains. Strike terror into wrongdoers and make heaps of mutilated limbs out of them. Visit the sick among Muslims, attend their funerals, open your gate to them and give heed in person to their affairs, for you are but a man amongst them except that God has allotted you the heaviest burden.[2]

In spite of the intimate relationship between the temporal and spiritual sides of the new dispensation, the Koran itself contains almost nothing that may be called civic or State legislation. The nearest approximation to anything of the kind is a general behest to the faithful to obey God and his apostle "and them that have command among you".[3] The commentators, of whom Bayḍāwī is typical, say that by them are meant the chief personages among the Muslims in Muhammad's own time and that they include caliphs, qāḍīs, commanders of troops and them that know the law; though another view considers the verse to be merely an exhortation to the troops of a particular commander setting out on a campaign at the time.[4]

The fact would appear to be that, since neither Muhammad nor his people seem ever to have envisaged the possibility of his

[1] There was nothing new in this. Ancient Israel was just such a community, and in Roman jurisprudence the *ius sacrum* was part of the *ius publicum*, while the emperor was also *pontifex maximus*.

[2] Ibn Qutayba, *Uyūn al-akhbār*, ed. Brockelmann (Berlin and Strassburg, 1900–8), p. 28.

[3] Koran 4^{62}.

[4] Bukhārī, *Ṣaḥīḥ*, ed. Krehl, III, p. 227 (*Kitāb Tafsīr al-Qur'ān*, 11).

dying, no provision was made for the continuance of government in the community and no successor was appointed to the man who was the head of the State as well as the spiritual guide of the community. He had, moreover, constantly proclaimed himself to be the direct and only agent of God upon earth, the last of the prophets and without heir.[1]

The consternation and confusion in Islam, therefore, when Muhammad finally did prove mortal was tremendous.[2] And here some little of history is necessary for a proper appreciation of the question of the Caliphate. Common sense was forced to take the place of immediate divine guidance, and the difficulties of the community in providing themselves with a chief were settled when Omar, son of al-Khaṭṭāb, the most outstanding personality in the prophet's tribe of the Quraysh, gave Abu Bakr the *bay'a*, the clap of palm on palm, which was the normal token of the settling of a bargain and came to be the sign of acknowledgment of sovereignty.[3]

Abu Bakr was a senior member of the Prophet's following, being also his father-in-law, and he had, according to tradition, been asked by the Prophet on his death-bed to lead the community in prayer as imām.[4] He was therefore a person with some claim to become the *khalīfa* (Caliph) or "substitute" of Muhammad, at any rate on the temporal side. Although as Caliph he would have certain religious duties to perform such as acting as imām to the faithful at prayer,[5] they did not endow him with any sacredness of character; for there has never been any dedication for specially sacred duties in Islam and there exists neither priesthood nor hierarchy. The Caliph consequently would not fill in Islam the place filled by the Pope in Christianity. It should be noted further that neither through his having acted as imām nor by his kinship with the Prophet, nor by any specific "right" at all did Abu Bakr become Caliph; indeed, he was to all intents imposed on the community by the action of Omar. He in turn was nominated Caliph

[1] Koran 33⁴⁰.

[2] Cf. Ṭabarī, I, 1816 f.

[3] *Ibid.* I, 1819. This formality of the *bay'a* or *mubāya'a* was never omitted by the Prophet when he made a new convert to Islam; cf. Koran 9¹¹², and Ibn Hishām, p. 296 f.

[4] Ṭabarī, I, 1811.

[5] This was in fact regarded as the Caliph's privilege (Shāfi'ī, *Kitāb al-Umm* (Būlāq, A.H. 1321), I, 139).

by Abu Bakr on his death-bed,[1] and became the "Commander of the Faithful" without any question being raised about the way in which he succeeded to office. He nominated a council of six to elect his successor, after a nominee of his own had refused the Caliphate. The council chose 'Uthmān ibn 'Affān, a member of the Umayyad clan, who had been one of Muhammad's sons-in-law. By this choice they passed over another of the Prophet's sons-in-law, 'Alī, who was also his cousin and who on that ground amongst others considered that he had a prior claim to be Caliph. Thereby were sown the seeds of a dissension which was to split the community of Islam permanently from top to bottom.

The result of the electors' action showed itself in the latter half of the reign of 'Uthmān, who, by his conduct, sometimes weak and sometimes unnecessarily harsh, antagonized the majority of his subjects, in particular the inhabitants of Egypt and Iraq. The dissatisfaction crystallized about 'Alī, and he was elected Caliph when 'Uthmān was ultimately assassinated. The latter's family, the Umayyads, however, were a powerful body. One of them, Mu'āwiya, was governor of Syria, and held sway there independently and in defiance of the Caliph at Medina, whom he held responsible for the death of his royal kinsman. At the first opportunity he proclaimed himself the true "Commander of the Faithful", with the result that, until 'Alī died, there were two Caliphs of Islam, the one at Damascus, the other at Medina.

'Alī's main support was at Medina, but he moved out of it to Kūfa on the Euphrates, in the hope of playing on the antagonism of Iraq for Syria and subduing his rival—or rebellious subordinate, as he considered him—from there. Propaganda was rife. On 'Alī's side a certain 'Abd-allāh ibn Sabā, a recent convert to Islam from Judaism, had during 'Uthmān's time been spreading abroad the doctrine that there had been a thousand prophets, each of whom had a *waṣī*, or executor. Muhammad, the last of the prophets, had 'Alī as his *waṣī*, and none could do greater wrong than to seize command of the community in opposition to one who held executorship to the apostle of God.[2] Such teaching had its effect, particularly in Iraq, which was still Persian in spirit and which was favourably disposed towards the hereditary principle in any form. 'Alī in the end met his death at the hands of a group of fanatics,

[1] Ṭabarī, I, 2137 f. [2] Ṭabarī, I, 2942.

the "Khārijīs", or "Seceders", who cared neither for him nor for Mu'āwiya but regarded both as usurpers, on the grounds that neither was ever raised to the chieftainship of Islam by that free choice which Arab custom demanded. These democratic Arab tribesmen detested both the sanguinary family rivalries of the aristocrats of Mecca and what they considered the hierarchical pretensions of those in power at Medina.[1] They, in fact, disputed any need at all for any imām, or head of the State, as long as the divine law was carried out, and they felt that the victory of either of the two rivals would mean the triumph of worldliness over the religion of Islam. They determined, therefore, on the assassination of both; but their attack on Mu'āwiya did not prove fatal, while 'Alī died of his wounds. His son Ḥasan was acknowledged Caliph at Kūfa, but soon abdicated to Mu'āwiya on hearing that the latter was launching an expedition against him.

In what light the Umayyad chieftain regarded the matter of elevation to the Caliphate may be gathered from the following anecdote:

Mu'āwiya once approached the Hāshimites, fellow-descendants with the prophet from his great-grandfather Hāshim, and asked them if they would not enlighten him about the grounds upon which they claimed the office of the Caliphate as their perquisite, to the exclusion of the rest of the Quraysh. He argued that it could only be on the grounds either that they had been universally approved and chosen by general consensus of believers or that they had kinship with the Prophet, or on both grounds together. If they based their claim on universal approval, then their kinship did not strengthen their right in any way. If, on the other hand, they argued from the fact of kinship alone, then there was nothing to prevent the Prophet's uncle 'Abbās from aspiring to the Caliphate; a man, moreover, who was one of the Prophet's heirs and had provided water for pilgrims and been the support of orphans. If, again, the Caliphate depended upon all three conditions of approval, general consensus and kinship together, then the latter was only one qualification out of the several required for the imāmate, or Caliphate. The Hāshimites, said Mu'āwiya, claimed office on the last qualification alone, and against them he held that

[1] See further A. von Kremer, *Herrschenden Ideen des Islams* (Leipzig, 1868), pp. 359 ff.

the member of the Quraysh who had most right to the Caliphate was he to whom all men stretched out their hands in acknowledgment, to whom men directed their steps in longing and towards whom their wishes flew in confidence of fulfilment. After various further arguments Mu'āwiya concluded by saying that it would not benefit them to see in themselves anything that the rest of the community did not see in them.[1]

Once he was securely at the head of Islam, however, Mu'āwiya, in spite of his democratic views, became ambitious to perpetuate the Caliphate in his own family, and fearing, as he said, "to leave the community of Muhammad like a sheep without a shepherd", he appointed his son Yazīd to be his *Walī al-'Ahd*, "Successor by virtue of a covenant", i.e. his heir apparent. The remark was made to 'Abd-allāh, son of the Caliph Omar, into whose mouth the reply was placed: "If you bring out your throne I will come and pay my allegiance to you, although I will concur, after you are dead, with anything that the community agrees upon. And, by Allah, if the community agrees together after you are dead upon a [black] Abyssinian slave, I will follow the course set by it."[2]

Arab indcpendence of spirit would not let Mu'āwiya's high-handed action go unchallenged. Two rivals to Yazīd appeared almost at once; one, 'Abd-allāh ibn Zubayr (a senior member of his own family) in the Ḥijāz, and the other, Ḥusayn (son of 'Alī by his marriage with Muhammad's daughter Fāṭima), at Kūfa in Iraq. Ibn Zubayr, with deep cunning, encouraged the young Ḥusayn to stand out in rebellion, and himself waited until Yazīd had crushed the feeble efforts of the Prophet's grandson and slain him on the field of Kerbelā. Not long afterwards, the pietists at Medina proclaimed him (Ibn Zubayr) their Caliph in opposition to the Umayyad ruler at Damascus, whom they regarded with detestation as a godless and impious libertine.

The results of the battle of Kerbelā linked themselves up with those brought about by the original rejection of 'Alī's claim to the Caliphate, and the main consequence was the foundation of a legitimist party, which held that the only persons having a claim to the succession were direct descendants of the Prophet.[3] This was the beginning of the "Shī'a", i.e. the "Partisans" (of 'Alī).

[1] Ibn Qutayba, *'Uyūn al-akhbār*, p. 22. [2] Ṭabarī, II, 176 f.
[3] I.e. through his daughter Fāṭima by his cousin 'Alī.

Another consequence was, as already said, that Islam for a time had two rival Caliphs; the Umayyad, acknowledged in Syria, and Ibn Zubayr, in the Ḥijāz and Egypt. The point is important in view of the theory of the Caliphate evolved at a later date.

Yazīd was able to win the support of the Umayyad army in favour of the succession of his own young son (Mu'āwiya II) to his part of the Caliphate. But the youth was a weakling who did not live long. He was followed, although the claims of a younger brother of his were put forward, by Marwān I, a brother of the first Mu'āwiya, founder of the dynasty. Marwān was raised to power by the faction at Damascus, who preferred strong leadership to the claims of heredity, but he himself created his own son 'Abd al-Malik his heir apparent. After nine years of struggle that prince was able to end the rule, together with the life, of Ibn Zubayr, and made himself sole Caliph in Islam. Like his father, he preferred to be followed on the throne by his son rather than by a brother, previously nominated, and he in his turn appointed two of his sons to be Caliphs in succession in place of his brother who was heir apparent, and who, fortunately for them, died before he could ascend the throne.

A significant token of the hold which democratic Arabian tribal custom had upon the Umayyads is that notice of the appointment was sent to the governors of the provinces, who almost everywhere obtained promises of adherence to the arrangement. The exception was at Medina, where the recusant Sa'īd b. al-Musayyab proclaimed that he would not acknowledge the two princes as future Caliphs, for reasons which are variously stated by the historians; namely, either because the whole community was not assembled to make its voice heard, or because he himself had not seen the persons nominated[1] or, according to a third version,[2] because he would acknowledge no one while the Caliph was still alive.

No less than four sons of 'Abd al-Malik came to the throne, although a cousin, Omar II, interposed between the first two and the second two. The members of the Abbasid dynasty, which followed that of the Umayyads, generally attempted by the method of preliminary nomination to secure the accession of their sons and exclude their brothers.[3] There were exceptions; as when

[1] Ṭabarī, II, 1170 f. [2] Ibn al-Athīr, IV, 410.

[3] Cf. *ibid.* A.H. 182, comment on Rashīd's act.

al-Saffāh, the first of the dynasty, having no son capable of succeeding him, nominated his brother Manṣūr and his cousin 'Īsā ibn Mūsā to follow him in order. Manṣūr came to the throne, but 'Īsā was compelled to abdicate his claim, although he was compensated with a large sum of money for so doing. The Caliph Ma'mūn also nominated a brother, Mu'taṣim, or, according to another account, it was Mu'taṣim's son Abu Isḥāq whom he nominated.

The appointment of a son as heir apparent was not always followed by his accession; for, in the absence of a principle of hereditary succession or of primogeniture and in face of the legal disapproval of such a principle, it was generally the most powerful member of the royal family who secured the throne for himself.

In the third century of Islam the already degenerate Abbasid monarchs fell into the power of their Turkish mercenary troops. They continued to remain in the hands of the same virile race, first the Buwayhid tyrant-princes, who came from the region south of the Caspian Sea, and then the Seljūqs, thus losing the power even to dispose of their own persons, let alone to appoint their successors. The "Commander of the Faithful" was then elected or deposed according to the whim of the Turkish *Amīr al-Umarā*, or "Supreme Commander", who happened to be in power, though he was always chosen from the Abbasid family. Thus the commander Tūzūn blinded and removed from the throne the Caliph Muttaqī (in 333/944) and set up the latter's cousin Mustakfī in return for a bribe of 100,000 dīnārs.[1] He, like his predecessor, was rendered incapable of occupying the throne by being deprived of his sight a year later. Indeed the Buwayhid princes, being Shī'ites, were quite prepared to destroy the Abbasid Caliphate, which by their tenets was the creation of mere usurpers. But the alternative would have been an 'Alid dynasty, and it was not to the interest of a lawless group like the Buwayhids to have a spiritual overlord who might destroy their independence and deprive them of their much-cherished power. They contented themselves therefore with keeping the Caliphs in a state of utter subjection and allowing them no political discretion whatsoever.[2] Nevertheless, as we have noted, they never ventured to make a Caliph of one who was not a member of the Abbasid family.

[1] Ibn al-Athīr, VIII, 313 (A.H. 333). [2] *Ibid.* VIII, 339 f.

The ultimate decline of the Buwayhid power coincided with the reign of the Caliph Qādir, a person who happened to be able and willing to assert himself against his overlords in spite of being their nominee. It is a mark of his character that he was one of the few Caliphs who died in their beds. Actually while on his death-bed he held an audience at which he consented to the petition of those present that he would choose his son al-Qā'im to be his successor.[1] That prince's only son died before his father, who secured the throne to his grandson Muqtadī. After him, and until the Mongols destroyed the dynasty, son followed father upon the throne with few exceptions.

Amongst the Umayyads of Cordova the sovereignty was handed down from father to son for the first six generations, i.e. from 'Abd al-Raḥmān I to Mundhir. The latter was succeeded by his brother 'Abd-allāh, and again son followed father upon the throne for four generations; after which various remote descendants of the famous 'Abd al-Raḥmān III held office.

Even more completely hereditary was the office in the hands of the Ottoman sulṭāns, who, although counting themselves rigid Sunnīs, for almost three centuries (from 'Uthmān, A.D. 1299, to Muhammad III, A.D. 1595) handed on their power from father to son. Thereafter brothers generally succeeded before sons. Further, amongst the Mogul emperors of Delhi the greatest efforts were made to keep the kingship to the line of Bābur, the first emperor.

As for the official ceremony which took place at the accession of a new monarch, that appears to have been very simple under the "Orthodox" Caliphs and the Umayyads of Damascus, though it was later made very elaborate. The historians describe in a few words what occurred at the first public appearance in Damascus, the capital, of the Caliph al-Walīd ibn 'Abd al-Malik. After the burial of his father he went directly, and without first going home, to the chief mosque in the city, where he mounted the pulpit and addressed the assembled congregation as follows: "We are in God's hands and to Him do we turn. God is He from whom we seek aid in our affliction, the death of the Commander of the Faithful. Praise be to God for the favour of the Caliphate which He has granted us. Rise and acknowledge me." The first who rose to acknowledge him was a certain 'Abd-allāh al-Sallūlī, who

[1] Ibn al-Athīr, IX, 55 f.

declaimed two complimentary verses and retired, after which the rest of the congregation paid their homage.[1]

The foregoing historical sketch has shown how each Caliph actually succeeded to the throne. Side by side with it there must be considered the theory of the Caliphate as it was evolved by the legists of Islam. The authority generally quoted is Māwardī, who wrote at Baghdad in the days when the Caliphs were being kept in a position of utter humility by the Buwayhid *Amīr al-Umarā*. Māwardī's work *al-Aḥkām al-Sulṭānīya*,[2] or "The Laws concerning Rulership", as its title implies, deals with the constitution of the Muslim state and more particularly with its head, the Imām, or Caliph, from the Sunnī, or "Orthodox", point of view.

According to Māwardī, the Imāmate, or Caliphate, was divinely appointed, in succession to the office of the Prophet, in order to defend the faith and secure the right government of the world. About its necessity there is no doubt, but there is dispute as to whether reason or law dictates the necessity. Those who point to reason as the dominant principle, declare that reasonable men naturally surrender to the authority of a prince, who forbids them to wrong each other and who decides between them in their disputes; but for their rulers men would be leaderless and go astray. A Bedouin poet[3] has said: "A folk that hath no chieftains cannot prosper, and it hath no chieftains if it be led by the vulgar in it."

They who hold that it is the law (*shar*ʻ) which demands the office declare that it is so because the imām's preoccupation is with the *shar*ʻ. Reason tells the reasonable being only that he must restrain himself from oppressing others and from dissent, and must regard justice and amity as essential. He reflects with his own personal mind and takes small account of the reasoning of others. The law, however, is administered by one who is divinely entrusted with the carrying out of its behests.[4] The Koran says: "Obey God and His apostle and them that have command over you." Obedience therefore is divinely imposed upon us to them that have authority over us. And they are the imāms.[5]

1 Ṭabarī, II, 1177 f.

2 Edited by M. Enger (Bonn, 1853).

3 Al-Afwah. See Nöldeke, *Delectus Veterum Carminum Arabicorum* (Berlin, 1890), p. 4.

4 4[62].

5 The appointment of an imām is a compulsory duty imposed on the community of Islam (cf. for example, Ibn Khaldūn, *Prolégomènes*, tr. de Slane, I, 388).

Various qualities are requisite in the imām, or Caliph, namely, that he must be just, have the knowledge to determine the significance of Koranic laws and their derivatives, be in full possession of all his senses and be sound in every member, free to act, of good counsel and high courage and, finally, of the right stock, i.e. a member of the Quraysh.[1] The historian and philosopher Ibn Khaldūn, when dealing with this last condition, holds it is not requisite for the Caliph to be actually of the Prophet's family, but he declares that those legists who dispute about the necessity for Qurashite birth base their arguments on false interpretation of various *ḥadīths* of the Prophet.[2] He interprets and expatiates upon the other qualities, and says that, although knowledge, justice and ability are matters about which opinions may differ, there is no discussing about bodily and mental soundness. Any defect whatsoever which prevents full employment of body and mind disqualifies a man from the Caliphate. Madness, blindness, dumbness, deafness are all reasons for exclusion from the imāmate. Parallel with the loss of a member is any hindrance, such as by *force majeure* or captivity, whether by a Muslim or a non-Muslim, which may deprive the imām of the power to carry out his duties. The Caliph would thus be incapacitated if he were held in submission by one of his servants who dominated him without coming to an open breach or rebellion. If, on examination, the general conduct of such a "guardian" is found to be in accordance with the precepts of the law and the faith, then the imām may be retained in his office. If the contrary be the case, Muslims are bound to call to their aid someone who can restore to the Caliph the powers he has lost. When the Buwayhids took possession of the Caliphate, the Abbasids of the Quraysh proved themselves too feeble to govern and were hence disqualified from office. If, however, the Quraysh had been able to provide a strong Caliph, they alone would have been qualified to be the heads of Islam.[3]

In view of what they required from the Caliph, the lawyers and theorists could not leave to chance the method by which he reached the throne. Māwardī assumes that election is the proper means to be adopted. According to him, when the need arises for an imām, the community of Islam divides into two bodies; the

[1] Māwardī, pp. 3 ff. [2] *Prolégomènes*, tr. de Slane, I, 395 f.
[3] *Ibid.* I, 392, and Māwardī, p. 25.

first comprising those qualified to choose a leader for Islam, and the second those persons from amongst whom he may be chosen. The qualifications requisite in the Caliph have been considered, and it remains therefore to consider those requisite in the electors. Three qualities are demanded in them; first, a character for justice in all respects, second, knowledge which will lead to recognition of the men eligible for the Caliphate, and third, the good judgment which will lead to choice of the person most deserving of the office. The persons having the necessary qualifications are those who possess real influence in the community, men with the power "to bind and to loosen". Those persons who reside in the same city as the imām who may be elected should have no advantage in the election over those living elsewhere. It is through recognized precedent (*'urf*), and not by the law (*shar'*), that those living about the palace have an advantage, and that merely because they are the first to learn of the death of the Caliph and because those most fitted to the office of Caliph live in his city.

As to the actual number of persons requisite to hold the election, there is dispute among the learned. Some say that the whole body of duly qualified persons in every city must agree on the choice, but the necessity for this general consensus is refuted by the precedent of the election of Abu Bakr, who was acknowledged only by those persons who happened to be in his company at the time. Others of the learned say that five electors only are necessary, because out of the council of six appointed by Omar, one, 'Uthmān, was appointed by the other five. Still others again hold that three electors only are necessary, in the same way that a *walī* and two witnesses are necessary to ratify a marriage. And there are even some (the Asha'rites) who maintain that the acknowledgment by one person alone is valid.[1]

When the persons having power "to bind and to loosen" are assembled, they scrutinize the character of those eligible for office, and then proceed to pay homage to the one who excels most in the qualities desirable and requisite and whom people will be inclined to obey. They must not delay, but as soon as their deliberations have led them to decide upon a particular person they must offer him the imāmate. If he accepts it, they acknowledge him as imām, and by their acknowledgment the office is confirmed in his hands.

[1] Māwardī, pp. 5 f.

It is then necessary for the whole of the community to pay homage to him and to submit themselves to his command. If, however, he refuses the office, he may not be compelled to it, for it is a voluntary contract into which compulsion does not enter.[1] The offer is then transferred to the next of those qualified. If there are two candidates equally qualified, then the elder is the one to be acknowledged. If there is no difference in age, then the circumstances of the period and its needs must be taken into consideration in the choice of the imām.

Should two different parts of the Caliphate each elect a Caliph, the election is invalid, for the reason that there cannot be two imāms in the community at one and the same time, though there are people who claim that the existence of more than one imām is lawful.[2]

There is, Māwardī acknowledges, a second method by which the community may be provided with a Caliph; namely, through appointment by the preceding Caliph.[3] This is a method approved by the *ijmā'*, which normally serves to give legal sanction to the accomplished fact and which here is based upon the precedents established by Abu Bakr, who appointed Omar to be Caliph, and by Omar, who appointed a conclave to elect his successor.

So much for the orthodox view of the qualifications and functions of the holder of the sovereignty, which for Sunnīs is represented by the Caliphate. As has already been to some extent indicated, the Shī'a view of the qualifications for the headship of Islam is a very different one. In the first place, the majority of the heterodox are strongly legitimist. The Imāmīya, divided into the

[1] Not all the legists agree with this. Thus, according to Shīrāzī (*Tanbih*, p. 311), the election of the imām is a duty incumbent upon the whole community. If there is only one man suitable, he must seek the office. If he refuses it he must be compelled to take it.

[2] There were actually, at the time Māwardī wrote, three Caliphates in existence, namely, that of the Abbasids at Baghdad, of the Fāṭimids in Egypt and Syria and of the Umayyads in Spain. Ibn Khaldūn (*Prolégomènes*, tr. de Slane, I, 391) was of the opinion that there might be two imāms at one and the same time provided that they were not in the same country or in contiguous ones, and that there was sufficient distance between them to prevent any conflict of authority. He ascribes the doctrine that no two imāms may hold office together to a tradition quoted in the *Ṣaḥīḥ* of Muslim in the section dealing with the leadership (*imāra*) of Islam. The learned of Andalusia and North Africa especially favoured the legality of there being more than one Caliph.

[3] *Op. cit.* pp. 6 and 12 ff.

Ithnā-'asharīya,[1] the Sab'īya[2] and the Zaydīya factions—for Shī'ism, like heterodoxy in general, is fissiparous—maintain that the head of Islam must be a descendant of Muhammad through his daughter Fāṭima, who married 'Alī. They, the Imāmīya, "agree in declaring that the nomination of the imām—the leader or principal of the community—is not amongst the ordinary affairs of life which can be left to the decision of the people. The imāmate is the mainstay of the faith and the foundation of Islam. The Prophet himself dared not leave it to the free choice of the community to appoint the holder of the office, and it was incumbent on him to make the appointment for them. . . . 'Alī was the person so appointed."[3] This view is based on certain Koranic texts which the Shī'ites interpret according to their own doctrines and certain other texts which do not occur in the Koran and which the Shī'a declare to have been deliberately omitted from it by those whose views differ from their own.

The point upon which the legitimists differ is that of the succession to 'Alī. The "Ithnā-'asharīya" hold that the descendants of Fāṭima in turn occupy the imāmate, and that each appoints his successor.[4] They are known as the "Twelvers" because they declare that twelve imāms—counting 'Alī as the first—appeared on earth, and that the last of them, Muhammad b. al-Ḥasan al-'Askarī, whom they call *al-Mahdī*, i.e. "the guided aright", entered an underground chamber at Ḥilla in the year 260/873–4 and there disappeared.[5] At the end of time he will reappear and fill the earth with justice.[6] Until then, the sovereignty of true believers, i.e. of the Shī'a, is held by persons who are simply guardians of public order; so that the Shāh of Persia, which country has been officially Shī'ite since the accession of the Ṣafawī dynasty in A.D. 1502, is from this point of view regarded as no more than a temporary holder of the sovereignty charged with the function of maintaining law and order.

The "Sab'īya" or "Seveners" agree with the "Ithnā-'ashar-

[1] I.e. the "Twelvers", for a reason to be explained. [2] The "Seveners".

[3] Ibn Khaldūn, *Prolégomènes*, ed. Quatremère, I, 355; tr. de Slane, I, 400. Cf. also Shahristānī, *Kitāb al-Milal*, ed. Cureton, pp. 2 f.

[4] Ibn Khaldūn, *Prolégomènes*, ed. Quatremère, I, 357; tr. de Slane, I, 402.

[5] The impostors who appear from time to time and call themselves the "Mahdī" are claimants to the honour of the twelfth imāmate.

[6] Ibn Khaldūn, *Prolégomènes*, ed. Quatremère, I, 359.

īya" about the list of imāms as far as Ja'far al-Ṣādiq, the sixth, but there the two factions part company. The origin of the division goes to the roots of the matter, but is simply explained. The "Twelvers" declare that Ja'far al-Ṣādiq nominated as his successor his second son Mūsā al-Kāẓim[1] for the reason that his eldest son Ismā'īl was a drunkard, unworthy of the honour, and, moreover, died before his father. This nomination the more rigid "Seveners" regard as futile, since each imām is the eldest son of his predecessor and has been divinely appointed from the beginning of time, and therefore Ismā'īl, after whom they call themselves "Ismā'īlīs",[2] is the seventh imām. According to them, further, he did not really die before his father, but disappeared; and he is the last of the imāms, who will one day reappear.[3]

The point on which the "Zaydīya"—adherents of Zayd, grandson of Ḥusayn—differ from the other factions is that of the qualifications required of the imām other than being descended from Muhammad through Fāṭima, his daughter. They hold democratically that the imām must be elected by the Shī'a, and that he must be a person of knowledge, an ascetic and a brave man, who comes forward to claim office.[4] In accordance with their doctrines, he may not himself appoint his successor, and they admit the possibility of there being two imāms living at the same time, provided their domains are far apart.[5] Amongst the Zaydīs are the rulers of San'ā in Yemen, who have always called themselves "Imāms".

Of other dissident groups it must suffice to mention the Khārijīs, who held that it was not essential to have an imām at all, provided that the laws of the faith were kept; but that if it were found necessary to have one, then a worthy believer was to be elected, and that without regard to his being either a slave or a free man, Arab or non-Arab.[6]

[1] One of the two imāms buried at Kāẓimayn, near Baghdad.

[2] To this faction belonged the "Assassins", who created so great a stir in Europe during the Crusades.

[3] See further, Levy, "An account of the Ismā'īlī doctrines" *J.R.A.S.*, July 1930, pp. 509–36, and B. Lewis, *The Orgins of Isma'ilism: a study of the historical background of the Fatimid Caliphate* (Cambridge, 1940).

[4] Ibn Khaldūn, *Prolégomènes*, ed. Quatremère, I, 357.

[5] Cf. R. Strothmann, *Das Staatsrecht der Zaiditen* (Strassburg, 1912).

[6] See further D. B. Macdonald, *Development of Muslim Theology, Jurisprudence and Constitutional Theory* (New York, 1926), pp. 23 ff., etc.

One may pause at this point to remark that Sunnī theory of the Caliphate agreed ill with its actual history. Nevertheless it must be noted that the persons who built up the theory were not entirely detached from reality, for it was they who interpreted, deduced and compiled the laws by which the Muslim theocratic State was administered, and hence held a position of importance, more particularly at the Abbasid court where the Persian ideal of religion as the sister of kingship[1] prevailed. Where the legists were forced to succumb to facts they called in aid the doctrine that *ijmā'*, the agreement, actually the acquiescence, of the community, justifies whatever happens in Islam. That the Caliphate became practically a hereditary honour was not to their advantage, for they would probably have gained opportunities as referees if the elective principle had prevailed. As it was, when it became the common practice for a Caliph to appoint his *walī al-'ahd*, or heir-apparent, the lawyers recognized it as legal, but only because they were compelled, and then pointed to *ijmā'* to justify their action.[2]

It is easy to see how the lawyers and theorists came to insist on membership of the Quraysh as a requisite in a Caliph, for in fact every Caliph, whether of the four "Orthodox" ones, the Umayyads or Abbasids, had belonged to some branch of the tribe. The Abbasids, with their Persian affinities, favoured the hereditary character of their office, and not being direct descendants of the prophet himself, tried hard through their court lawyers to make the community forget it, thus ignoring the fact that it was the acquiescence of the community, and not their own origin, which preserved them on the throne.[3]

Apart from being of Qurashite birth, few ruling Caliphs fulfilled the conditions demanded by the theorists.[4] Many of them,

[1] See Firdawsī, *Shāhnāma* (on *Dīn* and *Shāhī*), ed. Turner Macan, III, 1412, and also Ibn Qutayba, *'Uyūn al-Akhbār*, p. 30, l. 6 f.

[2] The pious of a later time called hereditary sovereignty *sunnat kisrā wa qayṣar*: "the practice of Chosroes and Caesar", i.e. the way of heathen empires.

[3] When Muntaṣir became Caliph (247/861), a certain Ḥusayn ibn Ḍaḥḥāk congratulated him in the following terms: "I felicitate you, Commander of the Faithful, on your Caliphate. The desires of the *umma* (the community) of Muhammad have agreed upon it." (*Agh* VIII, 177.) See further Goldziher, *Muhammedanische Studien* II, 98 ff.

[4] There came a time when only the members of a particular family of the Abbasid clan could be appointed, for the reason that all except that one family

though holding office as heads of the Islamic state, were yet tyrannous despots who persecuted fellow-believers for the most godless reasons; and after Ma'mūn, who died in 218/833, there was none amongst the degenerate line of Abbasids capable of the duties of defending the faith or administering the empire. The fact was recognized by the philosophers of Islam. But again *ijmā'*, as the embodiment of the common sense of the people, permitted the ordinary Muslim to continue his way of life without greatly disturbing himself over questions of state. Ghazālī, who died in A.D. 1111, speaks out on the matter and says: "There are those who hold that the imāmate is dead, lacking as it does the required qualifications. But no substitute can be found for it. What then? Are we to give up obeying the law? Shall we dismiss the qāḍīs, declare all authority to be valueless, cease marrying and pronounce the acts of those in high places to be invalid at all points, leaving the populace to live in sinfulness? Or shall we continue as we are, recognizing that the imāmate really exists and that all acts of the administration are valid, given the circumstances of the case and the necessities of the actual moment?"[1]

It is clear from the work of the theorists that they agreed with Ghazālī and preferred any kind of stable government, even if accompanied by tyranny, to civil war; and demanded obedience to the ruler, whoever he might be, from all subjects.[2] There is a *ḥadīth* to the effect that, if the Commander of the Faithful were a mutilated negro slave, he must be obeyed. Another *ḥadīth* says: "Obedience to me (the prophet) is obedience to God and obedience to the imām is obedience to me; also rebellion against me is rebellion against God and rebellion against the imām is rebellion against me."[3]

Every Caliph on accession to the headship of Islam claimed the prerogatives which were exclusively his as Commander of the

(Qādir's) had assimilated with the ordinary population, and no longer had the necessary prestige to command the respect of the population. (Ibn al-Athīr, x, 65, A.H. 467.)

[1] *Iqtiṣād fī 'l-i'tiqād* (Cairo, A.H. 1327), pp. 98 f. See further, Goldziher, *op. cit.* II, 93 ff.

[2] E.g. *Iqtiṣād fī 'l-i'tiqād*, p. 97.

[3] Abu Yūsuf, *Kitāb al-Kharāj*, pp. 5 f. Compare Ibn Qutayba, *'Uyūn al-akhbār*, p. 19: "If the man is just, then reward is due to him and gratitude from you. If he is tyrannous, then the burden of sin is his, and it is your duty to be patient."

Faithful. The first was that when he himself was not leading the prayer in the mosque as the imām, or foremost of the community, the person who led the prayer in his place should pronounce the sovereign's name in the *khuṭba*, the address delivered in the mosques on Fridays, in the course of which a prayer is recited for the welfare of the recognized head of Islam. Great importance was attached to mention of the ruler's name, for particularly when court intrigues were at work and there were clashing interests, it indicated to the general body of believers whom the persons in power regarded as the Caliph.[1] The omission of the Caliph's name from the *khuṭba* was taken as a sign of rebellion. When in the reign of Ma'mūn, Ṭāhir Dhu'l-Yaminayn, who was governor of Khurāsān, committed this fault of omission, Ma'mūn's intelligence officer, who was present in the mosque and in full expectation of being put to death for his act, promptly wrote a dispatch reporting that the governor had declared himself independent of the central authority.[2] If there was any difficulty about the appointment, or an attempt to hold back mention of the Caliph's name, as sometimes happened when power was in the hands of the Buwayhids, the *khuṭba* was recited, but a general title was inserted instead of the Caliph's personal name. This was so under the Abbasid al-Qādir.[3]

The second of the prerogatives claimed by the Caliphs was that of having their names on all coinage in the empire.[4] This privilege was generally, but not always, accorded them even by princes who were virtually independent of the central government, but who continued the practice out of a traditional loyalty or from some remains of pious feeling. In these cases, the name of the Caliph appeared on the coinage together with that of the prince who struck it; thus Maḥmūd of Ghazna and Saladin in Egypt

[1] Under non-Muslim rule, it is not usual to mention the name of the actual reigning prince.

[2] Ṭabarī, III, 1064.

[3] Ibn al-Athīr (A.H. 381), IX, 55 f. See further for the *khuṭba* Ibn Khaldūn, *Prolégomènes*, tr. de Slane, II, 71 ff.

[4] It would appear that the Umayyad Caliphs did not put their names on their coinage, and hence the advent of a new Caliph of that line caused no alteration in their coins. Seemingly the Abbasid Caliph Mahdī began the practice. (S. Lane-Poole, *The Coins of the Eastern Khaleefehs in the British Museum* (London, 1875), pp. viii ff. See also Ibn Khaldūn, *Prolégomènes*, tr. de Slane, II, 54 ff.)

inscribed both the name of the Caliph of Baghdad and their own name on their coins. Rival Caliphs, as for example the Fāṭimids in Egypt, had their own names exclusively upon their coinage.[1]

Another privilege of the Caliph was to have a special portion of the mosque railed off or enclosed for his exclusive use and with a private entrance from the street. This special enclosure is called the *maqṣūra*, i.e. "the confined part", and tradition connects its origin with an attempt made by the Khārijīs on the life of the Caliph Mu'āwiya during service in a mosque.[2] In the mosques also the early Caliphs alone used the *minbar*, or pulpit, a wooden structure which developed out of what in pre-Muslim times had been the raised seat of the tribal judge and became under the Umayyads the throne occupied by the Caliph.[3]

Less important symbols of office were the sceptre and the seal, which each of the Umayyad Caliphs transmitted to his successor on the throne, as well as the *burda*, the mantle of the Prophet, which the Caliph Mu'āwiya had, by purchase or otherwise, acquired from the man to whom Muhammad had presented it. Al-Saffāḥ, the first of the Abbasids, obtained possession of it, and it remained with the dynasty until the end.[4] This relic is said to have been preserved at Constantinople until comparatively recent times.

As for the functions which the lawyers and theorists lay down for the Caliphate, since it is a substitute for the office of the Prophet, those functions consist of the double task of defending the faith and administering the worldly affairs of the Muslim empire. In the same way that the Prophet, who revealed the law, was concerned with guiding men for their good to a knowledge of the sacred law both as it affects this world and the next, so the Caliphs, who are the representatives of the Prophet, must concern themselves with leading men towards observance of the laws so as to ensure their welfare in both worlds.[5] Succinctly put, the duties of the ruler in Islam are four: judgment, taxation, the Friday

[1] See the *Catalogue of Oriental Coins in British Museums*, vols. II and IV.

[2] See further Ibn Khaldūn, *Prolégomènes*, tr. de Slane, II, 71 ff.

[3] Cf. *Aghanī*, IX, 13; XVIII, 14, last line. See further Goldziher, *Muhammedanische Studien*, II, 40 f. and C. H. Becker, *Islamstudien* (Leipzig, 1924), I, 450 ff.

[4] *Fragmenta Historicorum Arabicorum*, ed. de Goeje, I, 82 and 208.

[5] Ibn Khaldūn, *Prolégomènes*, ed. Quatremère, I, 343 f.

service and the *jihād* (the "holy war").[1] These duties were increased and expanded by Māwardī under ten heads. According to him, the Caliph is bound to maintain the faith according to the *uṣūl* (principles) established and the *ijmā'*. If an "innovator", i.e. a creator of heresies, appears, or if a believer is seized with doubt, it is the Caliph's duty to direct him in the right path. He must, in fact, see that the faith is guarded against all injury and the community from all error. Further, he must make the laws effective and see that justice is done between disputants. He must defend the territory of Islam, and secure the inviolability of its inhabitants and their possessions, so that men may go abroad in safety on their lawful occasions. He must see that the penalties demanded by the law are inflicted upon wrongdoers, so that the prohibitions decreed by Allah may be protected from falling into disregard. He must keep the frontiers well guarded with forces enough to repel any sudden raid by an enemy on the sacred territory of Islam and any attack on the person of a Muslim or an ally. Against those who resist Islam after they have been summoned to adopt it, a *jihād* must be declared, unless they belong to the "protected" peoples. Within the empire, he is responsible for collection of taxes and the *ṣadaqa*, the "alms", as the law demands from him, and he must perform his duty without fear or regret. He must see that all grants and allowances due out of the public treasuries are paid. He must nominate trusty men to take charge of government posts and to have the care of the finances. And, lastly, the Caliph must personally have control of affairs and watch the progress of events, not delegating his duties to another on purpose to devote himself to his own pleasures.[2]

In modern western treatises dealing with authority in the State, it is customary to consider the powers of the king or of the government under the three heads of (1) the legislative, (2) the executive, and (3) the judicial. This scheme may with advantage be followed here in considering in greater detail the way in which the functions of the Caliph were actually performed.

So far as legislation for the community of Islam is concerned, the Caliph had in theory no powers at all, seeing that God is the

[1] Ibn Qutayba, *'Uyūn al-akhbār*, p. 18.

[2] Māwardī, pp. 23 f. See further, L. Gardet, *La Cité Musulmane: Vie sociale et politique* (Paris, 1954).

only lawgiver and that he had declared his will in the Koran as revealed by the Prophet Muhammad. Any seeming obscurity or inadequacy in the Koran was made good by the *ḥadīth*, which was the record of the Prophet's sayings and doings and was a sufficient guide to the will of Allah. Failing them, and where there remained still some uncertainty or some need for a new application of the revealed law, a number of authorities, namely, the imāms, the founders of the four "schools" of law, interpreted or expanded the laws as they stood. The Caliph was not endowed with any special privilege in this respect. He was in theory merely the representative and agent of the law, the person by whose efforts it was carried into effect. He had himself to observe it as well as to secure its being observed by others. Where it was explicit[1] and clear, he had to carry it out as it stood, not changing it in any particular, as for example in the case of the alms-tax, in which the lawyers demand that he must collect all that is prescribed by the text-books, without fear or favour. Even the theorists, however, allow great scope for the Caliph when the texts and precedents give no guidance on a question that concerns him. Thus, for example, he was allowed to declare in wars against infidels what the fate of the prisoners was to be and how conquered lands were to be distributed. Also he could make what laws he pleased with regard to the conferment of public office and in connection with his relations with foreign princes.

How in actual practice laws came into being after Muhammad's time has been to some extent demonstrated. Where no special legislation was required by the advent of Islam, long-standing local custom was generally permitted to continue without question. As a rule, the need for legislation arose when the Caliph in his capital, or the conqueror and governor of a province, was unexpectedly confronted with a case in which practical interests were at variance with the claims of Islam. A situation of that kind arose when the treasury in Khurāsān was depleted owing to the remission of taxes to the many inhabitants who became converts to the faith. Generally, it is obvious that legislation thus demanded by expediency cannot have been intended to have more than temporary validity.

As few of the Caliphs, particularly of the Abbasid dynasty,

[1] I.e. where there is a *naṣṣ*, or text, specifically covering any question.

were themselves competent either to adapt or to initiate legislation, they were assisted by *'ulamā* and *fuqahā*, "doctors" and "legists" trained in the study of the law, who performed these tasks for the sovereign. Abu Yūsuf the qāḍī fulfilled these functions of legal advisership for Hārūn al-Rashīd, for whom he compiled the work known as *Kitāb al-Kharāj*. It contains guidance on "Imposts, land-tax, tithes, poor-rate, poll-taxes and other matters which it is his business to supervise and enforce".[1] There is evidence, however, that the Caliphs did not always follow the counsel of their legal advisers. In the name of public expediency, *maṣlaḥa*, they could and did by their rescripts impose laws which were not in accordance with the *shar'* (the written law). At times they limited the jurisdiction of the qāḍīs, who had to interpret the law, by suspending the application of certain enactments or choosing the interpretation of the particular school which most favoured their own desires or was best adapted to the circumstances of the time or place.[2] On the other hand, once the religion of Islam came to be interpreted almost exclusively by the *'ulamā* and the legists, their influence over the community overruled that of the Caliph himself, and when the Caliphate disappeared the sovereignty often lay in their hands. It was they who in times of crisis indicated the way for the community to follow, and even powerful monarchs found it expedient to work through them. Thus when the Mongol conqueror Hūlāgū in 1258 destroyed Baghdad and the Caliphate with it, though not a Muslim himself he consulted the *muftīs* of the great Mustanṣirīya *madrasa* in the capital as to whether the just unbeliever or the unjust believer had a greater claim to respect. They gave their verdict in favour of the former and hence justified Hūlāgū's claim to rulership of the Muslim community.[3]

In the realm of administration, the main duties of the Caliph were, theoretically, to carry out the laws of Islam and to keep the

[1] *Kitāb al-Kharāj*, p. 2.

[2] Cf. D. Santillana, *Istituzioni di diritto musulmano*, I, 19.

[3] *Al-Fakhrī*, ed. Ahlwardt, pp. 19 f. A modern example is provided by the history of France in Morocco. When France asked the consent of the Sulṭān Mulay Ḥasan (1873–94) to have a consular representative at Fez, he submitted the question to the *'ulamā* at Mecca, and asked for a *fatwā*, declaring that, in spite of the French conquest, Algiers should be reckoned as *Dār al-Islām*, i.e. Muslim territory, and not *Dār al-Ḥarb*, i.e. hostile territory. (A. G. P. Martin, *Quatre siècles d'histoire marocaine*, p. 387.)

frontiers of its empire intact. We have seen that the regulations in the Koran applicable to the government of the State are negligible in quantity, and that consequently it was left to the individual Caliph, assisted if he thought fit by men learned in the law of Islam, to evolve such methods either as appealed to him or as seemed expedient. During the period of the expansion of the Islamic empire, the efforts of most of the Caliphs were directed to the preservation of what they already held and the acquisition of further territory. Within the frontiers, and more particularly in the capital and other large cities or in their neighbourhood, public works claimed the attention of some of the monarchs, who erected mosques and other buildings for general use and dug canals for the benefit of agriculture and trade, while others confined their attention to erecting magnificent palaces to satisfy their own private ambitions. Money was the first essential either for the maintenance of armies or for the carrying out of civil schemes, and we find that the centre of the system which slowly grew up was the revenue department.

Ibn Khaldūn, basing his theory upon what he had observed in his reading of history, laid it down that the prime necessities for the governance of a State are troops, money and means of communication with distant parts. More summarily he declared that the instruments of government are the sword and the pen.[1] Consideration of the first of these terms, "the sword", which represents the military side of the government, will be deferred until some attention has been paid to the functions of "the pen". This term represented during the history of the Caliphate a number of different functionaries and their duties. Under the first four successors of Muhammad, while the capital of the empire was at Medina, "the pen" was held in the hands of the Caliph himself. Those were the early days of conquest, when the Caliph and his agents were chiefly concerned in the acquisition of territory. Military exigencies predominated. The raising and organization of armies, the appointment of generals and the direction or operations were then the main tasks of the sovereign. But he had further to deal with the vast sums sent to the capital as tribute from the conquered territories. This had to be divided amongst the faithful, and "the pen" was employed by the Caliph

[1] *Prolégomènes*, ed. Quatremère, II, 19; tr. de Slane, II, 23.

Omar in compiling a *dīwān*, or register, of those Muslims about him entitled to shares.[1] The troops actually engaged in campaigning abroad needed little immediately, for they lived as conquerors on the lands they subjugated and enriched themselves by vast quantities of booty taken on every field of battle. When the necessity arose for the organized levying and collection of taxes, the duty was undertaken by the Caliph[2] in addition to the distribution of the proceeds. The idea of depositing any portion in the treasury to be held as a reserve against emergencies was alien to the first Caliphs. Omar looked upon the suggestion of it as blasphemous and as implying that Allah would not provide for every contingency; he severely rebuked the man who broached the matter.[3]

To their various duties, the early Caliphs added those of building mosques, maintaining law and order, and occasionally sitting as judges. At Medina, for example, Omar himself acted as qāḍī, and he further appointed the qāḍīs for places outside the capital. These tasks, though fully occupying the Caliph's time and energies, formed the sum total of their administrative efforts. Social amelioration in accordance with the behests of the Koran and its adjuncts was not the concern of the central government, but of each individual Muslim, to every one of whom the revelations of Allah were directed. Thus, the State as such made no effort at the regulation of labour or at specifying the conditions of employment, but each member of the community was aware of what the law—which at the same time regulated Islam and the State—required from him in his treatment of his slaves. Similarly, there was no State system of poor-law administration, but the mendicant could and did demand alms as a right because the Koran had imposed the giving of alms as a duty upon Muslims and there had of necessity to be recipients. Education was almost entirely the concern of the individual, for, though theoretically the administration of the greater mosques, to which the schools were attached, was in the hands of the Caliph, the vast majority of mosques were small places of worship, innocent of any school

[1] Ṭabarī, I, 2411 ff. The word *dīwān* changed and widened its significance to mean "Ministry" or "Office", as will be seen.

[2] *Ibid.* 2496.

[3] *Ibid.* 2414 f.

and maintained by local groups in the places where they were situated.[1]

The system of administration at the heart of the Caliphate remained simple even when the Umayyads succeeded to office and removed the capital to Damascus. Mu'āwiya, the first member of the new dynasty was, however, inclined to autocracy, and disliked the large measure of independence enjoyed by the generals who had charge of military operations and of the administration of the subjugated regions. A period of greater centralization now set in, and as, simultaneously, more settled conditions began to prevail the need arose for better organization of the government. Although the Caliph still exercised personal supervision and control of the affairs of the empire, he was now assisted in the more difficult and complicated duties of peacetime by a number of *dīwāns*, which had come to mean official departments or ministries. Mu'āwiya is said to have begun by establishing the *dīwān al-khātam*, whose duties corresponded to those of a chancellery, where outgoing messages from the Caliph were copied into a register and carefully sealed up before despatch.[1] Gradually there were added other offices. In the *dīwān al-rasā'il*, state missives were composed and put into elegant language; the *dīwān al-mustaghallāt* received rents for the use of state lands and government property, and in the *dīwān al hharāj*, the most important of all the duties of the treasury were carried out. Here were received all moneys remaining over in the various parts of the empire after payment of officials and other necessary expenditure, and it was from here, presumably, that payments were made for the public works which the Umayyads carried out.

A service which was of the greatest importance for the central administration, that of the *barīd* or postal system, was maintained hence throughout the empire. Its purpose was not the carrying of letters for the general public, but the conveyance of official messages between government agents in the provinces and the capital. The officers attached to its service in the provinces were, in fact, intelligence agents, whose business it was to keep watch on events in the various parts of the empire, and send in reports

[1] Cf. Ibn Khaldūn, *Prolégomènes*, ed. Quatremère, I, 395 f.; tr. de Slane, I, 446.

[1] *Al-Fakhrī*, ed. Ahlwardt, p. 130.

of any happenings worthy of note,[1] even in quite unimportant matters. "The king thereby becomes aware of all that passes, good or ill, so that, if a man should wrongly seize a sack of straw or a hen five hundred parasangs away, he (the king) thereby has news of it and commands the punishment of the culprit. Thereby others will know that the king is alert and has appointed men of experience in every place, so that oppressors will withhold their hands from wrong, and men may go about in security in the shade of his justice to gain their livelihood and cultivate their lands."[2]

This instrument of government was not new in Umayyad times, for its name is almost beyond doubt connected with the Latin *veredus*, "a post-horse", and from the fact, further, that many of the terms connected with it are of Persian origin, it may be assumed that the system was taken over from those in use in the Byzantine and Persian empires.[3] Traditionally, its institution is attributed, with other administrative measures, to the Umayyad 'Abd al-Malik ibn Marwān (65/685–86/705) and Omar II is said to have improved it by building caravanserais at suitable stages along the great Khurāsān highway. It was, however, under the Abbasids that the *barīd* achieved its greatest importance and performed its true function as an intelligence service. In their day, relays were placed at suitable stages on all routes leading to the capital, and the Caliph Mahdī in 165/781–2 established a new road supplied with relays from Yemen to Mecca and thence to Baghdad.[4] Messages were sent either by runners or by carriers mounted on horses or camels. In Persia, runners were employed, and the stages there were therefore shorter than in Syria or Arabia, where the postal messengers were mounted. Sometimes, too, pigeons were employed in the service.[5] As well as messages, officials or small bodies of troops, if required in haste at any particular point, were carried by the *barīd*, and during the Mamlūk

[1] Cf. the instance from Abbasid times quoted above (p. 292) of Ma'mūn's intelligence officer who reported to him the act of disloyalty committed by Ṭāhir the Ambidextrous in omitting the Caliph's name from the *khuṭba* (Ṭabarī, III, 1062).

[2] Niẓām al-Mulk, *Siyāsat-nāma*, ed. Schefer (Paris, 1891), p. 58.

[3] *Ibid.*: "Both in the *Jāhilīya* and in Islam, kings have received fresh news through the postmaster." There is a *ḥadīth* of the Prophet in which the *barīd* is mentioned (Bukhārī, *Ṣaḥīḥ*, ed. Krehl, *Kitāb al-Wuḍū'*, I, p. 69, no. 66).

[4] Ibn al-Athīr, VI, 49.

[5] Mas'ūdī, *Murūj al-dhahab*, VII, 127.

period in Egypt its services were even employed for carrying snow from Damascus to Cairo. In Egypt, the officer in charge of the *dīwān al-inshā*, or chancellery, was also responsible for the equipment of the various stages with horses and messengers. Each of the latter, at one time, when on duty wore round his neck a bag of yellow silk containing a copper token, on which was inscribed the Sulṭān's name and titles. At a later period the copper token fell into disuse, but the yellow bag remained as a badge of office.[1]

In course of time, the *ṣāḥib al-barīd*, chief master of the posts of the Caliphate, acquired political significance as supervisor of provincial functionaries. Dispatches from all districts were first directed to local *barīd* officials, who sent them on by the speediest routes to the capital. At the headquarters there, where a special *dīwān* was created for it, the chief master of the posts had the duty of presenting the messages of his subordinates, or reports compiled from them, to the Caliph. Other duties of the chief officer of the service were to appoint local officials in different cities, to nominate secretaries, to place suitable men at relay posts along the roads, to appoint couriers and to see that all received pay and supplies.[2] Seeing that his functions were in large measure those of a director of intelligence services,[3] he was required to have at his command not only the knowledge ordinarily available, but also special information about routes and stages, in case the Caliph ever had need to go on a journey or dispatch troops by the shortest way possible. The route-books compiled by officers of the *barīd* were the earliest Muslim geography books. They provide details of the various itineraries, together with short accounts of the towns on the way, and they also give information about revenues and products of the provinces through which the roads pass. The *barīd* was discontinued in the Eastern Caliphate by the Seljūq Sulṭān Alp Arslān (1063–72), in spite of the protests of the

[1] Qalqashandī, *Subḥ al-a'shā* (14 vols., Cairo, 1913 ff.), I, 114.

[2] Qudāma, *Kitāb al-Kharāj*, in Ibn Khurdādbih, ed. de Goeje (Leyden, 1889), p. 184 (tr. p. 144).

[3] In Manṣūr's day, the officer in charge of the *barīd* in each district was required each day to send reports (*a*) on the price of flour, grain and other food-stuffs, (*b*) on the decisions made in the district by the qāḍī, (*c*) on the activities of the *'āmil*, or governor, (*d*) on the returns of the local treasury, and (*e*) on any happenings of note (Ṭabarī, III, 435).

famous minister Niẓām al-Mulk, who saw in the institution a valuable means of keeping order in the empire.[1]

Of more immediate importance for the general welfare of the country was the work undertaken in connection with canals and irrigation. Under the Caliph 'Abd al-Malik, part of the Baṭā'iḥ, the great Tigris-Euphrates swamp, was drained by order of Ḥajjāj, viceroy in Iraq. Dykes were built up, and channels deepened and widened both for drainage purposes and to provide passage for shipping.[2] Al-Walīd also ordered the making and improvement of roads and the digging out of canals.[3] Further, under the Caliph Hishām, a canal was dug to supply Mosul with drinking water,[4] and another, the "Iraq canal", at Wāsiṭ, by the then governor of Iraq, Khālid al-Qasrī. In spite of the general advantages to be derived from such works, they were by no means always pleasing to the inhabitants of the territory through which they ran, the reason being that landowners were dispossessed to make room for them and local labour impressed for their construction. Thus the poet Farazdaq assailed Khālid al-Qasrī, who dug the "Iraq canal", with the following abusive couplet[5]:

> You have wasted the wealth of Allah without right upon this ill-omened and unblest canal,[6]
> You beat honest people on the back and leave what is due to Allah behind Mālik's[7] back.

[1] See further, Maqrīzī, *Histoire des Sultans Mamlouks de l'Égypte*, tr. Quatremère (2 vols., Paris, 1837–62), II, ii, 89 ff.

[2] Balādhurī, ed. de Goeje, pp. 293 f.

[3] *Frag. Hist. Arab.*, ed. de Goeje, p. 4.

[4] Ibn al-Athīr, v, 99.

[5] *Aghānī*, XIX, 61.

[6] The canal seems to have been called *al-Mubārak*, "the Blessed" (*Aghānī*, XIX, 18).

[7] Mālik was the superintendent of the *shurṭa*, the security (police) force at Basra. He had denied to a dispossessed owner the proprietorship of a village through the site of which the canal passed (*loc. cit.*). Another version of the passage, with the reading *ẓulm* for *ẓahr* in the second line, occurs in the *Dīwān* of Farazdaq, published by J. Hell (Munich, 1901), II, B, 147. There the story is that Mālik slew a certain 'Umar b. Yazīd, and that when the Banu Tamīm tribe came to Khālid, the governor of Iraq, to lay a charge against Mālik, he (Khālid) rejected their evidence. The murder is more fully described in Ṭabarī, II, 1495. For the references in this note I am indebted to the late Professor A. A. Bevan, who suggested that, in accordance with the original context, the word *ẓahr* in the last couplet should be read *ẓulm* as in Farazdaq, i.e.: "You neglect Allah's due demands against Mālik for his crime."

Al-Walīd is credited further with having written to his officers in the various parts of his empire to make provision for the crippled and for chronic invalids, also to build hospitals for the sick.[1]

An administrative reform, probably intended to reduce disorder in the matter of payment of revenues though the Arabic authorities ascribe it to religious pride, is attributed to ʻAbd al-Malik ibn Marwān. This was a change in the coinage of the Muslim empire brought about in 76/695–6.[2] Until that time the coins in circulation in the various provinces of Islam had been those of the various powers in possession before the Muslim conquest. Thus, in Egypt and Syria, Byzantine gold, silver and copper coins were in use, while in what was once Persian territory Sasanian drachmas were the currency. Both systems of coinage were in use together, and interchangeably. Moreover, the Persian coinage had become debased with the decline in the fortunes of the Sasanian kings, so that, in any transactions involving use of it, the parties generally had first to come to an agreement on the value of the money that passed.[3] The result was endless confusion, and a new set of coins was struck. They were on the old models, but were confined to gold *dīnārs* taken from the Byzantine system, and silver *dirhams* from that of the Persians, together with a few Ḥimyarite coins of silver.[4] In design little change was made, but Byzantine coins were adapted for Islamic use by the substitution of Arabic inscriptions (written in Kūfic characters) for the Latin ones on both sides,[5] and the substitution on the obverse of the figure of the Caliph, sword in hand, for that of the Byzantine emperor holding a staff with a cross on it, and, on the reverse, the alteration of the cross standing on four steps into a column with

[1] *Frag. Hist. Arab.*, ed. de Goeje, p. 4.

[2] Ṭabarī, II, 939; Balādhurī, pp. 465 ff.; Māwardī, p. 268, and Ibn al-Athīr, IV, 337. Cf. also von Kremer, *Culturgeschichte*, I, 168.

[3] Māwardī, p. 268.

[4] *Ibid.*

[5] *Obverse*:

In the name of Allah
There is no God but Allah alone
Muhammad is the apostle of Allah.

Reverse:

In the name of Allah. This
dīnār was struck in the
year 76.

a ball at its top.[1] Similarly, the silver coins were after the pattern of those struck by the last Sasanians ("The Chosroes"),[2] but were altered by the addition of crescents and stars and *Bismillāh* on the margins. According to Māwardī, the earliest silver coins, struck in 70/689–90, had a "blessing" on one side and the legend *Li'llāh* ("unto Allah") on the other, while the coins of Ḥajjāj, struck in Iraq a year later, bore the legend *Bismillāh* and the name of Ḥajjāj, the then governor of the province.[3] A study of the coins extant from the Umayyad period shows that the Caliphs of that dynasty did not put their names on the money, and a change of Caliph caused no alteration in the coinage even at Damascus itself.[4] With the introduction of the new coins it was made a penal offence to clip or cut them, though the doctors of Islam dispute the legality of punishment for the misdemeanour.[5]

The transfer of power from the Umayyads to the Abbasids, men in whose veins flowed a good deal of Persian blood and who owed their accession largely to Persian support, meant a change from the simplicity of Bedouin rule to the elaborateness of a system of government copied in many respects from the Persian. The Caliph was no longer a man of simple life accessible to all, but a personage who was surrounded by ministers and officials, and who was accustomed to the luxury traditionally associated with kingship in Persia. The period of the rise to power of the dynasty coincided with a time when acquisition of new territory, and incidentally of fresh supplies of booty, was slow, difficult and sporadic, and the Caliph had to look to the revenue from countries already settled to provide him with the vast sums needed to fill his own private treasury and to meet public expenditure.

The actual land in these countries fell into a number of categories. They might be (*a*) lands which paid either *'ushr* ("tithe"), or land which paid *kharāj*, a general tax; the distinction depending probably on what these lands paid before the Islamic conquest[6]

[1] See Keary, "The Morphology of Coins," *Numismatic Chronicle* (1885–6), quoted by O. Codrington, *Musalman Numismatics* (London, 1904), pp. 11 f.

[2] Māwardī, p. 269.

[3] Māwardī, *loc. cit.* and Codrington, *loc. cit.*

[4] Cf. S. Lane-Poole, *The Coins of the Eastern Khaleefehs in the British Museum* (London, 1875), pp. viii ff.

[5] Māwardī, p. 270.

[6] In theory, all lands are the possession of the whole body of Islam. Those which came into its possession by conquest are divided into three classes:

(*a*) Those in which the inhabitants had to be driven out. Of this, some legists say it is divided up like booty amongst the conquerors, whilst others hold it to

and Muslim legal terms being applied only for distinction. They might further be (*b*) lands comprising the personal estates of the Caliph which had originally been, in Iraq, the private domains of the Sasanian kings.[1] These lands correspond to the *Arāḍī Sanīya* ("the Sublime (i.e. Royal) estates") of the Sulṭāns of Turkey in Iraq, which paid rent at a specially high rate and not the ordinary government revenue. With other lands for which no owners could be found at the conquest, they became in the first place state property, to be disposed of by the Caliph as he saw fit. In Abbasid times, the royal estates, which were cultivated in the ordinary way, paid all their income into the private exchequer of the Caliph. Most of them lay in the rich *Sawād* district in the neighbourhood of Baghdad, and in Muqtadir's day there was a special *dīwān al-ḍiyā' al-khāṣṣa*, or office of the privy estates, to administer their affairs.[2] In still another class were (*c*) lands which in Buwayhid times and occasionally earlier[3] had been set aside for soldiers in return for services in war. These *qaṭā'ī'* (military fiefs) paid *kharāj*. They had at the Muslim conquest been the lands for which no owners could be found, and had hence become the property of the *Bayt al-Māl*, or Government Treasury. Finally there were (*d*) Uncultivated, unused or "dead" lands (*arāḍī mawāt*) which could be granted by the Caliph on special terms to persons who could put them into cultivation or make use of them otherwise.

For a picture of the general administrative duties in which the Caliph engaged, one may quote the historian Ibn al-Athīr, who, in describing Manṣūr, the second member of the Abbasid dynasty, says that he was constantly engaged in the task of commanding

be *waqf*, or mortmain, for the common benfit. If it is divided, the occupants pay *'ushr*; if the original inhabitants are allowed to return, they pay *kharāj*, "tribute".

(*b*) Those in which the inhabitants are permitted to stay. These pay *kharāj* as rent for occupancy, and the *kharāj* therefore continues to be payable even when the occupiers become Muslims. If the occupant did not cultivate his land, it could be sequestrated.

(*c*) Those with whose inhabitants treaties of peace were made on condition that they paid *kharāj* (Māwardī, pp. 237–9, 254).

[1] Abu Yūsuf, *Kitāb al-Kharāj*, p. 32.

[2] *Eclipse of the Abbasid Caliphate*, ed. and tr. H. E. Amedroz and D. S. Margoliouth (7 vols., Oxford, 1920–1), I, 152.

[3] See M. van Berchem, *La Propriété territoriale et l'Impot foncier sous les premiers Califs* (Geneva, 1886), pp. 43 ff.

the right and forbidding the wrong, allotting authoritative duties (*wilāyah*) to his officials, dismissing them, guarding frontiers and outlying regions of the empire, making roads secure, supervising taxation and expenditure and seeing to the welfare of his subjects.[1]

Of all these duties, that of supervising the revenue came easily first, for, if it was important before, it now governed the whole of the administration. In theory, there was a difference between the privy purse of the Caliph[2] and the State treasury.[3] Actually, since the Caliph had control of both, he made little distinction between them; or, at any rate, much that passed into the privy purse came from taxation or fines. Otherwise it is difficult to explain, if report is true, how the Caliph Hārūn al-Rashīd at his death left the enormous sum of 900,000,000 dirhams[4] in the treasury (*bayt al-māl*), while Muqtadir at one time owned a fortune of 500,000 dīnārs.[5] Their ancestor Manṣūr is reported once to have said that four officers were essential for the prosperity of the state: namely, an upright qāḍī, a just officer of the peace (*ṣāḥib al-shurṭa*), a revenue officer who will make thorough investigation without being extortionate ("seeing *I* am enriched by any extortion from my subjects") and, lastly, an officer of the *barīd* who will tell the truth about all of them.[6] The remark made in parenthesis concerning the revenue officer throws considerable light on the Caliph's attitude towards public funds. It was not always, however, to his advantage that he had charge of the State exchequer as well as his own. There were times during the troubled period preceding the arrival of the Buwayhid robber-princes—they were little more—when whole provinces of the Caliphate had fallen away and revenues were scanty, when the Commander of the Faithful had himself to provide money for the public account. The Caliph Muqtadir, when the treasury was empty, was once thus compelled to pay the sum of 300,000 dīnārs out of

1 Ibn al-Athīr, VI, 17 (A.H. 158).

2 *Bayt Māl al-Khāṣṣa*. Cf., for example, Hilāl al-Ṣābī, *Kitāb al-Wuzarā*, ed. H. F. Amedroz (Leyden, 1904), p. 139.

3 *Bayt Māl al-Muslimīn.*

4 Ibn al-Athīr, VI, 146 (A.H. 193). At a moderate estimate the sum was equivalent to £20,000,000 sterling. His grandfather Manṣūr was said to have amassed the sum of 960,000,000 dirhams, which Mahdī, Hārūn's father, dissipated. (Jahshiyārī, *Kitāb al-Wuzarā*, ed. H. v. Mžik (Leipzig, 1926), p. 93a.)

5 *Eclipse of the Abbasid Caliphate*, I, 181.

6 Ṭabarī, III, 398,

his own purse to mercenary troops who had mutinied for their hire.[1] Also the famous vizier 'Alī ibn 'Īsā, when required to defend his administration, said he had not caused the privy purse one-twentieth the expense of his predecessors.[2]

There is little call for sympathy with the Caliphs in this matter since nearly all of them practised extortion from their subjects, and particularly from their ex-ministers, in order to supply their own treasuries. Thus the sum of 700,000 dīnārs was extracted by Muqtadir's agent from the widow of his late minister, Muḥassin, and put into the private treasury,[3] though sometimes the spoils were divided between the public purse and the Caliph's own coffers.[4] Most Caliphs who had the power made similar exactions, often to the accompaniment of torture, from ministers they had dismissed from office, but the brutal and tyrannous Mutawakkil was notorious for this method of adding to his income.[5] It was considered no disgrace in the victim to be thus mulcted, and he was very often permitted to resume office.[6] Naturally it was not the Caliphs alone who practised these "official" acts of extortion. Instances of the kind are recorded of Sulṭān Mas'ūd of Ghazna, who once, after extracting a large sum of money from an official, Niyāl-tagīn the Treasurer, sent him as governor to India.[7] There was even in the third century of Islam a regular *dīwān al-muṣādarīn* or "office of the mulcted", to which ministers were appointed in the same way as to other dīwāns.[8] Its origin probably lay in the special treasury, the *bayt māl al-maẓālim* ("treasury of wrongful exactions"), which the Caliph Manṣūr founded in order to contain the sums of money and other property which he seized from every '*āmil* (provincial governor or revenue officer) whom he accused of extortion and dismissed from office. Each deposit there was carefully labelled for return to the owner on Manṣūr's death.[9]

This form of obtaining revenue was not without its justification in the circumstances in which it was obtained, for office was openly regarded as the path to wealth,[10] and those who were mulcted

[1] *Eclipse of the Abbasid Caliphate*, I, 142.
[2] *Wuzarā*, p. 284.
[3] *Eclipse of the Abbasid Caliphate*, I, 141.
[4] *Ibid.* p. 129.
[5] Cf. Ṭabarī, III, 1374 ff.
[6] Ibn al-Athīr, VI, 8 and VIII, 116, 162.
[7] Gardīzī, *Zainu'l Akhbār*, ed. M. Nāzīm (Berlin and London, 1928), p. 97.
[8] *Eclipse of the Abbasid Caliphate*, I, 21.
[9] Ṭabarī, III, 415 f.
[10] Cf. Ibn al-Athīr (A.H. 158).

recouped themselves by various methods from the unfortunate peasants, who were the actual payers both of the legal tax and its illegal supplement. Abu Yūsuf[1] describes various abuses which he advises the Caliph to abolish, amongst them the practice by revenue-officers of making the peasants supply food and the cost of paper used in official clerical work, and even of extorting a fee for the use of the scales employed in weighing out the government share of harvested grain. Exactions were also made when money was brought in payment of the government demands. It was not unknown for the officials to declare the proffered dirhams to be below the current value of the coins and to demand supplementary payment. If the taxpayer demurred, he was liable to be tied with ropes and exposed to the heat of the sun or even to have the *jarra* (? "garrotte") fixed upon him.

The public purse, the treasury or exchequer of Islam, as distinct from the Caliph's privy purse, was known as the *Bayt al-Māl*,[2] "The House of (Public) Property". The term had no reference to any particular building or locality, but was applied to that part of the Caliph's activities concerned with such wealth, either in specie or in kind, as belonged to the community of Islam as a whole and which passed through the hands of the *'āmils*, the agents or tax-gatherers of the community.

The sources from which, theoretically, the *Bayt al-Māl* derived its income were three: (i) *Fay'*, or tribute from lands conquered by Muslims: (ii) *Ghanīma*, the loot of battle; and (iii) *Ṣadaqa*, alms-tax.

(i) *Fay'*, except as to one-fifth, is the due of the *Bayt al-Māl* because the disposal of it is at the discretion of the imām, the Caliph.

(ii) *Ghanīma* is booty acquired on the field of battle. Four-fifths is divided up amongst the men who have won it, the remaining fifth, like the similar portion of the *Fay'*, is divided into three portions, of which one-third goes to the *Bayt al-Māl*. This is the Prophet's portion and is to be expended for the general welfare of Muslims according to the discretion of the imām. One-third goes to the kinsmen of the prophet, and hence the imām has no power over it and it does *not* go to the *Bayt al-Māl*; and one-third

[1] Cf. *Kitāb al-Kharāj*, p. 62.
[2] Māwardī, pp. 366 ff.

goes to the *Bayt al-Māl* for specified charitable purposes, such as relief of orphans, the poor and the wayfarer.

(iii) *Ṣadaqa* (alms-tax) is of two kinds:

(*a*) From property not disclosed by the owner—this kind may be disposed of immediately by the payer, in such fashion as he wills.

(*b*) From property openly acknowledged by the owner, namely agricultural lands, fruit trees and cattle. It is called *'ushr* ("tithe") when taken from the first two items, and alms-tax, *ṣadaqa*, or *zakāt*, from the last. The purposes for which the alms-tax is intended are specified in the Koran (9^{60}). It is to be used for the "poor and the needy, and those who labour to collect it, and those whose hearts are won to Islam and for [the ransom of] captives and those in debt and those [warring] on God's path, and for the wayfarer".

Apart from the *ghanīma*, the *Bayt al-Māl's* sources of revenue, namely the *kharāj*, *'ushr* and *zakāt*, are imposts on property situated within the boundaries of the Muslim empire. This is regarded as being owned by the community of Islam whether the occupier is a Muslim or a "protected" non-Muslim; because, according to theory, it was in the first place acquired by conquest. Traditionally, Omar is credited with having refused to sanction the division of the conquered lands, such as Iraq and Syria, amongst the men who had seized them, holding that, if that were done, there would be nothing left for the posterity of Islam, but that portable booty was a different matter.[1] The *fay'*, or tribute from these lands, according to theory,[2] was the *kharāj*, or produce, derived from them. *Kharāj* is not, however, to be levied on all lands, but only on two kinds. The first is territory in which the inhabitants have come to terms with Islam, one of the conditions being relinquishment of their sovereign.[3] Such land may not be sold, and the *kharāj* levied upon it is rent which does not cease with the conversion of its inhabitants to Islam, but is taken from both Muslim and "protected" peoples. The second kind is that in which the Muslims have come to terms with the inhabitants, one of the terms being that the native sovereignty shall continue.[4]

[1] Abu Yūsuf, *Kitāb al-Kharāj*, pp. 13–15. [2] *Ibid.* p. 13.

[3] E.g. parts of Persia whose ruler was cast from the throne when Islam gained power.

[4] This can only mean raiding territory not actually subdued, as, for example, in parts of the Byzantine empire or in India.

This second kind of land may be sold and the *kharāj* thereon is a tax (*jizya*) which ceases on conversion to Islam. It is taken from "protected" peoples, but not from Muslims.[1]

A slightly different version of what constitutes *kharāj* territory is provided by Abu Yūsuf,[2] who says that it comprises all non-Arabian lands left by the conquering Caliph in the hands of its original inhabitants, and all non-Arabian lands in which the inhabitants came to terms and put themselves under the "protection" (*dhimma*) of Islam. Other lands—such as those in which the inhabitants were converted to Islam, either peaceably or after having been offered it as an alternative to death, without the option of accepting the *dhimma*—are, with a few exceptions, liable to *'ushr* ("tithe") and not to *kharāj*. It was held further that the non-Muslim inhabitants of lands which paid *kharāj* had to pay the poll-tax (*jizya*).

The theory of *kharāj* as here set forth was formulated not earlier than the second century of Islam, by which time Muslims were being compelled to pay *kharāj* for any lands they held, in addition to the alms (*ṣadaqa* or *zakāt*) to which all members of the faith were liable. The earliest Muslims had paid no *kharāj*, and in Omar's day, when there was strict adherence to his rule that no Arab Muslim could own lands in conquered territory, the exchequer was sufficiently well filled by the tribute derived from non-Muslims in occupation of such land. When the rule fell into abeyance the public funds suffered, until the Umayyad governor of Iraq, Ḥajjāj, was compelled to enforce payment of the land-tax on holders of land under his control whether they were adherents of Islam or not. The pious Caliph Omar II (717–20) further precipitated matters in his attempt to encourage the spread of Islam by freeing Muslims from taxation. After a struggle—the course of which may be followed in the history of the conquest of Khurāsān[3]—between the claims of piety and the exchequer, *kharāj* came to be imposed on all land-holders whether Muslims or not, and the theory was invented that every inhabitant of Muhammadan territory paid "land-tax", i.e. *kharāj*, while, in addition, the *dhimmīs*, "protected peoples" (Jews, Christians and the like) were submitted to the ignominy of paying the poll-tax (*jizya*). There is little doubt that in origin *kharāj* and *jizya* were interchangeable

[1] Māwardī, p. 399. [2] *Kitāb al-Kharāj*, p. 39. [3] *Supra*, pp. 12–14.

terms. In the Arabic papyri of the first century A.H.[1] only *jizya* is mentioned, with the general meaning of "tribute", while later the poll-tax could be called *kharāj 'alā ru'ūs ahl al-dhimma*, i.e. "a tax on the heads of protected peoples".[2] The narrower meaning of the word is brought out in a saying attributed to the legist Abu Ḥanīfa, "No individual can be liable at the same time to the *zakāt* and to *kharāj*."[3]

Of the various sources of revenue which accrued to the *Bayt al-Māl* the *kharāj* was much the most important. It was levied in the separate provinces of Islam usually according to the different systems which had obtained in them before the coming of the invader, and it was not often that the theory of how it should be levied agreed with the actual methods practised. Ancient usage, further, could be modified at the caprice of the Caliph. Thus, it is recorded that the Caliph Ma'mūn reduced the share of the harvest payable as tax by the cultivators in the Sawād lands of Iraq from one half to two fifths—a reduction of twenty per cent.[4] On another occasion, in A.H. 203, he reduced the amount of tax payable by the city of Rayy (the ancient *Rhages*) by the sum of two million dirhams.[5] When, seven years later, the citizens of Qumm were encouraged by the example of Rayy to petition the Caliph for a reduction in the amount of *kharāj* levied on them, Ma'mūn rejected their plea. Thereupon they refused to pay any tax at all, but Ma'mūn brought them to their senses by dispatching an expedition against them, and in addition increased the amount of *kharāj* they had to pay from two million to seven million dirhams.[6] A further instance of the Caliph's control of revenue administration is quoted from the reign of Mahdī (775–85), the third Abbasid Caliph. Until his time the revenue had been collected in cash on the basis of the area of land under cultivation, but he was persuaded by his vizier 'Ubayd-allāh that his income would be increased if, instead, he levied the tax on the products of the land

1 C. H. Becker, *Papyri Schott-Reinhardt* (Heidelberg, 1906), I, 39; H. I. Bell, *Aphrodito Papyri* (London, 1910), pp. 167 f.

2 *Jami' al-ṣaghīr* (on margins of *Kitāb al-Kharāj*), p. 21. Cf. also *Tāj al-'Arūs*, II, 29: "The peasant paid *kharāj* on the produce of his land and the *dhimmī* (the 'protected' Jew, Christian, etc.) for his head."

3 Balādhurī, *Futūḥ al-buldān*, ed. de Goeje, p. 447.

4 *Al-Fakhrī*, p. 260.

5 Ṭabarī, III, 1030.

6 *Ibid.* III, 1092 f.

—whether in cash or in kind is not clear—and to apply the same system to date palms and other fruit trees.[1]

As a rule, the central government, as embodied in the Caliph, was slow to bring about measures of reform that would rectify abuses or remove hardships. Yet instances are not unknown of administrative advances. From its nature the *kharāj* was a tax levied after the harvest. The financial year, so far as this tax was concerned, was a solar one. In what had once been Persian territory, the date of payment was the Sasanian *Naw-rūz*, or New Year's Day, which originally was celebrated at the midsummer solstice, June 21st. By that date in Persia the barley and wheat harvests would have been gathered. The calendar in use, however, did not tally with the actual solar year, with the result that the date of *Naw-rūz* gradually advanced to a date in the spring. By the year 282/895 it was about seventy days in advance, and as the officials still went by the old calendar, considerable hardship was caused to cultivators, who were being made to pay the *kharāj* long before the harvest was due. To remedy this difficulty, the Caliph Muʻtaḍid in the year mentioned delayed the date of payment by sixty days, fixing it on the eleventh of Ḥazīrān (June) in the Rūmī (Syrian) calendar,[2] which was a solar one.[3] The reform also affected the Copts in Egypt, who had similarly kept the Persian New Year.[4]

Another reform attributed to ʻAlī ibn ʻĪsā, the vizier of Muqtadir (908–32), has special reference to the province of Fārs in Persia. There the system known as the *takmila* had been causing great hardship. It had been continued from Sasanian times, and consisted in assessing the *kharāj* in lump sums payable by the various districts. If any of the cultivators liable to tax in a particular district defaulted by fleeing to other and less severely taxed regions, the liability for their portion fell on those who remained, and as the assessments were generally heavy there were land-

[1] *Al-Fakhrī*, pp. 215 f.

[2] Ṭabarī, III, 2143.

[3] About half a century later, Barīdī, the unscrupulous minister of the Caliph Muttaqī, obtained an advance of funds by reverting to the old date in Ādhār (March) for his collection of *kharāj*. (*Eclipse of the Abbasid Caliphate*, II, 25.) Another vizier replenished the empty treasury by collecting in one year the *kharāj* due for that year and the next (*Wuzarā*, p. 10).

[4] Maqrīzī, *Khiṭaṭ*, I, 273 f. The Copts still celebrate *Naw-rūz* as their New Year. It now occurs, for them, on the 10th or 11th of September (Lane, *Modern Egyptians*, ch. XXVI, *ad fin.*).

owners who were compelled to sell part of their estates to meet the tax-gatherers' demands. Complaints were bitter, and the Caliph brought relief by discontinuing the *takmila*, though he maintained the total of his revenue by imposing a tax on fruit trees, which had hitherto been exempt.[1]

There is an interesting account extant of the inquiry held at the capital into the complaint of those burdened by *takmila*. The bolder ones amongst those who held grain lands submitted that, until the tax was assessed, they were compelled to keep their grain in jars, so that it rotted. In proof they produced specimens and complained that, being deprived of the value of it, they had to put themselves up for hire and even to sell the hair from the heads of their women-folk. At the same time they declared that the growers of fruits, of which they displayed various specimens (figs, apricots, almonds, pistachio-nuts, etc.) went scot free. The fruit-growers for their part submitted that they had sunk their capital in the purchase of fruit-trees, and that, if they were taxed, they would have spent their money for nothing. They claimed further that the Caliph Mahdī had abolished the tax on fruit-trees. However, the case of the *takmila*-payers was a strong one and the Caliph decided as we have seen.[2]

The theorists carry their delight in uniformity into the realm of taxation and describe in systematized form the different kinds of taxes, the persons liable to them and the amount due from each individual. According to Māwardī,[3] in some of the Sawād territory of Iraq (the rich territory in the lower Tigris-Euphrates basin), the earliest rate of *kharāj* imposed was one *qafīz*[4] of grain and one dirham in cash per *jarīb* (60 cubits by 60) of land. This was the rate which had been charged in Sasanian times. It was changed by Omar, who put an officer in charge of this territory with the command to measure it and impose a tax of 10 dirhams per *jarīb* on vines or thickly planted fruit-trees, 8 on date-palms, 6 on sugar-cane, 5 on clover, 4 on wheat and 2 on barley. Different rates were imposed in Syria, and instructions were given that *kharāj* there, too, was not to be imposed at any flat rate, but

[1] *Wuzarā*, pp. 340 ff. [2] *Ibid.* [3] Pp. 259 ff.

[4] The *qafīz* is described as being eight *raṭls*, but as the weight of the *raṭl* was different in each country and at different times, its equivalent cannot be estimated. In modern Egypt it is a weight amounting to about 2½ kilogrammes, or 5 lb. 10 oz.

according to the bearing capacities of each kind of land and the method by which it was irrigated, because land which required artificial means for irrigation, such as beasts of burden or water-wheels, could not bear the same amount of *kharāj* as land watered by streams or rain.[1]

The idealized regularity of the scheme attributed to Omar, although it is said to have been in force in the fourth century of Islam,[2] cannot, for reasons to be considered further, correspond so well to the actual incidence of taxation in Iraq as to that which is indicated as having prevailed in Syria. Māwardī, when he speaks of the varying rates levied on different kinds of lands, is undoubtedly setting down something that is familiar to him and is describing what must have been the practice long before his time, and which has, in fact, continued until the present. He is thereby deprived of the opportunity of setting down the ordered figures which are his delight. More suited to his theoretical methods is the scheme laid out for collection of *'ushr*, or tithe. Like the *kharāj*, its origin is attributed to Omar. As to the uses to which it is applied, when it is taken from Muslims it is treated in the same way as the alms-tax; when it is taken from *dhimmīs*, or from persons inhabiting enemy territory, it is treated as *kharāj*.[3] Further, if a (Muslim) merchant will declare on oath to the collector of *'ushr* that his goods have already paid the alms-tax, then they are exempt, and the inference is that *'ushr* and alms-tax are regarded as equivalent; and since none but a Muslim pays the alms-tax the exemption from *'ushr* cannot apply to non-Muslims.[4]

According to Abu Ḥanīfa, all products of the earth except wood, seeds and grass, pay tithe, which is calculated on what is left after the cost of all wages for labour and fodder for cattle has been deducted from the gross product of the harvest.[5] It would appear that the tax is, as a rule, only a nominal tenth of the value taxed.

[1] Māwardī, p. 258.

[2] By Maqdisī: 2nd ed. de Goeje (Leyden, 1906), p. 133.

[3] See above, p. 309.

[4] Abu Yūsuf, *Kitāb al-Kharāj*, pp. 76–8. The alms-tax came, in law, to be equivalent to *'ushr* when taken from Muslims, and in theory the collector of *'ushr* was not accountable for it to the *Bayt al-Māl*, or treasury, but to the *Ahl al-Ṣadaqāt*, i.e. the persons for whose benefits the alms was applied. (Māwardī, p. 365; *Eclipse of the Abbasid Caliphate*, II, 127 f.)

[5] *Jāmi' al-ṣaghīr* (on margins of *Kitāb al-Kharāj*), pp. 21 f. Abu Yūsuf is quoted as having exempted vegetables from *'ushr*.

The method of levying it is to add together the values of the various items to be taxed—"of all that passes before the tithe collector"—and then to exact the *'ushr* as follows: at one fourth of the standard rate from a Muslim owner, at one half of it from a *dhimmī* and at the full rate from an inhabitant of enemy territory. Goods less in value than 200 dirhams do not pay *'ushr*.[1] Even then, though it may have been that the city merchant paid an *'ushr* approximating to the provisions of the law-books, it is as little likely that the individual cultivator paid the legal proportion of his produce in "tithe" as that he paid the lawfully specified *kharāj* for the land he occupied. What is more probable is that he paid an agreed sum or portion of his crop to his shaykh or to the *mukhtār*, the recognized head of the district in which he lived, and that the latter paid the sum demanded by the person authorized to collect the taxes. He was not always an official of the government. From very early times it had been the custom of the central government to farm out the taxes of various regions to *concessionnaires* in return for a fixed sum to be paid in advance into the Treasury. The system obviously lent itself to abuses,[2] and the qāḍī Abu Yūsuf, in his work on the *kharāj*, advised his master, the Caliph Hārūn al-Rashīd, not to countenance it, for when the amount of *kharāj* failed to balance the sum paid by the tax-farmer under his *qabāla*, or contract, he practised extortion on the peasantry, and often by means of torture exacted from them more than was due. Abu Yūsuf does not, however, disapprove of a scheme by which the inhabitants of a particular town or agricultural district agree to pay their *kharāj* to some man of means or influence who is resident amongst them and is known to them for honourable dealing. He would be responsible to the government for the sums levied and be accompanied by an official of the *Bayt al-Māl*, who was to exercise supervision.[3]

In Egypt, quite certainly, the taxes were paid collectively, as they had been in the Byzantine era. Experts, after making an estimate of the amount of cultivation in the various districts, met the heads of the villages and settled what proportion of the total

[1] *Kitāb al-Kharāj*, p. 76.

[2] An instance is known where the tax-farmer obtained as his share double the amount that was due from the *kharāj*. (*Eclipse of the Abbasid Caliphate*, I, 100.)

[3] *Kitāb al-Kharāj*, p. 60.

tax was payable by each. The appropriate part of this sum was in turn imposed on the craftsmen and other wage-earners in each village, the share of any defaulter being paid by the rest.[1] One legist quoted in this connection was of the opinion that there were two kinds of *jizya*,[2] one levied on the individual *dhimmī* and the second on each village as a whole.[3]

The method of farming out taxes seems to have been resorted to in Iraq[4] more particularly when the Treasury was in need of funds,[5] but in Egypt it was for long the regular means of revenue collection. Contracts would be made for four years to permit of adjustments for drought or other difficulties, and allowances would be made for any dykes built or repaired, or channels dug out, at rates specified in the registers of *kharāj*. These contracts in effect amounted to the grant of lands (*qaṭā'i'*) in return for fixed sums which compounded for the yield of revenue. The system lasted until the sixth century of Islam. By that time the revenue derived from the ordinary *qaṭā'i'* had been very greatly reduced, while that derived from lands granted to the *umarā*, or military aristocracy, had more than doubled. The consequence was the rapid transformation of all *qaṭā'i'* in Egypt into military fiefs, which did not, however, continue for long to yield the increased revenues.[6]

In cases where there was no contract with a tax-farmer, the *Bayt al-Māl* did not receive the gross income of the *kharāj* tithe and alms-tax from the provinces, but only the surplus remaining after the cost of all local services in each province and the pay of the military[7] had been deducted. Since the taxes were payable some in kind and others in money, both were sent to the capital, and were included in the registers kept in the *Dīwān al-Kharāj*, or Revenue Office, which was created to deal with it. In spite of deductions, the value of what reached the Treasury remained for long very considerable, as may be gathered from a summarized

[1] Maqrīzī, *Khiṭaṭ*, I, 77 (first half of page).

[2] Here meaning "tax" as a general term.

[3] Maqrīzī, *loc. cit.* (second half of page *ad fin.*).

[4] The contract was known as *iltizām* more commonly than *qabāla* and the tax farmer was known as the *multazim*. Various municipal and other minor taxes are in Iraq farmed out to the *multazim* to the present day.

[5] Cf. *Wuzarā*, pp. 10 f.

[6] Maqrīzī, *Khiṭaṭ*, I, 83.

[7] *Eclipse of the Abbasid Caliphate*, I, 107 f.

estimate of the treasury receipts for a year during the reign of Hārūn al-Rashīd (A.H. 170–93 = A.D. 786–809) which has been preserved.[1]

I.—Eastern Provinces

		Dirhams
From grain-lands (*ghallāt*) in the Sawād of Iraq ...		80,780,000
From other items of revenue in the Sawād ...		14,800,000
Goods in kind:		
Najrānī cloaks (*raṭls*)	200	
Terra sigillata (*raṭls*)	240	
From Kaskar (the region of the Wāsiṭ)		11,600,000
From Kūr Dijla (the region of the Shaṭṭ al-'Arab)...		20,800,000
From Ḥulwān...		4,800,000
From Ahwāz		25,000,000
Goods in kind:		
Sugar (*raṭls*)	30,000	
From Fārs		
Goods in kind:		
Black raisins (*raṭls*)	20,000	
Pomegranates and quinces (*raṭls*) ...	150,000	
Rose-water (*bottles*)	30,000	
Preserved fruits (*raṭls*)	15,000	
Sīrāfī clay (edible)[2] (*raṭls*)	50,000	
Raisins, Hāshimī (*kurrs*)	3	
From Kirmān		4,200,000
Goods in kind:		
Yamanī goods (*cloaks*)	500	
Dates (*raṭls*)	20,000	
Cumin	100	
From Mukrān		400,000
From Sind and neighbouring territory		11,500,000
Goods in kind:		
Kayrakh (? food-stuffs) (*qafīzs*) ...	1,000,000	
Elephants	3	
Ḥashīshī robes	2,000	
Waist wrappers	4,000	
Indian aloes-wood (*manns*)	250	
Other kinds of aloes-wood (*manns*) ...	150	
Sandals (*pairs*)	1,000	

This in addition to cloves and nutmeg.

[1] Jahshiyārī, pp. 179b–182b. [2] Cf. le Strange, *Eastern Caliphate*, p. 258.

I.—Eastern Provinces—*continued*

		Dirhams
From Sijistān		4,600,000
Goods in kind:		
Special robes	300	
Sugar (*raṭls*)	20,000	
From Khurāsān		28,000,000
Goods in kind:		
Ingots of silver	2,000	
Pack-horses	4,000	
Slaves	1,000	
Cloaks	27,000	
Myrobolans (*raṭls*)	300	
From Jūzjān		12,000,000
Goods in kind:		
Silk (*manns*)	1,000	
From Qūmis		1,500,000
Goods in kind:		
Ingots of silver	2,000	
Dresses	70	
Pomegranates	40,000	
From Ṭabaristān, etc.		6,300,000
Goods in kind:		
Ṭabarī carpets	600	
Dresses	200	
Cloaks	500	
Kerchiefs	300	
Glass vessels	600	
From Rayy		12,000,000
Goods in kind:		
Pomegranates	100,000	
Peaches (*raṭls*)	1,000	
From Iṣfahān		11,000,000
Goods in kind:		
Honey (*raṭls*)	20,000	
Wax	20,000	
From Hamadhān, etc.		11,800,000
Goods in kind:		
Robb (*manns*)	1,000	
Honey (*raṭls*)	20,000	

I.—Eastern Provinces—*continued*

		Dirhams
From the two Māhs of Baṣra and Kūfa (i.e. Nihāwand and Dīnawar)		20,700,000
From Shahrazūr, etc.		24,000,000
From Mosul, etc.		24,000,000
Goods in kind:		
White honey (*raṭls*)	20,000	
From Jazīra, the Diyārs and the Euphrates ...		34,000,000
From Ādharbayjān		4,000,000
From Mūqān and Karakh		300,000
From Jīlān		
Goods in kind:		
Slaves	200	
From Babr and Taylasān		
Goods in kind:		
Honey (*skins*)	12	
Falcons	10	
Robes	20	
From Urmiya		13,000,000
Goods in kind:		
Maḥfūrī carpets	20	
Embroidery (*pieces*)	580	
Salt (*raṭls*)	10,000	
Ṭarīkh (salt fish)	10,000	
Falcons	30	
Mules	200	

II.—Syria and Egypt

		Dīnārs
From Qinnisrīn and frontier towns		490,000
From Ḥims		320,000
Goods in kind:		
Raisins (*camel-loads*)	1,000	
From Damascus		420,000
From Urdunn		96,000
From Filastīn		310,000
From all the stations in Syria		
Goods in kind:		
Raisins (*raṭls*)	300,000	
From Egypt (apart from Tinnīs, Damietta and al-Ashmūn, the revenues of which are set aside to provide for expenditure)		1,920,000

III.—Western Provinces

		Dirhams
From Barqa		1,000,000
From Ifrīqiya		13,000,000
Goods in kind:		
Carpets	120	

IV.—Arabia

	Dīnārs
From Yemen (in addition to cloaks)	870,000
From Mecca and Medina	300,000

The contributions in kind are to the value of 5,000,000 dīnārs, which, at the rate of 22 dirhams to the dīnār,[1] are equivalent to 125,532,000 dirhams.

The coined (silver) money amounts to 404,780,000 dirhams. The money plus the value of the deliveries in kind amount to 530,312,000 dirhams.[2]

It will be noted that the receipts from the eastern provinces, which were originally Persian territory and where silver was plentiful, are given in silver dirhams, while the erstwhile Roman provinces of Syria and Egypt, with the adjacent Arabia, paid their *kharāj* etc. in gold dīnārs. At first the silver standard was the official one under the Abbasids, and expenditure was reckoned in terms of dirhams. We are told, for example, that the cost of the building of Baghdad by Manṣūr was 4,833,000 dirhams.[3] But by Hārūn's day gold was so plentiful, having been received in great masses as tribute and spoils of battle, that the chief payments such as those made for emoluments of governors and important officers, for gifts and especially luxuries, were in gold, and only minor officials continued to be paid in silver.[4] Gold, therefore, became the standard of the currency, rapidly ousting silver, seeing that no attempt was made either to check the flow or to maintain any reserve of the more precious metal. By the reign of Muqtadir

[1] Theoretically, the gold dīnār was equivalent to 10 (silver) dirhams. Under Hārūn the dīnār was normally worth 20 dirhams, though in government transactions, as here, its value was reckoned at 22 dirhams. See further A. von Kremer: "Ueber das Einnahmebudget des Abbasiden Reichs vom Jahre 306", in *Denkschrift d. Phil.-hist. Kl. d. Wiener Academie*, XXXVI, 287.

[2] It is not apparent how these sums are arrived at.

[3] Ibn al-Athīr, V, 440 (A.H. 146). [4] *Ibid.* VIII, 113.

(295/908–320/932) the huge expenditure of the Caliph and his entourage was no longer balanced by sufficient receipts from the provinces,[1] and deficiencies in the Exchequer became chronic. Before two more reigns were over (those of Qāhir and Rāḍī), the Caliphate had sunk to its lowest ebb, and during the supremacy of the Buwayhid princes silver was once again restored as the standard.

With the budget-estimate above may be compared that of the year 306/918–9 (in the reign of Muqtadir), which includes such miscellaneous items as the proceeds of the alms-tax (*ṣadaqa*) on various lands, i.e. Baṣra and the Sawād, ship tolls at Baṣra, sheep-market dues at Baghdad, Sāmarra, Wāsiṭ, Baṣra and Kūfa; profits from the mints in these cities and taxes on *dhimmīs* at Baghdad and elsewhere.[2] Both at the capital, moreover, and in outlying parts of the empire, various local and municipal taxes (*mukūs*) were imposed, in some places regularly and in others as occasion demanded. In Baghdad, during the time when the fortunes of the Caliphate had sunk very low, a tax was imposed by the Caliph's vizier Barīdī of 70 dirhams on every *kurr*[3] of wheat imported into the city, and heavy duties were levied on all goods sold by measure, including even oil.[4] The Buwayhid prince 'Aḍud al-Dawla, in addition to increasing by 10 per cent the assessment of each holding of *kharāj* land in the Sawād of Iraq, imposed a number of fresh taxes, such as on the profits of flour-mills, and on the sale of horses, asses and camels in the markets. He further opened a *dīwān* to deal with taxation on pastures and the prescribed alms-tax. In the year 389/999, the Ḥamūdī palace at Baghdad was burnt down in a riot caused by the imposition of tithe on all silken and cotton garments manufactured in the city. The riot was quelled after a concession had been made that the tax would be levied only on silken goods and not on cotton ones. This was announced by criers on both sides of the city; overseers and inspectors were appointed who stamped every piece of goods that paid the tax and an office was set apart to deal with it which continued until "the last days of 'Amīd al-Juyūsh".[5]

[1] Cf. *Wuzarā*, p. 339. The vizier 'Alī ibn 'Īsā writes to the revenue officer of a district on the Khurāsān highway: "You know how great the need is for revenue. Let the need urge you to greater effort in the gathering of taxes. . . ."

[2] See reference in note 1, p. 320.

[3] "Six ass loads" (Lane, *Arabic-English Lexicon*, s.v.).

[4] *Eclipse of the Abbasid Caliphates*, II, 25 f.

[5] *Ibid.* III, 336.

Taxes could be levied for a special purpose. Thus the Caliph Mustarshid, in 517/1123, imposed a tax on all exports from Baghdad in order to pay for the extension of a wall which he was building round the royal precincts in east Baghdad. The impost was so generally unpopular that it had to be removed and the money returned to those who had paid it.[1] Mustarshid's ancestor Manṣūr had, for a similar purpose to be carried out at Kūfa, levied a toll of 40 dirhams on every male in the city, after having first distributed the sum of 5 dirhams to every one and so carried out a rough census. This method of numbering the people and its results were celebrated in popular rhyme.[2] At Judda (Jedda), the port of Mecca, in the tenth century A.D., import taxes were laid on wheat, cloth, wool and saffron, while slaves paid an export tax. So also at various land control-posts there was a customs bureau. It was estimated by the local merchants that one third of their wealth went into the government treasury.[3] In Egypt, these extra taxes (*mukūs*) were collected each month and were hence called the "monthly" (*hilālī*) imposts, as distinct from the *kharājī*, which were collected annually from lands and agricultural products. The *mukūs* seem to have formed a regular item of the *Bayt al-Māl's* income until they were abolished by Saladin, who regarded them as illegal.[4]

Another item of revenue which enriched the *Bayt al-Māl* until it was pronounced unlawful by the legists was that obtained from escheated property. Where persons died intestate the statutory "shares" of their estate, as laid down by the Koran ($4^{12\text{ ff.}}$), were paid to the specified relatives if there were any, and such balance as remained reverted to the *Bayt al-Māl*, of which a special department, the *Dīwān al-Mawārīth al-Ḥashrīya*, or "Office of Escheated Estates", was established in order to deal with the revenue thus accruing. The *Bayt al-Māl* was, in theory, never the beneficiary of non-Muslims dying intestate, it being unlawful for Muslims to inherit from unbelievers and vice-versa.

[1] Ibn al-Athīr, x, 435. [2] Ṭabarī, III, 374. [3] Maqdisī, p. 104.

[4] Maqrīzī, *Khiṭaṭ*, I, 103 f. They reappeared after Saladin's death, but apparently the proceeds of them did not go into the provincial *Bayt al-Māl* but into the pockets of the Coptic officials. Amongst the *hilālī* revenues were the taxes on the rents of buildings, such as large houses, shops, baths, ovens, flour-mills, as well as tolls on fish caught in the sea and in the Nile, and other imposts. (*Ibid.* p. 107.)

In the reign of Mu'taḍid, the dīwān was entirely abolished, and the vizier Ibn al-Furāt sent to all provincial governors a circular letter announcing the abolition on the grounds that none of the authorities—Koran, *sunna* or consensus of the imāms—had ever declared that the *Bayt al-Māl* was the proper recipient for the property of deceased Muslims. Thereafter, if any surplus remained after payment of all "shares", the residue was to be divided amongst blood-relations of the person deceased.[1]

The objects on which public money was spent and with which the public treasury dealt were comparatively few, and they differed with time and circumstances. From the earliest days of the Caliphate the largest drain on the *Bayt al-Māl* was caused by the expenses of the royal household, with all its numerous branches, together with the cost of the buildings required to house them and their harems and huge retinues. As an item in the same account was to be reckoned the great number of persons, professing all kinds of talents and arts, who besieged the Caliph's gates, in the hope, often justified, of attracting his attention and stimulating his generosity towards themselves. Apart from them was the large and usually discontented clan of Hāshimites, who claimed kinship with the Prophet and the Caliph and were therefore entitled to State pensions, which were regularly paid to them; though payments would appear not to have been made automatically but required an order (*ṣakk*), that might on occasion be withheld.[2]

By comparison with the vast amount spent on the royal household (*al-Dār*) generally, the item concerned with the pay of the Caliph's bodyguard during the height of his power was a small one. When, soon after the beginning of the third century of Islam, that power showed indications of decline, and the Caliph Mu'taṣim (A.H. 218–27 = A.D. 833–42) introduced the practice of having a bodyguard composed of Turkish, Berber and other mercenaries, the expenditure under this head increased by leaps and bounds. In the year 252/867, their cost at the capital alone, which was then temporarily at Sāmarrā, amounted to 200,000,000 dīnārs, a sum equivalent to two years' yield of *kharāj* from the whole empire.[3] The cost could only be met by exactions from officials and

[1] Ṭabarī, III, 2151; *Wuzarā*, pp. 236 f.; Quatremère, *Mamlouks*, II, i, 133.
[2] Ṭabarī, III, 1371.
[3] *Ibid.* III, 1685.

occasionally from other wealthy citizens, in the same way as that by which the Caliph Amīn, during the first siege of Baghdad, had squeezed the rich merchants and others to provide him with means for payment of troops.

How the income of the *Bayt al-Māl* was normally expended may be gathered from the budgetary estimates for 306/918–9, which have been preserved with curious particularity.[1] The main items of public expenditure are as follows:

	Dīnārs
On the Holy Cities[2] (Mecca and Medina) and the pilgrim routes thereto	315,426½
On the frontier posts	491,465
Stipends of qāḍīs in the empire	56,569
Police officers and magistrates in the empire	34,439
Officers of the *barīd* (post)	79,402

The total cost of these public undertakings and other State expenditure was less than one million dīnārs, while the expenditure on the royal household, the minor officials in government dīwāns, the security police at the capital and other items[3] accounted for over fourteen and a half millions.

[1] *Wuzarā*, pp. 11 ff., and von Kremer, *Einnahmebudget*, pp. 303 f. The passage quoted from al-Waṣṣāf in the latter work, after a list of the items of expenditure, contains a statement to the effect that expenditure exceeded income by over 2,000,000 dīnārs.

[2] The expenditure on the Holy Cities and the pilgrim roads was not merely a work of piety, but helped to retain a close connection between the civil and religious capitals of the empire, a fact which had an appreciable effect on its history. As early as the Caliph Mahdī, in 161/778, military stations had been built on the road from Baghdad to Mecca, milestones set up and wells dug for this purpose. (Ṭabarī, III, 486.)

[3] The detailed list is as follows:

Watchmen and others of like station, such as gate-keepers; white provincial and foreign mercenaries; negroes (mostly slaves bought in Egypt, Mecca, etc.); freedmen of the Caliphs (they acted as chamberlains at the palace and as escort on journeys); private bodyguards—foot and mounted; officials, seventeen classes, employed about the *Dār* and including messengers, Koran readers, muezzins, astrologers, cup-bearers, jesters, etc.; security police at Baghdad, jailers, patrolmen, etc.; chosen slave-troops; royal private kitchens and bakeries; public ditto for troops, slaves, etc.; water-carriers for the palace, bakeries, etc.; private servants at the palace; craftsmen and artisans (tailors, fullers, shoemakers, furriers, etc.); courtiers, physicians, huntsmen, etc.; watermen on the royal boats; Hāshimite pensions, etc.; *khaṭībs* (preachers) in the Friday mosques at Baghdad; senior scribes in the dīwāns, treasurers, porters, *mudīrs*, etc.

The moneys and other revenues that flowed into the *Bayt al-Māl* were checked by the *Dīwān al-Kharāj*. Primarily, its function was to have control of the revenues from the rich Sawād lands of Iraq, the central province of the empire. At a later date, under the Caliph Mu'taḍid (279/892–289/902) it came actually to be called the *Dīwān al-Sawād*, but it also concerned itself with the finances of the more distant provinces. For them it prepared the revenue demands, checked the items of their receipts and expenditure and in addition kept the general accounts of the Exchequer.[1] Closely connected with this office was the *Dīwān al-Nafaqāt*, or "Office of Expenditure", actually the office of the comptroller of the royal household.

As early as the reign of Mahdī (A.D. 775–85), control of income and expenditure, additional to that provided by these dīwāns, was found necessary, seeing that all the offices had by this time been concentrated under a single authority—that of the vizier. He decided to have a special office for the control of departmental accounts, the *Dīwān al-Azimma*, in which the register (*zimām*) of each dīwān was to be in charge of an official, with an overseer to have control over all.[2] Thence onwards every government department that had financial dealings appears to have had a register of control, for which a special dīwān was created with an official in charge.[3] Thus the *Dīwān al-Kharāj* had its *Dīwān Zimām al-Kharāj*[4] which supervised all dealings affecting revenues and revenue-bearing lands,[5] and so also the *Dīwān al-Nafaqāt* had its *Dīwān Zimām al-Nafaqāt*.[6] A similar office existed in Egypt, where every official in charge of a dīwān submitted his accounts to the *mutawallī*, or chairman of the council, who acted as controller of the joint offices.[7]

Other dīwāns arose at Baghdad as necessity or the Caliph's whim demanded. A very important one was the *Dīwān al-Jaysh*, or Military Department, which dealt with the recruitment and

1 Cf. Khwārazmī: *Mafatīḥ al-Olûm*, ed. van Vloten (Leyden, 1895), p. 54.

2 Ṭabarī, III, 522; Jahshiyārī, p. 98 b.

3 Māwardī, p. 369 *ad fin.*: "As for the official in charge of the dīwān he was the person responsible for its *zimām*." (Reading *zimāmihi* for the present text *dhimamati*.) Cf. Dozy s.v. *zimām*.

4 Ṭabarī, III, 2274, l. 6.

5 Cf. *Wuzarā*, p. 183.

6 Ṭabarī, III, 1379, l. 5.

7 Maqrīzī, *Khiṭaṭ*, I, 99, last line, and I, 82 *ad fin.*

pay of the army.[1] Its functions were intermittently exercised, and the very existence of the office would appear to have depended on the character of the ruling Caliph or of his vizier, an official of whom we shall have something further to say.

The lesser posts, under the Caliph Manṣūr, founder of Baghdad, included that of the Seal (*al-Khātam*), that of the Chancellery and Secret Records (*Kitābat al-Rasā'il wa'l-Sirr*), that of the royal estates and that of the "outgoings" department. Not all of these had then reached the dignity of being regarded as regular dīwāns. The offices greatly multiplied in the following reigns, presumably without adequately facilitating the course of government affairs, for the Caliph Mu'taḍid, who gained distinction as an able administrator, combined them all into one central office, the *Dīwān al-Dār*, the "Palace Dīwān", with three departments, (*a*) the *Dīwān al-Mashriq*, a survival from Mahdī's day,[2] dealing with the affairs of the eastern provinces; (*b*) the *Dīwān al-Maghrib*, dealing with the western provinces; and (*c*) the *Dīwān al-Sawād*, or *Dīwān al-Kharāj*, whose function is indicated by its title.[3] This restriction of the dīwān system did not work satisfactorily; or at any rate it discontented the many candidates for public office and emoluments, and in the reforms carried out by the vizier 'Alī ibn 'Īsā in the reign of the Caliph Muqtadir (295/908–320/932), a list of appointments to not less than a dozen dīwāns was made, of which the *Dīwān al-Dār* was only one, while its three departments now had separate existences.[4]

As for the emoluments of the officials in charge of dīwāns, they were modest enough at the beginning of the Abbasid period; heads of departments and governors of provinces alike receiving 300 dirhams per month, a salary which had been usual under the Umayyads.[5] About a century and a half later, under the Caliph Muqtadir, the highest-paid minister—he who had charge of the dīwān of the Sawād—drew a monthly salary of 11,000 dirhams, which was for a time reduced to 5000 dirhams, while less exalted officials had to be content with 100 dīnārs (2200 dirhams).[6] In

[1] Māwardī, pp. 351 ff.

[2] Jahshiyārī, p. 179 a.

[3] *Wuzarā*, pp. 79 (*ad fin.*), 131, etc. It was regarded as "the most important of the dīwāns." (*Eclipse of the Abbasid Caliphates*, I, 151.)

[4] *Eclipse of the Abbasid Caliphate*, I, 151 f.

[5] Jahshiyārī, p. 71 a.

[6] *Wuzarā*, p. 314.

theory, the stipends of all officials came from the *Bayt Māl al-Muslimīn*, or common treasury, for since they performed the tasks of the community they had to be paid from the common purse.[1] Sometimes, however, as we have seen, the emoluments of officials were a charge on the revenues of particular provinces.[2]

One of the dīwāns which under one name or another had a permanent existence was that in which official letters were composed and sealed for dispatch. Some note of its existence in Umayyad days as the *Dīwān al-Khātam* has already been made. It became under the Abbasids the *Dīwān al-Tawqī*ʻ,[3] so called from its principal duty, which was to expand into the proper form of a letter the Caliph's decision (*tawqī*ʻ) written down by his secretary on petitions and other documents presented for the royal consideration. Sometimes the Caliph himself inscribed his *tawqī*ʻ with his signature on the document, and the *tawqī*ʻ therefore at times meant the royal signature. An instance of the working of this dīwān was provided when the Caliph Muʻtaḍid decided to postpone the date of payment of *kharāj*. A petition having been presented to the Caliph, he gave his answer to the scribes, who, in as concise yet elegant language as possible and in a fine and delicate script, wrote it down on the document. The inscribed petition was passed on to the officers of the dīwān, who drew up the formal document, made several copies of it (of which one was entered into a register), added the royal seal and motto, and then sent the copies out as circular letters to all provincial governors and other officials concerned.[4] When the secretary of the Caliph happened to be a person of political tastes or desirous of intrigue, the office could exert considerable political power and control over the governors of provinces and the revenue officials with whom the chief correspondence was conducted. It was hence sometimes called "The Office of Decision and of Supervision over Governors".[5]

Behind all the dīwāns and in close relationship with the Caliph

[1] Abu Yūsuf, *Kitāb al-Kharāj*, p. 115.

[2] Cf. *Wuzarā*, p. 178.

[3] It was sometimes known as the *Dīwān al-Rasā'il* or, in Egypt, as the *Dīwān al-Inshā*. (Qalqashandī, I, 110 ff.)

[4] Maqrīzī, *Khiṭaṭ*, I, 274; Qalqashandī, I, 93. Another instance of the function of the *tawqī*ʻ is given in *Wuzarā*, p. 183.

[5] *Dīwān al-Tawqī*ʻ *wa'l-Tatabbu*ʻ *ʻalā 'l-ʻUmmāl* (Ṭabarī, III. 1440).

stood the official known as the vizier. His function, which was to begin with that of secretary and adviser, had existed even under Muhammad. Both he and all the Caliphs preceding the Abbasids had had confidential scribes, and, when occasion demanded, had had resort for advice to men who could be relied upon for their experience and wisdom. With the Abbasids, however, there was introduced, under Persian precedent, the regular office of the vizierate, whose first occupant was Abu Salama, "the Vizier of the House of Muhammad".[1] Its importance fluctuated according to the personality of the Caliph and of the official himself. A strong Caliph such as Manṣūr or Mahdī could delegate authority to his viziers and yet keep control of the administration, while a domineering, but not particularly capable, monarch, such as Hārūn al-Rashīd let his ministers, the famous Barmecides, have too much power and then attempted to regain control by violence. Appointment to the vizierate did not always go by merit, and instances are recorded when a grasping Caliph would grant the office in return for money. Thus Mahdī is said to have accepted the sum of 100,000 dīnārs, on the suggestion of a courtier, in return for appointing a certain Ya'qūb ibn Dā'ūd to be his vizier.[2]

As a rule, the earlier and more competent Caliphs appointed both the viziers and the officers in charge of the dīwāns. On occasion, as under Mahdī, the vizier was himself placed in charge of one or more of the dīwāns,[3] and when dismissed from the vizierate might yet hold some other office.[4] In the troubled days of al-Muqtadir, on the other hand, though the Caliph appointed the vizier, the latter appointed the officers of the dīwāns.[5] Thus the vizier Ibn Khāqān filled various offices with his own nominees and in addition determined the status of each.[6] Normally, a good vizier exercised a general supervision over the affairs of the empire,[7] so that within the scope of his activities there came the

[1] Ṭabarī, III, 20, l. 11.

[2] *Al-Fakhrī*, p. 219.

[3] Cf. Jahshiyārī, pp. 81 a, 84 a.

[4] Thus 'Alī ibn Yaqṭīn, who, when Mahdī appointed another vizier, was permitted to retain the *Dīwān al-Rasā'il*. (*Ibid.* p. 91 b; and cf. Qalqashandī, I, 93.)

[5] Miskawayhi and *Wuzarā*, *passim*.

[6] *Eclipse of the Abbasid Caliphate*, I, 20 (Miskawayhi, V, 82).

[7] Cf. *Ibid.* I, 108, where Ibn al-Furāt, in cross-examination of his predecessor, 'Alī ibn 'Īsā, remarked that for five years he had "administered the government of the kingdom".

administration of border districts, of the dīwāns and the provinces.[1] In the fourth century of Islam, moreover, the vizier, as chief official of the government, had charge of the capital province of Iraq. From his important official duties and from his great powers of patronage he filled a position akin to that of a modern Prime Minister. But often enough he neglected the duties of his office, and for the sake of bribes appointed to the dīwāns persons with no qualifications but the capacity to pay what was demanded of them. The vizier himself therefore did not usually depend on his stipend for his income, although, during the middle period of the Caliphate, the emoluments of the office were considerable and might include a *qaṭīʿa* (fief) as part of them.[2]

The office of the vizierate was temporarily suspended during the period of the decline of the Caliphate and the subjection of the Caliph to the Buwayhid princes. Actually, it was under the Caliph al-Rāḍī that the vizier yielded up his position as the highest official in the land to the *Amīr al-Umarā*, or "Supreme Commander".[3] Under the Buwayhids it was their chief official who became the real vizier, while the Caliph's minister, who was now little more than his private secretary, took the title of *Ra'īs al-Ru'asā*. When the Caliphate once more revived to some extent under the Seljūqs, the vizier was at the same time restored to his original office and functions.

We turn now to the third of the Caliph's governmental functions, namely, that concerned with the administration of justice and policing. Before Islam, law and order had been maintained within each tribe by the power which it possessed of expelling members who offended its canons of morality[4] and by the practice of the *talio*. As protection against outside aggression, there was the recognized understanding that the tribe avenged a wrong done to any of its members, and thus men hesitated to shed blood when the whole of their immediate society might be involved. At Mecca there was a confederacy of the Quraysh, the *Ḥilf al-Fuḍūl*, which set itself to repress acts of violence by the tribesmen of the neighbourhood, to prevent oppression in the city

[1] *Eclipse of the Abbasid Caliphate*, I, 352 (Miskawayhi, v, pp. 533 f.).

[2] *Ibid.* I, 155.

[3] *Ibid.* I, 352.

[4] Cf. *Aghānī*, XIX, 75, for an instance of expulsion for drunkenness and debauchery.

and to ensure his rights to every man, whether he was a citizen or a stranger, a free man or a slave.[1]

Muhammad, in his Medina charter, as has been seen, perpetuated the main features of the system; but he strengthened the hand of the law-abiding, and made retaliation for offences more certain, by making the whole community responsible for delivering up to the victim or his avenger any man who had committed wrong against another out of private rancour and of set purpose. Even the kinsmen of the wrongdoer were laid under this obligation. The change which this wrought in the older system was that *talio* was now regularly to be inflicted on the actual offender and not simply on any member of his family who could be reached, the object aimed at being to prevent vengeance for bloodshed from turning into long-continued vendettas within the community. The right of blood-feud outside the *umma*[2] was continued. It was still, however, exaction of vengeance by the individual, and not punishment by the community for an offence committed against it; for the penalty continued to be inflicted by the injured person or, if he were slain, by his *walī* (nearest kinsman), who had it within his discretion to choose whether he would exercise his right or forgo it in return for material compensation. This continued to be the law in Islam. If a man is brought before the imām having of set purpose killed another person, and the fact is notorious or proven by evidence, then the murderer is handed over to the slain person's *walī*, who either slays or pardons, at his discretion. This is so even if the murderer has voluntarily confessed his crime.[3] Similar is the case of those who commit other offences for which retaliation may be exacted, or which are liable to *ḥudūd* (penalties specified by the law) or a discretionary penalty (*taʿzīr*); and so also are wounds, for which *talio* is inflicted unless the victim pardons the offender.

It is to be observed that before the penalty was exacted the offender was brought before the imām (i.e. the Caliph or his agent) for his decision, and it was not always left to the victim or his *walī* to avenge an injury. Even when the imām had conceded the justice of a claim for vengeance there were occasions—e.g. in the case of a head wound[4]—when the individual was precluded

[1] *Aghānī*, XVI, 65 f.; Māwardī, pp. 132–4.
[2] I.e., the community.
[3] Abu Yūsuf, *Kitāb al-Kharāj*, p. 91.
[4] *Ibid.* pp. 89 f.

from exacting the *talio*. The community then intervened, in the person of the imām or his agent. In that case, the offender paid compensation to the victim and was beaten and imprisoned until he was manifestly penitent.[1] Something would appear to depend on whether the offence was caused against a particular individual for a reason personal to him and the culprit. If a man committed highway robbery, presumably choosing his victims at random, it was the imām who had to carry out the sentence passed on the criminal.[2] These instances imply public action, or at any rate that vengeance is not always the concern purely of the individual who has been wronged. Theory, indeed, has it that the penalties specified by the law are punishments which Allah established in order to deter men from committing what He forbade and from neglecting what He commanded.[3] That is in keeping with the general spirit of Islam, in which Allah is the ultimate power in the world both politically and spiritually, and it forms an element new to the idea of justice which had been prevalent before Islam.

With the coming of Muhammadanism, the Prophet and his successors (the Caliphs) made themselves responsible for the internal discipline of the realm of Islam. As the empire expanded, the viziers and governors of provinces took their share of the responsibility, but the actual duty of maintaining order amongst the subjects of the realm devolved in the last resort upon officials appointed by the Caliph or the more important of his agents. In each city, there was a *ra'īs*, or "chief", who was held responsible for its orderly conduct and sometimes also for the payment of dues. In Baghdad, each quarter had its representative, who made it his duty to know what was going on in his district and who could be relied upon, like his modern counterpart the *mukhtār*, to lay his hands on any person required by the authorities. When disturbance broke out, or matters went beyond control of these officials, the military took charge.

There was always in the capital a body of troops whom the Caliph kept for his own protection. At first they were the pick of the Arab tribesmen who formed the bulk of the army; later the force was composed of foreign (Turkish and North African)

[1] Abu Yūsuf, *Kitāb al-Kharāj*, p. 90.
[2] *Jāmi' al-ṣaghīr* (on margin of *Kitāb al-Kharāj*), p. 72.
[3] Māwardī, p. 378 *ad fin.*

mercenaries who could be trusted not to be influenced by local intrigues and to remain loyal to their master. These were known as the *shurṭa*[1] and they normally kept order in the capital. In time, the *shurṭa* came to be regarded primarily as a police force, so that, to take an example, during the troubled period at the beginning of the reign of Muqtadir, it was Mūnis, the royal treasurer, who kept order in the capital Baghdad, which he patrolled with a force of nine thousand men, mounted and foot.[2] Similar bodies of the *shurṭa* were to be found in the other main cities, the capitals of provinces and the like, in which governors or other high officials resided. In lesser places, there was the *ma'ūna* force, which had similar duties without the special guard of the sovereign or his representative. The officer in charge of this force was the *sāḥib al-shurṭa*, or *saḥīb al-ma'ūna*; in Egypt, he was called the *wālī*, and, according to Maqrīzī,[3] he was the officer charged with the policing of the city and with making nocturnal rounds for the purpose of suppressing malefactors. It was part of his duties each day to learn from his subordinates about all the happenings in the city and to compile a written report of them for the sulṭān.[4] In general, the duties of the ṣāḥib al-shurṭa werc, says Ibn Khaldūn,[5] concerned with the law. He had to repress crime, to investigate offences committed and to punish those guilty of them.[6] In describing the origin of this special office, the author declares that, in those lands where people pretended to have forgotten the authority of the Caliph, the review and examination of *maẓālim* (grievances) fell to the sulṭān, whether power had been delegated to him by the Caliph or not. In these circumstances, the duties of policing and legal administration were divided amongst the ṣāḥib al-shurtā and the qāḍī. The former acted and made his decisions in accordance with the "political" law (i.e. the *'urf*, or "customary law", which had sprung up or been preserved in every land), which was concerned with the material welfare of the State as distinct from the *shar'ī* law, which concerned religious matters and was derived by interpretation of the Koran and other "roots" of *fiqh*. To the qāḍī fell the other duties, namely, the determination

[1] Seemingly a word of foreign (? Greek) derivation.

[2] *Eclipse of the Abbasid Caliphate*, I, 20.

[3] *Khiṭaṭ*, II, 220.

[4] Quatremère, *Mamlouks*, I, 109, n. 140.

[5] *Prolégomènes*, ed. Quatremère, I, 400 f., and II, 30 f.

[6] This summarizes Māwardī, pp. 375–8.

of fitting punishments and the sentencing to the prescribed legal penalties of those who had offended the *shar*ʿ, or specifically religious code.

The ṣāḥib al-shurṭa had wider powers than the qāḍī, or ordinary judge concerned with *sharʿī* affairs. The latter had no authority to go outside his own court for investigation of crimes reported or suspected, nor could he attempt to extract a confession by force from an accused person. Furthermore, he could act only on the complaint of interested parties, for example in cases of theft or adultery, and then only according to the ordinary procedure.[1] The prefect of police,[2] as also the amīr who had military command of a province, on the other hand, had power to act on the reports of subordinate officers about persons suspected of crimes, and the rule laid down for them was that, where there was any doubt, the previous character of the accused was to be taken into consideration. The amīr and the police prefect also, but not the qāḍī, could imprison a suspected person in order to make investigations about him and could threaten him or subject him to torture in order to force a confession;[3] they could imprison for life a habitual criminal, or one whose crime inflicted great suffering on the community; they could hear the evidence of non-Muslim witnesses belonging to the "protected" faiths,[4] and of other persons whose evidence was not valid in the qāḍī's court; and, finally, they could hear complaints of assaults for which the penalties were legally specified.[5] The men who filled the post of ṣāḥib al-shurṭa are generally described as notorious for their cruelty and unscrupulous character. An extreme example of their type was ʿAbd al-Raḥmān ibn ʿUbayd, who had been appointed to be prefect of police at Kūfa by the famous Ḥajjāj,[6] governor of Iraq under ʿAbd al-Malik the Umayyad. Of him a contemporary said:

I never saw a ṣāḥib al-shurṭa like him. He never imprisoned anyone except for a debt. When a man who was a *naqīb* (head of a

[1] See below under "Procedure". He could not order imprisonment simply on a charge by another person and without trial. (Shāfiʿī, *Umm*, VI, 240.)

[2] *Wālī al-aḥdāth wa ʾl-maʿāwin*, i.e. the officer having charge of police affairs; another name for the ṣāḥib al-shurṭa.

[3] This in spite of the rule that confession under duress was invalid. (Abu Yūsuf, *Kitāb al-Kharāj*, p. 107.)

[4] In the qāḍī's court, the evidence of Muslims alone was accepted.

[5] Māwardī, pp. 376–8. [6] Died 95/714.

section of the community) was brought before him, he transfixed him with a piercing instrument (*manqiba*). If a man who was by trade a digger came before him, he dug a grave for him and buried him in it; if it was a man who had attacked or threatened another with some sharp weapon, he cut off his hand; if it was someone who had burnt a house over the head of its occupants, he burnt him; and if it was a dubious character suspected of robbery, even though there was no direct evidence against him, he would inflict three hundred lashes on him. Often a period of forty nights would pass without any criminal being brought before him, and Ḥajjāj ultimately gave him the police control of Baṣra in addition to that of Kūfa.[1]

It was in keeping with the dual, religio-political, character of the Islamic state that, for the purpose of ensuring the maintenance of the law, there came into existence alongside the ṣāḥib al-shurṭa another officer, the *muḥtasib*, who was concerned with the less secular side of it, and whose business it was to see that the religious and moral precepts of Islam were obeyed.[2] He was appointed by the Caliph or his vizier, and, like other holders of public office, had to be a Muslim and a free man of respectable character. Generally he was a legist, and, in addition to his specifically police duties, he performed those of a magistrate. In this respect, his functions stood midway between those of the qāḍī and the *nāẓir al-maẓālim*, or "reviewer of torts"[3]; but in rank and powers he was subordinate to both these officers.[4] In some respects, his duties were parallel with those of the qāḍī, since both officers were, for example, empowered to consider pleas. But the muḥtasib's jurisdiction was limited to matters connected with defective weights and measures, fraudulent sales and non-payment of debts. Even here he could only try cases summarily, and when the truth was not in doubt. As soon as evidence had to be sifted and oaths to be administered, cases were referred to the qāḍī. Mainly, his

[1] Ibn Qutayba, *'Uyūn al-Akhbār*, p. 33.

[2] Maqrīzī, *Khiṭaṭ*, I, p. 463 *ad fin.*: "Only the principal men in Islam should be appointed to the *ḥisba* [i.e. the office of the muḥtasib] because it is a religious duty." Cf. Ibn Khaldūn, *Prolégomènes* (ed. Quatremère), I, 405 *ad fin.*; tr. de Slane, I, 458. For a detailed description of his powers and duties see *Ma'ālim al-qurba fi aḥkām al-ḥisba* (Gibb, N.S. XII, London, 1938).

[3] See below, pp. 347–50.

[4] If, however, he found the qāḍī neglectful of his duties, it was the duty of the muḥtasib to express his disapproval. (Māwardī, p. 429.)

functions were those of a censor, and he thus had power to enforce right dealing and prevent wrongdoing on his own initiative and without requiring the complaint of any interested party. He had to see that, in a place where there were Muslims, they did not neglect to hold a Friday service in the mosque, and that, if they numbered a quorum of at least forty, they were to form themselves into a community; though if they were a larger number and differed on the question of worshipping together, the authority of the muḥtasib might be disputed. (In this connection, the muḥtasib's function included the insistence on the *adhān*, or call to prayer of the muezzin (*mu'adhdhin*), whom he could summon to pass an examination in the subject of the times lawful for the *adhān*.[1]) It was not, however, his business to insist on the individual Muslim's attendance at the mosque unless he made a practice of absenting himself, and then the officer might not go beyond chiding the delinquent. So far as the mosques themselves were concerned, if they were not in the care of private individuals, and repair became necessary, the muḥtasib was charged with the duty of calling attention to it. He had, further, to check persons who contravened the religious laws, such as those whom he saw eating during the fast of Ramaḍān, but he might not act on suspicion and had first to inquire the reason for any contravention.[2] It was his duty to see that widows and divorced women observed the law with regard to the period of waiting (*'iddāt*) before remarriage, and to encourage the marrying of unmarried girls with men among their peers.

The actual doctrines of Islam and the spiritual welfare of the faithful were also under the care of the muḥtasib. Thus, if he found a person who had not normally belonged to the class of legists suddenly engaging in the study of the law and thus possibly misleading persons who might apply to him, the muḥtasib had power to turn him from this pursuit after making investigation of the man's motives. Similarly, if a person regularly engaged in the study of theology propounded views which were contrary to those agreed upon by *ijmā'*, then the muḥtasib had power to check him.

[1] Tanūkhī, *Nishwār al-muḥāḍarah*, ed. D. S. Margoliouth, p. 250. The muḥtasib could also warn an imām whose prayers in the mosque were of such length as to inconvenience worshippers. (Māwardī, p. 428.)

[2] A man seen eating during Ramaḍān may be an invalid, or on a journey, and so excused from observing the fast.

If he repented, then all was well; if not, then it was the duty of the sovereign—presumably on the muḥtasib's report—to maintain the purity of the faith. Schools too had to be visited by the muḥtasib, though not so much for the purpose of inspecting the character of the teaching as to ensure that the teachers did not beat their pupils too severely.[1]

Public morals had a large share of the muḥtasib's attention. He had to see that men did not consort with women in public, and it was his duty to chastise anyone who appeared abroad in a state of drunkenness and gave false reasons for his condition. He had to prevent wine-drinking in public; if the offender was a Muslim it was his duty to admonish him and spill the wine on the ground[2]; if he belonged to one of the "protected" religions he was to be warned not to offend again in public. The playing of musical instruments forbidden by the law also came under the muḥtasib's ban, and he had to maintain supervision over games and toys, for though they were not directly counter to the law,[3] yet they might be associated with causes of offence. Thus, dolls, which are of use in encouraging the maternal instinct in children, may lead to the portraiture of married women or the representation of idols.[4]

It must be emphasized that the offences mentioned had to be committed in public before the muḥtasib could take action about them. He had no right to go beyond closed doors or penetrate the veil of decency. In the markets and other public places he had to prevent frauds of all kinds. Commercial knavery was especially within his jurisdiction, and in the markets he had supervision over all traders and artisans, amongst whom his assistants had to patrol every day[5] and about whose arts some of the text-books[6] provide instruction in order to enable the officer to cope with any trickery. Usury could only be dealt with by him if it was

[1] Maqrīzī, *Khiṭaṭ*, I, 464.

[2] Abu Ḥanīfa, who was the most liberal of the imāms, denied to the muḥtasib the right thus to destroy private property.

[3] There is a tradition that the Prophet once found his wife 'Ā'isha, whom he married when she was nine years old, playing with dolls in the company of some other girls, and he did not disapprove.

[4] Māwardī, pp. 420 f.

[5] Maqrīzī, *Khiṭaṭ*, I, 463.

[6] E.g. *Nihāyat al-rutba fī ṭalāb al-ḥisba* by 'Abd al-Rahmān ibn Naṣr al-Shayzarī, ed. Al-Bāz al-'Arīnī (Cairo, 1365/1946); tr. by W. Behrnauer in *Journal Asiatique*, 5me Sér. XVI, 347–92, and XVII, 1–76. See also *Kitāb al-Ishāra, ilā maḥasin al-tijāra*, by Abu'l-Faḍl Ja'far b. 'Alī al. Dimashqi (Cairo, 1318).

interest charged on a credit transaction, for the reason that the lawyers were unanimous that usury of that kind was illegal. If the usury, however, was for a sum paid in cash it did not concern him, legal objection to it, though it occurred, being only slight. Another matter which came within his cognizance was cruelty to servants and animals either by underfeeding or overburdening them with tasks beyond their powers.[1]

Amongst the many miscellaneous duties with which the muḥtasib was charged, a number were concerned with public amenities rather than with morals or religious institutions. Thus, in towns where the source of drinking-water was fouled, or there was no provision for poor wayfarers, or the walls threatened collapse, he could order the townsmen to rectify matters at their own expense, if there were no money in the public treasury for these purposes. If the place was situated on a frontier where the collapse of the walls might be a menace to Islamic territory, the governor was not allowed to permit any emigration, and, as in other cases of danger, the rich and powerful of the place were called upon to assist. But it was the duty of the muḥtasib to bring the matter to the notice of the government and invoke the aid of the notables. If anyone built a house or other building, the muḥtasib had to see that, even if it were a mosque, it did not encroach on a frequented public thoroughfare, however wide, and also that any encroaching part of the building was demolished. He had further to ensure that no house[2] was raised above another belonging to a Muslim so as to overlook the women's quarters,[3] and that no house had projecting rain-spouts or open drain-pipes which might in winter or summer drench or befoul wayfarers in the street.[4] To prevent any hindrance or inconvenience to traffic was indeed one of the principal duties of the muḥtasib; but the traffic, it must be remembered, was that of pedestrians. In the narrow market-streets of the cities he had to forbid merchants to deposit their goods so as to impede free passage,[5] and he had to protect the clothes and persons of purchasers and others by forbidding the driving of animals laden with piles of wood or straw, or with offensive

[1] Māwardī, p. 429.

[2] Particularly if it belonged to a Jew or Christian (Māwardī, p. 428).

[3] Māwardī, p. 430.

[4] *Nihāyat al-rutba*, ch. III, *Journal Asiatique*, XVI, (1861), 361.

[5] Māwardi, p. 430.

matter, through the bazaars. Also it was his duty to see that those who traded there kept their place cleaned.[1]

In general it may be said that the theory of the function of the ṣāḥib al-shurṭa and the muḥtasib is that it lay in preventing and detecting offences against the law and in the punishment of offenders on conviction. The intermediate stage, namely that of judging persons accused and allotting punishment, is the function of the qāḍī. In theory, he exercised authority in all legal matters. Naturally enough, the head of Islam is also regarded in law as the judge of the whole Muslim community[2]; he is the authority who decides disputes and to whom persons aggrieved carry their plea for justice or vengeance when they are themselves incapable of exacting it. The Prophet himself and the early Caliphs often decided cases in person where the parties had access to them. Omar is usually credited with having been the first to appoint qāḍīs to assist him in this part of the Caliph's duties.[3] The judges at Medina, Kūfa and Baṣra are mentioned as having been so appointed by him, but under the Umayyads Hishām and Walīd II their appointment was made, not by the Caliphs, but by the governor of the province of Iraq. It is known indeed that provincial governors frequently exercised a right to appoint and, in fact, elected and dismissed the judges as they pleased.[4] Although there was a reversion to the system of direct appointment by the Caliph under the early Abbasid Manṣūr[5], viziers[6] and governors at a later time again appointed their own qāḍīs, who were endowed with equal power with those elected by the Caliph. Without such appointment by the Caliph or his representative no qāḍī had authority,[7] and once endowed with it, he regarded himself as independent of any other control. The point is illustrated by the report that when an agent of the *barīd* (the intelligence service) in Egypt attempted to sit with a qāḍī in his court, the judge informed him that that was the court of the Commander of the Faithful,[8]

[1] *Nihāyat al-rutba, loc. cit.*
[2] Cf. Ibn Khaldūn, *Prolégomènes*, ed. Quatremère, I, 397.
[3] *Ibid.* and Ibn Qutayba, '*Uyūn al-akhbār*, pp. 82 f.
[4] Cf. Ibn al-Athīr, V, 106, 115, 180, etc.
[5] Ya'qūbī, *Historiae*, ed. Houtsma (Leyden, 1883), II, 468.
[6] Eg. Ibn al-Furāt, *Nishwār al-muḥādara*, p. 115.
[7] Shīrāzī, *Tanbīh*, p. 313.
[8] At that time the Caliph Ma'mūn (A.H. 198–218).

without whose command none might occupy the judicial seat.[1]

In the principal cities of Islam there was a chief qāḍī, known as *Qāḍī al-Quḍāt* in Baghdad,[2] Cairo and other cities of the eastern Caliphate, while he was known as *Qāḍī al-Jamā'a*, or "community qāḍī", in North Africa and Spain.[3] In early times in Spain, in the days when the personage who filled the office had belonged to the military aristocracy, he had been known as *qāḍī al-jund*, or "qāḍī of the army", and there remained a *qāḍī al-'askar* in North Africa. His functions, however, were restricted to the army, even though he had authority in it wherever it was stationed, except in the capital.[4]

Under the Fāṭimid dynasty in Egypt, the Caliph usually appointed a representative to have charge of the judiciary. He too was called *Qāḍī al-Quḍāt* and held high rank. When the real power in the State passed to the vizier, who also had command of the army,[5] the appointment was made by him.[6] In Ibn Khaldūn's day[7] each of the four "schools" of law at the great Cairene mosque and university of al-Azhar had its own *qāḍī al-quḍāt*, but the head of the Shāfi'ites, owing to the great numbers who acknowledged his jurisdiction, held pre-eminence.[8]

The conditions of the qāḍī's office are that the holder must be a male—since women are incapable of carrying out the duties of a public position[9]; he must be of full age and free, for otherwise he

[1] Al-Kindī, ed. R. Guest (Gibb Series, Leyden, 1912), p. 444, ll. 13–15. Cf. also *ibid.* p. 524 where the qāḍī Ibn Ḥarbawayhi (third century A.H.) is reported, on his appointment to Egypt, to have refused to call and pay his respects to the governor, Ibn Bistām. For judicial administration in Islam generally, see E. Tyan, *Histoire de l'Organisation Judiciaire en Pays d'Islam* (Paris, 1938).

[2] The appointment of this official is mentioned more than once in Ṭabarī, e.g. III, 1421 and 1684 (A.H. 240 and 252). Previously the appointment of the more important qāḍīs is regularly noted.

[3] Dozy, *Supplément aux Dictionnaires arabes*, II, 363 b.

[4] De Slane, "Autobiographie d'Ibn Khaldoun", *Journal Asiatique*, 4me Série, III, 327, n. 2.

[5] This began with the vizier Badr al-Jamālī (466/1074).

[6] Maqrīzī, *Khiṭaṭ*, I, 403 f.

[7] A.D. 1332–1406.

[8] De Slane, "Autobiographie d'Ibn Khaldoun", p. 328.

[9] Abu Ḥanīfa is quoted by Māwardī as being of the opinion that women may lawfully act as judges in matters where their evidence is valid. Other authorities deny the eligibility of women in any circumstances and hold that the Koran (4^{38}) forbids the placing of women in a position of authority over men.

will not be legally responsible for his actions, and he must be a Muslim, since a non-believer cannot be placed in authority over true believers.[1] Moreover, he must be a person of good understanding and perception as well as of sound eyesight and hearing.[2]

A qualification that would seem indispensable is that he should be of honourable character. It is clear, however, that appointments to the judgeship as to other offices were usually made for personal or monetary reasons,[3] and men of honour, such as the imām Abu Ḥanīfa, consequently refused the office as degrading.[4] In fact, if records and satires are to be credited, the administration of justice under Islam has not always approached the high standards set for it by the law-books. A satirical story by Jāḥiẓ describes every official engaged in the administration, from the highest to the lowest, as being corrupt.[5] Even Hārūn al-Rashīd's qāḍī, Abu Yūsuf, expressed his doubts whether the judges of his day carried out their duties honourably.[6] The law-books make provision for the trial by a qāḍī of a corrupt predecessor, though his oath is accepted as proof of innocence.[7]

Amongst the qualifications demanded by theory is one that the qāḍī must be a person filled with knowledge of the four *uṣūl*, the principles or "roots" of the *fiqh* ("law"). Thus qualified he is entitled to employ *ijtihād*, or the effort whereby he may deduce and enunciate authoritative answers (*fatwās*) to questions of law propounded to him.[8] In this process, he is entitled to apply his own intelligence, if, when excogitating a problem, he can find no precedent either in the Koran, or the *sunna* of the Prophet; he must then adduce parallels and analogies in deciding.[9]

As for the scope of the qāḍī's jurisdiction,[10] that may be either general or restricted. If it is general, it comprises the settling of disputes, either by arbitration on lawful terms[11] between the

[1] Abu Ḥanīfa holds that a non-believer may act as judge in his own community.

[2] Māwardī, pp. 107–9.

[3] E.g. *Wuzarā*, p. 131, and *Nishwār al-muḥāḍara*, p. 115.

[4] See Ibn Khallikān, tr. de Slane, III, 555 ff.

[5] The story of Jamīla (Jāḥiẓ, *Maḥāsin*, ed. van Vloten (Leyden, 1898), pp. 264 ff. See also Ibn Qutayba, *'Uyūn al-akhbār*, p. 87.

[6] *Kitāb al-Kharāj*, p. 115 *ad fin.*

[7] Shīrāzī, *Tanbīh*, p. 316.

[8] Māwardī, pp. 109 f.

[9] *Ibid.* p. 120.

[10] *Ibid.* pp. 117–22. Cf. Amedroz, *J.R.A.S.*, 1910, 761 ff.

[11] Without permitting the unlawful or forbidding what is legally permitted.

parties, or by enforcing liabilities by judgment in favour of those entitled upon persons who dispute them; but only after proof, which may be either by admission or by evidence. This was originally the sole duty of the qāḍī.[1] In course of time other duties accrued. These were: the perpetual control over persons forbidden to have charge of their property by reason of madness, infancy or insolvency and enforcement of rights and obligations in their favour; the charge of *awqāf* (pious foundations); the carrying out of testamentary conditions of wills, if lawful; the giving in marriage of unmarried women, if they desire it, to men who are their peers[2]; inflicting specified legal penalties[3]; securing the welfare of the district under his jurisdiction by preventing encroachment on roadways and spaces open to the public and the exclusion of buildings from them.[4]

The qāḍī is not concerned with *kharāj*, "which comes within the province of the military authorities". But some say that the alms-taxes (*ṣadaqāt*), if there is no one appointed to have charge of them, may come within the jurisdiction of the qāḍī, and he may collect and expend them for proper objects as being included amongst religious matters. Others say, however, that even if the qāḍī have general jurisdiction, he is precluded from concerning himself with them, since they come within the province of the Treasury and must be left to the effort of the Caliphs.

Restricted jurisdiction is when the qāḍī is allowed to decide on admission but not on evidence, or in cases of debt but not of marriage, or in valuations for purposes of tithes. Also the qāḍī may have general jurisdiction over a restricted area; thus he may have authority on one side only of a city like Baghdad, situated on both banks of a river, or he may have jurisdiction only in a particular quarter of the city.

[1] Ibn Khaldūn, *Prolégomènes*, ed. Quatremère, I, 397.

[2] Abu Ḥanīfa denied that this was a duty of the qāḍī, holding that women are themselves capable of dealing with the question of marriage.

[3] If they are incurred for offences against what is due to Allah, then he may act on his own initiative and without any person making a claim; if they are incurred for offences against what is due to men, then a claim must be made. Abu Ḥanīfa says that both require a complaint to be made.

[4] He may act here on his own initiative. Abu Ḥanīfa holds that a complaint is necessary. This particular duty, however, concerns divine rights, and must be carried out whether there is a complainant or not. This and the two foregoing notes are from the text of Māwardī, *op. cit.* pp. 117–22.

In practice, the qāḍī in the early days of Islam was appointed only to large cities, for the reason that there alone were there any large bodies of Arab Muslims. The non-Muslims had for a considerable period to deal with their own disputes, and were compelled to obtain justice in any way possible to them. This is not to say that they did not receive justice when it was due. When a Christian complained to the pious Umayyad sovereign Omar II ibn 'Abd al-'Azīz that his kinsman Hishām had robbed him (the complainant) of an estate, the Caliph commanded Hishām to restore the seized property and destroyed the documents with which he had bolstered up his case.[1] So far as the qāḍī's real jurisdiction is concerned, only those matters are referred to him which are popularly connected with religion—e.g. marriage and divorce, inheritance and *awqāf* (pious foundations). Other matters have nearly always come before the lay authorities, who decide, not by *fiqh* (the law as elaborated by the religious authorities), but by '*āda* (in Persia known as '*urf*), which is customary law, differing (sometimes considerably) from place to place. In reaching his decisions, moreover, the qāḍī, except in the earliest times, has been deprived of all power of independent decision by *ijtihād*, and he is bound by the text-books of the *madhhab*, or school of law, to which he owes allegiance.[2]

Even in theory the qāḍī is not concerned with anything beyond making decisions, all executive functions of the law being left to the amīr, the secular ruler.[3] Where their jurisdictions clashed, it would appear that the amīr could override the decisions of the qāḍī when it was expedient. Amongst the rare cases quoted is one from Egypt. In that particular instance, the *walī* of a married woman sought before a qāḍī to have the marriage annulled on the grounds that the husband was not the woman's peer as the law demanded. The qāḍī refused the application, saying that the marriage was legal. Thereupon the case was taken to the amīr, who did not himself quash the verdict but ordered the qāḍī to change it and grant an annulment.[4]

[1] *Fragmenta Historicorum Arabicorum*, ed. de Goeje, p. 60.

[2] An exception is regarded as notable. Thus the qāḍī Ibn Ḥarbawayhi of Baghdad followed his own counsel when acting as qāḍī in Egypt (Kindī, p. 528, ll. 14 f.).

[3] Māwardī, p. 378 *ad fin.*

[4] Kindī, p. 36.

In a civil dispute, the qāḍī was the first resort, the parties coming before him and presenting their suit orally. Strict rules of procedure are enunciated by the law-books for the trial of cases before him. Thus it is laid down as desirable that he should sit for judgment in a spacious and open place in which he is readily accessible to all, and he should not seclude himself except for a good reason. He should not try cases in the mosque[1]; and this probably for the reason that certain persons might not have access to him there. His first duty is to examine prisoners and to release anyone who is wrongfully detained. When actually sitting in judgment, his case of books of reference should be before him, and, near enough for him to supervise, the clerk who writes down the record. He should not deliver judgment except in the presence of the witnesses and of learned lawyers, whom he should consult in difficult cases. If the truth is clear to him, he must pronounce judgment according to it; if not, then he must delay until the verdict is evident. He may not depute another to make the decision. If there are a number of litigants, he must begin with the first arrived, except when there are wayfarers. If a number of litigants arrive at the same time, he must cast lots amongst them to decide the order of precedence.

To the two parties in a dispute, he must accord equal treatment in their entering, the place accorded to them for sitting, their presentation and the hearing accorded to them. If one is a Muslim and the other a non-believer, then the Muslim shall be given precedence in entering and a more honourable seat. But the qāḍī must not defend either party, nor whisper promptings in his ear nor dictate to him how he shall plead; though some say it is permissible. When the parties are seated before him, he shall decide when they are to speak, and he should keep silence while they are speaking. If each has a claim against the other, precedence is given to the party who first preferred his claim. If either of the parties interrupts the other or is quarrelsome or ill-mannered, the judge must check him, and punish him if he persists.[2]

The judge shall not hear an obviously unjustifiable claim. If a

[1] In spite of this instruction, the qāḍī frequently held his court in the mosque, particularly in early times. Cf. *Aghānī*, x, 123, and Tanūkhī, *Nishwār al-muḥāḍara*, ed. D. S. Margoliouth, p. 164.

[2] Shīrāzī, *Tanbīh*, pp. 315 f. Cf. Shāfi'ī, *Umm*, vi, 201.

claim is justifiable, however, the judge shall ask the defendant what answer he has to it. Some say that he shall not do so until requested by the plaintiff, but this is a matter of no importance. If the defendant admits the claim, judgment shall be given against him; but not until the plaintiff requests it. If the claim is denied, the judge shall ask the plaintiff if he has evidence of it and shall maintain silence while it is produced. If the plaintiff has no evidence, then the word of the defendant is accepted on oath, but the judge shall not swear him until the plaintiff requests. If the defendant refuses to swear, the oath passes to the plaintiff, and if he swears it the verdict is his. If he too refuses, the judge dismisses them both.[1]

If the plaintiff brings witnesses in proof of his claim, the defendant may be granted three days in which to produce rebutting evidence, and the plaintiff has the right of insisting on his (the defendant's) appearance in court at the end of that period. If he fails to bring the required evidence the plaintiff has the right to the verdict. If the witnesses are men unknown to the judge[2] and there is a doubt of their being Muslims, their word on the point is accepted; if it is doubtful whether they are free men, they must produce proof.[3] Should it be challenged that the witnesses are *'udūl*, "just" and competent men, and time is needed for inquiries—which are made secretly by persons known as *Aṣḥāb al-masā'il*[4]—then the plaintiff may demand their detention during the

[1] According to Shāfi'ī, *Umm*, VI, 237, the person who is in actual possession of the object of claim needs no proof of ownership but his word.

[2] "When the witnesses give evidence before the qāḍī—they being unknown (to him)—he writes down the description of each, his family relationships or the person to whom he owes allegiance as a *mawlā*, his honorific title (if he has one), his home address, his trading address and the name of his mosque or other place of worship." (Shāfi'ī, *Umm*, VI, 208 ff.)

[3] The Koran (2^{282}) requires for proof two men. In default of two men, then one man and two women will suffice; though the latter, according to Bayḍāwī, are acceptable witnesses only in civil claims. The commentators declare that the witnesses must be Muslims of full age, free and of good character.

[4] Lit. "Possessors of the Questions," i.e. inquiry agents. Ghawth ibn Sulaymān, qāḍī in Egypt (A.H. 140–4), was the first to make secret inquiries about witnesses. Before his day judges used to accept without question the evidence of witnesses, known to be honourable, who came before them. The evidence of persons known to be the contrary was rejected. If the witness was entirely unknown, neighbours were asked about him and the report they gave, good or bad, was acted upon. This was so until the time of Ghawth, who made inquiries in secret. "In those days the witness (after giving his evidence)

period that then elapses. If the plaintiff says he has evidence not present in court, then it is within the judge's discretion either to swear the defendant or detain him until the plaintiff brings his evidence.

In the case of claim for debt the defendant may refresh his memory from an account book, but the plaintiff cannot compel its production. The defendant's word, however, that he has not incurred a debt or has paid it, is not accepted without proof. Claims against the estate of a deceased person, or an infant, or a person absent from the court are valid if supported by proof. It is disputed whether a claim may be heard against a citizen not present in court.

If the plaintiff invokes the judge's assistance in bringing the defendant into court to answer a claim, the judge may send for him to appear, if he is in the city. If he refuses to appear he (the plaintiff) shall produce two witnesses to swear to the fact and shall then approach the chief of police[1] with the request to enforce his attendance. If the defendant is absent from the city and in a place where there is no judge, the qāḍī shall write to a man of understanding to mediate between the parties. If there is no such

returned amongst men as an ordinary individual again. No one was ever called a witness (by profession) or was ever referred to as one." (Kindī, p. 361.)

"Ibn Naṣruwayhi said: Tamīmī, who was once qāḍī at Baṣra, accepted 36,000 men as witnesses. I said to him, 'That was a great number. How was it?' He replied: 'The qāḍīs were of the belief of Abu Ḥanīfa and other legists that all men satisfying the conditions you know of were competent to give evidence.' All men could give evidence before Tamīmī and when he heard their evidence he would question them, and if they were respectable men he accepted their evidence. Men used to give evidence for one another—neighbours and people in the same street. We knew nothing of any system by which certain persons only were appointed to act as witnesses, until Ismā'īl took office." (*Nishwār al-muḥāḍara*, pp. 128 f.)

Nevertheless there appear to have been officials known as "witnesses" as early as the reign of Ma'mūn (Ibn al-Athīr, VI, 298, who does not here agree with Ṭabarī, III, 1112). The office of professional "witness" came to be regarded as corrupt and degrading. On one occasion a chief qāḍī is reported to have said that if the "witness" was without a certain three "hellish" qualities he would himself become an inhabitant of Hell. He went on to ask, "What think you of a city of 10,000 men of whom only about ten are 'witnesses'? Every other inhabitant of the town schemes to outwit them. How can they prosper if they are not very demons in alertness, perspicacity, wariness and understanding?" (*Nishwār al-muḥāḍara*, p. 240). Normally the evidence of drunkards, imaginative poets (who are regarded as liars), and persons who indulge in gaming and other reprehensible pursuits, is not admissible. (Shāfi'ī, *Umm*, VI, 21.)

[1] *Ṣāḥib al-shurṭa.*

person, then the qāḍī cannot compel the defendant's appearance unless the plaintiff proves the claim. A free woman who does not go out of doors need not appear in person when a claim is made against her but may appoint a deputy, and he may, if necessary, administer an oath to her.[1]

In coming to a decision the qāḍī may take into consideration only such evidence as is open and obvious. He may not guess at a hidden motive or cause (of action) or thought.[2] It is disputed whether the judge may decide a case on his own personal knowledge. The different opinions are (1) that he may so decide, (2) that he may not, and (3) that he may if the *ḥudūd Allāh* (statutory penalties stated in the Koran for the offences of adultery, theft, war against believers, and the drinking of wine) are not involved.[3]

The difference between law and equity in decisions was not unknown. Ibn Qutayba gives the following example: "To take a life for a life is legal and equitable; to slay a free man for a slave is equitable but not legal, and a legal but not equitable ruling is that a slayer's clan is responsible for paying blood-wite."[4]

In theory, the qāḍī's decision, however reached, was final, and no appeal from it could lie. In practice, as we have seen, the qāḍī might be compelled by a governor to reverse his decision, and the successor of an unjust qāḍī did, on occasion, reverse his judgments.

Though the text-books make no mention of fees, it is fairly certain that they were paid to the qāḍī by the plaintiff and probably also by the defendant, or at any rate by the successful party.[5] The text-books lay it down that the qāḍī's emoluments should come from the public Treasury, seeing that he performs a public duty,[6] and the inference therefore is that fees were not legally payable by litigants. There is, however, frequent mention of qāḍīs who achieved wealth while in office and of some who paid for the privilege of being appointed. Some, conversely, are pointed out as men of honour, and poor.[7]

The procedure in cases of wounding is the same as in civil

[1] Shīrāzī, *Tanbīh*, pp. 316–20. [2] Shāfi'ī, *Umm*, VI, 202.

[3] Shīrāzī, *Tanbīh*, pp. 318 f.

[4] *'Uyūn al-akhbār*, ed. Brockelmann, p. 84.

[5] For modern practice see Lane, *Modern Egyptians*, ch. IV, pp. 116 f.

[6] E.g. *Kitāb al-Kharāj*, p. 115.

[7] For references see A. Mez, *Renaissance des Islams* (Heidelberg, 1922), pp. 211–14.

actions. If a man accuses another of wounding him he must bring proof before the qāḍī. If he can produce satisfactory evidence the verdict is his; otherwise, the accused is made to swear his innocence. If he swears, he is acquitted; if not, the plaintiff is entitled to the verdict.[1] In a case of murder, fifty oaths are required from (i.e., probably, in support of) the man accused.[2]

In every action except one[3] in fact, the procedure is the same: the plaintiff brings proof,[4] or, if he cannot make good his claim, the defendant is discharged, on swearing an oath of his non-liability.

The oath has always been, in Muhammadan legal procedure, a feature of extreme importance, its significance being due to religious and eschatological reasons. Illustrations of its force are frequently encountered. When the Bahz clan of Medina complained to the Caliph 'Uthmān (A.H. 23–35) that the poet Shammākh had satirized and slandered them and driven them out of the city, he denied it. Thereupon he was made to ascend the Prophet's pulpit in the mosque at Medina and swear an oath in support of his assertion. The official who admonished him used the following words: "Shammākh, you are swearing upon the pulpit of the apostle of God, and he who there swears falsely shall have his abode for everlasting in Hell."[5] In modern times, and even under alien and non-Muslim administration, an oath, particularly if it is sworn at a sacred shrine, will determine a suit.[6]

Side by side with the qāḍī's court, as a means by which persons who felt themselves the victims of injustice or oppression could obtain redress, was the audience of the vizier at the capital or of the governor in the provinces. Under the first four Caliphs the qāḍīs were given jurisdiction in all legal matters, but their authority soon waned, and 'Alī himself sat to hear complaints when acts

[1] Shāfi'ī, *Umm*, VI, 240. [2] *Ibid.*

[3] Where a person notoriously free claims to be a slave. This is true even if evidence is produced.

[4] This principle is perhaps borrowed from Roman law, *affirmanti incumbit onus probandi.* [5] *Aghānī*, VIII, 103.

[6] The present writer, while engaged in lower Iraq on the duty of determining boundary disputes, was often assured by litigants that they were prepared to accept the statements of the opposing party if supported by an oath, *bi'l-Ḥusayn*, i.e. at the sacred shrine of Ḥusayn, at Kerbelā. Similarly the evidence of witnesses was tested by their readiness or otherwise to swear to it at that shrine or others in the neighbourhood.

of lawlessness made it necessary.[1] This more powerful court for what was called *naẓr al-maẓālim* ("review of wrongs") "combined the justice of the qāḍī with the power of the sovereign", and was instituted by the later Umayyads, who sat in person to receive petitions from all comers. The early Abbasids, from Mahdī to Muhtadī, followed their example,[2] but after them—although the Caliph Qāhir, for one, promised to preside at the review of *maẓālim*[3]—the duty was undertaken by the vizier, whose failure to carry it out was regarded as a serious fault.[4] Sometimes the Caliph appointed deputies to act for him, either in a provincial city or in the various quarters of the capital. At Baghdad the Caliph Muqtadir ordered the chief of police to nominate lawyers who were to sit for the hearing of pleas in each of the city quarters. Those who attended the courts were not even required to pay for the paper on which their petitions were written, so desirous was the prince to see justice done.[5] The same prince was persuaded by his mother to appoint a stewardess named Thumal to hear plaints in the Ruṣāfa quarter every Friday. The public showed its disapproval of her by absenting itself on the first occasion when she presided. On the second Friday she brought a qāḍī with her and matters then took their ordinary course.[6] The appointment by Mutawakkil of a poet, 'Alī ibn Jahm, to fill the office at Ḥulwān[7] would appear to have been less suitable.

The court of the "Reviewer of Wrongs" concerned itself with (*a*) acts of oppression of the Caliph's subjects by those in authority over them; (*b*) injustice in the levying of taxes;[8] (*c*) the acts of

[1] Māwardī, pp. 129 ff.

[2] Māwardī. *loc. cit.*; Bayhaqī, *Maḥasin wa'l-masāwi*, ed. F. Schwally (Giessen, 1902), p. 577; Mas'ūdī, *Murūj*, VIII, 21; Ṭabarī, III, 1736.

[3] Ibn al-Athīr, VIII, 193.

[4] 'Arīb (*Ṭabari Continuatus*), p. 25, l. 18.

[5] *Ibid.* p. 71.

[6] *Ibid.*

[7] *Aghānī*, IX, 108 (middle).

[8] An example given by Māwardī (pp. 136 f.) is that of Muhtadī (Amedroz, *J.R.A.S.* (1911), 639, has made it clear that this prince is meant and not Mahdī, as given in Enger's text) who had occasion to review the payment of revenue in Persian and Byzantine coins. In Omar's day, revenue from certain conquered provinces had been accepted in their own local currency, and attention was paid only to the number and not the weight of the coins, which differed considerably in this particular. When, with the decay of virtue, people offered only the lighter coins, those charged with collection of revenue demanded extra payments to make up for the deficiency. This led to injustice and the consequent impoverishment of the Sawād and other rich lands until, under Manṣūr, some cultivators were able to pay only in kind on certain crops, while tax on others was remitted. Muhtadī brought about a reform by allowing payments to

scribes in public offices. In these matters, he could take action without any initial step by a person entitled to complain. Other matters proper for the cognizance of the court were (*d*) complaints by those in receipt of official stipends that these had been reduced in amount or had not been paid; (*e*) claims for restoration of property wrongfully seized; (*f*) the interests of *awqāf* (pious endowments), whether public or private; (*g*) the enforcement of decisions made by qāḍīs not sufficiently strong to see their judgments carried out against defendants occupying high rank or powerful positions; (*h*) the suppression of evil-doing and the enforcement of regulations within the jurisdiction of the *muḥtasib* (the "censor") but beyond his power to apply; (*i*) the care of public worship and religious practices in general and seeing to their due performance; (*j*) the hearing and decision of disputes generally, when the rules of procedure which govern cases that come before the ordinary qāḍīs and judges will prevail.[1]

The difference between the qāḍī and the reviewer of *maẓālim* was that the latter had much wider powers. He could check unsupported denials on the part of litigants and restrain acts of violence on the part of wrongdoers; he could use intimidation (*irhāb*) to overawe a defendant into an admission and obviate the calling of unnecessary evidence; he could take time to investigate evidence and consider all sides of a case—action not permitted to ordinary judges, who are compelled to settle cases out of hand; he could refer litigants to persons of responsibility who would act as arbitrators—a proceeding not open to the qāḍī, except by consent of both parties; he could compel the attendance of parties in court where it was apparent that one or other was putting forward a claim or a defence without support, and he could require a security where that was admissible in order to bring the parties to an understanding. He could administer an oath to witnesses if he was doubtful of their veracity, and he could summon as many of them as he pleased to free him from doubt, a step which an ordinary judge could not take; and, finally, in the matter of procedure,

be made without regard to weight of coin, even though the loss to the revenue was calculated at 12,000,000 dirhams per annum.

Other examples are mainly fiscal; e.g. a complaint of the basis on which an estate was taxed and an oppressive assessment. (*Wuzarā*, pp. 143 and 345.)

[1] Māwardī, pp. 135–41; Amedroz, *art. cit.* pp. 635 f. Examples of such cases: a dispute about shops (*Wuzarā*, p. 143), and another about the width of the arches of a bridge (*ibid.* p. 256).

he could begin the trial by summoning the witnesses and questioning them about their knowledge of the dispute, whereas the practice of the qāḍīs was to require the plaintiff to bring forward his proofs, which were not considered until after he had made a request to that effect.[1]

In other respects, however, the qāḍī and the reviewer of *maẓālim* were equal in authority. As it was possible on occasion for a qāḍī to act as reviewer of *maẓālim*, the two courts might have concurrent jurisdiction. Thus, in the *Maqāmāt* of Ḥarīrī, Abu Zayd (the "hero") describes how he assaulted a persistent creditor in order to be brought before a lenient "officer [of the court] of offences" rather than before a harsh and greedy "judge of *maẓālim*" (i.e. of civil wrongs), who would have tried the claim for debt. Shārīshī, the commentator of Ḥarīrī, explains that by "the officer of the court of offences" is meant the prefect of police, while Ḥarīrī obviously identifies the "judge of *maẓālim*" with the qāḍī.[2]

The officer presiding at the review of *maẓālim*, if he was the vizier or other highly placed official, who counted this amongst other duties, set aside a special day for this task[3]; if he was specially appointed to have charge of this office and no other, then he sat every day.[4] In Egypt during the Fāṭimid rule, the vizier, when he was the chief officer of the State or else the "Lord of the Gate" (*Ṣāḥib al-Bāb*), sat on two days in the week at the Golden Gate at the palace of Cairo to dispense justice and review cases of civil wrong. Before him sat the chief representatives of the various communities, and the royal chamberlains, and a crier summoned those who had plaints. These were made orally, if the complainants lived at Cairo or Miṣr, and each plaint received was sent for necessary investigation to the lieutenant of police or the qāḍī of the quarter concerned. If the person against whom complaint was made lived outside of the two cities, the plaintiff sent in his plaint in writing. A chamberlain received all the written plaints and took them to the official known as "the Inscriber with the Fine Pen", who wrote on each a decision, and transmitted them to the

[1] Māwardī, pp. 141 f.

[2] *Maqāmāt*, ed. de Sacy, 2nd ed., I, 311 (1st ed., p. 270), and Amedroz, *art. cit.* p. 663.

[3] Niẓām al-Mulk (*Siyāsat-nāma*, p. 10) regarded it as essential for the king to sit two days a week for this purpose.

[4] Māwardī, p. 134.

"Inscriber with the Broad Pen". He, in turn, supplied details which could only be indicated by the other, and all were then sent to the Caliph for his confirmation and approval. That done, the plaints were put into a sack and given back to the chamberlain, who at the palace gate gave each petitioner his own document, the decision upon which was carried out by the dīwān concerned.[1]

There has been occasion to refer often to statutory penalties for offences against the law. They are those which the Koran laid down, and of which the most important were the penalties for apostasy, homicide, adultery, mutilation and theft. The penalty for adultery has already been dealt with in a previous chapter[2] and it remains now to deal with the others. All but theft are punishable by death, and it may be assumed that only if he is guilty of one of the specified offences is it legal for a Muslim to be put to death by the Caliph or his agent. The historians, however, constantly report the killing of Muslim subjects, often of high rank, for political offences or merely out of spite, and generally it would appear that criminals were punished, if at all, as expediency or caprice dictated rather than as the theory of the *fiqh* demanded.

It is in agreement with the character of the Islamic State that apostasy by one who has been a believer should be regarded amongst the most heinous of crimes.[3] The legists[4] demand that the apostate be given three chances to repent, and he is not to be killed until he has definitely refused.

The matter of homicide is not so simply determined. Deliberate slaying of a believer is forbidden,[5] and the Mosaic rule of a life for a life holds in Islam also.[6] But the question of motives must be brought into consideration, and it is the duty of the Caliph or his representative to decide whether the slayer acted of set purpose or slew the victim by accident.[7] When it is found that the killer has acted of set purpose and without excuse,[8] the victim's *walī*, or

[1] Maqrīzī, *Khiṭaṭ*, I, pp. 402 f.; S. de Sacy, *Chrestomathie arabe* (2nd ed.), I, 132 ff.

[2] Pp. 119 ff.

[3] Cf. Koran 2^{214}.

[4] E.g. Abu Yūsuf, *Kitāb al-Kharāj*, pp. 109 ff.

[5] Koran 4^{94}.

[6] *Ibid.* 5^{49}. "A free man for a free woman, a slave for a slave, a woman for a woman." (*Ibid.* 2^{173}.)

[7] *Kitāb al-Kharāj*, p. 91.

[8] "A man who threatens Muslims with a weapon may be killed by them with impunity. A man who enters another's house at night and robs it may be followed by the owner and slain with impunity. A man who kills another after threatening him with a weapon and being dealt a blow is guilty and liable to retaliation." (*Jāmi' al-ṣaghīr* (in margins of *Kitāb al-Kharāj*), p. 119.)

male next of kin, has power to avenge him,[1] but he may not act outrageously,[2] i.e. by mutilating or slaying anyone other than the murderer.[3] Yet it is not essential for retaliation to be exacted; indeed, the Koran regards pardon as commendable, on payment of generously reckoned compensation by the slayer.[4] The vagueness of the Koran's language about the alternative, and the recommendation to mercy, give the legists ample room for discussion and difference of opinion. On the general principle laid down by the Koran, of a life for a life, Abu Ḥanīfa and his school hold that the *walī* of the victim has no choice but to exact vengeance, and that he may not take the *diya*, or blood-money, unless he wishes especially to favour the slayer.[5] Holding strictly to the text of the Koran, the Ḥanafī school further maintains that a man who has slain another, the victim being a Muslim or a member of one of the "protected" religions, free man or slave, shall himself be slain. Also, a man shall be slain for a woman and an old woman for a young one. But no man shall be slain for his own son nor an owner for his slave or his son's slave.[6] The Shāfi'ites hold that the *walī* of the slain person shall be entitled to choose between *talio* and blood-money, provided that victim and slayer are equal in standing.[7] This implies that no Muslim shall be slain for an unbeliever and no free man for a slave; nor is it required to inflict *talio* on a father or grandfather for slaying his son or grandson.[8] The Mālikites interpret the law as a general principle that a man, whether bond or free, shall be slain for murdering another. If, however, the slayer "stands superior to the victim by reason of religion or liberty", i.e. by being a Muslim and the victim an unbeliever, or by being a free man and the victim a slave, then there is no need for *talio*. According to this principle, therefore, Mālikites would exact vengeance from a man who kills his son or

[1] Koran 17^{35}. In pre-Muslim and early Muslim times it was possible, when a man had slain another who belonged to a hostile tribe, for the *walī* of the victim to capture the slayer and hold him to ransom. In *Aghānī* II, 188, we are told how, while they were watering camels, Hilāl b. As'ar, of the Māzin tribe, threw a *miḥwar* (an implement used for cauterizing) at Buhays of the hostile 'Anaza and slew him. His son captured Hilāl and held him imprisoned while negotiations for his ransom were carried on.

[2] Koran, *loc. cit.*

[3] Bayḍāwī *ad loc.*

[4] Koran 2^{173}.

[5] Māwardī, p. 392.

[6] Qudūrī, *Mukhtaṣar*, p. 172; Nasafī, *Kanz al-daqā'iq*, II, 300–2.

[7] Māwardī, *loc. cit.*

[8] Shīrāzī, *Tanbīh*, p. 262.

grandson.[1] In spite of the rule of a life for a life, it is held by the Mālikites that since the *walīs* are the male heirs of the dead man, they must be in entire agreement on the question of exacting the *talio*. If even one of them will forgo it, then blood-wite is payable.[2] The Ḥanbalites would appear to agree with the Mālikites on the general principle of *talio* for deliberate killing.[3]

If a man slays another unintentionally and entirely by accident, there is no question of *talio*. Blood-money is, however, payable, and it is the duty of the whole of the slayer's clan[4] collectively to compensate the heirs of the victim, whereas the fine for deliberate killing is paid out of the slayer's own property.[5]

If a man is found slain by an unknown hand within the territory of a tribe not his own, they are liable to pay the blood-wite to the victim's *walī*. This practice is obviously of long standing, but it is based by the legists on a tradition of the Prophet.[6]

The amount of the *diya* varied. There is a tradition that the Prophet determined it according to the means of the slayer's family and in terms of what they regarded as wealth. Thus he imposed on a camel-owner a *diya* of a hundred camels for slaying a man and on a sheep-owner a thousand sheep. If the slaying was unintentional and the *diya* payable by the slayer's clan, then it could be paid in three years by instalments.[7] The law-books generally contain elaborate details of the value of the *diya* payable in various circumstances. Abu Yūsuf, for example, declares that the blood-money for a woman accidentally slain is half that for a man[8]; accidental killing by a slave requires from his owner half the *diya* payable by a free man.[9] It was also the practice to pay for a *mawlā* (freed man) half the *diya* payable for a free and pure-blooded member of an Arab tribe.[10] If a free man kills a slave by accident he must pay the owner the value which the slave had on the day of his death.[11]

[1] Khalīl, *Mukhtaṣar*, tr. Guidi and Santillana, II, 662.

[2] Māwardī, *loc. cit.* See further, *Kitāb al-Kharāj*, p. 91 (middle).

[3] *Kanz al-daqā'iq*, II, 300.

[4] His *'āqila*, i.e. his "party, who league together to defend one another, consisting of the relations on the father's side, who pay the blood-wite (apparently in conjunction with the slayer) for him who has been slain unintentionally". (Lane, *Lexicon*, s.v.)

[5] Shāfi'ī, *Umm*, VI, 81; Māwardī, pp. 393 f.; *Kitāb al-Kharāj*, pp. 92 f.

[6] Cf. Bayḍāwī on Koran 4[95].

[7] *Kitāb al-Kharāj*, pp. 92 f.

[8] *Ibid.* p. 95.

[9] *Ibid.* p. 92.

[10] Cf. *Aghānī* II, 176.

[11] *Kitāb al-Kharāj*, p. 95.

The law of the *talio* was applied for mutilations as for murder —a limb for a limb, an eye for an eye and a tooth for a tooth. But compensation might be offered and accepted and the *talio* forgiven, particularly for wounds inflicted in the head, where no precise equivalent could be exacted.[1] Though a woman is slain if she kills another person, the *talio* is not inflicted on her if she mutilates a man or another woman, but she must pay monetary compensation.[2] If a woman herself suffers mutilation resulting in the loss of a limb or an eye, the compensation paid to her is half that payable to a man for a similar loss.[3] Between free men and slaves there is no *talio* for mutilation unless loss of life ensues. If a free man mutilates a slave, for example by striking off a hand or an ear, the master of the slave will assess the damage and the culprit must pay him compensation.

The thief, for a first offence, has his or her right hand cut off.[4] For a second offence the left foot is amputated and so forth. Theft is defined as taking by stealth property to the value of at least one-quarter of a dīnār from a place which is without any doubt private and reserved.[5] Punishment is to be inflicted on all thieves alike, men or women, free men or slaves, Muslims or unbelievers. But no boy suffers it, no slave stealing from his master and no parent stealing from his son.[6]

Imprisonment seems to have been at the will of anyone in power. Habitual criminals might by law be imprisoned for life, but they must be fed and clothed at the expense of the *Bayt al-Māl* (the public Treasury) if they have no means of their own, though often they went out in chains to beg for charity.[7] No Muslim prisoner might by law be put into bonds which would prevent his standing for prayers.[8] There is evidence, finally, that imprisonment was not entirely casual and haphazard, and that though often enough it was the result of official wantonness, yet some record of prisoners was kept during the Caliphate in a special dīwān. On one occasion this was plundered and burnt during an outbreak of rioting at Baghdad, some of the registers being destroyed.[9]

[1] *Kitāb al-Kharāj*, pp. 91 f. [2] *Ibid.* p. 93. [3] *Ibid.* p. 95.
[4] Koran 5[42]. [5] Bayḍāwī on Koran 5[42]. [6] Māwardī, p. 388.
[7] *Kitāb al-Kharāj*, pp. 88 f. [8] *Ibid.* [9] Ṭabarī, III, 1510 f.

CHAPTER VIII

GOVERNMENT IN THE PROVINCES OF THE CALIPHATE AND IN THE SUCCESSION STATES

For the first century and a quarter of its history the whole of the territory subjugated to Islam acknowledged the headship and authority first of Muhammad the Prophet and then of his "Orthodox" and Umayyad successors in turn. During the century of swift expansion which had followed the Prophet's death, successive Caliphs at Medina or Damascus were proclaimed sovereigns and chiefs of Islam from the Oxus and the frontiers of India, across Persia, Arabia and the north of the African continent to the Pyrenees and the Atlantic Ocean.

Records of the first period of Islamic history are scanty, a few papyri being all the written monuments that remain, for even the earliest extant Muslim annals date only from the second century of Islam. In those of them that deal with the events of the first century, much reliance is necessarily placed upon tradition and report, the authentic character of which is by no means certain. Yet there remains, after the application of the tests of criticism, sufficient to provide a not unsatisfactory account of how government and administration were carried on.

Tradition says that the Prophet himself in his lifetime had appointed agents, *'ummāl* (singular *'āmil*), to collect the alms-taxes in every part to which Islam had penetrated. With these officers he sent amīrs, who, presumably, were in command of troops intended to enforce payment.[1] The system became established, and on the heels of each general who conquered a province and became its amīr, there followed an 'āmil to collect tribute, although there were times, in the absence of an amīr, when the 'āmil was the Caliph's agent for all purposes, military as well as civil. In Arabia, the Prophet's immediate successor, Abu Bakr, stationed 'ummāl in all the principal towns. Outside the peninsula also, in Syria, more than one 'āmil was appointed, of whom the victorious Khālid ibn

[1] Ṭabarī, I, 1750.

Walīd had charge,[1] and in Iraq two were appointed to have charge respectively of the lands watered by the Euphrates and the Tigris, while additional officers were sent to be in command of Baṣra and Kūfa.[2]

Upon the officers mentioned there rested the burden of provincial government in the early days of conquest. The first amīrs naturally wielded powers that were all but supreme in the territories they took by the sword, and it may easily be understood that for a considerable time the only positive measures of administration had for their objects the gathering of revenue and the suppression of any tendency to rebellion. Abu Yūsuf speaks of Omar's having sent three officers to Iraq, one to lead in prayer and war, another to have charge of the administration of justice and of the treasury, and a third to measure the newly acquired lands for revenue purposes.[3] Once the first rush of conquest had abated and the Muslims had turned their attention to consolidating their acquisitions, the 'āmil began to advance in importance until he became the equal of the amīr; where the interests of the treasury were concerned, his opinion might even be the decisive one.[4]

Before the consolidation of the occupied territories that came with the Umayyads, the armies in the field were sufficiently independent of the central authority to insist on governors of their own choice in the newly conquered regions. Ṭabarī, enumerating the provincial officers at the time of 'Uthmān's death (35/656), says that his governor at Baṣra, founded as a military station, had been forced to leave it, and that no one was sent to succeed him. At Kūfa, similarly, the Caliph's nominee had been ejected, while in Egypt various claimants competed for authority without reference to the Caliph. In Syria there was the strong arm of Mu'āwiya to maintain his personal independence. He appointed his own subordinates, placing lieutenants of his choice in the cities of the province.[5]

The machinery of provincial government remained simple during the Umayyad regime, though the varying fortunes of the Caliphate determined the actual number of officers appointed to

[1] Ṭabarī, I, 2136. [2] *Ibid.* I, 2636 f. [3] *Kitāb al-Kharāj*, p. 20.
[4] For instance, on the question of *kharāj* in Khurāsān, see above, p. 310.
[5] Ṭabarī, I, 3057 f.

each province and the extent of their powers. The annalists (e.g. Ṭabarī) chronicle new appointments year by year, and the records indicate that the extent of territory allotted to an official varied with his personal capacity. Two officers of equal powers might sometimes be sent to a province where one alone had governed before, or a single one might, at the will of the Caliph, be given charge of two provinces.

In the yeaı 41/661–2 'Abd-allāh ibn 'Āmir succeeded to the governorship of Baṣra, and was given charge of the campaign against Sīstān and Khurāsān.[1] Two years later 'Abd-allāh dismissed his agent in Khurāsān, to which he appointed a certain 'Abd-allāh ibn Khāzim.[2] In the next year 'Abd-allāh ibn 'Āmir was himself removed from the governorship of Baṣra.[3] His successor, al-Ḥārith, was dismissed after only four months,[4] and then Ziyād "Ibn Abīhi", whom Mu'āwiya claimed for his half-brother, was given the office, together with the governorship of Khurāsān and Sīstān, as well as the more or less nominal control of India, Baḥrayn and 'Umān.[5] Five years later, Kūfa, too, was placed under his jurisdiction,[6] and in the same year the whole of North Africa was put into the charge of Maslama b. Mukhallad, who was also invested with authority over Egypt,[7] although previously it had had a governor of its own.[8] On the other hand, Mu'āwiya is reported (A.H. 58) to have made two brothers joint 'āmils of Khurāsān, which, as one of them remarked, was a province wide enough to support a double governorship.[9] More frequently, however, one man had supreme charge in all the eastern provinces; for, to add another instance, the famous

[1] Ṭabarī, II, 15. [2] *Ibid.* II, 65. [3] *Ibid.* II, 67. [4] *Ibid.* II, 71
[5] *Ibid.* II, 73. [6] *Ibid.* II, 88. [7] *Ibid.* II, 94. [8] *Ibid.* II, 84.

[9] *Ibid.* II, 188 f. A sidelight on the aims and objects of provincial government is provided by an incidental report in Ṭabarī on one of these two brothers, who had returned to Damascus after three years of office with 20,000,000 dirhams in his possession. Yazīd, the reigning Caliph, on discovering the fact, gave him the alternative either of surrendering the total sum to the royal treasury and returning to the province—in order, presumably, to amass another fortune for himself—or else of paying one million dirhams to the man who was to be his successor (in addition, one may understand, to a large sum for the Caliph himself), and being removed from office.

A similar instance is given by Jahshiyārī (*Kitāb al-Wuzarā*, ed. Hans v. Mžik (Leipzig, 1926), p. 11A), who declares that Khālid, a controller of *kharāj* in Iraq in Mu'āwiya's day, received at the Persian feasts of *Nawrūz* and *Mihrgān* gifts amounting to 10,000,000 dirhams for the year.

Ḥajjāj ibn Yūsuf was regarded as capable of bearing on his own shoulders the burden of governing not only Iraq but Khurāsān and Sīstān in addition,[1] though he employed in the Persian provinces lieutenants whom he changed as he desired.[2]

Difficulties of communication must always have embarrassed the central control of the more distant provinces. Once in power the official in charge was assured of virtual independence until he was dismissed. On the other hand, although the initial appointment of the chief governors during Umayyad days was always made from Damascus, the royal nominee might encounter opposition when he reached his province. When Khālid al-Qasrī, for example, went to take charge of Sind, the local potentate disputed his authority, claiming that he had himself been permitted to retain his hereditary control of internal affairs by the Caliph Omar ibn 'Abd al-Azīz.[3] Khālid actually remained in Sind for a very short time, for he is reported as governor of Baṣra soon afterwards.

At the opposite extreme of the empire, Spain, which had been conquered in 92/711, was governed by a series of 'ummāl who were subordinate to the viceroy in North Africa, and, as a rule, held office for very short periods. The viceroys themselves were often transferred from similar employment in Egypt.[4] But the Umayyad capital, Damascus, was too far away for the Caliph's authority in the west ever to have been very strong. In the year 125/743 one Abu'l-Khaṭṭār entered Spain as amīr, but his power was disputed by a self-appointed rival, 'Abd al-Raḥmān, over whom he was successful, though he himself was dismissed two years later by his Andalusian subjects, who appointed their own governor.[5]

As for Egypt, the papyri contain a mass of details supplementing the accounts given by later historians of the governmental regime followed in the Umayyad period. At the head of the province stood the amīr, or *walī*, who was appointed by the Caliph and changed with every change of monarch. Generally his charge was called that of leadership in prayer (*'alā'l-ṣalāt*),[6] with which he might combine the function of revenue administration (*kharāj*).[7]

[1] Ṭabarī II, 1032 ff.
[2] *Ibid.* II, 1138.
[3] Ibn al-Athīr, A.H. 107.
[4] Cf. Ibn al-Athīr, A.H. 113 and 117.
[5] *Ibid.* A.H. 127, 129.
[6] See Kindī, ed. Guest (Gibb Series), under Umayyads *passim.* In practice it almost came to mean "civil authority".
[7] Cf. Kindī, pp. 58, 83.

If he were not placed in charge of the *kharāj* he could himself appoint an officer for the purpose.[1] More often there was a *ṣāḥib kharāj*, who was independent of him and communicated directly with the Caliph.[2] The amīr, as head of the military organization, was nominally the chief officer in the province, but as the functions of the 'āmil who was responsible for the revenue increased in importance, he advanced in status until he was equal with the amīr, in some respects the treasury officer having greater power. A token of their equality in Abbasid times was the fact that the famous vizier Ibn al-Furāt addressed both officers by the same titles of honour.[3]

Following historical precedent, the Muslim invaders at their first coming into new territory, and for a considerable period afterwards, left the details of administration, which in practice consisted mainly of collecting taxes, to the minor native officials of the older regimes displaced in the different provinces. It was the rule for the governors to have the appointment of their own subordinate officials, including, in addition to those who were kept to continue the business of the old revenue system, those who filled the newer offices made necessary by Islam. Yazīd ibn Muhallab, who succeeded Ḥajjāj as governor of Iraq, appointed the officer of the *kharāj*,[4] and Khālid al-Qasrī, governor of Iraq and Khurāsān in A.H. 107, had one lieutenant for the organization of prayer at Baṣra, while another was in charge of the administration of justice, and a third was officer of the *shurṭa*.[5] At Samarqand another officer (in charge of police) was responsible both for military duties and the collection of revenue.[6] In the year 110/728 Khālid al-Qasrī entrusted all the public offices at Baṣra, except that of the revenue, into the hands of a single individual, who was accordingly charged with the combined duties of prayer-organization, policing and judicial administration.[7] On the whole, the actual number of officials on the government pay-rolls was small, for the tribal chieftains and village headmen were in the majority of cases held responsible for maintaining law and order, and for enforcing payment of taxes. In Khurāsān, for example, each *balad*

[1] Cf. Kindī. pp. 65 f.
[2] *Ibid.* pp. 73, 85, 93.
[3] Hilāl al-Ṣābī, *Wuzarā*, ed. Amedroz, p. 156.
[4] Ṭabarī, II, 1138.
[5] *Ibid.* II, 1487.
[6] *Ibid.* II, 1507 f.
[7] Ibn al-Athīr, A.H. 110.

or township was allowed to choose its own representative, who would be responsible for it to the government.[1]

In Syria the old Byzantine officers continued to be employed; the revenue system remained what it was before the coming of Islam, and the tax-lists remained in Greek. Similarly in Iraq, at Kūfa and Baṣra, there were two dīwāns, or tax-registers, the one in Arabic, to keep account of the Arab invaders and of the pay and pensions due to them, and the other in Persian for recording the revenue due from the native inhabitants.[2] The latter register continued to be written in Persian according to one tradition until A.H. 81, in the reign of the pious Caliph 'Abd al-Malik ibn Marwān,[3] though another tradition ascribes the change to the governor Ḥajjāj ibn Yūsuf.[4] According to Maqrīzī,[5] the Egyptian revenue registers were written in Coptic at the Muslim conquest, and remained so until a reform was introduced by the governor 'Abdallāh, son of 'Abd al-Malik ibn Marwān (in A.H. 87). The Copts, who filled the majority of the revenue offices in Egypt in the first century of Islam, undoubtedly (and naturally) used their own language for their accounts, but some records certainly were kept in Greek by officials of the old régime.[6]

Of the systems of administration followed in the various Umayyad provinces, we have the most reliable information about that of Egypt. Whether amīr or 'āmil was the chief of the revenue department, the actual work of financial administration was carried on by the Coptic advisers, who had been trained in the Byzantine system and were appointed by the head of the department, although immediately after the conquest the appointment was

[1] Ṭabarī, II, 1481.

[2] Jahshiyārī, *Wuzarā*, ed. Mžik, p. 17A; Māwardī, ed. Enger, p. 349; Ibn Khaldūn, *Prolégomènes*, ed. Quatremère, II, 18; tr. de Slane, II, 21.

[3] Jahshiyārī, *loc. cit.*

Maqrīzi (*Khiṭaṭ*, I, 98) says the change from Persian to Arabic was made by Walīd b. Hishām b. Makhzūm b. Sulaymān, who died in 222/837. "But most say that it was the scribe of Ḥajjāj who made the change at some date after A.H. 80." He says the change from Greek to Arabic (in Syria) is attributed both to 'Abd al-Malik and his son Hishām.

[4] Balādhurī, ed. de Goeje (Leyden, 1866), p. 300. In the tenth century A.D. Arabic was the official language of Fārs, although the natives spoke Persian. (Ibn Ḥawqal, p. 205.)

[5] *Khiṭaṭ*, I, 98.

[6] Cf. C. H. Becker, *Papyri Schott-Reinhardt* (Heidelberg, 1906); *Greek Papyri in the British Museum*, vol. IV, ed. H. I. Bell (London, 1910).

made directly by the Caliph.[1] There were two of them, and they had joint control of the revenue in Upper and Lower Egypt,[2] which were, for purposes of their system, divided into *kūras*, or districts. Each *kūra* consisted of a chief town or large village with the surrounding territory of which it formed the economic centre. The lesser units that went to make up this larger division were the *qaryas*, or villages, each in charge of a local head known as a *māzūt*. This basic division into *kūras* was continued until the Fāṭimid period, when the revenue system of the country was reorganized into *a'māl* (singular *'amal*), "parishes".[3]

Under the agrarian system in force in Byzantine days and continued under the Caliphate, the land belonged to the State and was rented out to the peasant cultivators who tilled it. After harvest the grain was gathered into heaps, of which the contents were determined by a government official known as a *qabbāl*, who took the amount due as rent to the Caliph and gave what remained to the cultivators.[4] There appears to have been no special tax called *kharāj* levied on individual cultivators, as there was in other provinces of the Caliphate.[5] Taxation, indeed, was collective, specified groups being responsible for particular amounts. There was in addition, however, a money-tax, which had something of of the nature of a capitation fee.[6] The demands for this were prepared at Fustāt, the headquarters of the province, and it was collected in each *qarya* by the local chief, who forwarded it to headquarters. At all times the country was liable to be burdened with "extraordinary" dues. These were levied on each *kūra*, whose chief was made responsible for their delivery, and generally consisted of materials in kind, such as timber for shipbuilding, or implements, though demands might also be made for craftsmen or

1 Cf. the case of Theodore, who held office between A.D. 661 and 677 (*Patrologia Orientalis*, ed. Evetts, v, 1, 5; and Becker, *Islamstudien*, pp. 248 f.).

2 They were ultimately replaced by Muslims, who held charge separately over the respective divisions of the country (see Becker, *Zeitsch. f. Assyriologie*, xx (1907), 101). So far as the inhabitants were concerned, the change of tax-gatherers brought little relief, for the new ones seem to have imposed cesses of their own immediately upon arrival. Cf. Severus, *History*, in *Patrologia Orientalis*, v, 188. "After a while there arrived two men of the dīwān, officers from the king to Miṣr, and they were Muslims . . . and they imposed two [extra] taxes on Lower Egypt and one [extra] tax on Upper Egypt."

3 Maqrīzī, *Khiṭaṭ*, 1, 72.

4 Cf. Becker, *Papyri*, pp. 70 f.

5 Maqdisī, ed. de Goeje (2nd ed.), p. 212.

6 Maqrīzī, *Khiṭaṭ*, 1, 98.

sailors. In either case the whole community was liable for satisfaction of the demands exactly as they were made, money not being accepted in substitution.[1] The money and materials received from rents and other levies in the province were first applied in the province itself for the payment of troops and officials, and the purchase of necessary military supplies. What remained was sent to the Umayyad treasury at Damascus.[2]

With the overthrow of the Arab dynasty of the Umayyads by the semi-Persian Abbasids, and their foundation of the new capital Baghdad, the territory of Islam ceased to have a single temporal centre. From then onwards a process of disintegration set in, although for over a century the Islamic world was divided between two powers only, the Eastern Caliphate of the Abbasids and the Amīrate of Andalusia under the Umayyads of Cordova. The provinces of the Eastern Caliphate all had some feature of government in common, generally in having their administration placed in charge of an amīr and an ʿāmil appointed from Baghdad. In detail, however, there were considerable differences in provincial government, the results of different local traditions or of accidental circumstances. Thus Iraq from its closeness to the capital stood in special relationship to the administrative headquarters, so that the fertile region known as the Sawād of Iraq was in charge of ministers of State and not of ordinary governors. The dīwān of the Sawād was, in fact, regarded as the most lucrative of the ministries, and was in consequence eagerly sought after.[3] Similarly, the district of Bādurayya, on the right bank of the Tigris, having Baghdad touching its north-eastern corner, was inevitably endowed with special interest. Anyone capable of administering it well was regarded as suitable for the ministry of *kharāj*, an office which was, in its turn, a qualification for the vizierate.[4] In the chief remaining districts of Iraq there was put a *walī*[5] or an ʿāmil—not necessarily both—appointed by the Caliph in the

[1] Cf. Maqrīzī, *Khiṭaṭ*, I, 77, and *Greek Papyri in the British Museum*, IV, 435 ff.

[2] Maqrīzī, *Khiṭaṭ*, I, 98 f.

[3] Miskawayhi, *Eclipse of the Abbasid Caliphate*, I, 151; Hilāl, *Wuzarā*, ed. Amedroz, p. 314.

[4] Tanūkhi, *Nishwār al-muḥāḍara* (British Museum MS. Or. 9586, f. 7A).

[5] Tabarī, III, 465, l. 12.

days when he still concerned himself with the details of government,[1] or by the vizier, when that official had powers of patronage.[2]

In the other provinces of the Caliphate—namely, the holy cities of Arabia, Yemen, Syria, Ādharbayjān, Armenia, the Jazīra or Mesopotamia proper, North Africa, Egypt, Sind, and the several divisions of Persia—there was, in the earlier years of the Abbasids, a viceroy (*'āmil*) of the Caliph in charge.[3] Upon occasion, however, in later times, particularly in Egypt, two officers were appointed to have charge of the province, the amīr to hold military command and someone else to be responsible for revenue.[4] Thus in 304/916–17 there was at Iṣfahān, owing presumably to its importance, a special official in charge of the military organization (*mutawallī 'l-ḥarb*), and another who was overseer of revenue (*mutawallī 'l-kharāj*).[5]

In Egypt, under the earlier Abbasids as under the Umayyads, the governors were appointed to have charge of prayer and *kharāj*.[6] Some were entrusted only with the nominal headship which was implied in the prerogative of acting as *imām* at prayer,[7] another officer having control of the finances.[8] The duties were somewhat differently distributed in the second century of Abbasid rule, when one of the two chief officers was appointed to lead in war and prayer and the other controlled the revenue administration.[9] Afterwards, when Egypt achieved independence under Aḥmad ibn Ṭūlūn in 254/868, that competent and ambitious statesman held all the reins of office himself, as also did al-Ikhshīd,[10] who after a short interval in which Baghdad regained a precarious footing in Egypt, made himself master in the country to which he had been sent as amīr in 323/935.

Appointments to governorships were sometimes made for purely political reasons, and the Caliph Ma'mūn appointed natives of Persia to offices in that country in return for services rendered to

[1] Jahshiyārī, pp. 52b, 86b, 99a, etc.

[2] Hilāl, *Wuzarā, passim; Eclipse of the Abbasid Caliphate*, I, 16, 28, etc.

[3] Ṭabarī, III, 459.

[4] *Ibid.* III, 501.

[5] Ibn al-Athīr, VIII, 36, A.H. 304.

[6] Kindī, ed. Guest (Gibb Series), pp. 101, 120, 129, etc.

[7] *Ibid.* pp. 117, 118, 142, etc.

[8] E.g. *ibid.* p. 108; Jahshiyārī, p. 81a.

[9] Ibn Sa'īd, *Kitāb al-Mughrib*, ed. K. N. Tallquist (Leyden, 1899), p. 15, ll. 21–23 (tr. p. 37).

[10] *Ibid.* p. 16 (Arabic).

him against his brother Amīn. One appointment thus made was that of Faḍl ibn Sahl, who claimed descent from the kings of Persia, and whose father, Sahl, had been the first convert of the family from Zoroastrianism to Islam.[1] Ma'mūn granted to Faḍl the charge of "the East, from Hamadān mountain to the mountain of Siqīnān and Tibet in length, and from the Sea of Fāıs and Hind (i.e. the Persian Gulf) to the Sea of Daylam and Jurjān (i.e. the Caspian Sea) in breadth. And he allotted to him a stipend of 3,000,000 dirhams . . . and he called him 'Lord of Two Headships' "—the latter, it is explained, in reference to his having command both of military power and of the civil administration.[2]

Purchase was a common means of acquiring a governorship, though an offer might, for political reasons, be refused. Thus Yūsuf ibn Abi 'l-Sāj, who was in supreme control of Ādharbayjān and Armenia, was ambitious of adding Rayy to his territory, and marched there with a body of troops. The Caliph Muqtadir, however, refused to confirm him in the desired office in spite of a large sum which Yūsuf offered him; whereupon the interloper withdrew, though only after plundering the unfortunate inhabitants of the city.[3]

Kinship with the sovereign provided a natural claim to a governorship. Thus Ma'mūn had as a prince been made 'āmil of Khurāsān by his father Hārūn, and, further, the Caliph Mu'tamid in 261/875 made his two sons, Ja'far and Abu Aḥmad governors of the western and eastern provinces respectively.[4] The fact that colleagues of some experience were appointed to act with these two princes indicates that the honour in their case was titular. In so far also as their appointment concerned Egypt and Persia, it was in large measure a formality without significance, for Aḥmad ibn Ṭūlūn then held independent power in Egypt, while Naṣr ibn Aḥmad, the Sāmānid, was in an equally strong position in Transoxiana and Khurāsān. In the case of the Sāmānids the Caliphs continued to address them as their viceroys, sending each new Sāmānid prince a patent of confirmation long after the act lost its significance.[5]

[1] *Al-Fakhrī*, ed. Ahwardt, p. 265.
[2] Ṭabarī, III, 841.
[3] Ibn al-Athīr, A.H. 304.
[4] Ṭabarī, III, 1890.
[5] *Ibid.* III, 1889, 2279.

For the system of revenue administration under the Abbasids, that followed in the Sawād may be regarded as typical. It was divided into two *kūras* (districts), each of which consisted of several divisions known as a *tassūj*.[1] Bādurayya was the richest, and it was composed of twelve *rustāqs* (rural areas), of which the best was that of al-Karkh, comprising twelve *qaryas* (villages).[2] The part of Iraq known as Ṭarīq Khurāsān ("The Khurāsān Highway"),[3] with Ba'qūba as its centre, was similarly divided into a number of *tassūj*.[4] Another part, that centred about Wāsiṭ, had as the revenue unit the '*amal*.[5] which may be regarded as equivalent to the *tassūj*. Like the larger administrative units under the control of an 'āmil, the *kūra* was not of fixed dimensions, and it could be expanded or made part of others at the will of the central government.

Often the 'āmil appears as a tax-farmer rather than a salaried official of the *Dīwān al-Kharāj*, and he was granted his position in return for a fixed sum of money—paid in advance or guaranteed to the treasury—which permitted him to extort what sums he could from the inhabitants of the province.[6] Ibn al-Athīr speaks of one instance in which it was not the 'āmil but the amīr, already in charge of military affairs, prayer and administration of governmental decrees (*aḥkām*) in Ādharbayjān and Armenia, who was responsible for the dispatch of revenue to the capital.[7]

Buying and selling of the tax-farms, with consequent oppression of the subject peasantry, was the main feature of provincial government in Abbasid days, although before Baghdad completely lost control the Caliph might appoint an overseer (*mushrif*),[8] or a responsible minister might consider it his duty to pay a visit of inspection to a province in order to audit revenue accounts.[9] Since the 'āmil and the amīr in command of the troops between them managed the affairs of the province, they were able, if they could come to terms, to arrange matters almost to their liking

[1] Yāqūt, *Mu'jam al-buldān*, I, 241 (under *Istān al-'Alī*).
[2] Hilāl, *Wuzarā*, p. 258.
[3] Cf. *Nuzhat al-Qulūb*, ed. le Strange, p. 42.
[4] Hilāl, *Wuzarā*, p. 339.
[5] Yāqūt, *Mu'jam al-buldān*, IV, 882.
[6] Cf. Hilāl, *Wuzarā*, passim; *Eclipse of the Abbasid Caliphate*, I, 16, 45, 57, etc.
[7] Ibn al-Athīr, A.H. 304.
[8] Cf. Ṭabarī, III, 377.
[9] Cf.Hilāl al-Ṣābi, *Wuzarā*, pp. 319 f.

under a weak central government.[1] This was particularly true if the officer of the *barīd*, whose function it was to act the spy on the provincial governors on behalf of the authorities at the capital, was venal or incompetent. Sometimes matters were facilitated for an ambitious governor when he was powerful enough to demand control both of the army and *kharāj*,[2] although a strong Caliph like Ma'mūn could with confidence entrust both to the same individual.[3]

The extent of territory covered by Islam after the first century was greater than could be effectively controlled by an individual ruler, for means of communication were inadequate to enable even a powerful monarch to supervise adequately the doings of governors and subjects in provinces distant from the capital. As has been seen, the governors appointed by the Umayyads from Damascus to have charge of the extremities of the empire in Andalusia and Khurāsān were virtually their own masters. But even when Islam was well established, there were among the conquering people jealousies and rivalries in which the inhabitants of the subdued provinces were compelled to take sides, although they cared little which party won. The situation was such that a man who combined determination with ambition was assured of support if he had effective reasons—such as those of religion, sentiment or military strength—for claiming it. Thus in Andalusia a certain Umayyad nobleman, who had escaped the general massacre of his kinsmen by the Abbasid forces, was adroit enough to employ to his advantage any traces of loyalty that were still felt for his family. He set up a kingdom which claimed to carry on the rightful succession to the Caliphate, and thus brought it about that Andalusia never in any way acknowledged the rule or suzerainty of the Abbasids.

Shortly after the foundation of Baghdad also there broke out at Medina a revolt of the supporters of the 'Alid claimant to the

[1] For a case of the kind, where the amīr and the financial officer of the joint provinces of Fārs and Kirmān refrained for three years from sending revenue to Baghdad, cf. Ibn al-Athīr, VIII, 165 f. (A.H. 319).

[2] E.g. when Bajkam, the ambitious Turkish general, refused to proceed to Ahwāz unless he were entrusted with both charges (Ibn al-Athīr, VIII, 252, A.H. 325).

[3] Ṭabarī, III, 375, l. 7.

rulership of Islam. The revolt was suppressed and the ringleaders were forced to flee. One of them, Idrīs ibn 'Abd-allāh, a descendant of 'Alī, came to Morocco, where he founded a Shī'ite kingdom which lasted for over a century and a quarter (788–922), in rivalry to the Abbasid Caliphate. The Berber population of North Africa has always been susceptible to propaganda, particularly when flavoured with schism and heresy. When, therefore, with the decline of the Idrīsids, and of their neighbours the Aghlabids in Tunis, the missionaries of one 'Ubayd-allāh came to spread the doctrine that he was the Mahdī and a descendant of the Imāms—and hence also of the Prophet's daughter Fāṭima—their efforts met with success. 'Ubayd-allāh founded the Fāṭimid Caliphate, which spread with Shī'ism into Egypt and Syria, and robbed the Abbasids of some of their richest possessions. The Fāṭimid rule lasted from 297/909 until the year 567/1171, when Saladin came to power and restored the name of the Abbasid Caliph to the *khuṭba* and the coinage[1] in territory from which it had been absent for over two and a half centuries. Egypt once more became Sunnite, and its rulers called themselves by the title of sulṭān.[2] Ifrīqiya (Tunis) was the actual country in which the Fāṭimid propaganda had begun. At the coming of 'Ubayd-allāh it was in the hands of the Aghlabids, descendants of Ibrahīm ibn Aghlab, who had in 184/800 been appointed governor of the whole of the province of North Africa by Hārūn al-Rashīd. In spite of being Sunnīs and nominally vassals of the Caliph of Baghdad, they acknowledged allegiance to no one, and some of them omitted the formality of inscribing the name of the Caliph on their coinage.

The outward sign of absolute and defiant independence of the Baghdad Caliphate, as a rule, lay in the usurpation of the title of *Khalīfa* or *Amīr al-Mu'minīn* ("Commander of Believers"), or of some close approximation to it. The early Fāṭimid dynasties, such as the Idrīsids of Morocco and the 'Alid rulers of Ṭabaristān, it is true, used the title of *Sayyid*,[3] which was the token of their descent from the Prophet, but the Fāṭimids of Egypt and Syria

[1] Cf. S. Lane-Poole, *Catalogue of Oriental Coins in the British Museum* (London, 1875–82), IV, 67–9.

[2] Cf. Abu'l-Maḥāsin ibn Taghri-Bardī, *Annales*, ed. Juynboll (Leyden, 1855–61), II, 252.

[3] Cf. Ibn Isfandiyār, *History of Ṭabaristān*, tr. E. G. Browne (Gibb Series, II), pp. 162 ff.

called themselves Caliphs.[1] In Spain, the Umayyad rulers of Cordova were content with the title of Amīr, or of "Son of the Caliph",[2] until the accession of the famous 'Abd al-Raḥmān III. He, however, in the seventeenth year of his reign (317/929), was encouraged by the feebleness of the Baghdad Caliphs, then at the nadir of their powers, to follow the example of the 'Alid rulers of North Africa and assume the title of *Amīr al-Mu'minīn*.[3] The precedent he established was followed by his successors, not only of his own line but also of the *Mulūk al-Ṭawā'if*,[4] the petty rulers who shared the Umayyad territories amongst themselves on the fall of the dynasty, and each of whom proclaimed his own lordship and mastery from the pulpits of his country.[5] The Almorāvids, who ousted them in their turn, called themselves *Amīr al-Muslimīn*, which was parallel, for all intents and purposes, with *Amīr al-Mu'minīn*.[6] In Egypt the Ikhshīdids called themselves *Amīr*,[7] while the Ayyūbid princes and the Mamlūks were called *Sulṭān*, and "Soldan" was normally recognized in Europe of the middle ages as the title of the Egyptian ruler.[8]

Some of the more humbly born of these rulers demanded formal and public recognition of their office. Thus the negro slave Kāfūr, who had for long held the reins of government under the Ikhshīdids, when he himself succeeded to the throne in 355/966 asked the acknowledgment of the Egyptian amīrs and the army. So also the Mamlūk Sulṭān al-Malik al-Nāṣir, who came to the throne at a troubled period in the history of Egypt, summoned the nobles of the country in order to have his sovereignty formally acknowledged and established according to law. Some of them refused him, with the result that serious strife broke out, but

[1] Cf. *al-Fakhrī*, ed. Ahlwardt, pp. 308 f.

[2] Maqqarī, *Nafḥ al-ṭīb* (4 vols., Būlāq, n.d.), I, 202.

[3] Ibn al-Athīr, A.H. 350. Cf. S. Lane-Poole, *Coins of the Mohammadan Dynasties in the British Museum* (London, 1876), II, 14–28.

[4] I.e. "tribal kings". This is the title given by Muslim historians to the rulers of provinces and towns, who, after the fall of their suzerain, divided his lands amongst themselves and ruled as despots until they were all dethroned by the Almoravids. Cf. S. Lane-Poole, *Coins of the Mohammadan Dynasties*, pp. 29 ff.

[5] Cf. Marrākushī, *History of the Almohades*, ed. Dozy (2nd ed., Leyden, 1881), p. 63.

[6] *Ibid.* p. 122 *et al.*

[7] The negro Kāfūr called himself modestly *Ustād* ("Master"). (Ibn Sa'īd, *Kitāb al-Mughrib*, p. 124.)

[8] Cf. Abu 'l-Maḥāsin, ed. Juynboll, II, 152.

finally the qāḍīs formulated a decree that he was in fact and of right the sulṭān.

It is a fact worthy of note that no independent ruler in Persia ever usurped the title of "Caliph". The dynasties founded in that country by the governors who were appointed by the Umayyads and Abbasids all owned at least nominal allegiance to them, while other reigning families had reasons of their own for so acknowledging them. Of these others the Ghaznawids, Buwayhids and Seljūqs are outstanding. The first and last of the three, pious Sunnīs, were loyal out of religious feeling to the Commander of the Faithful, while the Shī'ite Buwayhids declared him their suzerain because it gave them a freedom which acknowledgment of a Shī'ite Imām would have curtailed. After the destruction of the Caliphate of Baghdad the gradual increase of nationalism in Persia, together with the attendant growth of Shī'ism, directed Persian sentiment inwards, and culminated in the foundation of a national dynasty—that of the Ṣafawid shāhs. During the existence of the Baghdad Caliphate no Persian prince, though he might be entirely his own master and paid only nominal service to the *Amīr-al Mu'minīn* (by mentioning him in the *khuṭba* and on coins), claimed a higher title than that of sulṭān. Even Maḥmūd of Ghazna called himself no more than *amīr* on his coins,[1] and it is said that Khalaf ibn Bānū, ruler of Sīstān and a vassal of Maḥmūd's, was the first to call him sulṭān.[2]

Persian governors and rulers after the earliest period wielded none the less real independence for their show of allegiance. It has been seen that under the direct authority of the Umayyads and earlier Abbasid Caliphate, the principal officers in the Persian provinces, and particularly those like Khurāsān and Transoxiana, which lay furthest from the capital, were changed almost annually. This prevented any governor—free from control as he was—from achieving too great power, though the cost was the absence of settled government. When, however, the authority of Baghdad weakened to such an extent that its orders could be ignored or defied with impunity, governors began to transmit their office to their sons, and so established autonomous dynasties. The first

[1] See S. Lane-Poole, *Coins of the Mohammadan Dynasties in the British Museum*, p. 132.

[2] Cf. Mīrzā Muhammad Qazwīnī's note, Niẓāmī 'Aruḍī Samaroandī, *Chahār maqāla* (Gibb Series), p. 163.

declared attempt at self-assertion was made by Ṭāhir Dhu'l-Yamīnayn, to whom the governorship of Khurāsān had been allotted by Ma'mūn in 205/821. Ṭāhir's attempt is usually regarded as having failed, so far as he himself was concerned, for he died suddenly, having been in office for only a year, after a report from the *ṣāḥib barīd* of the province that the governor had omitted the Caliph's name from the *khuṭba*. Whether the two events are to be associated remains a matter for speculation, but it is a fact that Ṭāhir was succeeded as amīr by two sons, a grandson and a great-grandson, who yielded to the Caliph's authority to the extent only of paying a small proportion of their revenues to him in annual tribute.[1]

The last member of the Ṭāhirid dynasty was forced (in 259/872) to surrender his dignities to Ya'qūb ibn Layth Ṣaffār (the "Coppersmith"), who had compelled the Caliph Mu'tamid two years earlier to recognize his amīrate of Balkh, Tukhāristān and the neighbouring regions, as well as that of Kirmān, Sīstān and Sind, which he already held.[2] It was not for another three years that the Caliph would acknowledge in addition Ya'qūb's *de facto* governorship of Khurāsān and the adjoining territories.[3] His brother 'Amr, who succeeded him, was a man of greater distinction and administrative ability, and it is probable that he made some effort to keep on friendly terms with the Caliphate in order to gain the support of such subjects as were loyal to the head of Islam.[4] The fact, however, that he usurped the Caliph's prerogative of inscribing his name on the coinage of the province would indicate that he regarded himself as free of control from Baghdad. 'Amr's downfall came about through his excessive ambition. At his own request he had received from the Caliph Mu'taḍid the governorship of Transoxiana, but, advancing to take possession of his new domains, he was met and defeated, much to the Caliph's relief, by Ismā'īl ibn Aḥmad, the Sāmānid, who held the province as governor.[5]

The Sāmānid marched into Khurāsān,[6] and was in his turn recognized as its governor by the Caliph, who sent him a patent of appointment and a banner.[7] The family to which he belonged

[1] Cf. Barthold, *Turkestan*, p. 220.
[2] Ṭabarī, III, 1841, 1881 f.
[3] Ṭabarī, III, 1892.
[4] Cf. Gardīzī, *Zain al-Akhbār*, ed. Nazim, p. 15.
[5] Ṭabarī, III, 2194 f.
[6] *Ibid.* III, 2204.
[7] Gardīzī, p. 21.

traced descent from the Sasanian shāhs, and various members of it, almost as soon as they had embraced Islam, were presented by Ma'mūn to offices subordinate to the amīr of Khurāsān in Transoxiana and elsewhere in northern Persia. Although the Caliph regarded the Sāmānids as his vassals,[1] they were permitted, without interference from Baghdad, to make their appointment hereditary, and at times of need they were capable of showing their loyalty to the Caliph by carrying out military duties.[2] But apart from the performance of these voluntary services and inclusion of the Caliph's name in the *khuṭba* and on the coinage, they owned no vassalship or inferiority.

So far as their position in their own country was concerned, the Sāmānids were absolute monarchs, except that they left the government of certain remote districts in the hands of local families in which chieftainship was hereditary, and whose ruling members sent no more than nominal tribute to Bukhārā, the capital.[3] Amongst these families were the Ṣaffārids, who continued to lead a practically autonomous existence in Sīstān, though acknowledging their vassalage to the Sāmānids.

As for the succession, the strongest male of the dynasty seized the throne, while the others were frequently in rebellion.[4] If there was a doubt concerning the heir-apparent when a Sāmānid sovereign died, his intimates and the elders of the capital met to decide upon a new ruler, as happened when Aḥmad ibn Ismā'īl died leaving an eight-year-old son.[5]

The position of the Ghaznawids, who succeeded to the empire of the Sāmānids, was a parallel one to theirs in relationship to the Caliphate. As good Sunnīs they were on terms of friendliness with the Abbasid Caliph, and Maḥmūd, the most powerful member of the dynasty, was acknowledged amīr of Khurāsān by al-Qādir

---

[1] "Naṣr ibn Aḥmad, *Mawlā-i Amīr al-Mu'minīn*" is inscribed on a coin of Alptagīn (S. Lane-Poole, *Coins of the Mohammadan Dynasties in the British Museum*, p. 128). Nūḥ ibn Manṣūr Samānī is similarly described in Abu Muti' al-Balkhī's *'Ajā'ib al-Ashyā* (E. G. Browne MS., Cambridge G. II, 12, fol. 1), and his brother, Aḥmad ibn Manṣūr, is called by the same title on a coin of his father, Manṣūr ibn Nūḥ (S. Lane-Poole, *op. cit.* p. 111).

[2] E.g. Aḥmad ibn Ismā'īl's war against the non-Muslim Turks at the Caliph's request ('Arīb, p. 43).

[3] Cf. Maqdisī, pp. 337, 340, and *Bibl. Geog. Arab.* IV, 343.

[4] Cf. E. de Zambaur, *Manuel de Généalogie . . . de l'Islam* (Hanover, 1927), p. 203.   [5] Gardīzī, pp. 25, 43.

(381/991–422/1031) almost as soon as news of the overthrow of the Sāmānids had reached Baghdad.[1] The good feeling between Caliph and amīr was indeed reciprocal, for when al-Qādir died, the envoy who announced the enthronement of his successor was received with great ceremony at Ghazna, al-Qā'im's name being coupled with that of the amīr (then Mas'ūd, son of Maḥmūd) in the *khuṭba*, and a message of loyalty sent to the new Caliph.[2]

In the account that is extant of the ceremonies which took place at the accession of Mas'ūd ibn Maḥmūd, much is made of the *manshūr*, the patent of appointment, sent by the Caliph and assigning to the new amīr all the territories which his father had held, or which he himself might acquire. It was read out in the original Arabic before a large assembly, for whose benefit a short translation in Persian was added. The ceremony concluded with the amīr's donning a *khil'a* (a robe of honour) sent by the Caliph, and his recitation of two parts of the formula of worship. Subsequently, copies of the *manshūr* were sent to all the more important cities in the Ghaznawid empire.[3]

Although, like the Sāmānids, they were regarded by the Caliph as no more than the amīrs of Khurāsān, the Ghaznawids were supreme and absolute rulers in their own territories, and visited with their extreme displeasure any subordinate ruler who refused to acknowledge them as such.[4]

Of other dynasties which held sway at one period or another in Persia, the Buwayhids in the fourth century of Islam, and the different branches of the Seljūqs in the fifth and sixth centuries, stood in a peculiar relationship to the Caliph, of whom they were not merely independent, but the masters and controllers. Both dynasties nevertheless—though for different reasons, as has already been explained—made a show of acknowledging his suzerainty, so that in the coinage of both dynasties the name of the Caliph is found coupled with that of the reigning Buwayhid or Seljūqid.

With the destruction of the Baghdad Caliphate in 1258 there disappeared the symbol of the vanished alien power which had

[1] Gardīzī, p. 62.

[2] Bayhaqī, *Ta'rīkh-i Mas'ūdī*, ed. W. H. Morley (Calcutta, 1862), pp. 353 ff.

[3] *Ibid.* pp. 48–50.

[4] Thus Maḥmūd treated with violence the Khwārazm-shāh who omitted his name from the *khuṭba* (Bayhaqī, *op. cit.* pp. 841 ff.).

once dominated the land, and all need ceased for even a pretence of vassalship to one who might claim the headship of Islam. For two and a half centuries thereafter the Mongol conquerors and their successors held sway, but there was slowly coming about a revival of an ancient sense of nationality and of corporate feeling. It manifested itself in the enthusiasm which greeted Ismāʿīl the Ṣafawid when, at the end of the fifteenth century, he swept away the numerous minor dynasties of Mongol origin in Persia, and himself claimed the sovereignty of the land. It manifested itself further in the success of his efforts to satisfy the particular religious susceptibilities of himself and the majority of his people by establishing Shīʿism as the national faith. He belonged to a family of *pīrs* or *murshids*, hereditary Ṣūfī leaders who traced descent from Shaykh Ṣafī al-Dīn, who, in his turn, claimed to be of the stock of the seventh Imām, Mūsā al-Kāẓim. While Ismāʿīl did not claim to be an Imām, yet he spoke of being divinely aided in his task of making Shīʿism the faith of his country. Divine honours were there accorded to him, and his own prestige and that of his descendants amongst the Persians must be attributed in part to the religious character of the dynasty and its claim to hereditary greatness.[1]

Concerning the methods of government in the earliest independent or semi-independent states, details are for the most part lacking. In Persia a certain process of development can be traced from the primitive stage in which the ruler held all the reins in his own hands, being personally in command of military forces as well as supervising the business of finance in the country, to that in which there was an elaborate system of officials in numerous grades. An example of the simple form of rule is that ascribed to ʿAbd-allāh ibn Ṭāhir in Khurāsān.[2] Such autocracy did not necessarily mean oppression or bad government as reckoned by the standards of the time and the people, although the degree of benevolence shown towards the subject varied with each despot. It is reported that in Khurāsān, Ṭāhir's son ʿAbd-allāh interested himself in agriculture, and endeavoured to put an end to the

[1] Cf. E. G. Browne, *History of Persian Literature in Modern Times* (Cambridge, 1924), pp. 49 ff.

[2] Ṭabarī, III, 1338 f.

constant disputes concerning water-rights, which are endemic in lands where water is scarce. 'Abd-allāh, finding no guidance either in the books of *fiqh* or in the Prophet's *ḥadīth* about the rules governing the distribution of water from the underground channels (*qanāt* or *kārīz*) characteristic of Persia, summoned the *faqīhs* of Khurāsān and Iraq to compile a manual (*Kitāb-i Quniy*) on the subject. The work was still in use two centuries afterwards, in the days of Gardīzī, who reports the matter. 'Abd-allāh, moreover, encouraged the production of grain, and appears to have believed in the value of universal education.[1]

It may be presumed from the early history of Ya'qūb ibn Layth Ṣaffār—he began his military career as a brigand—that he did little for the civil administration of Khurāsān and the lands he held, and he appears, with little foresight, to have extorted money wherever and whenever the opportunity presented itself, in preference to waiting for regular collections of revenue.[2] His brother 'Amr, who succeeded him, went to work with more method to establish order and financial stability.[3] The geographer Ibn Ḥawqal has preserved the name of one of 'Amr's officers, Ḥasan ibn al-Marzubān, who was in charge of the *Dīwān al-Istidrāk* ("The Office of Requisition"), and belonged to a family in which public service was traditional.[4] For the benefit of his troops 'Amr had a magazine of arms, together with a treasury—filled from the proceeds of alms-taxes and certain special levies—that was employed exclusively for military pay and equipment. For his own private use he had another treasury out of which he paid for foodstuffs or lands to produce them, while still a third treasury was filled by money from taxes, and was used for the support of retainers and palace officials.

The amīrate of the Sāmānids, which succeeded that of the Ṣaffārids, covered a far greater expanse of territory, and it was, in fact, the largest independent kingdom that had existed in Persia since the beginning of the Caliphate. Its government had stability, and the administration was well organized. The capital, and the centre of the government, was at Bukhārā, but the *sipāh-sālār*, the general commanding the royal forces, acted as the amīr's viceroy in Khurāsān, and was stationed either at Merv or

[1] Gardīzī, p. 8. [2] *Ibid.* p. 11. [3] *Ibid.* pp. 14 f.
[4] Ibn Ḥawqal, *Masālik wa'l-mamālik*, ed. de Goeje (Leyden, 1873), p. 208.

Nīshāpūr.[1] For the administration of civil affairs in the amīrate the capital was equipped with an elaborate system of dīwāns which recalls that of Baghdad and was well established in the time of Naṣr (II) ibn Aḥmad.[2] That prince had offices built at his palace gates for his principal state functionaries—the vizier, the *mustawfī* (the treasurer), the *'amīd al-mulk* (the king's confidential secretary and head of the *Dīwān-i Risālat* or Chancery),[3] the *ṣāḥib shuraṭ* (police commandant), the *ṣāḥib mu'ayyad* (literally "The Officer Assisted"—his duties are not described), the *muḥtasib* (the censor), and the qāḍī, as well as for the administrators of his private domains and the funds of the *awqāf* (pious endowments).[4]

The sovereign appointed the more important officers, and sometimes he retained the chief appointments within his family. Thus Naṣr ibn Aḥmad made one of his sons vizier and another the *sipāhsālār*.[5] A distinction must normally be drawn between the officers of state and the functionaries of the *dargāh* (the palace), whose concern was with the ceremonial of the court and the administration of the royal household. The chief palace official was the *ḥājib al-ḥujjāb*, "the chamberlain-in-chief", who was placed extremely high in the ranks of public employees, and regarded his importance as far exceeding that of an 'āmil or provincial revenue officer.[6]

The chief civil officer in the state was the vizier, and it was he who shouldered the responsibilities of government when the king was incapable by reason of youth or otherwise of undertaking the necessary duties. During the minority of the Prince Naṣr ibn Aḥmad it was the vizier Abu 'Abd-allāh al-Jayhānī, therefore, who administered the affairs of the state.[7] A powerful vizier could appoint and dismiss other officials, and even military commanders of the highest rank.[8] If the fifteenth-century historian Mīr-

[1] Gardīzī, pp. 30, 35, 39, 43.

[2] The fourth prince of the line.

[3] Cf. Bayhaqī, *Ta'rīkh-i Mas'ūdī*, ed. Morley (Calcutta, 1862), p. 163. On p. 21, Ṭāhir the Secretary—previously (p. 6) described as head of the Chancery—is "Master '*Amīd*", by whom all business was transacted.

[4] Narshakhī, *Ta'rīkh-i Bukhārā*, ed. Schefer (Paris, 1892), p. 24.

[5] Gardīzī, p. 39.

[6] *Ibid.* p. 42.

[7] *Ibid.* p. 25. Cf. p. 32 for Abu'l Faḍl, who was *ṣāḥib tadbīr* (administrator) and vizier to Nūḥ ibn Naṣr.

[8] Narshakhī, *op. cit.* p. 134.

Khwānd is correctly informed, the vizier could himself hold the chief army command.[1]

Administration under the Ghaznawids resembled that of their predecessors. The great officials of the state were the *sipāh-sālār*, the Great Chamberlain (*ḥājib-i buzurg*), who was, strictly speaking, a palace official,[2] and the vizier.[3] In Ghazna, however, even more than elsewhere under the Islamic system, the quality and importance of any office depended almost exclusively on the character and desires of the sovereign. Thus in the interim between Sulṭān Maḥmūd's death and the accession of his son Muhammad, the government was carried on by 'Alī, the Great Chamberlain.[4] It was possible, moreover, for an outsider who held no official post to be called in and be entrusted with great power and responsibility.[5] As a rule, however, the vizier was the officer most regarded in the state after the amīr himself.[6] Not only were the lives of the general mass of the population in his hands,[7] but the fortunes of all other officers of the state, so that, to take an instance, when Abu Sahl Zawzanī became vizier, the head of the Chancery (*Dīwān-i Risālat*), although an official of some importance, absented himself from duty out of fear of the new chief minister.[8]

At the head of the treasury was the *mustawfī*, who appears to have corresponded to the *ṣāḥib dīwān al-kharāj* at Baghdad and under whom were a number of *khāzins* (treasurers) in charge of specie and various classes of valuable stores. They were responsible for keeping accounts, a task in which they were assisted by a number of *kātibs* (scribes) and *mushrifs* (overseers).[9] As under the Sāmānids an important place was held by the *Dīwān-i Risālat*, the Chancery, from which there issued all letters of state, patents of office and royal proclamations.[10] The importance of this dīwān has been exaggerated by officials employed in it, from whom, incidentally, much of our information is obtained; but it undoubtedly had a considerable measure of influence in the making and unmaking of political careers, comparable in some measure with that of the *dīwān-i barīd*, which was the headquarters of the intelligence service of the State.[11]

[1] Mīr-Khwānd, *Historia Samanidarum*, ed. Fr. Wilken (Göttingen, 1808), pp. 72, 84.
[2] Bayhaqī, *op. cit.* pp. 4, 13.
[3] *Ibid.* pp. 176 f.
[4] *Ibid.* pp. 4, 11 f.
[5] *Ibid.* pp. 26, 170.
[6] *Ibid.* p. 176.
[7] *Ibid.* p. 500.
[8] *Ibid.* p. 67.
[9] *Ibid.* pp. 312, 314.
[10] *Ibid.* pp. 164 f. and *passim*.
[11] *Ibid.* p. 165.

When the Buwayhids came into power in the fourth century of Islam, they held sway not only in Fārs, in which they had their headquarters, but in the adjacent provinces and Iraq too, with Baghdad itself reduced to the humble rank of a provincial capital. The early members of the family held all the reins of government in their own hands, although for the details of administration they employed a vizier, who might act on occasion as commander of an army. 'Aḍūd al-Dawla had two viziers, one of whom he left as his deputy in Fārs, while the other fought rebels in the marshes of Iraq.[1] The Caliph's minister who had been called vizier before the advent of the Buwayhids was now reduced to being the Caliph's secretary, with the title of *ra'īs al-ru'asā*. As their history progressed, the members of the dynasty who ruled in Fārs left an increasing amount of the work of administration to their ministers, so that the famous vizier, the Ṣāḥib Ismā'īl ibn 'Abbād, was permitted by his master, Mu'ayyad al-Dawla, to have charge even of his finances—a token of confidence remarkable in this dynasty.[2]

Seljūq administration of the state, in its main features, resembled that of the Sāmānids. The description of it given by Niẓām al-Mulk relates rather to an ideal than to the actual conditions which prevailed; but a good deal must have been based on fact. All that need here be said is that the vizier was the officer of greatest importance in the organization, and upon his efficiency and that of his subordinates in the provinces—the *'amil*, the *qāḍi*, the *ṣāḥib barīd* and the *ra'īs*—depended the prosperity of the land.[3]

The Mongol administrative system owed little to Islam, and therefore lies outside the scope of this work.[4] It was not until the establishment of the Ṣafawī dynasty that Persia resumed a form of government which may be described as being of the Islamic pattern, or, rather, in the Islamic tradition. The early Ṣafawī shāhs delegated few of their duties at the capital. Shāh Ṭahmāsp (1524–76) employed a council of advisers, who were generally

[1] Cf. Ibn al-Athīr, A.H. 382 (IX, 66), and A.H. 369 (VIII, 515 f.). Their high office did not protect ministers from physical violence at the hands of their master if they offended him; but, as was normal in Persia, a beating implied no disgrace, and they might resume office after it (cf. Ibn al-Athīr, A.H. 341, *ad fin*).

[2] Yāqūt, *Irshād al-arīb*, ed. Margoliouth (Gibb Series), II, 275.

[3] Cf. Niẓām al-Mulk, *Siyāsat-nāma*, ed. Schefer, pp. 18, 43, 57 and *passim*.

[4] See Barthold, *Turkestan*, pp. 382 ff. for a discussion of the system.

"sulṭāns",[1] i.e. provincial governors whose main function was to be answerable to the sovereign for the conduct of affairs in their provinces, of which the actual government, such as it was, lay in the hands of the "khāns", who were their deputies.[2] "The grand councillors", however, had no vote, and could say nothing unless called upon by the king.[3]

The shāh also employed a vizier,[4] who, to judge from the qualities belauded in him, was little more than a private secretary. In later times the Grand Vizier, who bore the title of *I'timād al-Dawla*, "the Pillar of the State",[5] was the chief of the provincial governors, who had come to be known as viziers. It was the shāh, however, who at all times decided matters of importance, whether concerned with foreign relationships or the government of the chief provinces, and the Grand Vizier, in spite of his titles and dignities, was actually no more than the intermediary between the sovereign and the outer world.

The best accounts of the government of Persia during the Ṣafawī period are given by the European travellers who were attracted to the country for political or commercial reasons. According to Olearius,[6] who was in Persia between November, 1636, and February, 1638 (i.e. in the reign of Ṣafī, the son of Shāh 'Abbās the Great), the *I'timād al-Dawla*, or Chancellor, at the time

> was president of the King's Council, the Soul of Affairs, the principal Minister of State, and, as it were, Viceroy of Persia. . . . He hath oversight of the King's Revenues and Treasury. This was the most self-concerned person of all that ever had the management of publick affairs, as a Minister of State. For there was no business done at Court, whereof he made not some advantage; and there was no charge or employment to be gotten, but the person

[1] Cf. *Tadhkira-i Shāh Ṭahmāsp*, "Kāviānī" ed. (Berlin, A.H. 1343), p. 18.

[2] Cf. John Fryer, *A New Account of East India and Persia* (1672–81: Hakluyt Society, 1915), III, 21 f.

[3] *A Narrative of Italian Travels in Persia* (Hakluyt Society, 1873), p. 220.

[4] *Tadhkira-i Shāh Taḥmāsp*, p. 9.

[5] Cf. Iskandar Munshī, *Ta'rīkh-i 'Ālam-ārā'i 'Abbāsī* (E. G. Browne MS., Cambridge, H. 13 fol. 5b).

[6] Adam Olearius (Oelschläger), secretary to the embassy which was "sent by Frederick, Duke of Holstein, to the great Duke of Muscovy and the King of Persia". His account was "Faithfully rendered into English by John Davies of Kidwelly", and published in London in 1669. The references in the text are to this edition.

petitioning for it must have made his agreement with the Chancellor; whose exactions were, in this particular, excessive, not only upon the accompt of the Presents, which being made by him twice every year to the Court, rendered the King himself in a manner a complice of his concussions [extortions], but also upon this consideration, that being an Eunuch, all the wealth he got was at his death to fall to the King.[1]

Sometimes, in addition to his duties in attendance on the shāh, the *I'timād al-Dawla* was given charge over the less important provinces of the state, the more important ones coming under the control of the sovereign himself.[2]

Of the other principal offices of state, the *Dīwān-i Risālat* (Chancery) of earlier dynasties was continued by the *Wāqi'a-nawīs* ("Writer of the Minutes"), who was "secretary of state and of the king's revenue". He was the instrument by which orders and dispatches were issued and sent into the provinces, and by which account was kept of goods and moneys received from the treasury for the maintenance of the royal household.[3]

In the component provinces of the Persian State, government resembled on a lower plane that of the central administration, the main difference being that in the smaller unit the revenue officer held a rank commensurate with his real importance. His duties were closely bound up with the prevailing system of land tenure, in which long-standing local custom maintained continuity and prevented any significant change. Under the early Sāmānids and the Ghaznawids the constituent provinces were placed in the charge of *wālīs*,[4] each of whom had his own officers[5]—a vizier, a *sipāh-sālār*[6] to have command of troops, and a *wakīl-i dar*, who was a confidential assistant or chamberlain.[7] The Ghaznawids normally made the *wālī* himself responsible for the revenues, but gave him a *ṣāḥib-dīwān* as a financial assistant.[8] Under their predecessors the Sāmānids, however, there might be an 'āmil in each

[1] Olearius, *op. cit.* p. 272.

[2] John Fryer, *op. cit.* III, 21 f.

[3] Olearius, *loc. cit.* In more modern times, under the Qājārs, the ministries increased in number, partly under European influence. The Shāh's viziers formed a council, of which the chief members were the *Ṣadr-i A'ẓam* (Chancellor), the *Wazīr-i A'ẓam* (Prime Minister), the *Mustawfī al-Mamālik* (Minister of the Interior), and the *Wazīr-i Niẓām* (War Minister).

[4] Bayhaqī, *op. cit.* pp. 16, 320.

[5] Gardīzī, p. 21.

[6] *Ibid.* p. 49.

[7] Gardīzī, p. 43.

[8] Bayhaqī, *op. cit.* p. 509.

province who had charge of the finances independently of the *wālī*.[1]

As had been the case from time immemorial in Persia, actual and immediate responsibility for the collection of revenue and for the maintenance of law and order, particularly in the districts outside the towns, devolved upon the *dihqāns*. They were essentially cultivators and owners of land, which might be great or small in extent, and much of the substantial wealth of the country was in their hands. Much, also, it may incidentally be said, of the traditional lore of Īrān was preserved by them, and it was of their stock that Firdawsī, the author of the *Shāh-nāma*, was derived.

The governors, both then and in later times, regarded their office as hereditary and the territory under their control as part of their own property.[2] Yet they were liable to be dismissed by the shāh, and remembered therefore to secure his favour by gifts, to which he replied at New Year with a robe of honour.[3] The more powerful of the tribal chiefs never yielded to the shāh's authority as represented by his agents, and in many districts the *ḥākim*, or military governor, was often compelled in the course of his duties to proceed against rebellious nobles, as well as to defend the frontiers of his province against outside aggression.[4]

Ordinarily the acting governor, or *khān*, in each province undertook duties of the kind, and was, in addition, obliged to pay certain fixed sums of revenue into the coffers of the shāh, by whom alone he was appointed or dismissed.[5]

Under the Qājārs the governors frequently were members of the royal family, and bore distinctive titles according to their own personal rank. The most important provincial areas, the *iyālats*,[6] were placed in their hands, but the method of government in the provinces had little system or regularity about it. The *wilāyat*, which is the area, great or small, placed in the charge of a *wālī* or a *ḥākim*, was in general the district attached by geographic or

[1] Narshakhī, *Ta'rīkh-i Bukhārā*, ed. Schefer, pp. 81 f.

[2] Cf. *Tadhkira-i Shāh Ṭahmāsp*, p. 12.

[3] Cf. *Don Juan of Persia*, ed. G. le Strange (London, 1926), p. 46.

[4] *Tadhkira-i Shāh Ṭahmāsp*, p. 10, and *passim*.

[5] A comprehensive account of the Ṣafawī administration is provided by V. Minorsky in his commentary on the *Tadhkirat al-Mulūk* (Gibb Memorial Series, n.s. XVI. London, 1943), by an unknown author.

[6] Ādharbayjān, Fārs, Khurāsān and Kirmān; but the area classed as an *iyālat* might have additional territory added to it, or a portion removed as expediency demanded.

economic links to some large village or township (the *qaṣaba*, or centre), and for which the governor principally was responsible. He did not administer the internal affairs of the *qaṣaba*, since the inhabitants themselves had the right to elect their own magistrates, to make rules for the bazaars, and to set up their own civil and commercial tribunals.

Purely local government under the early dynasties was entrusted to a *ra'īs* or *shiḥna*,[1] whose main function appears to have been to represent his community on ceremonial occasions, and to act as the instrument for the transmission of royal commands to his fellow-townsmen.[2] Within each *maḥalla* (quarter) and bazaar of the town there was, further, a locally elected elder who saw that the orders of the *ra'īs* were fulfilled.[3] In the towns probably lived the lesser provincial officials, such as the *bundār*, who kept account of the revenues levied in kind and of government stores generally, and the *ṣāḥib ma'ūna*, whose prime concern was with emergency stores for military purposes, but who might also be responsible for certain police duties.[4] These district officers were under the authority of the provincial chief of their own department, who in their turn were answerable to the amīr.[5] Amongst the local functionaries, as amongst the *dihqāns*, office was often hereditary, having been transmitted from father to son from Sasanian times.[6]

Away from the larger towns much of the population then, as now, was nomadic or semi-nomadic, and it was upon the tribal chieftains that the central government relied, as often as was possible, to act as its agents. If a bargain could be struck between the amīr and the chiefs, the latter became responsible for the peace and good order of the district over which their respective tribes roamed, and they might even act as tax-gatherers for the government.

The tenth-century geographer, Ibn Ḥawqal,[7] describes the

[1] Bayhaqī, *op. cit.* pp. 9, 289.

[2] *Ibid.* pp. 45 f., 352. In Ṣafawī days his place was filled by the *kalantār* (R. du Mans, *Estat de la Perse en* 1660, ed. C. Schefer (Paris, 1890), p. 14).

[3] Bayhaqī, *op. cit.* p. 46.

[4] Ibn Ḥawqal, *Masālik wa'l-mamālik*, ed. de Goeje (Leyden, 1873), pp. 307, 309.

[5] *Ibid.* p. 309.

[6] Cf. *ibid.* p. 205; Iṣṭakhrī, *Masālik wa'l-mamālik*, ed. de Goeje (Leyden, 1870), p. 147.

[7] *Masālik wa'l-mamālik*, p. 185.

relationships which existed in his day between the central authorities and the Kurdish sheep-owning tribes of Fārs. Every *zumm* or pastoral group had within its *nāḥiya*, or grazing territory, a number of towns or large villages, in which was a more or less settled population that lived by trading or cultivation. In each *nāḥiya* the tribal chief had powers of control, and might be persuaded or coerced into paying revenue, maintaining order, and securing the safety of solitary travellers and caravans. Persuasion was, as the geographer hints, the better course for the government to pursue in dealing with the tribes, for they were strong numerically,[1] and were at all times capable of resisting successfully an order they disliked.[2]

The province of Khurāsān, which had a more settled population than that of Fārs, was classed as a single *kūra*, divided for revenue purposes into thirty *a'māl* (parishes). Under the later Sāmānids and the Ghaznawids a number of 'āmils shared in it the work of assessing and collecting the government revenue.[3] In the more important parts of the province were petty governors who acted as administrators (*ḥākims*), while in each '*amal* there was a qāḍī and an officer of the *barīd*. The latter was appointed by the amīr himself, and it might go ill with anyone who attempted to deter this agent from his duties.[4]

Under Mas'ūd, son of Maḥmud, the whole kingdom was divided into four districts, each under the supervision of a *mushrif* ("inspector"),[5] and spies were everywhere, so that even the members of the royal household were not exempt from their activities.[6]

For the system of taxation employed under the Sāmānids, that which was in existence in the province of Fārs may be regarded as typical. In its essentials it was probably a survival from Sasanian times, though it may have acquired some characteristics with the

[1] He puts their strength at over half a million *bayts* (tents). The number is probably an exaggeration, and he admits that only the registers of the *ṣadaqāt* (alms-taxes) could provide accurate figures.

[2] *Ibid.* p. 186.

[3] Bayhaqī, *op. cit.* pp. 289, 295.

[4] *Ibid.* pp. 165 f. The Ghaznawids attached special importance to their intelligence service. Punitive expeditions were always in communication with the capital, and an important official, such as the minister of the Chancery (*Dīwān-i Risālat*), was on occasion deputed to accompany a force in order to send daily dispatches to the amīr. (*Ibid.* p. 500.)

[5] *Ibid.* p. 166.

[6] *Ibid.* pp. 135, 154.

spread of Islam. Fārs then was divided for revenue purposes into five *kūras*, each with its *qaṣaba* (market centre), and the *kūra* again into *nāḥiyas* (districts), which comprised the grazing areas of tribes above mentioned.[1]

The sources of revenue were, first, the taxes from the Kurdish pastoral tribes in such measure as was agreed upon between them and the officials of the State treasury; second, *kharāj* from agricultural lands and, finally, a number of miscellaneous items. These were alms-taxes, a "tithe" levied on ships (presumably on the cargoes landed at the Persian Gulf ports), a "fifth" levied on mines and (? the rents of) pastures, poll-taxes on non-Muslim free men, profits on the mint, taxes on watch-towers erected on private lands, the hire of public properties, an "eighth" levied on irrigation rents and, lastly, imposts on salt-pans and watering-pools.

The *kharāj* was generally levied in one of three ways: on the basis of (*a*) the area under cultivation, (*b*) an agreed division of the crops, or (*c*) an annual payment to the treasury, made irrespective of whether the land occupied was put under cultivation or allowed to lie fallow. The last was a well established practice, and the sum paid was calculated according to the area of the land and the value of the crop over a series of years.

In the province of Fārs the *kharāj* was assessed by the first method, except where the lands were cultivated by the nomad *zumūm*, the Kurdish pastoral tribes, who paid an agreed annual sum or proportion of the crop. The rate of this tax levied on the basis of area was not uniform, but differed—as it still does—according to the method of irrigation and the crop cultivated. One great *jarīb*[2] of land irrigated by a natural stream, and sown with wheat or barley, paid 190 *dirhams*; if planted with fruit trees it paid 192 *dirhams*; with dates or cucumbers, 237½ *dirhams*; with

[1] Iṣṭakhrī, *op. cit.* p. 97.

In modern Persia, the *wilāyats* are divided into *bulūks*, which are made up in turn of a number of villages (*qarya* or *dih*). In each of the villages there is a headman or elder (*kedkhudā* or *rīshi-i safīd*), whose prime responsibility is the payment of the revenue demanded by the government from his village. See G. Demorgny, *Essai sur l'Administration de la Perse* (Paris, 1913), pp. 48 f., 136. The work deals in general with proposed reforms rather than with the actual situation of the time in which it was written.

[2] One great jarīb = 3⅗ little jarībs.

One little jarīb = 60 × 60 king's cubits.

One king's cubit = 9 *qabḍas* (the *qabḍa* being the closed fist). (Iṣṭakhrī, *op. cit.* p. 157; Ibn Ḥawqal, *op. cit.* p. 216.)

cotton, 256 *dirhams* 4 *dānqs*; and with vines, 1425 *dirhams*. These were the rates in the neighbourhood of Shīrāz, the capital. In the *kūrās* generally the rates were lower by a third.[1] On land which depended on rain the tax was one-third of that levied on land watered by a natural stream, while crops of melons, cucumbers and green vegetables irrigated from a well paid two-thirds of the latter rate. Land through which a river or other natural stream flowed paid an additional one-fourth of the tax, which went as a perquisite to the ruler.[2]

The amīr's private estates were taxed for the public treasury, surrendering for general purposes a proportion of the crops raised on them. Also rents paid for *mustaghallāt*—i.e. urban properties such as the ground on which the bazaars were built, flour-mills and rose-water manufactories—went to the central exchequer; under the Sāmānids, therefore, to Bukhārā. The money which the Sāmānids derived from the revenues was not all spent on their own requirements. A considerable sum went to endow public institutions. According to tradition, the Amīr Ismā'īl purchased agricultural lands, the income from which was used to build and maintain a hostel for the use of wayfarers in Bukhārā.[3] Other pious endowments were provided for the maintenance of students and impoverished descendants of 'Alī—the Prophet's son-in-law and a national hero—as well as for the poor of the capital.[4]

Although it is declared that taxation was light under the Sāmānids in Transoxiana and Khurāsān,[5] and that cultivators in bad years when lands were flooded escaped taxation altogether,[6] the *kharāj* was not the only burden on the cultivators. Villages given as grants to favourites of the court might be heavily burdened with dues for the new owner. The instance is quoted of a village near Bukhārā, in which a prosperous local industry was carried on. It had at one time been part of the royal estates, but had been bestowed as a gift on a courtier who drew from it an annual revenue of 10,000 *dirhams*. This was a burdensome tax,

[1] Iṣṭakhrī, *loc. cit.* Cf. Ibn Ḥawqal, *loc. cit.*
[2] Ibn Ḥawqal, *loc. cit.*
[3] Narshakhī, *op. cit.* p. 13.
[4] Narshakhī, *op. cit.* p. 14.
[5] Ibn Ḥawqal, *op. cit.* pp. 341 f., says that taxes under Manṣūr ibn Nūḥ amounted to not more than 20,000,000 *dirhams* in six months, while he paid out, in salaries and allowances to officials, at least 5,000,000 *dirhams* each 90 days (i.e. each quarter).
[6] Narshakhī, *op. cit.* p. 31.

and after suffering it for a number of years the inhabitants protested to the amīr Ismā'īl ibn Aḥmad. A long dispute followed, and the landlord finally agreed to forgo his claims for a lump sum of 170,000 *dirhams*.[1]

In Fārs, when taxation threatened to become unduly heavy, the smaller landowners surrendered their property to chieftains in Iraq, under an arrangement which permitted the virtual owners to retain the power of selling or bequeathing their property as they wished.[2]

Of taxation under the Ghaznawids few details have survived, but that it was heavy may be gathered from the fact that the governor of Iṣfahān, under Mas'ūd son of Maḥmūd, was called upon to pay the sulṭān annually 200,000 gold dīnārs in cash and 10,000 pieces of locally made cloth, in addition to the substantial gifts expected by the ruler at the feasts of *Naw-rūz* (the New Year festival celebrated at the spring equinox) and *Mihrgān* (the festival of the autumn equinox).[3] The sovereign could on occasion show his pleasure by remitting taxation, as occurred when the 'āmil and *ra'īs* of Ṭirmidh congratulated Mas'ūd on a victory. He made it clear that all citizens were to share equally in the relief. Maḥmūd, above all else a warrior, looked on his subjects as little more than providers of revenue, and his agents exploited them mercilessly in order to provide him with rich gifts and win his favour.[4] On one occasion when the men of Balkh had ventured in his absence to repel an attack from Qarākhānī raiders, he rated them angrily, telling them that it was not their function, and that as a penalty he would make them pay for the bazaars of their town, which he had built at great expense for them.[5] Actually the bazaars were in the first place paid for either out of taxes or the proceeds of plunder taken on his Indian expeditions.

The incidence of taxation has varied within certain limits in the course of the history of Persia, but land has at all times provided most of the revenues. Under the Ṣafawīs all land was in theory *mulki shāhī*, i.e. the property of the shāh; but in fact, much had from time immemorial been in private hands (hence known as *arbābī*, i.e. "belonging to owners"). Shāh Ṭahmāsp, the Ṣafawī, took a sixth part of agricultural produce and of the value of

[1] Narshakhī, pp. 11 f.
[2] Iṣṭakhrī, *op. cit.* p. 158.
[3] Bayhaqī, *op. cit.* p. 16.
[4] *Ibid.* p. 510.
[5] *Ibid.* p. 688.

grazing land, and also levied a tax on sheep and cattle[1]—a tax which Shāh 'Abbās abolished. The latter monarch relieved Shī'ites from all taxation during the month of Ramaḍān, and also for that month relieved all Muslims from payment of *aḥdāth* (i.e. "new taxes", not specified by the Koran or *shar'*).[2] His successor Shāh Ṣafī reimposed the taxes on cattle and sheep, making the owners pay, for the privileges of watering and pasture, the annual dues known as *āb-khurī* and *'alaf-khurī* ("water-drinking" and "grass-eating"). These are local taxes still collected in some districts. Further revenue was raised from a duty on the sales of cattle, from tolls on roads and bridges, from rents of caravanserais, as also from the proceeds of farming out "the fishing of rivers, the baths and stores, the places of publick prostitution and the springs of Nefte [naphtha]".[3] The author from whom this is quoted goes on to say that the ṣhāh "sells also the water which comes into the fountains, and raises only from the river Zindarut at Iṣfahān [then the capital] the yearly sum of 16,000 crowns. All the Armenian Christians, whereof there is a great number in Persia, pay yearly a Poll-money of two crowns for every head".[4]

According to the Père du Mans, who wrote in 1660, there was in each region a tax-farmer who held all state lands at his disposal, and from whom villagers rented what they could, paying one-half to two-thirds of the produce into the king's treasury.[5]

The system of taxation thus described has remained, with few changes, until the most recent times. Of the public domains (*khāliṣa*), a large part is leased out to individuals in return for a percentage of the crops grown or cash in lieu. Privately owned (*arbābī*) lands pay a tithe of the owner's share if any official assessment of the property has been made; otherwise the tax is levied according to a traditional calculation, of which the details are entered in the books of the local *mustawfī*, or district treasurer, who would appear, incidentally, to regard his books as his stock-in-trade, and in a large measure his own property. As has generally been the rule, the revenues from these sources are

[1] *A Narrative of Italian Travels in Persia* (Hakluyt Society, 1873), p. 226.

[2] Iskandar Munshī, *Ta'rīkhi 'Ālam-ārā'i 'Abbāsī* (E. G. Browne MS., Cambridge, H. 13, Part I, f. 109b).

[3] Olearius, *op. cit.* pp. 177, 272.

[4] *Ibid.* p. 272.

[5] *Estat de la Perse en 1660*, p. 226.

farmed out, or are collected by the provincial governors or tribal chiefs.[1]

Egypt is the country which next claims attention. It achieved complete independence of the Eastern Caliphate under the Fāṭimids, who held power in Syria for over two centuries after Jawhar, lieutenant of the Caliph Mu'izz (reigned 952–75), had founded Cairo (969). Like the other princes of Islam, the Fāṭimids, while themselves retaining control, left the details of administration to a number of ministers and dīwāns, of which some were concerned with the palace and others with the State. The vizier was the chief personage in the State after the Caliph, being in charge of all the civil administration and the finances. Until the time of the Caliph Mustanṣir, the office was held by a "Man of the Pen", a civilian official. In 467/1074–5 that Caliph appointed as his principal minister Badr al-Jamālī, who was a "Man of the Sword" and commander-in-chief of the armies as well as director of the civil administration, in which latter capacity he had the duty of appointing such high officers of state as chief qāḍīs.[2] Thenceforward it was normal for the vizier to be a soldier, and he was generally, therefore, entitled *Amīr al-Juyūsh*, i.e. "Commander of the Armies", instead of vizier, while as token of their office the latest holders of the position under the Fāṭimids were called *Malik* (literally, "king") in addition to their other titles. When, in 530/1136, Riḍwān ibn Walakhshī was appointed vizier to al-Ḥāfiẓ, he received the titles of *al-Sayyid al-Ajall al-Malik al-Afḍal* ("The most puissant lord, the most excellent king").[3]

In practice the powers of the vizier or *Amīr al-Juyūsh* were not always commensurate with the magnificence of his titles. The rapid dismissal of a succession of viziers under Mustanṣir led to a decline in their authority,[4] and under al-Ḥāfiẓ there were periods when no vizier was appointed at all, the Caliph transacting the business of state either in person or through the agency of his son, who was heir to the throne.[5] In his attempts to find a competent

[1] For a comprehensive review of the Persian revenue system and its history, see A. K. S. Lambton, *Landlord and Peasant in Persia* (Oxford, 1953).

[2] Maqrīzī, *Khiṭaṭ*, I, 440. Cf. Qalqashandī, *Subḥ al-a'shā* (Cairo, 1913 ff.), III, 482 f.

[3] Maqrīzī, *loc. cit.* [4] Maqrīzī, *op. cit.* I, 356 (middle). [5] *Ibid.* 357.

minister he at one time employed a Christian as vizier, but that officer was deposed by a riotous mob.[1] A previous ruler, al-Ẓāhir, had once appointed a chief qāḍī to be vizier, an appointment rare under the Abbasids. This minister was Abu Muhammad, who was allowed to act in both the judicial and ministerial capacities, and was called by the title of *Sayyid al-Wuzarā* ("Master of the Viziers").[2]

The steps by which the vizierate was reached are mentioned in an account of two of al-Ẓāhir's ministers: both had been in charge of the Chancery (*Dīwān al-Inshā*), while one had also held the captaincy of the *shurṭa*, which was at one and the same time the royal bodyguard and the police force of the capital.[3]

Second in importance to the vizier was the Chief Chamberlain or *Ṣāḥib al-Bāb* ("Lord of the Gate"), who was sometimes also known as the Lesser Vizier. His function was in general that of a palace official, except that he had the privilege of presenting ambassadors. Both the vizier and the *Ṣāḥib al-Bāb* are classed as "Men of the Sword" by Qalqashandī, the fourteenth-century chancery official, who has left an account of the government offices of Egypt as they existed in his own day and earlier.

Of the other civil officers the principal was the chief qāḍī, who was not only head of the judiciary but also the overseer of the mint.[4] Next in rank came an official peculiar to the Fāṭimid organization, though one of great importance under a government which owed its power to missionary effort. He was the *Dā'i al-Du'āt*, the Chief Propagandist, whose function was to answer questions on matters of law and religious doctrine, and to elucidate difficult passages of the Koran.[5] He presided for official and state purposes in the *Dār al-'Ilm*, which combined the functions of a library, university, record office and bureau of information.[6] But he also sat for the general body of believers in two other places, for men on the "Chair of Propaganda" in the Great Hall (*Aywān al-Kabīr*), and for women in the *Majlis al-Dā'ī* ("The Propagandist's Place of Session"). The office was hereditary in the family of the Banu 'Abd al-Qawī, the last of whom also held the office of chief qāḍī.

[1] Maqrīzī, *loc. cit.* [2] *Ibid.* 536 (line 3). [3] *Ibid.* 354.
[4] Qalqashandī, *loc. cit.*, and Maqrīzī, *op. cit.* I, 404.
[5] Maqrīzī, *ibid.* 391. [6] *Ibid.* 458 f.

Personality remained always the ruling factor in the State, and at times of crisis it was not necessarily the highest officials who held power. During the period of severe famine which broke out during the reign of the Caliph al-Ẓāhir and was at its height in 415/1024, when there was a danger of the business of the State falling into utter confusion (since the Caliph was entirely occupied with his own pleasures), the black eunuch Mi'ḍād, who had been appointed *qā'id*, or general of the royal forces, determined to carry on the government on his own resources. Accordingly, he summoned to his aid three civilian notables, with whom he agreed that no one but themselves should have access to the Caliph, although before that crisis it had been the practice of the high officials of State to visit the Caliph once in every twenty days. These dignitaries had been four in number, the *Ṣāḥib al-Miẓalla*[1] (a military official and Carrier of the Parasol of State), the *Ṣāḥib al-Inshā* (the head of the Chancery), the *Da'ī al-Du'āt* (the Chief Propagandist), and the *Naqīb Nuqabā al-Ṭālibiyīn* (the spokesman and chief representative of the 'Alid clan).[2] During the period of disturbance they retired into the background.

Of the ministries, the dīwān of the *Majlis* was primarily concerned with the privy purse and Civil List, keeping account of all gifts customarily made by the sovereign at established seasons, and, of all allowances made to members of the royal family and its retainers, but also keeping a record of *iqṭa'āt*, the grants of land made on guarantee of an annual return of revenue to the treasury.[3]

The various departments of the public *Bayt al-Māl* were under the control of the *Dīwān al-Naẓar* ("Ministry of Supervision"), whose director had power to appoint and dismiss subordinates, and was himself answerable only to the Caliph and the vizier. To them at stated times he submitted documents and reports concerning the activities of his department. Ambassadors, viceroys, and other representatives of the sovereign also communicated with this officer in the first instance.[4]

There existed still another financial department of State, the *Dīwān al-Jaysh wa'l-Rawātib* (the "Dīwān of the Army and Emoluments"), which, as its name implies, was primarily an

[1] Thus C. H. Becker, in his *Beiträge zur Geschichte Egyptens* (Strassburg, 1902), I, p. 33. The text read *maẓlama*, which does not make adequate sense.

[2] Maqrīzī, I, 354, 24 ff.

[3] *Ibid.* I, 397 ff.

[4] *Ibid.* I, 400.

army pay office. It had charge of all the muster-rolls, keeping a record of all men on the active service list and of all who for any reason fell out; it had the ordering of equipment and decorations, and kept a register of military fiefs and of all—whether men or women—who drew pay from funds assigned to military purposes. In this latter connection the emoluments of different officials are mentioned: the vizier is shown as receiving 5000 *dīnārs* per month, while the officers next in importance—the director of the palace, the treasurer, the bearer of the state parasol, etc.—received only 100 *dīnārs*.[1]

The Fāṭimids did not hesitate to employ non-Muslims when it suited their purpose.[2] In their *Dīwān al-Inshā* ("Chancery") both Jews and Christians held office, and a Jew named Manasseh was appointed to be governor of Syria by the Caliph al-'Azīz (975–96), who was, however, compelled to withdraw his nominee because of the offence it gave to the Muslims of Egypt.[3]

The country was divided into four regions for administrative purposes: Qūṣa (Upper Egypt), the principal one of the four: Sharqīya (the East), Gharbīya (the West) and Alexandria. Revenue was obtained by a system of tax-farms. It is reported that in 363/974, about a year after his entry into his new capital of Cairo, Mu'izz appointed two officials, Ya'qūb ibn Killīs and 'Aslūj ibn Ḥasan, to be responsible for the revenue of the State. Their method was to invite contracts (*qabālāt*) for the taxes due from private estates and other forms of property, and to allot them to any person who could guarantee sufficient payment in advance to the exchequer. Certain public lands, generally *mawāt* (dead)—i.e. derelict and uncultivated lands—were given as grants for specific purposes, such as provision of military funds or some other item of public expenditure.[4] It may here be added that in course of time valuable private lands, which for one reason or another had escheated to the crown, began to be added to the *mawāt* as military fiefs. The result was that by Maqrīzī's day a great part of the land in Egypt was possessed by the sulṭān or his military commanders, with consequent impoverishment of the land and the treasury owing to the conversion of a free peasantry into bond-slaves, tied to the soil as chattels of the fief-holders, who

[1] Maqrīzī, I, 401; Qalqashandī, III, 492.
[2] Qalqashandī, I, 96.
[3] Ibn al-Athīr, IX, 81.
[4] Maqrīzī, I, 97.

cared little what happened so long as they had sufficient supplies themselves.[1]

Incidental taxes (*aḥdāth* or *mukūs*)[2] formed a considerable part of the revenue in Egypt, although there, as elsewhere in Islam, their legality was always disputed,[3] and their abolition regarded as an act of piety by religious princes. They were imposed either by the central government on imports and exports, or by municipalities on the profits of sales or on goods brought for sale into the markets. The traveller Ibn Jubayr, who visited Egypt in Sulṭān Saladin's day, says that alms-tax (*zakāt*) was taken from all Muslims entering the country, a percentage being levied on all merchandise and money found in their possession. These exactions were not countenanced, he says, by the sulṭān, but went into the pockets of the officials.[4] Those *aḥdāth* current under the Fāṭimids included tolls on drugs and spices, general merchandise, cotton, timber, salt and matting, as well as on the caravans which imported or transported them. They also included dues from buildings of public utility, such as the "sugar-factory", flour-mills, slaughter-houses, bazaars and hot baths.[5] Saladin, it has been indicated, abolished these dues, with the result that at Alexandria, as Ibn Jubayr found, the Muslim citizens paid no taxes except the Koranic alms, of which the government received actually only three-eighths, the rest being applied to swelling *awqāf* and charitable funds.[6] The relief to the citizens lasted only the length of Saladin's reign. His son and successor not only reimposed the cesses, but increased the amounts payable.

Amongst the more permanent sources of revenue not already mentioned were the profits from various monopolies, death-duties (or escheated estates), tolls on ships and bridges, profits from the mint and fees from the assaying office.[7] *Zakāt* was, of

[1] Maqrīzī I, 83, 85 f., 97.

[2] They were known as *hilālī*, i.e. "monthly" taxes, as opposed to *kharājī*, which were imposed on annual crops (Maqrīzī, I, 103, 107).

[3] The *makkās*, the official who collected the *mukūs*, was proverbially regarded with detestation. See, for references, Goldziher, *Muhammedanische Studien*, I, 19 n. 2.

[4] Ibn Jubayr (ed Wright and de Goeje, Gibb Series), pp. 39 f.

[5] Maqrīzī, I, 103 f.

[6] The numerous Jews and Christians of the city paid a poll-tax (Ibn Jubayr, *op. cit.*, p. 42).

[7] Maqrīzī, I, 107–11.

course, normally taken from every Muslim who was free and not physically incapacitated, and was levied on his monetary capital, livestock, and garden or orchard produce; monetary capital being defined as gold coin, securities or merchandise.[1] Non-Muslims paid *jizya* if they were free men and of full age; not, however, if they were women, boys, slaves or lunatics. "As for decrepit old men and monks, there is dispute of opinion about them." The tax was in Saladin's day levied in three rates—upper, middle and lower—according to the estimated wealth of the payer. The upper rate amounted to $4\frac{1}{6}$ *dīnārs*, the middle to $2\frac{1}{12}$, and the lower to "a *dīnār* and a third and a fourth and two grains"—i.e. slightly less than $1\frac{1}{2}$—and the tax was payable annually at the New Moon of the month of Muḥarram.[2] A special class of *jizya* payer was constituted by certain Armenians in Upper Egypt and at Aswān. They paid a *dīnār* and 2 *qīrāṭs* per head, but no official was at liberty to demand the tax without the express permission of the sulṭān. In general, if a person liable to *jizya* was absent from his town or village for a long period, but was the owner of a house there, the tax could be deducted from the rent of the house. Decision on this point rested, however, with the chief revenue officer of the district.[3]

Once the Fāṭimid regime was well established, governors were appointed for the three main divisions of the empire—Egypt, Syria, and the territory bordering on Asia Minor—the western provinces in the Maghrib having been lost to usurpers soon after the departure of Mu'izz for Egypt. In the government of the subordinate provinces, a large measure of initiative must always have remained in the hands of the officials, even after allowing for occasional checks from the central administration. The point is well illustrated by the report of an interview between the Caliph Mu'izz, when he was about to leave Ifrīqiya for his new dominion of Egypt, and Ja'far ibn 'Alī, whom he proposed to leave behind as his lieutenant. Ja'far's reply to the proposal was: "Leave with

[1] The taxable minimum sum for gold was 20 *mithqāls*, which paid half a *mithqāl*. Larger sums paid in proportion. Securities less than 200 *dirhams* in value paid nothing. If of 200 *dirhams* value they paid 5 *dirhams*, and so on in proportion. Goods bought for resale paid similar percentages of their value (Ibn Mammātī, *Kitāb Qawānīn al-dawāwīn*, Cambridge MS., Qq. 244/6, fols. 40 ff.).

[2] *Ibid.* fol. 43 b.

[3] *Ibid.*

me one of your sons or brothers to sit in the palace while I conduct affairs. And question me not about money, because what I shall impose in taxation shall equal what I expend. And if I desire any object, I shall achieve it without awaiting the arrival of your command—there being so great a distance between Egypt and the Maghrib. Also appointment to the judgeship and the revenue office (*kharāj*) . . . must be in my hands." Mu'izz angrily rejected these terms, and appointed the Berber al-Sanhājī, with such checks as he deemed efficient.[1]

The number of subordinate revenue officials employed in Egypt under the Fāṭimids and their successors was comparatively large, and they ranked in grade from the *nāẓir* (the overseer) and *mutawallī al-dīwān* (the officer in charge of the district dīwān) down to petty scribes and storekeepers. The *nāẓir* was the chief provincial officer, whose chief duty was to scrutinize the accounts of the *mutawallī*. He in his turn, or else an official known as the *mushārif* ("inspector") of the region, was charged with keeping a record of the main items of income and expenditure of his department. He was appointed on certain terms, which might be (*a*) that he was trusted to transmit all revenues as he received them (this was known as *imāna*); (*b*) that he undertook to bring in more than his predecessor (this was known as *badhl*); or (*c*) that he bound himself to produce a sum specified (this was known as *ḍamān*).

The work of recording the details of revenue collection was in the hands of the '*āmil* (sometimes also of the *mutawallī*), who was responsible to the *nāẓir* and the *mushārif*, and upon whom appears to have been laid the drudgery of the task.[2]

There was considerable expansion and elaboration of the administrative system under the Mamlūk Sulṭāns, after a period (564/1169–650/1252) in which Saladin and his successors, the Ayyūbids, ruled with a comparative economy of officials. The training of the earlier Mamlūks,[3] who were brought up to serve as soldiers,[4] led to a militarization of the state. There had been some tendency towards this process under the Fāṭimids, the later members of which dynasty always appointed a soldier as chief

[1] Maqrīzī, I, 352 f.

[2] Ibn Mammātī, *op. cit.*, British Museum MS., Or. 3120, fol. 9 ff.

[3] The name means "owned", and was generally applied to a white, Turkish or Circassian slave.

[4] Cf. Maqrīzī, II, 213.

administrator. Under several of the Mamlūks, the first officer in the kingdom was the *nā'ib al-kāfil* (the "deputy plenipotentiary"), who was given extremely wide powers. He had supreme military command, being able in all routine matters except the appointment of generals to act on his own initiative and without reference to the sulṭān. Further, he discharged many of the civil functions normally regarded as being reserved for the sulṭān himself. All civil officers but those of the highest rank were appointed by him, and no appointment was made without his approval. The vizier, now considerably reduced in status, though still important, and either a soldier or a civilian, was subordinate to the *nā'ib*, who was "the sulṭān in brief—nay, the second sulṭān".[1] To distinguish him from the sulṭān's *nā'ib* (lieutenant) in Syria he received the title of *Kāfil al-Mamlakati 'l-sharīfati 'l-Islāmiyati*.[2] The office was intermittent. Sulṭān al-Nāṣir ibn Qalā'ūn abolished it, together with the vizierate, in 737/1336–7, but it was restored in the next reign. Thereafter it lapsed several times, coming finally to an end in the days of al-Nāṣir Faraj ibn Barqūq.[3]

The *ḥājib al-ḥujjāb* ("chamberlain-in-chief") ranked next in importance. His function was to see that amīrs and army officers behaved with justice and regard towards the mass of the people, and he had a voice in ordering promotions and in mustering the troops. When there was no *nā'ib* he was supreme in these matters. Military disputes and cases concerning military fiefs came within his jurisdiction, though he was in theory barred from exercising authority in matters that fell within the province of the *shar'*.[4] This theoretical limitation of the powers of the *ḥājib* was by no means effective in practice, and in describing that officer's functions the historian Maqrīzī utters a complaint of a kind that is rare amongst men of his craft, who usually regarded the qāḍī with suspicion. We have always [in the past] understood, he says,

that if any civil official or tax-farmer took refuge with the qāḍī from the jurisdiction of the *ḥājib*, he could not be removed from out of the qāḍī's protection. . . . Today the *ḥājib* has jurisdiction over

[1] Qalqashandī, IV, 17.
[2] "Plenipotentiary of the noble Islamic kingdom."
[3] Maqrīzī, II, 214 f.; Qalqashandī, IV, 16 f.
[4] Maqrīzī, I, 219.

everyone, great and small alike, both those subject to the *shar'* and what they call the political law. No qāḍī dare take an offender out of the *ḥājib's* power. Yet the *ḥājib's* agent today, in spite of being of low estate and of insignificant rank and his associating with others for unlawful purposes in unheard-of fashion, . . . may take a person charged with an offence out of the qāḍī's hands and inflict at his discretion a beating or fine without anyone to say him nay. [What is called] "political law" was in the first instance the Chamberlain's rules. It is a devilish term, of which most people of our time know not the origin. Yet they make facile use of it, and say: "This affair does not concern the *shar'ī* laws; it comes under the 'political law'." They regard that as a simple matter, but in the eyes of God it is a grave one.[1]

The elaborations of the Mamlūk system as a whole may be pictured from the account of Cairo in the fifteenth century as presented by the historian Ibn Taghri-Bardī. In describing the reign of the Sulṭān al-Malik al-Nāṣir al-Faraj, he begins by enumerating the office-holders of the day [801/1398–9]. First come the qāḍīs-in-chief of the four *madhhabs*, then the Atābeg of the Armies (the *Amīr al-Kabīr*, the Commander-in-Chief), the *Amīr Silāḥ* ("the Chief Ordnance Officer"), the *Amīr Majlis* ("Steward of the Audience Chamber"), the *Amīr Ākhur al-Kabīr* ("Chief Groom of the Royal Stables"), the *Ḥājib al-Ḥujjāb* ("the Lord Chamberlain"), the *Rās Nawbat al-Nuwwāb* ("Captain of the Chief Guard"), the *Dawādār al-Kabīr* (the "Principal Scribe"—in this case Baybars, nephew of the Sulṭān Malik al-Ẓāhir), the *Khazānadār* (the "Treasurer"), the *Shādd* ("Controller") of the wine-houses, the *Ustādār* ("Director of the Royal Household"), the *Kātib al-Sirr* (the "Private Secretary"), the Vizier, the *Nāẓir al-Jaysh wa 'l-Khāṣṣ* ("Overseer of the Army and of Privy Estates"), the *Muḥtasib* of Cairo, and finally the *Wālī* or Superintendent of Police.[2]

A large number of subordinate official are mentioned by Qalqashandī as having made up the administrative hierarchy; most, as might be expected, being employed in the service of the revenue department. "There was not a village great or small",

[1] Maqrīzī I, 219 f.

[2] Ibn Taghri-Bardī, *Nujūm al-Ẓāhira*, ed. W. Popper, VI (California, 1915), 2 f. Many of the titles mentioned are of Persian origin but come immediately from Turkish, the mother-tongue of the Mamlūks.

says Maqrīzī, "in which there was not a number of scribes, foremen, and the like". Many were Copts, and they lived on the peasantry, transferring the proceeds of many imposts into their own pockets. In the year 715/1315–16 the Sulṭān Nāṣir Muhammad ibn Qalā'ūn abolished a number of irregular *mukūs* and monopolies—one of which prevented the open sale of chickens and another collected dues from brothels—and instituted reforms by which, after a survey of taxable lands, specific sums were allotted for payment by each village or agricultural area. The reforms are said to have remained effective almost until the end of the Qalā'ūnid dynasty.[1]

A peculiar feature of the administration in Egypt was the presence of a pseudo-Caliph. After the destruction of the Baghdad Caliphate by the Mongols (in 1258), a member of the Abbasid family escaped to Cairo, where he and his descendants continued, until the Ottoman conquest of Egypt, to exercise an authority even more unsubstantial than that at Baghdad in the years following its decline. In this second stage of their history they were acknowledged on the coinage of the sulṭāns of Delhi,[2] although it was not for eighty years that the resurrection of the Caliphate at Cairo was acknowledged in the Indian capital and that the name of the contemporary holder of the office was inserted.[3] In the meantime the Sulṭān Mubārak Shāh had himself assumed the title of Caliph, and after 795/1393 the coins struck by the Delhi sulṭāns simply acknowledge the Amīr al-Mu'minīn without specifying his name. The same may be said of the kings of Bengal,[4] but the kings of Jawnpūr often mention the name of the Caliph of the day.[5] In Egypt the Mamlūk Sulṭān Baybars paid homage to the first member of the re-established line (Mustanṣir) and inserted his name, and later that of his successor al-Ḥākim, on the products of the mint.

The later Mamlūks did not continue the formality, and in

[1] Maqrīzī, I, 87–91, 111.

[2] Cf. S. Lane-Poole, *The Coins of the Sultans of Delhi* (London, 1884), pp. 69 ff.

[3] *Ibid.* p. xxvi.

[4] S. Lane-Poole, *The Coins of the Mohammadan States of India* London, 1885), pp. xxxiii, 13 ff.

[5] *Ibid.* pp. 89 ff.

Egyptian history of the period the Caliph's name generally appears only in conjunction with that of the qāḍīs in cases where the authority of the *shar'* was required to determine some matter at issue. Thus he is mentioned once as having concurred with the qāḍīs on the question of the legal status of Sulṭān Malik al-Nāṣir,[1] and on another occasion as having been summoned with the qāḍīs and nobles to determine whether it was lawful, in case of necessity, to make a seizure of the property of the merchants and *awqāf*. Only the answer of the qāḍīs is recorded.[2] At the Ottoman conquest in 1517, the last of the Abbasids, al-Mutawakkil III, is said, on disputed authority, to have transferred his office, together with the symbols of it, to Sulṭān Salīm "the Grim". Thereafter he and his successors claimed to be the Commanders of the Faithful until modern times, when events in Turkey led to the renunciation of the Caliphate by the Ottoman ruler in 1924.

Closely resembling the elaborate, militarized system of the Mamlūk sulṭāns was that which grew up under the Ottoman Turks. The earliest of their rulers probably managed most of their affairs themselves, with little assistance from officials.[3] With the taking of Constantinople the necessity for appointing ministers to share the duties of the State became obvious, and Muhammad II, the Conqueror, is said to have appointed a number of his slaves to office. They remained slaves, even though acting as Grand Viziers, Beylar-beys,[4] Sanjāq-beys,[5] and other high officers of state,[6] for they were utterly within the power of their master, and received no salaries for their work, although from the beginning they were given annual presents of considerable value. The "pillars of the State" mentioned as being in receipt of these presents were the *Ṣadri A'ẓam* (the Prime Minister) and the *Shaykh al-Islām* (the chief religious dignitary of the State), who received 30,000 *āqcha* (about £300) each; the viziers, who received 20,000 *āqcha* each; the *qāḍi-'askars* (chief judges) of Rūm-īlī (i.e. European Turkey) and Anatolia, who received a like sum; the

[1] Ibn Taghri-Bardī, *Nujūm al-Ẓāhira*, VI, 13, 95.

[2] *Ibid.* p. 47.

[3] See Qūchī Bay, *Risāla* ("The Letter on the Organization of the Government, sent to Sulṭān Murād IV"), Constantinople, A.H. 1303, p. 1; tr. W. Behrnauer, *Z.D.M.G.*, XV, (1861), 272 ff.

[4] Governors of provinces.

[5] Deputy-governors of provinces or governors of provincial sub-divisions.

[6] Qūchī Bey, p. 12.

Nīshānjī (Lord Privy Seal), who received 30,000 *āqcha*; and the *Chā'ūsh-bāshī*, who received 15,000.[1]

The Grand Vizier[2] was chief in every department of the State, and had charge of all its affairs—civil, military, financial and political—and in the numerous cases where the law specified no penalties he had power to inflict what punishment he wished. Being the only person that had unrestricted access to the sulṭān, who remained secluded from his subjects except when he rode abroad, the minister acted as the intermediary between him and the outer world. All reports from other officials were made to the minister, who compiled from them his own "notes" for presentation to the sulṭān. These were of two kinds, dealing either with current affairs, on which he gave his comments and requested guidance,[3] or with matters already decided, but which required formal approval of the monarch.[4] As a rule, further, the Grand Vizier held the seals of the sulṭān, had power to enter the treasury in case of need, saw to the policing of the capital, and, during the frequent absences of the prince in war, presided over the dīwān.[5]

First after the Grand Vizier came the *Kiahyā Bey*,[6] who attended to the details of internal administration, and through whose hands passed all royal *firmāns* and dispatches affecting the country, as well as incoming documents and reports from the provinces and departments of state. In general, he was the deputy of the Grand Vizier, and was regarded as being responsible in particular for the security and policing of the capital. With him acted the *Ra'īs Efendī*, who was minister for foreign affairs and head of the Chancery, and the *Chā'ūsh-bāshī*, the chief of the executive arm of the judiciary and marshal of the court. These three, with a number of subordinates, formed the official staff of the *Bāb-i 'Ālī*, the "Sublime Porte", which became the Turkish Foreign Office.

[1] 'Ayn 'Alī Efendī, *Qawānīn-i Āl-i 'Uthmān* (Constantinople, A.H. 1280), pp. 198 f.

[2] *Wazīr-i A'ẓam.* 'Alī Pasha, son of Khayr al-Dīn Pasha, was the first to hold the title, under Murād I. ('Alī Chelebī, *Kunh al-akhbār*, Constantinople, n.d., v, 73.)

[3] This kind was known technically as *taqrīr*.

[4] The second kind was known as *talkhīs*. See further M. D'Ohsson, *Tableau général de l'empire othoman*, VII, 136.

[5] Von Hammer, *Des osmanischen Reichs Staatsverfassung und Staatsverwaltung*, 2 vols. (Vienna, 1815), I, 578.

[6] Persian *ked-khudā*. He held the rank of Pasha, with three *tūghs* (horse-tails).

The conqueror of Constantinople is generally credited with having instituted the two dīwāns which existed until comparatively recent times, the first at the royal palace (the *Sarāy*) and the second in the house of the Grand Vizier. The first was at once the Council of State, the Supreme Court and the central seat of the administration, where the principal business of state was dispatched. Sulaymān I had a special chamber built for the dīwān in the palace, and after this chamber, which had a *qubba* ("dome"), the ministers—apart from the Grand Vizier—who sat in it were called *Qubba Wazīrlar*, i.e. "Viziers of the Dome", and had the title of Pasha. Under Muhammad II there were only three, in addition to the Grand Vizier. Later their number was increased to eight, distinguished by the titles of second vizier, third vizier etc. In wartime they served as generals under the orders of the sovereign or the Grand Vizier, who, in accordance with their military tradition, acted as the commanders-in-chief of the country. The subordinate viziers acted in various capacities,[1] serving in some manner as apprentices to the Grand Vizier. Their mutual jealousies led, in course of time, to a reduction in their numbers, and finally to their suppression under Aḥmad III (1115/1703–1143/1730), after which only one minister with the title of vizier sat in the council.[2]

Under Sulṭān Muhammad II ("The Conqueror") and his successors down to Sulaymān I (the Great), government was carried on by the dīwān which was under the presidency of the Grand Vizier,[3] though the sulṭān looked on at its deliberations when he was present in the capital. It sat at the Sarāy, the royal palace, and in early times considered any questions—legislative, judicial or political—that required decision.[4] Gradually the judicial duties of the dīwān were transferred to the other dīwān attached to the Sublime Porte. That now received the petitions asking for justice, and either dealt with them or sent them to the courts of the *shar'*, for action to be taken. Even then the ministers of State were expected to be within call in order to answer questions.

The military form of the State organization is well illustrated by

[1] Cf. Wāṣif, *Ta'rīkh-i Wāṣif* (Constantinople, A.H. 1219), I, 10 f. and *passim*.

[2] See D'Ohsson, *Tableau général de l'empire othoman*, VII, 211 ff.

[3] He is called *Dīwān Humāyūn Qulī*, "the Slave of the Imperial Dīwān". Cf. D'Ohsson, *ibid.* VII, 156 ff.

[4] Qūchī Bey, *Risāla*, p. 10.

the offices and titles of those present at a dīwān held by Sulṭān Salīm I in 921/1515. They were the Aghā (Master) of the Janissaries, the Pashas (i.e. the Viziers) and the Qāḍī 'Askars.[1] The Sulṭān himself was commander-in-chief of the forces; the Aghā of the Janissaries represented the corps formed by Murād I in imitation of the Mamlūk system, and originally recruited by force from the Christian subjects of the empire in Macedonia and Thrace; the Pashas were the *Sanjāq-beys*, "the Lords of the Standard"—i.e. the military governors of the chief provinces—who held their offices and fiefs on condition of marching to war with armed forces from their territories when occasion demanded; while the original duties of the two Qāḍī 'Askars—one for the European provinces and the other for Anatolia—were to follow the sovereign on his expeditions and act as judge-advocates among the troops. The Qāḍī 'Askar of the European Provinces (Rūm), after the inclusion of Constantinople in the empire, was given jurisdiction in all '*askarī*, "military" (i.e. Muslim) cases, so called as being between Muslims, who were all liable to military service while the Qāḍī 'Askar of Anatolia filled the subordinate task of dealing with *baladī*, "civilian" (i.e. non-Muslim) cases.

Under Sulṭān Murād IV, the dīwān was composed of the Grand Vizier, the Muftī (i.e. the *Shaykh al-Islām*, the highest exponent of the Islamic law), the *Qapūdān Pāshā* (the Grand Admiral), and the *Daftardār* (the chief financial officer). They are enumerated with other high functionaries who, in 1063/1653 gathered at the invitation of the monarch to take counsel together on the condition of affairs in the country.[2]

An official known as the *daftardār* was employed, it would appear, even by the earliest of the Ottoman sulṭāns. When the empire had been established in Europe for some time a second *daftardār* was appointed, by Bāyazid II, to have charge of the European provinces, while the first was occupied with those of Asia Minor. Salīm I nominated still a third to be responsible for the finances of Egypt, Syria and Diyār Bakr, and a fourth became necessary under Sulaymān I for Hungary and the Danube provinces. His office was suppressed after the loss of the provinces with which he was concerned, and in the general process of

[1] Firidūn Bey, *Munsha'āt al-salāṭīn* (Constantinople, A.H. 1274), I, 465.
[2] Ḥājji Khalīfa, *Dastūr al-'amal.* Tr. Behrnauer, *Z.D.M.G.*, XI (1857), 111 ff.

centralization which took place in the following years, only one *daftardār* remained as Grand Treasurer. He received nightly an account, which he communicated to the Grand Vizier, of each day's transactions of the public treasury, though perhaps his most important duty was to ensure that the troops in the capital received their pay at the times—twice a year—at which it was due.[1]

For purposes of revenue and local government, two great divisions were recognized in the empire, probably as a survival from Byzantine times. They were Rumelia (i.e. European Turkey) and Anatolia (i.e. Turkey in Asia). At the head of each of these great divisions was a *Beylar-bey* or *Mīr-mīrān* (governor-general), who was given as a badge of his authority a standard with two or three *tūghs* (horse-tails). In the system which ruled under the early sultāns, there was under him a *sanjāq-bey*, i.e. lord of a *sanjāq* (standard) or *mīr liwā* (with the same meaning), whose badge was a single *tūgh*, and who had command of a subdivision of the greater unit.

Following Islamic custom generally, all the land in the realm was regarded as being in theory the property of the sulṭān.[2] Some of the more valuable portions were reserved for the benefit of the privy purse, the right of user (*taṣarruf*) of the rest being granted to his warrior subjects or on terms to the old Christian occupiers. Land so granted could be *kharājīya*, i.e. liable to payment of *kharāj* in such proportion as long-standing local custom sanctioned, or *'ushrīya*, which paid "tithe"; or else it could be retained as *arḍ mamlakīya* ("State land"), to be assigned as fiefs to soldiers of high rank and to certain civil officials. Normally the terms of these grants were that the holder of the fief had the right to receive from it the proceeds of any cesses that would ordinarily have accrued to the State Treasury, and that in return he did military service in time of war,[3] providing men and horses to a number varying according to the value of the fief.[4] Sometimes he might be

[1] D'Ohsson, VII, 261 ff.

[2] It was *raqaba*, i.e. the land as opposed to its "user" or employment.

[3] Cf. Qūchī Bey, *Risāla*, p. 46.

[4] It was called *qilīj zī'āmat* "sword-fief", or *zi'āmat* for short, if its value was over 20,000 piastres per annum, and a *tīmār* if it was worth less than that. ('Ayn 'Alī Efendī, *Qawānīn*, pp. 61–3.) Originally, however, there would appear to have been no distinction in meaning between the two terms.

allowed to pay a certain sum of money in lieu of these dues.[1] In peace time the feudatories maintained law and order in their territories, in which they had both military and administrative authority. The latter was not often exercised. Public works, such as they were, were carried out by the administrators of *awqāf*, and the primitive form of municipal government was in the hands of the qāḍī, or in those of the *muḥtasib* in more important places. The feudatories were mainly interested in collection of taxes, due either to themselves or the central government.

The subordinate officers, ranking between the *sanjāq-bey* or *mīr-liwā* and the ordinary feudatory or trooper (*sipāhī*), were first the *alāy-bey*, who was subordinate to the *sanjāq-bey*, and then the *ṣū-bāshī*, who was a district commander, and also had immediate responsibility for apprehending offenders and seeing that order was kept.

After the taking of Constantinople (1453), the number of pashas of the rank of two or three *tūghs* was increased by Muhammad II, whose successors created still more pashas as the empire grew. Under Sulaymān I (Qānūnī, reigned 1520–66) it was enacted that the *sanjāq-beys* were to rank according to the value of their fiefs, except that when a deposed Grand Vizier was amongst them he took precedence. The value of the first fief granted to a *sanjāq-bey* was calculated at 200,000 piastres, which was increased as his period of service lengthened, until he became *beylar-bey* or *mīr-mīrān*. The Aghā of the Janissaries, if appointed to be *sanjāq-bey*, received a fief of the annual value of 500,000 piastres, while other high officers, such as the *Nīshānjī-bāshī* (Lord Privy Seal) and the Grand Master of the Horse, received an additional 100,000 piastres over their old income. Such *beys* or notables as distinguished themselves in war received vacant *tīmārs* in reward.

For each 5000 piastres of his revenue the *sanjāq-bey* was expected to furnish a man ready equipped with arms for military service. The lowest number of men brought on to the field by a *sanjāq-bey*, therefore, was forty, since the fief allotted to a man of his rank was of the annual value of at least 200,000 piastres.[2]

As for the mass of the subject population, although they were

[1] 'Ayn 'Alī Efendī, *ibid.* pp. 61 f.

[2] Evliyā Chelebī, *Narrative of Travels*. Tr. J. von Hammer, 2 vols. (London, 1834–50), I, 89 ff.

in theory exempt from taxation if they were natural-born Turks, actually, in addition to being called upon to do military service, they were liable to taxation both direct and indirect. For his agricultural land each cultivator paid *jizya* or *kharāj*, as well as an impost on the products and a tax on his flocks (*rasm ghanam*), while officials took other minor tolls. Those households which sent no soldiers to war paid *khāna-'awāriḍi*, corresponding to the *khāna-wārī* of Persia.[1] Merchants paid toll for their merchandise, including slaves, animals and wine, at the *gumruk* (*comerchio*, customs-house) in the larger cities and at the frontiers, and dues were generally payable in addition on the sale of commodities. The method of farming out these government dues is reported to have been in practice from the very earliest times of the empire. Thus the story is told that after 'Uthmān Ghāzī, the eponymous founder of the Ottoman dynasty, had seized the town of Qaraja Ḥiṣār, he had the *khuṭba* proclaimed and coinage issued in his name, and provided for local administration by appointing a qāḍī and a *ṣū-bāshī*. When this had been done, there approached him an individual from a neighbouring town who requested permission to purchase the taxes imposed in the bazaar. The sulṭān at first refused to listen to him, but was finally persuaded to farm out the tax, which was 2 aspers (piastres) per load on all goods brought to market.[2]

Christians and Jews paid a capitation tax.[3] It was imposed only on males, and was payable at the beginning of every month. If it remained unpaid for more than a certain number of months, the claim of the State was regarded as having lapsed.[4]

[1] Qūchī Bey, *Risāla*, p. 64 f.

[2] Nöldeke, Auszüge aus Nešris Geschichte des Osmanischen Hauses, *Z.D.M.G.*, XIII (1859), 209 f.

[3] Known as *kharāj*. The Venetian ambassadors to Turkey transliterated the word as *caraz*. Cf. E. Alberi, *Relazioni degli Ambasciatori veneti*, III, 1 (Florence, 1840), p. 15.

[4] Cf. D'Ohsson, *Tableau général*, v, Ch. II. In this distinction between Muslim and non-Muslim subjects of the state lay the origin of the famous Capitulations now abolished. After the treaty of Paris (1856), by which Turkey was admitted to the Concert of Europe, the Sublime Porte issued a royal rescript which professed to banish all distinction between the tributary non-Muslim and the Muslim subjects (*ra'īyat wa bī-ra'īyat*) of the sulṭān. The idea of nationality, *taba'īyat*, hitherto foreign to Islam, was thus introduced, and the phrase *taba'a'i shāhāna* ("imperial subjects") or *taba'a'i dawlat-i 'Uthmānīya* ("Subjects of the Ottoman State") came into use. The poll-tax was thereby

The system of fiefs worked with some success until the death of Sulaymān I (Qānūnī), under whom and his predecessors Turkey's great imperial expansion east and west had taken place. After Sulaymān degeneration set in. The fiefs, which had never in the first place been hereditary, became so; the pashas extorted from their subjects more than they could bear, and they themselves failed to perform their allotted duties, whether consisting of military service or the payment of due revenues.[1] Fiefs, moreover, were allotted at the capital to tax-farmers, whose only concern was to fill their own pockets.

Under Murād III (1574–95) the system was reorganized. He divided the empire into *iyālats*, provinces under the governorship of a *wālī*, who received the title of vizier in addition to that of pasha, and had as his badge of rank a standard of three *tūghs*. The *iyālat* was divided into *liwās*, whose governors were raised to the rank of *mir-mīrān*, and were distinguished by badges of two *tūghs*. The importance of the reform lay in the fact that the offices and the accompanying fiefs were granted for fixed periods, which ultimately were as little as one year, whereby it was made more difficult for governors to acquire too great power or to enrich themselves unduly at the expense of their subjects or the royal treasury.[2] Even with these restrictions, at a distance from the capital there were pashas strong enough to defy the sulṭān and openly assume virtual independence as *dere-beys* (feudal seigneurs). Notable examples at the beginning of the nineteenth century were Sulaymān Pasha and Dā'ūd Pasha at Baghdad, and Muhammad 'Alī in Egypt. It was Sulṭān Maḥmūd II (1808–39) who finally realized the futility, from the point of view of the central government, of keeping alive the feudal institution, and he introduced the beginnings of a military and administrative system which was borrowed from those prevailing in Europe.

At the western end of the Islamic world, in Spain, the prime function of revenue collection was, as elsewhere, the duty of local

abolished, although the practice arose of exacting a commutation fee (*bedel*) from those who did not carry out the military service to which, theoretically, they thus rendered themselves liable.

[1] Qūchī Bey, *Risāla*, pp. 46, 64 f.

[2] D'Ohsson, *op. cit.* VII, 274 ff.

chieftains.[1] As for the officials of the government there, they were not greatly different, in the early days of the Umayyads of Cordova, from those at Baghdad. The chief lieutenant of the sovereign was the vizier. Under the later Umayyads he fell from his high position, and his title was given to the heads of the several branches of the administration, namely, those of the treasury, the chancery, the justiciary, and frontier defence.[2] The *ḥājib* (the chamberlain) was now endowed with the powers formerly held by the vizier, a change later seen in Egypt.

In North Africa, on the other hand, the vizier remained the chief minister and the *ḥājib* was a palace official, generally a eunuch.[3]

Indian history provides other examples of the working of the Muslim system of land-ownership and taxation, combined with local government. Under the Slave Kings of Delhi, Shams al-Dīn (A.D. 1210–35) had inaugurated a system of granting fiefs to warrior chieftains in return for military services. Within half a century, the defects of the system had begun to be apparent, and a reform was instituted by Sulṭān Ghiyāth al-Dīn Balban. He permitted the original grantees to retain their villages, while other holders were divided into two classes: those capable of fighting, and those who were the female relatives or children of the original feudatories. Those of the first class were permitted to stay in their villages, out of the revenues of which a proportion had to be paid to the government treasury; while the women and children who were heirs of the original grantees were deprived of their holdings and given maintenance allowances instead.[4]

'Alā al-Dīn Khaljī, who came to the throne in 695/1295–6, seized for the exchequer all property which had thus been granted as free gift (*in'ām*) or was in private ownership (*mulk*), though he maintained the system—which continued until Humāyūn's day—of granting fiefs for military services. Seeing that land was the

[1] Cf. Dozy, *Recherches sur l'histoire ... de l'Espagne* (Leyden, 1881), I, Appendix II, p. vii.

[2] Ibn Khaldūn, *Prolégomènes*, ed. Quatremère, II, 9 f.; Muḥammad Lisān al-Din, *Al-Iḥāṭa fī ta'rīkh Gharnāṭa* (Cairo, A.H. 1319), I, 352.

[3] Marrākushī, *The History of the Almohades*, ed. Dozy (2nd ed., Leyden, 1881), pp. 176, 226 f.

[4] H. M. Elliot and J. Dowson, *The History of India as told by its own Historians*, 8 vols. (London, 1867–77), III, 107 ff.

main source of his revenue, 'Alā al-Dīn introduced survey and assessment as a means of arriving at a clearer estimate of his income from it.[1] Of the assessed produce he took one-half, and his *nā'ib wazīr al-mamālik* (deputy vizier), who had been placed in control of the finances, exerted a constant pressure on the revenue officials, whose collections had to tally with the records kept by the *patwārīs*, the village accountants. Yet he appears to have adhered to the letter of the law in the matter of the *aḥdāth*, the "new" taxes, which he abolished, also banishing from Delhi the "vintners and gamblers and beer-sellers" from whom heavy taxes had been taken.[2] He refused, however, to accept poll-tax from Hindus on the ground that none of the *imāms* but Abu Ḥanīfa had consented to include them in the category of *dhimmīs*,[3] people who remained under the "protection" of Islam and paid *jizya*. He nevertheless decided that since the Hindu gentry were wealthy and contributed nothing to the state, either by *kharāj* or *karhi* (house-tax) or *charā-ī* (pasture-tax), they should be deprived of their lands.[4] In general the sulṭāns of Delhi left the landowners, whether Muslim chiefs or Hindu Rajahs, in peace, so long as they paid the tribute due from them. The earliest Mughal emperors, Bābur and Humāyūn, followed their example, so that under Bābur, for example, the landowners administered the country as well as guaranteeing the revenues.[5] Akbar, however, brought a change by introducing measures which were more likely to further his own aims and ambitions and which had lasting effect.[6]

[1] Cf. R. C. Temple, "Sher-Shah", *The Indian Antiquary* (1922), LI, 189 f.

[2] Elliot and Dowson, *ibid.* III, p. 179. The *aḥdāth* never remained absent for long. We find that they were again "abolished" in the reigns of Muḥammad (II) ibn Tughlaq and of his successor, Fīrūzshāh III (Ibn Baṭṭūṭa, *Voyages*, III, 116 f.). For a full list of these taxes, see E. Thomas, *Revenue Resources of the Mughal Empire* (London, 1871), pp. 5 f, note.

[3] In spite of the inaccuracy of the term when so applied, it is used by Muslim historians in India in reference to Hindus.

[4] Elliot and Dowson, *ibid.* III, 185.

[5] *Bābur-nāmah*, "The Memoirs of Bābur", tr. A. S. Beveridge (London, 1912–21), ii, 520.

[6] See further, E. Thomas, *ibid.* pp. 5 ff.

CHAPTER IX

MILITARY ORGANIZATION IN ISLAM

Warfare in pre-Muslim Arabia was waged regularly for a certain part of each year as an ordinary part of the routine of tribal life, the ostensible motive being the desire for plunder or revenge, although an underlying inducement was the necessity for relief from the monotony of desert existence. Islam added a new motive which combined with the old ones to lead men to warlike activities.

The first Muslims to undertake warlike tasks were the *muhājirs*, Muhammad's fellow-emigrants from Mecca, of whom small groups were, during the struggle with the Prophet's tribe of the Quraysh, sent out to intercept enemy caravans. These expeditionary forces of the first or second[1] year of the *hijra* were weak in numbers; thirty men taking part in the first, which proved abortive, sixty in the second and about twenty in the third.[2] However, at the battle of Badr, in which the objective was the famous Quraysh caravan under Abu Sufyān, the number of Muslims engaged was more than three hundred, of whom over seventy were *muhājirs* and the rest *anṣār*, loyal converts of Medina.[3] A year later, by the time of the battle of Uḥud, in which Muhammad suffered a reverse, his force had increased to a thousand, of whom three hundred deserted before the actual engagement. The opposing Quraysh in that battle, according to tradition, numbered over three thousand, and had two hundred horses as against the Muslims' two, while seven hundred of their men wore armour to the Prophet's one hundred.[4] Subsequent diplomacy and piecemeal destruction of his opponents re-established Muhammad's prestige, and his following gathered strength from the Quraysh, the Medinese and other tribes. Three thousand men are said to have been sent on the Mu'ta expedition in A.H. 8.[5] and several Arab tribes of the Ḥijāz are enumerated as having taken part in the siege and capture of Mecca in the same year,[6] which was the last before the Prophet's death.

The men who engaged in the battles were ordinary members of

[1] Cf. Ṭabarī I, 1266.
[2] *Ibid.* I, 1365–7.
[3] *Ibid.* I, 1297.
[4] *Ibid.* I, 1390.
[5] *Ibid.* I, 1610.
[6] *Ibid.* I, 1637.

the Arabian tribes whose normal life consisted in tending camels or sheep, and who, after their military services were ended for the season, returned to their accustomed everyday tasks.

The expeditions sent out by Abu Bakr and Omar from Arabia after the defections and other troubles consequent on Muhammad's death were not strongly manned, but the men who took part were prepared for long absence from home and took their families with them. The army sent by Abu Bakr against Syria in A.H. 13 consisted of seven thousand men.[1] But there are said to have been 27,000 men on the Muslim side by the time of the battle of the Yarmūk in the same year, and they were reinforced by nine thousand more under Khālid ibn Walīd.[2] Tradition appears to have exaggerated these figures, for the strength of the opposing Byzantine army is given as 140,000.[3]

The numbers allotted for the march on Iraq in the same year are somewhat smaller. Omar is said to have put Abu 'Ubayd b. Mas'ūd at the head of five thousand men,[4] who, in spite of some reinforcements, were defeated at the battle of the Bridge.[5] On receiving news of the reverse Omar sent to various tribes of Arabia demanding recruits, who were supplied and sent to Muthannā at Ḥīra.[6] At the decisive battle of Qādisīya the force for whom provision was made by headquarters is estimated at about seven thousand strong,[7] although others probably attached themselves as volunteers or were sent as reinforcements. How many Muslims there were in all is doubtful, since according to Balādhurī[8] the number of those who marched on Persia was between nine and ten thousand, while Ṭabarī[9] reports six thousand slain at Qādisīya and in the raids preceding. He puts the number present at Madā'in (Ctesiphon) two years later as twelve thousand men, all

[1] Ṭabarī, I, 2079.

[2] *Ibid.* I, 2089. Balādhurī (*Futūḥ al-buldān*, p. 107) says that originally three parties numbering 3,000 each under separate commanders were dispatched to Syria and that later the force was increased to 24,000, in addition to Khālid ibn Walīd's auxiliary army.

[3] Ṭabarī *loc. cit.*

[4] Dīnawarī, *Akhbār al-ṭiwāl*, ed. Guirgass (Leyden, 1888), p. 118.

[5] Ṭabarī I, 2174 ff.

[6] Dīnawarī, p. 119.

[7] Ṭabarī I, 2236. The tribe of the Bajila constituted one-fourth of the total Muslim army at this battle (Balādhurī, p. 267).

[8] Balādhurī, pp. 255 f.

[9] Ṭabarī I, 2337.

mounted.[1] These figures may to some extent be checked from Ya'qūbī[2] who puts the numbers present at Qādisīya as five thousand full-blooded Arabs (of the Muḍar and Rabī'a confederacies) and one thousand other Muslims.

For the conquest of Egypt the force allotted by Omar to 'Amr b. al-'Ās amounted to no more than four thousand men, although he was compelled to reinforce them by a like number.[3] By Mu'āwiya's day the force recognized as entitled to draw allowances numbered forty thousand.[4]

As Islam advanced and the number both of its Arab and non-Arab adherents increased, its armies also obtained fresh accretions. In Iraq, the garrison which grew into the city of Baṣra was formed originally of eight hundred men whom Omar sent, accompanied by their wives and families, to guard his eastern frontiers. They settled at first in tents, but as their numbers grew, villages were built which developed and ultimately coalesced to form a large city.[5] Less than a quarter of a century after the arrival of the garrison, a census taken in the governorship of Ziyād ibn Abīhi declared the numbers of the population capable of bearing arms to be eighty thousand, with one hundred and twenty thousand women and children. The figures given for Kūfa, which was established as a garrison at about the same time as Baṣra, were sixty thousand and eighty thousand respectively.[6] The Kūfans were employed especially against Rayy and Ādharbayjān, against which two objectives ten thousand men were engaged in 24/645, while forty thousand more are said to have been available at Kūfa.[7] In 51/671, in the governorship of Ziyād, Iraqī "colonists" are reported in Khurāsān,[8] and for continuing the advance into Persia Ḥajjāj ibn Yūsuf in 80/699, during his governorship of Iraq,

[1] Ṭabarī, I, 2451. A similar number is reported to have been opposing the Persians at the battle of Jalūlā on the way to Persia in A.H. 16. (Balādhurī, p. 264.)

[2] Ya'qūbī, *Historiae* (ed. Houtsma) II, 164 *ad fin.*

[3] *Ibid.* II, 168.

[4] Maqrīzī, *Khiṭaṭ* I, 94. The authority is late but the number is a probable one.

[5] Balādhurī, p. 342.

[6] *Ibid.* p. 350. Cf. Mas'ūdī, *Murūj al-dhahab*, IV, 194.

[7] Ṭabarī, I, 2805. It is there reported that each warrior took part every four years in the raids on these objectives, but the statement appears to be due to the desire to systematize the earlier history of Islam.

[8] Balādhurī, p. 410.

dispatched drafts of twenty thousand men from Kūfa and Baṣra.[1] Against the eastern part of Khurāsān there was being employed in 96/714–5 a force which contained forty thousand men of Baṣra belonging to the five different tribal confederacies of the 'Alīya, Bakr, Tamīm, 'Abd al-Qays and Azd. They were known as the *akhmās*[2] ("fifths"), each *khums* forming a separate unit under its own chief. There were also in the force seven thousand Kūfans and a like number of *mawālī*, non-Arab converts.[3]

Long before Persia was uniformly subjugated, large regions of it had recognized and accepted the fact of Arab domination, and a considerable time before the end of the first century of Islam numerous Persians were enrolled in the advancing armies, some undoubtedly as volunteers, but many also as forced levies from the conquered territories. Thus, of the army of five thousand men who crossed the Oxus to invade Tukhāristān, a fifth were Persians[4] and in 94/713, after crossing the Oxus, Qutayba compelled the inhabitants of Bukhārā, Kash, Nasaf and Khwārazm (Khiva) to supply him with twenty thousand men, whom he sent on to Shāsh (Tashkent).[5] Four years afterwaıds, Yazīd b. Muhallab assembled an army of a hundred thousand (a figure seemingly chosen to represent a large, round number), comprised of Syrians, Iraqīs and Khurāsānīs, for the conquest of Jurjān and Ṭabaristān. This force also had a number of other *mawālī* and "volunteers" (*mutaṭawwi'a*) in its train.[6]

In directions other than Persia also the comparatively small forces originally sent out were augmented by the newly converted non-Arab subjects of the Caliphs. In the reign of 'Uthmān, Mu'āwiya, who was then governor of Syria and the Jazīra (Mesopotamia), despatched a force of about eight thousand men from these two provinces against Armenia, reinforcing them later when they encountered opposition with men from Kūfa.[7] Natives of these provinces were also sent on the summer and winter campaigns which the Umayyads despatched against the Greeks beyond the frontiers of Syria and the Jazīra, and it would appear that when Sulaymān b. 'Abd al-Malik launched his ill-fated expedition under his brother Maslama against Constantinople, the

[1] Ibn al-Athīr, A.H. 80 and 83.

[2] Cf. Zabīdī, *Tāj al-'arūs* (Cairo, A.H. 1287), IV, 141.

[3] Ṭabarī, II, 1290 f.

[4] Balādhurī, p. 407.

[5] Ibn al-Athīr, A.H. 94.

[6] *Ibid.* (A.H. 98), V, 19.

[7] Balādhurī, p. 197.

new non-Arab Muslims formed the main strength of the army.[1] The case was similar in the west. Ṭāriq ibn Ziyād's invasion of Andalusia in 92/711 was carried out by a force of seven thousand men,[2] most of whom were Berbers or *mawālī* of other stocks, only a minority being Arabs.[3]

The number of men engaged in the civil wars which raged before the Umayyad accession, and in the expeditions to suppress the rebellions which broke out during that regime, was little less than those employed abroad. The reports must be treated with caution, for the figures given of those who took part in the battle of Ṣiffīn are so large as to arouse suspicion of their accuracy, 'Alī being said to have had ninety thousand men in the field and his opponent Mu'āwiya eighty-five thousand.[4] Yet a point to be noted is that Hāni' b 'Urwa—shaykh of the āl-Murād tribe and one of the supporters of 'Ālī's son Ḥusayn—who was beheaded in the intrigues against his hero, could, if his tribe had been loyal, have put into the field four thousand mounted men, and twice as many more on foot, and with his allies of the Kinda could have mustered a force of thirty thousand.[5]

The long series of battles against the Khārijīs, and in particular against the redoubtable Shabīb al-Azraqī tried the resources of the State to the utmost. In 76/695, Ḥajjāj sent against him an Iraqī force of six thousand picked men, whom he defeated.[6] In the following year Ḥajjāj sent to the Caliph 'Abd al-Malik asking for Syrian troops, seeing that the Kūfans and others in Iraq were incapable of subduing the rebel. The Caliph sent six thousand men in two detachments,[7] with whom Ḥajjāj strengthened his force of Kūfans amounting to forty thousand warriors of the Quraysh and other Arab tribes and ten thousand camp followers, this being the total male population of Kūfa of any fighting value.[8]

In the earliest period of the faith there were many who had fought in the ranks of Islam on the inducement of spiritual rewards to be attained in the hereafter. Not a few, of whom 'Uthmān is picked out for special mention,[9] contributed generously towards the cost of the Prophet's campaigns. Then, when

[1] Balādhurī, p. 162; *Fragmenta Historicorum Arabicorum*, I, p. 24.
[2] Ṭabarī (II, 1235) says 12,000.
[3] Ibn al-Athīr (A.H. 91), IV, 444.
[4] Mas'ūdī, *ibid.* IV, 344.
[5] *Ibid.* V, 140.
[6] Ṭabarī, II, 1930.
[7] *Ibid.* II, 943 f.
[8] *Ibid.* II, 948.
[9] *Ibid.* I, 1694.

the foreign expeditions began under the first Caliphs, the motives inspiring the tribes to flock to the standards were combined with anticipations of plunder from the fabled riches of the lands to be invaded.[1] During the reigns of Abu Bakr and Omar, such hopes were realized, and what were to the recipients large sums were distributed not only amongst the men who actually took part in the campaigns but also amongst the members of the community who remained in Arabia. To Omar, from whom Islam claims to have received the greater part of its formal organization, is attributed a scheme whereby every warrior received annually four thousand dirhams to be used in equal parts for the care of his family during his absence in the field, the provision of his equipment at home and his maintenance abroad and for the payment of a companion at arms.[2] To Omar also is ascribed the first dīwān, or register of troops, by which an *'aṭā*, or stipend, was granted to each warrior who had taken part in the battle of Qādisīya and subsequent engagements.[3]

For the actual distribution of pay, the army was divided into *'irāfas* or groups, which varied in strength at different times. At first they contained ten men under their own leader,[4] but later were enlarged. Omar is said to have included in each *'irāfa* forty-three men who fought at Qādisīya, with an equal number of women and children, and to each such *'irāfa* he allotted one hundred thousand dirhams. Those who had joined Islam later and had fought only in battles subsequent to Qādisīya were in still larger groups, although the allotment of money to each *'irāfa* remained the same.[5]

In Abbasid times, to anticipate, the *'irāfa* was changed again and there is a report that the "Turkish" mercenaries in Muhtadī's day (256/870) demanded a return to the earlier system in vogue under Musta'īn, when there was an *'arīf* over every nine men, a *khalīfa* over fifty men and a *qā'id* over a hundred. They further demanded that no women should be included nor any charges made for equipment etc.[6]

During the time that plunder continued unrestricted the troops were paid out of the proceeds of it. When that source was

[1] Cf. Ṭabarī, I, 2815 f., 2913, l. 12.
[2] Ibn al-Ṭiqṭaqā, *Al-Fakhrī*, ed. Derenbourg, p. 117.
[3] See above, p. 57; and cf. Ṭabarī I, 2412, Balādhurī, pp. 265 ff.
[4] Ṭabarī, I, 2224 f. [5] *Ibid.* I, 2496. [6] *Ibid.* III, 1799.

exhausted, recourse was had to the taxes brought in to the treasury from the subjugated lands.[1] But grants of land (*iqṭā'āt*) were also made, when this was convenient, even in the days of the earliest Caliphs,[2] although the institution of these grants, because of the mischief they produced, is frequently ascribed by Muslim historians to "foreign" dynasties, especially the Seljūqs.[3]

Under the Umayyads the pay of the troops engaged in the various provinces was regarded as the first charge on the local revenues. In Egypt in Mu'āwiya's day there were forty thousand men who are said to have been paid two hundred dīnārs each (? annually), so that the Caliph received from the province no more than a comparatively small surplus of revenue. He kept a close check upon the numbers of the garrison and their families and appointed an Arab official for the sole purpose of inquiring into arrivals and departures. In Syria, the capital province of the dynasty, each *jund* (district)[4] had its garrison which was paid from local taxation.[5]

In order to ensure a constant supply of men for their armies, the Umayyads subsidized various tribal chiefs and made terms with them for the provision of warriors.[6] The first four Caliphs of the dynasty received a standing draft of two thousand men from the Qaḥṭān confederacy of tribes in Syria. In return they paid the successive chiefs two million dirhams each and guaranteed to each the succession of his nominee, whether son or nephew, as well as granting complete independence in the management of the internal affairs of the tribes.[7] So also Yazīd II allotted stipends for three thousand men at 'Umān to come up for service when called upon.[8] The early Abbasids granted similar subsidies to tribes for special services. The Caliph Manṣūr, after building Malaṭya

[1] Cf. Maqrīzī, *Khiṭaṭ*, I, 95.
[2] Cf. Balādhurī, pp. 128, 255 f.
[3] Cf. Maqrīzī, *ibid.*, and see below, p. 419.
[4] The name *jund* would appear to have been applied to a military district of this kind and the local force was called *jund* after the district. (Cf. Balādhurī, pp. 131 f.) The name, however, was also used for the personal bodyguard of the sovereign or of a chieftain, as opposed to the '*askar*, which was a term applied to the army as a whole. (Cf. Ṭabarī, II, 1970, l. 6; Ibn al-Athīr, VII, 102.) The same term was applied also to the standing army as distinct from the *mutaṭawwi'a* or from the general body of the population. (Cf. Balādhurī, p. 166; *Fragmenta Hist. Arab.*, I, 102, and Ṭabarī, I, 2090.)
[5] Maqrīzī, *ibid.* I, p. 94.
[6] Cf. Ibn al-Athir, III, 242; IV, 162 ff., 230 ff.
[7] Mas'ūdī, *Murūj*, V, 200.
[8] *Fragmenta Hist. Arab.*, I, 66.

(Melitene) on the Byzantine frontier, settled four thousand warriors from Mesopotamian tribes there—the city being nearest them—and gave each man a special grant of ten dīnārs over and above his stipend as well as an extraordinary allowance of a hundred dīnārs. Any tribe which failed to send the full complement of men demanded from it paid in compensation a sum[1] which was used for the hire of substitutes.[2]

There is clear evidence that after the first enthusiasm of the faithful had evaporated, the men whose business it was to serve in the armies of Islam were reluctant to carry out their duties even though they were in receipt of stipends. A capable and ruthless administrator such as Ḥajjāj ibn Yūsuf, who was governor of Iraq under the Umayyad Caliph ʻAbd al-Malik, used compulsion; but not all had the same power and forcefulness of character. In 80/699 he raised a compulsory levy of twenty thousand men from each of the two garrison cities of Baṣra and Kūfa[3] for the reinforcement of the armies advancing in Persia. Three years later he required a like number from Kūfa for the campaign in Khurāsān and on this occasion announced that he had been commanded to pay stipends to men who were enrolled, but that he would put to death any man who delayed joining the force for more than three days after receipt of his pay.[4] In the years before, he had raised troops under compulsion at Kūfa for his campaigns against the Khārijī rebels. Of a force of three thousand men sent in 76/695 against the redoubtable Shabīb, one thousand are described as of the "first fighters" and the remainder as of the force which Ḥajjāj had levied on Kūfa.[5] Another army, consisting of six thousand "knights and notables", was raised under the threat of terrible penalties for any failure to comply with the order to mobilize.[6] The rebel was victorious against these troops as also in the next year against a much stronger detachment which Ḥajjāj raised by forcing every available male in Kūfa out into the field. They are said to have numbered forty thousand "warriors" and ten thousand "youths".[7]

The troops owing allegiance directly to the sovereign, and the

[1] It was called technically *juʻl*.

[2] Balādhurī, pp. 187 ff.

[3] Ibn al-Athīr, A.H. 80, cf. A.H. 83.

[4] Mubarrad, *Kāmil*, ed. Wright, p. 216.

[5] Ṭabarī, II, 890.

[6] *Ibid.* II, 930.

[7] *Ibid.* II, 948. See below, p. 418.

tribesmen and others in receipt of subsistence-money and supplies (*arzāq*),[1] made up the nucleus of the armies raised for the purposes of war by the central authority. They were expected to come up for service when called upon and could be compelled, as has been seen, when they held back. In addition to them were others who were not in receipt of regular allowances but gave their services in return for special grants in case of need,[2] and still others who were purely volunteers (the *mutaṭawwi'a*) moved to fight by zeal for their faith.[3] They came at their own expense, and on occasion might even be made to contribute towards the cost of the campaign in which they were taking part, out of any booty which they might acquire.[4] The distinction between the volunteers and the *jund* is clear from the fact that the former could make terms with the Caliph with regard to the period of their service. In one of the last battles of the Umayyads (in 130/747–8) there fought on the side of the Caliph Marwān II four thousand knights from Syria and Mesopotamia in whose terms of service was included the condition that they should be permitted to return home once the object of the campaign had been attained.[5]

At the close of the Umayyads' rule their military strength, so far as numbers were concerned, was considerable. In the revolt that broke out in the Ḥijāz under the last Caliph, Marwān II, the force sent by him against the recalcitrant Meccans consisted of eighty thousand men made up of detachments from the Quraysh, the *anṣār* and ordinary "merchants",[6] while in the struggle against the rising Abbasid forces, an Umayyad army, estimated variously at one hundred thousand and one hundred and fifty thousand and consisting almost entirely of Arab tribesmen of Syria or their kinsmen domiciled in Khurāsān, was in 131/748–9

[1] The recipient was the *murtazaq*. There were 60,000 of them in Iraq alone in A.H. 64 and the allowances for them and their families amounted annually to 60,000,000 *dirhams*. (Mas'ūdī, *Murūj* v, 194.)

[2] Cf. Ṭabarī, III, 492.

[3] Cf. Ibn al-Athīr, v, 19.

[4] Cf. Balādhurī, p. 410. Ziyād b. Abi Sufyān in A.H. 51 appointed Rabī' b. Ziyād governor of Khurāsān. "He was the first to order the *jund* to make contribution towards the expenses of the campaign." The term for such contribution is *tanāhud*.

[5] *Fragmenta Hist. Arab.*, I, 171. Cf. Ṭabarī, I, 2807 f.

[6] *Fragmenta Hist. Arab.*, I, 167.

put into the field. They were, however, defeated by a force of twenty thousand Abbasid troops.[1]

The strength of the early Abbasid military force lay in the Khurāsānī tribesmen raised by Abu Muslim, the propagandist to whom the new dynasty owed its rise to power. From very small beginnings he had by 129/746–7 collected an army of seven thousand men, who were persuaded to keep their loyalty by occasional small gifts of money.[2] A year later many thousands more had joined him not only from amongst the natives of Khurāsān,[3] but also from troops who had deserted from the Umayyad armies.[4]

Natives of Khurāsān continued for nearly a century (until the accession of Mu'taṣim in 218/833) to form the main portion of the Abbasid armies and of the Caliph's personal bodyguard.[5] It was they who were chiefly employed in the raids against the Byzantines.[6] But they were used in other directions also,[7] thirty thousand of them being engaged in the expedition of 162/778–9 and various numbers at other times. They were not, however, the only forces employed in the Caliphate. Manṣūr, founder of Baghdad, kept in his army a number of Arabs, some being the deserters from the Umayyads while the rest belonged to the north-Arabian confederacy of the Muḍar, the southern tribes of the Yemen and the confederacy of the Rabī'a.[8] Troops from other Arab lands were used as they were available. Thus, in 159/776, an expedition launched by sea against India was composed of two thousand men of Baṣra made up from the various *ajnād* or tribal corps, seven hundred Syrians under their own leader, four thousand "knights" of Persian origin[9] domiciled at Baṣra and a number of volunteers. Of the latter, fifteen hundred were men who had served as frontier guards and a thousand more were ordinary citizens who went

[1] Ṭabarī, III, 5.

[2] Three *dirhams* per man and an extra gift of four are mentioned. (Ṭabarī, II, 1968 ff.)

[3] Ṭabarī, II, 2002.

[4] *Ibid.* III, 3.

[5] A token of the long-continued relationship between Khurāsān and Baghdad is provided by the fact that in 255/869, in the reign of Muhtadī and long after the Khurāsānīs had been ousted by the "Turkish" troops, warriors of the province came to the city of the Caliphs in the expectation of finding there a fund, which, until a swindler decamped with it, had existed there for their benefit. (Ibn al-Athīr, VII, 136.)

[6] Ṭabarī, III, 493 f.; III, 459, 712 etc.

[7] *Ibid.* III, 843.

[8] *Ibid.* III, 366.

[9] See Balādhurī, p. 280.

taking their money with them.[1] The Caliph Amīn also raised an army in Syria when he was engaged in fighting his brother Ma'mūn's force under Ṭāhir, but although one chieftain after another brought his men they could not agree with the Khurāsānī troops from Baghdad and ultimately dispersed to their homes.[2]

Under the events recorded for the year 193/808–9 there is the first mention by the historian Ṭabarī of the "Turkish"[3] mercenaries who were afterwards to play so important a part as a standing army in the history of the Abbasid Caliphs. On this occasion they fought on the side of the rebellious Rāfi' ibn Layth against Ma'mūn, who was in command of the government troops. Two years later, Turks and men of Khwārazm and of Bukhārā are mentioned as having fought for Ma'mūn in the struggle against his brother Amīn.[4] On the accession of the Caliph Mu'taṣim in 218/833, the Persian *jund*[5] at Baghdad rose in favour of his nephew 'Abbās, son of Ma'mūn, but he himself acknowledged Mu'taṣim and was able to quell the disturbance.[6] The Caliph, however, continued distrustful of the Persian force and by purchase and other means recruited a large force of men originating from the Turkish-speaking provinces of eastern Persia and Transoxiana. In 219/834 he determined to leave it behind at Baghdad while he himself with his now enormous slave bodyguard of "Turks" moved his court from the city,[7] going first to Qāṭūl and then to Sāmarrā.[8]

In his mistrust, and possibly also to find money for his Turkish guards, the Caliph ordered that the names of all Arabs were to be removed from the pay-rolls in Egypt. A year after his accession, consequently, Arab troops ceased to be employed there and were replaced by "foreigners" until Aḥmad ibn Ṭūlūn seized power.[9]

Mu'taṣim did not confine his army strictly to Turks, but he acquired for it men, bond and free,[10] of different origins, a number from the West (*Maghrib*) being formed into a separate corps. Both corps were used against the Byzantines at the siege of Amorium in 223/838[11] and it is a mark of the confidence he placed

[1] Ṭabarī, III, 460 f.
[2] Ṭabarī, III, 841 ff.
[3] The term is often used generically to designate foreign soldiery.
[4] Ṭabarī, III, 775.
[5] *Ibid.* III, 799 ff. Cf. III, 815[9], and 891.
[6] *Ibid.* III, 1164.
[7] *Ibid.* III, 1179 f.
[8] Hārūn al-Rashīd had similarly moved his place of residence from Baghdad to Raqqa, and for a similar reason. (Ṭabarī, *ibid.*)
[9] Maqrīzī, *Khiṭaṭ*, I, 94.
[10] Cf. Ṭabarī, III, 1370.
[11] *Ibid.* III, 1250.

in the Turks that in the invasion of Asia Minor the chief command under Mu'taṣim was held jointly by Ashnās and Afshīn, of whom at least the former was a Turk.[1]

The mercenary corps were increased by the addition of men from Farghāna, negroes and Egyptians.[2] Even under Mutawakkil, who came to the throne in 232/847, they were sucking the treasury dry,[3] and the Caliph was storing up trouble for himself by favouring some of the corps at the expense of others in the matter of pay. At his accession he gave the recruits (*shākirīya*)[4] eight months' stipend, the older Turks and the Maghribīs considerably less.[5] The latter refused what was offered, but he was able to satisfy the malcontents by allowing the slaves amongst them to be sold out of the army and by promising the freemen that they would be formed into a model corps.[6]

The loyalty of the standing army was assiduously fostered and great care was taken by sovereigns who wished to assure the succession for their own nominees to win for them the allegiance of these troops.[7] Their pay was a first charge on the treasury and when it was for any reason not forthcoming they rioted dangerously,[8] although their loyalty was not always to be depended upon even when they were paid, if they had other cause for dissatisfaction.[9] Many a man deserted to become a highway robber, and to have worn military garb seems frequently to have been synonymous with brigandage.[10]

Mutawakkil was murdered at Sāmarrā by one of his Turkish

[1] According to Michael Syrus, Mu'taṣim's army was 80,000 strong, and there were with him 30,000 merchants and providers. Cf. J. B. Bury, *A History of the Eastern Roman Empire* (London, 1912), p. 263, n. 3.

[2] Al-Ṣābī, *Kitāb al-Wuzarā*, ed. Amedroz, p. 11.

[3] Cf. Ṭabarī, III, 1544.

[4] The word *shākirīya* has been derived from the Persian *chākir* ("servant" or "apprentice"). They are spoken of in connection with the "youth" (Ṭabari, III, 1510, 1534) as opposed to the *jund*, and this makes it probable they were recruits.

[5] Ṭabarī, III, 1369 n. (*d*).

[6] *Ibid.* III, 1369 f.

[7] Cf. *ibid.* III, 545, 647, 764 f., 768, 796, etc. *Fragmenta Hist. Arab.*, II, 436.

[8] Ṭabarī, III, 814.

[9] *Ibid.* III, 546, 892 f., 934, 998, etc.

[10] Cf. Qiftī, *Ta'rīkh al-ḥukamā*, ed. Lippert (Leipzig, 1903), p. 441. It is here said that the father of the Banu Mūsā, the famous scientists employed by Ma'mūn, was not himself a *savant*, but rather "a brigand and highwayman, who wore the garb of the *jund*."

chiefs, Bāghir by name,[1] and thereafter the Caliph was a creature of his guards, of whom rival parties in turn secured his person and derived what advantage they could from the loyalty owed him by his people.[2] One section of the guards moved back to Baghdad, and in the quarrels of the hostile factions the ordinary citizen suffered greatly. Some verses composed on the murder of Bāghir himself, who was assassinated by rivals, contain a bitter description of the plight of the innocent inhabitants of the capital while Turks, Maghribīs and Farghānese went about in armed bands, mounted and afoot, and laid the city in ruins with their strife.[3]

In 251/865 the Turkish guard that remained at Sāmarrā elected Mu'tazz to be Caliph in succession to Mutawakkil, whereas those at Baghdad gave their acknowledgment to Musta'īn. In the account of the new officers appointed by Mu'tazz there is mention of one officer who was put over the *ḥaras*, the personal bodyguard, another who was in charge of "the war-office of the Turks" and a third who had charge of "the treasuries, and moreover of the stipends of the Turks, Maghribīs and the *shākirīya*".[4]

Mu'tazz, when he had for a time maintained the upper hand, refused to acknowledge any responsibility for the Turks at Baghdad and, when informed that they were rioting for their pay, declared that he had no need of them and would do nothing to help them.[5] Thereafter when the activities of the Turks or other members of the bodyguard are reported, it is more often than not in connection with disturbances they created when their pay was delayed.[6] There is no record of their having taken part effectively in any foreign campaigns and they left the defence against Byzantine attacks to be carried out by private effort.[7] Even at home they did little to earn their pay. An army of eighty thousand sent against a small force of the Qarmaṭī heretics advancing on Baghdad and numbering well under three thousand[8], was routed.[9] Nevertheless the Caliph Muhtadī, in his last illness, complained that his dīwān contained the names of a hundred thousand such men in receipt of pay.[10]

[1] Ṭabarī, III, 1535 ff.
[2] *Ibid.* III, 1512 f.
[3] *Ibid.* III, 1540 f. Cf. Ibn Al-Athīr, VII, 80.
[4] *Ibid.* III, 1550.
[5] Ibn al-Athīr, VII, 113 f.
[6] *Ibid.* VII, 136, 150, 154, 185; VIII, 149, 160, etc.
[7] Cf. Ṭabarī, III, 1511.
[8] Variously given as 1500 or 2700 men.
[9] Ibn al-Athīr, VIII, 127.
[10] *Ibid.* VII, 307.

In part their feebleness may have been due to poor leadership. Under the efficient generalship of Muwaffaq and his son Abu'l-'Abbās well-equipped forces of them were effective against the Zanj rebels in difficult territory in the southern Iraq marshes, and they undertook the heavy task, when labourers were not available, of undermining the walls of besieged towns with no more than their ordinary weapons.[1]

To maintain these standing forces, in the days when the central authority was strong and taxes flowed into the treasury, stipends and allowances were as a rule drawn from it, although in special cases military fiefs might be granted instead or in addition. Manṣūr is said to have given to the garrison at Maṣṣīṣa (Mopsuestia) grants of land over and above their stipends, but his successor Mahdī put a stop to the practice.[2] In later times, when the treasury was unable to meet the demands for pay, lands in the provinces were assigned to the chiefs of the "Turkish" guards on condition that they kept order and remitted certain annual sums to the capital. A well-known instance of this arrangement is that in which Bāyakbāk (Bābakyāl) received a large tract of Egypt as his fief. He himself remained at Baghdad, leaving the estates to be managed by agents, one of whom was the famous Aḥmad ibn Ṭūlūn. After the death of his master, who was killed by command of the Caliph Muhtadī, Aḥmad continued in control of the Egyptian estates and succeeded finally in making himself the independent ruler of the country.[3]

It was the Seljūqs later, it may here be added, who made the greatest use of the system of grants. An important instance is the grant by the Seljūq Sulṭān Maḥmūd in 515/1121 of the town of Mosul and the adjoining lands to the Amīr Āqsunqur for his services in war.[4] The Seljūqs were not wealthy and at times were hard put to it to pay their men,[5] but they introduced certain safeguards for the protection of the peasants, from whom only specified sums might be exacted and whose wives and children were not, under penalty, to be molested.[6]

[1] Ibn al-Athīr, VII, 234 ff.
[2] Balādhurī, pp. 165 f.
[3] Ibn al-Athīr, VII, 126 f. Cf. *ibid.* VII, 89 and see further (for the case of Ahmad b. Sa'lūk in Rayy), Ibn Khaldūn, *Kitāb al-'Ibar* (Būlāq, A.H. 1284), III, 370.
[4] Ibn al-Athīr, X, 1415.
[5] Rāwandī, *Rāḥat al-ṣudūr*, ed. Md. Iqbāl (London, 1921), p. 127.
[6] Niẓām al-Mulk, *Siyāsat-nāma*, ed. C. Schefer (Paris, 1891), p. 28.

Owing to the abuses of the system, it fell into great disrepute amongst the common soldiery and the peasants, for although the chiefs managed their properties well the common run of the men had no notion of agriculture, and by neglecting watercourses and paths they soon reduced their land to ruin and were compelled to demand other forms of compensation for their services.[1]

The "Turks" were finally ousted from their position by the Buwayhids, who, being themselves well organized, were able to disperse the Baghdad *jund*, at that time and for long afterwards no more than a leaderless rabble of brigands preying on the citizens.[2]

For practical purposes any central army which could be called upon to fight for Islam, as represented by the Muslim empire under the Caliphate, disappeared with the domination of the Turkish bodyguard. Yet there remained, it must be remembered, numbers of men inspired by their faith who would come to its aid when danger threatened. Mention has been made of the volunteers who fought even under the Umayyads, who were regarded as a worldly and irreligious dynasty. Many more gathered about the Abbasid standards when there was need to help in the defence of Muslim territory and in the raids into the territory of the Byzantines in Asia Minor.[3] When the enemy in his turn attacked the frontier cities (*thughūr*) of Islam in Syria, Mesopotamia and elsewhere, it was not the army of the Caliph but the local inhabitants to a man who gave their services, "save those who had neither horse nor weapons".[4] Furthermore, in the days when the Caliph was unwilling or unable (as, for example, in the case of Musta'īn) to take action against the infidel, Muslims living far from the scene of aggression would send assistance in men and materials to their co-religionists who were defending the frontiers.[5]

If it was necessary to fight a rebel or a heretic nearer home, the Caliph or the officer charged by him with command of a punitive

1 Ibn al-Athīr, VIII, 342. This refers to the Buwayhid Mu'izz al-Dawla, who made grants of land in 334/945–6, when he was either unwilling or unable to pay his troops otherwise. But long before then there had been dissatisfaction with the system. (Cf. Ṭabarī, III, 1799.)

2 Ibn al-Athīr (363/973–4), VIII, 474 ff., 483; (417/1026), IX, 248, 254 ff.

3 Cf. Ṭabarī, III, 709.

4 *Ibid.* III, 1235. Cf. Ibn al-Athīr, VIII, 172 ff., 399, 460.

5 Cf. Ibn al-Athīr, VII, 80.

force, could often rely upon local aid, as when the Caliph Muʿtamid in 257/871, after a regular force under his chamberlain had been defeated,[1] sent Aḥmad al-Muwallid to Baṣra against the Zanj. There a great number of men "gathered about him",[2] presumably volunteers, whose lack of training and skill led to their being easily routed by a determined force more accustomed to fighting. A further disadvantage in the employment of the *mutaṭawwiʿa* was that they were not altogether subject to the common discipline imposed by military exigencies, for if they followed their own feelings about coming, they also used their own judgment about departing. An occurrence of this nature under the Umayyads has already been described above. Another instance is given by Ṭabarī, who, in his account of the long fight against Bābak, the Khurramī heretic, says that when, one campaigning season, victory was seen to be impossible, the "volunteers" determined to return home.[3]

In the days when the power of the Caliph was supreme, with his authority and influence intact, the organization of the military side of the State possessed a considerable measure of efficiency. Nominally the central authority worked through the *Dīwān al-Jaysh* (Ministry of the Army) which was declared responsible for recruitment and pay of troops.[4] Actually the Caliph himself or his vizier were concerned with these matters, which were amongst the most important in the State. Military policy was decided in the last resort by the Caliph, and he was responsible for war and peace. To him personally, as has been seen, was attached a body of warriors who did duty as his bodyguard whether in war, which was the normal state, or peace, which was the period of the year when campaigning was not possible. When it was necessary to proceed against a powerful enemy, whether a foreign infidel or a rebellious vassal, the bodyguard was increased by the addition of men from the tribes. In the recruitment of them the chiefs performed an important office, for it was they who roused their tribes to war and it was about its own *ra'īs* that each tribe rallied, marched and fought.[5] Provision for war and general organization were as a rule left to the central authority.[6]

[1] Ibn al-Athīr, VII, 166. [2] *Ibid.* VII, 170. [3] Ṭabarī, III, 1214.
[4] See Māwardī, *Constitutiones Politicae*, ed. Enger (Bonn, 1853), pp. 351 ff.
[5] Cf. Ṭabarī, I, 2224, 2815 f., 2985, 3153 ff.; III, 843.
[6] Ibn al-Athīr, III, 242.

The organization of the Buwayhids, who held the central authority in the eastern Caliphate after they had ousted the "Turkish" bodyguard, was definitely a military one, but not much is to be gleaned from the historians to throw light upon it. Thus many pages of his chronicle are filled by Ibn al-Athīr with the exploits of the Buwayhids, but he rarely gives details to explain either the organization of their military system or of their methods of war. It may be assumed that the Daylamite tribesmen fought under their Buwayhid chieftains on condition of receiving a share of the plunder gained, for, like other men of their kind, they rioted when their pay was not given them.[1] As the armies advanced, they were joined at various periods by men from the conquered territories, and by tribal chiefs and their retinues in search of gain, but volunteers had no significant place in their system.[2]

The Buwayhids in their turn were ousted by the Seljūqs, of whom considerably more is known. They are reported as having, in 420/1029, been engaged in battle with Maḥmūd of Ghazna, who attempted to drive them out of his territories which they had invaded, and attacked them in the open country outside Bukhārā. They then numbered two thousand tents and were making for Iṣfahān. Another branch of these Ghuzz Turks, under Tughril Beg, Dā'ūd and Yabghū, were then in Transoxiana and were moving south and west.[3] This branch must even then have been very strong numerically, for there is a legend to the effect that when Maḥmūd heard of them he entered into negotiations with "the four sons of Seljūq ibn Luqmān", and to gain some idea of their resources pretended to them that he might require their help for his raids into India and asked what would be forthcoming. The Seljūq representative carried a bow and had two arrows stuck in his girdle. One of them he handed to Maḥmūd, saying: "When you have need of help send this to my host and a force of a hundred thousand mounted men will come to your assistance." Maḥmūd then asked what would happen if he needed further auxiliaries and was told to send the second arrow, when he would receive a further fifty thousand horsemen. "What if they are still

[1] Ibn al-Athīr, VIII, 342.

[2] Cf. *ibid.* VIII, 520, where a number of the allies of 'Aḍud al-Dawla are mentioned.

[3] *Ibid.* IX, 266.

insufficient?" persisted Maḥmūd. The Seljūq general in reply handed over the bow and said: "Send this as a token to Turkistān, and if you require two hundred thousand men you shall have them."[1]

For that early stage of their career the figures given are doubtless exaggerated, but once their conquests began in earnest the Seljūq armies obtained accretions of men from the various tribes, both kindred and foreign, whom they subjugated or with whom they allied themselves. Thus, the princes who submitted to Tughril Beg in Ādharbayjān and elsewhere offered him the services of their *junds*,[2] and some years later, Tughtagīn, a Turkoman amīr who had been engaged in raiding Byzantine territory, persuaded the Seljūq Sulṭān Alp Arslān to join forces with him. Alp Arslān subjugated a number of cities in Asia Minor and their inhabitants became part of his *jund* and his following.[3] Similarly, when, in the decisive battle of Manzikert (463/1071), which brought the Eastern Roman domination in Asia Minor to an end, the Byzantines were defeated and their emperor Romanus Diogenes was captured, one of the conditions of peace was that a specified number of troops should be sent to the conqueror on his demand.[4]

The admixture of foreign soldiery with the Seljūq warriors seems to have formed part of a settled policy, for Niẓām al-Mulk, the famous minister of three successive sulṭāns, in his *Siyāsat-nāma* ("Treatise on Government") declares that the army ought to be composed of troops of different nationalities to prevent any danger from concerted rebellion. Thus, he suggested, the guard at the palace should consist of two thousand Daylamīs and Khurāsānīs, with sections composed of Georgians and men of Fārs.[5] Some part of Niẓām al-Mulk's theory was based upon the practice of Maḥmūd of Ghazna, who employed in his army men of numerous different peoples, such as Turks, Khurāsānīs, Arabs, Hindus, Daylamīs and others. On the march, each "nation" was warned of the number of men required from it for guard-duty at night. The station of each was precisely allotted, and through fear of report by the others no group dared move from its appointed

[1] Rāwandī, *Rāḥat al-ṣudūr*, p. 89.
[2] Cf. Ibn al-Athīr (A.H. 446), IX, 410 f.
[3] *Ibid.*, X, 25.
[4] Ibn al-Athīr X, 45.
[5] *Siyāsat-nāma*, ed. Schefer, pp. 92 f.

place until relieved at dawn. If, during the daytime, there was a battle, each group fought as a separate unit.[1]

Since the Seljūq State was conducted upon a military basis, it need occasion no surprise when Niẓām al-Mulk mentions four hundred thousand troopers as the strength of his master's army and declares that a reduction to seventy thousand, which a courtier had proposed to the sovereign during a spell of peace, would mean ruin to the State, while an increase to seven hundred thousand would mean its greatly heightened prosperity.[2]

Not all these numbers of men were ever employed together in the same quarter. Forty-six thousand troopers are mentioned as having formed the army of the Sulṭān Malikshāh against the Ghaznawids on one occasion[3] and at the battle of Manzikert the Sulṭān Alp Arslān was able to muster no more than fifteen thousand troopers, although the enemy were said to have been two hundred thousand strong.[4]

The Caliph, like the Prophet, was always, if not actually then in theory, in supreme command of the forces of Islam. To him belonged the authority to use troops and the power to dispose as he wished of all military equipment and supplies. When Hārūn al-Rashīd determined to make his son Ma'mūn heir to the throne he was in Khurāsān, where he summoned the qāḍīs and men of standing and made them bear witness that everything in his army, including money, treasure, arms, horses and other equipment, was in the hands of his son Ma'mūn, and of no one else.[5] Hārūn himself was more than once in command of armies against the Byzantines and even as a child he had been in nominal command under the tutelage of a member of the Barmecide family.

Next to the Prophet or the Caliph came the generals appointed by him. Sometimes the Caliph gave command to his own sons, but more often the commanders were men who had had experience of warfare, and they in their turn appointed their own officers, for whom the first qualification required, except in special circumstances,[6] was military skill. Ṭāriq ibn Ziyād, who conquered Andalusia, was a freedman,[7] and at a later time even slaves could

[1] *Siyāsat-nāma*, ed. Schefer, pp. 92 f.

[2] *Ibid.* p. 144.

[3] Rāwandī, *Rāḥat al-ṣudūr*, p. 131.

[4] Ibn al-Athīr, x, 44 f.

[5] See Ṭabarī, II, 510^{1}. Dīnawarī, *Akhbār al-ṭiwāl*, p. 118.

[6] *Ibid.* (A.H. 189), VI, 130.

[7] *Ibid.* II, 1235.

be given command, although more often they seized it.[1] Under the commander-in-chief, normally, the tribal chiefs led their men in battle, but he might appoint competent substitutes if they themselves were for any reason absent.[2] After the death of the Prophet, the old feelings of tribal independence and equality were amongst some communities temporarily revived. Thus, the tribal chiefs, at the battle of the Yarmūk, when there was confusion about the command of the Muslim forces, were prepared each independently to go into battle with their own men, without any consultation or co-operation with one another.[3]

The institution of a system of military gradation is ascribed to Omar, who went on the basis of a practice of Muhammad. It is said to have originated when Omar wrote to the commander of the force advancing into Persia, who was then at Qādisīya, ordering him to divide his army into ten, to appoint *'arīfs* and amīrs and to arrange the whole force into *ta'bīya*, which is a military formation perhaps best described as parade order.[4] He was further commanded that the whole army was to be divided into tens and that each ten (*'irāfa*) was to be in charge of a man of their own people and known as an *'arīf*.[5]

In order of precedence the amīr or commander-in-chief came first; the commanders of the divisions of the *ta'bīya* held rank next to the amīr, next to them came the commanders of the tenths, then the standard-bearers, who would appear to have held high rank,[6] and lastly the tribal chiefs. There were also separate commanders for the infantry and the cavalry, but their position in the list is not specified.[7]

[1] In the fight between the "Turkish" chiefs Bajkam and al-Barīdī, the latter gave command of his army to his slave Abu Ja'far. (Ibn al-Athīr, VIII, 257.) Aḥmad ibn Ṭūlūn, who seized the reins of government in Egypt, was a slave, and the case of the Mamlūks in that country is well known.

[2] Cf. Ṭabarī, I, 2116.

[3] *Ibid.* I, 2091 f. Cf. Dozy, *Supplément*, s.v. *sanada* (VI).

[4] See below, p. 427.

[5] The "ten" (*'irāfa*) was regarded as an institution of the Prophet's (Ṭabarī, I, 2225). It was considered under Omar as a convenient group for purposes of the distribution of pay. (See above, p. 412.)

[6] Ṭabarī, I, 1616. Khālid ibn Walīd made himself an amīr although he had not been appointed, when he took charge of one of the Prophet's standards.

[7] A similar system was employed by the rabble army of the Caliph Amīn at the siege of Baghdad. Each group of ten was commanded by an *'arīf*, ten *'arīfs* by a *qā'id* and ten *qā'ids* by an amīr (Mas'ūdī, *Murūj al-dhahab*, VI, 452).

Apart from the fighting officers there were also appointed to the force physicians, a qāḍī, who was in charge of the booty before it was distributed and saw to its equitable division, a *dāʿiya* or advocate to put forward the claims of the men, a *rāʾid*, whose duty it was to find camp-sites, an interpreter and, lastly, a scribe.[1]

The general organization for war seldom included any specific training of the army. However, most of the operations in which the men were engaged were little more than raids on a large scale, and in the art of raiding the tribesmen required little instruction. The Caliph's personal bodyguard which formed the backbone of the fighting service was in a different position. It was reviewed and tested frequently, and one Caliph at least, Muʿtaḍid, carried out these duties in person. At certain periods he mustered his corps on the parade ground of the capital, where a target was set up and each man's skill in archery and horsemanship was tested. The results (good, medium or bad) were entered into a register, and upon them depended the nature of the duties assigned to each man.[2]

The recognized military formation, whether on parade, on the march, or in battle, was the *taʿbīya*. In it the army was divided into five main divisions,[3] namely centre, right and left wings, van (*muqaddama*) and rear-guard (*sāqa*). The men forming each division consisted of men of the same tribes or otherwise known to each other. The centre was the position of the amīr and his retinue, and in the wings on either side were subordinate commanders. Separate from them and in front of the centre went the vanguard with its own commander and flag. The *sāqa* acted as rear-guard and also had charge of baggage, supplies, arms and heavy siege engines.[4] In addition there were light-armed troops separate (*mujarrada*) from the rest of the formation and also bodies of scouts or advanced guards (*ṭalāʾiʿ*). The various parts of the formation might be close together or at a distance from one another, as circumstances demanded.[5]

[1] Ṭabarī, I, 2223 ff. [2] Al-Ṣābī, *Kitāb al-Wuzarā*, p. 13.

[3] Whence an army is sometimes in Arabic called *khamīs*, "Five". Ibn Khaldūn (*Prolégomènes*, ed. Quatremère, II, 67) assumes that this formation was learnt from the Greeks and Persians. (Cf. Ṭabarī, I, 2266, for Persian formation.)

[4] Ṭabarī, III, 1238; *Fragmenta Hist. Arab.*, II, 485 f.

[5] Ibn Khaldūn, *loc. cit.*

The "five" formation was in use as early as the Prophet's own time, e.g., at the battles of Badr and Mu'ta,[1] and to its invention and introduction has been attributed much of his success against opponents who were still using the old irregular methods of attack. With such variations as shall be noted, it continued for centuries to be the recognized formation in Islam on the road or the parade-ground, although it appears in the actual conflict to have kept no more than its name.

The ordinary method of fighting in vogue in Arabia at the beginning of the Prophet's career was that of the raid, in which a sudden charge was followed by prompt retreat and a sudden return to the onslaught.[2] This method was retained by the Prophet's earliest converts when they went out against the Quraysh caravans. There was at most an interchange of arrow shots and the men returned without achieving their object and without doing or receiving much harm.[3] By the time of the battle of Badr (A.H. 2) the Prophet had acquired some military sense[4] and then introduced the new formation of the *ta'bīya* for the first time, with great success. He had very few more than three hundred men, of whom only one was mounted.[5] He arranged them in straight, regular ranks, which he put in order himself, walking along the ranks with an arrow in order to push back any man who was out of line with the rest.[6] Behind the fighting line was the *sāqa*, in charge of the baggage and transport-animals.[7] A verse of the Koran (61⁴), if it may be taken literally, would seem to imply that the Prophet intended this new formation to be permanently adopted, and colour is lent to the possibility by the fact that in 145/762 when the Caliph Manṣūr sent 'Īsā ibn Mūsā to fight the 'Alid pretender Ibrahīm ibn 'Abd-allāh (who claimed to be of the kin of the Prophet), the 'Alid was advised to meet the onslaught with his men in a broken line of cohorts rather than in the old formation. He refused, however; saying that the change was an

[1] Ṭabarī, I, 1299, 1614.

[2] The method known as *karr u farr*, literally "return and flight". (Cf. Ibn Khaldūn, *Prolégomènes*, ed. Quatremère, II, 66.)

[3] See Ṭabarī, I, 1365–7.

[4] His strategy even at Badr was not approved by those of more military experience. (Cf. *ibid.* I, 1309.)

[5] Ṭabarī, I, 1297.

[6] Ibn Ḥishām, ed. Wuestenfeld, I, p. 444; Ṭabarī, I, 1319.

[7] Ibn Ḥishām, I, 433.

unlawful innovation in Islam and quoting the verse of the Koran cited above.[1]

In spite of the permanence thus implied, changes were inevitable after the Muslims had had experience with enemies more accustomed than themselves to pitched battles and with the improvement in their own means of warfare.

An important change was brought about by the introduction of horses. At Badr there had been only one mounted man and the Prophet was compelled to wait for the attacks of the enemy, although he followed sound military practice when he kept an unbroken wall of infantry to receive the enemy's cavalry. On that occasion he attended the battle in a litter.[2]

At the battle of the Yarmūk, less than ten years later, the Muslim army faced the Byzantines with forty-six thousand men, all mounted.[3] Nearer home, unmounted men were not entirely discarded, and at the battle of Ṣiffīn there were both arms, under separate commanders, on the side both of 'Ali and of Mu'āwiya. The value of the infantry and cavalry as a support to each other was clearly recognized by the Umayyads, who used them both when they could, as in 65/684–5 against the Shī'ite rebels of Kūfa under Sulaymān ibn Ṣurd, who demanded vengeance for the death of Ḥusayn.[4] Infantry were also used in support of cavalry in the penetration of Persia by Qutayba, who, meeting with resistance before Bukhārā, laid siege to the city. A sally by the Turkoman horse was driven back, but they rallied on some raised ground across the river which had to be crossed and they were able to impede Qutayba's advance. After a good deal of hesitation on the part of the tribesmen, the Muslim cavalry swam over, leaving a small force of infantry to cross by a hastily constructed bridge. While the cavalry created a diversion the infantry attacked and the Turkomans were put to flight.[5]

With the Abbasids, infantry came to be more rarely used. The effective forces, except in the campaigns against the Zanj in the marshes of lower Iraq, were all cavalry,[6] and if it was necessary to take infantry they were not seldom mounted behind the cavalry.

[1] Ṭabarī, III, 312. [2] *Ibid.* I, 1318. [3] *Ibid.* I, 2091, 2096.
[4] Cf. *ibid.* II, 554. [5] *Ibid.* II, 1201.
[6] Some others were present. A prisoner taken at the battle of the Zāb said he was merely a slave belonging to one of the soldiers (Ṭabarī, III, 39).

At the battle of the Zāb, in which the Umayyads were finally routed, the Abbasid cavalry were ordered to dismount and meet the enemy's charge, kneeling with their lances held out in front of them.[1] Where the country was unfavourable for the movement of horses, the cavalry had to fight on foot.[2]

Another important change in the established formation was introduced at the battle of the Yarmūk, when the Byzantine army advanced in a line of squadrons. This so impressed the Arabs that at the suggestion of their commander, Khālid ibn Walīd, they proceeded immediately to dispose their own force in the same manner. Centre, right and left wings consequently were divided up into a number of squadrons (estimated at thirty-six or forty), each composed of men of the same tribe and under its own leader.[3] This is the first occasion on which the *karādīs* (singular *kardūs*) in the Muslim army are mentioned, but Ṭabarī in a later passage[4] declares that it was Marwān II, the last of the Umayyad Caliphs, who abolished the unbroken line-formation and introduced instead that consisting of a number of the compact bodies of troops known as *karādīs*.[5] This would imply that the *kardūs* was a temporary expedient at the Yarmūk and that for a time there was a reversion to the traditional practice of putting the men into line of battle consisting of an elongated and unbroken oblong. However that may be, it appears that the *kardūs* was simply a detachment or subsection of the larger divisions, for the arrangement into centre and wings was maintained, each being divided into a number of *karādīs*, as in the attack on Amorium under Mu'taṣim.[6] In that campaign there was a distance of two parasangs between the centre and the wings, and each of these divisions was itself divided into right and left wings.[7] As a general rule, however, the divisions remained in close contact and if one of them was being hard pressed, men from the others might easily be detached so as to go to its help.[8]

In early times a common preliminary to the battle, in continuance of the pre-Muslim custom, was to harangue the men and to

[1] Ṭabarī, III, 40.
[2] Ibn al-Athīr, VII, 240.
[3] Ṭabarī, I, 2091 ff.
[4] *Ibid.* II, 1941.
[5] It is upon this passage that the statement of Ibn Khaldūn, *Prolégomènes*, ed. Quatremère, II, 81, appears to be based.
[6] Cf., for example, Ṭabarī, III, 1247^{12}.
[7] *Ibid.* III, 1244.
[8] Cf. *Fragmenta Hist. Arab.*, I, 218, and Ibn al-Athīr, XII, 23 f.

rouse their martial ardour by the recital of verses reminding them of the exploits of their kinsmen. "You are poets and orators and Arab knights", said the commander at the battle of Qādisīya to his lieutenants: "Go amongst the tribes and the regiments [banners] and stir the men to war."[1]

Another frequent preliminary to the general onslaught was the fight between champions from either side. Thus at Badr, before the order came to attack, the herald of the still pagan Quraysh challenged the Muslims to send out men for single combat. Three citizens of Medina came out in reply to the challenge, but the Quraysh would have nothing to do with them, demanding men who were the equal of themselves in birth and prowess. The Prophet accordingly nominated three of his companions to go out, and they were accepted. Two of the Muslims killed their opponents outright, the third had some difficulty and his comrades rushed to his aid, so that the battle began in disorder.[2] A similar method of beginning by single combat between picked warriors of either side was practised even in foreign campaigns. In 115/733, in a summer raid against the Byzantines, a young Greek who had slain five men was finally opposed by the Muslim commander, who went forward himself and having killed the youth called on his own men to charge.[3] The most common way, perhaps, in which battles began was in engagements of outposts or advanced guards who met each other before the main bodies came up. An instance is recorded where the Seljūq forces first met those of the Ghaznawids in this fashion.[4]

Tactics in the battle naturally varied with circumstances. At Badr, the Prophet commanded his men that they were not to attack until he gave the order, though they might beat off with arrows such of the enemy as came inconveniently close.[5]

At Qādisīya the Persians were in thirteen ranks, one behind the other, while the Arabs were much inferior both in numbers and equipment. Their three ranks suffered much from the Persian arrows, against which their only defence was a barrier of palm-branches stuck upright into their baggage, the leather thongs from

1 Dīnawarī, *Akhbār al-ṭiwāl*, p. 128.
2 Ṭabarī, I, 1317 ff.
3 *Fragmenta Hist. Arab.*, I, 91.
4 Cf. Bayhaqī, *Ta'rīkh-i Mas'ūdī*, ed. Morley, p. 714.
5 Ṭabarī, I, 1318.

which they employed to bind round their heads in substitution for helmets.[1] Their own arrows were lacking both in quantity and quality and the Persian jibe at the thin Arab arrows as "spindles" has been preserved.[2] But the day was won in spite of this ill equipment. The Muslims stood firm until the order was given to charge, and then came on with their lances until they were in amongst the Persians. They then threw away the more unwieldy weapons and used their swords to good effect.[3]

When, at Ṣiffīn, 'Alī fought Mu'āwiya, he put his infantry into a single *ṣaff*, i.e., the unbroken line of the Prophet's devising, with men in armour in the front rank.[4] His instructions for the attack were that the line was to advance until the men's lances were almost at the chests of the Umayyad troops, when they were to halt for further orders.[5] In the charge, he told his men, they were to lean forward over their spears for better effect.[6] His cavalry were formed into *karādīs* and were armed with bows and swords, but once they got in amongst the enemy after their charge the bows were useless and the men took to their swords.[7]

The Umayyad line of battle, as illustrated in the conflict with Shabīb the Khārijī heretic, had the usual division into centre and wings, but the whole line was formed of three ranks, of which the first consisted of infantry armed with swords and under separate command from the rest, the second of mounted men with lances and the third of archers, presumably mounted also. The line was subdivided into regiments (*rāyāt*, literally "banners") under subordinate commanders, but it is not clear whether each *rāya* was composed of all arms or contained only men from a single arm.[8]

No variation of the traditional order of battle is reported from early Abbasid times. Yet it was not always rigidly maintained. In a battle between two Abbasid forces, those of Ma'mūn and Amīn, in Khurāsān in 195/810, their respective generals Ṭāhir and 'Alī ibn 'Īsā disposed their troops in different formations. Alī ibn Īsā had the usual prime distribution into centre and wings, but decided that his men were too few to advance in an unbroken line. He accordingly subdivided them under banners, a thousand men to each, and attacked with the wings, sending forward the

[1] Ṭabarī, I, 2353 f.
[2] *Ibid.* I, 2236; Balādhurī, *Futūḥ*, p. 260.
[3] Dīnawarī, *ibid.*
[4] Ṭabarī, I, 3290.
[5] Mas'ūdī, *Murūj al-dhahab*, IV, 374.
[6] Ṭabarī, *ibid.*
[7] Mas'ūdī, *ibid.* IV, 376.
[8] Ṭabarī, II, 950.

rāyāt one at a time at intervals of a furlong,[1] the men in armour in the van of each, with the order to the commanders that they were to attack in rotation, retire, and attack again when they were rested. 'Alī himself remained in the centre with his guards and the "notables". Ṭāhir, on the other hand, arranged his men in smaller divisions (*katā'ib* and *karādīs*), and these were unable to withstand the attack of the heavier bodies. The day would have gone against him if he had not rallied his men in an interval and launched a surprise attack on 'Alī's centre, which had remained in position and which fled before the sudden onslaught.[2]

A variation on the usual order of battle is illustrated by the formation used in 517/1123 by Dubays, the rebellious vassal of the Caliph Mustarshid, in opposing the government force sent against him. He put his whole army into one unbroken line, with centre and wings under separate commanders as usual. His infantry, however, was placed in front of his cavalry, which being thus immobilized was rendered useless, and he was defeated.[3]

The tactics of the Seljūqs was conditioned by their being nearly all mounted men. Their line of battle was in the normal centre and wings order, but it was much deeper than under the Abbasids, so that in each division there was more than one subordinate commander. In the battle between Sulṭān Mas'ūd and his uncle Sulṭān Sanjar near Dīnawar in 526/1131, Sanjar remained in the centre with the flower of his army, while on each wing the men were in charge of three subordinate commanders and thrown out in front of the centre was a line of elephants. Mas'ūd's formation was similar, although he had but two commanders on each wing.[4]

The "five" formation was used within the boundaries of the Eastern Caliphate by so great a warrior as Maḥmūd of Ghazna, but he was able to make it more effective by the use of elephants in the battle. In a letter to the Caliph al-Qādir reporting how he conquered Khurāsān and defeated the Sāmānids he says that he gave command of the right to one of his brothers. In it were ten thousand men—infantry—and thirty elephants, while on the left wing were twelve thousand cavalry and forty elephants. Maḥmūd himself was in the centre with seventy elephants and twenty

[1] Ibn al-Athīr, VI, 168, calls it a bowshot.

[2] Ṭabarī, III, 823; Ibn al-Athīr, *ibid.*

[3] Ibn al-Athīr (A.H. 517), X, 428 f. [4] *Ibid.* X, 476.

thousand cavalry, equipped with swords and lances, shields and armour.[1]

Concerning the theory of battle, the Spanish essayist, Abu Bakr Ṭurṭūshī (i.e. of Tortosa), who died in 520/1120, has something to say in his work entitled *Sirāj al-mulūk*.[2] According to him, the leader in battle must be a bold and courageous man, experienced in war and knowing the positions of the centre, right wing and left wing in battle.[3] As for the disposal of the force in battle, the author gives it as his opinion that the best order for the line is in three ranks. The first should be composed of infantry armed with good shields, long lances and sharply-pointed javelins; the (butts of the) lances to be fixed in the ground behind with the points inclined towards the enemy, while the men themselves kneel on the left knee with their shields upright in front of them. The second line should be composed of picked archers "whose arrows can pierce armour", and behind them again should come the cavalry. In the attack—it is presumed that the enemy move first—the infantry keep their position and formation, while they and the bowmen transfix the advancing enemy, the first with their javelins and the others with their arrows. When the enemy come close enough the lances are brought into use and as they scatter right and left the cavalry come forward and "obtain from them what God wills".[4]

In general the "five" formation was effective. Its danger lay in the difficulty of control if the force was large or too widely scattered, and especially so if the divisions lost sight of one another, as might happen during a dust-storm,[5] seeing that orders had to be sent by messenger or to be signalled by trumpets or flags.

It was the common practice that the signal for the attack was given by the waving of a flag or by trumpet blast or both.[6] Flags

[1] Al-Ṣābī, *Wuzarā*, p. 374.

[2] Ed. Cairo, A.H. 1289. See *infra*, p. 456.

[3] *Op. cit.* p. 299.

[4] *Op. cit.* p. 308. The author implies that he has seen in action the formation he describes.

[5] Cf. Bayhaqī, *Ta'rīkh-i Mas'ūd*, ī, p. 717 *ad fin.*

[6] Balādhurī, *Futūḥ*, p. 303. At the battle of Nihāwand Nu'mān the 'āmil said: "I noticed that when the Prophet failed to give battle in the morning he would wait until the sun set and the wind blew." He added: "I shall now shake the standard I carry three times. At the first shake let each man perform his ablutions and satisfy his natural wants; at the second let each attend to his sword (or he may have said sandal-thong) and prepare himself. When the third shake comes, charge; and let no man heed his neighbour." Cf. Ibn al-Athīr, VII, 281.

had another significance in Muslim warfare. Each tribe had its own and regarded it as the rallying centre in battle, for near it was the position of the commander.[1] An example is provided by an incident that occurred in one of the battles between the force of Saladin and Safadin (Sayf al-Dīn). The latter's general in the field had set up his standard in a low-lying part of the plain, where it was out of sight of the men engaged in the battle. At a crucial point in the fight the absence of the flag was noted and the rumour promptly spread that the commander had fled.[2]

The importance of the symbol may be gauged from the prominence given to the names of those who bore the Prophet's banner and that of the *Anṣār* at the battle of Badr,[3] also of the standard-bearers in other, later, engagements. The phrase used for sending out an expedition is "to bind on a banner",[4] and the granting of a banner was regarded as the sign of conferring command. When the Caliph Mahdī was in Khurāsān he was faced by a rebellion under the Persian chieftain Ustādhsīs. A certain Khāzim ibn Khuzayma offered to quell it, but only on condition that no flag should fly except his own or such as he had "tied on". When he received command he lowered the flags of all others of whom he disapproved.[5]

On the Abbasid military system in general some additional information is to be obtained from an important non-Muslim source, namely the *Tactica* of the Byzantine Emperor Leo VI ("The Wise"). Leo did not himself fight the Saracens and his information is not at first-hand, but he used for his work the materials provided by his father, the Emperor Basil, and by generals who had fought on the frontiers. The Byzantine emperor reigned from 886–912 and was a contemporary therefore of the Caliphs Mu'tamid, Muktafī and Muqtadir, under whom the Abbasid régime had begun its decline. But the old system was still in great part retained, having had a considerable measure of success under Mu'tamid, in particular when the royal forces in command of Muwaffaq, the Caliph's brother, operated against the Zanj rebels in southern Iraq.

[1] Cf., for example, Ṭabarī, II, 498: "You cannot dispense with an amīr to whom you may have recourse and a flag about which you may rally."

[2] Ibn al-Athīr, XI, 283.

[3] Ṭabarī, I, 1297.

[4] *Ibid.* I. 2080.

[5] *Ibid.* III, 355. A distinction is here made between *liwā*, "banner" and *'alam*, which is normally translated "standard".

The *Tactica*, amongst much else that is of interest, shows what importance the Saracens attached to speed and mobility. Their infantry were carried on horseback or rode behind the cavalrymen.[1] It was effective tactics, therefore, to attack the horses as well as the men, since it decreased their mobility, and the best defence against Saracens and Turks was an abundance of bows and arrows "for their whole hope of victory is based on arrows".[2] For transport they used camels, horses, asses and mules, and in battle they clanged cymbals and used their camels in order to terrify the horses of the enemy. The camels and all the other sumpter-beasts had a further use in battle, for they were so placed in the midst of the troops as to give the appearance of large and important forces.[3] In front of the troops was thrown out a screen of Ethiopians, whose effect upon the enemy, although they were lightly-armed and unprotected, was considerable. The knights themselves were armed with bows and arrows, two-edged swords (*spatha*), lances, shields and axes. They bore as armour helmets, breastplates, arm-pieces and greaves and had other equipment, too, like that of the Romans.[4]

In battle they never broke their formation (*acies*) either in attack or defence. If, however, it was broken, it was not easily reconstituted.[5] This formation, which they kept both on the march and when at close quarters with the enemy, was an elongated, solid oblong, which was very safe and difficult to counter in the attack.[6] They met the enemy's charges steadily and quietly, waiting till they saw he was exhausted before themselves attacking. This they did also in their naval battles.[7]

Leo, or his informants, very well understood Arab mentality. "They are bold," he says, "when hopeful of victory, but easily frightened if they are in despair of it."[8] They were always in fear of night attacks, especially in foreign territory, and took great precautions against them. Guards were on duty all night, or else the camp was carefully fortified so as not to be taken by surprise.[9]

Much of what Leo says is borne out, it will have been seen, by what can be derived from the Muslim historians themselves and his general statements can be further supplemented from them.

1 *Tactica* (in Migne, *Patrologia Graeca*, vol. 107), § 115.
2 *Ibid.* §§ 22 f.
3 *Ibid.* §§ 112 f.
4 *Ibid.* §§ 114 f.
5 *Ibid.* §§ 116 f.
6 *Ibid.* §§ 118 f.
7 *Ibid.* §§ 121 f.
8 *Ibid.* § 117.
9 *Ibid.* § 117.

Let us now turn to other aspects of Muslim military organization. It will have been gathered that in the earliest part of their career the fighting forces of Islam were as ill equipped with arms as with men. Contact with Greeks and Persians, however, taught them much. After the first stages the chief weapons of the infantry were spears or lances and swords, while the mounted men had bows and either lances or swords. Slings are sometimes mentioned but not as part of the regular equipment of the warrior.[1] For protection each man wore a helmet with a flap at the back[2] and a breastplate[3] and carried a round shield.[4] On distant expeditions also a man carried needles and thread, an awl, scissors etc. as part of his kit.[5] In battle, commanders and others of high rank wore coats of mail which proved on occasion too heavy for the wearer.[6] A fully-equipped man might wear two breastplates and a full suit of armour (*tannūr*, literally "oven").[7] In single combat the champion carried a sword and shield only[8]; and in general, desperate fights at close quarters meant that bows and arrows were discarded in favour of the sword or (?) dagger (*dabbūs*).[9] Cavalry in a charge used lances and swords.[10]

Although the invention of gunpowder is popularly ascribed to the "Arabs" there appears to be no record of the use of fire-arms by Muslims for some time after the adoption of the new weapons in the west.

Defence of its frontiers was one of the most urgent and obvious duties of the early empire of Islam. On the Byzantine borders in particular, where attacks were most commonly to be countered, a series of fortresses or strong points (*'awāṣim*) was very early raised and garrisoned either from amongst local tribes or by foreign mercenaries. Experience of Greek methods of attack and defence taught the Muslims a great deal, but knowledge of the simpler forms of defence was acquired by them even before they came into serious contact with the Greeks. The Prophet himself is said to have learnt the art of entrenchment from a Persian, Salmān al-Fārisī, and employed it in his defence of Medina

[1] Ibn al-Athīr, VII, 245.
[2] Cf. *ibid.* (A.H. 92), where the warlike equipment donned by the Muslim envoys to the emperor of China is described.
[3] Ṭabarī, I, 1315.
[4] Balādhurī, p. 318.
[5] *Ibid.*
[6] *Ibid.* p. 303.
[7] Ṭabarī, II, 2014.
[8] *Fragmenta Hist. Arab.*, I, 91.
[9] Cf. Ibn al-Athīr, X, 44 f.
[10] *Ibid.* IV, 163.

against a threatened attack from the Meccans.[1] In the field, trenches came to be in common use, sometimes for long periods.[2] Thus the Baṣra force which was sent out to combat the Zanj rebels remained entrenched for six months before being driven out.[3]

In the more strongly fortified cities the trench was dug as an additional defence in front of the walls, which were especially thickened and protected with baulks of timber to withstand missiles from siege-engines.[4] Gates and other vulnerable parts of the defences were guarded by mangonels and catapults, which are mentioned as having been used by Mustaʿīn when Baghdad was besieged by the hostile forces of Muʿtazz.[5] Both for the digging of the defence trenches and for the heavy work of undermining the walls of besieged cities and fortresses, special bodies of labourers were taken with the army, although when they were not available the troops themselves were compelled to undertake tasks of this kind.[6]

For the attack on fortresses and strongly defended points in general, the early Muslim expeditionary forces carried with them engines of war such as mangonels and catapults, the use of which—to judge at least from the name of the mangonel in Arabic—was acquired from the Greeks.[7] As early as A.H. 13 they were in use at the siege of Damascus, seemingly, however, without any great effect, for the city was finally entered by men who swam the moat on inflated skins, flung on to the turrets ropes with running nooses and so climbed the walls and opened the gates.[8]

[1] Ṭabarī, I, 1465. Cf. *ibid.* III, 228.

[2] *Ibid.* III, 355. The art of using concealed pits as defence against cavalry was well known. (Cf. Ibn al-Athīr, VII, 236.)

[3] Ibn al-Athīr (A.H. 256), VII, 163.

[4] Cf. for use of cypress-wood by the Greeks at Kamachon, Balādhurī, p. 184.

[5] Ibn al-Athīr, VII, 94 f.

[6] Ṭabarī, III, 1199; Ibn al-Athīr, A.H. 267.

[7] The Arabic *manjanīq* or *manganīq* would appear to be derived from the Greek *manganikon*, but it is not impossible that the original of the Muslim machine was the *monankon*, a "one-arm" catapult less elaborate than the ordinary torsion catapult, which had two arms moved by twisted ropes or hair. (See further J. Kromayer and G. Veith, *Heerwesen und Kriegsführung der Griechen und Römer* (Berlin, 1928), especially plates 16 ff., and W. W. Tarn, *Hellenistic Military and Naval Developments* (Cambridge, 1930), pp. 12 ff.) I am indebted to Mr Richard Barnett of the British Museum for this reference.

[8] Ṭabarī, I, 2152.

The Umayyads and Abbasids used siege engines as far afield as India and eastern Persia. At the siege of Daybul, in Sind, Muhammad ibn Qāsim had a mangonel set up which he called *al-'Arūs* ("the Bride") and which was manned by no less than five hundred people.[1] As a rule these engines threw stones[2], but some also threw fire and naphtha,[3] the latter of which was carried as part of the stores of war.[4] At the siege of Heraclea, Hārūn al-Rashīd, who was in command, had sulphur and white naphtha placed with the stones. The whole was wrapped round with tow and set into the holder, where it was set ablaze and shot against the walls, to which it clung, so that they split with the heat.[5] A special body of troops, known as *naffāṭūn* ("naphtha men") was employed to prepare and use the naphtha,[6] and also to deal with it when it was used against the Muslims. On one of Hārūn's campaigns in Asia Minor he found his way barred by the Emperor Nicephorus who had had trees cut down across the road and set on fire. The *naffāṭūn*, who wore special fire-proof garments, plunged in amongst the burning timber and made a way for the army.[7]

At the siege of Amorium the mangonels used were "as wide as four men" and were moved about by being placed on wheeled platforms. These might be used close up against the walls, the intervening moat being filled with sheepskins (taken from the flocks brought for food) stuffed with earth. Where it was not possible to fill in a moat a smaller engine known as an *'arrāda* was brought into use. It could be loaded on to a barge or boat and moved to any suitable place along the wall.[8]

For the shooting of arrows in quantity or for shooting larger and heavier arrows than could be managed by the archers, the Muslim troops under Saladin at the siege of Sihyūn used a machine known as a *ziyār*, which was composed of a number of crossbows, three being the number mentioned in one instance.[9] According to Ibn-al-Athīr a hail of arrows was kept up against the fortress by means of hand-bows, "wheels" (i.e. crossbows),

[1] Balādhurī, p. 437. Cf. *ibid.* p. 390.
[2] *Ibid.* p. 184.
[3] Ibn al-Athīr, VII, 98.
[4] *Fragmenta Hist. Arab.*, I, 24 f.
[5] *Aghānī*, XVII, 82. Cf. Ṭabarī, III, 79, and the vocabulary of the de Goeje edition s.v. *mushāqa*.
[6] Ṭabarī, III, 1511. Cf. Ibn al-Athīr, VII, 270.
[7] *Aghānī*, XVII, 45.
[8] Ibn al-Athīr, VII, 98.
[9] Quatremère, *Histoire des Mongoles de la Perse*, p. 286.

zambūraks (literally "little bees", probably for firing large arrows and so called from the humming of the thick bowstring[1]) and these *ziyārs*.[2]

Another engine of war which was designed for direct attack on city walls was the *dubbāba*. It was a movable tower built in several stages or stories, on each of which were stationed a number of men able to make their onslaught simultaneously at different levels. Those below were armed with picks and drills while the others used bows and arrows both to protect their own men and to inflict damage on the defenders on the walls. One such *dubbāba* is mentioned as having been in use at the siege of Kamachon in 149/766[3] and Mu'taṣim, at the siege of Amorium had a number of them to hold ten men each. The main difficulty in employing them was that as they were extremely cumbersome they were liable to become immovably imbedded amongst the sheepskins stuffed with earth which were used for filling in moats and across which they had to be dragged. Particularly if the defenders kept up a fire of arrows and stones, as the Greeks did at Amorium, the men in any *dubbāba* which was thus brought to a standstill in the ditch, could be rescued only with great difficulty.[4]

At the siege of Kerak in 580/1184, after Saladin had captured the outer works he found a deep trench separating him from the citadel. His attempts to fill it being for a long time hampered by a heavy fire of arrows and flaming naphtha from the defenders, he was compelled to find some method of protecting his men at work and ordered the erection of a penthouse of beams and bricks under cover of which his men were enabled to proceed with their task.[5]

When there was no moat or when it was possible to attack a defensive wall directly, tunnelling was resorted to and a specially trained body of men known as *naqqābūn* ("piercers") who used picks and drills[6] was brought into action. They were protected while at work by a barrage of arrows from the bowmen in their

[1] In modern times the same name was given in Persia to a small cannon.

[2] Ibn al-Athīr, XII, 5 f.

[3] Balādhurī, *Futūḥ*, p. 184.

[4] Ṭabarī, III, 1248. Cf. Quatremère, *ibid.* p. 284 b, and Dozy, s.v. *dubbāba*. See also M. Amari, *Biblioteca Arabo-Sicula*, second Appendix (Leipzig, 1887), p. 22.

[5] Ibn al-Athīr, XI, 333 f.

[6] Cf. *ibid.* X, 25.

rear.[1] Sometimes also a *kabsh*, or ram, was employed. Where the wall was too strong to be pierced, scaling ladders were brought into use.[2]

Another way of storming a strong point was by keeping up an unremitting onslaught and giving the defenders no rest. This was Saladin's method at the siege of Barzīya (584/1188), when he divided his force into three sections, each of which attacked in turn and without any interval until the Frankish defenders were compelled to surrender. The method was especially effective in this case because the Franks sallied out at the first attack and were greeted by a destructive hail of arrows from the men kept unexpectedly in reserve.[3]

A properly equipped force carried all the requisite engines of war with it. In the war against the Zanj rebels, who inhabited the marsh lands of southern Iraq, the army of Muwaffaq brought not only mangonels and catapults with it, but must also have carried much of the ammunition, for stones are unobtainable locally in that region of Iraq.[4] They also carried naphtha and requisite tools such as axes,[5] and further took with them the necessary craft for transporting men across rivers and up the narrow channels which are the only approaches to the numerous villages of the marsh. Long canoes of shallow draft, made of local reeds pitched over with bitumen, probably formed the major part of these craft, but there were also larger boats equipped with rudders and yet with sufficiently low freeboard to be concealed among the reeds.[6] For the handling and navigation of these vessels, boatmen were employed, as distinct from the ordinary fighting force.[7] In the chief attack on the city of the Zanj leader, al-Khabīth, there were as many as ten thousand of these watermen drawing pay, in addition to the crews of the transports which carried men and supplies.[8]

When they are desirous of emphasizing the importance of any particular campaign, the Muslim historians stress the fact of the army's being particularly well provisioned. Thus we are told that for the Zanj campaign, Muwaffaq, who was in command, had

[1] Ibn al-Athīr (A.H. 268), VII, 254; XI, 285, etc.
[2] *Ibid.* (A.H. 462), X, 25, and (A.H. 567).
[3] *Ibid.* (A.H. 584), XII, 8.
[4] *Ibid.* VII, 244.
[5] *Ibid.* VII, 270.
[6] *Ibid.* (A.H. 266, 267), VII, 234 ff, 274.
[7] *Ibid.* VII, 244 (?).
[8] *Ibid.* VII, 274.

arranged with the Baṣra merchants to supply him with stores in large quantities which were kept in a depot (the town of Muwaffaqīya) specially built for the purposes of this long war against the Zanj, who had proved themselves a determined foe.[1] Another occasion on which the army was well supplied was for the invasion of Asia Minor by Muʿtaṣim in 244/838. The army is said by Michael Syrus to have had with it thirty thousand "merchants and providers" as well as thousands of camels and mules.[2]

Ibn al-Athīr reports further how in the reign of Mutawakkil a Sudanese tribe kept up a series of attacks on the workers of a Muslim-owned mine which was situated in their territory and paid a royalty of about one-fifth of the proceeds to the Egyptian treasury. As the attacks persisted, work and the consequent payments ceased, and complaint being made to the Caliph, he took counsel on the matter and was told that access to the territory of the culprits was difficult since it lay across desert country, and that any force which was sent against them would have to be sufficiently well supplied to make the journey outwards and back again on its own resources. The Caliph's ʿāmil in charge of military operations in Egypt was thereupon told to bring up his force to full strength and to dispatch it equipped with all that would be required. The commander of the expedition marched towards a point on the Red Sea where seven ships laden with meal, olives, dates, barley and fine flour had been ordered to be in waiting for him and supply him with necessaries as they were required. In the meantime the chief of the Sudanese tribe, not knowing of the ships, evaded direct attack and planned to wipe out the Muslims, as he had destroyed other forces, when their food and drink were exhausted. But on this occasion his plan miscarried, for he was forced to give battle to an enemy well supplied and capable of defeating him.[3]

The historians do not in general concern themselves with mentioning the important question of supplies, and these reported instances would appear to be exceptional. The fact is that as a rule the Muslim forces lived, or hoped to live, on the country they invaded, sometimes with disastrous consequences for themselves,

[1] Ibn al-Athīr, VII, 246.
[2] J. B. Bury, *Eastern Roman Empire*, p. 263 n. 3.
[3] Ibn al-Athīr, VII, 50 ff.

as in the unsuccessful attempts, made during the Umayyad period (in 673 and 718) to take Constantinople, and in the early Abbasid period (under Hārūn al-Rashīd in 806 and under Mu'taṣim in 838) to gain a permanent footing beyond the Taurus.

It remains now to deal with the army on the march and in camp. The early campaigns, it must be remembered, were not mere raiding forays but were in part "colonizing" expeditions so that the warriors were accompanied by their families when they set out for Persia, Syria and Egypt. In Umayyad times and earlier[1] the commanders had taken their wives with them on ordinary plundering raids and even where serious fighting was in contemplation,[2] but for the more distant expeditions the transport of the men's families was encouraged as part of a definite policy of colonization. For this reason the drafts sent by Ḥajjāj from Baṣra and Kūfa went with their women and children to Khurāsān[3] and similarly when Qutayba marched on Kāshghar, those of the troops who had families were accompanied by them so that they could be settled at Samarqand and other places on the way. Once the army had crossed the Oxus, guards were stationed at the fords to prevent anyone returning without leave.[4]

Generally the women and children were carried in litters[5] accompanying the *sāqa* or rear-guard following in the wake of the main force. The value of their presence is variously estimated both as an encouragement to the men in battle and as a drawback, but the former appears to be more generally to have been true, for on occasion the women could give a good account of themselves, as they did at the battles of the Yarmūk and elsewhere,[6] and also at the siege of Bukhārā in 90/709, when a body sallying out from the beleagured city broke right through the rear of the besiegers.[7] When a forced march was necessary, either to take the enemy by surprise or for some other reason, the impedimenta and presumably with them the women and children, were left behind under guard. This happened in the first raid on Samarqand when Qutayba advanced with the cavalry and archers only.[8]

On the march the "five" formation was kept, with the advanced

[1] Cf. Wensinck, *The Muslim Creed* (Cambridge, 1932), p. 42.

[2] Cf. Ṭabarī, I, 2888 f. and *Aghānī*, XVI, 33.

[3] Ibn al-Athīr (A.H. 80 and 83).

[4] *Ibid.* (A.H. 96), V, 2.

[5] Cf. Balādhurī, p. 167.

[6] Ṭabarī, I, 2100 and 2347.

[7] *Ibid.* II, 1201.

[8] Ibn al-Athīr (A.H. 93).

guard going ahead and with the centre and right and left wings forming the main body. The *sāqa*, as indicated, brought up the rear and usually contained the baggage, siege engines, heavy equipment and supplies.[1] Normally also, as has been shown, the women and children accompanied it, as well as the slow-moving flocks and herds intended for supplies. But this was the case apparently only in earlier times, for in the Crusading era it appears to have been the practice to send the animals and impedimenta ahead under a light guard, which on occasion proved insufficient to prevent their capture by the enemy.[2]

The column marched to the beating of drums. When that ceased the column halted wherever it happened to be.[3]

Camp sites in war were carefully chosen by an official especially appointed for the purpose.[4] As a rule, when a halt of any length was proposed, camps were surrounded by a trench for defensive purposes,[5] and as additional protection in enemy territory the warriors stood to arms in their proper formation.[6] When for any reason the digging of a trench was omitted, still further precautions were taken to ensure safety. On the march against Bābak, the rebellious Khurramī heretic, Afshīn, the commander of the Caliph's army, by his orders placed the main body in the midst of a ring of calthrops[7] when he encamped, while a mounted patrol kept circling, night and day, about the camp at a distance of a league.[8] Within the camp shelter was provided, at any rate for senior officers, by large tents in which they ate their meals and slept, interviewed prisoners and performed other duties.[9]

In peacetime troops of a garrison were billeted on the townspeople where possible. Frequently, the exactions and misbehaviour of the soldiery led to local unrest, and where that occurred separate camps had to be set up. This was the case when Ḥajjāj ibn Yūsuf billeted his Syrian troops on the Kūfans, whose protest led to the evacuation of the army and the building of the garrison city of Wāsiṭ;[10] and also much later, when the Seljūqs at Baghdad

[1] Ṭabarī, III, 1238, *Fragmenta Hist. Arab.*, II, 485 f.
[2] Cf. Ibn al-Athīr (A.H. 517), X, 428 f.
[3] Ṭabarī, III, 1203.
[4] Cf. Ibn al-Athīr, IV, 162 f.
[5] See above, p. 438.
[6] Ṭabarī, III, 355, 1202.
[7] The text (Ṭabarī, III, 1197) has *fī-'l-ḥasak*.
[8] *Loc. cit.* Cf. *ibid.* III, 1200.
[9] *Ibid.* III, 1350.
[10] Ibn al-Athīr (A.H. 83).

quartered themselves on the citizens, to their great disturbance,[1] although in other places the army had camps of their own.[2] In the frontier city of Malaṭya (Melitene) the Caliph Manṣūr quartered four thousand men, who were divided into *'irāfas* ("squads") of from ten to fifteen men each. For each *'irāfa* there was built a two-storied house with a stable, and provision was made locally for their keep.[3]

We have dealt so far in the main with the army of the Eastern Caliphate at Baghdad. Something must also be said concerning the Muslim armies which existed outside it and, in particular, concerning the important military organizations of the Fāṭimids, Ayyūbids (especially under Saladin), Mamlūks and Turks, all of which had characteristics in common.

The Fāṭimid forces took their rise in North Africa when 'Abd-allāh, the chief propagandist of the 'Alid claims, gathered an army of forty thousand men, "leaving no brave man in Ifrīqiya whom he did not attach to his armies".[4]

The numbers increased rapidly during the dynasty's period of power in Egypt and Syria. According to the Persian traveller Nāṣir-i Khusraw, who visited Egypt in 1047, there was a large and well disciplined army in Cairo at the time. In his *Safar-nāma* he describes the army as it stood in parade order on the occasion of the ceremony of the opening of the Nile sluices.[5] The whole army was present, he says, mounted or afoot, regiment after regiment, each with a name and title. The cavalry regiments comprised twenty thousand men from Qayrawān in North Africa, fifteen thousand Bāṭilīs from north-west Africa and thirty thousand mixed mercenaries, negroes and others. Of infantry there were twenty thousand black Maṣmūdīs, also from North Africa, men of good stature but of hideous appearance, who fought with sword and spear and could use no other weapon;[6] there were also ten thousand men known as "orientals", men born in Egypt but of Persian or Turkish origin. There was further a regiment known as the "Bought Slaves", who, as their title shows, were acquired in the market-place. They are set down as being thirty thousand

1 Ibn al-Athīr, (A.H. 446), IX, 430 f.
2 *Ibid*. IX, 432.
3 Balādhurī, pp. 187 f.
4 Ibn al-Athīr (A.H. 296), VIII, 30.
5 Ed. and tr. Charles Schefer (Paris, 1881), pp. 45 f.
6 *Ibid*. p. 42.

strong. A large body was that of the Bedouins, fifty thousand men of the Ḥijāz who fought with the spear. Moreover there was, under separate command, a large palace guard of infantry, said to number ten thousand men, drawn from numerous different countries and arranged in detachments by nationalities, each man fighting with the weapons to which he was accustomed in his own land. Lastly, there were thirty thousand *Zanj*, or Ethiopians, men who fought with the sword. The numbers given total two hundred and fifteen thousand, a figure which was at times increased or diminished. Yet even towards the end of the sovereignty of the Fāṭimids their army still numbered forty thousand horsemen and thirty thousand foot, nearly all negro slaves.[1]

The scheme of military organization adopted by the Fāṭimids was an elaborate one, although it may be doubted whether in practice it was as efficient as the ideal intended. The Caliph settled matters of policy with the help of his viziers and paid his troops, through the agency of the *Dīwān al-Jaysh*,[2] with money derived from the taxation of lands rented out to various classes of the community and from the crops raised, one-third of the total sum accruing being devoted to military purposes. The pernicious system of granting fiefs to the soldiery was not yet in force.[3]

The vizier had charge of the dīwān and military affairs generally unless he was a "Man of the Pen", and under him and in immediate command of the army was the *isfāh-sālār*. The ranks below him were the amīrs in order, namely, the gold-chain amīrs, the sword-bearers and the regimental officers. Of the regiments there was a great number, each called after a Caliph or vizier, but sometimes also after the nationality of the men composing it: e.g. Ḥāfiẓīya (after a vizier named Ḥāfiẓ), Rūmīya (Greeks), Saqāliba (Slavs) etc.

The Fāṭimid régime was finally displaced by that of Saladin and the Ayyūbids. His army, even at its best, did not, in spite of the admiring comments of the historians, surpass that of his predecessors in numbers, though in efficiency it was far higher. It is recorded under the events of the year 567/1171 (Muḥarram), that after a proclamation from him ordering a general mobilization of

[1] Maqrīzī, *Khiṭaṭ*, I, 86, 94. [2] See above, p. 422.
[3] See Maqrīzī (*Khiṭaṭ*, I, 86), who quotes Ibn Mammātī.

the forces owing him allegiance, multitudes came "such that no king of Islam had ever mustered the like of them". Actually 147 *ṭulbs* came, the *ṭulb* in the Ghuzz (Turkish) language representing a chieftain entitled to a banner and a trumpet salute, together with his own company of mounted men, numbering between seventy and two hundred. This was not the total number of *ṭulbs* available, for twenty were absent, and the *ṭulbs* present were not at full strength, seeing that the estimated number of troopers mustered at the date mentioned was only fourteen thousand.[1] Most of these were paid free-men, known as *ṭawāshīya*, the *ṭawāshī* being a knight in receipt of an allowance, normally of between seven hundred and one thousand *dīnārs*, although it might be as low as one hundred and twenty, out of which sum he had to provide ten baggage-animals for common use and also a slave to carry his own arms and equipment.[2] The whole force was supplemented by a number of black slaves and presumably by volunteers.

At his accession to power, Saladin had abolished the army of negro slaves, officered by Egyptians, Arabs and Armenians, which the Fāṭimids had maintained in Egypt, and had substituted a special force of Kurds and Turks, who numbered no more than twelve thousand horsemen.[3] The reason for this step appears to have been one of finance. In the year 577/1181 Saladin was forced to investigate the question of military fiefs and determined upon a strength of about nine thousand troopers, one hundred and eleven amīrs, about seven thousand *ṭawāshīya* and fifteen hundred or so negro slaves (*qarāghulāmīya*).[4] Six years later, at the siege of Tiberias, his army numbered twelve thousand knights in receipt of allowances.[5] But he had further a number of volunteers, and in case of need he could always summon supporters to do voluntary service. Against the Crusaders he had the help of fellow-Muslims in Mosul and Mesopotamia generally, as well as in Egypt and Syria.[6] Even he, however, could not entirely control their movements. When, after the fall of Jerusalem, the Muslim force was held in check before Tyre, a portion of the volunteer army, represented by the richer and more powerful chiefs, were for

[1] Maqrīzī, *Khiṭaṭ*, I, 86.
[2] Cf. Quatremère, *Mamlouks*, I, i, 253.
[3] Maqrīzī, *Khiṭaṭ*, I, 94.
[4] *Ibid.* I, 86.
[5] Ibn al-Athīr (A.H. 583), XI, 350 f.
[6] *Ibid.* XI, 349 ff.

departing home. The ostensible reason was that the siege was likely to prove abortive, but actually many of them, knowing that Saladin's field coffers were empty, were afraid that he might force loans from them in order to carry on the campaign. In the end the general was compelled to abandon the siege and permit his troops to return to their homes for the winter on condition that they returned in the spring. The men "from the East and Mosul", as also those of Syria and Egypt, therefore departed, leaving him at Acre with no more than his personal following.[1]

Something has already been said of Saladin's battle and siege tactics. For his order of battle he retained the "five" formation, but he varied it by employing a picked force of archers for the vanguard (the *jālishīya*)[2] instead of keeping all the best troops for the centre. It was upon these archers that the commander relied for his opening assaults, the wings and centre playing their part at the appropriate situation in the battle. The *sāqa* as usual was present in the rear.

With the death of Saladin his army dispersed, although his son al-Malik al-'Azīz could still command the services of over eight thousand knights, each of whom had a more or less considerable following, making a total which Maqrīzī, doubtless with some exaggeration, puts at two hundred thousand.[3]

When power passed from the Abbasids to their Turkish mamlūks ("slaves") who turned themselves into sulṭāns, there came into being a national military system which has perhaps been equalled only in Europe in modern times. It was unique in Islam, although their kinsmen, the Ottoman Turks, created one that approached it when they founded their corps of Janissaries. Like Saladin, the Mamlūks limited their recruiting to Turks and a comparatively small number of Kurds. It is said that the number of Turkish slaves in Manṣūr Qalā'ūn's retinue was between seven and twelve thousand, a number which afterwards increased until the army in the days of al-Nāṣir Muḥammad ibn Qalā'ūn comprised twenty-four thousand knights.[4]

When the Qalā'ūnids fell from power in 784/1382, the new sulṭān, al-Malik al-Ẓāhir Barqūq, disbanded the so-called

[1] Ibn al-Athīr, (A.H. 583), XI, 368.

[2] *Ibid.* XI, 350 f. For the *jālishīya* cf. Quatremère, *Mamlouks*, I, pp. 225, n. 1; 226 f.

[3] Maqrīzī, *Khiṭaṭ*, I, 94.

[4] *Ibid.* I, 94.

Ashrafī (Turkish and Kurd) army of his predecessors and formed a new bodyguard for himself consisting of Circassian slaves either bought or enlisted, and numbering in all about four thousand men. These, too, were the nucleus of a force which rapidly increased its numbers.

The system followed was similar under both parts of the Mamlūk régime. The army was divided into three classes; the first enlisted soldiers (*mustakhdimūn*), the second *mamlūks* or slaves proper, both of which classes received fixed pay and allowances from the sulṭān, and a third class to which the other two might not belong. This was the company of the feudatories, the so-called "company-soldiers"[1] who received lands in return for their services.[2] Each member of this privileged class received a separate fief, of which the annual value might be as high as thirty thousand *dirhams* and as low as ten thousand, and was granted in addition an allowance for maintenance which might amount to five thousand *dirhams* where the calls on any particular fief were heavy. Thus the leader of a company might go out to battle at the head of ten men who ate at his table, while their slaves, who formed the rank and file of the troopers, were also supplied from his kitchen. The numbers varied, but it was for their maintenance that the chief part of his allowance was expended.

At the time (A.D. 1296), when the Mamlūk Sulṭān Manṣūr Lājīn succeeded to the throne, the territory of Egypt was divided into twenty-four parts, of which four formed the private estate of the sulṭān, ten belonged to the "company-soldiers" and ten to the amīrs or officers in high command. The latter, however, had seized the best lands, with the result that the subordinate soldiers were reduced to poverty and brigandage. Lājīn brought about a reform which consisted in redistributing the available lands so that eleven out of the twenty-four parts went to the amīrs and other officers of high rank, and nine to the rest of the army. But this led to unrest amongst the amīrs, and in spite of changes in subsequent reigns the system was never established to the satisfaction of all those whose living depended on it.[3]

The troops as a whole were divided into four grades, of which

[1] *Ajnād al-ḥalqa* (lit. "soldiers of the ring").

[2] See Quatremère, *Mamlouks*, I, i, 161, and Maqrīzī, *ibid.*

[3] Maqrīzī, *Khiṭaṭ*, I, 94.

the chiefs were known as "chiefs of thousands".[1] They had command of at least one hundred troopers or were in charge of detachments of craftsmen. Their number after the time of al-Nāṣir Muḥammad ibn Qalā'ūn was restricted to twenty-four for the whole of Egypt. Next to them came the "drum-commanders",[2] unlimited in number and each in command of forty troopers. In this group were reckoned the lesser departmental heads, revenue officers and other officials. They were followed by the "commanders of tens"[3] and the "commanders of five" who were no more than upper-grade troopers.[4]

Maqrīzī describes the training of the young *mamlūk* recruit. As soon as he was brought as a child by the slave-dealer he was placed before the sulṭān for his approval and then consigned to his proper class. The first part of his course was undergone in the school, where he was taught his letters and the reading of the Koran, as well as being instructed in the duties of religion and the ritual of prayer. On reaching puberty the more strictly military part of his training began. This consisted of horsemanship, archery, manipulation of the lance and throwing of the javelin. Those who showed ability were advanced grade by grade until they became military amīrs. Others whose talents lay in other directions might become legists, poets or accountants, but all were submitted to the strictest military discipline and might be called upon for military duties.[5]

Closely modelled upon the system devised by the Mamlūks was that of the Janissaries (*Yenī Cherī*) "the New Corps" of the Ottoman army whose foundation is ascribed to Sulṭān Murād I in 763/1361.[6] They formed at first only a small force selected from amongst the '*ajam oghlu* ("sons of foreigners"), who were levied from the sulṭān's Christian subjects in Thrace. The training of those taken for Janissaries resembled in essentials that of the *mamlūks* and was carefully supervised.[7] Those who showed no particular military ability were left to become army tradesmen.

[1] Tukish *bīn-bāshī*.

[2] *Umarā al-ṭabal-khāna*.

[3] Turkish *ōn-bāshī*.

[4] Qalqashandī, *Ṣubḥ al-a'shā*, IV, 14 ff.

[5] Maqrīzī, *Khiṭaṭ*, II, 213.

[6] Thus von Hammer (*Staatsverfassung*, II, 192), who does not give the authority for his statement. D'Ohsson, *Tableau général* (VII, 308), says the corps was founded by Orkhān in 1330.

[7] F. Babinger, *Hans Dernschwam's Tagebuch einer Reise nach Konstantinopel* (Munich, 1923), p. 60.

The better men were promoted by slow and regular stages, and picked ones could reach high rank, for it was from amongst them and their kind that the reigning sovereign took his chief ministers. The rank and file were infantry. They were divided into regiments and companies which varied in size and numbers according to the totals of men recruited. Under the old recruiting law (the *devshirme*) of Murād I (by which Christian boys alone were taken for the corps of Janissaries although the rest of the army was reserved for Muslims), the numbers remained comparatively small, so that under Sulaymān I (Qānūnī) there were not more than twelve thousand Janissaries. Under Murād III the numbers had reached forty-five thousand men, who, however, being never regularly paid, had become a hotbed of intrigues and agitations and were closely linked with the Bektashī dervishes.[1] They were finally disbanded, many being treacherously slaughtered by Sulṭān Maḥmūd II in 1241/1826.[2]

In addition to the military arm, a navy has at one time or another in the history of Islam played an important part in the machinery of attack and defence employed by the Caliphate or its successors. The desert Arabs who made up the earliest Muslim forces, being unfamiliar with the sea, feared and detested it, and pious legend makes Omar refuse to entrust any Muslim lives to its terrors when he was urged by Mu'āwiya to attack the Byzantines from the sea.[3] That competent warrior was later able to persuade the Caliph 'Uthmān to permit a sea-raid, although even he stipulated that no man was to be compelled to go to sea against his will, but that all who took part should be volunteers.[4] Mu'āwiya is said to have been the first to attack the enemy by sea and to have made fifty summer and winter raids, the objectives of which are not

[1] See Barbier de Meynard, *Considérations sur l'Histoire ottomane* (Paris, 1886), p. 61.

[2] Cf. Khiḍr Ilyās Efendī, *Ta'rīkh-i Andarūn* (A history of the imperial household during the reign of Maḥmūd II) (Stambūl, A.H. 1276), pp. 367–71. For further details concerning the Janissaries, see the works just quoted and Eugenio Alberi, *Relazioni degli Ambasciatori Veneti al Senato*, 15 vols. (Florence, 1839–63), especially III, 3, 263 ff.; A. H. Lybyer, *The Government of the Ottoman Empire in the Time of Suleiman the Magnificent* (Cambridge, Mass., 1913); H. A. Gibbons, *The Foundation of the Ottoman Empire* (Oxford, 1916); J. K. Birge, *The Bekteashi Order of Dervishes* (London, 1937).

[3] Cf. Ṭabarī, I, 2820 ff.

[4] *Ibid.* I, 2824. (Cf. Ibn Khaldūn, *Prolégomènes*, ed. Quatremère, II, 33.)

specified,[1] though Cyprus is mentioned as having been one of the earliest of them. That raid was made from the Syrian coast in 28/643, in which year also an attack was launched against the island from Egypt.[2] Then, as later, the ships' crews, including rowers, helmsmen etc., were distinct from the actual warriors,[3] being Greeks or Copts, while the latter were Muslims, either true Arabs or *mawālī*. From the Greek and Arabic papyri of about 710–11 (discovered in Egypt and dealing with that country as an Umayyad province), it is clear that the annual raids against the Bzyantines were carried out by sea as well as land, the naval raids being designated by the names of the places from which the fleets set out, e.g. Egypt, Anatolia, Africa or "from the sea". The crews were raised by conscription in the same way as the armies were in the various territories subjugated by the Muslims, being drawn from the classes of the community which supplied the ordinary crafts and trades; and they, like the impressed soldiers, received pay and an allowance of food.[4]

In 34/654–5[5] a large fleet, said to have numbered over two hundred ships, was sent by Mu'āwiya to attack the Byzantines, who had over five hundred ships, and gained a decisive victory.[6] An eye-witness's report of the encounter is that the wind at first was against the Muslims, who anchored for a time not far from the shore, with the enemy fleet close by. The wind then dropped and the Muslims appear to have given the Byzantines the alternative of fighting out the battle either on land or sea. Eventually the fleets engaged on the sea, ship grappling with ship and the men fighting at close quarters with daggers.[7] The sailors, who were Copts,[8] as distinct from the Muslim warriors, appear to have taken no part in the actual struggle.

In A.D. 717, on the occasion of the combined attack by the Umayyad land and sea forces on Constantinople, the Muslim

[1] Tabarī I, 2824. (Cf. Ibn Khaldūn: *Prolégomènes*, ed. Quatremère II, 33).

[2] Ṭabarī, I, 2826.

[3] Cf. Ibn al-Athīr, VII, 244, 274.

[4] Cf. *Greek Papyri in the British Museum*, IV (*Aphrodito Papyri*, ed. H. I. Bell), xxxii ff.

[5] Some historians place the event in A.H. 31. Cf. Ṭabarī, I, 2865.

[6] From the large number of vessels engaged the battle was called "the Raid of the Masts". It may be that the Muslim historians confuse this battle with one in which the Byzantine fleet was wrecked by a great storm. See L. Caetani, *Annali dell 'Islam*, VIII (Milan, 1918), 92 ff.

[7] Ṭabarī, I, 2868; Maqrīzī, *Khiṭaṭ*, I, 169.

[8] Ṭabarī, I, 2870.

navy, which, according to the Greek historians numbered eighteen hundred vessels, was utterly routed by the Byzantines. The Muslim annalists do not report the full extent of the disaster which overtook this expedition, and the details have to be culled from the records of their enemies.[1]

Although there were some vessels in the service of the Caliphs of Baghdad,[2] the raids upon the various Mediterranean cities and the capture of the larger islands were in general directed from North Africa and Spain. But Egypt also maintained a fleet under the Fāṭimids, and warships were built at Cairo, Alexandria and Damietta.[3] The Byzantine emperor Leo speaks[4] of the large and heavy *cumbaria*, slow-moving because of their weight, which the Saracens used to good effect at close quarters. At one time there were five thousand sea-captains employed under command of ten admirals, of whom one was in supreme command. These higher commanders had fiefs allotted to them in like fashion with the generals of the army.

With the decline in the fortunes of the Fāṭimid dynasty their navy fell into decay, although there were still some vessels of war left at the very end.[5]

The Egyptian fleet was revived under Saladin, who created a special dīwān for it and allotted special sources of revenue for its maintenance. In 569/1173, on the occasion of the Sicilian attack on Alexandria, the harbour is said to have been crowded with war-craft and merchant vessels.[6] On Saladin's death decline once more set in; interest in the fleet disappeared, and men had to be pressed into its service. They were seized in the streets, those who could not free themselves by bribery or other means being chained to their posts during the day and kept in prison at night. As a result of the degeneracy and corruption that prevailed in consequence of this method of recruiting, the word *uṣṭūlī* ("naval man") became a term of abuse.[7]

It was in Spain that the greatest interest was taken in naval matters. Muhammad I in 266/879–90 had ships built on "the

[1] Tabarī, II, 1314 ff. and cf. J. B. Bury, *A History of the Later Roman Empire* (London, 1889), II, 401–3.

[2] Cf. Ibn al-Athīr, VII, 98.

[3] See Maqrīzī, *Khiṭaṭ*, II, 193 f.

[4] *Tactica*, XIX, 67.

[5] Maqrīzī, *ibid.* I, 94 *ad fin.*

[6] Amari, *Biblioteca Arabo-Sicula*, second Appendix (Leipzig, 1887), p. 21.

[7] Maqrīzī, *Khiṭaṭ*, II, 194.

river of Cordova" (i.e. the Guadalquivir) for use in the Atlantic against the refractory province of Galicia, which was more vulnerable from that side. But his sailors were unaccustomed to the open sea, and in this expedition the ships separated as soon as they emerged into the Atlantic, and only a few ever returned.[1] Within the Mediterranean, however, the Moorish fleets assisted for centuries in preserving most of the islands and much of the coast-lands as Muslim territory and provided the nautical vocabularies of Europe with numerous Arabic words.

When the Moors had been driven out of Spain, the Turks and the Barbary corsairs remained to carry on the Muslim nautical tradition in the Mediterranean.[2] They dominated the inland sea for over three centuries, until well into the nineteenth century, being only subjugated when the French empire in North Africa came into being.[3]

To the record provided of the practical details of the Muslim system of attack and defence must be added, for its comprehension as a whole, some account of the Muslim theory of war and military organization. In large measure it was derived, like much of the practical side, from the experience gained against the Persians and Byzantines, but it was elaborated in ways peculiar to the Muhammadan mind, under the joint influence of the precepts of Islam and the reported sayings and doings of the Prophet. The great Muslim philosopher, Ibn Khaldūn, states the facts clearly in his treatment of the subject of war and military organization.[4] His view of the art of war, namely, that it means the way to fight battles successfully, is in essence correct, although lacking in all particularity. Under the Caliphate, he says, there were two methods of doing battle; the first being the Persian way of attacking in line, and the second, that of the Bedouin Arabs and of the Berbers, which consisted of raids by unorganized groups, their speedy retreat and sudden return. He claims that the method of advancing in line and organized formation is more certain of victory and

[1] Ibn al-Athīr, VII, 232.

[2] See Ibn Khaldūn, *Prolégomènes*, ed. Quatremère, II, 34 ff, where some facts are to be gained, although the confused generalities of the chapter are not characteristic of the author's usual precision.

[3] See further, S. Lane-Poole, *The Barbary Corsairs* (London, 1890).

[4] *Prolégomènes*, ed. Quatremère, II, 65 ff.

more formidable than the other, for the reason that the lines of the attackers are well ordered and regular, in the same way that arrows are arranged or the ranks of the Muslims in prayer. Being thus properly marshalled the troops stand more steadily in the battle and are to the enemy as impregnable as a continuous wall or a strongly constructed fort. And this opinion is confirmed by the verse of the Koran (64) already quoted above.

Although the pagan Arabs knew only the raiding (*karr u farr*) method of attack, they soon learnt to attack in line; and for two reasons. One was that since their enemies fought in line formation they were compelled to do likewise, and the second was that they were desperate fighters in their *jihād* (struggle against infidels) and the line formation is more suited to men engaged in a struggle to the death.[1]

The books of *fiqh* are not without their chapters on war, although they naturally deal with its legal aspects. But from the list of the duties for which the commander of an army is responsible some idea may be gained of the Muslim view of the military art. According to Māwardī, the law demands that the commander of a force shall be responsible for its security. He must guard his men against surprise, investigating all places in which an ambush is possible, and he must so protect his main body with outposts and guards on all sides that they shall have security for their persons and their belongings when they are not fighting. If any property is left behind in a campaign, that too must be made secure. The commander is responsible for choosing the site on which the enemy shall be offered battle. It should be a place as level and as well supplied as possible with water and pasture. Also it should be guarded by such natural features (as mountains or streams) on the flanks and outskirts that the site is of use in the actual battle and a source of security. He must ensure adequate supplies of food for his men and of fodder for the animals. Moreover, he must inform himself of the movements and strength of the enemy so as to be secure against their tactics and have sufficient power for his attacks on them. He must dispose his troops both for the battle-line and for the reserves and have sufficient to guard his flanks. In the battle he must urge his men to victory, by making light of the enemy for them, by promising

[1] *Prolégomènes*, ed. Quatremère, II, p. 70.

those who are steadfast the rewards of Allah if they should reach the next world, and, if they remain alive in this world, tribute and an extra share of booty. He must apply his forces for such purposes only as Allah has ordained and such as come within the laws of Allah. He may not permit any of his troops to engage in trade or agriculture, either of which may seduce them from their real duty of combating the infidel.[1]

In the actual battle the commander-in-chief may not himself go out in single combat against a champion from the enemy side.[2] As to those whom it is lawful to slay, the *fiqh* declares that a Muslim in war may slay any unbeliever (idolator) whether combatant or not, although there is dispute whether old men and monks may be slain. Yet women and children are not to be slain, nor slaves and other menials. No man, moreover, may hamstring or otherwise destroy a horse, for it may be a source of strength in furthering God's purposes and of use in the struggle against His enemies.[3]

Somewhat more in accord with practical experience are the principles of war laid down by the Moorish essayist, Abu Bakr of Tortosa, already quoted. According to him war means deception,[4] and only in the last resort is it necessary to set troops to fight at close quarters or to launch army against army. To gain the victory the commander must use strategy, and when he has used it to the best advantage he must clinch matters with his troops.

As for the order of battle, it is a principle well known, he says, amongst men experienced in wars, that the boldest fighters and stoutest warriors should be stationed in the centre. Then, even if the wings are driven back, all eyes will look to the centre, and if its banners are flying and its drums beating it will become a rallying-point for the wings, so that every fugitive will take refuge therein. But if the centre is broken, the wings will be destroyed. Many a time has victory been achieved by the centre after the wings have been routed, but seldom has the contrary occurred.

The most effective stratagem in war is the ambush. Not too many men must be employed in it; one good one being better than ten thousand others. A multitude destroys the possibility of

[1] Māwardī, *Constitutiones Politicae*, ed. Enger, pp. 71 f.

[2] *Ibid.* p. 67.

[3] *Ibid.* p. 70.

[4] It was a view not uncommonly held. Muhallab, the Umayyad governor in Persia, in his death-bed counsels told his sons that foresight and cunning were of more avail in war than bravery (Ṭabarī, II, 1083).

surprise, and in surprise lies destructive effect. The best number for a guerilla expedition is four hundred, and the best army is four thousand strong.

The best battle-formation which the author says he ever saw in his own country, was where the infantry with various rallying-points formed the first line, with good shields, long lances and sharply pointed javelins. Each man knelt on his left knee with his shield upright before him, while his lance was fixed by the butt in the ground behind him and inclined forwards towards the enemy. Behind the infantry were the picked archers, "whose arrows pierced all shields", and behind them again were stationed the cavalry. When the Christians (*Rūm*) advanced, no Muslim stirred until they came within range, and then the archers transfixed them with their arrows and the infantry with their javelins, while at closer quarters still the spear-points met them. As the enemy broke the cavalry came forward "and obtained from them what God willed".[1]

Abu Bakr's treatise on the art of war is but one chapter of his "Lamp for Kings". Other works exist which are devoted entirely to the subject. One such work, which is based upon Aelian's *Tactics* (although containing other things dictated by Muslim precept and experience) is a practical manual[2] by 'Īsā ibn Ismā'īl al-Āqsarā'ī, who wrote in the seventh century of Islam, giving instruction in archery, the use of the spear, sword, and other weapons, the disposition of troops on the march, in camp and on the battlefield. Chapters are devoted to the question of military intelligence and the agents to be used for obtaining reliable information, to guards and outposts, days propitious for beginning a march (the Prophet favoured Thursday, which is therefore a day to be chosen), the proper equipment for the various branches of the army, and to other subjects of military interest.[3]

[1] Abu Bakr al-Ṭurṭūshī, *Sirāj al-mulūk*, ch. 61, 298 ff.

[2] It is entitled *Kitāb fi Faḍl al-jihād wa ta'līm al-furūsīya* (A book on the Excellence of the Holy War and on Instruction in Horsemanship), *Nihāyat al-sūl wa'l-umnīya fī ta'līm al-furūsīya* ("The Aim of Ambition and Desire in Instruction in Horsemanship"). Brockelmann, *Geschichte d. Arab. Litteratur* (I, 496), mentions two separate works with these titles by Najm al-Dīn Ḥasan al-Rammāḥ al Aḥdab, who died in 694/1294.

[3] Cambridge University Library MS. Qq. 277. See Ḥājjī Khalīfa, VI, 126. Wuestenfeld's *Das Heerwesen der Muhammedaner* (Göttingen, 1880) is based on this work.

CHAPTER X

ISLAMIC COSMOLOGY AND OTHER SCIENCES

The sciences to which men in cities devote themselves, either in study or teaching, fall into two divisions. The one comprises those "natural" in man, who is guided thereto by his reason, while the other contains those which are "traditional", being acquired by transmitted report from those who instituted them. In the first division are included the philosophic sciences, which are those which a man may acquire by his inborn power of cogitation, while in the second are the transmitted institutional sciences, all of which are based upon information derived from the lawgiver who founded them and in which there is no room for reason except in so far as is necessary for the deduction of practical applications.

In these words the historian and sociologist Ibn Khaldūn[1] expresses his view of the division of the sciences, a view which is the reflection of that generally adopted in Islam. The earliest Islamic acceptance of the word *'ilm* ("knowledge") did not however extend beyond the limits of what was known to Muhammad and his interpreters who were nearest to him in time. To them the results of Greek philosophy were not as yet familiar and their conception of science was therefore a very different one. An aphorism attributed to the Prophet declares that "Knowledge is twofold; knowledge of religions and knowledge of bodies",[2] the face value of which is that knowledge lies in theology and medicine,[3] although it has been interpreted to mean that science is divided into two branches dealing respectively with the abstract and the concrete.

It is clear from these classifications that in Islam, science, in the sense of "natural" science, far from being contrasted with religion is not at all to be distinguished from it, and includes it within its scope. From the point of view, indeed, of the ordinary believer who is convinced that Islam covers the whole of life, his

[1] *Prolégomènes*, ed. Quatremère, II, 385.

[2] *Al-'ilm 'ilmān, 'ilm al-adyān wa 'ilm al-abdān.*

[3] Cf. Ibn Abi Uṣaybi'a, *'Uyūn al-anbā*, ed. A. Müller (Cairo, 1882), p. 2.

religion, as being the greater, includes all that is known as natural phenomena. This aspect of the matter is illustrated by the well-known legend of the Caliph Omar and the library at Alexandria, which he ordered to be destroyed because the learning which it represented was either to be found in the Koran or it was not; in the one case it was superfluous and in the other harmful.[1] The story is almost certainly apocryphal,[2] but it represents the spirit of certain classes of Muslims who were prepared to maintain that the whole of knowledge was contained in the Koran or the Traditions of the Prophet; an attitude parallel to that of the Rabbis who declared that all wisdom was to be found in the Torah. According to Ibn Ḥazm,[3] "Any fact whatsoever which can be proved by reasoning is in the Koran or in the words of the Prophet, clearly set out." Those who took up this attitude declared that since Islam superseded all the religions that went before, it also abolished all the accumulated learning that was associated with them.[4] But this unbalanced view was adopted only at a comparatively late stage in the history of Islam, when the predominant influence of the *'ulamā* had made it rigid and exclusive. If the fact had been otherwise it is difficult to conceive how the study of Greek science could have been so eagerly pursued and so generously encouraged as it was under the ninth-century Abbasid Caliphs at Baghdad, at the courts of the Persian rulers of that century and the next, in Egypt under a number of the Fāṭimid Caliphs and in Spain under the Umayyads; for in all these places Islam was sternly and sometimes fanatically maintained as the only true religion.

In the earliest stage of its history, the faith was engaged in establishing itself and could not have permitted any recognition of so distracting and unsettling a study as that of Greek philosophy,[5] even if the materials had been available. But with the

[1] See Gibbon, *Decline and Fall*, ch. LI (ed. Bury, V, 452 ff.).

[2] Ibn Khaldūn, *Prolégomènes*, III, 89 f., ascribes the event to the conquest of Persia, without specifying the locality of the library.

[3] *Kitāb al-Fiṣal* (Cairo, A.H. 1317), II, 95.

[4] Cf. Ibn Khaldūn, *ibid.* II, 387.

[5] Yet even during that period, it is reported, the Umayyad prince Khālid ibn Yazīd ibn Mu'āwiya studied alchemy, medicine and astronomy with a Greek monk. (See Ibn Khallikān's life of the prince.) Ibn al-Nadīm, *Fihrist*, ed. Flügel (Leipzig, 1871), I, 354, mentions only his interest in alchemy, "the Art" (*al-ṣan'a*); cf. Qiftī, *Ta'rīkh al-ḥukamā*, ed. Lippert, p. 440. Some doubt was thrown on the report by J. Ruska, in his *Arabische Alchemisten*, I (Heidelberg, 1924).

emergence of the Mu'tazilīs, who sought to establish their faith on a rationalist basis, outside influences began to be felt. It became impossible to exclude from consideration the ideas of the Greeks and others who had elaborated "philosophic" or "scientific" systems based on observation and reason. Nevertheless, even after the existence of philosophy had been recognized, *'ilm*—which corresponds in its original significance to the Latin *scientia*—continued to embrace theology and the learning which is concerned with the fundamentals of Islam. Apart from a small number of investigators inspired by Greek philosophic ideals, the Muslims who engaged in the pursuit of science did so, like the Hebrews, in order to discover in the wonders of nature the signs and tokens of the glory of God.[1] But those who, like the Greeks, were eager for abstract truth for its own sake, did not cease to remain true believers; so that the philosopher Avicenna, whom the learned Shahristānī places for discussion among the *Ahl al-Ahwā* (those who stood outside positive religion and evolved their ideas out of their own "desires"), confesses in his autobiography that he repaired to the mosque for prayer and inspiration when he was at a loss in the working out of his problems.[2]

It is necessary now to examine in greater detail the Islamic conception of "science". The prime division, it has been seen, is into the religious and the secular studies. The former are concerned with the Koran, the *ḥadīth* and theology, the language of which is Arabic. For that reason they are called *'Ulūm al-'Arab*, "The Arab Sciences", while the secular sciences, being derived mainly from foreign (Greek) and ancient sources are known as *'Ulūm al-'Ajam*, "The non-Arab Sciences" or *'Ulūm al-Awā'il*, "The Sciences of the Ancients".

Of the "Arabic" or "traditional" branches of science, that which made the Koran its subject-matter was evidently of paramount importance. The language and thought of the sacred book, regarded as literally and verbally the word of Allah, were made the object of intense study and investigation, for every word and letter was endowed with significance. This led to research into the Arabic language and in particular into the vocabulary and grammar of the dialect spoken by the Prophet's own tribe of the Quraysh.

[1] Cf. Koran 50^6, with which cf. Psalms XIX^2, and see also Job, XXXVIII ff. See further Qiftī, *ibid.* p. 50, ll. 3 ff.

[2] Qiftī, *ibid.* p. 415, ll. 6 ff.

As an aid to this study, collections were made of surviving specimens of ancient Arabic verse, which had been the more easily retained in the memory by reason of their rhythm and rhyme, and to these verses reference was made for the explanation of Koranic and other words which were unfamiliar or rare. From other sources, likewise, materials which had a bearing on the significance of words were assembled, ultimately to form the basis of dictionaries. Grammar was associated with lexicography and formed an important subject of study, particularly in Iraq, where the schools at Baṣra and Kūfa became famous. Both these disciplines were ancillary to the study of Koranic exegesis.

Next in importance to the Koran as a subject of study, and, for the practical purposes of Islam as a religion, equal with it in importance, came the Traditions of the Prophet. They not only formed one of the "roots" of the *fiqh* but provided most of the materials for Muḥammad's biography. The work of writing his life and describing his campaigns was early undertaken, and its ramifications included accounts of the various peoples, Arab and foreign, with whom he came into contact. His companions too became the objects of research, so that genealogy, which had been a species of knowledge greatly esteemed in pre-Muslim days, was able to retain its importance, but with the difference that now it was relationship with the Prophet or his tribe of the Quraysh which investigators sought to establish. The rise of the early Caliphs and the beginning of foreign conquests gave the first impulse to more general history, which was not confined to the Arabs but concerned itself with all those nations with whom the Prophet's victorious successors were concerned.[1]

At the same time more general literary pursuits, such as poetry (a survival from pre-Muslim days), rhetoric and *adab*, which latter corresponds in a general fashion to *belles lettres*, were not neglected, particularly since, as the influence of Islam grew, their subject-matter drew increasingly upon apostolic tradition or was treated in such method as to provide religious edification. By Ibn Khaldūn[2] they are included with lexicography and grammar

[1] Cf. the contents of Khwārazmī's *Mafātīḥ al-'ulūm*, composed in A.D. 976, and of the *Fihrist* of Ibn al-Nadīm, composed in A.D. 988 (ed. Flügel, Leipzig, 2 vols., 1871–2). For a description of these works see E. G. Browne, *Lit. Hist. of Persia*, I, 378 ff.

[2] *Prolégomènes* (text), II, 385.

amongst the philological sciences which are the necessary preliminaries to the study of the Koran and are therefore regarded as belonging peculiarly to the "Muslim" sciences. Based upon the Koran and *ḥadīth* are the science of the principles of the *fiqh* and that of the practical applications of them, and, finally, that of *kalām*, or scholastic theology, which is concerned with the nature of God, with His manifestations, the Resurrection, the reward of Paradise and the punishment of Hell, with Destiny, and with the rational proofs of them all.

Although the primary concern of all these studies was the elucidation of the religious and legal content of the Koran, they incidentally throw light upon the scientific conceptions, in the more technical sense, of the Prophet and of those who undertook to interpret his words. There were already in existence amongst the Arabs of the *Jāhilīya* a number of arts and crafts such as horse-breeding, farriery and camel-rearing, the technical terminology of which was the result of long study. There was also a body of locally acquired knowledge concerning the fixed stars, the movements of the planets and the changes of the weather, all carefully observed for the purposes of travel, whether peaceable, as when flocks and herds were being moved to fresh pastures, or warlike, as when raiding was afoot. In a like class were the names of the plants and wild animals of the desert. A further branch of knowledge was that of local and tribal history, with which was associated the study of genealogy, of considerable practical importance in matters of inheritance, and even more when there was a question affecting prestige, either tribal or individual. Such lore as this provided the background of the Prophet's teaching.

In the Koran the aspects of Nature which are mentioned are usually associated with descriptions of the Creation, and the reference to them is of a rhetorical character. It may, however, be gathered that the Prophet conceived of the universe as geocentric. The earth itself also is constantly spoken of as having been "stretched out" at Creation[1] or "spread out" as a carpet,[2] whence it may be inferred that the Prophet conceived of it as flat,[3] although orthodoxy denies this.[4] As a rule the earth is spoken of in the

[1] Koran 79^{30}, 84^{3}. [2] *Ibid.* 51^{48}, 71^{18} f. [3] Cf. *ibid.* 78^{6}.

[4] The commentator Bayḍāwī, on Koran 2^{20}, declares that it does not follow from the Prophet's utterances that he thought of the earth as flat, for the extent of the surface of the globe is vast enough to justify the idea of its being "spread out".

singular, but in one passage[1] it is declared that Allah created the earth to correspond with the seven heavens[2] with which before Creation it formed one piece.[3] On to the earth the mountains were "cast down" to act as tent-pegs[4] in order to hold it in position and prevent its movement,[5] presumably upon the primeval waters,[6] and on the surface of the earth also were created "the two seas", the one fresh and the other salt,[7] which meet but are yet kept unmingled with one another.[8] They would appear to have been distinct from the primeval waters over which floated the Throne of Allah.[9]

Over the earth the sky is built up as a roof[10] and is held aloft by Allah's power without the need for any supporting columns.[11] It consists of seven heavens,[12] firmly constructed[13] in layers one above the other.[14] No hint is given of the estimated distance between them, or of the distance between the heavens and the earth, but the commentators attribute to the Caliph Omar the opinion that the latter distance is equivalent to that which lies "between the east and the west" and would be a five hundred years' journey at the pace of a traveller upon a level road.[15]

1 65^{12}.

2 Cf. Bayḍāwī on 6^{1}, 39^{67} and Ṭabarī, *Ta'rīkh*, I, 38.

3 Koran 21^{31}.

4 *Ibid.* 78^{7}.

5 *Ibid.* 21^{32}, 31^{9}, 16^{15}. Bayḍāwī, on the last verse, remarks that before the mountains were created on the earth, it was a smooth sphere and that, true to its spherical character, it revolved like the heavens, or moved for other causes, even the slightest. When the mountains were created in it, the "sides", i.e. the "cardinal points", of the earth were differentiated and the mountains by their weight settled towards the centre and became equivalent to tent-pegs to prevent its moving.

6 The commentators speak of the *Nūn* (the "Fish" of Babylonian mythology) which they distinguish from the waters beneath. Cf. Ṭabarī, *Ta'rīkh*, I, 49 f.

7 Koran 25^{55}.

8 Koran 55^{19}, 27^{62}, 35^{13}.

9 *Ibid.* 11^{9}. Ṭabarī, *Ta'rīkh*, I, 37 f., *Tafsīr*, XII, pp. 4 f., quotes an opinion describing this as the "surrounding" sea which lies about the heavens and the earths and divides off the seven "earths" from each other.

10 Koran 21^{33}.

11 *Ibid.* 13^{2}.

12 *Ibid.* 23^{16}, 2^{27}.

13 *Ibid.* 78^{12}.

14 *Ibid.* 71^{14}, 23^{16}, 67^{3}, 2^{27}. The heavens began as vapour. Traditionally, the lowest heaven is made of green emerald, the second of white silver, the third of red coral, the fourth of white pearl, the fifth of red gold, the sixth of yellow coral and the seventh of light. (Mas'ūdī, *Murūj al-dhahab*, I, 47 ff.) Commenting on Koran 2^{27} Bayḍāwī reconciles the Koranic conception with the Babylonian-Ptolemaic theory of nine spheres by declaring that there is a doubt about the latter, but alternatively that if it is true, the *'Arsh* and the *Kursī* (both meaning the "Throne") make up the nine.

15 Ṭabarī, *Ta'rīkh*, I, 2822.

In separate heavens float the sun and the moon,[1] and in the lowest heavens are other luminaries,[2] presumably the fixed stars and the planets.[3] The sun journeys each day to an abode determined for its rest,[4] "as though the sun had a halting-place",[5] and to reveal the splendours of the night the day is stripped away from it as though it were a curtain.[6] The moon has amongst the signs of the zodiac[7] its appointed stations, to which it comes on successive nights,[8] but the heavens as a whole return after each revolution to the same positions,[9] and the sun may not outstrip the moon nor the night the day in their regular succession.[10]

In the heavens is stored up the rain[11]; the clouds, driven by the winds, cover the sky, and by means of them and through their interstices the water pours down to fertilize the earth.[12] Hail also descends from mountainous clouds sent down from the heavens,[13] clouds like those which harbour "darkness, thunder and lightning".[14]

Of the ultimate constitution of matter the Koran itself has nothing to say, although the commentators, as will appear, make their own inferences from the text. But in his revelations the Prophet specifically declares that all living things were created from water,[15] although man, according to another idea, was created of clay[16] and the *jinn* of fire.[17]

By the commentators of the Koran the question of the composition of matter was treated in the spirit characteristic of the ancient sages who aimed at presenting knowledge in the form of concise aphorisms put into the mouths of the heroes of the people and given the authority of great names. Thus there is a story that,

[1] Koran 36^{40}, 21^{34}, 71^{15}. [2] *Ibid.* 67^{5}. [3] *Ibid.* $81^{15\text{ f.}}$

[4] *Ibid.* 36^{38}. [5] Bayḍāwī *ad loc.* [6] Koran 36^{37}.

[7] *Ibid.* 15^{16}.

[8] *Ibid.* 36^{39}. The phases of the moon are appointed in order to acquaint men with times and seasons (*ibid.* 2^{185}, 105).

[9] *Ibid.* 86^{11}. [10] *Ibid.* 36^{40}. [11] *Ibid.* 15^{22}.

[12] *Ibid.* 30^{47-49}, 2^{159}, 7^{55}. 'There is, under the Throne, a sea whence descends the sustenance of all living creatures. What God wills rains down from one heaven to another until it reaches the place called *al-Abram*. And God sends to the wind which bears it to the cloud, and that sifts it down." (Mas'ūdī, *Murūj*, I, 49 f.)

[13] *Ibid.* 24^{43}.

[14] *Ibid.* 2^{18}. Bayḍāwī on this verse says, "It is known that the cause of it [thunder] is the collision of the masses of the clouds when the wind drives them together."

[15] *Ibid.* 21^{31}, 24^{44}, 25^{25}. [16] *Ibid.* 23^{12} ff., 35^{12}. [17] *Ibid.* 15^{27}.

in the course of Omar's wars against the Greeks, the emperor wearied of battle and engaged the Caliph in a duel of wits. In one bout he sent his adversary a bottle with the request to him to "fill it with all things". Omar replied by sending back the bottle filled with water and accompanied by a message which said that it contained "all things in the lower world".[1]

According to Bayḍāwī,[2] God could create absolutely, *ex nihilo*, as He created the heavens and the earth, or from matter already existing, as He created all that lies between the heavens and the earth. The new creation need not be of the same genus as that from which it was derived; thus Adam and the animals were different from the matter of their origin (water or clay); and living creatures might come from the male alone, as Eve from Adam, or from the female alone, as Jesus from Mary, or from the male and female together, as in the generality of mankind. In this connection it may be observed that the Koran speaks of human beings that were transformed into apes and swine.[3]

The Koranic declaration (of Biblical origin) that the world was created in six days[4] was discussed by the Muslim commentators in much the same way as the Rabbinical commentators discussed the original of the statement in the Book of Genesis, and the conclusion reached concerning the age of the universe and the probable period of its duration (namely, six or seven thousand years in all) was little different.[5]

Simultaneously with the rise of the Mu'tazilīs[6] and their interest in a rational explanation of their beliefs, a desire for knowledge beyond that supplied by the "Arabic" sources of the Koran and the *ḥadīth* began to grow in Islam. The effect was that under some of the early ninth-century Abbasids, Greek learning as contained in the philosophy and "natural science" of Aristotle,

[1] Ṭabarī, *Ta'rīkh*, I, 2822. Mas'ūdī, *Murūj*, I, 47, states that men of science were agreed that the first thing God created was water. The reason is an obvious one.

[2] On Koran 5^{20}.

[3] *Ibid.* 2^{61}, 5^{65}.

[4] *Ibid.* 41^{8-10}, $50^{32\,ff}$.

[5] Cf. Ṭabarī, *Ta'rīkh*, I, 8 ff.

[6] The "seceders"—a sect particularly active during the reign of the Caliph Ma'mūn (813–33). They differed from the orthodox theologians in holding that the Koran was the creation of Allah and was not co-eternal with Him, also that his attributes had no separate entity.

the mathematics of Euclid and the medicine of Hippocrates and Galen was made available, in translation, to the lettered amongst Muslims who interested themselves in such matters. The Koranic conceptions of "natural" science had indeed been expanded and elaborated by the transmitters of *ḥadīth* and by those who regarded the description of worldly phenomena as a vehicle for the reporting of edifying anecdotes concerning the Prophet and his companions or others of high rank in the hierarchy of Islam. But the more philosophic standards and methods of the Greeks had their attraction for those whose conception of religion did not exclude the possibility of studying the products of foreign thought. The imported ideas spread rapidly, and those of the learned who had a taste for theory and speculation turned to them eagerly, not as to revealed truth but in the hope of finding answers to questions newly arisen in their minds and not touched upon in the works available to them.

The most famous name in the early period when Greek influences began to work upon Islamic thought is that of al-Kindī, "the Philosopher of the Arabs", who died about A.D. 850. His work, however, is, except for a negligible quantity, not available in the original and we may turn, as an alternative, to the work of his contemporary, the Mu'tazilī Jāḥiẓ of Baṣra, who died in 255/869. He was an enlightened *mawlā* who read widely and whose discursive writings bear frequent evidence of an independent mind working upon traditional materials in the endeavour to find a satisfactorily rational explanation of the universe. In his *Kitāb al-Ḥayawān* ("Book of Animals")[1] the ostensible purpose of which is to be a text-book of zoology, he roams over a vast number of subjects, in the course of discussing which he discloses a knowledge of the Aristotelian doctrine of the four elements (*al-arkān*) which go to compose the sublunar world; namely water, earth, air and fire. He accepts this doctrine and, still under Aristotelian influence, divides the universe into two parts, that which grows (and has life) and that which does not grow. That which grows he subdivides into animals and plants, after which he devotes himself to the various genera of animals. For them he creates four classes—corresponding in general to the Aristotelian classification but reached by applying a wholly divergent system

[1] Ed. Cairo (7 parts), 1325/1907; part i, p. 14.

of differentiae[1]—in which they are arranged according as they walk, fly, swim or move along on their bellies. He is aware that the classification is not a satisfactory one, for he knows, for example, that creatures which fly also walk, but he claims that he will not be misunderstood, because those creatures which walk and do not fly will not be called flying things. The class which walks is further subdivided by him into four genera, namely, men, domestic animals, wild animals and creeping things; and the division stands, as being comprehensible "to hearers of this speech and those who have this tongue", even though the things that creep may also come into the classes of the domestic animals or of the wild animals.[2]

In another part of his discursive work on animals, the author returns to discuss the question of the four elements. Some of the "materialists" (i.e. the secularist philosophers), he says, declare that the world is composed of the four elements: heat, cold, dryness and fluidity (all existing things being compounded of these four, which they call "substances"[3]); others, he says, declare that the four elements are earth, air, water, fire, the other four being mere attributes of these essentials. The question was one which greatly exercised his contemporaries, and those who held that the "natural" bodies were heat, cold, dryness and fluidity considered that fire, earth and the rest of the series were their compounds.[4]

The spirit of the science of the day may be appreciated from Jāḥiẓ's exposition of the nature of compounds. As the basis of his

[1] Cf. W. D. Ross, *Aristotle* (London, 1923), pp. 114–17.

[2] *Ḥayawān*, I, 13 f., IV, 90.

[3] *Ajsām*.

[4] The *Firdaws al-ḥikma* ("Paradise of Science"), written by 'Alī ibn Sahl Rabban al-Ṭabarī about 850 propounds this view and also the view that these compounds (the "natural" qualities) had within them the power of being changed into each other. Thus water was potential air, air was potential fire, and so on through the series. The result of a change was not absolute in so far as quantity went but was only so in respect to the nature of the substance. The example is given of water, which turns to "air" ("e.g. in the hot baths where the water rises as 'air' to the roof and there condenses to form water again; also the fire of a lamp newly quenched may turn into 'air' and this back into fire"). See the edition by M. Z. Siddiqi (Berlin, 1928, pp. 11 ff.). Al-Kindī is said to have written a treatise on the Aristotelian theme that the heavens were composed of a fifth "natural quality" (*ṭabī'a*) different from the four sublunar ones. (Ibn Abi Uṣaybi'a, *'Uyūn al-anbā*, I, 211.) About a century later, Mas'ūdī took Aristotle's "fifth" essence to refer to the series heat, cold, etc., and not to the series earth, air, etc. See *Kitāb al-Tanbīh*, ed. M. J. de Goeje, Leyden, 1894, p. 8.)

discussion he takes the luminous and combustible substances and proceeds to inquire whether the fire in them was actually in existence before coming into view and whether in that case it existed alongside or within the body in which it appeared. He goes on then to inquire into the means of its coming into being if it is not hidden within the body; also how it is that air transforms fire and wood into charcoal, if the fact of transformation be admitted and if the fact of the persistence of qualities (accidents) be proved. Further he inquires into the constitution of the combustible matter that appears in trees, and into the sparks that appear from stones, into the colour of fire and other allied questions.[1]

Another example of the critical character of the man, less probably of his age, is to be found in his discussion concerning the existence of the fabulous bird known as the *'anqā*, which corresponds in some of its features to the phoenix. There are people, he says, who hold that the bird exists, but he declares that to him the thing is so much "red sulphur", i.e. a fiction. Whilst on this subject of fabulous reports he discusses the question of the rhinoceros and of the birth of its young, about which Indians make statements which, he says, men of science would sweep aside as nonsensical if the Indians did not so persistently repeat them. They are to the effect that the young animal puts out its head from the mother's belly to feed on the surrounding vegetation before being actually born and withdraws it again when it is satisfied. Jāḥiẓ remarks on this, "I do not consider this to be impossible, nor outside God's power. . . . We do not find that the Koran denies it nor that *ijmā'* rejects it; neither do I therefore venture to reject it, but my heart strongly inclines to refuse belief in it. This is something which man cannot know by analogy, nor know at all except by actual seeing."[2]

Most of the Muslim philosophers of note confined themselves more rigidly to the Aristotelian scheme[3] and were content to follow the Stagirite without substantial modification from other sources. A part of his system, which accorded well with their liking for analysis and subdivision, was his classification of the sciences. This consisted primarily of a division into two groups, the theoretical and the practical, in the first of which he included

[1] *Ḥayawān*, part V, p. 2 ff. [2] *Ibid.* VII, 40 f.
[3] Cf. Qiftī, *Ta'rīkh al-ḥukamā*, p. 29, ll. 6 f.

first philosophy (metaphysics), physics and mathematics, while in the other were gathered those arts or sciences which comprehend action in addition to reasoning. Subsequent elaboration divided the latter group into the practical, which have no other result than the action itself, and the constructive or artistic, which leave as their result, when the action is completed, some substantial product.

Of the learned in Islam, the first, according to tradition,[1] to concern himself with the question was the Turkish *savant* Abu Naṣr al-Fārābī (died at Damascus in 339/950), who, as his name indicates, was a native of Fārāb in Transoxiana. In his work entitled *Iḥsā al-ʿulūm* ("The Enumeration of the Sciences") he groups the sciences with which he proposes to deal or has dealt, as follows: I. The science of language (in seven parts); II. The science of logic (in eight parts); III. The science of mathematics (in seven main parts, which are: arithmetic, geometry, optics, astrology, music, "weights" and mechanics); IVA. Theological and natural science (in eight parts, which are: that which all natural bodies share in common, the simple bodies, the coming to be and passing away of bodies (*de Generatione et Corruptione*), the beginnings of "accidents" and changes which concern the elements, the bodies compounded of the elements, the mineral bodies,[2] plants and animals); IVB. The science of "theology", comprising politics, *fiqh* (law) and *kalam* (scholastic theology).[3]

In another work, *De Ortu Scientiarum*, which is ascribed to him but which exists only in a Latin translation, there is a brief exposition of his philosophy in a rather different form. This declares that nothing exists but substance, accident and the Creator of substance and accident. Accidents may be perceived by the senses; substances only by reason, accidents being the means of their being perceived. Natural science deals with the occasions and causes of changes in substances; it is the science of action and passivity. The origins of all substances under the sphere of the moon[4] lie in

[1] Cf. Qiftī, *ibid.* pp. 277 f.

[2] Al-Fārābī would appear to be the originator of the division of substances into mineral, vegetable and animal. Aristotle contented himself with treating the "soul-less" substances as a background to the rest.

[3] M. Bouyges, "Sur le *de Scientiis* d'Alfarabi" (*Mélanges de l'Université Saint-Joseph*, IX (1923–4), 41–96).

[4] He follows Aristotle strictly in believing that there is a fifth element (the quintessence), of which the sky is composed.

the four elements, fire, air, water, earth, from the four qualities of which, namely heat, cold, fluidity (moisture) and dryness, arise the accidents as well as action and passivity. Out of these roots, together with the four mathematical sciences (*al-'ulūm al-riyāḍīya*) of numbers, mensuration, astronomy and music, arises all knowledge under the sphere of the moon. The component parts of natural science, as here given, are as follows: judicial astrology (*de judiciis*), medicine, divination (*de nigromantia*), (interpretation of) visions (*de imaginibus*), agriculture, navigation, alchemy ("which is the science of transforming things into other species") and optics (*de speculis*).[1]

Al-Fārābī's great successor Ibn Sīnā (Avicenna) (d. 1037) went back beyond him to Aristotle himself, although making certain changes which accorded with his special purposes. In a short treatise[2] which he devoted to the subject of the classification of the sciences, he makes a primary division of wisdom or philosophy (*ḥikma*)[3] into two parts, the one theoretical or speculative and the other practical. The aim of the theoretical is the acquisition of established beliefs concerning existing things whose existence in no wise depends upon man's activity; its purpose indeed being merely the forming of reasoned views (*ra'y*), as, for example, in the "science" of belief in the unity of God or in the "science" of predestination (*qisma*). In the practical the aim is not merely the acquisition of settled beliefs concerning existing things but rather the acquisition of reasoned views in matters by which a man may attain to what is good; it is opinion acquired with a view to action.

A different division is into three parts, namely, the lower science, which is called "natural" science (*al-'ilm al-ṭabī'ī*), the middle science, which is called "propaedeutic" (mathematical)

[1] Clemens Baeumker, *Alfarabi, Ueber den Ursprung der Wissenschaften* (*De Ortu Scientiarum*), in *Beiträge zur Geschichte des Mittelalters*, XIX, iii. Munster i. W., 1916.

[2] *Risāla Taqsīm al-'ulūm*, British Museum MS. Add. 16,659, fol. 342 b–345 a.

[3] He defines it as "a speculative art whereby a man may attain to a realization of the purpose of existence as such, and also of the end to which his own actions should be directed in order that his soul may be ennobled and perfected and that he may become wise and understanding, conforming with the existing world but preparing for the ultimate felicity of the next world, in so far as lies in human power".

science (*al-'ilm al-riyāḍī*), and the upper science, which is called "theological" science (*al-'ilm al-ilāhī*).

"Original" natural science is subdivided into two parts, of which the first,[1] which may be regarded as the root (or principle), is concerned with the qualities possessed by all substances in nature—namely matter, form, motion, character and causes (or conditions of production), whether to an end or not. The second part, which may be regarded as the branch or derivative, is that whereby there are made known the conditions of those substances which are the essential constituents of the world—namely of the heavens and what is in them and of the four elements and their natural properties, their movements and their stations.

The derivative part is subdivided into the various "departmental sciences"; medicine, astronomy, physiognomy, "interpretation of ideas" (*ta'bīr*), magic (*'ilm al-ṭilismāt*) and alchemy.

Intermediate in time between Al-Fārābī and Avicenna come the so-called *Ikhwān al-Ṣafā*, "The Brethren of Purity", an "academy" or society which flourished at Baṣra in the latter part of the fourth/tenth century. From their work, consisting of a number of treatises covering the whole field of contemporary knowledge, it may be gathered that they were rationalists interested in educating their fellow-Muslims in ideas of the universe which were not to be gathered from orthodox doctrine. On this and other grounds—such as that their work is mainly anonymous—the assumption has been made that they were a group of Shī'ite or Mu'tazilī origin inspired by a definitely political object, namely, the overthrow of the Abbasid dynasty. It is stated that they derived their title[2] from their declaration that the law (*sharī'a*) had become defiled with ignorant teachings and polluted with errors and that the only way to "purify" it was by means of philosophy.

Other members of their faith were not disposed to agree with the "Brethren" and characterized their treatises as superficial efforts to cover every branch of knowledge without satisfaction or efficiency, and containing falsehoods and errors in abundance. When the treatises were submitted to Abu Sulaymān al-Manṭiqī (the Logician) he returned them with very unfavourable

[1] This corresponds to Aristotle's First Philosophy.

[2] In full it is *Ikhwān al-Ṣafā wa Khullān al-Wafā wa Ahl al-'Adl wa Abnā' 'l-Ḥamd*, "Brethren of Purity, Friends of Honour, Men of Justice and Sons of Praiseworthy Conduct". *Ikhwān al-Ṣafā, Rasā'il*, ed. Cairo, 1928/1347, I, I.

comment, declaring that the authors had attempted to conceal philosophy under the cloak of the *sharī'a*, and had failed, even as cleverer men before them had failed. When asked his reasons for his opinions he replied that the *sharī'a* was derived from Allah by means of an inspired intermediary and that submission to its contents was demanded without question of why, or of how. The talk of an astrologer-astronomer (*munajjim*) about the influences of the stars and the movements of the heavens, he declared, has no place in the *sharī'a*, nor has any discourse of any "natural scientist" observing their phenomena and the facts concerning heat, cold, fluidity and dryness, or concerning what is the agent and what the patient and what their unions and antipathies are, nor is there any place for the discourse of geometrician or logician. How therefore, he asked, could the "Brethren" permit themselves to claim that they could combine philosophy with the *sharī'a* despite the fact that others beside them might lay claim to their methods; men, for example, like the enchanter, the alchemist, the talisman-maker, the interpreter of visions and the magician? If all these plied their professions lawfully Allah would have declared them lawful and the Giver of the *sharī'a* would have made use of them to make good any deficiency there may be in it. But He did not do so. On the contrary, He denounced them all and prohibited the Muslim from concerning himself with them, saying that he who consults a wizard or soothsayer seeks to discover God's secrets. Moreover, Allah sent a perfect religion by His Prophet and left no need, after the clear exposition provided by inspiration, for any recourse to the expositions of reason. Muslims in the past, he concluded, had been able to discuss their religious differences and difficulties without recourse to philosophy, just as Jews, Christians and Magians had been independent of it for the purposes of their religion, and there was no need now to apply to it.[1].

These were reactionary views of the kind which, with certain reservations, Ghazālī about a century later set himself to combat in his *Tahāfut al-Falāsifa*[2] ("The Confusion of the Philosophers") and other writings. It was in the face of such opinions

[1] Qiftī, *ibid.* pp. 82 ff.

[2] This was itself combated by the twelfth-century philosopher Averroes in his *Tahāfut al-Tahāfut*. Cf. M. Bouyges, *Bibliotheca Arabica Scholasticorum*, III (Beyrouth, 1930); and the translation by S. van den Bergh, 2 vols. (London, 1954).

that the Brethren did their work, which was undertaken in an endeavour to teach Muslims some of the facts, derived from foreign sources, concerning the world of phenomena. It is clear from their object that the treatises[1] were not intended for professed *savants* but for a more popular audience. They nevertheless cover a wide field and illustrate what the Brethren regarded as the capacity for scientific knowledge possessed by their better informed fellow-members of Islam in the fourth century of its history. The original Aristotelianism of the Treatises is strongly coloured by neo-Platonism and they are marked by endeavours to harmonize the Greek with the Muhammadan thought, but the source of their inspiration remains clear throughout.

The first treatise (on Number) states in an introductory paragraph the general scheme of the whole and declares that philosophy, or science, is divided into four parts, comprising respectively the mathematical, the logical or dialectical, the "natural" and the theological sciences. The mathematical group is made up of arithmetic, geometry, astronomy and music, the division later adopted by the Schoolmen, to whom it was known as the *quadrivium*. In the chapter on arithmetic the main interest lies in the theory of numbers. They are represented as being in four grades, namely, units, tens, hundreds and thousands; they are not so of necessity, as part of the "nature" of number, in the way that numbers must be either odd or even, but they have been so classified by the sages in order to make numerical matters accord with "natural" matters, most of which were arranged by Allah in fours, e.g. the four natural qualities (*ṭabā'i'*)—heat, cold, etc., the four elements (*arkān*)—fire, air, etc., the four humours—blood, phlegm, yellow bile and black bile[2]—the four seasons of the year, the four "directions" (points of the compass) and the four classes of created things—minerals, plants, animals and man.[3] A description of the special characteristics of the individual numbers forms part of the Treatise; thus that two is the first real "number", three the first odd number, four the first square number, five the first "round" number, seven the first "perfect" number, and so forth up to twelve and beyond. Then come successively a description of the arithmetical processes, a section

[1] Their number is given as either 51 (Qifṭī, *ibid.*) or 52 (*Rasā'il*, 11).
[2] A doctrine derived immediately from Galen. [3] *Rasā'il*, 1, 27.

on the reason for prefacing the whole work by the Treatise on Number—namely, that this science is present potentially in every soul and only requires study to be known, and a section explaining that the science of Number is a guide to the "science of the soul".

Geometry is the subject of the second treatise and is defined as the knowledge of quantities and dimensions and their properties, beginning with the point and advancing through line and plane to the solid. The two parts of the science are the practical and the theoretical; the first dealing with figures and bodies perceptible by the senses, and the second with the theory of the subject, employing imaginary things such as the line between sunshine and shadow, or the line that may persist in the mind when both sunshine and shadow have disappeared. The use of theoretical geometry is stated to be a guide from the perceived to the imagined and from the concrete to the abstract.

The third treatise is a lengthy one, as befits the importance of its subject, astronomy. Three divisions are allotted to the subject, the first deals with the structure of the heavens, the number of the stars, the signs of the zodiac, the distances of the stars, their size, their motions and whatever else appertains to this subject, which is called *'Ilm al-Hay'a*, "The Science of 'Formation' [i.e. of the heavens]". The second division deals with the calculation of astronomical tables, the making of calendars and similar tasks, while the third has as its subject-matter the prognostication of sublunar events from the revolution of the heavens, the signs of the zodiac in the ascendant and the motions of the planets. This third division of the science is known as *'Ilm al-Aḥkām* ("Judicial Astrology").

The stars are described as spherical luminous bodies, of which 1920 large ones can be perceived by observation. Seven of them are called "planets"; namely, Saturn, Jupiter, Mars, the sun, Venus, Mercury and the moon, and the rest are called "fixed" stars. Each of the seven planets has a sky proper to itself. The skies are spherical bodies, transparent and hollow, nine[1] in number and contained one within the other like the layers of an onion. The nearest of them to us is the sphere of the moon, which surrounds the atmosphere on all sides while the earth is in the centre of the atmosphere. Next to the sphere of the moon is that of Mercury,

[1] Only eight are enumerated; but see below, p. 478.

beyond which are the spheres respectively of Venus, the sun, Mars, Jupiter, Saturn. Beyond is the sphere of the fixed stars and lastly comes the "all-encompassing" sphere.[1] This last sphere is in constant revolution, like a water-wheel, turning from east to west above the earth and from west to east below it once in every day and night.[2] It moves the other (the orbital) spheres together with the planets, and it is divided into twelve *burūj*[3]—the signs of the zodiac.[4]

The sun annually passes through all the twelve signs of the zodiac, describing an imaginary circle (the ecliptic) in its course. Of the signs,[5] six (Aries, Taurus, Gemini, Cancer, Leo, Virgo) are northern, and while the sun is among them the nights are shorter and the days longer; the other six signs are the southern ones and when the sun is amongst them the nights are longer and the days shorter. The two points where the northern and southern signs meet are known as the "poles" of the zodiacal sphere.[6]

[1] This arrangement of the (orbital) spheres was borrowed by the Brethren from Ptolemy, but appears to have come in the first instance from the Babylonians. The same scheme is given by Mas'ūdī (d. 956) in the *Murūj al-dhahab*, I, 186 f. In his *Kitāb al-Tanbīh* (p. 12) he says that both the ancients and the moderns have disputed about the order of the spheres, Ptolemy Claudius in the Almagest and in his book on astronomy declaring that it was not clear to him whether Venus and Mercury were above the sun or below it, while Johannes the Grammarian reported Plato as having been of the opinion that the sphere of the moon is nearest to us, that of the sun next, then those of Venus and Mercury and then the others in the order set down in the text. In another passage of the *Tanbīh* (pp. 9 f.) Mas'ūdī speaks of a sphere outside that of the fixed stars actuating all the other spheres. It was called "The Sphere of the Equator" but, the author adds, it was identified by some astronomers with the sphere of the fixed stars.

[2] "The sphere revolves continuously with a motion inherent in it, and by its motion and that of the stars in it the four 'essential' qualities [heat, cold, etc.] are worked upon and the four elements [fire, water, etc.] are distributed. . . ." By the movements and amalgamations of elements and qualities winds are caused to blow, clouds gather, rain descends and meteorological conditions are set up in the heavens affecting the welfare of living creatures on the earth. (Mas'ūdī, *Tanbīh*, p. 9.)

[3] Each *burj* or sign of the zodiac is divided into 30 degrees each composed of 60 minutes. The minute is subdivided into 60 seconds, the seconds into thirds and so continuing.

[4] *Rasā'il*, I, 73–5.

[5] "The signs are merely a number of fixed collocations which have been given names so that the positions of stars in the universal sky may be determined by them." (Mas'ūdī, *Murūj*, I, 187.)

[6] "Aristotle and the Indian, Persian, and Chaldean philosophers before and after him believed that . . . the sky was a round, spherical, hollow body turning

The orbit of the sun in its passage through the ecliptic intersects the orbit of each of the other planets at two points known as the nodes (*jawzahr* or *'uqda*). When the sun and moon together are at one of the nodes of the same sign, and in the same degree of it, the sun is eclipsed. This can occur only at the end of a month, when the moon's position is opposite to (and in line with) that of the sun so that the sun's light is cut off from our vision and we see it eclipsed in the manner in which a cloud passing before the sun will prevent our seeing it. When, however, the sun is at one of the nodes and the moon at the other, the moon is eclipsed; and this can occur only in the middle of a month, for the moon is then in a sign facing that in which the sun lies and the earth is between them, thus preventing the sun's light from shining on the moon.[1]

The sun circles once through the twelve signs of the zodiac in three hundred and sixty-five days and a quarter, remaining in each sign thirty days and a fraction and in each degree a day and a night and a fraction. In the day-time it is above the earth and at night below it. In the summer it is amongst the "northern" signs in the atmosphere and is near to the point which is over our heads,[2] whereas in winter it is amongst the "southern" signs and is lower in the atmosphere and at a distance from the point over our heads. At apogee[3] (*awj*) it is high in the sphere and furthest from the earth, while at perigee it is low in the sphere and nearest to the earth.[4]

At the entry of the sun into four specified and well-known signs of the zodiac the four seasons begin. Thus when the sun descends into the first minute of the Sign of Aries, nights and days are equal in length, the weather becomes equable, winter departs and spring enters, while the entry of summer, autumn and winter is at the descent of the sun into the first minutes of Cancer, Libra and Capricornus respectively.[5]

about two pivots which are the Poles, the one being at the head of Cancer and the tail of the Plough, opposite the point of South, and the other at the head of Capricornus, wherein are stars resembling those of the Plough, opposite the point of the North." (Mas'ūdī, *Tanbīh*, p. 8.)

1 *Rasā'il*, I, 78–80.

2 Lit. "the direction (*samt*, whence 'zenith') of our heads".

3 Formerly used of any planet, now usually of the moon.

4 *Rasā'il*, I, 84.

5 *Ibid.* I, pp. 87 f. Mas'ūdī (*Tanbīh*, pp. 14 ff.) gives the length of spring as 93 days 23¼ hours, beginning when 10 days remain of Ādhār (March) and continuing until the twenty-fourth of Hazīrān (June). The length of summer is given as 92 days 23⅓ hours, of autumn as 88 days 17$\frac{1}{15}$ hours, and of winter as 89 days 14 hours.

The last section of the treatise is concerned with astrology, which deals with the influences of the heavenly bodies on terrestrial affairs. Briefly stated the function of astrology is to show that when the planets are in harmonious relationship, affairs in the sublunar world of "Generation and Corruption" go well; and that when the planets are out of harmony affairs go ill. Furthermore, certain conjunctions of the planets point to the occurrence on earth of specified situations and conditions.[1]

In this connection the statement of Ibn Ḥazm of Cordova (994–1064) is noteworthy. According to him[2] the stars have no influence on terrestrial affairs. If there appears to be any such influence it is not that of a dominant and independent force, for the stars are themselves under control and have no ruling power. If it were otherwise, they and their spheres would be able to move as they wished and would not be confined to the single form of motion (the circular) to which they are now compelled. If they have an influence it is no greater than that of fire in the processes of burning or of water in the processes of cooling.

In one of the other treatises (the sixteenth) of their series, the Brethren return to the subject of the cosmos but approach it from a different angle. They quote and expound in it the statement of the ancient philosophers that the universe, the macrocosm, which consists of the seven heavens and the seven earths and what lies between, bears a resemblance to the individual human being, the microcosm, with all his parts and members.[3] The universe is, moreover, endowed with a single spirit which directs the powers of each part of it in the same way that the soul of the individual man directs all his members.

[1] *Rasā'il*, I, 100 ff. Mas'ūdī (*Tanbīh*, p. 13) complains that the men of his day who were learned in the science of the skies neglected mathematical astronomy, which deals with the structure and composition of the heavens, and confined themselves to the study of astral influences. He declares that the two branches of the science are inseparable, since the influences are generated by the movements of the planets, and to be ignorant of the one branch means ignorance of the other also.

[2] *Kitāb al-Fiṣal* (Cairo, A.H. 1317), II, 96.

[3] "Man is called the microcosm because his members are divided according to the twelve signs of the zodiac, and the seven planets. In him also is yellow bile, product of fire, black bile, product of earth, blood, product of air, and phlegm, product of water." (Jāḥiẓ, *Ḥayawān*, I, 100.)

The parts of the universe which compose what is extra-terrestrial are the seven spheres in which the seven planets move, together with the sphere of the fixed stars and the sphere of the outermost heaven, which is the Throne of Allah. Between the lowest celestial sphere and the earth lies the atmosphere. As for the earth, it is—with all that exists upon its surface: mountains, seas, deserts, rivers and lands both inhabited and uninhabited—a single globe, and it is situated, by Allah's favour, at the centre of the universe, in the midst of the air.[1]

This series of spheres, eleven in all, fits closely together, the inner surface of the containing sphere being in immediate contact with the outer surface of that which is contained. There is consequently no empty space or vacuum between them, the cleavage being perceptible only to the imagination. The writer of the treatise declares that those scholars who believe in the existence of a vacuum in the heavens or between the atoms of the "elements" are labouring under a misapprehension, for they imagine, when they see the celestial bodies moving from place to place that there must be empty space there, for otherwise any matter that occupied the space would prevent movement. That would only be true if all bodies were solid and their atoms firmly adherent to one another as in the case of stone or iron. But some bodies are soft, subtile and fluid, like water; and the atmosphere, being of that kind, does not prevent the passage of other bodies.

Beyond the eleven spheres that make up the universe there exists neither matter nor endless vacancy as has been thought,[2] for, says the author of the treatise, it has been shown that no vacuum is possible either inside or outside the universe, "and as for him who claims that there is another body outside the universe, the burden of proof lies upon him".[3]

Except for the earth, which is solid, each of the spheres comprising the universe consists of two concentric hollow spheres

[1] The sun is, however, declared to lie in the middle of the universe because its sphere lies in the middle of the system of spheres (*Rasā'il*, II, 25).

[2] Al-Bīrūnī (d. 1048) declares in his *Kitāb al-Tafhīm*, ed. and tr. R. Ramsay Wright (London, 1934), pp. 44 f., that, "A number of people consider that beyond the eighth sphere there is a ninth entirely quiescent; . . . because the prime mover must not be moved, and it is on this account that they describe it as motionless."

[3] *Rasā'il*, II, 20–4.

between which is a certain depth.[1] The atmosphere, which surrounds the earth and extends from its surface to the inner surface of the moon's orbital sphere, has a depth seventeen and a half times greater than the earth's diameter, and its diameter is twice its depth. The diameter of the moon's sphere equally is twice its depth, which is also that of the atmosphere. The depth of the orbital sphere of Mercury is one hundred times the diameter of the earth, and twice its depth is equivalent to one-fifth its diameter (i.e. the diameter is ten times the depth). Dimensions of an equally speculative kind are given for the orbital spheres of all the remaining planets. The depth of the sphere of the fixed stars is given as "nearly" twelve thousand times the diameter of the earth and its diameter as twice the depth.[2]

In order to account for the varying positions of the planets in relation to one another a differentiation in the rates of motion of the spheres is assumed. The prime moving sphere—which is itself set in motion by the Divine Spirit—rotates about the earth once in twenty-four hours. The sphere[3] immediately within, being in contact with it, is made to move in the same direction at a slightly lower rate of speed; the amount of difference being one degree in a hundred years. The next sphere, that of Saturn, moves at a lesser rate still, the decrease amounting to two minutes a day, and each successive sphere moves more slowly than the one containing it until the orbital sphere of the moon is reached. That moves most slowly of all and rotates about the earth once in twenty-four hours and six-sevenths of an hour.[4]

The apparent retrograde movement of the planets is explained as follows. When the (five) planets other than the sun and the moon appear at some times to retrograde and at others to halt this does not actually occur, and the phenomenon is due to optical illusion. The reason for it is that each of these planets moves in a small sphere (epicycle) sunk within and compounded with the

[1] The depth and diameter of the earth are the same, namely, 2167 parasangs, and its greatest circumference is 6800 parasangs.

[2] *Rasā'il*, II, 26 f.

[3] The text (*ibid.* II, 29, l 4) reads *kawkab* ("star"), but this would appear to be an error for *falak* ("sphere"). It is the sphere of the fixed stars.

[4] The author claims that his explanation of the differential rates of the planetary motions refutes those "who have no training in scientific study of geometry" and who maintain that the planets move from west to east in a sense contrary to that of "the surrounding sphere" (*ibid.* II, 32 f.).

thickness of the great one (deferent), so that at one point of its course it touches the outer surface and at another the inner surface. The planet, therefore, is sometimes retreating from the earth (i.e. when ascending) and sometimes approaching it (i.e. when descending). In the upper part of its revolution it appears to be moving amongst the signs of the zodiac in a direction contrary to theirs,[1] and in the lower part it appears to be moving with them, whilst in the actual ascent and descent it appears from the earth to be stationary.[2]

As for the composition of the heavens, the philosophers claim it is of a fifth essence (element),[3] but that means only that the heavenly bodies are not susceptible to the changes wrought by generation and corruption, nor to any change, increase or diminution to which sublunary bodies are liable. It also means that their motion is perpetually circular. Some believe the philosophers' statement to have meant that the skies are different in essence from the sublunary bodies, but that is an error. The evidence of our eyes proves it, seeing that the moon shows the same variation in the capacity to receive light and shade as the earthly bodies, and it throws a shadow as they do. All the heavenly bodies are associated with air, water, crystal and glass in their transparency; the sun and the stars generally are associated with fire in their luminosity and with earth in their dryness. It appears, therefore, that the philosophers meant by their fifth essence no more than that it is the nature of the heavens to move in circles and to be exempt from the changes characteristic of sublunary bodies.

Furthermore the heavens are neither light nor heavy, nor hot nor cold nor moist.[4] The explanation given is that those parts of the universe which are in the rightful places allotted to them by

[1] Lit. "from the first towards the last of them."

[2] *Rasā'il*, II, 36.

[3] See above, p. 467, n. 4.

[4] Mas'ūdī (*Tanbīh*, p. 8) on this question says, "Philosophers both before and after Plato have disputed about the nature of the sky. Some declared that it is composed of the four 'natural qualities' [heat, cold, etc.], the fiery being dominant, but only as it is to be found in bodies naturally and not burning (as fire). Others declared the sky is composed of fire, air and water; earth being absent. Aristotle and most philosophers both before and after him, as well as Indians, Persians and Chaldeans believed it to consist of a fifth 'natural quality' [essence] apart from the others and having neither heat, cold, dryness nor moisture."

Allah are without the qualities of lightness or heaviness,[1] and thus the heavens, being for ever established in the positions appropriated to them by Allah, are neither light nor heavy. The earth, similarly, being in the place appointed for it at the centre of the universe, is not heavy; nor is the water upon it nor the air above it. And the fire which lies at the top of the atmosphere[2] is not light. But there are parts of the universe outside their own element, which they seek to regain. Thus when earth is in water or in the air it is in a strange element. Meeting an obstacle in the way to its return it exerts effort and is then called heavy. Air within water similarly and fire in air seek to regain their own element. Those things which seek to gain the centre of the universe are called heavy, and those which seek to gain the encompassing sphere (of the atmosphere) are called light.[3]

Coming to the configuration of the earth, the Brethren expand their description of it as a globular body situated in the centre of the atmosphere, and declare that its greatest circumference is 25,455 miles or 6855 parasangs and the corresponding diameter approximately 6551 miles or 2167 (*sic*) parasangs.[4] The centre of the earth is an imaginary point at the middle of the diameter and equidistant from any point on the surface whether the surface at that point be land or water. No part of the surface of the earth can be said to be the lowest, for the lowest part is that which is nearest the centre. The external surface of the earth, namely, the surface in contact with the atmosphere, is upward ("above"), and wherever a man may be standing on the earth's surface he has his feet upon ("above") the earth, pointing downwards to the centre, and his head pointing upwards towards the heavens. He sees but one half of them, the other half being hidden by the earth's curvature, and when he moves from one place to another there

[1] Cf. *Rasā'il*, I, 113 f. [2] See above, p. 484. [3] *Rasā'il*, II, 40 f.

[4] "Authorities concerned with the measurement of the earth and its conformation declare that its circumference is nearly 24,000 miles. That is the full circumference, taking into account all waters and seas; for the waters are curved with the earth and the lines of their configuration correspond. Thus where there is a gap in the earth's curvature [sphericity] either longitudinally or latitudinally, it is filled by a stretch of water of which the longitude and latitude are continuous with those of the land. The extent of a degree was ascertained thus: the latitudes of two cities, Kūfa and Baghdad, were taken, the less subtracted from the greater and the result divided by the number of miles between the two cities. According to Ptolemy a degree corresponds to 66 miles of the earth's surface." (Mas'ūdī, *Tanbīh*, p. 26.)

becomes apparent to him part of the sky previously hidden from him.[1]

Of the earth's surface, one half is covered by the great circumambient ocean in such fashion that one-half of each hemisphere is submerged; like an egg half in the water and half out. Of the half which emerges from the water, a half, comprising land adjacent to the equator[2] and to the south of it, is desert, while the other half, lying to the north of the equator is the habitable quarter of the globe. In the northern habitable quarter are seven great seas[3] which are bays and gulfs of the circumambient ocean and the water of which is salt. In this quarter also there are fifteen small seas of varying size. But as for the Sea of the West,[4] the Sea of Gog and Magog[5], the Seas of Zanj[6] and of Zābaj,[7] the Green Sea[8] and the circumambient ocean, they are outside the habitable quarter of the earth.

In this quarter there are as many as two hundred mountain ranges of varying descriptions and extending from the east to the west or from the south to the north, some being in inhabited lands and others in deserts. In this habitable quarter also there are about two hundred and forty rivers, long or short, flowing in various directions. These rivers rise in the mountains, and on their course down to the sea or the marshes supply cities and cultivated lands with water. The surplus water mingles with the seas. In time it becomes vapour and ascends into the air to form the

[1] *Rasā'il*, I, 112 f.

[2] "The equator is an imaginary line going from east to west under the orbit of the head of Aries. Along this line day and night are always equal. There the two poles are directly on the horizon, the one, nearest the pivotal point of Canopus, in the south, and the other, nearest Capricorn, in the north." (*Rasā'il*, I, 114).

[3] The Sea of the Greeks (the Mediterranean), the Sea of the Slavs (? the Baltic), the Sea of Jurjān (the Caspian), the Sea of Qulzum (the Red Sea), the Sea of Fārs (the Persian Gulf), the Sea of Sind and Hind (the Indian Ocean), and the Sea of China (*loc. cit.*). For other accounts, see Yāqūt, *Mu'jam al-buldān*, ed. F. Wuestenfeld (Leipzig, 1866), I, 499 ff.; Ḥamdallāh Mustawfī, *Nuzhat al-qulūb* (tr. G. le Strange, Gibb Series, London, 1919), pp. 221 ff.; *Ḥudūd al-'ālam* (tr. V. Minorsky, Gibb Series, London, 1937), pp. 54, 181 f.

[4] The (Western) Mediterranean. Cf. Yāqūt, *ibid.* I, 504 f.

[5] (?) Mythical.

[6] Below Zanzibar. Yāqūt, *ibid.* I, 501 f.

[7] Java. The text reads, erroneously, *Zānaj*, cf. Yāqūt, *ibid.* sv. *Zābaj*.

[8] A name sometimes given to the circumambient ocean (Yāqūt, *ibid.* I, 504). Apparently not the sea of that name mentioned by Mustawfī. See Mustawfī, *ibid.* p. 224.

cloud masses which are driven by the winds to the mountain summits and bare heights there to condense and fall as rain. This in its turn forms the rivers.[1]

The habitable quarter has been marked out into seven climes, each like a carpet with its length spread from east to west. They vary in their dimensions, the longest and widest being the first clime,[2] and the shortest and narrowest the seventh.[3] The climes are not natural divisions but are imaginary lines set out by the ancient kings that the boundaries of lands and kingdoms might be ascertainable.[4] Each nevertheless is allotted to the influence of one or other of the planets. The characteristics of the seven climes are, briefly stated, that the first, which is nearest the equator, is the home of the negroes; the next to the northward, containing the cities of Mecca and Medina, is inhabited by men between brown and black in colour; the third, which contains such important cities as Qandahār, Shīrāz, Baṣra, Damascus, Jerusalem, Alexandria in Egypt, Qayrawān and Tangier, is inhabited mainly by brown people. The fourth is the clime of prophets and sages because it is the middle one of the seven and is under the influence of the sun. Its inhabitants are between brown and white in colour and are in constitution and character the best balanced of men. Its cities include Kāshghar, Herāt, Merv, Nīshāpūr, Rayy, Iṣfahān, Baghdad, Mosul and Aleppo. The fifth is the clime of white men, and it passes through the lands of the Turks, across the Oxus, through northern Persia and across the north of the Mediterranean Sea, and after passing through the middle of Andalusia ends in the Sea of the West. The sixth lies in a belt which passes to the north of the "Lands of Gog and Magog", the south of Sagistān (Sīstān), the north of Jurjān, Ṭabaristān and Gīlān, through Armenia to the north of Constantinople and through Macedonia and the middle of North Africa to the Sea of the West. Its inhabitants are between ruddy and white in colour. The seventh

[1] *Rasā'il*, I, 114 ff.

[2] 3000 parasangs long by about 150 wide.

[3] 1500 parasangs long by about 70 wide.

[4] According to Mas'ūdī (*Tanbīh*, p. 34), scholars and sages dispute whether the climes are confined to the region north of the equator, and some hold that they cover the territory both north and south of it. Most are of the former opinion "because of the scanty population of the south". The division of the earth into seven circular climes is known. The fourth and middle one was that containing Babylon.

and most northerly clime lies in territory of which the names, except for a few like the Sea of Jurjān and the land of Sagistān, are more related to myth than to identifiable realities.[1]

After the treatise on astronomy (including geography), come others on the remaining branches of mathematics, on the speculative and practical arts in general, on ethics and manners, and on the *Isagoge*, the six formulas used in logic and dialectic by the philosophers and bearing the same relation to correct thought as grammar to correct speech.[2] Then follows a treatise introducing the section on the "natural" sciences by a discourse on the common (Aristotelian) factors of "physics", namely, form, matter, motion, time and space. The properties of matter are then described and also the four elements (earth, air, fire, water) together with their compounds, the animal, the vegetable and the mineral.

The first "physical" treatise deals with meteorology and begins by describing the atmosphere. This, it is stated, is divided into three distinct layers, of which that nearest the moon is a fire of the intensest heat and is called the "aether", that which comes next is of the intensest cold and is called the *zamharīr*, and that which is nearest the earth is of moderate temperature in the generality of places and is known as the *nasīm* (the "zephyr"). Although the layers are distinct it is possible for them to interpenetrate.

The atmosphere as a whole is subject to change from a variety of causes which include light and darkness, heat and cold, winds and terrestrial vapours. As consequences of them there arise haloes, clouds, thunder, lightning, rain, dew, snow, hail, rainbows and comets together with such earthly phenomena as the overflowing of rivers and the rise and fall of the tides. The wind is no more than a wave-like motion of the air resembling the motion of waves in the sea. One of the causes of atmospheric movements is the rising of moist vapours from bodies of water on the earth and of dry air from arid regions. They ascend to the intense cold of the *zamharīr* and being driven back from it displace various parts of the atmosphere and so cause the winds.

If there should be a mountain range in the way of vapours of which the pressure happens to be great, the cold of the *zamharīr*

[1] *Rasā'il*, I, 115–30.

[2] *Ibid.* I, 132–362.

at its summit will drive the vapour down to mingle with any vapours at the foot of the range, their coalescence bringing about the formation of clouds. These rise, and any dry air is turned into wind by their movement while moist vapour becomes water, the particles of which become compacted and form drops of rain. If the ascent of the moist vapour occurs at night, the extremely cold air will prevent its upward movement, condensing it into a wet precipitation such as dew. Any vapour which is permitted to ascend will be acted upon by the extreme cold and, becoming congealed amongst the interstices of the clouds, will turn into ice or snow. These are congealed particles of water which, mingled with particles of air, fall gently to the ground. In spring and autumn, when the clouds are piled high, the topmost layers are in contact with the *zamharīr* and the moisture, becoming congealed in large drops by the great cold, falls as hail, while the lower parts fall as rain.[1]

Lightning and thunder occur simultaneously, but the lightning reaches the vision before the sound to the hearing because the light is "spiritual" in form whereas the sound is "physical". They originate when the cold of the *zamharīr* compresses the dry hot emanations ascending from the earth within the moist vapours that are mingled with them in the atmosphere. The dry emanations are heated and in their effort to escape burst the envelope of vapour, which emits spluttering sounds as moist objects do when fire is piled about them. A rumbling sound, which is diffused in all directions, is thereby set up in the air, and at the same time the dry heated emanations bursting forth from the moist vapours set up an illumination which is called lightning. This occurs in the same way that the smoke from a lamp recently extinguished will light itself if brought near to a flame.[2]

As for the rainbow, that originates in the lowest layer of the atmosphere when the air is moist to saturation. Its position is always vertical, with the curve at the top in proximity to the layer of the *zamharīr*, and it can appear only at the beginning or at the end of the day opposite to the rising or the setting sun. It appears usually as less than a semicircle; when, however, the sun is level with the horizon, the rainbow appears as a complete semicircle. The reason for this is that the centre of the rainbow lies along the

[1] *Rasā'il*, II, 60–5.   [2] *Ibid*. 66.

line drawn (at right angles) from the centre of the body of the sun, and the higher this is in the heavens the less does there appear of the rainbow, which lies below and facing it. The appearance of the rainbow is due to the shining of the sun upon the particles of moist vapour in the atmosphere and the reflection of its rays. The colours are four in number, corresponding to the number of essential qualities, the elements, the seasons, the humours and the colours of flowers and blossoms. The reason is that when the rainbow appears in its full colours it is an indication of the moistness of the atmosphere and of the consequent abundance of grass and herbage, and it is a general token to living creatures of the fertility of the season.[1] The order of the colours is always red above the yellow and blue below the green; and if there is a second bow below the first one the colours will be in the reverse (reflected) order.[2]

The phenomena that originate in the *zamharīr* are the meteors and the falling stars. The matter and substance of them is the dry, subtle, vapour which rises from mountains and arid places. On reaching the line of division between the *zamharīr* and the aether it turns back and the fire of the aether is kindled within it as the fire of lightning is kindled in the dry oil-like smoke compressed in the moist vapour of the cloud, or as fire is kindled in white naphtha.[3] These falling stars appear sometimes to be revolving in a small circle which is itself carried upon the circumference of a large one, for we see them sometimes travelling from the east across the zenith to the west, sometimes from the west to the east, sometimes beginning their journey in the south and passing across the zenith to the north, and in various other directions. They might be imagined by beholders to be balls of cotton set alight and thrown into the air, where the fire burns them away and they throw off sparks until they are consumed.

[1] "The common people say that excess of red points to bloodshed, of yellow to sickness, of blue to famine and of green to fertility."

[2] *Rasā'il*, II, 67 f.

[3] It is an error, say the Brethren, to suppose that the words of the Koran (67[5]), "We have adorned the heaven with lamps and allotted them to be missiles against demons", refer to these falling stars, which some people believe to be cast from heaven into the air, so to fall on to the earth. The meteors, so the Brethren maintain, do not even originate in the heavens, but near the earth, as may be proved from the swiftness of their transit, for if they began in or near the orbital sphere of the moon or higher their passage would take much longer.

The falling of these stars is only apparent, because the light matter of which they are composed must seek the heights, and their being aflame merely increases their lightness. Those which actually fall to the earth originate in the *nasīm*, the lowest layer of the atmosphere, and are caught and pressed downwards by the clouds. The circular motion of them all is due to the fact that fluid bodies by their nature take a form (namely that of the circle) which offers least resistance. Raindrops in the air take this shape, which is essentially the most perfect.

The comets (literally "stars with tails") that sometimes appear in the sky before sunrise or after sunset, originate in the layer of the atmosphere nearest the moon, the proof being that in their movements they resemble the planets. They are composed of subtle dry and moist exhalations which are condensed by the influence of Saturn and Mercury until they become transparent as crystal. In their course they revolve with the heavens, rising and setting until they are dissipated and vanish.[1]

After the treatise on meteorology follows the section on the composition and formation of minerals, introduced by an explanatory chapter dealing with geology. This begins with some general comments on the characteristics of matter and on its changes. Amongst them are included the changes in the configuration of the earth, such as the gradual transformation of mountains into plains, of plains into the beds of seas and rivers, and of these into marshes, desert sands and mountains.[2] The reason for the existence of mountains and other irregularities in the earth's surface is to prevent the lands being covered entirely by the sea, an event which would occur if the earth were entirely smooth. Rivers and torrents flow down from the mountains but are gradually dried by the desiccating power of the sun, moon and stars. The mountains, deprived of moisture, split and crumble—a process assisted by the action of thunderbolts— and become rocks and stones, gravel and

[1] *Rasā'il*, II, 70–4.

[2] The principle of change also affects the stars. Every 3000 years, the Brethren declare, the fixed stars alter their position and the planets the degree of their apogee and their position with relationship to the signs of the zodiac. The change amounts in 9000 years to one-fourth of the circuit of the sky; in 36,000 years therefore to a complete circuit. Thereby the place of incidence of the planets' rays varies constantly, the result being changes in day and night, summer and winter. Climatic changes in the four quarters of the globe also are to be referred to these celestial changes (*Rasā'il*, II, 80).

sand. These are carried by rain and streams down to the seas and lakes, upon the beds of which they are deposited, layer upon layer, by the action of waves and storms, until in the course of ages mountains are formed in the depths of the ocean in the same way that hills of sand accumulate in the desert through the action of the winds.[1]

The mountains vary in their composition, some being of hard granite and rock or of smooth stone upon which little vegetation grows, as in the mountains of Tihāma (near Mecca), some of soft rocks, light clay, soil, sand and gravel in layers. In mountains of this kind there are numerous caves, hollows, torrent beds (*wādīs*), springs, and streams, and they abound as in Palestine and Ṭabaristān in vegetation of all kinds. In the caves and hollows of the mountains, water gathers, remaining imprisoned when there is no outlet, and, if the earth near it is hot, becoming heated in contact with it and so turning into steam. In seeking an outlet for expansion, the steam may burst open the earth, which quakes and in places subsides. If no outlet is found, the earthquakes continue until the interior of the caves and hollows is cooled and the steam is condensed. The resultant liquid remains in these places for long periods of time, in the course of which its purity and density are increased and it ends by becoming (unstable) quicksilver.[2] In a later passage this "mineral" is described as the product of moisture compounded at high temperature with earth-like atoms. It forms with sulphur (itself described as the product of moisture compounded at high temperature with oil-like atoms) the basis of the other metals, the character of which depends upon the precise conditions of heat and cold to which the compound has been subjected and upon the proportions of the two constituents. Gold, silver, copper, lead, iron and antimony are thus formed and the

[1] *Rasā'il*, II, 81 f. The Brethren here insert a passage giving their theory of the rise of human civilization. They declare that as the mountains are built up in the ocean depths, the seas rise and overflow plains and steppes until in the course of time the plains become seas and the seas dry land. Upon the land raised out of the sea, rain falls, and streams are formed which bring down soil and sand. In this, plants, herbage of various kinds and trees grow. They become the lurking-place of wild animals and attract the attention of man, who comes in search of timber and game. He remains to cultivate the land so that it bears crops of various kinds. Then villages and towns grow up and men make their homes there.

[2] *Rasā'il*, II, 83–5.

jewels (literally "the stone-like minerals") similarly, fire being the decisive factor for them.[1]

Gold is the mineral substance possessing the most perfectly balanced composition and the purest constituents, whose spirit is one with its soul and its soul one with its body—by the spirit being meant the air atoms, by the soul the water atoms and by the body the earth atoms. Fire is the determining element in minerals, and gold is the noblest of the metals, as jacynth amongst the jewels, because fire cannot resolve it into its constituent parts. In the place of its origin, gold was subjected to a constant and equable heat for a long period of time, and that too was a factor in its perfection.[2] Next to it is silver, which might have become the more precious metal if there had not occurred a sudden cooling in the mine.[3] A similar theory is propounded for the formation of the other "minerals" of all classes.[4]

The minerals form the lowest stage in an ascending series which culminates in man and the angels. Above the stage of the minerals is that of the vegetables, the connecting link being a compound of mineral and vegetable, and above the vegetable stage is that of the animals, whose noblest member is man.[5] In the treatise on the vegetable kingdom, the various plants are attributed to special regions of the earth, each with its own character. The minerals are similarly attributed. Thus, gold is formed only in sandy deserts and mountains and amongst soft rocks; silver, copper, iron and the like only in the heart of mountains and of rocks compounded with soft soil; sulphur only in moist earth and soft soils; oily liquids, copperas (green vitriol) and gum benzoin[6] (*aklāḥ*) in marshes and water-logged places; gypsum and ceruse in sandy soils which are mixed with gravel, and the alums and vitriols only in sour and barren soils.

There are innumerable kinds of minerals, some of them unknown to man; but experts recognize about nine hundred varieties, differing in their nature, colour, taste, smell, and mass, and

[1] *Rasā'il* II, 91 ff. [2] *Ibid.* II, 99. [3] *Ibid.* II, 101.

[4] *Ibid.* II, 100 ff. The theory has its place in the history and practice of alchemy. See below, p. 500.

[5] All the three kingdoms are compounds of the four elements acted upon by "Nature", which is the power of the Universal Spirit working through the agency of the skies and the stars. (*Rasā'il*, II, 112 f., 128.)

[6] The identification is not certain.

in their good and harmful qualities. Some are stone-like and hard, but are fusible with fire and harden when cold. Such are gold, silver, copper, iron, lead, glass and the like. Others of the kind are not fusible except by the most extreme heat and are not to be fractured except by use of a diamond. Such are the jacynth and the cornelian. Another variety is earth-like and not fusible but friable (e.g. the salts, the vitriols and talc), and another is fluid, moist and averse to fire (e.g. quicksilver), while still another is aetherial, oil-like and consumable by fire (e.g. sulphur and the arsenics).

There is further a vegetable class, comprising such minerals as coral, both white and red, and there is also an animal class, which includes the pearls. Certain substances produced by congelation form a further class in which are to be found such substances as ambergris and the bezoars. The former is by origin dew which falls upon the surface of the sea and in certain places and at particular times becomes congealed. The bezoars also are congealed dew which has fallen on particular kinds of rocks and become solidified in their interstices. And pearls too have the same origin, for they are formed from drops of dew caught by oysters, sea creatures within which the dew congeals and hardens.

After a restatement of their theories concerning the world of matter and the influence of the astral upon the terrestrial, the Brethren turn to the vegetable kingdom. In introducing their treatise on this subject the Brethren declare their object to be an exposition of the genera of plants; of their origins and growth; of the causes of their differentiation in form, colour, taste, smell, and the shape of their leaves, flowers, berries (grains) and seeds; of their growth (i.e. habit); of their roots and branches and of the principles of their beneficial qualities.[1]

Every kind of plant has a germ ("origin") which is a chyme (*kaymūs*) or mixture of a particular kind. From a given mixture (of elements) a particular chyme is produced, and from it there should grow only one particular kind of plant. Now if the original

[1] "Although plants are obvious and visible creations, the cause of their existence is hidden and veiled from the perception of man. It is what the philosophers call 'the natural forces', what the *sharī'a* calls the 'angels and troops of Allah appointed for the nurture of plants and the generation of animals and the composition of minerals' and what we call the 'partial spirits'." (*Rasā'il*, II, 130.)

matter were always irrigated by the same water, planted in the same kind of soil, fanned by the same breeze and ripened by the same uniform heat from the sun, it would be capable of receiving any form. But there are secondary kinds of matter with it, capable from the nature of their origin of producing only particular forms. Thus, although earth and water are the materials from which the plants both of wheat and cotton grow, yet from the cotton plant there comes nothing but fibre (whence are produced cloth and garments), and from the wheat plant nothing but flour (whence are produced dough and bread). This comes about by the fact that when moisture and the subtile parts of the soil reach the roots of plants, they are changed and become chymes of a particular composition, from which a special plant is produced. The same rule holds for the varieties of leaf, blossom, root and grain.[1]

The genera of the plants are formed under the influence of the various powers[2] of the universal celestial spirit, the partial spirit which is particularly concerned with plants being known as the "vegetable spirit". To this Allah has assigned seven powers; namely, the attractive, the retentive, the digestive, the propulsive, the nutritive, the expansive and the formative. Their functions are respectively to draw the distilled essences of the four elements, in a form suited to the requirements of each genus, to the roots of each plant, to retain them there, to digest them, to propel them to the different parts of the plant, to bring about their assimilation, to encourage growth and to form the variety of shapes and colours.

The first of the plant genera comprises the trees. Amongst them are included all plants possessing an erect stem. There are perfect and imperfect forms of them. The perfect form is that which possesses root-fibres, main root, shoots, branches, leaves, blossoms, fruit, bark and resin: the imperfect form is that which lacks one or more of these parts. The second of the plant genera includes the stemless plants; for example, those which trail along the ground or which cling to trees and are raised into the air. Such are the grape-vine, the gourd and the melon.

A different classification of the plants ranges them according to their habitat, i.e. according as they are to be found in deserts and wildernesses, on mountain-tops, on river-banks, sea-shores, or in

[1] *Rasā'il*, II, 132.
[2] "The prophet calls them 'angels'." (*Ibid.* II, 134.)

pools and hollows. To a special class belong those which are sown and cultivated by men, in towns or arable lands and gardens.

The majority of plants grow on the surface of the soil; some, like the sugar-cane and rice, will grow only under water, others on the surface of water and still others on rocks.[1]

Of the various grades of plants the humblest are the insignificant growths to be found on the rubbish heaps of encampments, and the noblest are those, the palms, which come nearest in their qualities to the animal kingdom. The former spring up in the cool moisture of a night and are withered by the noonday sun, while the palms stand far higher in the natural scale. Individuals of them are either of the male or the female sex, in the former being the active power and in the latter the passive; in other plants the powers do not lie in distinct individuals. Since these phenomena are elsewhere to be found only amongst animals, the palm is animal in spirit but vegetable in body.[2]

Plants, like the lowest of the animals,[3] have only a single sense, that of touch. This is proved by the fact that they send out roots towards moist places and refrain from any approach to rocks and dry places. Further, plants which have been set in a restricted place turn aside in the endeavour to find more room, and plants which have been covered with a roof will find a way through any hole within their reach. These are facts which show that plants have a sense of touch and sufficient discrimination for their needs.[4] Their creation preceded in time that of the animals, for they provided the substance of animal nourishment, being able by their construction to absorb the elements in a form suitable for animal consumption. But for them, animals would have had to obtain their food directly from the soil[5]

The characteristic which distinguishes the animals from the plants is stated by the Brethren to be the capacity to change position in the search for food, and man differs from the other

[1] *Rasā'il*, II, 136 f. [2] *Ibid.* II, 142 f.

[3] This is declared to be the *ḥalazūn*, a small slug which inhabits certain reeds growing on river-banks and sea-shores. When in search of food this creature puts out a part of its body and expands when it touches moisture, but contracts when it meets a dry patch.

[4] *Ibid.* II, 143 f. The Brethren declare that it would not be in accord with Divine wisdom to inflict pain upon plants without having endowed them with the power to escape it or with the means of warding off danger.

[5] *Ibid.* II, 154.

animals in possessing the faculties of speech and reason. All created things are alike in having been created from the four elements (the *arkān*); plants are superior to minerals in being able to absorb nourishment, to grow and feel; animals in addition to these powers have one or more of the five senses, and man, while of the animal kingdom in other respects and possessing all the senses, also speaks and reasons.[1]

The animals are divided into those which are perfect and those which are imperfect in their creation. In the perfect class are included those which have sexual congress, conceive, bear and suckle their young; in the imperfect class are those which originate in putrescences. Between the two classes is that of the creatures which lay and incubate eggs and feed their young. The animals of imperfect creation precede the perfect ones in origin; also they are brought into being in a shorter space of time. Further, the marine animals precede the land animals in order of creation, seeing that the water preceded the earth in origin. The perfect animals originated in the clay, being produced by male and female in the earth beneath the equator, where day and night are equal, the climate always uniform (between hot and cold) and the matter susceptible of receiving form is always to be found. It was there that Adam was brought into being. In the order of creation the animals preceded man, for whom and because of whom they exist.

Of the grades of animals, the lowest is that which has only one sense. The next grade is that of the grubs, which originate and crawl about on the leaves, blossom and fruit of trees and plants. They have two senses, namely those of taste and touch. The third grade, which includes the marine and aquatic animals and those which inhabit dark places, has three senses, adding the sense of smell to the two mentioned. The fourth grade, which includes the insects and creeping things which crawl about in dark places, has all the senses but that of sight, which is unnecessary to it. The most perfect grade is that which possesses all the senses, and it is the grade of the animals of perfect creation.

Another classification of the animals is according to their habitat. There are those which live in the water, namely creatures such as fishes, crabs, frogs, oysters and the like; those which inhabit the air, namely the majority of birds and the swarming

[1] *Rasā'il*, II, 153.

insects; those which dwell on land, namely domestic cattle and wild beasts; and those which dwell in the soil, namely the worms. Of all these animals some are consumers and the rest the consumed.[1]

The animals most perfect in form are those which have the most complete structure. Their external features are a number of limbs and members, each composed of bones put together at symmetrically constructed joints and held together by nerves and ligatures, the interstices being filled with flesh interwoven with veins and the whole protected by skin covered with hair, fur, wool, feathers, shell or scales. Within the body are contained the vital organs, namely, the brain, lungs, heart, liver, spleen, kidneys, bladder, intestines, stomach, crop, gizzard and the rest.[2]

There is no member of the body which does not serve some other, either by protecting or supplementing it or by enabling it to function. An example of this is the brain, which dominates the human body as sovereign. It is the place of origin of the senses, the source of thought, the abode of consideration, the treasure-house of memory, the dwelling-place of the soul and the seat of the reason, and it is served by the heart and the other parts of the body. The function of the heart is to be the controller and regulator of the body: it is the starting-point of the pulsating veins (the arteries) and the source of the body's natural heat. The heart in its turn is served by three members; the liver, the pulsating veins and the lungs, and the liver is assisted in its functions by five other members. The chief of them is the lungs, "the house of breath", which are themselves served by the chest, diaphragm, windpipe and nostrils. Here the Brethren find a suitable place for a description of the function of breathing. In this, they say, the air sucked in through the nostrils enters the windpipe, where its temperature is made normal, and thence reaches the lungs, in which it is purified. It then enters the heart, where it cools the natural heat (of the body), and from there issues into the pulsating veins and so reaches all those parts of the body known as *nabḍ* ("pulse").[3] From the heart also the burnt-up air emerges into the lungs and

[1] *Rasā'il*, II, 167 f. [2] *Ibid.* II, 159 f.

[3] This was the commonly accepted theory in the western world until Harvey's discoveries concerning the circulation of the blood.

so by way of the windpipe into the nostrils or the mouth. The chest serves the lungs by expanding when air is sucked in and contracting when the air is exhaled.[1]

Similar illustrations are provided for the organs concerned in the digestive processes.[2]

In the course of their treatise, the Brethren point out how various animals are provided with special organs suited to their habits of life. Thus the herbivorous land animals have been granted wide mouths to enable them to seize their food, sharp incisor teeth for cutting it and hard molars for grinding the hard parts of herbage, grain, leaves, bark and kernels; also they have a wide smooth gullet, through which the masticated food is swallowed down, and a capacious stomach in which it is contained. Some animals bring back what they have swallowed, in order to masticate it a second time. The product of the second mastication is received after it is swallowed in a second stomach distinct from the first. It is so constructed that it may separate the coarser parts of the food, which are sent to the bowels, from the more subtile, which are sent to the liver, and that it may mature (cook) and purify a second time. What remains passes to vessels adapted to receive it. These are the spleen, the gall-bladder, the heart, the kidneys and the hollow veins, the latter acting as the channels and ducts through which the purified blood passes to all parts of the body. In the body of the male, for the surplus of the nutrient materials, there are divinely provided certain organs, vessels and channels into which it passes. It forms the semen, which, at the time of mating, flows from these organs into the womb of the female, through certain channels and organs in her body which have been prepared to receive it and be the seed-bed in which the young originate and grow.

The wild beasts which eat flesh are by nature and in the structure of some of their organs different from the herbivorous animals. Seeing that they derive their nutriment by eating the bodies of other animals, they have been provided by the Creator with hard incisor teeth, strong curved claws and powerful forearms (*zanadāt*), and further they have a lightness of spring and the power to leap far in order to pounce upon and rend their prey.

The Creator in His wisdom in providing animals with perfection

1 *Rasā'il*, II, 161–3. 2 *Ibid.* II, 163.

of form, distinguished the two halves, the right and the left, whereby they correspond to the first real number ("one" being merely a unit and not a "number") and the combinations of the elements. The body's three divisions, namely, two sides and middle, make it correspond with the first odd number, and its four humours with the first square number. The five senses accord with the first "round" number and the five "qualities", of which four are the "natural" (sublunar) qualities and the fifth the "celestial" quality. In its power to move in six directions (towards the four points of the compass and upwards and downwards) it possesses something which corresponds to the first "complete" number and the number of the faces of a cube. The seven physical faculties correspond to the first "perfect" number and the number of the planets, while the eight possible mixtures (of the elements) correspond to the first cubed number. The structure of the body is in nine layers corresponding to the number of the spheres which surround the earth, and there are in the body twelve openings which are as doorways to the perceptions and correspond to the twelve signs of the zodiac. The twenty-eight vertebrae, upon which depends the erect carriage of the body, correspond to the number of the stations of the moon, and the three hundred and sixty veins of the body are the same in number as the degrees of the zodiac and the days of the year. Thus, he that counts and considers the parts of the body in general will find that they all correspond in number with particular existing phenomena. "This establishes the declaration of the Pythagoreans that all existing things are grouped according to the nature of number."[1]

To complete the picture of science as presented by the Brethren it is necessary to state that they included magic, astrology, and divination within its scope, and in their study of these arts used Indian and Persian as well as Greek authorities.[2] They were careful, however, to proclaim that these arts were only for the initiated,[3] and that parts were true and parts false.[4]

Two works almost contemporary with those of the Ikhwān provide a concise conspectus of science as known to Islam in

[1] *Rasā'il*, II, 168 f.
[2] *Ibid.* IV, 320 ff.
[3] *Ibid.* IV, 340.
[4] *Ibid.* IV, 347.

the fourth and most fruitful century of its history, and serve in some measure to supplement what, in spite of the wide scope of their work, the Ikhwān have not adequately covered. These are the *Mafātīḥ al-'ulūm* ("The Keys of the Sciences") composed in 976 by Muhammad ibn Aḥmad ibn Yūsuf "the Scribe" of Khwārazm, and the *Fihrist* ("Index"), composed in 988 by Ibn al-Nadīm al-Warrāq, the "Paperseller" or "Copyist", of Baghdad.[1]

The *Mafātīḥ al-'ulūm* deals chiefly with the terms employed in the two branches of science, namely the "Arab" and the "foreign", and defines these terms with some attention to the detail of what they represent. The first discourse on the "Arab" sciences has six chapters dealing respectively with *fiqh*, *kalām*, grammar, secretaryship, poetry and prosody and history. Each chapter makes extensive digressions, so that that concerned with *fiqh*, for example, in dealing with the *zakāt* (the alms-tax), gives the names used technically for large and small cattle at various stages of their existence, and the chapter on *kalām* enumerates the various Islamic sects and, moreover, the various Christian, Jewish and "heretical" sects with which the author was familiar. The second discourse deals with philosophy, and includes theology (in the Aristotelian sense), philosophic terminology, logic, medicine, arithmetic, geometry, astronomy (with judicial astrology), music, mechanics and alchemy.

It is in the second part that this work most supplements the treatise of the Ikhwān. The chapter on medicine has sections dealing with anatomy (in which the names, positions and functions of different parts of the body are set out), with diseases and sicknesses, foods, medicaments, both simple and compound, physicians' weights and measures, and, finally, with a number of technical terms. The chapter on arithmetic is of some importance for the history of the subject, because it explains, as though it were dealing with an unfamiliar topic, the functions of the "Indian" numerals[2] and that of the "cipher" in particular. It is described

[1] E. G. Browne, *Literary History of Persia*, I, 382 ff.

[2] Our "Arabic" numerals. (Carra de Vaux sees in the Arabic adjective *Hindī* a corruption of *Handisī*, i.e. "geometric".) Researches into the calculations made to determine legal shares in inheritance (*'ilm al-farā'iḍ*), into the origins of the algebraic terms *māl* (square) and *shay'* (square root, the familiar x of the text-books) and into the terminology of quadratic equations make it probable

as a small circle whose use is to preserve the order of the columns, so that it may be known that a numeral which is not in the first column will belong to the "tens" if followed by a single cipher, to the "hundreds" if followed by two ciphers, and so forth to any degree desired. In the chapter on alchemy the apparatus, processes and the substances used in "The Art" are described.

The *Fihrist* may be said in general terms to deal with the same topics as the *Mafātīḥ al-ʿulūm*, but it is historical and bibliographical rather than descriptive. Its main interest in the present context is for the ideas prevalent concerning the introduction of "foreign" learning into Islam, and for the life and work of the most outstanding figures both Muslim and non-Muslim, in the realm of science.

Except in the fields of astronomy and medicine, where practical observations were added to (although they did not modify) Greek theories, there is little trace of advance made by Muslim science in the centuries after the fourth. Even in astronomy, Ibn Khaldūn (eighth century) declared that scientific observation of the stars had been very little practised after the death of the Caliph Ma'mūn, and that for practical purposes the observations of the ancients were commonly relied upon.[1] Ibn Khaldūn, however, was not in possession of all the facts, and even if no greater practical use was made of astronomy in his day[2] than it is at the present, and if the authority of the past masters was so great that no new theories were evolved,[3] yet for centuries study of the heavens was continuous, new observatories were built and new forms of the old

that all these too were derived from Indian sources. (See J. Ruska, *Zur ältesten arabischen Algebra und Rechenkunst* (on the Algebra of Muḥammad ibn Mūsā al-Khwārazmī), Sitzungsber. d. Heidelberger Akad. d. Wissenschaften (Phil.-Hist. Klasse) 1917, 2te Abhandlung).

[1] *Prolégomènes*, ed. Quatremère, III, 105 f.

[2] For determining, for example, the beginning and end of Ramaḍān. To this day it is not astronomical calculation which determines the date but actual observation of the new moon's rising.

[3] Speculation continued even if it resulted in no new theory. Yāqūt in the *Muʿjam al-buldān* (begun in Muḥarram, 625 = December 1227) reports how the ancients disputed about the shape of the earth, some declaring it was a plane, others that it was drum-shaped, others that it had the shape of a dome set up on its rim, others that it was cylindrical. As for the revolution of the stars, some said that it was due to the rotation of the earth itself and not to the revolution of the heavens. (*Muʿjam al-buldān*, ed. F. Wuestenfeld, I, 14.)

astronomical instruments were constructed. By this activity the foundations of modern astronomy were laid, a fact which is made obvious by the Arabic nomenclature still in use.

The regard for authority is more obvious in medicine where "the mighty name" of Galen has kept some Muslim practitioners of that art in subjection to this very day. Even the greatest of them, Rhazes and Avicenna, were content to follow the Greeks for their anatomy, physiology and pathology, although occasionally an accident enabled first-hand observation to correct theory. A widely quoted instance of this is to be found in the diary of the physician 'Abd al-Laṭīf al-Baghdādī (d. 629/1231), who, during his travels in Egypt discovered a great collection of skeletons, accumulated during a pestilence, on the hills at Maks, and was there able by the evidence of his own eyes to correct Galen's description of the structure of the human mandible.[1] It had never occurred to him (he flourished during the latter half of the sixth and the beginning of the seventh century of Islam) previously to examine a subject for himself in order to discover the truth, nor had there been any dissection of the human body by even the most eminent of his predecessors, or by any amongst his fellow-practitioners. This was not in any measure due to prohibitions of the Islamic authorities, but rather to age-old prejudice against interference with the dead. Islam itself had no scruples about mutilation of the human body, when alive at any rate, for mutilation was the punishment recognized by the *shar'* for theft. The importance of "Arab" medicine lies in the evidence of original experiment in treatment and exact empirical observation of the aetiology and symptoms of disease. As Professor Browne remarks in his *Arabian Medicine*,[2] the clinical notes of these old "Arabian" physicians are of much greater interest and importance than their obsolete physiology and pathology or their second-hand anatomy."[3] Their success as physicians probably lay in their

[1] *Kitāb al-Ifādah*, ed. J. White (Oxford, 1788), pp. 272 ff.; tr. S. de Sacy (*Relation de l'Égypte*, Paris, 1810), p. 418.

[2] Cambridge, 1921, p. 50.

[3] There are evidences even in the *Arabian Nights* of the study of disease symptoms as reported in the examination of the learned slave-girl Tawaddud. Her reply to a question on diagnosis is that the physician may diagnose by palpation hardness, heat, dryness, cold and moisture. By ocular perception he notes the tokens of internal affections; yellowness of the eyes indicating jaundice, twisting of the back, pleurisy, and so forth. Symptoms of internal complaints may be diagnosed from six sources, namely, from the patient's reactions, from

ignoring theories and their employment of means suggested by experience and common sense.

One further branch of "science", namely, alchemy, occupied a considerable place in the attentions of the Muslim *savants*, although its claim to be regarded as a serious branch of knowledge was often in dispute. The subject was of foreign derivation, having been introduced into Islam from Egypt or Greece, but, like other new subjects of promise, it was taken up with avidity. At no time in its history can it be said to have had fixed and universally accepted principles such as appear in medicine. The philosophic basis of the art rested on the Aristotelian theory that all things ultimately were composed of the four "matrices", namely, fire, air, water and earth. It has been seen that according to the Ikhwān al-Ṣafā mercury and sulphur were the more immediate bases of the minerals, and the belief of the alchemist was that elixirs might be discovered which would transmute less noble minerals or metals, such as lead, tin, copper, mercury or even iron, into the precious metals such as gold and silver. But the method followed by the individual investigator depended upon his answer to the question whether the metals differed from each other in their essence or only in their accidental qualities.

Abu Naṣr al-Fārābī held that all metals belong to the same species and that it is therefore possible to convert one metal into another. Another authority, Al-Ṭughrā'ī, held that they differed only in accidentals and nevertheless that the secret of transmutation lay not in creating or discovering the substance through which the more precious metal differed from the less precious one, but in careful preparation of the elemental materials which would display the appropriate differences once the desired combination was successfully achieved.

Both the theory and the practice were denounced as false and dishonest by men of authority in Islam, although alchemy continued to flourish in spite of them until the rise of modern chemistry. Avicenna held that metals were distinguished from one another by specific differences and that each formed a species by itself and distinct from the rest.[1] His view therefore was that it

bodily evacuation, from pain, from the locality, from swellings and external symptoms. (*Alf layla wa-layla*, ed. Macnaghten (Calcutta, 1831–42), II, 514 f.)

[1] Cf. Ibn Khaldūn, *Prolégomènes*, ed. Quatremère, III, 200 f., 229, 233 f.

was impossible to change one metal into another and that the practitioners of the "Art" merely produced colourable imitations of the precious metals, the essential character of the base ones being retained in them.[1] According to Mas'ūdī[2] alchemy bred deceit and trickery, and it was denounced by the philosopher al-Kindī in a treatise which proved man's incapacity to rival Nature in its workings. Ibn Khaldūn held similar views and refused even to recognize that alchemy was a branch of "natural science". Its pretensions he declared to be false and asserted that if it were possible to change one thing into another essentially different then the art belonged to the realm of magic, since it meant the creation of something out of materials not appropriate to it.[3]

It will have been made apparent that the debt which science in Islam owed to the Greek philosophers, and in a lesser degree to the Indians and Persians, for its general theories, was a great one. The Muslim *savants* accepted the theories as they stood, and on the whole left the field of the physical science much as they had found it. Yet, during the period when their activities were encouraged, they enriched the subjects in which they engaged by the accumulation of numerous observed facts and by their vigorous pursuit of knowledge for practical ends. After the fifth century of Islam, as has been indicated, it is evident that the spirit of inquiry was dulled, for the outstanding figures in the scientific world were no longer Muslims although working under Muslim protection and encouragement. In large measure this would appear to be due to the growing influence of the '*ulamā* and the hardening of dogmatic feeling in the various "schools" of the faith. Rigid orthodoxy disapproved of philosophers (even of those "natural" philosophers whose researches into the works of Creation led them to acknowledge the omnipotence of the Creator), the reason being that they declared man to be no different from other creatures, that his soul perished like his body and that there was

[1] *Avicennae de Congelatione et Conglutinatione Lapidum* (an extract from the *Kitāb al-Shifā*), (ed. E. J. Holmyard, Paris, 1927), p. 95. He nevertheless recognized alchemy as a branch of "natural science" and says its object is to deprive the "mineral essences" (i.e. the metals) of their particular character and to give them other characters, so that it may lead ultimately to the derivation of gold and silver from other bodies. (*Risālah Taqsīm al-'ulūm*, B.M. MS. Add. 16,659, fol. 349 a.)

[2] *Murūj al-dhahab*, VIII, 175-7.

[3] *Prolégomènes*, ed. Quatremère, III, 208.

no resurrection in the hereafter.[1] For that reason orthodoxy branded them as heretics and was careful to declare whether any Muslim who devoted himself to philosophy could be regarded as a true believer or not,[2] and it was on that account also that the scientific side of *'ilm* was always kept distinct from the religious, with no attempt made to harmonize the two.

Ghazālī,[3] in his exposition of the duties of the true believer, discusses the question of how far it was necessary for him to inquire for himself into the facts of religion and natural phenomena. At the outset the author quotes two *ḥadīths*, of which one makes it the bounden duty of every Muslim to seek "knowledge", while the other is the widely-quoted counsel of perfection which bids man "seek knowledge, even if it be in China". The difficulty lies in the definition of *'ilm*: the scholastic theologians say it is their *kalām*, the *faqīhs* that it is *fiqh*, and the Ṣūfīs that it is Ṣūfīsm, while Abu Ṭālib al-Makkī[4] maintained that it was the learning which concerned itself with the five fundamental requirements of Islam.

Without saying more to determine the question than that only such knowledge is requisite as will enable the believer to perform the essential duties imposed on him by his faith, Ghazālī proceeds to a classification of the various aspects of knowledge. Knowledge, he says, is divided into that which is connected with the *shar'* and that which is unconnected therewith. In the first class is comprised all the science which is derived from the Prophets and is not acquired by reasoning, like arithmetic, or by experience, like medicine, or by the hearing, like language. In the second class is contained all the rest and it is divided into three parts, the recommended, the deprecated, and the permitted (indifferent). The first part comprises those branches of knowledge which concern the

[1] Cf. al-Qifṭī, *Ta'rīkh al-ḥukamā*, p. 50. For the attitude of Ghazālī on the question in his *Tahāfut al-falāsifa* and other works, see below, pp. 503 ff.

[2] Cf. the case of 'Abd al-Salām, who studied the "Sciences of the Ancients", was accused of heresy and had his books publicly burned (Qifṭī, *ibid.* pp. 228 f.), and the case also of 'Umar Khayyām, who "taught the science of the Greeks" and the inward meanings of whose works were "serpents stinging the *sharī'a*" (*ibid.* p. 244), while Rhazes, "the physician of the Muslims" (*ibid.*, p. 271), and al-Fārābī, "the philosopher of the Muslims" (*ibid.*, p. 277), are carefully described as "unobjectionable" (*ghayru mudāfa'*). The latter is described as having distinguished between divine inspiration (*waḥy*) and philosophy.

[3] *Iḥya*, I, 12 ff.

[4] Died 996. Best known for his treatise on Ṣūfīsm, the *Qūt al-qulūb*.

welfare of the world, such as medicine and mathematics; and each science of this kind must be practised by at least one member of the community (i.e. it is *farḍ al-kifāya*), the rest of whom are exempt. In the same class as these sciences are certain fundamental crafts such as husbandry, weaving, the tending of beasts and certain arts such as cupping and tailoring. But deep research into the minutiae of mathematics and the laws of medicine is unnecessary and superfluous, as being of no immediate practical value. The blameworthy sciences are those concerned with magic, talismans and jugglery, for the reason that they rely for their validity upon reference to powers other than Allah.[1] The permitted arts (i.e. those towards the practice of which the law is indifferent) are such studies as poetry and history.[2]

In his autobiographical work entitled *Al-Munqidh min al-ḍalāl*[3] ("The Deliverer from Error"), Ghazālī indicates that fanatical adherents of Islam believed they were helping the faith by declaring false all knowledge derived from the philosophers, so that they went to the extent of denying what was said about the eclipses of the sun and moon. He protests that the function of the "natural" sciences is to deal with the celestial "spheres" and the stars, with the elements which exist below the "sphere" of the moon (namely water, air, earth, fire), with their compounds (which are animals, plants and minerals) and with the causes of their changing and combining. Religion therefore does not demand that this science should be denounced any more than that medicine should be denounced, except in particular questions which are specified in the book called *Tahāfut al-falāsifa*, "The Confusion of the Philosophers", for the root purpose of all these sciences is to make it known that "Nature" is subordinated to Allah, and does not act alone but is directed by its Creator. As for the conceptions of the ancients which have been transmitted by the philosophers, some, he says, may arise spontaneously in any mind, others may be found in works which are concerned with the *shar'*, and the principles of most are to be found in the books of the Ṣūfīs. Even if they are not so to be found, provided that the subject-matter is in itself in conformity with reason, susceptible of proof by argument and not contrary to the Book and the *sunna*, then

[1] Thus Ibn Khaldūn, *Prolégomènes*, ed. Quatremère, III, 136.
[2] Ghazālī, *Iḥya*, I, 14.
[3] Ed. Cairo, A.H. 1309, pp. 9 ff.

there is no need to denounce and forbid it. Otherwise if all ancient truths had to be rejected, then the Koran itself and the Traditions of the Prophet and authentic historical material would have to be rejected merely because the Ikhwān al-Ṣafā had cited them. On the other hand those who, like the Ikhwān al-Ṣafā, make a study of philosophy are apt also to fall into error, for they mingle what they approve of philosophy with prophetic wisdom and Ṣūfī lore and then hasten to accept the falsehood mingled with the truth. The reading of their books should for this reason be discouraged.

It was only in the unlearned that Ghazālī discouraged inquiry. He himself was fully acquainted with the scientific thought of his day and much of it he accepted as true. In the *Tahāfut* there is a clear exposition of the various branches of "Natural Science", in the course of which the author explains what he would retain and what reject. He proclaims that certain of the beliefs of some of the philosophers (al-Fārābī and Ibn Sīnā being singled out for special mention) do not offend the principles of Islam and there is no necessity for the confirmation of these beliefs by prophets and apostles. An example of such beliefs is that the eclipse of the moon is due to the fact that its light is blotted out by the intervention of the earth between it and the sun, from which the moon receives its light. These and similar beliefs may be left without question because they can be mathematically proved.[1]

In recounting what he regards as acceptable, Ghazālī provides a conspectus of the subjects of scientific study in his day, which show little change from those of the Ikhwān. They include the general principles of Aristotelian physics (the ideas of motion, change etc.), the composition of the heavens and the four elements and their "natural qualities", "Generation and Corruption", the conditions of the elements which produce the meteorological phenomena such as clouds, rain, thunder and the rest, the "mineral essences", the laws of plants, zoology, "the animal spirit and the perceptive powers and the fact that the human soul does not die with the death of the body and that it [the soul] is a spiritual essence".

The foregoing are regarded as the principal subjects. Derivative

[1] *Algazel Tahafot al-Falasifat*, ed. M. Bouyges, S.J. (Beyrouth, 1927), pp. 10 f.

from them are a number of subjects which form the "departmental" sciences, of which the first is medicine. Its object is defined as the knowledge of the beginnings of the human body, its condition in health and sickness, the causes and symptoms of the latter and the means of warding it off and preserving good health. The second derivative subject is judicial astrology, which has for its aim the prognostication of terrestrial events from the positions and combinations of the stars. The third subject is physiognomy, which concerns itself with the diagnosis of character from physical qualities; the fourth is the interpretation of dreams; the fifth is that of talismans ("the connection of celestial influences with certain terrestrial objects so as to produce a force which shall work in unfamiliar fashion in the terrestrial part of the universe") and the sixth that of "white magic", which is "the mingling of the earthly essences in such fashion as to produce unfamiliar things". The seventh and last of the derivative sciences is that of alchemy, the purpose of which is to "change the character of the 'mineral essences' and so achieve the production of gold and silver by a species of devices".[1]

To these "natural sciences" Ghazālī takes no exception, and it is on more general and metaphysical questions that he joins issue with the philosophers. This is not the place in which to discuss them but they are summarized in the *Tahāfut* under four headings: (1) The decision of the philosophers that the association which is apparent in the world of phenomena between causes and effects is a necessary one and that it is not within the bounds of possibility to find the cause without the effect nor the effect without the cause; (2) the assertion of the philosophers that the human soul has an independent existence; (3) the statement of the philosophers that the destruction of the human soul is impossible; and (4) that the human soul cannot return to the body (after death).[2]

Orthodox Islam has not moved from the position assumed by Ghazālī in the fifth century of its history, but individual Muslims have at various times adopted the results of the scientific investigations of their day rather than those of scholastic theology, and by their work made their place in the history of science one of recognized importance.

[1] This seems to bear evidence of Avicenna's definition. See above, p. 501.
[2] *Algazel Tahafot*, pp. 268 ff.

BIBLIOGRAPHY

Abd-el-Jalil, J. M., *Brève Histoire de la Littérature Arabe*, Paris, 1947.

Abd al-Laṭīf al-Baghdādī. *Kitāb al-Ifāda wa'l-i'tibār*. Ed. J. White (*Compendium memorabilium Aegypti*). Oxford, 1788. Tr. S. de Sacy (*Relation de l'Égypte*). Paris, 1810.

Abdur Rahim. *The Principles of Muhammedan Jurisprudence*. London, 1911.

Abu Bakr al-Ṭurṭūshī. *Sirāj al-mulūk*. Cairo, A.H. 1289.

Abu'l-Qāsim b. Ḥasan al-Jīlānī. *Qawānīn al-uṣūl*. Tabriz, 1858.

Abu Tammām. *Ḥamāsa*. Ed. G. Freytag. 2 vols. Bonn, 1828–47.

Abu Yūsuf (Ya'qūb b. Ibrāhīm). *Kitāb al-Kharāj*. Būlāq, A.H. 1302.

Adams, C. C. *Islam and Modernism in Egypt*. London, 1933.

L'Afrique et l'Asie. Paris, 1952 ff.

Aghababian, R. (or Aghababoff). *Législation Iranienne*. 2 vols. Teheran, 1939; Paris, 1951.

Kitāb al-Aghānī. 20 vols. Būlāq, A.H. 1285.

Aḥmad b. Ḥanbal. *Musnad*. 6 vols. Cairo, A.H. 1313.

Alberi, Eugenio. *Relazioni degli Ambasciatori Veneti al Senato*. 15 vols. Florence, 1839–63.

Alf layla wa-layla. Ed. W. H. Macnaghten. 4 vols. Calcutta, 1831–42.

'Alī Chelebī. *Kunh al-akhbār*. Constantinople, n.d.

'Alī b. Sahl Rabban al-Ṭabarī. *Firdaws al-Ḥikma*. Berlin, 1928.

Amari, M. *Biblioteca Arabo-Sicula*. Leipzig, 1887.

Ameer Ali. *Personal Law of the Mahommedans*. London, 1880.

'Āmilī, Ḥasan b. Zayn al-Dīn. *Ma'ālim al-dīn*. Lucknow, 1301.

'Āmilī, Muḥammad al-Ḥurr. *Bidāyat al-Hidāya*. Lucknow, 1885.

Anderson, G. N. D. *Islamic Law in Africa*. H.M.S.O. London, 1954.

André, P. J. *L'Islam Noir*. Paris, 1924.

Annuaire du Monde Mussulman. Ed. L. Massignon. Paris, 1925–1955.

'Arīb. *Ṭabarī Continuatus*. Ed. M. J. de Goeje. Leyden, 1897.

Arnold, T. W. *Preaching of Islam*. London, 1913.

Arnold, T. W. *Painting in Islam*. Oxford, 1928.

'Aṭṭār (Farīd al-Dīn). *Tadhkirat al-awliyā*. Ed. R. A. Nicholson. 2 vols. Leyden, 1905–7.

Averroes (Ibn Rushd). *Tahāfut al-Tahāfut*. Tr. S. van den Bergh. 2 vols. London, 1954.

Avicenna. *De Congelatione et Conglutinatione Lapidum*. Ed. E. J. Holmyard. Paris, 1927.

Avicenna. *Risāla Taqsīm al-'ulūm*. B.M. MS. Add. 16,659.

'Ayn 'Alī Efendī. *Qawanīn-i Āl-i 'Uthmān*. Constantinople, A.H. 1280.

Babinger, F. *Hans Dernschwam's Tagebuch einer Reise nach Konstantinopel, 1553–55*. Munich, 1923.

Bābur, *Babūr-nāmah*, "The Memoirs of Bābur". Tr. A. S. Beveridge. London, 1921.

Baeumker, C., *Alfarabi, Ueber den Ursprung der Wissenschaften. Beiträge zur Geschichte des Mittelalters*, XIX, iii. Münster i. W., 1916.

Balādhurī. *Futūḥ al-buldān*. Ed. M. J. de Goeje. Leyden, 1866.

Barbier de Meynard. *Considérations sur l'Histoire Ottomane*. (Publications de l'École des Langues orientales vivantes.) Paris, 1886

Barthold, W. *Histoire des Turcs d'Asie Centrale*. Paris, 1945.

Barthold, W. *Turkestan down to the Mongol Invasion*. (E. J. W. Gibb Memorial. n.s. v.) London, 1928.

Bayḍāwī. *Anwār al-tanzīl* (Commentarius in Coranum). Ed. H. O. Fleischer. 2 vols. Leipzig, 1846.

Bayhaqī. *Ta'rīkh-i Mas'ūdī*. Ed. W. H. Morley. Calcutta, 1862.

Bayhaqī. *Maḥāsin wa'l-masawī*. Ed. F. Schwally. Giessen, 1902.

Becker, C. H. *Beiträge zur Geschichte Egyptens*. Strassburg, 1902.

Becker, C. H. *Islamstudien*. 2 vols. Leipzig, 1924.

Becker, C. H. *Papyri Schott-Reinhardt*. Heidelberg, 1906.

Bell, Sir Charles. *People of Tibet*. Oxford, 1928.

Bell, H. Idris. *Aphrodito Papyri*. London, 1910.

Bell, R. *The Origin of Islam in its Christian Environment*. Edinburgh, 1926.

Bennigsen, A. *L'Afrique et l'Asie*. Paris, 1952–3.

Berchem, M. van. *La Propriété territoriale et l'Impot foncier sous les premiers Califs*. Geneva, 1886.

Birge, J. K. *The Bektashi Order of Dervishes*, London, 1937.

Bīrūnī. *Kitāb al-Tafhīm* (Elements of the Art of Astrology). Ed. and tr. R. Ramsay Wright. London, 1934.

Blunt, Lady Anne. *Bedouins of the Euphrates*. 2 vols. London, 1879.

Bouyges, M. *Sur le* de scientiis *d'Alfarabi*. Mélanges de l'Université S. Joseph, IX (ii). Beyrouth, 1922–3.

Bouyges, M. *Bibliotheca Arabica Scholasticorum*. Vol. III. Beyrouth, 1930.

Brockelmann, C. *Gesch. d. Arabischen Litteratur*. 2 vols: Vol. I, Weimar, 1898; vol. II, Berlin, 1902. Supplement. 3 vols. Leiden, 1937–42.

Browne, E. G. *Literary History of Persia*. 2 vols. London, 1909, 1915; reissued (4 vols.) Cambridge, 1928.

Browne, E. G. *Persian Literature under Tartar Dominion*. Cambridge, 1920.

Browne, E. G. *History of Persian Literature in Modern Times*. Cambridge, 1924.

Browne, E. G. *A Year Amongst the Persians*. London, 1893.

Browne, E. G. *Arabian Medicine*. Cambridge, 1921.

Bukhārī. *Ṣaḥīḥ*. Ed. L. Krehl. (*Le Recueil des Traditions Mahometanes.*) 3 vols. Leyden, 1862–8.

Burckhardt, J. L. *Notes on the Bedouins and Wahabys*. London, 1831.

Burton, R. F. *The Book of a Thousand Nights and a Night*. 12 vols. London, 1894.

Burton, R. F. *Pilgrimage to Al-Madinah and Meccah*. 2 vols. London, 1893.

Bury, J. B. *A History of the Later Roman Empire*. 2 vols. London, 1889.

Bury, J. B. *A History of the Eastern Roman Empire*. London, 1912.

de Busbecq. *Turkish Letters of Ogier Ghiselin de Busbecq*. Tr. E. S. Forster. Oxford, 1927.

Butler, A. J. *The Arab Conquest of Egypt*. Oxford, 1902.

Caetani, L. *Chronographia Islamica*. Rome, 1912 ff.

Caetani, L. *Annali dell' Islam*. 10 vols. Milan, 1905 ff.

Cahun, L. *Introduction à l'Histoire de l'Asie. Turcs et Mongols*. Paris, 1896.

Caussin de Perceval. *Essai sur l'histoire des arabes avant l'Islamisme*. 3 vols. Paris, 1847–8.

Central Asian Review. London, 1953 ff.
Chan, Wing-tsit. *Religious Trends in Modern China*. New York, 1953.
Chardin. *Voyages du Chevalier Chardin en Perse*. Ed. L. Langlès. 10 vols. Paris, 1811.
Chardin, J. *Travels in Persia*, with an introduction by Sir P. Sykes. London, 1927.
Chatelier, A. le. *Les Confréries musulmanes du Hedjaz*. Paris, 1887.
China Handbook. Taipei, Taiwan, 1953.
Clavel, E. *Droit Musulman*. 2 vols. Paris, 1895.
Clot Bey, A. B. *Aperçu général sur l'Égypte*. Paris, 1840.
Codrington, O. *Musalman Numismatics*. London, 1904.
Coon, C. S. *Caravan*. New York, 1951.
Cromer, Lord. *Modern Egypt*. 2 vols. London, 1908.
Crooke, W. *Islam in India*. Oxford, 1921.
Curzon, W. *Persia and the Persian Question*. 2 vols. London, 1892.
Damīrī. *Ḥayāt al-ḥayawān*. 2 vols. Cairo, A.H. 1311.
Darling, M. L. *Rusticus Loquitur*. Oxford, 1930.
Demorgny, G. *Essai sur l'Administration de la Perse*. Paris, 1913.
Dimashqī [Ja'far b. 'Alī]. *Kitāb al-Ishāra ilā maḥāsin al-tijāra*. (?) Cairo, 1318.
Dīnawarī. *Akhbār al-ṭiwāl*. Ed. Guirgass. Leyden, 1888.
Don Juan of Persia. Tr. G. le Strange. London, 1926.
Doughty, C. M. *Arabia Deserta*. 2 vols. Cambridge, 1888.
Dozy, R. *Recherches sur l'Histoire et la Littérature de l'Espagne*. 2 vols. (3rd ed.) Leyden, 1881.
Dozy, R. *Spanish Islam*. Tr. F. G. Stokes. London, 1913.
Dozy, R. [ed.] *History of the Almohades* by al-Marrākushī. 2nd ed. Leyden, 1881.
Dozy, R. *Supplément aux Dictionnaires arabes*. 2 vols. Leyden, 1881.
Dunne, J. Heyworth. *Introduction to the History of Education in Modern Egypt*. London, 1939.
Dunne, J. Heyworth. *Religious and Political Trends in Modern Egypt*. Washington, 1950.
Eclipse of the Abbasid Caliphate. Ed. and tr. H. E. Amedroz and D. S. Margoliouth. 7 vols. Oxford, 1920–1.
Elliot, H. M., and Dowson, J. *The History of India as told by its own Historians*. 8 vols. London, 1867–77.

Evans-Pritchard, E. E. *The Sanusi of Cyrenaica.* Oxford, 1949.
Evliyā Chelebī. *Narrative of Travels.* Tr. J. von Hammer (Oriental Translation Fund.) 2 vols. London, 1834–50.
Firīdūn Bey. *Munsha'āt al-salāṭīn.* 2 vols. Constantinople, A.H. 1274.
Fragmenta Historicorum Arabicorum. Ed. M. J. de Goeje. 2 vols. Leyden, 1869–71.
Fryer, John. *A New Account of East India and Persia.* [Hakluyt Society.] 3 vols. London, 1915.
Fyzee, Asaf A. A. *Outlines of Muhammadan Law.* Oxford, 1949. 2nd ed. Oxford, 1955.
Gardet, L. *La Cité Musulmane: Vie sociale et politique.* Paris, 1954.
Gardīzī. *Zayn al-Akhbār.* Ed. M. Nazim. Berlin, 1928.
Gaudefroy-Demombynes, M. *Muslim Institutions.* London, 1950.
Gautier, E. F. *Les Siècles obscurs du Maghreb.* (*L'Islamisation de l'Afrique du Nord.*) Paris, 1927.
Ghazālī, M. *Iḥyā 'ulūm al-dīn.* 4 vols. Cairo, A.H. 1289.
Ghazālī, M. *Al-Munqidh min al-ḍalāl.* Cairo, A.H., 1309.
Ghazālī, M. [*Algazel*] *Tahafot al Falasifat.* Ed. M. Bouyges, S.J. Beyrouth, 1927.
Ghazālī, M. *Ayyuhā 'l Walad* (*O Kind!*). Ed. Hammer-Purgstall. Vienna, 1838.
Ghazālī, M. *Al-Durrat al-fākhira.* Ed. and tr. L. Gautier. Geneva, 1878.
Ghazālī, M. *Al-Iqtiṣād fī 'l-i'tiqād.* Cairo, A.H. 1327.
Gibb, H. A. R. *The Arab Conquests in Central Asia.* London, 1923.
Gibb, H. A. R. *Modern Trends in Islam.* Chicago, 1947.
Gibb, H. A. R. *Mohammedanism.* London, 1949.
Gibbon, E. *Decline and Fall of the Roman Empire.* Ed. J. B. Bury. 7 vols. London, 1896–1900.
Gibbons, H. A. *The Foundation of the Ottoman Empire.* Oxford, 1916.
Goldziher, I. *Muhammedanische Studien.* 2 vols. Halle, 1889–90.
Goldziher, I. *Vorlesungen über den Islam.* 2nd ed. Ed. Fr. Babinger. Heidelberg, 1925.
Goldziher, I. *Die Ẓâhiriten.* Leipzig, 1884.
Greek Papyri in the British Museum. (Vol. IV. *Aphrodito Papyri*, ed. H. I. Bell. London, 1910.)

Grundriss der Iranischen Philologie. Ed. W. Geiger and E. Kuhn. 2 vols. Strassburg, 1895 ff.

Ḥājjī Khalīfa. *Kashf al-Ẓunūn*. Ed. and tr. G. Fluegel. 7 vols. Leipzig and London, 1835–58.

Halide Edib. *Inside India*. London, 1937.

Ḥamdallāh Mustawfī Qazwīnī. *Nuzhat al-qulūb*. Ed. and tr. G. le Strange (Gibb Series XXIII, i and ii). London, 1915, 1919.

Hamilton, C. *The Hedaya*. Ed. C. S. Grady. London, 1870.

Hammer-Purgstall, J. von. *Des osmanischen Reichs Staatsverfassung und Staatsverwaltung*. 2 vols. Vienna, 1815.

Ḥarīrī. *Maqāmāt*. Ed. S. de Sacy. Paris, 1822. 2nd ed. (Reinaud and Derenbourg), 2 vols. Paris, 1847–53.

Harris, M. *Egypt under the Egyptians*. London, 1925.

Hartmann, M. *Zur Geschichte der Islam in China*. Leipzig, 1921.

Ḥasan b. ʿAlī al-Ṭabarī. *Kāmil-i bahāʾī*. Bombay, A.H. 1323.

Hasanein, A. M. *The Lost Oases*. London, 1925.

Hasluck, F. W. *Christianity and Islam under the Sultans*. 2 vols. Oxford, 1929.

Herklots, G. A. *Islam in India*. Ed. W. Crooke. London, 1921.

al-Ḥillī. *Al-bâbu 'l-ḥâdî ʿashar*. Tr. W. M. Miller. London, 1928.

Ḥudūd al-ʿālam. Tr. V. Minorsky. (Gibb Series.) London, 1937.

Hujwīrī. *Kashf al-maḥjūb*. Ed. V. Zhukovsky. Leningrad, 1926. Tr. R. A. Nicholson (Gibb Series XVII). London, 1911.

Hurgronje, Snouck. *Mekka*. 2 vols. Leyden, 1888.

Hurgronje, Snouck. *Verspreide Geschriften*. 6 vols. Bonn, 1923.

Hurgronje, Snouck. *The Achehnese*. Tr. A. W. S. O'Sullivan. 2 vols. Leyden and London, 1906.

Ibn Abi Uṣaybiʿa. *ʿUyūn al-anbā*. Ed. A. Müller. Cairo, 1882.

Ibn ʿAbdūn. [*Un Document sur la vie urbaine . . . à Séville an début du XIIe siècle*.] *Le Traité d'Ibn ʿAbdūn*. Ed. E. Lévi-Provençal. Journal Asiatique, t. 224 (1934).

Ibn al-Athīr. [*Al-*]*Kāmil*. Ed. C. J. Tornberg. 14 vols. Leyden, 1851–76.

Ibn Bābūyah al-Qummī. *Man lā yaḥḍuruhu al-faqīh*. B.M. MS. Add. 19,358.

Ibn Baṭṭūṭa. *Voyages d'Ibn Batoutah*. Ed. C. Defrémery et B. Sauguinetti. 4 vols. Paris, 1874 ff.

Ibn al-Faqīh. *Kitāb al-Buldān*. Ed. M. J. de Goeje. Bibliotheca Geographorum Arabicorum, V. Leyden, 1885.

Ibn Ḥawqal. *Kitāb al-Masālik wa'l-mamālik*. Ed. M. J. de Goeje. Leyden, 1873.

Ibn Ḥazm. *Kitāb al-Fiṣal*. 5 parts. Cairo, A.H. 1317.

Ibn Hishām. *Sīrat Saiyidnā Muḥammad*. Ed. F. Wuestenfeld. 2 vols. Göttingen, 1858–60.

Ibn Isfandiyār. *History of Ṭabaristān*. Tr. E. G. Browne. (Gibb Series II.) London, 1905.

Ibn Jubayr. *Travels*. Ed. W. Wright and M. J. de Goeje. (Gibb Series V.) Leyden, 1907.

Ibn Khaldūn. *Kitāb al-'Ibar*. 7 vols. Būlāq, A.H. 1284.

Ibn Khaldūn. *Prolégomènes*. Ed. M. Quatremère. 3 parts. Paris, 1858.

Ibn Khaldūn. *Prolégomènes*. Tr. MacGuckin de Slane. Notices et Extraits, vols. 19–21. Paris, 1863–8.

Ibn Khaldūn. *Histoire des Berbères*. Tr. MacGuckin de Slane. 4 vols. Algiers, 1852 ff.

Ibn Khallikān. *Wafayāt al-a'yān*. Tr. MacGuckin de Slane. 4 vols. Paris and London, 1843–71.

Ibn Khurdādbih. *Kitāb al-Masālik wa' l-mamālik*. Bibliotheca Geographorum Arabicorum. Vol. VI. Ed. M. J. de Goeje. Leyden, 1889. [2nd ed. Ed. J. H. Kramers. Leyden, 1938–9.]

Ibn Mammātī. *Kitāb Qawānīn al-dawāwīn*. Cambridge MS. Qq. 244/6; B.M. MS. Or. 3120.

Ibn Miskawayhi. *Tahdhīb al-akhlāq*. Cairo (?), A.H. 1298.

Ibn al-Nadīm al-Warrāq. *Fihrist*. Ed. G. Flügel. 2 vols. Leipzig, 1871–2.

Ibn al-Qiftī. *Ta'rīkh al-ḥukamā*. Ed. J. Lippert, Leipzig, 1903.

Ibn Qutayba. *'Uyūn al-akhbār*. Ed. C. Brockelmann. Berlin, 1900–8.

Ibn Qutayba. *Kitāb al-Ma'ārif*. Ed. F. Wuestenfeld. Göttingen, 1850.

Ibn Sa'd. *Kitāb al-Ṭabaqāt al-kabīr*. Ed. E. Sachau *et al.* 9 vols. Leyden, 1904–28.

Ibn Sa'īd. *Kitāb al-Mughrib*. Ed. K. N. Tallquist. Leyden, 1899.

Ibn Taghri-Bardī. *Annales*. Ed. T. G. J. Juynboll. 2 vols. Leyden, 1855–61.

Ibn Taghri-Bardī. *Nujūm al-Ẓāhira*. Ed. W. Popper. California, 1909–29.
Ibn Taymīya. *Al-Qiyās fī'l-shar' al-Islāmī*. Cairo, 1346.
Ibn al-Ṭiqṭaqā. *Al-Fakhrī*. Ed. W. Ahlwardt. Gotha, 1860.
Ibn al-Ṭiqṭaqā. *Al-Fakhrī*. Ed. H. Derenbourg. Paris, 1895.
Ibshīhī. *Al-Mustaṭraf*. 2 vols. Cairo, n.d.
Ikhwān al-Ṣafā. *Rasā 'il*. 4 vols. Cairo, 1347/1928.
The Indian Antiquary. London, 1872–1933.
Indian Census Reports, 1901, 1911, 1921, etc.
International Review of Missions. Edinburgh, 1912 ff.
'Īṣā b. Ismā'īl al-Āqsarā'ī. *Kitāb fī Faḍl al-jihād*. Cambridge University Library MS. Qq. 277.
Der Islam. Strassburg, Berlin, 1910 ff.
Islamica. Ed. A. Fischer. Leipzig, 1925 ff.
The Islamic Review. Woking.
Iṣṭakhrī. *Kitāb al-Masālik wa'l-mamālik*. Ed. M. J. de Goeje. Leyden, 1870.
Jacob, G. *Die Bektaschijje*. Munich, 1909.
Jāḥiẓ. *Kitāb al-Bayān wa'l-tabyīn*. 2 vols. Cairo, A.H. 1313.
Jāḥiẓ. *Tria Opuscula*. Ed. G. van Vloten. Leyden, 1903.
Jāḥiẓ. *Kitāb al-Tāj*. Ed. Ahmed Zéki Pasha. Cairo, 1914.
Jāḥiẓ. *Kitāb al-Maḥāsin wa 'l-aḍdād*. Ed. G. van Vloten. Leyden, 1898.
Jāḥiẓ. *Kitāb al-Ḥayawān*. 7 parts. Cairo, 1325/1907.
Jāḥiẓ. *Manāqib al-Atrāk*. Tr. C. H. Walker. *J.R.A.S.*, 1915.
Jahshiyārī. *Kitāb al-Wuzarā*. Ed. Hans von Mžik. Leipzig, 1926.
Jalāl al-Dīn Rūmī. *Dīvāni Shamsi Tabrīz*. Ed. and tr. R. A. Nicholson. Cambridge, 1898.
Jalāl al-Dīn Rūmī. *Mathnawī-i Ma'nawī*. Ed. and tr. R. A. Nicholson (Gibb Memorial Series). 8 vols. London and Leyden, 1925–40.
Jāmī. *Nafaḥāt al-uns*. Ed. W. Nassau Lees. Calcutta, 1859.
Jaussen, A. *Coutumes palestiniennes: Nablus*. Paris, 1927.
Jaussen, A. *Coutumes des arabes au pays de Moab*. Paris, 1908.
Jenkinson, Anthony, *et al. Early Voyages and Travells to Russia and Persia*. Hakluyt Society. London, 1886.
Jīlānī (Abu' l-Qāsim). *Qawānīn al-uṣūl*. Tabrīz, 1858.
Jomier, J. *Le Commentaire Coranique du Manar*. Paris, 1954.
Journal of the Central Asian Society. London.

Journal of the Royal Asiatic Society. London, 1834 ff.
[Sharīf] al-Jurjānī. *Ta'rīfāt*. Ed. G. Fluegel. Leipzig, 1845.
Juwaynī. *Tarīkh-i Jahān-gushā*. Ed. Muhammad Qazwīnī (Gibb Memorial Series). 3 vols. London and Leyden, 1912–37.
Juynboll, A. W. T. *Handbuch des Islamischen Gesetzes*. Leyden, 1910.
Kai Kā'us b. Iskandar. *Qābūs-nāma*. Ed. R. Levy (Gibb Memorial Series n.s. XVIII). 1951.
Kai Kā'us b. Iskandar. *Qabūs-nāma*. Tr. (under title *A Mirror for Princes*), R. Levy. London, 1951.
Kennet, A. *Bedouin Justice*. Cambridge, 1925.
(Sidi) Khalīl b. Isḥāq. *Mukhtaṣar*. Tr. I. Guidi and D. Santillana. 2 vols. Milan, 1919.
(Sidi) Khalīl b. Isḥāq. *Mukhtaṣar*. Trans. A. Perron, in *Exploration Scientifique de l'Algérie*, vol. XIII.
Khwārazmī [Muḥammad b. Yūsuf]. *Mafātīḥ al-'ulūm*. Ed. G. van Vloten. Leyden, 1895.
Khiḍr Ilyās Efendi. *Ta'rīkh-i Andarūn*. Stambūl, A.H. 1276.
Kindī. *Kitāb al-Wulāt*. Ed. R. Guest (Gibb Memorial Series). Leyden, 1912.
Kremer, A. von. *Culturgeschichtliche Streifzüge auf dem Gebiete des Islams*. Leipzig, 1873.
Kremer, A. von. *Culturgeschichte des Orients unter den Chalifen*. 2 vols. Vienna, 1875–7.
Kremer, A. von. *Die herrschenden Ideen des Islams*. Leipzig, 1868.
Kromayer, J., and Veith, G. *Heerwesen und Kriegsführung der Griechen und Römer*. Berlin, 1928.
Lambton, A. K. S. *Landlord and Peasant in Persia*. Oxford, 1953.
Lammens, H. *L'Islam, Croyances et Institutions*. Beyrouth, 1926. [English translation Sir E. D. Ross. London, 1930.]
Landon, H. *Nepal*. 2 vols. London, 1928.
Lane, E. W. *The Manners and Customs of the Modern Egyptians*. (Everyman ed.). London, n.d.
Lane, E. W. *One Thousand and One Nights*. 3 vols. London, 1841.
Lane-Poole, S. *The Coins of the Eastern Khaleefehs in the British Museum*. London, 1875.
Lane-Poole, S. *The Coins of the Mohammadan Dynasties in the British Museum*. London, 1876.
Lane-Poole, S. *The Coins of the Sultans of Delhi*. London, 1884.

Lane-Poole, S. *The Coins of the Mohammadan States of India.* London, 1885.
Lane-Poole, S. *The Barbary Corsairs.* London, 1890.
Lane-Poole, S. *The Mohammadan Dynasties.* London, 1894.
Lane-Poole, S. *The Moors in Spain.* London, 1887.
Lane-Poole, S. *Saladin.* New York, 1898.
Laurent, J. *L'Arménie entre Byzance et l'Islam depuis la conquête arabe jusqu'en* 886. Paris, 1919.
Layard, A. H. *Nineveh and Babylon.* London, 1853.
Law in the Middle East. Ed. M. Khadduri and H. J. Liebesny. Vol. I. *Origin and Development of Islamic Law.* Washington, D.C., 1955.
The Legacy of Islam. Ed. Sir T. W. Arnold and A. Guillaume. Oxford, 1931.
Leo (Emperor) VI. *Tactica*, in Migne, *Patrologia Graeca-Latina*, vol. 107.
le Strange, G. *The Lands of the Eastern Caliphate.* Cambridge, 1905.
Levy, R. *A Baghdad Chronicle.* Cambridge, 1929.
Levy, R. *A Mirror for Princes* (translation of the *Qābūs-nāma*). London, 1951.
Lewis, B. *The Origins of Isma'ilism: a study of the historical background of the Fatimid Caliphate.* Cambridge, 1940.
Lisān al-Dīn, Muḥammad. *Al-Iḥāta fi ta'rīkh Gharnāta.* 2 vols. Cairo, A.H. 1319.
Little, K. L. *The Mende of Sierra Leone.* London, 1951.
Luke, H. C. *A Bibliography of Sierra Leone.* Oxford, 1925.
Luke, H. C., and Jardine, D. J. *The Handbook of Cyprus.* Oxford, 1921.
Lybyer, A. H. *The Government of the Ottoman Empire in the Time of Suleiman the Magnificent.* Cambridge, Mass., 1913.
Macdonald, D. B. *Development of Muslim Theology, Jurisprudence and Constitutional Theory.* London, 1913; New York, 1926.
Mālik b. Anas. *Muwaṭṭa'*, with commentary of Zurqānī. Cairo, A.H. 1280.
Malouf, L. [Ed.]. *Traités inédits d'anciens philosophes arabes.* Beirut, 1911.
du Mans, R. *Estat de la Perse en* 1660. Ed. C. Schefer. Paris, 1890.
Maqdisī [Al-Mokaddasi]. *Descriptio Imperii Moslemici.* Ed. M. J. de Goeje. Leyden, 1877; 2nd ed. 1906.

Maqqarī. *Nafḥ al-ṭīb*. 4 vols. Būlāq. n.d.
Maqrīzī. *Khiṭaṭ*. 2 vols. Būlāq, A.H. 1270.
Maqrīzī. *Histoire des Sultans Mamlouks de l'Égypte*. Tr. M. Quatremère. 2 vols. Paris, 1837–62.
Margoliouth, D. S. *Early Development of Mohammedanism*. London, 1914.
Marrākushī. *History of the Almohades*. Ed. R. Dozy. 2nd ed. Leyden, 1881.
Martin, A. G. P. *Quatre siècles d'histoire marocaine*. Paris, 1923.
Massignon, L. *Annuaire du Monde mussulman*. Paris, 1925–55.
Mas'ūdī. *Murūj al-dhahab*. Ed. and tr. Barbier de Meynard and Pavet de Courteille. 9 vols. Paris, 1861 ff.
Mas'ūdī. *Kitāb al-Tanbīh*. Ed. M. J. de Goeje. Leyden, 1894.
Māwardī, Abu'l Ḥasan al-. *Constitutiones Politicae*. Ed. M. Enger. Bonn, 1853.
Māwardī, Abu'l Ḥasan al-. *Kitāb Adab al-dunyā wa'l-dīn*. Stambūl, A.H. 1299.
The Mejelle (*Ḥanafī Code*). Tr. C. R. Tyser *et al.* Nicosia, 1901.
Meynard, Barbier de. *Considérations sur l'Histoire ottomane*. Paris, 1886.
Mez, A. *Die Renaissance des Islams*. Heidelberg, 1922.
The Middle East. A Political and Economic Survey. 2nd ed. Royal Institute of International Affairs. London and New York, 1954.
Mīr-Khwānd. *Historia Samanidarum*. Ed. Fr. Wilken. Göttingen, 1808.
Miskawayhi (*et al.*). *The Eclipse of the Abbasid Caliphate*. Ed. and tr. H. E. Amedroz and D. S. Margoliouth. 7 vols. Oxford, 1920–1.
Migne, J. P. *Patrologia Graeca*. Paris, 1857–66. Vol. 107.
Miller, W. *The Ottoman Empire*. 4th ed. Cambridge, 1936.
Mitteilungen d. Seminars für Orientalischen Sprachen. Berlin, 1898 ff.
Morier, James. *Hajji Baba of Ispahan*. [Introduction by E. G. Browne.] 2 vols. London, 1895.
The Moslem World. New York, 1911 ff.
Moubray, G. A. de C. *Matriarchy in the Malay Peninsula*. London, 1931.
Mubarrad. [*Al-*] *Kāmil*. Ed. W. Wright, Leipzig, 1864 ff.

Musil, Alois. *Arabia Petraea*. 3 vols. Vienna, 1907–8.
Mustawfī. (Ḥamdallāh) *Nuzhat al-qulūb*. Ed .and tr. G. le Strange. London, 1915–19.
Nachrichten von d. Königl. Gesellschaft d. Wissenschaften zu Göttingen.
Nallino, C. A. *Raccolta di Scritti*. 6 vols. Rome, 1940 ff.
Narshakhī. *Tārīkhi Bukhārā*. Ed. C. Schefer. Paris, 1892.
Nawbakhtī. *Firaq al-Shī'a*. Ed. H. Ritter (Bibliotheca Islamica). Constantinople, 1931.
Nasafī. *Kanz al-daqā'iq*. 2 vols. Būlāq, A.H. 1285.
Nasā'ī. *Sunan*. Cairo, A.H. 1313.
Naṣīr al-Dīn Ṭūsī. *Akhlāq-i Nāṣirī*. Lucknow, 1891.
Nāṣir-i Khusraw. *Safar-nāma*. (*Relation du Voyage de Nassiri Khosrau.*) Ed. and tr. C. Schefer. Paris, 1881.
Nawawī. *Minhādj aṭ-Ṭālibīn*. Ed. Van den Berg. 3 vols. Batavia, 1882–4.
Nicholson, R. A. *Elementary Arabic, Second Reading Book*. Cambridge, 1909.
Nicholson, R. A. *Literary History of the Arabs*. Cambridge, 1930.
Nicholson, R. A. *Studies in Islamic Mysticism*. Cambridge, 1921.
Nicholson, R. A. *Studies in Islamic Poetry*. Cambridge, 1921.
The Nigeria Handbook. (Crown Agents for the Colonies.) London, 1953.
Niẓām al-Mulk. *Siyāsat-nāma*. Ed. and tr. C. Schefer. Paris, 1891–3.
Niẓāmī 'Aruḍī Samarqandī. *Chahār maqāla*. Ed. Muhammad Qazwīnī (Gibb Memorial Series, XI). London and Leyden, 1910. Tr. E. G. Browne (G.M.S. XI, 2). London, 1921.
Nöldeke, Th. *Delectus Veterum Carminum Arabicorum*. Berlin, 1890.
Nöldeke, Th. *Geschichte der Perser und Araber zur Zeit der Sasaniden*. Leyden, 1879.
Nöldeke, Th. *Geschichte des Qorans*. Ed. F. Schwally [2nd ed.]. Leipzig, 1909–19.
D'Ohsson [Mouradja]. *Tableau général de l'empire othoman*. 7 vols. Paris, 1788–1824.
Olearius, Adam (Oelschlager). *Voyages and Travells*. Tr. John Davies. London, 1669.
d'Ollone, G. *Recherches sur les Mussulmans Chinois*. Paris, 1911.

Olufsen, O. *The Emir of Bokhara and his Country*. London, 1911.
Oriente Moderno. Rome, 1923 ff.
Palgrave, W. G. *A Year's Journey through Central and Eastern Arabia*. 5th ed. London, 1869.
Philby, H. St J. *The Heart of Arabia*. 2 vols. London, 1922.
Polak, J. E. *Persien, das Land u. seine Bewohner*. 2 vols. Leipzig, 1865.
Polo, Marco. *Travels*. Ed. H. Yule. 3rd ed.; 2 vols. London, 1903.
Poole, S. L. *Catalogue of Oriental Coins in the British Museum*. London, 1875–82.
Qalqashandī. *Subḥ al-aʿshā*. 14 vols. Cairo, 1913 ff.
Qiftī. *Ta'rīkh al-ḥukamā*. Ed. W. Lippert, Leipzig, 1903.
Quatremère. *Histoire des Mongoles de la Perse*. Paris, 1836.
Quatremère. *Histoire des Sultans Mamlouks de l'Egypte*. 2 vols. Paris, 1837–45.
Qūchī Bey. *Risāla*. ("The Letter on the Organization of the Government, sent to Sulṭān Murād IV.") Constantinople, A.H. 1303. Tr. W. Behrnauer, *Z.D.M.G.* Vol. xv (1861), 272 ff.
Qudāma. *See* Ibn Khurdādbih.
Qudūrī. *Mukhtaṣar*. Bombay, 1886.
Querry, A. *Droit Musulman. Recueil des lois concernant les Musulmans Chyites*. 2 vols. Paris, 1871.
Qushayrī. *Risāla*. Būlāq, A.H. 1287.
Rāwandī. *Rāḥat al-ṣudūr*. Ed. Muhammad Iqbāl (Gibb Series n.s. II). London, 1921.
Rein, G. K. *Abessinien*. 3 vols. Berlin, 1918.
Reinaud, M. *Invasions des Sarrazins en France*. Paris, 1836.
Rescher, O. *Studien über den Inhalt von* 1001 *Nacht*. (Der Islam, IX, 1918.)
Revue des Études Islamiques. Paris, 1927 ff.
Revue internationale de Législation musulmane. Cairo, 1954.
Risley, H. H. *The People of India*. Calcutta, 1915.
Rodd, F. R. *People of the Veil*. London, 1926.
Rose, H. A. *The Darvishes*. Oxford, 1927.
Ross, W. D. *Aristotle*. London, 1923.
Royal Anthropological Institute, Journal. London, 1872 ff.
Ruska, J. *Zur ältesten arabischen Algebra und Rechenkunst*. Sitzungsber. d. Heidelberger Akad. d. Wissenschaften (Phil.-Hist. Kl.), 1917.

Ruska, J. *Arabische Alchemisten*. Heidelberg, 1924.
Rutter, E. *The Holy Cities of Arabia*. 2 vols. London, 1928.
Ruxton, F. H. *Mālikī Law*. London, 1916.
al-Ṣābī, Hilāl. *Kitāb al-Wuzarā*. Ed. H. F. Amedroz. Leyden, 1904.
Sachau, E. *Muhammedanisches Recht*. Berlin, 1897.
Sa'dī. *Būstān*. Ed. C. H. Graf. Vienna, 1858.
Santillana, D. *Istituzioni di diritto musulmano malichita*. 2 vols. Rome, 1926–38.
Sarton, G. *Introduction to the History of Science*. 2 vols. Baltimore, 1927–9.
Sauvaget, J. *Introduction à l'Histoire de l'Orient Musulman*. Paris, 1946.
Schacht, J. *Bergsträsser's Grundzüge des Islamischen Rechts*. Berlin 1935.
Schacht, J. *Der Islam (Religionsgeschichtliche Lesebuch)*. Tübingen, 1931.
Schacht, J. *Origins of Muhammadan Jurisprudence*. Oxford, 1950.
Seligman, C. G., and B. Z. "The Kababish". *Harvard African Studies*, II. Cambridge, Mass., 1918.
Shāfi'ī. *[Kitāb al-]Umm*. Būlāq, A.H. 1321.
Shahristānī. *Kitāb al-Milal wa'l-niḥal*. Ed. W. Cureton. London, 1846.
Sha'rānī. *Mīzān (Traduit de l'Arabe par le Dr Perron)*. Algiers 1898.
Shaybānī. *Jāmi' al-ṣaghīr*. Lucknow, 1893.
Shayzarī ['Abd al-Raḥmān b. Naṣr]. *Nihāyat al-rutba fī ṭalab al-ḥisba*. Ed. Al-Bāz al-'Arīnī. Cairo, 1365/1946.
Shīrāzī. *Tanbīh*. Ed. A. W. T. Juynboll. Leyden, 1879.
Skrine, C. P. *Chinese Central Asia*. London, 1926.
Skrine, F. H., and Ross, E. D. *Heart of Asia*. London, 1899.
Smith, Margaret. *Rābi'a the Mystic*. Cambridge, 1928.
Smith, W. Robertson. *Kinship and Marriage in Early Arabia*. Cambridge, 1885. [2nd ed. Cambridge, 1903.]
Strothmann, R. *Das Staatsrecht der Zaiditen*. Strassburg, 1912.
Subkī. *Jam' al-jawāmi' fi 'l-uṣūl*. 2 vols. Būlāq, A.H. 1285.
Subkī. *Mu'id al-ni'am*. Ed. D. W. Myrhman. London, 1908.
Subkī. *Ṭabaqāt al-Shafi 'īya*. Cairo, A.H. 1324.
Sudan Notes and Records. Khartoum, 1918 ff.

Ṭabarī (Muḥammad b. Jarīr). *Annales.* Arabic text, ed. M. J. de Goeje *et al.* 15 vols. Leyden, 1879–1901.
Ṭabarī (Muḥammad b. Jarīr). *Tafsīr.* 30 parts. Cairo, A.H. 1320–1.
Ṭabarī (Ḥasan b. 'Alī). *Kāmil-i bahā'ī.* Bombay, 1323.
Tadhkirat al-mulūk. Tr. V. Minorsky. (Gibb Series, n.s. XVI). London, 1943.
Tanūkhī. *Nishwār al-muḥāḍarah.* Ed. D. S. Margoliouth. London, 1921.
Tarn, W. W. *Hellenistic Military and Naval Developments.* Cambridge, 1930.
Tha'ālibī. *Qiṣaṣ al-anbiyā.* Cairo, A.H. 1310.
Thomas, B. *Arabia Felix.* London, 1932.
Thomas, E. *Revenue Resources of the Mughal Empire.* London, 1871.
Thorning, H. *Beiträge zur Kenntnis des islamischen Vereinwesens.* Berlin, 1913.
Toynbee, A. J. *The Islamic World since the Peace Settlement.* (Survey of International Affairs, 1925.) Vol. I. Oxford, 1927.
Trimingham, J. S. *Islam in Ethiopia.* Oxford, 1952.
Trimingham, J. S. *Islam in the Sudan.* Oxford, 1949.
Tupper, C. L. *Punjab Customary Law.* 4 vols. Calcutta, 1881.
Ṭurṭūshī (Abū Bakr). *Siraj al-mulūk.* Cairo, A.H. 1289.
Tyan, E. *Histoire de l'Organisation Judiciaire en Pays d'Islam.* Paris, 1938.
'Ubayd-i Zākānī. *Laṭa'if.* (Kaviani edition.) Berlin, A.H. 1343.
Übach, E., and Rackow, E. *Sitte und Recht in Nordafrika.* Stuttgart, 1923.
Vambéry, A. *Sketches of Central Asia.* London, 1868.
Van Vloten, G. *Recherches sur la domination arabe.* Amsterdam, 1894.
Wāṣif. *Ta'rīkh-i Wāṣif.* 2 vols. Constantinople, A.H. 1219.
Weil, G. *Geschichte der Chalifen.* 3 vols. Mannheim, 1846 ff.
Wellhausen, J. *Das arabische Reich und sein Sturz.* Berlin, 1902.
Wellhausen, J. *Die religiös-politischen Oppositionsparteien in alten Islam.* Berlin, 1901.
Wellhausen, J. *Muhammed in Medina,* Vakidis *Kitāb al-Maghazi.* Berlin, 1882.
Wellhausen, J. *Die Ehe bei den Arabern.* Nachrichten von d. Königl. Ges. d. Wissenschaften. Göttingen, 1893.

Wellhausen, J. *Medina vor dem Islam*. Berlin, 1889.
Die Welt des Islams. Berlin, 1913 ff.
Wensinck, A. J. *Handbook of Early Muhammadan Tradition*. Leyden, 1927.
Wensinck, A. J. *The Muslim Creed*. Cambridge, 1932.
Westermann, D. "Islam in the Sudan". *International Review of Missions*, I (1912).
Westermarck, E. *Marriage Ceremonies in Morocco*. London, 1914.
Wills, C. J. *In the Land of the Lion and the Sun*. London, 1893.
Wills, C. J. *Persia as it Is*. London, 1886.
Wilson, R. K. *Digest of Anglo-Muhammadan Law*. London, 1908.
Winstedt, R. O. *Malaya and its History*. London, 1948.
Winstedt, R. O. *The Malays: A Cultural History*. London, 1950.
Wuestenfeld, H. F. *Das Heerwesen der Muhammedaner*. Abhand. d. K. Gesellsch. der Wiss. zu Göttingen. Bd. 26, 1880.
Ya'qūbī. [*Kitāb al-*]*Buldān*. Ed. M. J. de Goeje. Leyden, 1892.
Ya'qūbī. *Historiae*, ed. M. T. Houtsma. 2 vols. Leyden, 1883.
Yāqūt. *Irshād al-arīb*. [*Mu'jam al-udabā*]. Ed. D. S. Margoliouth (Gibb Series). 7 vols. London, 1908–27.
Yāqūt. *Mu'jam al-buldān*. Ed. F. Wuestenfeld. 6 vols. Leipzig, 1866–70.
Yule, H. *Cathay and the Way Thither*. 2nd ed. 3 vols. (Hakluyt Series). London, 1913.
Zayd b. 'Alī. *Majmu' al-fiqh*. Ed. E. Griffini. Milan, 1919.
Zabīdī. *Tāj al-'arūs fi sharḥ al-Qāmūs*. 5 vols. Cairo, A.H. 1286–7.
Zamakhsharī. *Kashshāf*. Ed. W. H. Lees. 2 vols. Calcutta, 1856–9.
Zambaur, E. de. *Généalogie de l'Islam*. Hanover, 1927.
Zaydān, J. *Umayyads and 'Abbāsids*. Tr. D. S. Margoliouth (Gibb Memorial Series). Leyden, 1907.
Zaydān, J. *Ta'rīkh al-tamaddun al-Islāmī*. 5 vols. Cairo, 1902–6.
Zeitschrift der deutschen Morgenländischen Gesellschaft. Leipzig, 1847 ff.

INDEX

"—" before a name indicates *al;*
"b." indicates *ibn.*

INDEX

expenditure, public, 298, 302, 323 f.
extortion (for revenue), 307 f.

Faḍl b. Sahl, 364
faith the criterion of good, 196
faqīh, 259, 296
—Fārābī, 223, 469–71, 500, 502 n.
Farazdaq, 302
farḍ, 155, 202, 251, 503
Fārs, 312, 377, 382 f.
fasting, 160 f., 184
father, legal powers of, 143 f.
—*Fātiḥa*, 184
Fāṭima (the Prophet's daughter), 280, 288 f.
Fāṭimids, 288, 293, 339, 350, 367 f., 387
Fāṭimid armies, 445 f.
fay', 308
feudatories, 449
Fihrist, 497 f.
fiqh, 150–91 *passim*, 192 f., 202, 222, 242 f., 462
Firdawsī, 253, 380
Firdaws al-ḥikma, 467 n.
fiṭra, 252
flesh, the, see *nafs*
foods, lawful and unlawful, 156, 162, 172 f., 174, 175, 184, 185, 247, 250 f.
France, 18
fraternities, 89
free will and predestination, 205–7, 209, 237
Fūla, 49 f.
Fusṭāṭ, 24
futuwwa, 213 f.

Gabriel, angel, 156, 215
Galen, 466, 499
gambling, 203, 204
Gaul, 181, see also France
genealogy, science of, 461
geography, 481–4
geology, 487–9
geometry, 474
Georgians, 38
ghanīma, 308 f.
Ghazālī, 196–8, 204 f., 214–22, 259, 291, 472, 502–5
Ghazna, 14, 32, 41, 372
Ghaznawids, 74, 263, 369, 371 f.
Ghiyāth al-Dīn Balban, 405
Ghūrids, 41
Ghuzz Turks, 423
Gibraltar, Straits, 17
Golden Horde, 38
good and evil, 194 f., 196, 206 f., 217, 223, 227
Greek, language of tax-registers, 360
Greek philosophy and Islam, 458–60, 466, 468–98 *passim*, 504
Greeks and Muslims, 25 f., 24, 36, 37, 360, 452
guardian, see *walī*
guilds, trade, 89
Gujarāt, 41

ḥadīth, 129, 133, 168, 170–81 *passim*, 196, 234, 253, 291, 295, 461
Haḍramaut, 43 f.
Ḥāfiẓ, 251
ḥājib, 261, 405
ḥājib al-ḥujjāb, 375, 376, 394 f.
Ḥajj, see pilgrimage
Ḥajjāj b. Yūsuf, 21, 58, 302, 304, 333, 358, 360, 411
Ḥājjī Khalīfa, 223
ḥalāl, 213
Ḥallāj (Ḥusayn), 211
Hamadān, 11, 12
Ḥanafī school, 166–91 *passim*
Ḥanbalī school, 180, 182, 183
happiness, 225, 227, 229 f.
ḥaram, 203, 213
Hārūn al-Rashīd, 133, 146, 167, 296, 306, 328, 364, 367, 425, 443
harvests, date of, 312
Ḥasan (b. 'Alī), 68, 279
Hāshimīs, 65, 279, 323
Hausa, 50
Hell, 205 f.
Hellespont, 9, 10
heretics, 254
Ḥijāz, 280
hijra, 2, 5
Ḥilf al-Fuḍūl, 329
Hindus as *dhimmīs*, 254 f., 406
—intermarriage with, 244 f.
Hippocrates, 466
Ḥīra, 6, 8, 408
homicide, 351, 353
horse-racing, 204
hospitals, 303
ḥudūd, 330, 346, 351–4

Shaykh al-Islām, 265, 268–70, 400
Shī'a, and children, 136, 140, 147
  and women, 109, 116, 247
Shī'a doctrine and practice, 70, 171, 185, 207 n., 209 f., 252, 287–9
shighār, 105
shiḥna, 381
Shī'ites, 171, 180 f. (see also Shī'a)
ships and boats, 441, 442, 451–4
Shuhda bint al-Ibarī, 133
shurṭa, 306, 332
Sicily, 17, 26 f.
siege engines, 438–40
Sierra Leone, 50
Ṣiffīn (battle), 411, 429, 432
ṣīgha, 117
Sihyūn, 439
sin, 203, 211, 214
Sind, 358
sipāhsālār, 375, 376
Sīstān, 21, 357
Siyāsat-nāma, 74 f., 424 f.
slaves, adoption of, 77
  as army officers, 425 f.
  conduct towards, 221, 298
  emancipation of, 80
  emasculation of, 80
  marriage with, 79, 124
  right of marriage, 102
  (female), marriage of, 105, 111 f., 117 f.
  legal status of, 75, 76, 77 ff., 102
  as soldiers, 74 f., 445 f., 447, 448–50
  as state officials, 397
Slave Kings of Delhi, 41, 74, 405
slave-trade, 81–8, 124, 188, 322
slavery, 60 f., 63 f., 73–90, 154
  by capture, 76
  by inheritance, 76
  by sale, 76
  modern, 85–9
society, divisions of, 66
"Soldan", see *Sulṭān*
soul, the, 211, 215, 216 f., 223 f., 225, 228–30, 239, 505
sovereignty, succession, 371
Soviet Republics, Muslim, 44, 101, 107, 128
Spain, Moorish, 17, 27, 29–31, 37 f., 182, 206, 339, 358, 368, 404 f., 453 f., 459
speculation, commercial, 204, 255–7
spoils, division, 56 f.
State, the, 226, 242, 248, 258–70 *passim*, 274 f., 294–354 *passim*
Straits Settlements, 88
"Sublime Porte", 398
suckling of children, 139 f.
Sūdān, 48 f., 86, 246
Sufism, 90, 210–14, 219, 234, 238
suicide, 207
Sulaymān the Magnificent (Qānūnī), 35, 267, 402, 404, 451
Sulaymān Pasha, 404
sulṭān, 265, 269 n. (see also State, the)
Sulṭān (title), 32, 367, 368, 369, 378
Sulṭānate (Ottoman), 269, 283
Sumatra, 43
sunna, 202
Sunna, 150, 170 f., 176, 212, 234, 242, 254
Sunnites, 171, 247
Sunūsīs, 86 f., 89, 254
"sword, (Man of the)", 297, 387, 388
synagogues, 184 f.
Syria, 5, 6, 7, 10, 101, 142, 187, 278, 309, 313, 314, 355, 360, 408, 413, 443

Ṭabarī, 180 and *passim*
Ṭabaristān, 367
tactics, Saracen, 431–6
Tahāfut al-falāsifa, 472, 503
Ṭāhir Dhu'l-Yamīnayn, 292, 370
Ṭāhirids, 370
taḥlīl, 121, n. 5
Ṭahmāsp Shāh, 264, 377
takmila, 313
Ṭalḥa, 171
talio, 78 f., 190, 241, 274, 329, 330 f., 346, 352–4
talismans, 505
Tamerlane, 34
Tanbīh of Shīrāzī, 187–91
Tanganyika, 182
Tangier, 16
taqīya, 207
taqlīd, 204
Ta'rīkh-i Fīrūz-Shāhī, 262
Ṭāriq b. Ziyād, 16 f., 411, 425
ṭarīqa, 89 f.
Tartars, 38, 45
tashrī', 269